COMPANION
to the
HYMNAL

TEXTS: *Fred D. Gealy*
TUNES: *Austin C. Lovelace*
BIOGRAPHIES: *Carlton R. Young*
GENERAL EDITOR: *Emory Stevens Bucke*

COMPANION
to the
HYMNAL
a handbook to the 1964 Methodist Hymnal

Nashville   **ABINGDON PRESS**   New York

COMPANION TO THE HYMNAL

Copyright © 1970 by Abingdon Press

ISBN 0-687-09259-0

Library of Congress Catalog Card Number: 76-98899

The translation of the two additional stanzas of
"How Great Thou Art," quoted on p. 323, was
made by Stuart K. Hine, copyright 1958, and is
used by permission of Mr. Hine.

Scripture quotations noted RSV are from the Revised Standard Version of the Bible, copyrighted
1946 and 1952 by the Division of Christian Education, National Council of Churches, and are used
by permission.

SET UP, PRINTED, AND BOUND BY THE
PARTHENON   PRESS   AT   NASHVILLE,
TENNESSEE, UNITED STATES OF AMERICA

HOW TO USE THIS BOOK

Anticipating the use of this book by both layman and professional, the publisher has kept the format simple. The abbreviations are few and those generally used. In the interest of saving space, st (s). has been adopted for stanza (s), and Arabic numbers are used in the comments on texts, tunes, and biographies. With the exception of the indexes, all numbers in **bold face type** refer to the numbers in *The Methodist Hymnal*. Those in light face type refer to page numbers in the *Companion*. Tune names are set in SMALL CAPITALS.

As noted in the Publisher's Preface, the arrangement of the book is alphabetical. After the general articles, comments on hymn texts and tunes are placed first, followed by comments on canticles with music, service music, and Communion music. Biographies are last. This alphabetical arrangement makes an additional index of first lines and titles of hymns unnecessary. There is an index of first lines of service music, Communion music, and canticles with music, as well as an index of tune names. The latter index includes the several names a particular tune is known by, as well as the name used in *The Methodist Hymnal*. In addition, the general index, one of the most complete to be found in a reference book of this type, will provide useful information to layman and professional alike.

Frequently, reference to the different Methodist hymnbooks is made by date only. For further clarification, the reader is asked to consult the general articles in this book and the chart "American Methodist Hymnals," found on pp. 52-53 in this book.

PUBLISHER'S PREFACE

Companions to the Methodist hymnal have been produced before. In 1848 David Creamer did his valuable book, *Methodist Hymnology,* and while it is now a collector's item, Creamer's work is careful and authentic and is quoted often by historians of church music. Following the publication of the 1935 hymnal, Robert G. McCutchan wrote *Our Hymnody,* which has served as a standard work for understanding the backgrounds of the tunes and texts of that collection.

In this *Companion to the Hymnal* we have taken a whole new approach. Instead of designing a book of interest to Methodists only, we think we have a book of general interest to the whole ecumenical church. Three excellent writers have arranged their work alphabetically. In dealing with the texts of the hymns, we have the careful work of Dr. Fred D. Gealy; the tunes have been handled by Dr. Austin C. Lovelace; the biographies of authors and composers have been written by Dr. Carlton R. Young. Since most of the material is common to all hymnody, this means that the book will be of excellent value to anyone who needs information in these three categories of study. We have had the excellent editorial services of Mrs. William Mills in coordinating the work of the three writers. We believe that the work will commend itself to many future generations of pastors, laymen, musicians, and historians who will want this careful reference work in their study of hymnology.

Methodists have been producing hymnals since 1737 when John Wesley published his *Collection of Psalms and Hymns* at "Charlestown," South Carolina. However, official hymnals did not come until 1790, when the Methodist Publishing House was just a year old. Wesley had tried to impose his several collections on the American Methodists, but there was considerable resistance to them—notably his 1784 *Collection.*

The 1964 edition of *The Methodist Hymnal* is an official book of the church. The hymnal is authorized by the General Conference and published by the Methodist Publishing House exclusively. This means that the editorial content of the volume is the responsibility of the church, and the format and method of publication are the responsibility of the publisher.

Long before publication—indeed almost eight years—many people began to work on this project. The Commission on Worship had already developed its proposed revision of *The Book of Worship,* which it also presented to the General Conference of 1964 for approval, and it was obvious during all of that work that the church would need a new hymnal that would serve the greater church. Because a merger between the Evangelical United Brethren Church and The Methodist Church was in the offing, it was clear that consultants from the Evangelical United Brethren should be involved in the consideration. Because the pastors and church musicians were the people who could give the commission the most practical advice on what should be built into the new hymnal, a most thorough research project was carried out, and more than 11,000 local church leaders participated in that process. Indeed, there was some honest scoffing from some of the professional hymnologists who said that the democratic process was being carried much too far in determining what to do to the new hymnal!

The Commission on Worship elected the Reverend Carlton R. Young to serve as its full-time editor for the hymnal, and he accepted that responsibility in the fall of 1960. As a member of the staff at Abingdon Press, where he was manager of its church music publishing department, he had familiarized himself with the graphic arts and thus was able to work efficiently with the Production Department in the publishing of the hymnal.

Organizing the basic consideration of tunes and texts meant more than forty-five subcommittee meetings in preparation for the general meetings of the commission. Some 1,500 original hymn tunes and texts were considered. Demands from the many varieties of people called Methodists were ministered to in an amazing way, and their needs were served. The all but unanimous approval of the commission's work by the 1964 General Conference was a thrilling event.

The publisher was most fortunate in having an excellent copy editor available for the detailed work of manuscript preparation so that the production of the hymnal could proceed on schedule. Mrs. William Mills coordinated the work of Dr. Young, in manuscript preparation, and his colleague, the chairman of the tunes committee, Dr. Austin Lovelace. A battery of artists under the direction of Mrs. William Bozeman in Abingdon's Production Department carried out the painstaking retouching and correcting of page proofs for the 539 hymn texts and the 402 hymn tune harmonizations in this book.

The new hymnal went into production at once, and by the time it was ready for delivery, more than two and one-half million copies had been ordered. Five years after publication approximately four million copies were in use throughout The United Methodist Church.

In order to meet the initial demand for two and one-half million copies, the manufacturing division of the Methodist Publishing House had to be ready with 13,146 miles of paper; 332.2 miles of cloth; 27.3 miles of 23″ width genuine gold foil; 7,500 pounds of ink; and 13.2 freight car loads of binder boards. It took 58,404 man hours of work to put it all together.

CONTENTS

Part I
GENERAL ARTICLES

The Psalms and Hymns of the Church
Fred D. Gealy

The prose of praise rises quickly to poetry. Proclamation becomes acclamation becomes exclamation. Staccato shouts of joy, crisp confessions of faith, ecstatic cries of thanksgiving of themselves fall into rhythmical patterns, the form varying with the type and intensity of emotional expression. As monotone moves toward melody, prose rhythms move toward meter and rhyme. Phrases repeated become regularized and stabilized, both rhythmically and melodically. Thus music and poetry, unintended twins, come into existence as ordered sequences of sounds, accents, rhythms.

As the Christian church confessed its faith, it sang; as it sang, it confessed its faith. John Wesley described his 1780 *Collection of Hymns for the Use of the People Called Methodists* as "a little body of experimental and practical divinity." If lyricism has been overly subjected to the control of dogma, it is because like the windows in a cathedral the intent of hymnody has been to delineate the story of salvation, not to entertain.

The Beginnings

Colossians 3:16, so frequently printed on the title page of hymnals throughout the centuries, is itself a summons to poetry: "Let the word of Christ dwell in you richly, as you teach and admonish one another in all wisdom, and as you sing psalms and hymns and spiritual songs with thankfulness in your hearts to God" (RSV). "Psalms" (φάλμοι) "hymns" (ὕμνοι), and "spiritual songs" (ῷδαὶ πνευματικαί) are not to be distinguished absolutely, and in some circles not at all. Yet the main body of "psalms" sung in the early church would be from the Old Testament psalter, well established in both liturgical and private worship. The "hymn (s) " sung at the Last Supper, Mark 14:26, would be psalms; likewise those sung by Paul and Silas in prison, Acts 16:25. To "sing praise" (ψάλλειν), James 5:13, probably means no more.

If "psalms" refers primarily to the psalter, "spiritual songs" may in the first instance refer to such spontaneous and ecstatic outbursts as the sounds uttered in glossolalia, without meaning, or, preferably to Paul, songs which one could sing "with the mind" (I Corinthians 14:15). Sometimes in the excitement of the service, unpremeditated hymnlike phrases might come to expression, themselves becoming the nucleus of such a hymn (ψαλμός) as could later be brought to the assembly (I Corinthians 14:26). But since all Christian praise was inspired by the Spirit, there was no need precisely to distinguish the categories. The terms, common in Judaism of the diaspora and in the pagan world, could be and were used interchangeably.

Many New Testament phrases sound so hymnlike that one is tempted to see a veritable ground swell of hymnody underlying the prose of its praise and to conclude that the hymn form, whether doxological, a hymn to God, or to Christ, was and is the most potent form of Christian speech. Therefore, hymns may have formed a basic part of the catechetical instruction given to converts.

The simplest and most frequent formula of rhythmical praise is the doxology, usually addressed to God, sometimes to Christ, sometimes ambiguous, e.g., Romans 11:36; Galatians 1:5; Ephesians 3:20-21; Philippians 4:20; I Timothy 1:17, 6:16; II Timothy 4:18; Hebrews 13:21; I Peter 4:11, 5:11; Jude 25; Revelation 1:6, 5:14, 7:10, 12, 19:1, 4. The hymns in Revelation 11:17-18, 15:3-4, 19:5, 6-8 are notable. Hymnlike addresses to God can be seen in Acts 4:24-26; Romans 11: 33-36; II Corinthians 1:3-4; Ephesians 1:3-14; Colossians 1:13-14; I Peter 1:3-5; Revelation 4:8, 11. Addresses to or about Christ are Philippians 2:6-11; Ephesians 5:14; Colossians 1:15-20; I Timothy 3:16; Hebrews 1:3; Revelation 5:9. See also I Timothy 1:15 and II Timothy 2:11-13.

The three great canticles in the Lukan infancy narratives, the *Magnificat,* 1:46-55, the *Benedictus,* 1:68-79, and the *Nunc dimittis,* 2:29-32, done in Old Testament or Rabbinic poetic style, would suggest the presence of a distinctive Christian hymnody at the time Luke's Gospel was written, if not earlier.

Thus the New Testament itself confirms the statement of Pliny, governor of Bithynia, written c. 112 to Emperor Trajan, that Christians in his area "sang antiphonally hymns to Christ as to a god." Pliny, indeed, writes "say" (*dicere*) not "sing" (*cantare*). Luke also, 2:13, uses "say" (λέγειν), not "sing" (ὕμνειν) for the praise of the heavenly host, as well as for introducing the canticles. Further, we are nowhere told in the New Testament that the canticles were sung in the worship services. Yet, given the widespread practice of singing (chanting) among Jews and Greeks, as well as its continuation in the New Testament churches, it could well be that the singing of the canticles preceded their incorporation into Luke's Gospel.

Though I Corinthians 14:14, 26 and the term "spiritual songs" suggest that the way was open for newly inspired texts, doubtless in actual practice most such spontaneous expressions would be biblically based. In the main, hymnody would be centered in psalms and canticles of the canonical scriptures, including also such apocryphal hymns as the ·Benedictus es (668) and the Benedicite (616).

The prayer form and hymn form have always been intimately related. Since both address God directly, the one easily issues into the other. Just as the language of prayer tends to become hymnlike, so most hymns begin or end as prayers. Most notable of the early prayer hymns are the eucharistic prayers in the Didache, or Teaching of the Twelve Apostles, a second-century treatise. These prayers turned into meter appear in our hymnal (307). The most important of the hymns from the first four centuries are found in part or in whole in the Liturgy of St. James, c. 200, or in the seventh and eighth books of the Apostolic Constitutions, fourth or fifth century: the Ter Sanctus (Thrice holy), Isaiah 6:3, with the Hosanna and Benedictus of Matthew 21:9 sometimes added (830B); "Let all mortal flesh keep silence" (324); the Trisagion, common in the Eastern liturgies, "Holy God, Holy and Mighty, Holy and Immortal, have mercy on us"; the Gloria in excelsis (830A); the evening hymn, "Hail, gladdening light" in John Keble's translation (see 1935 hymnal, No. 637); and the great Te Deum laudamus (665). These hymns are all of Greek origin except the Te Deum, which is Latin, and all except the Te Deum seem to have been fashioned for use in the Eastern liturgies: Palestine and Syria, Jerusalem and Antioch, and later Edessa, became flourishing centers of liturgical chant. Of the few Syriac hymns translated, none appears in our hymnal.

Of the early Gnostic hymns the most extended are the hymn in the Acts of Thomas, A.D. 250-300, beginning "When I was a little child," and the "Hymn of Jesus" in the Acts of John, c. 150, beginning "Glory to Thee, Father." The latter is best known to us in the musical setting by Gustav Holst. The historical importance of the Gnostic hymns,

17

however, is owing to their freedom from conventional Hebrew literary forms and to the incentive they gave the orthodox to provide hymns with which to counter Gnostic heresies.

Greek Hymns

Authentic Greek hymnody begins with Clement of Alexandria, c. 160-215. In his book of instructions for catechumens, the *Paidagogos,* he includes a "Hymn to Christ the Savior," beginning "Bridle of colts untamed." Two adaptations of this hymn appear in our hymnal (84, 86). A second writer from this early period represented in our hymnal is Synesius of Cyrene, c. 375-430 (284).

The high point in Greek hymnody came in the seventh and eighth centuries in Palestine and Syria. The two greatest names are Andrew of Crete, c. 660–c. 740, who wrote his "Great Kanon," a poem of 250 stanzas modeled on the nine canticles, in Jerusalem (238), and John of Damascus, c. 675–c. 749 (437, 446, 448), who with Cosmas founded the school of hymn writers at the monastery of St. Saba, between Jerusalem and the Dead Sea. Although the Arab conquest of Palestine, Syria, and Asia Minor drove thousands of monks from their monasteries causing them to flee to Constantinople and Thessalonika, and on to Italy, France, and Spain, the interest of the Eastern Church in singing hymns remained undiminished.

Our hymnal also prints translations of three anonymous Greek hymns (99, 353, 491).

Latin Hymns

Hilary, bishop of Poitiers, c. 310-366, was the first prominent Latin hymn writer. Exiled in Phrygia by his theological opponents, the Arians, he found them using hymns to promote heresy. On his return he wrote hymns to express the orthodox faith. However, it was Ambrose, c. 337-397, bishop of Milan, who was the real originator of the medieval Latin hymn as known to us. He too had learned the use of hymns on his travels in the East and like Hilary wrote hymns to support the orthodox faith. It was Ambrose who created the classical form of the Latin hymn. Some eighteen hymns ascribed to Ambrose are extant, at least four of which are undeniably his. "O splendor of God's glory bright" (29) in our hymnal is "almost undoubtedly" his.

The story of hymns in Milan is best told by Augustine, *Confessions,* ix. 7:

The church of Milan had only recently begun to employ this mode of consolation and exaltation with all the brethren singing together with great earnestness of voice and heart. . . . This was the time that the custom began, after the manner of the Eastern Church, that hymns and psalms should be sung, so that the people would not be worn out with the tedium of lamentation. This custom, retained from then till now, has been imitated by many, indeed, by almost all the congregations throughout the rest of the world.

The singing of hymns became widely popular in the monasteries where the seven canonical hours or offices of daily prayer were observed. Among others, Benedict, d. 543, ordered hymns to be sung at the hour services of his rule. In these early lists throughout western Europe, from thirty-four to sixty hymns appear, all "Ambrosian" in style, a style which dominated hymnody for the next five or six hundred years.

The Spaniard Prudentius, 348–c. 413, a contemporary of Ambrose and the greatest Latin poet of his age, is represented in our hymnal by hymns **357** and **405**; Pope Gregory the Great, 540-604, by hymn **504**; Fortunatus, c. 530–c. 609, bishop of Poitiers, by hymn **452**; and Theodulph, bishop of Orleans, c. 750–c. 821, a Goth by race, a Spaniard by birth, has contributed the noble Palm Sunday processional, hymn **424**. "Christ is made the sure foundation," hymn **298**, is part of the regular Latin cycle in the Western Church. It occurs in the oldest extant hymnals of the ninth century but is probably a century or two older. Our hymnal retains two centos from the famous twelfth-century hymn *Jesu dulcis memoria,* long attributed to Bernard of Clairvaux, but perhaps of English authorship, hymns **82, 329**; and one from the long poem, *De Contemptu Mundi* by Bernard of Cluny, twelfth century, hymn **303**. Some one hundred hymns of Peter Abelard, 1079-1142, of France were discovered in the mid-nineteenth century, of which hymn **427** is one. The most recent Latin hymn in our hymnal is *Adeste fideles* (**386**), the oldest text of which dates c. 1743.

By the eleventh and twelfth centuries the ordinary usage of hymns in the various offices of the Western Church had become fixed. The clergy and the monks had become the principal poets. In contrast to the early Greek and Latin hymns, the texts were no longer confined to the praise of the Creator and of the persons of the Trinity, but had become more mystical, subjective, devout. They became meditations on the Passion and wounds of Christ (see **418**), on the sweet name of Jesus (**82**), in praise of the Virgin, especially the moving thirteenth-century *Stabat Mater,* on the joys of Paradise (**303**), and on the terrors of judgment, notably the great thirteenth-century *Dies Irae.*

Under the enervating and over-sentimental influence of conventual life, Latin hymnody in the late Middle Ages suffered the same decadence which Reformation hymnody was later to experience at the hands of the Pietists and as English hymnody was to experience in the gospel song movement in America. Most of the extensive deposit of Latin hymnody down through the eighteenth century remains unknown except to specialists.

Translations of anonymous Latin hymns dating from the seventh to the eighteenth century are hymns **78, 82, 298, 354, 386, 391, 418, 443, 447,** and **814.**

The two most important translators of Latin and Greek hymns were Edward Caswall, 1814-1878, an Anglican become Roman Catholic, and John Mason Neale, 1816-1866, both of whom made conspicuous contributions to the Oxford Movement. Caswall published about two hundred translations of Latin hymns in his *Lyra Catholica,* 1849. Our hymnal retains 3: hymns **82, 91,** and **405.**

John Mason Neale was the most learned and capable hymnologist of his day. As a translator of Latin and Greek hymns he surpasses all others. His translations from the Latin appeared in his *Mediaeval Hymns and Sequences* in three editions: 1851, 1863, 1867; in *The Hymnal Noted,* in two parts, 1851 and 1854, in which Neale translated ninety-four out of the 105 hymns; and in *Hymns, Chiefly Mediaeval, on the Joys and Glories of Paradise,* 1865. Our hymnal reprints nine of Neale's Latin translations: hymns **78, 298, 303, 354, 357, 391, 424, 451,** and **814.**

Neale's Greek translations appeared in his *Hymns of the Eastern Church,* 1862. Like his Latin translations, these are adaptations rather than translations, some of them indeed being virtually original hymns. In any case, they are a priceless heritage. Our hymnal reprints five of these Greek translations: hymns **99, 238, 437, 446,** and **491.**

The five most recent translations of Latin and Greek texts in our hymnal are one from the Greek of Clement of Alexandria, by Kendrick Grobel, made in 1962 for this hymnal (84); two by F. Bland Tucker, one from the Latin of Abelard (427) and one from the Greek of the Didache (307) done in 1938 and 1939 respectively; one by Percy Dearmer of a hymn attributed to Gregory the Great (504), translated for *The English Hymnal,* 1906; and one by Robert S. Bridges from the Latin of Ambrose (29), done for his *Yattendon Hymnal,* 1899.

German Hymnody

The church hymn as commonly understood, that is, as a religious lyric sung by the congregation in public worship, was born with and popularized by the Lutheran Reformation. Before the hymn as we know it could become possible, three developments had to take place: (1) Poetry had to move away from the irregular rhythms of prose toward the carefully regulated recurring accents of the lyric poem. The use of a rhyme scheme itself brought poetry nearer to music. (2) Music itself had to move from the restlessness of modality to the security, even secularity, of tonality with its full cadence and home note, so making possible the repetition of the same melody for any number of stanzas. (3) The centrality of the congregation or the rediscovery of the laity in worship, the priesthood of all believers, had to be affirmed and insisted upon. This required hymns in the vernacular language set to familiar secular tunes.

In the late Middle Ages indeed, the use of hymns was widespread, but they were sung in Latin, usually at high festivals and predominantly by clergy and choir. Luther democratized the use of music in church by restoring the hymn to the whole body of believers, giving it a place of honor in the service and even substituting his metrical paraphrase of the Creed "We all believe in one God" (see e.g. 463) for the prose form in his "German Mass." Further, by opening the way for poets to create fresh statements of the Lutheran faith and for musicians to make use of the native folk song already intelligible to and fervently enjoyed by the people, Luther made the chorale stand for the believer's direct access to God, the very symbol of the layman's rights and privileges in the gospel, a formidable weapon for the promotion of the faith.

Luther himself was the first of the Reformation hymnists. He began writing in 1523, soon after he had completed his translation of the New

Testament. In 1524 he wrote no less than twenty-one of his thirty-seven hymns, and the last two in 1543. Our hymnal prints three (20, 438, 526) of his hymns, two of which are psalm paraphrases (20 and 526). His "A mighty fortress" remains one of the most powerful statements of faith in the entire range of Christian literature.

The first German Reformation hymnal, *Etlicher christlicher Lieder Lobgesänge,* or the *Achtliederbuch,* appeared in 1524. Four of the eight hymns were by Luther. The Erfurt *Enchiridion,* also 1524, contained twenty-five hymns, of which eighteen were Luther's. So rapid was its growth that the fifth edition (1553) of Klug's *Geistliche Lieder* (Wittenberg, 1529) contained 131 hymns.

Two of the greatest chorales come out of the very end of the sixteenth century. Philipp Nicolai's "Wake, awake" (366) and "O Morning Star" (399). The second of these is somewhat of a departure from the bold, confident, objective hymns of Luther and introduces the series of German Jesus hymns in which the sentiment of the love of the soul for the heavenly bridegroom finds fervent expression.

Our hymnal prints three important hymns from the tragic period of the Thirty Years' War, 1618-1648: hymn 412 by Johann Heermann, hymn 363 by Georg Weissel, and hymn 49 by Martin Rinkart.

German hymnody now moves from the churchly and confessional to the pietistic and devotional type of hymn. From the period from Paul Gerhardt to Philip Jacob Spener, 1648-1676, four hymn writers have hymns in our hymnal: Paul Gerhardt, Johann Franck, Johann Rist, and Georg Neumark. Gerhardt, the ablest German hymn writer of the seventeenth century, credited with 123 hymns, has contributed five (51, 132, 259, 379, 418); Franck, two (220, 318); and Neumark, one (210). Although Rist is said to have produced some 680 hymns, not too many have been translated into English. "Break forth, O beauteous heavenly light" (373) has been popularized by its inclusion in Bach's *Christmas Oratorio.*

John Wesley was sufficiently interested in Johann Scheffler, 1624-1677, a mystic who later became a Roman Catholic, to translate four of his hymns. The most widely used of these is "Thee will I love, my strength, my tower," which may be seen in *The Methodist Hymn-Book* (London, 1933).

In the late seventeenth and eighteenth centuries the Pietist and Moravian movements produced a great number of hymn writers.

Both movements represented a reaction against the scholasticism and formalism of the Lutheran Church in favor of a more personal, experiential, lushly devotional type of Christian life. As was later to be the case with Methodism in England, the founders of all these Reformation revivals were themselves hymn writers: Philip Jacob Spener, 1635-1705, and August Hermann Francke, 1663-1727, the founders of Pietism, who remained within the state church; and Nicolaus Ludwig Count von Zinzendorf, 1700-1760, who organized the Moravian movement as a separate community on the remnant of the Bohemian and Moravian Brethren or *Unitas Fratrum.*

Of the large number of Pietist hymn writers only Benjamin Schmolck, 1672-1737, finds recognition in our hymnal. Hymn 13 is included for the first time in an American Methodist hymnal. Hymn 167, in our hymnals since 1878, has long been a favorite, perhaps made popular by Carl Maria von Weber's romantic tune from *Der Freischütz,* discarded in 1964. Among John Wesley's thirty-three translations from the German, eight lyrics come from the Pietist group, from C. F. Richter, Johann A. Freylinghausen, Gottfried Arnold, Joachim Lange, Ernst Lange, and W. C. Dessler.

Count von Zinzendorf was the most productive of the Moravian hymn writers, writing some two thousand hymns. He is often compared to Charles Wesley in fervor, intensity, and productivity. For the English hymnbook of the Moravians 205 of his hymns have been translated. John Wesley translated eight of Zinzendorf's hymns, two of which (127, 213) have been included in all Methodist hymnals. Wesley also translated one hymn of A. G. Spangenberg, 1704-1792, bishop of the Moravians and long resident in America.

Two very important hymn writers from this period belonged to the German Reformed Church, Joachim Neander of Bremen and Gerhardt Tersteegen, who published 111 of his hymns in his *Geistliches Blumengärtlein,* 1729. Neander's fine hymn "Praise to the Lord, the Almighty" (55) entered our hymnal in 1935. John Wesley's translation of Tersteegen's *"Verborgne Gottesliebe du"* (531) has been included in all Methodist hymnals. Hymn 105 is a second Tersteegen hymn printed in our hymnals beginning with 1878. The opening hymn 788 offers one stanza of "Gott ist gegenwärtig." John Wesley translated this hymn also, beginning "Lo, God is here! Let us adore."

Of the remaining translations of German originals in our hymnal, one hymn is from the sixteenth century (**389**), five from the seventeenth century (**91, 258, 257, 463, 4**), three from the eighteenth century (**513, 209, 124**), and two from the nineteenth (**91, 393**).

That there should be only two translations of nineteenth- and no twentieth-century German hymns does not of itself indicate a dearth of German hymn writing in these latter centuries. It is always the translators who determine which foreign language hymns get Englished. That "Silent night" and "When morning gilds the skies" are the two indicates the rather limited sentimental tastes which prevailed among nineteenth-century English-speaking churchmen. Further, the great wealth of native hymns in England and America left little room for translations from other languages. The hymnbooks were full of homemade products.

The importance of the translator in selecting originals and creating English hymns out of them merits a brief consideration of the translators who have done the most in making the temper of German hymns an important part of our tradition. Of special interest for us are the thirty-three translations of German hymns which John Wesley made while in Georgia, between February 6, 1736, and December 2, 1737. As we have already noted, five of the thirty-three are included in our 1964 hymnal.

The two German hymnals available to Wesley were (1) the hymnal of the Brethren, the *Herrnhut Gesangbuch,* the first edition of which in 1735 had 991 hymns and (2) Freylinghausen's *Neues geistreiches Gesangbuch,* 1714, with 815 hymns. In selecting hymns from these collections, Wesley brought together representatives of Lutheran orthodoxy and the Pietism of both Halle and Herrnhut. Although these hymns were heavily weighted with the subjective devotional type of Jesus hymn, Wesley was sufficiently well schooled in the psalms and in the Anglican liturgy to maintain God as the center, to insist on grace as God's activity on man, and to prune the over-lush accounts of inner feelings, even erotic language, from some of Zinzendorf's hymns. Wesley's chief concern was to enable the objective doctrines of the church to become actualized in the experience of Christians.

Because of the formative influence of the German hymns on the Christian understanding and experience of the Wesleys, John's translations and the two brothers' promotion of these hymns were to have very far-reaching effects on subsequent English hymnody. Although

Calvin was to determine that the psalms, not hymns, should be the prevailing song of the English Reformation, Isaac Watts and the Wesleys together brought to an end the reign of the metrical psalter, making the free hymn the prevailing type of congregational song. It was through the Wesleys that the warmth and personal intensity of the German hymns first became an important ingredient in English hymnody.

The most important nineteenth-century promoters of German hymns include Frances E. Cox, *Sacred Hymns from the German,* 1841 (4), Henry J. Buckoll, *Hymns, Translated from the German,* 1842 (258), Arthur T. Russell, *Psalms and Hymns, Partly Original, Partly Selected,* 1851 (389), Richard Massie, *Martin Luther's Spiritual Songs,* 1854 (438), the Borthwick sisters, Jane and Sarah (Mrs. Eric J. Findlater), *Hymns from the Land of Luther,* first and second series, 1854, 1855 (105, 167, 209), and above all Catherine Winkworth, who published *Lyra Germanica* in two series, 1855, 1858, and her *Chorale Book for England,* 1863. More Winkworth translations are more widely used than any other translations from any other language. Our hymnal prints fourteen (13, 49, 55, 210, 220, 257, 318, 363, 366, 379, 399, 463, 526, 784).

The only American translators of German hymns included in our hymnal are J. W. Alexander (418), F. H. Hedge (20), and J. F. Young (393).

The Metrical Psalters

Although Luther was well aware of the importance of the psalms in Christian worship and continued their use, he likewise cherished the hymn tradition established in the Latin Church and proceeded to foster new hymns of free composure. Calvin, however, excluded from public worship all nonbiblical materials. Aware of the unbroken continuity of the use of the psalms from temple and synagogue on down through the historic churches, both east and west, he wanted nothing else. But if the public worship needs of the newly discovered laity were to be met, the psalms had to be turned to meter and provided with tunes. Therefore, where Calvin prevailed, at Geneva, Strassburg, England, and Scotland, the popular music of the Reformation took the form of the metrical psalm, not the hymn. Calvin tried his own hand at versifying but was not happy with his work. Fortunately

Clément Marot, an accomplished poet who had adopted Huguenot views, was available in Paris. Some thirty of his psalms, published in 1542, quickly gained great popularity. On fleeing from Paris to Geneva under indictment for heresy, Marot completed his *Fifty Psalms*, a collection published posthumously in 1544. Theodore de Bèze, at Calvin's request, versified the remaining one hundred, thus completing the French Psalter by 1551-52. These psalms with their new tunes, particularly those by Louis Bourgeois and Claude Goudimel, became quickly popular, even to the extent of playing an important part in shaping the metrical psalters of England and Scotland.

In the meantime, English Protestants, whether at home or as refugees on the continent, were experimenting with English versions of the psalter. Thomas Sternhold started a psalter a little later than Marot. Sometime before his death in 1549 he had done nineteen psalms. After his death thirty-seven were published. John Hopkins continued this work and in 1551 added seven.

With the accession of Queen Mary to the throne, the leaders of the Reformation took refuge in Geneva (1553), and while there, in 1556, published a collection of *One and Fifty Psalms of David in English Metre*. This collection contained the forty-four psalms of Sternhold and Hopkins then available and seven others done by William Whittingham. The next edition, 1558, contained twenty-four versions by William Kethe, among them the important version of Psalm 100, "All people that on earth do dwell." Kethe continued the work of translation in Geneva until the entire psalter became versified. Published in 1562, it became popularly known as the Sternhold and Hopkins Psalter. Licensed for use in public worship, it was bound with the Bible and continued to be printed as the authorized version until the second decade of the nineteenth century. For further information on the early psalters, see comments under "All people that on earth do dwell," pp. 79-80.

However, the making of psalters did not cease, and before the end of the seventeenth century, two Irishmen, Nahum Tate and Nicolas Brady, were given the task of preparing a new version. They completed this in 1696. Although this version met with much hostility, it gained prestige by assuming the name "New Version," thereby fixing the sobriquet "Old Version" on Sternhold-Hopkins.

The important Scottish Psalter of 1650, a separate offshoot from the earlier Sternhold-Hopkins Psalter and used to this day in Scotland, has its own importance. And of special interest to Americans is the *Bay Psalm Book* of 1640, the first book printed in English on the North American continent. The purpose of the New England Puritans was to secure a version of the psalms which would be more close-fitting to the Hebrew than the Sternhold-Hopkins Psalter was. This psalter went through some fifty editions in New England, Scotland, and England itself.

Some idea of the long and widespread use of metrical psalms in English may be gained from observing the list of complete and partial versions of the psalms in English from 1414 to 1889 as printed in the *Dictionary of Hymnology*. John Julian lists 326 items.

Our hymnal includes psalms from the following psalters: Sternhold and Hopkins, 1562 (21); the Scottish Psalter, 1650 (68, 295); Tate and Brady, 1696 (54, 56, 255); *The Complete Psalmodist*, 1749 (443, stanza 2); Scottish *Translations and Paraphrases*, 1781 (361); the United Presbyterian *Book of Psalms*, 1871 (65, 216); and the United Presbyterian Psalter, 1912 (44, 57, 512).

A complete list of psalm hymns in our hymnal is given in the index of the hymnal under No. 847.

Isaac Watts

Isaac Watts belonged to that group of Puritans known as Independents and later as Congregationalists who rejected the authority of both the presbytery and the episcopacy. Confronted with the fact that in the churches of his time congregational participation in public worship was limited to singing, Watts set out to see that this "sacrifice of praise" should be made as meaningful as possible. At this time, hymn singing was strictly opposed in the established and dissenting churches alike, both in England and Scotland. Although Watts was not the first to write English hymns of "free composure," he deserves to be called the "father of the English hymn" because he proved able to write free hymns so effectively that eventually the hymn displaced the metrical psalm as the basic form of congregational praise. The "reign of Watts" lasted for 150 years.

The epoch-making work of Watts rests, first, upon his bold repudiation of the Calvinist principle that only scripture should be sung in church and that the psalter alone was adequate for Christian worship. Second, being a better poet than previous psalm versifiers, he rejected

27

the practice of making the psalm paraphrases "close-fitting" to the Hebrew. And third, of chief importance was his theological boldness in rejecting portions of the psalms as unfit for Christian use, in christianizing some psalms by teaching David "to speak like a Christian," and even more important, in writing hymns which made no pretense to being psalm paraphrases. Thus his insistence was that the church song should be fully evangelical and not just a supplement to the psalms, that it should be freely composed and not just hold to the letter of scripture, and that it should give straightforward expression to the thoughts and feelings of the singers and not merely recall events of the distant past.

Only a poet who could write so noble a hymn as "When I survey the wondrous cross" could have successfully built a bridge from psalmody to hymnody and set the church free to create a living body of Christian praise in song. Although Watts's hymns are not "arrayed in the purple and fine linen of glittering diction," their simple, direct language, their plain words of one syllable, their glad healthful faith in God as Creator and Redeemer have given them enduring value.

Watts's first volume of verse, *Horae Lyricae,* bears the date of 1706. Book I contains twenty-five hymns and four psalm paraphrases together with other religious pieces. The body of his hymns appeared in *Hymns and Spiritual Songs in Three Books. I Collected from the Scriptures. II Compos'd on Divine Subjects. III Prepared for the Lord's Supper* (London, 1707). The hymns numbered 210, followed by a group of doxologies, at least three of which may be termed hymns. There were seventy-eight paraphrases in Book I, 110 "free composures" in Book II, and twenty-two hymns in Book III. In 1709 a second corrected and enlarged edition was published to include 145 additional hymns.

By 1719 Watts was able "to see a good part of the Book of Psalms fitted for the use of our Churches, and *David* converted into a Christian," for in that year he published *The Psalms of David, Imitated in the Language of the New Testament, and Apply'd to the Christian State and Worship.* The book contained versions of 138 psalms, excluding twelve and some passages of those rejected as unfit for Christian use.

Of much interest and great historic importance is Watts's *Divine Songs Attempted in Easy Language, for the Use of Children,* 1715, a book which was constantly reprinted for a century. John Wesley's last published collection, *Hymns for Children,* 1790, chosen from his brother's *Hymns for Children and Others of Riper Years,* 1763, represents the continuation of the work in hymns for children begun by Watts.

Our 1964 hymnal includes twenty hymns by Watts: none from *Horae Lyricae;* six from *Hymns and Spiritual Songs,* 1707 (5, 31, 134, 415, 435, 810), and one from its second edition, 1709 (533); one from *Divine Songs,* 1715 (37); eleven from *The Psalms of David,* 1719 (9, 14, 22, 24, 25, 28, 39, 365, 392, 472, 789); and one (239) from the end of Sermon No. 31, date unknown. Of these twenty hymns, twelve are psalm paraphrases.

In the seventeenth century in English-speaking lands the psalms alone were authorized for use in church song, with a few hymns tolerated in an appendix. In the next stage of development, the psalms still have priority, but only selected psalms are used, while hymns have rather equal place. In the third stage, hymns have risen to the dominant position with such psalms as are used being treated as hymns and in the organization of hymnals are conformed to the Christian year rather than to the psalter.

If Watts is to be credited with opening the doors to the free hymn, it was the Wesleys who were to be the major factor in crowding the gates with thankful praise.

John and Charles Wesley

Although the Wesleys were born into a family of poets and poetry-lovers and were well aware of the epoch-making work of Watts, they first discovered the power of congregational hymn singing from the Germans on that memorable voyage to Georgia in 1735. The immediate result was John Wesley's publication in 1737 of his *Collection of Psalms and Hymns,* Charleston, S.C., the first hymnal printed in America and described by Winfred Douglas in *Church Music in History and Practice* as the "first real Anglican hymnal." The book included forty hymns for Sunday, twenty for the fast days, Wednesday, and Friday, and ten for Saturday. Of the seventy, thirty-five are from Watts, seven from John Austin, six adapted from George Herbert, five from John's elder brother Samuel, Jr., six from their father, five translations from the German done by John, and three from Addison. It is notable that the 1737 hymnal contained no hymn by Charles. His hymns first began to appear in the third of the Wesleyan collections, *Hymns and Sacred Poems* (London, 1739). Once Charles began to write, his output ceased only with death. Year after year, between 1738 and 1785 the Wesleys kept publishing large and small collections to the number of some sixty-four separate collections, edited either by John or Charles or put out under both names. These are listed in John Julian's *Dictionary of Hymnology,* pp. 1259-60.

John's main contribution to the work was his translations from the German and his lifelong devotion to selecting, editing, and publishing hymns, mostly those of Charles, although he himself wrote an undetermined number of original hymns. Charles was the poet of the Methodist revival, some say the great hymn writer of the ages, being credited with at least 6,500 hymns.

The most important of the Wesley hymnals is *A Collection of Hymns for the Use of the People Called Methodists* (London, 1780), sometimes called the "Large Hymnbook." It included 525 hymns all taken from the brothers' previous publications and all but ten written by members of the Wesley family. The preface to this hymnal so well sets forth John's understanding of the nature and function of a hymnal that it deserves printing in full.

For many years I have been importuned to publish such a hymn-book as might be generally used in all our congregations throughout Great Britain and Ireland. I have hitherto withstood the importunity, as I believed such a publication was needless, considering the various hymn-books which my brother and I have published within these forty years last past; so that it may be doubted whether any religious community in the world has a greater variety of them.

But it has been answered, 'Such a publication is highly needful upon this very account; for the greater part of the people, being poor, are not able to purchase so many books: and those that have purchased them are, as it were, bewildered in the immense variety. A proper collection of hymns for general use, carefully made out of all these books, is therefore still wanting; and one comprised in so moderate a compass, as to be neither cumbersome nor expensive.'

It has been replied, 'You have such a collection already, (entitled "Hymns and Spiritual Songs,") which I extracted several years ago from a variety of hymn-books.' But it is objected, 'This is in the other extreme; it is far too small. It does not, it cannot, in so narrow a compass, contain variety enough:

not so much as we want, among whom *singing* makes so considerable a part of the public service. What we want is, a collection not too large, that it may be cheap and portable; not too small, that it may contain a sufficient variety for all ordinary occasions.'

Such a Hymn-Book you have now before you. It is not so large as to be either cumbersome, or expensive: and it is large enough to contain such a variety of hymns, as will not soon be worn threadbare. It is large enough to contain all the important truths of our most holy religion, whether speculative or practical; yea, to illustrate them all, and to prove them both by Scripture and reason; and this is done in a regular order. The hymns are not carelessly jumbled together, but carefully ranged under proper heads, according to the experience of real Christians. So that this book is, in effect, a little body of experimental and practical divinity.

As but a small part of these hymns is of my own composing,* I do not think it inconsistent with modesty to declare, that I am persuaded no such hymn-book as this has yet been published in the English language. In what other publication of the kind have you so distinct and full an account of scriptural Christianity? such a declaration of the heights and depths of religion, speculative and practical? so strong cautions against the most plausible errors; particularly those that are now most prevalent? and so clear directions for making your calling and election sure; for perfecting holiness in the fear of God?

May I be permitted to add a few words with regard to the *poetry?* Then I will speak to those who are judges thereof, with all freedom and unreserve. To these I may say, without offence, 1. In these hymns there is no doggerel; no botches; nothing put in to patch up the rhyme; no feeble expletives. 2. Here is nothing turgid or bombast, on the one hand, or low and creeping, on the other. 3. Here are no *cant* expressions; no words without meaning. Those who impute this to us know not what they say. We talk common sense, both in prose and verse, and use no word but in a fixed and determinate sense. 4. Here are, allow me to say, both the purity, the strength, and the elegance of the English language; and, at the same time, the utmost simplicity and plainness, suited to every capacity. Lastly, I desire men of taste to judge, (these are the only competent judges,) whether there be not in some of the following hymns the true spirit of poetry, such as cannot be acquired by art and labour, but must be the gift of nature. By labour a man may become a tolerable imitator of Spenser, Shakespeare, or Milton; and may heap together pretty compound epithets, as *pale-eyed, meek-eyed,* and the like; but unless he be *born* a poet, he will never attain the genuine spirit of poetry.

And here I beg leave to mention a thought which has been long upon my

* The greater part was composed by the Reverend Charles Wesley.

mind, and which I should long ago have inserted in the public papers, had I not been unwilling to stir up a nest of hornets. Many gentlemen have done my brother and me (though without naming us) the honour to reprint many of our hymns. Now they are perfectly welcome so to do, provided they print them just as they are. But I desire, they would not attempt to mend them: for they really are not able. None of them is able to mend either the sense or the verse. Therefore, I must beg of them one of these two favours: either to let them stand just as they are, to take them for better or worse; or to add the true reading in the margin, or at the bottom of the page; that we may no longer be accountable either for the nonsense or for the doggerel of other men.

But to return. That which is of infinitely more moment than the spirit of poetry, is the spirit of piety. And I trust, all persons of real judgment will find *this* breathing through the whole Collection. It is in this view chiefly, that I would recommend it to every truly pious reader, as a means of raising or quickening the spirit of devotion; of confirming his faith; of enlivening his hope; and of kindling and increasing his love to God and man. When Poetry thus keeps its place, as the handmaid of Piety, it shall attain, not a poor perishable wreath, but a crown that fadeth not away.

JOHN WESLEY

London, *Oct. 20, 1779.*

The Wesleys are credited with bringing into existence two new kinds of hymns, the evangelistic hymn and the hymn of Christian experience. If Watts's hymns were consistently and gloriously objective, free from introspection, the Wesley hymns were often autobiographical, bringing to moving expression the rapture of the soul in its response to the wonder and love of God as proclaimed in the gospel. It is revelatory of the genius of the Methodist movement that for many years the first hymn in Methodist collections was "O for a thousand tongues" and the second, "Come, sinners, to the gospel feast."

Of importance also are the many hymns written for celebration of the festivals of the Christian year, preparing the way for a liturgical hymnody. Charles has contributed enduring hymns on the Nativity, Resurrection, Ascension, Pentecost, and for many other special occasions. Of particular importance is his collection of *Hymns on the Lord's Supper,* 1745, the eleventh edition of which was published in 1825. This collection included 166 hymns, some of them being among Wesley's finest.

Our 1964 hymnal lists ten hymns under John's name, of which five are translations from the German, one (492) an original hymn, one (812) a reprint of the doxology in hymn 492, and three (9, 22, 28) John's alteration of Watts. The hymns of Charles number seventy-three. This contrasts with 54 in 1935, 120 in 1905, 307 in 1878, and 558 in 1849.

The Broadening Stream of English Hymns

Watts and Wesley are the giants of English hymnody, but of course they were not the first nor the last English hymn makers. The tributaries of the ever-widening river run far back into the seventeenth century. The translation of *Veni, Creator Spiritus* (467) by John Cosin, 1594-1672, is the most widely used translation of that Latin hymn, having found a secure place in the ordination service. As a poet, George Herbert, 1593-1633, is without a peer in the earlier group. He was, indeed, not a hymn writer, but we have seen that John Wesley had already adapted six of his lyrics for hymn use in the 1737 Charleston *Collection*. And in Wesley's third collection, *Hymns and Sacred Poems* (London, 1739), these were increased to forty-two adaptations. But exquisite as Herbert's lyrics are, Wesley's alterations could only injure them as poems without making them acceptable as hymns. Only "Antiphon" (10) survives in our present hymnal.

Thomas Ken, 1637-1710, is known for his straightforward morning and evening hymns (180, 493) and especially for the most widely used of all Long Meter doxologies. John Bunyan, 1628-1688, did not intend to write hymns, but his "He who would valiant be" (155) from *Pilgrim's Progress* has a place in many hymnals. Richard Baxter, 1615-1691, is represented by "Lord, it belongs not to my care" (218). Our three hymns by Joseph Addison, 1672-1719, first appeared in the *Spectator* (43, 52, 70).

Philip Doddridge, 1702-1751, a friend of Watts, who welcomed Wesley's hymns, wrote some four hundred hymns, most of which were first published posthumously by Job Orton, 1755. John Julian affirms that some eighty of his hymns are in common use. Our hymnal retains seven (53, 128, 249, 312, 325, 335, 509). John Cennick, 1718-1755, has contributed two hymns to our hymnal (300, 518). He also provided the inspiration and some of the words for Charles Wesley's "Lo, he comes with clouds descending" (364).

Edward Perronet has written one immortal hymn—"All hail the

power of Jesus' name" **(71, 72, 73)**. Augustus Montague Toplady, 1740-1778, an intense and cantankerous Calvinist associated with the chapels of the Countess of Huntingdon, has written one hymn which historically has vied with all others as the most popular hymn in the English language, "Rock of Ages" **(120)**. See also hymn **147.**

But none of the Calvinist hymn writers were so richly productive as William Cowper, 1731-1800, and John Newton, 1725-1807. Their joint venture, *Olney Hymns, in Three Books,* 1779, containing 348 hymns, of which Cowper contributed 67, is one of the truly great collections. Rough-hewn and powerful, yet tender and moving, the best of these hymns have been greatly cherished. Our hymnal includes five from Cowper **(98, 215, 231, 268, 421)** and five from Newton **(81, 92, 293, 334, 489)**.

Four nineteenth-century women writers may be mentioned: Charlotte Elliott **(119, 144)**, Jeannette Threlfall **(423)**, Elizabeth Clephane **(417)**, and Frances Ridley Havergal, the most productive of the group. John Julian lists some sixty of her hymns in common use. Our hymnal includes hymns **179, 187, 195, 274.**

Born in the eighteenth century but whose hymns were published in the nineteenth was Thomas Kelly, 1769-1854, a fiery Irishman whose archbishop forbade him to preach in a consecrated building, who wrote 765 hymns over a period of fifty-one years. John Julian lists about ninety of these in common use, but his two best hymns are those in our hymnal **(453, 458)**. Of greater importance was the Moravian James Montgomery, 1771-1855, whose hymns were variously published in his *Christian Psalmist,* 1825, his *Original Hymns,* 1853, and other collections. It has been written of him that "there is no writer, Charles Wesley himself not excepted, who has ranged so widely and with such unerring touch over the whole gamut of hymnody." Julian lists more than one hundred of his four hundred hymns in common use. Our hymnal prints ten **(16, 211, 237, 252, 313, 316, 337, 359, 382, 434)**.

Two well-known Scotsmen, both clergy of the Free Church of Scotland, may be mentioned: Horatius Bonar, 1808-1889, and George Matheson, 1842-1906. Julian's *Dictionary of Hymnology* lists some ninety of Bonar's hymns in common use. Our hymnal includes two **(117, 326)**. Matheson's two popular hymns **(184, 234)** have been widely enjoyed.

Reginald Heber, 1783-1826, is of particular importance to Anglican hymnody. He has been described as the "creator of the modern church hymn-book." For his parish at Hodnet he provided a collection containing from one to four hymns illustrative of the Gospel and Epistle lessons for every Sunday and principal holy days and for other church occasions. The scope of this book is essentially the same as that of modern church collections. Published posthumously in 1827, the book was entitled *Hymns Written and Adapted to the Weekly Service of the Church Year.* Heber wrote fifty-seven of these hymns himself. Of these, five are retained in our hymnal: hymns **26, 320, 400, 419, 497.** Henry Hart Milman, 1791-1868, contributed thirteen hymns to the collection, of which one is retained for our hymnal **(425).**

Of three important hymn writers associated with the Oxford Movement, John Keble, 1792-1866, John Henry Newman, 1801-1890, and Frederick W. Faber, 1814-1863, the latter two became Roman Catholics. Three hymns of Keble **(276, 499, 502)** have long been printed in our hymnals. Newman is represented by "Lead, kindly light" **(272)** included in all hymnals. Of Faber's 150 hymns, two only are in our present hymnal **(69, 151).**

The most ambitious undertaking in hymn collections in the second half of the nineteenth century in the Church of England was the making of the important hymnal *Hymns Ancient and Modern,* 1860-61, an attempt to make a hymnal to suit high church needs. Begun under the chairmanship of Henry Williams Baker, 1821-1877, it has recently celebrated its one hundredth birthday, its last revision being done in 1950. Three hymns in our hymnal **(67, 99, 357)** have Baker's name attached to them. Baker was able to enlist the aid of other accomplished writers such as William C. Dix, 1837-1898 **(385, 397, 524),** William W. How, 1823-1897 **(108, 181, 372, 536),** Mrs. Cecil F. Alexander, 1818-1895 **(34, 107, 414),** and John S. B. Monsell, 1811-1875 **(62, 178, 240, 398).**

Hymns Ancient and Modern is still probably the most widely used hymnbook in the Church of England. In the present century, a new publication, *The English Hymnal,* of Anglo-Catholic sympathies, edited by Percy Dearmer and Ralph Vaughan Williams, 1906 and 1933, has gained wide circulation. A new type of hymnal, *Songs of Praise,* edited also by Percy Dearmer with Martin Shaw and Ralph Vaughan Williams as music editors, 1925 and 1931, was designed as a national hymnal. It includes many poems not found in previous hymnals, with some older hymns considerably altered and more humanitarian hymns introduced. On both text and tune side it has had an important influence on recent American hymnals. In 1965 a well-edited hymnal entitled *Anglican Hymn Book* was published to take the place of *The Hymnal Companion to the Book of Common Prayer* and *The Church Hymnal for the Christian Year*. And in 1967, a quite superb collection of hymns, both lyrically and musically, named *The Cambridge Hymnal*, was published, primarily suitable for use in universities.

A brief list of twentieth-century nonconformist hymnals in Britain would include *The Church Hymnary* (Presbyterian), 1927, *The Methodist Hymn Book* (London, 1933), *Congregational Praise*, 1951, the *BBC Hymn Book*, 1951, and *The Baptist Hymn Book*, 1962.

Hymns in America

When the Protestant English-speaking colonists came to the New World, they brought with them the prevailing psalters used at home, namely the "Old Version," Sternhold and Hopkins, of 1562; Henry Ainsworth's Psalter, printed in Holland in 1612, used by the Plymouth Colony; and the psalters of Francis Rous, 1643, and William Barton, 1644, in use among the Presbyterians in New York and to the South. The Puritans of the Bay Colony, however, wanted a more "close-fitting" translation and in 1640 produced the *Bay Psalm Book*, referred to earlier. This psalter reigned supreme in New England for more than a century.

After 1696 the "New Version," Tate and Brady, claimed recognition. Watts's *Horae Lyricae* and his *Psalms of David, Imitated in the Language of the New Testament* were known in New England almost as soon as they were published. His *Psalms* were reprinted in the colonies in Philadelphia by Benjamin Franklin in 1729. They sold slowly, however, and a later edition was not called for until 1741, the same year in which the first Boston edition appeared. *Hymns and Spiritual Songs* was printed first in Boston in 1739, in Philadelphia in 1742, in New York in 1752. It was John Wesley who first introduced Watts to church use by including thirty-five of his psalms and hymns in the 1737 *Collection*.

The controversy over the various psalters proved to be long and acrimonious, splitting congregations and synods. In the end, Watts generally prevailed. When Timothy Dwight, the president of Yale, under sponsorship of the Connecticut Association and the General Assembly of the Presbyterian Church prepared a new edition of Watts's *Psalms of David,* versifying the psalms Watts had omitted and altering others, he wrote in the "Advertisement" printed in the book:

Dr. Watts was a man of great eminence for learning, wisdom, and piety; and in usefulness to mankind has had few equals. As a poet, in writing a flowing happy stanza, familiar without affectation or obscurity, he has perhaps never been excelled. The design of evangelizing the Psalms, if I may be allowed the expression, was one of those happy thoughts which rarely occur, and will give his version a decided superiority over every other, as a vehicle for the praise of Christians.

Dwight's own paraphrase of Psalm 137, "I love thy kingdom, Lord" **(294)** is probably the earliest American hymn in use.

When the evangelist Asahel Nettleton responded to the demand to prepare a hymnal more suitable for the revivals sweeping the country, he wrote in the preface to his *Village Hymns for Social Worship,* 1824, designed as a supplement to the *Psalms and Hymns* of Watts:

With great satisfaction and pleasure have I often heard the friends of the Redeemer express their unqualified attachment to the sacred poetry of Dr. Watts. Most cordially do I unite with them in the hope, that no Selection of Hymns which has ever yet appeared may be suffered to take the place of his inimitable productions.

According to Louis F. Benson, this was the finest evangelical hymnbook yet made in America. It contained many standard English hymns and some by American authors. " 'Tis midnight, and on Olive's brow" **(431)** by William B. Tappan first appeared here.

For a discussion of American Methodist hymnody and the various hymnbooks, see the article by Carlton R. Young, "American Methodist Hymnbooks," pp. 54-61.

The Methodist movement from the beginning was meant to be an evangelistic movement, not to result in an established church. Its preachers were "traveling elders," itinerants. Their saddlebags were the symbol of the movement. As loyal as the General Conferences meant to be to Wesleyan hymnody, the camp meetings, which after

1800 spread like wildfire across the South and the West, were to demand a new type of song, untutored, lively, revivalistic, often coarse, without subtlety or depth of thought, and lacking in literary graces. Already in 1824 Asahel Nettleton had noted the problem. In the preface to his *Village Hymns,* mentioned above, he wrote:

There is a numerous class of hymns which have been sung with much pleasure and profit in seasons of revival, and yet are entirely destitute of poetic merit . . . I am satisfied from observation, as well as from the nature itself of such hymns, that they must be ephemeral. They should be confined to seasons of revival: and even here, they ought to be introduced with discretion; for on this, their principal utility must depend. A book, consisting chiefly of hymns for revivals, however important in its place, would be utterly unfit for the ordinary purposes of devotion—as prescriptions, salutary in sickness, are laid aside on the restoration of health.

In spite of Nettleton's directives, however, those who entered the Christian life through the camp meetings and revivals were by no means ready to abandon the songs which carried them into faith on entering the church door. Their joy in the gospel would have been quenched had they been denied the very hymns which mediated their ecstasy. The revivalistic type of the Christian faith came to its most intense and rapturous expression in the emotionally lush and oversentimental songs. And when the church in its official hymnals refused to recognize camp-meeting songs, and later gospel songs, the official hymnals would be stacked in the corner, and the paperback collections of "ephemeral" songs, often enough given status by hardback bindings, would take over. In the "nonliturgical" churches, at least, the history of hymnody in the American nineteenth and twentieth centuries has been characterized by this struggle between the "standard" hymns and "pop art" of one kind or another. In "advance guard" circles today, the "hardback" hymnal is as suspect as it was in the early years of the nineteenth century. If at the beginning of this century pop art took the form of camp-meeting songs, at the end of the century it took the form of the gospel song; now it is guitar music.

The two most prominent earlier promoters and fashioners of the gospel song, Ira David Sankey, 1840-1908, and Fanny Crosby, 1820-1915, were both Methodists. This type of hymn was born at New Castle, England, 1873, during the Moody-Sankey evangelistic campaign there. Sankey's *Sacred Songs and Solos* became successively enlarged from twenty-three numbers in 1873 to 1,200 in the last edition, 1903. His *Christian Choir* was issued in 1884 with seventy-five hymns and in 1896 with 281. Fifty million copies of Sankey's books were said to have been sold.

Fanny Crosby's hymns began to be published in 1864, and from that time until her death a stream of hymns numbering over 8,000 dropped from her pen. Our 1905 hymnal carried five of her hymns; the 1935 hymnal, seven; our present hymnal increased these to nine (110, 145, 159, 175, 176, 205, 224, 226, 443). Among American hymn writers in our hymnal, Fanny Crosby leads in the number of contributions.

Gospel song texts and tunes were born together. They satisfied both the common musical and religious desires of the times and so were multiplied like the loaves and the fishes. It is estimated that some 1,500 songbooks of this kind were published before 1900.

A quite distinctive type of song, a true folk song in that its origins cannot be precisely traced, is the "spiritual" or "American folk hymn" as the genre is called in our hymnal. Transmitted orally and sung by Negroes in slave days and after, some may be white spirituals, others black spirituals in origin. In any case, both texts and tunes constitute a unique body of folk song, simple and powerful, poignant and profound. Six of these now enter our hymnals for the first time (212, 286, 330, 404, 436). Hymn 40 is a Dakota Indian hymn; hymn 432 seems to be an early nineteenth-century southern folk hymn.

But if for more than a century the churches in which revivalistic patterns have prevailed—and this includes those which have supported the influential charismatic figures of Dwight L. Moody, Billy Sunday, and now Billy Graham—have been committed to the gospel song type, nevertheless, throughout the nineteenth century and beyond there has been a restrained but important production of "standard" church type hymns, many of which find an appropriate place in our hymnals. Our esteemed nineteenth-century poets have served us well, if sparingly. Our hymnal lists William Cullen Bryant with one hymn (345), John Greenleaf Whittier with five (157, 199, 235, 290, 347), Oliver Wendell Holmes with two (64, 270), and James Russell Lowell with one (242).

Samuel Longfellow, 1819-1892, and Samuel Johnson, 1822-1882, whose most important publication was the Unitarian hymnal

Hymns of the Spirit, 1864, deserve special mention. Our hymnal includes more of Longfellow's hymns than those of any other American writer except Fanny Crosby. The 1935 hymnal printed two of Johnson's hymns, "Life of ages, richly poured" and "City of God, how broad and far," the latter of which has found important use in England.

Theologically these hymns are congruent with most late nineteenth- and twentieth-century hymns which have increasingly become concerned with the redemption of the social order—"we"-hymns rather than "I"-hymns, hymns of the Christian community, and this-worldly rather than other-worldly. The best examples are those of Washington Gladden (**170**), Frank Mason North (**204, 407**), Milton S. Littlefield (**197**), William P. Merrill (**174, 548**), Calvin W. Laufer (**203, 482**), John Haynes Holmes (**200**), Walter Russell Bowie (**355, 481**), Ozora S. Davis (**189, 202**), S. Ralph Harlow (**173**), Earl Marlatt (**413, 462**), and Georgia Harkness (**161, 542**).

Nineteenth- and twentieth-century hymnals have become increasingly eclectic and ecumenical. This is spectacularly demonstrated by the makeup of recent Roman Catholic hymnals in which, e.g., Martin Luther's "A mighty fortress" is accepted as a favorite. Although in the changing emphases of the times some objections are made to hardback hymnals which are anthologies of 2,500 years of psalm and hymn making, the church can hardly do with the loss of its great tradition. It will undoubtedly continue to reappraise and preserve its significant past at the same time that it refuses to quench the Spirit and welcomes the good gifts yet to come.

The watchman still needs to stand upon the mountaintop to see what the signs of promise are. It is too soon to despair in tagging guitar music as "liturgical and artistic degeneration," as a throwing "out of the window more than 2,000 years of beauty." Such hymns as those in the Roman Catholic *Hymnal for Young Christians,* issued by F. E. L. Publications, 1967, and quantities of others like them will most certainly prove a significant stimulus to the creation of new hymns of praise which may give more significant expression to the Christian faith in forms yet to be made known than did the pop art of the nineteenth century. In any case, in the Father's house there are many rooms.

A Survey of Tunes
Austin C. Lovelace

Without a tune a poem cannot become a hymn; therefore, the tune, while subordinate to the text, is very important in determining whether a text will come to life through song.

Usually the text comes first, created by the poet in a particular meter or metrical pattern. Then, unless the poet was also a musician and composer, it is the job of a hymnal editor to find a tune which is created in the same meter and will match the mood of the text.

The Metrical System of Hymnody

The most common metrical designs are Common Meter (listed in the hymnal as CM), Short Meter (SM), and Long Meter (LM). When "D" is added to any of these (or any series of numbers), it stands for "Double" and means that the pattern is repeated. In Common Meter there are eight syllables in the first line of poetry, six in the second, eight in the third, and six in the fourth. Short Meter consists of six, six, eight, and six syllables, while Long Meter has four lines of poetry with eight syllables in each line. All of these meters, along with numerous others, use iambic movement; that is, the first syllable is unaccented, and the second is accented in any pair of syllables (∪/). The reverse of this pattern is called trochaic and begins with an accented syllable followed by a weak syllable (/∪). All hymns in 77.77. are trochaic, along with other meters which are based on the "falling foot." When an accent is followed by two weak syllables, the pattern is called "dactyllic" (/∪∪); when the two weak syllables precede the strong accent, the movement is called "anapestic" (∪∪/). AZMON (1) is an example of iambic; RATISBON (401) is trochaic; LOBE DEN HERREN (55) is dactyllic; and TRUE HAPPINESS (227) is anapestic.

A wide variety of meters is possible in poetry using only these four patterns because of the varying number of syllables in each line of poetry. It takes fourteen syllables to sing the first line of "Praise to the Lord, the Almighty" (55) but only three for the last line of "Angel voices, ever singing" (2). Where the text is none of the three basic patterns (CM, SM, or LM), numbers are used (at the upper right hand of the page) following the tune name to indicate the meter. A period is used to indicate which lines go together to make up a rhyme scheme or a grouping of lines which carry a single thought. For example, OLD 113TH (9) is listed as 888.888. since the rhyme scheme is AABCCB (breath–death, powers; past–last, endures—which is a false rhyme with "powers"). Yet ST. PETERSBURG (89) also with six lines of poetry is listed as 88.88.88. because of the rhyme scheme ABABCC (pose–vine; foes-mine; shame-name). Therefore the text of hymn 9 cannot be sung conveniently with the tune for hymn 89 although there are the same number of syllables in each line and the same number of lines. Likewise, an iambic tune such as AURELIA (297) cannot be substituted for ST. KEVIN (446) which is trochaic, though both are 76.76.

There are 140 different meters listed in the Metrical Index (850), ending with two categories listed "Irregular"—which means that the designs are so unusual that they refuse to fit into any standard pattern. (For a fuller study of the relation of meter to hymns and hymn tunes see Austin C. Lovelace, *The Anatomy of Hymnody,* 1964.)

Most hymns in the hymnal have a time signature, which indicates the number of pulses in a measure and what kind of note value receives a pulse. But in a few instances time signatures have been omitted. In general, none of the tunes from the Genevan Psalter have any time signature since most are conceived as proceeding with a steady pulse until the end of a line of poetry with varying numbers of pulses in the measures. Sometimes there may be three pulses in one measure, sometimes only two, but the pulse remains constant (see OLD 107TH, 468; and GENEVA 124, 469). Measure two of COMMAND-MENTS (307) should be sung as a syncopated three pulses, not two groupings of three quarter notes; but it would be impossible to indicate this properly with a time signature. Likewise, in plainsong, where every note is pulsed according to the word rhythm, no time signatures have been used (see ADORO TE, 326). To find the correct tempo of such tunes one need only determine what note value is pulsed and then choose a tempo which allows a single line to be sung in one breath without hurrying or dragging.

While hymn tunes must be able to stand alone as rhythmic melodies, harmonizations add a larger and new dimension. Where a tune occurs several times, different harmonizations have often been provided for variety. ITALIAN HYMN has two different versions at hymns 3 and 292. LASST UNS ERFREUEN has two harmonizations at hymns 19 and 60, and also appears with two different keys (D and E flat). Where tunes appear several times, two keys are often included—a higher key for a brighter text of praise and a lower key for a quieter, more meditative text. However, the organist should not hesitate to transpose to other keys when they will be more suitable for a given group of singers. The organist's edition and all hymnals copyrighted with an "F" or later letter include listings of the different keys.

For some hymns alternate tunes are printed side by side and given separate numbers (see hymns 71, 72, 73; 157, 158). But to save space in most instances suggested alternate tunes are merely listed. While "Stand up and bless the Lord" (16) is set to ST. MICHAEL, it also sings well to the familiar tune ST. THOMAS (5), and some congregations may prefer the alternate tune to that printed. Where a tune has been changed from the 1935 hymnal, the old tune is usually listed as an alternate (cf. hymn 42).

Plainsong

The simplest tunes in the hymnal are those of the psalm tones and ancient chants. Examples may be seen at the Opening Sentences beginning at 773, with Tone V and Tone II, only two of many chant formulae used to present prose text in orderly fashion. The intonations (opening notes) and inflections (closing notes) give the unique quality to each. Other examples may be seen at 670, 793, and 826. An example of Thomas Tallis' harmonization of a psalm tone is 805. Although chants have been included in most Methodist hymnals, many Methodists have not had much experience in chanting. Instructions on chanting may be found at 662 and should be used in teaching choirs and congregations how to chant the canticles, opening sentences, and other similar materials.

As these tones were further developed into more extended melodic patterns, plainsong developed. At first only one note was used for each syllable, but later development added melismatic passages containing several notes for one syllable, allowing the emotional nature of the text to unfold in purely musical terms. In general, however, the music was subservient to the text, and the inflections of the words were reflected in the rise and fall of the music, and there was no precise steady pulse of rhythm other than the rhythm of the text. Since plainsong was conceived as pure melody, ideally it should be sung without accompaniment.

JAM LUCIS (814) and CONDITOR ALME (78) have only one note per syllable and are relatively easy for any congregation. DIVINUM MYSTERIUM (357) is a bit more florid, while ADORO TE (326) is almost modern sounding with its basic major tonality. VENI EMMANUEL (354) and VENI CREATOR (467) are examples of adaptations of plainsong, maintaining the essential character but lacking the rhythmic freedom of the originals. The various Communion settings by John Merbecke originally were plainsong, but were arranged by him one note per syllable as directed by Archbishop Thomas Cranmer.

Anglican chants developed out of psalm tones. As previously noted, Thomas Tallis harmonized the tones (805), and the result was an emphasis on harmony rather than on melody. Settings by Boyce, Crotch, Farrant, and Aldrich may be seen at **664, 666, 667,** and **669** as examples of Anglican chant.

During the eighteenth century there developed French church melodies, an attempt among Catholics to use plainsong in a modern form. The result was a type of tune which does not sound very much like plainsong, but more like a regular hymn tune. Examples are DEUS TUORUM MILITUM (194) and CHRISTE SANCTORUM (504), the latter in the typical Sapphic Meter of 11 11 11.5.

German Tunes

The sources for the German chorale are plainsong, secular and popular song, and the music of the troubadours, trouvères, minnesingers, and meistersingers, who derived their forms from the litanies, hymns, and sequences of the Roman Catholic Church. A basic pattern of a phrase repeated (*Stollen*) followed by an answering phrase (*Abgesang*) may be seen in NUN FREUT EUCH (58) and even in Martin Luther's EIN' FESTE BURG (20). The Bohemian Brethren tune MIT FREUDEN ZART (4) also uses the same pattern but has a more modern tonal center. An example of the laudi spirituali, popular songs sung by the Flagellants of northern Italy, c. 1260, may be seen in a much abridged and altered form in ALTA TRINITA BEATA (815).

Popular dance tunes such as IN DULCI JUBILO (391), GREENSLEEVES (385), THE FIRST NOEL (383), and O FILII ET FILIAE (451) are all in triple time and come from Germany, England, and France. GOD REST

YOU MERRY (378), FRENCH CAROL (441), and TEMPUS ADEST FLORIDUM (395) are representative of other folk tunes which found their way into the church.

When Luther gave hymn singing back to the people, he borrowed tunes from many sources, but he also composed some tunes himself, of which EIN' FESTE BURG (20), VOM HIMMEL HOCH (281), and AUS TIEFER NOT (526) are typical. Johann Walther's tune CHRIST LAG IN TODESBANDEN (438) is based on a phrase of the plainsong Easter sequence "Victimae Paschali." Nicolaus Hermann's tune LOBT GOTT, IHR CHRISTEN (389) is the first German tune in ballad meter (Common Meter) and repeats its fourth phrase. Its form suggests that it may have been borrowed from a secular song.

Most early German chorales have had their rhythm altered (and often emasculated) by the substitution of even note values for the more interesting original. Philipp Nicolai's WACHET AUF (366) in original rhythm should be compared with his WIE SCHÖN LEUCHTET DER MORGENSTERN (399) in Bach's harmonization and altered rhythm. Of interest to Methodists is the tune VATER UNSER (531), used by Luther for his versified form of the Lord's Prayer and included by John Wesley in his first tunebook for his translation of Tersteegen's hymn "Thou hidden love of God, whose height."

Other German tunes are Hassler's PASSION CHORALE (418), originally a secular love song; the subdued CHRISTUS, DER IST MEIN LEBEN (44); the exuberant GELOBT SEI GOTT (449) by Melchior Vulpius; and Teschner's strong tune ST. THEODULPH (424). AVE VIRGO VIRGINUM (448) from Leisentritt's *Catholicum Hymnologium Germanicum*, 1584, is a fine example of a German Catholic tune with its interesting original rhythms.

Psalter Tunes

Paralleling the earliest German chorales are the Genevan Psalter tunes, starting with Matthew Greiter's OLD 113TH (9) in abbreviated form and including such strong, rhythmic tunes as OLD 100TH (21), COMMANDMENTS (307), and GENEVA 124 (469). OLD 107TH (468), while Genevan in origin, was taken over into the Scottish Psalter tradition, as was ST. MICHAEL (16), an extremely truncated and altered form. All of the Genevan tunes were intended to be sung in unison without any accompaniment, and the rhythmic design consisted of a whole pulse, two half pulses, a double pulse for closing notes, and a syncopated pattern (♩ ♪ ♪) which carried the important role of adding variety.

The English and Scottish churches borrowed the psalter tune as a result of their contacts in Geneva, France, and the Lowlands during exile under Queen Mary, but with the exception of a few irregular meters such as GENEVA 124 (469) and OLD 107TH (468), they created a body of tunes largely in Short, Common, and Long Meters. Examples are ST. FLAVIAN (313), SOUTHWELL (284), WINCHESTER OLD (54), DUN-FERMLINE (57), CAITHNESS (52), and DUNDEE (FRENCH) (215). Thomas Tallis composed several tunes in the same idiom, of which TALLIS' CANON (180) and TALLIS' ORDINAL (316) have continued in popularity. Orlando Gibbons also wrote a series of tunes from which have been adapted CANTERBURY (135) and SONG 46 (229), in similar style but with un-psalter type meters.

The austere and strong psalter tunes were followed after the restoration of the English monarchy in 1660 by tunes such as those of Jeremiah Clark (ST. MAGNUS, 458) and William Croft (ST. ANNE, 28; and ST. MATTHEW, 457) and the exuberant anonymous EASTER HYMN (439).

The Evangelical Period

During the evangelical period of the eighteenth century, tunes ranged from fairly straightforward tunes such as ST. BRIDE (51), DUKE STREET (14), and ST. THOMAS (5), to the more suave RICHMOND (12), KENT (350), and ST. STEPHEN (296), to the unabashedly florid IRISH (56), ST. MARTIN'S (507), MILES' LANE (73), and DIADEM (72). John Wesley also included in his collections SAVANNAH (309) and AMSTERDAM (15), taken from other sources but filled with typical evangelical fervor and exuberance.

During the same period German composers were contributing excellent tunes in a variety of meters and styles. Johann Crüger is represented in the new hymnal by five tunes, of which GRÄFENBERG (134) is perhaps the most popular and well known, although all are excellently crafted. The 1625 *As Hymnodus Sacer* is the source for HERR JESU CHRIST, MEIN'S LEBENS LICHT (127) and ACH GOTT UND HERR (532), both new to the Methodist hymnal. Ebeling's WARUM SOLLT ICH MICH DENN GRÄMEN (379) is almost carol-like. LOBE DEN HERREN (55) with its 14.14.4.7.8. meter is one of the most exuberant tunes ever written (it is hard to imagine that the same composer, Neander, could have written ARNSBERG, 788). UNSER HERRSCHER (7) gains its excitement through rhythm and wide melodic range; and WER NUR DEN LIEBEN GOTT (210) is returned to its original triple time after appearing in the 1935 hymnal in 4/4.

While earlier German tunes had used many meters and much rhythmic variety, in the harmonizations of Johann Sebastian Bach the move was toward stodgier rhythm and more florid harmonization, the movement and coloration coming from the supporting voices beneath the melody. In general the congregation should sing the melody and let the choir sing the moving parts. A comparison of WIE SCHÖN LEUCHTET DER MORGENSTERN (399), with Bach's harmonization, and WACHET AUF (366), with its original rhythm, will indicate the difference between early German chorales and the later harmonizations by Bach. One original tune by Bach is included, ICH HALTE TREULICH STILL (253).

Later German tunes of the eighteenth and nineteenth centuries, while tuneful and useful, do not have the individuality and fine craftsmanship of earlier chorales. Examples are RATISBON (401), STUTTGART (63), FRANCONIA (141), O JESU (219), and ALLGÜTIGER, MEIN PREISGESANG (285).

English Tunes

Since 1900 most American hymnals have borrowed heavily from the nineteenth-century English tunes. William H. Havergal made adaptations of old tunes, giving us FRANCONIA (141) and WINCHESTER NEW (102), while Richard Redhead published a collection of his own tunes, of which only REDHEAD 76 (113) has survived. Thomas Helmore is responsible for presenting for modern use DIVINUM MYSTERIUM (357) and VENI EMMANUEL (354) in altered form.

The Oxford Movement, which looked back to Greek and Latin hymnody for knowledge and inspiration, also looked ahead in the field of hymnody. The book which has made the greatest impact on contemporary tune usage is the famous *Hymns Ancient and Modern* (1st music ed. in 1861), which went through many editions, the last in 1950, and has sold more than 100,000,000 copies. William H. Monk (eight listings in the new hymnal) was the original musical editor, whose keen insight first wedded EVENTIDE (289), NICAEA (26), MELITA (407), RATISBON (401), DIX (35), ST. THEODULPH (424), and ST. ANNE (28) to the texts to which they are still almost inseparably wedded.

It has been fashionable for many years to condemn all Victorian tunes of the nineteenth century, but to do so is musically dishonest. While it is true that their tendency toward saccharine melody and harmony is typical of "the flight from reason, and from the tensions and controversies to which reason leads," it is also true that some of their tunes are eminently singable and "right" for the texts which they serve. Erik Routley, quoted above, has given an honest and fair appraisal of their work in his *Music of Christian Hymnody,* Chapter 17. It is recommended that all of the tunes by John B. Dykes, Arthur Sullivan, Samuel S. Wesley, Henry J. Gauntlett, Henry Smart, Edward J. Hopkins, William H. Monk, Joseph Barnby, George J. Elvey, and John Goss be examined for a full view of the nineteenth-century hymn tune scene.

With the turn of the century there came several English composers who turned the tide toward a more honest type of hymn tune. *The English Hymnal,* 1906, and *Songs of Praise,* 1925, led the way with men like Ralph Vaughan Williams, Martin Shaw, Geoffrey Shaw, Walford Davies, and Gustav Holst contributing original tunes and folk tune arrangements. Of these Vaughan Williams is the towering genius. His original tunes, SINE NOMINE (74), RANDOLPH (540), KING'S WESTON (76), and DOWN AMPNEY (466), along with his folk tune arrangements, KING'S LYNN (484), FOREST GREEN (33), and his reworking of LASST UNS ERFREUEN (19) are some of the most refreshing in the hymnal. Holst's CRANHAM (376) is not typical of the austere tune for which he is most famous in England but is a classic example of a contemporary harmonization with simple melody. Joseph Parry's tune ABERYSTWYTH (125) is a combination of Welsh and English cultures, while WYLDE GREEN (62) by Peter Cutts is representative of tunes by younger English composers. AYRSHIRE (157) and GLENFINLAS (791) by Kenneth G. Finlay are attractive contemporary Scottish tunes in a folk idiom.

Folk Tunes

Most modern hymnals have included more and more folk tunes, and the 1964 Methodist hymnal is no exception. From the English material comes ROYAL OAK (34), in addition to the arrangements already listed by Vaughan Williams and the English carols. From Wales come ST. DENIO (27), ARFON (112), AR HYD Y NOS (497), LLANGLOFFAN (260), and LLANFYLLIN (136) in addition to Prichard's HYFRYDOL (132), Williams' EBENEZER (242), and Hughes's CWM RHONDDA (271), all of which are strongly folklike in nature.

Ireland contributes CLONMEL (189), SLANE (256), GARTON (375), and CORMAC (534); Sweden, TRYGGARE KAN INGEN VARA (521) and O STORE GUD (17), a tune which is much stronger in the original triple meter than in the version made popular in the Billy Graham crusades; Holland, IN BABILONE (69); Bohemia, MIT FREUDEN ZART (4) and FAR-OFF LANDS (85); Thailand, the charming SRI LAMPANG (214); Finland, NYLAND (230); Norway, NORSE AIR (304); China, WIANT (519), LE P'ING (490), and SHENG EN (317), composed by Su Yin-Lan; India, BINTI HAMARI (803); France, PICARDY (324) and the carols GLORIA (374) and FRENCH CAROL (441); Poland, W ZLOBIE LEZY (396); Scotland, CANDLER (529), better known as "Ye banks and braes of Bonnie Doon"; and from Nigeria, a Yoruba tune by A. T. O. Olude, NIGERIA (487), with fascinating rhythm and accompanying drum patterns. From traditional Hebrew sources come LEONI (30) and ROCK OF AGES (11).

While the first American settlers sang psalter tunes, they early turned to singing their hymns to folk tunes, many of which had English, Irish, and Scottish ancestry. Many of these tunes were collected by singing teachers who conducted singing schools, using as material their own collections of familiar tunes (with rough-hewn harmonizations), generally printed in shaped notes for ease in teaching reading music. Some used only four shapes:

◣　●　■　◆

Fa　Sol　La　Mi

while others used seven:

▲　♥　◆　◣　●　■　♥

Do　Re　Mi　Fa　Sol　La　Ti

The famous *Sacred Harp* collection is still used in singing sessions in the south.

The new hymnal has borrowed freely from this body of excellent material, including PLEADING SAVIOR (104), DETROIT (32), CLEANSING

FOUNTAIN (115), AMAZING GRACE (92), KEDRON (191), COMPLAINER (398), CHARLESTOWN (426), FOUNDATION (48), CAMPMEETING (111), DAVIS (129), PISGAH (142), MORNING SONG (190), WEDLOCK (211), TRUE HAPPINESS (227), PROMISED LAND (291), and WONDROUS LOVE (432)—tunes which are as fine as any folk hymnody of other lands.

Also a part of the folk tradition are the spirituals which developed before and after the Civil War. Of these GO, TELL IT ON THE MOUNTAIN (404), LET US BREAK BREAD (330), I WANT TO BE A CHRISTIAN (286), BALM IN GILEAD (212), JACOB'S LADDER (287), and WERE YOU THERE (436) have been included in a Methodist hymnal for the first time. Another interesting inclusion is the tune LACQUIPARLE (40) from the Indian mission station in the Dakotas.

American Tunes

There also were early American composers including Oliver Holden, Lewis Edson, and Daniel Read, whose tunes CORONATION (71), LENOX (100), and WINDHAM (80) were extremely popular. Composers of the early nineteenth century included Lowell Mason, Thomas Hastings, and William B. Bradbury, whose tunes were more polished but less strong. Lowell Mason in particular leaned toward European music and made many arrangements of material which he collected on his European tours. It was largely through his efforts and those of editors like William Gardiner and Edward Hodges that tunes by Haydn (HAYDN, 258), Schumann (CANONBURY, 195), and Handel (CHRISTMAS, 249; ANTIOCH, 392; and HALIFAX, 456) have been mined from symphonies, quartets, and operas for the hymnal. Beethoven's HYMN TO JOY (38) seems to be limited to America in its usage and came into popularity here with Henry van Dyke's text, "Joyful, joyful, we adore thee," written for the tune. Haydn's AUSTRIA (42) was written originally as a national song, but found use as a hymn tune in the *Foundling Hospital Collection* as early as 1796. Sibelius' FINLANDIA (209) was arranged as a hymn tune as late as the 1930's. Mendelssohn's tune for "Hark, the herald angels sing" was taken from a cantata celebrating the invention of the printing press and has become popular in spite of the composer's statement that it would never go with a sacred text. In general the best tunes for hymns have not come from the composers who work in larger forms, but from lesser individuals who have created tunes closer to smaller folk idioms.

The Protestant Episcopal *Hymnal 1940* was a leader in introducing new American tunes. Several have gained wide acceptance, and Graham George's THE KING'S MAJESTY (425), Bates G. Burt's SHADDICK (186), and C. Winfred Douglas' ST. DUNSTAN'S (155) have been included in our 1964 hymnal. Annabeth Gay's SHEPHERDS' PIPES (202) first appeared in *The Pilgrim Hymnal,* 1958. The Canadian composer, Graham George, reworked the manuscript tune GRACE CHURCH, GANANOQUE (240) for inclusion with "Fight the good fight." From the Baptists comes the new tune SIMS (533) by William J. Reynolds, their foremost hymnologist.

Twelve other tunes appear for the first time in a hymnal in the new book. Three are by Katherine K. Davis: WACHUSETT (96), MASSACHUSETTS (485), and SURETTE (408); three by V. Earle Copes: KINGDOM (314), VICAR (161), and EPWORTH CHURCH (422); and two by Lloyd Pfautsch: EUCLID (280) and WALDA (238). Single contributions are AUTHOR OF LIFE (315) by Robert J. Powell, PERRY (321) by Leo Sowerby, COVENANT HYMN (508) by Thomas Canning, and HIGH POPPLES (511) by Samuel Walter.

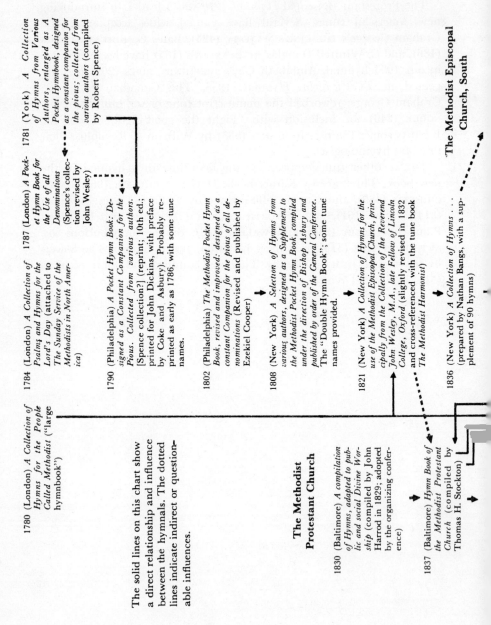

1780 (London) *A Collection of Hymns for the People Called Methodist* ("large hymnbook")

1781 (York) *A Collection of Hymns from Various Authors, enlarged as A Pocket Hymnbook, designed as a constant companion for the pious; collected from various authors* (compiled by Robert Spence)

1784 (London) *A Collection of Psalms and Hymns for the Lord's Day* (attached to *The Sunday Service of the Methodists in North America*)

1787 (London) *A Pocket Hymn Book for the Use of all Denominations* (Spence's collection revised by John Wesley)

1790 (Philadelphia) *A Pocket Hymn Book: Designed as a Constant Companion for the Pious. Collected from various authors.* [Spence collection?] (reprint; 10th ed.; printed for John Dickins, with preface by Coke and Asbury). Probably reprinted as early as 1786, with some tune names.

1802 (Philadelphia) *The Methodist Pocket Hymn Book, revised and improved: designed as a constant Companion for the pious of all denominations* (Revised and published by Ezekiel Cooper)

1808 (New York) *A Selection of Hymns from various authors, designed as a Supplement to the Methodist Pocket Hymn Book,* compiled under the direction of Bishop Asbury and published by order of the General Conference. The "Double Hymn Book"; some tune names provided.

1821 (New York) *A Collection of Hymns for the use of the Methodist Episcopal Church,* principally from the Collection of the Reverend John Wesley, M.A., late Fellow of Lincoln College, Oxford (slightly revised in 1832 and cross-referenced with the tune book *The Methodist Harmonist*)

1836 (New York) *A Collection of Hymns . . .* (prepared by Nathan Bangs, with a supplement of 90 hymns)

The Methodist Episcopal Church, South

The solid lines on this chart show a direct relationship and influence between the hymnals. The dotted lines indicate indirect or questionable influences.

The Methodist Protestant Church

1830 (Baltimore) *A compilation of Hymns, adapted to public and social Divine Worship* (compiled by John Harrod in 1829; adopted by the organizing conference)

1837 (Baltimore) *Hymn Book of the Methodist Protestant Church* (compiled by Thomas H. Stockton)

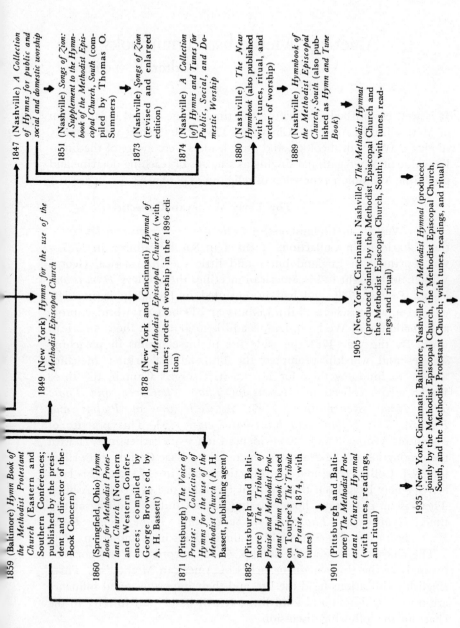

1847 (Nashville) *A Collection of Hymns for public and social and domestic worship*

1851 (Nashville) *Songs of Zion: A Supplement to the Hymnbook of the Methodist Episcopal Church, South* (compiled by Thomas O. Summers)

1873 (Nashville) *Songs of Zion* (revised and enlarged edition)

1874 (Nashville) *A Collection [of] Hymns and Tunes for Public, Social, and Domestic Worship*

1880 (Nashville) *The New Hymnbook* (also published with tunes, ritual, and order of worship)

1889 (Nashville) *Hymnbook of the Methodist Episcopal Church, South* (also published as *Hymn and Tune Book*)

1859 (Baltimore) *Hymn Book of the Methodist Protestant Church* (Eastern and Southern Conferences; published by the president and director of the Book Concern)

1849 (New York) *Hymns for the use of the Methodist Episcopal Church*

1878 (New York and Cincinnati) *Hymnal of the Methodist Episcopal Church* (with tunes; order of worship in the 1896 edition)

1860 (Springfield, Ohio) *Hymn Book for Methodist Protestant Church* (Northern and Western Conferences; compiled by George Brown; ed. by A. H. Bassett)

1871 (Pittsburgh) *The Voice of Praise: a Collection of Hymns for the use of the Methodist Church* (A. H. Bassett, publishing agent)

1882 (Pittsburgh and Baltimore) *The Tribute of Praise and Methodist Protestant Hymn Book* (based on Tourjee's *The Tribute of Praise*, 1874, with tunes)

1901 (Pittsburgh and Baltimore) *The Methodist Protestant Church Hymnal* (with tunes, readings, and ritual)

1905 (New York, Cincinnati, Nashville) *The Methodist Hymnal* (produced jointly by the Methodist Episcopal Church and the Methodist Episcopal Church, South; with tunes, readings, and ritual)

1935 (New York, Cincinnati, Baltimore, Nashville) *The Methodist Hymnal* (produced jointly by the Methodist Episcopal Church, the Methodist Episcopal Church, South, and the Methodist Protestant Church; with tunes, readings, and ritual)

1964 (Nashville) *The Methodist Hymnal*

American Methodist Hymnbooks
Carlton R. Young

It is well established that before the time of the formal organization of Methodism in America (Christmas, 1784), Methodists were already singing a Wesleyan theology, and their leaders were aware of the limitless value of congregational singing as a means of teaching doctrine and providing a common expression of religious experience.

The Early Wesleyan Collections

John Wesley's first hymnbook, *A Collection of Psalms and Hymns*—the "Charles-town Collection," printed in South Carolina in 1737—was reprinted in England but found little use in America. George Whitefield brought to his American meetings the Wesleys' *Hymns and Sacred Poems*, 1739, and had it reprinted in Philadelphia in 1740. The Irish lay preachers, Philip Embury and Robert Strawbridge, probably made use of Wesleyan hymns and hymnbooks in their American work. By the year 1781 the wide use of these hymns in preaching services and worship prompted the Philadelphia printer Melchior Steiner to bind together, for use in St. George's Church, the three Wesley hymn collections: *Hymns for Those That Seek, and Those That Have, Redemption*, 1747; *A Collection of Psalms and Hymns*, 1741; *Hymns and Spiritual Songs*, 1753. This practice of reprinting Wesley hymns was evidenced ten years earlier in 1771 with the production of the exact same material by Isaac Collins in Burlington, N.J. Collins reprinted the collection again in 1773, and this later activity may have been the result of the influence of Francis Asbury. There is no indication, however, that Asbury did any editing at this time. *Hymns for Those That Seek, and Those That Have, Redemption* was also reprinted by James Adams in Wilmington, 1770.

The chart of hymnbooks (see pp. 52-53) records the "authorized" hymnals of the three main branches of American Methodism. Three English publications head the list, and their importance and influence are traced by dotted and solid lines. It will be helpful to refer to the chart for the following discussion.

The first and earliest publication, *A Collection of Hymns for the Use of the People Called Methodists*, 1780, commonly called the "Large Hymnbook," was not to influence American hymnody until after the 1820's, and more fully in 1849. The second collection, the hymns that were bound with the 1784 *Sunday Services*, never found popular use and soon fell into oblivion. The third, *A Pocket Hymn-Book*, was issued by John Wesley (London, 1785) as a digest of the 1780 *Collection*. The fourth seems to have had the most influence on the first forty years of the young church's life. This was the "renegade" collection of 1781—*A Pocket Hymn-Book*, compiled by Robert Spence. This last fact goes far to explain the apparent lack of interest on the part of early American Methodism for the definitive 1780 *Collection* and, by virtue of this, the bulk of Wesley hymnody, which proved to be the mainstay of British Methodists for almost one hundred years.

The Methodist Episcopal Church was quick to make use of the Spence *Pocket Hymn-Book*, 1781, and various editions and variations of this basic publication sufficed until 1821. An interesting sidelight is seen in a comparison of the preface to Wesley's 1780 hymnbook (first American reprint, 1814) and Bishops Asbury and Coke's preface to the 1790 edition of the Spence *Pocket Hymn-Book*. Wesley maintained that English Methodists needed a collection that was "neither cumbersome or expensive." The bishops felt that the Wesley collection was too large and expensive for American use and thus justified the reprint of the smaller *Pocket Hymn-Book*. No doubt the bishops' rejection of both the 1784 collection (*Sunday Service*) and Wesley's 1780 "Large Hymnbook" needs to be studied along with the rejection by the young church of other direct Wesley influences.

The 1780 *Collection* was studied in detail by the compilers of the 1821 hymnbook, and the next generation saw more use of basic Wesleyan hymnody. These additions are reflected in the 1836 and 1849 editions.

Early Tune Collections

There was limited use of the Wesley *Foundery Collection*, 1742, and Thomas Butts, *Harmonia Sacra*, c. 1756, reprinted at Andover in 1816. In addition, the names of the tunes appropriate for each hymn began to appear in hymnbooks as early as the 1790 *Pocket Hymn-Book*. Andrew Law and others published tune collections related to the *Pocket Hymn-Book*.

A bold attempt to produce an authorized and standardized book of hymn tunes, *David's Companion,* part of which was printed in 1807, was given tacit approval by the 1808 General Conference. Reflecting the musical activity of John Street Methodist Church in New York City, it was revised in 1810 and 1817, but never enjoyed official sanction. The chaotic situation was somewhat improved with the publication of *The Methodist Harmonist* in 1821. This tune collection, revised in 1833 and 1837, cross referenced the 1821 hymnal. *The Devotional Harmonist,* 1849, also was used with official hymnals.

Methodist Episcopal Hymnbooks

Having the advantage of both printing facilities and more "settled" church situations, the Methodist Episcopal Church, North continued to expand its use of a common hymnal. Content was broadened to the extent that the 1849 book contained 1,148 hymns. Nine years later a tune edition was produced, but apparently it came too late to prevent the hymnbook from escaping the criticism that it was more an anthology of devotional poetry than a practical congregational hymnal. Within the next twenty years, particularly in post-Civil War times, the church was flooded with hymnbooks and songbooks that sought to please those who so strongly objected to the "official" hymnal of the church. Books for all occasions—camp meetings, social singing, sabbath schools, and revivals—competed in the open market. The General Conference of 1876 finally opened the canon of the official hymnal, and a new edition was authorized. A group of fifteen was charged with the responsibility and presented its work to the bishops of the church in an extensive printed report containing a thorough-going exposition of both the rationale and the content of the proposed revision. A reading of this report indicates that the committee not only was aware of the popular material, so much a part of the "unofficial" books, but also included material from the ecumenical church (translations from Greek, Latin, and German).

Tunes were provided with each hymn page. The hymnal contained 1,138 hymns, and the 1896 printing of this 1878 edition also included an Order of Worship, a first for American hymnals.

Methodist Protestant Hymnbooks

At the time of the separation, the Methodist Protestant group adopted John Harrod's 1830 collection, already in common use among the "protesting" ministers and people. Their next collection, dated 1837, was to serve as the basic source material for the several hymnals that followed, including the three books produced by the two divisions of the denomination, the Methodist Protestant Church and the Methodist Church. An interesting feature of the 1859 hymnal is the cross-reference of tunebooks in the appendix, containing the tune name of the musical settings suggested for each hymn. If a song leader wished to select and lead hymns from the whole hymnal, he would have to be knowledgeable in the use of a dozen tunebooks.

A unified Methodist Protestant Church adapted the already published hymnal, Eben Tourjee's *Tribute of Praise,* in 1882. This inclusive book sufficed until the 1901 hymnal. The 1901 hymnal was published in only one format, tunes and texts together on a page, one hymn to one tune, with most of the texts between the lines of music. A large section of the book was devoted to Scripture readings and ritual. It is paradoxical that the final hymnal produced by this branch of Methodism would in retrospect be looked upon as the most influential from the standpoint of publishing style and format.

Hymnbooks of the Methodist Episcopal Church, South

Immediately upon separation from the other major segment of American Methodism, the Methodist Episcopal Church, South went to work on its own hymnbook. Northern hymnologists, including David Creamer of Baltimore, assisted. Creamer, among other distinguished accomplishments, put together the first commentary on Wesleyan hymnody, *Methodist Hymnology* (New York, 1848), and he also assisted in the preparation of the Methodist Protestant hymnbook, dated 1859.

Exhibiting a bold realism, the Methodist Episcopal Church, South hymnal of 1847 was coupled with an unofficial *Songs of Zion,* 1851, a book widely heralded in the official life of the church. As a supplement to the first hymnal of the Southern Church, it no doubt served the large section of the church that would have nothing to do with the finer collection containing 600 hymns of the Wesleys and 150 by Isaac Watts out of a total of 1,047. The shortlived 1874 edition, with tunes, was an attempt to "get everything into one book," and while not as successful as hoped, it did, through the work of Rigdon M. McIntosh, music editor, pave the way for the full music editions of a generation later and provided for a time "one official book" for the Methodist Episcopal Church, South. Action of the General Conference requested the publishers to produce a book of not more than 800 hymns, and the 1889 edition contained 918 hymns. This was not a bad compromise when one considers that the large hymnbook of 1847 had contained 1,047 hymns and the *Songs of Zion* somewhat in excess of 500.

The Pan-Methodist Hymnal of 1905

Louis Benson in *The English Hymn,* 1915, identifies the hymnal jointly prepared by the Northern and Southern Churches as a "Pan-Methodist" hymnbook. This term originated in the Southern Church's General Conference of 1886 and aptly described the "growing together" of the two churches in matters of common interest. Both churches were unhappy with the large size of their hymnals, and both had been hard pressed to compete with the mass appeal of publications of the "gospel hymn" movement. Beginning in 1902, joint authorized work commenced, resulting in the 1905 book. With a few more than 700 hymns against the Southern Church's 1889 book containing 918 hymns and the Northern Church's 1878 containing 1,138 hymns, the new hymnal had unprecedented success. Carl F. Price has carefully reconstructed the path that led to the production of this joint hymnal in *The Music and Hymnody of the Methodist Hymnal,* 1911. Nutter and Tillett edited an annotated edition of the hymnal the same year, and this companion or handbook was published in both New York and Nashville.

A comparison of the Methodist Protestant hymnal of 1901 with the jointly produced book illustrates that the Methodist Protestants' successful efforts in producing a small handsome volume had at last brought the church and its publishers, though perhaps too late, to the realization that inclusiveness of content need not necessarily be reflected in size.

The 1935 Edition

The joint hymnal of 1905 was a "beloved" book. For many Methodists it could have been maintained as the official hymnal for a longer period of time than any previous book.

Agitation for a new hymnal officially began in 1928, with the creation of a revision committee by the Northern Church. In time a joint North-South effort was once again started; then finally the addition of the Methodist Protestant group rounded out the structure of the full revision committee. Space does not allow for a full discussion of this committee's work.* If anyone has ever doubted the earnestness of the committee's desire to produce a representative hymnal, he need only think upon the fact that the entire revision was accomplished at a time when the three branches of the church were still separate and the country was in the throes of economic disaster. Enormous physical energy was expended and basic study undertaken amidst the most trying and frustrating conditions to face a hymnal committee since the pre-Civil War days of the Methodist Protestants. When one is fully aware of their task and their accomplishments, it should be apparent that the 1935 hymnal is much better in every detail than might have been expected.

Still a smaller book than the 1905 hymnal, the 1935 edition nevertheless reflected the trends in post-Victorian English hymnody. It included some of the rich heritage of American as well as universal folk hymnody and generally upgraded the musical level. On the negative side, much biblical symbolism and many fine eighteenth-century evangelical texts were deleted or altered. Other criticism was leveled at the inclusion of too many so-called "gospel hymns." Experience proved that the book probably did not contain nearly enough "of the right ones" to suit the broader needs of the church.

The 1964 Edition

The present Methodist hymnal is the first to be authorized by a united Methodism since 1821. The General Conference of 1960 was informed by its Commission on Worship of the need for a new hymnal and authorized revision to begin, but only by a majority of thirty-one votes. The commission was directed to report back to the 1964 General Conference its recommendations for the revised hymnal.

Upon adjournment of the 1960 General Conference, the Commission on Worship had two major tasks: to perfect revisions of *The Book of*

---

* The Methodist Publishing House library in Nashville houses the minutes and papers of their labor along with the correspondence carried on in behalf of the committee by the hymnal editor, Robert Guy McCutchan, and the then book editor of the church, John W. Langdale.

Worship and to revise the hymnal. The commission was enlarged into a specially constituted hymnal committee. This group, by action of the General Conference, was composed of the regular commission members plus certain consultants, some of whom were named by virtue of their positions in various boards and agencies of the church. Others were appointed at the jurisdictional conferences of 1960. The hymnal committee was comprised of twenty-nine members: six bishops, five general board secretaries and staff members, and the eighteen members of the Commission on Worship. From time to time the committee called in consultants, swelling the total working membership to forty-five.* Only twenty-nine were voting members. The hymnal committee substructure was:

THE HYMNAL COMMITTEE

Psalter and Ritual Service Music	Tunes	Texts	Executive- Editorial

Subcommittee chairmen formed the nucleus of the executive-editorial group. The editor** was elected in 1960 and was ex-officio on all committees.

The full hymnal committee, in the years before the 1964 General Conference, met during the months October and February. Subcommittee meetings were held between meetings of the full committee. The basic work of the parent committee was to act on recommendations from the several subcommittees. When possible, the work of subcommittees was mailed to the full hymnal committee two weeks ahead of each meeting. Simple majority rule passed or rejected recommendations. A two-thirds rule prevailed on matters of reconsideration.

During the meetings sixty-five hymnbooks were studied. Manuscripts and suggestions were received from thousands of Methodists. An eighty-nine point questionnaire was sent to 22,000 pastors in charge of local churches. Eleven thousand of these questionnaires were returned; the results were tabulated and made available to the hymnal committee at its February, 1961, meeting. The membership of the

* See the preface to the hymnal for listing of the committee.
** The editor's correspondence and working files are housed at Bridwell Library, Perkins School of Theology, Southern Methodist University, Dallas, Texas.

National Fellowship of Methodist Musicians also received a questionnaire dealing with the music of the 1935 hymnal.

The results of the hymnal committee's work were recorded in a 515-page report * and sent in January to the delegates of the 1964 General Conference which met in Pittsburgh in April. The first major business session of the General Conference was devoted to the hymnal committee's report. After an hour's presentation and discussion, the conference adopted the report without a negative vote.

Two years were spent in editing and producing the new hymnal. Well over two million hymnals were distributed in the first year of publication, an event unprecedented in American publishing.

* Most Methodist college and seminary libraries have copies of the report.

A Charge to Keep I Have (150)

CHARLES WESLEY, 1707-1788

The text was first published in Wesley's *Short Hymns on Select Passages of Holy Scripture,* 1762, 2 volumes containing 2,030 hymns prompted by texts from Genesis to Revelation. Of the hymns inspired by the 16 Leviticus texts, "A charge to keep," 8:35, and "O Thou who camest from above," 6:13 (172), alone survive in current usage. The hymn was printed under the text "Keep the charge of the Lord, that ye die not."

Included in John Wesley, *A Collection of Hymns for the Use of the People Called Methodists,* 1780, it has maintained its place in all subsequent Methodist hymnals. Though Wesley printed the hymn in two 8-line sts., it seems to have been sung always in four 4-line sts. Without exception the hymn has been printed unaltered in Methodist collections.

Boylston

LOWELL MASON, 1792-1872

The tune first appeared in *The Choir,* 1832, set to "Our days are as grass." Armin Haeussler states, "This tune is based on a Gregorian formula," and William J. Reynolds notes the similarity to HOBART in I. B. Woodbury, *New Lute of Zion,* 1853, which is marked "arranged from an Ancient Chant."

Boylston is the name of a famous street in Boston and of a town in Massachusetts.

A Mighty Fortress Is Our God (20)
Ein' feste Burg ist unser Gott

MARTIN LUTHER, 1483-1546
Trans. by FREDERIC H. HEDGE, 1805-1890

Luther's magnificent battle hymn, extravagantly acclaimed "the greatest hymn of the greatest man in the greatest period of German history," was written sometime during the years 1527-29, probably shortly before Luther published it in his first church hymnal containing both texts and tunes (Wittenberg, 1529). Though the text seems to have been printed in a variety of hymnals in these early years, variously dated from 1529-31, our earliest extant source for Luther's text appears to be Michael Blum (e) 's printing of *Enchiridion geistlicher Gesänge und Psalmen für die Laien,* 1530 (?).

In a painstaking analysis of the hymn, Markus Jenny, in an article in *Jahrbuch für Liturgik und Hymnologie,* 1964, shows that though the first 3 sts. correspond precisely to the 3 strophes of Psalm 46 as separated by the sign *Selah,* st. 4 is unrelated to the psalm and must be regarded as an addition to it. The arguments are (a) the first 3 sts. complete the psalm; (b) the lyric is structurally complete without st. 4; (c) in general, Luther prefers the 3-st. hymn form; (d) Luther's first concern here was to provide comfort and assurance to individuals and churches in time of trial without reference to any concrete opponents such as st. 4 refers to; and (e) in st. 4 the more general concern of sts. 1–3 is narrowed down to such specific hostile acts as to reject the Word and to destroy body, goods, honor, children, and wife. The enemy here is no longer the devil as in sts. 1–3 but "they," which here can refer only to the pope and the Roman Church—hardly to the Turks or others.

Furthermore, st. 4 remains a crux for us. Line 2 (*und kein' Dank dazu haben*) is absolutely unintelligible, and the defiant self-assurance of the conclusion suggests the tone of a patriotic song rather than the mood of a Christian undergoing severe temptation or under immediate threat of martyrdom. Indeed, this st. would hardly have been given a place in our hymnals had it not borne the name of Luther, and Jenny concludes that it should be struck from the hymn, or not sung. Whatever the reaction to Jenny's analysis of the hymn may be, the origin and meaning of Luther's great hymn appear to be much more complex than is commonly supposed. More than 50 years of rather vigorous discussion have left the problems unsolved.

More than a hundred English translations have been made, the first probably that of Miles Coverdale, "Our God is a defense and towre," in his *Goostly Psalms and Spiritual Songs,* 1543 (?). The 2 English translations now usually printed are those of Thomas Carlyle and Frederic H. Hedge.

Though British hymnals prefer Carlyle's text, American hymnals print almost exclusively the Hedge translation, which first appeared in *Hymns for the Church of Christ,* 1853, a hymnal edited by Hedge and F. D. Huntington. It was in this form that Luther's hymn first entered official American Methodist hymnals in 1878 with its appearance in the Methodist Episcopal hymnal. Both the Carlyle and the Hedge translations continue to be printed unaltered.

Ein' feste Burg

MARTIN LUTHER, 1483-1546

The tune was probably first printed in Joseph Klug, *Geistliche Lieder* (Wittenberg, 1529), but no copy has survived. However, it appeared in A. Rauscher, *Geistliche Lieder* (Erfurt, 1531), as well as in *Kirchengesänge, mit viel schönen Psalmen und Melodien* (Nuremberg, 1531).

The original form of the melody was:

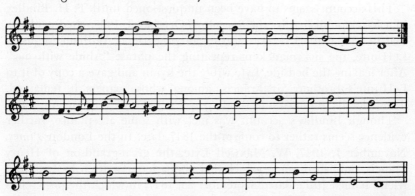

The form in common use today is based on J. S. Bach's version. The closing phrase is a formula common to many German chorales (e.g. see WIE SCHÖN LEUCHTET and VOM HIMMEL HOCH).

Ursula Aarburg in an article in *Jahrbuch für Liturgik und Hymnologie*, 1960, suggests that 4 of Luther's hymn melodies, including EIN' FESTE BURG and VOM HIMMEL HOCH, may be related to a twelfth-century troubadour song. As is the case with German chorales, the tune name comes from the opening words of the original German text.

Abide with Me; Fast Falls the Eventide (289)

HENRY F. LYTE, 1793-1847

The historical problem of the date of composition of the text remains unresolved. It was first published in leaflet form in 1847 (with a now discarded tune by Lyte himself) and then in the *Remains of Henry Francis Lyte,* 1850, with a prefatory statement by his daughter.

According to tradition, which is an elaboration of his daughter's account, Lyte, required by failing health to give up his parish in Lower Brixham, rallied to preach one last sermon and to celebrate one last Holy Communion, September 4, 1847. On the evening of that day, before seeking health in the milder climate of France, he walked out to the cliffs overlooking the sea at the end of his garden. There the setting sun reminded him of Luke 24:29: "Abide with us: for it is toward evening, and the day is far spent." He returned to his study and in less than an hour wrote the hymn "Abide with me." Final revision of the hymn, it is said, was done in France, where, on November 20, he died.

This account seems to have been unquestioned until T. H. Bindley in a letter published by the *Spectator,* October 3, 1925, cited evidence that in 1820 while Lyte was visiting a dying friend, William Augustus LeHunte, the sick man kept repeating the phrase "Abide with me." After leaving the bedside, Lyte wrote the hymn and gave a copy of it to LeHunte's brother, Sir Francis, among whose papers it remained. These details were given to Bindley by a nephew of William Augustus.

Though Bindley's account was met with some acceptance, further evidence seems rather to confirm the 1847 date. In the London *Times,* November 1, 1947, W. Maxwell Lyte, the great-grandson of Henry Francis, published a note which describes a letter written by Lyte to a friend named Julia, dated September 25, 1847, in which the poet refers to the hymn as "my latest effusion." Thus, the later date seems more probable, and it is not likely that the hymn which has been acclaimed as "the most popular hymn in the English language" could have been laid aside and forgotten for 27 years.

In any case, it is an end-of-life hymn; that it has become a funeral hymn is evidence enough of this. It is now generally and properly placed with the eternal life hymns, not with the evening hymns as was the case 50 years ago.

As most commonly sung now, the first 2 and last 3 sts. of the original make up the hymn, with 3 others being omitted. The hymn entered the Methodist Episcopal hymnal in 1878.

Eventide

W. H. MONK, 1823-1889

Written for this text, the tune first appeared in the first edition of *Hymns Ancient and Modern* (London, 1861). Lightwood quotes a letter from the composer's widow: "The tune was written at a time of great sorrow—when together we watched, as we did daily, the glories of the setting sun. As the last golden ray faded, he took up some paper and pencilled that tune, which has gone all over the world." There is a conflicting story, however, that the tune was written in 10 minutes at the conclusion of a meeting concerned with compiling the hymnal, for which Monk was responsible for tunes.

According to Thy Gracious Word (316)

JAMES MONTGOMERY, 1771-1854

The hymn was first published in Montgomery's *Christian Psalmist* (Glasgow, 1825) in 6 sts., with the motto "This do in remembrance of me," Luke 22:19. It has been printed in Methodist collections since 1847. Since the 1905 hymnal, sts. 3 and 4 of the original have been omitted.

The phrase "testamental cup" (2:1), though based on Luke 22:20, has seemed awkward. Some hymnals following *The Salisbury Hymn-Book,* edited by Earl Nelson, 1857, alter the line to read "The cup, thy precious blood, I [or, "I'll"] take"; however, most hymnals print the text in the original form.

Tallis' Ordinal

THOMAS TALLIS, c. 1505-1585

The tune was the ninth in the musical Appendix to Matthew Parker, *The Whole Psalter* (London, 1561-67), with tunes by Tallis. Erik Routley states in *Companion to Congregational Praise,* "It is the first C.M. hymn-tune in history and the simplest of all hymn-tunes."

The tune was originally associated with "Veni Creator Spiritus," the longer of 2 hymns in the 1549 *Book of Common Prayer* for ordinations—hence the tune name.

Ah, Holy Jesus, How Hast Thou Offended (412)
Herzliebster Jesu, was hast du verbrochen

JOHANN HEERMANN, 1585-1647
Trans. by ROBERT S. BRIDGES, 1844-1930

This text is deeply rooted in the piety of the Middle Ages. The ultimate source of the Latin is now believed to be Jean de Fécamp

69

(d. 1078). It is found embedded in the seventh chapter of the pseudo-Augustinian *Meditationes,* which itself is now known to have been taken over from the twelfth-century *Orationes,* in part correctly attributed to Anselm of Canterbury. The sentiment and the style of the hymn, so similar to the twelfth-century "Reproaches," could easily, if mistakenly, be identified with Anselm or Augustine.

Heermann's hymn in 15 sts. first appeared in his *Devoti Musica Cordis,* 1630. Bridges' translation appeared first in his *Yattendon Hymnal,* 1899, in meter well suited to the tune HERZLIEBSTER JESU, which Crüger composed for Heermann's hymn. With nobility of phrase he movingly recaptured both the sense and the spirit of the Latin and German texts.

Some hymnals unfortunately alter "holy Jesus" (1:1) to "dearest Jesus," perhaps in order to reproduce more literally the sense of the German "herzliebster." While this accords well enough with the piety of the Latin *Orationes* which delight in addressing God as "amabilissime, amantissime, benignissime, carissime, dulcissime," etc., Bridges used better judgment with the stronger and less cloying adjective.

The hymn is printed as Bridges wrote it. This is its first appearance in a Methodist hymnal.

Herzliebster Jesu

JOHANN CRÜGER, 1598-1662

First appearing in Crüger's *Neues vollkommlenes Gesangbuch* (Berlin, 1640), the tune has some similarities to another tune by Nicolaus Hermann in Johann Schein, *Cantional oder Gesangbuch Augsburgischer Konfession* (Leipzig 1627), and to Bourgeois' setting of Psalm 23. The meter is Sapphic, and the present form of the tune is a superior setting. Bach used it in his *St. Matthew Passion* and *St. John Passion.* Ellinwood suggests that the tune may also be based on Psalm 23 from the Genevan Psalter (which is Psalm 18 in the Ainsworth Psalter used by the Pilgrims). The harmonization in the hymnal is taken from *Chorale Book for England* (London, 1863).

Alas! and Did My Savior Bleed (415)

ISAAC WATTS, 1674-1748

The hymn was published first by Watts, *Hymns and Spiritual Songs,* Bk. II, "Composed on Divine Subjects," July, 1707. It appeared under the heading "Godly Sorrow arising from the Sufferings of Christ." Originally containing 6 sts., the hymn was printed in later editions by Watts with the st. 2 bracketed to indicate that it might be omitted. The hymn with the accepted 5 sts. entered American Methodist hymnals very early and is to be found in all the official hymnals of the church.

While the accepted sts. are on the whole printed as Watts wrote them, some words have offended editors. In 1:4 the words remained "For such a worm as I" until the 1935 hymnal changed it to "For sinners such as I." In 2:1 the 1935 hymnal changed "crimes" to "sins." Both of these alterations have been accepted by some other hymnals. In 2:1, though Watts wrote "had done," "had" is changed to "have" in all hymnals, and in 2:2, "groaned upon" was altered to "suffered on" in the 1935 hymnal.

The most troublesome line has been in 3:3: "When God, the mighty maker died." The paradox is powerful if the language is accepted as figurative: to say that God the creator should die for man the creature is a bold and moving affirmation. But fearing that the words might be taken literally, already in the Methodist hymnal of 1821 and in the Methodist Episcopal, South hymnal of 1847 and the Methodist Episcopal hymnal of 1849, "God" was altered to read "Christ." "Christ, the mighty maker" was retained until the 1935 hymnal altered it to read "Christ, the great Redeemer." This phrase is found previously only in the Methodist Protestant hymnal of 1837.

Martyrdom

HUGH WILSON, 1764-1824

The tune, originally in common time, first appeared on leaflets in the late eighteenth century. It was changed to triple time in R. A. Smith, *Sacred Music Sung in St. George's Church* (Edinburgh, 1825) where it was called an "old Scottish melody."

A lawsuit, after Wilson's death, proved without doubt that he was the rightful owner of the copyright, but Anne Gilchrist in the *Choir*, July, 1934, has traced similarities in the tune to the air "Helen of Kirkconnel," which indicates that Wilson may have borrowed from a traditional melody and copyrighted the tune.

Many other names have been used: FENWICK, DRUMCLOG, AVON, among many others.

71

All Beautiful the March of Days (33)

FRANCES W. WILE, 1878-1939

First published in the 1911 revised edition of *Unity Hymns and Carols*, the hymn was written at the suggestion of the editor, Dr. William Channing Gannett, minister of the First Unitarian Church in Rochester, N.Y. Noting that no hymn in celebration of winter was available, he secured the aid of a former parishioner, Mrs. Wile.

The hymn was originally in 4 sts. The third is usually omitted. This is the first appearance of the hymn in the Methodist hymnal.

Forest Green

Traditional English Melody
Harm. by RALPH VAUGHAN WILLIAMS, 1872-1958

Called "The Ploughboy's Dream," this English folk tune was drafted into *The English Hymnal* (Oxford, 1906) with a harmonization by Vaughan Williams, who noted the tune at Forest Green, Surrey, in 1903. In ballad meter (fourteeners) and AABA form, it is an attractive and simple melody.

All Creatures of Our God and King (60)

FRANCIS OF ASSISI, c. 1182-1226
Trans. by WILLIAM H. DRAPER, 1855-1933

The "Canticle of the Sun," or the "Song of Brother Sun and of All Creatures," was composed in Italian, in Francis' own Umbrian speech. It is said to be the first genuine religious poem in the Italian language, "the first greetings of the Italian Renaissance to the Nature she had found again." The original text may be found in Vlastimil Kybal, *Francis of Assisi* (Notre Dame, 1954).

According to tradition, the canticle was written by Francis during the last months of his life from July, 1225, to October, 1226, in times of intense pain and prolonged suffering and in the presence of death. The st. on forgiving others derives from Francis' distress over the quarrels between the secular and spiritual powers in Assisi and Perugia, and when he was informed that his illness was incurable, he sang, "Praise to thee, my Lord, for our Sister bodily Death." Ascetic and mystic though Francis was, his whole life was an expression of irrepressible and boundless joy in both God and his world.

Though the text of the canticle itself seems to praise God *for* all his creatures, Draper's hymn paraphrase summons the creatures themselves to praise God. Draper composed the hymn sometime during his pastorate at Adel, Yorkshire, 1899-1919, for use of children at a Whitsuntide festival at Leeds. It seems to have been first published in 1926.

The hymn entered the Methodist hymnal in 1935, but without st. 6, "And thou, most kind and gentle death," now properly restored.

Lasst uns erfreuen

Geistliche Kirchengesänge, Cologne, 1623
Arr. and Harm. by RALPH VAUGHAN WILLIAMS, 1872-1958

Composed of a rising and falling melodic line plus descending four notes, the tune was originally set to an Easter text, "Lasst uns erfreuen herzlich sehr." Vaughan Williams harmonized and lengthened the tune for Athelstan Riley's "Ye watchers and ye holy ones" for *The English Hymnal* (Oxford, 1906).

Erik Routley in *Companion to Congregational Praise* suggests that it may be a member of a family of tunes based on the major triad: MIT FREUDEN ZART, OLD 113TH, etc. In its extended form it is essentially jubilant and expressive of universal praise.

It has also been called VIGILES ET SANCTI. A more recent harmonization by Carlton R. Young may be found at **19**.

All Glory, Laud, and Honor (424)
Gloria, laus et honor

THEODULPH OF ORLEANS, c. 750-821
Trans. by JOHN M. NEALE, 1818-1866

According to the legend as told by Clichtoveus, in his *Elucidatorium*, 1516, the hymn was composed and first sung on a certain Sunday when Theodulph was in prison in Angers. The Emperor Louis was present that day as the procession moved through the city and halted beneath the tower where the saint was imprisoned. Suddenly, to his astonishment, the Emperor heard from above the *Gloria, laus,* chanted loudly and melodiously. Being charmed he asked the name of the singer and was told that it was his own prisoner, Theodulph. Moved with compassion for him, the Emperor pardoned the saint, returned him to his see, and ordered that henceforth the hymn which Theodulph had composed be sung on Palm Sunday. Ancient Palm Sunday use of the hymn is well attested in the French, Roman, and English rites.

The original Latin hymn consisted of 39 couplets, which may be found in *Hymns Ancient and Modern*, 1907. Though Julian lists some

8 English translations of the hymn made between 1849 and 1874, the familiar Neale version has displaced all others. Actually Neale made 2 translations, one published in his *Mediaeval Hymns and Sequences,* 1851, in the meter of the Latin; one in his *Hymnal Noted,* also 1851.

In *The Hymnal Noted,* the hymn is in eight 4-line sts., the first and last being identical and used as a refrain before each of the other 6. Neale's original st. 7 is commonly omitted.

The first st. originally began "Glory, and laud, and honour." With Neale's approval it was altered to its present form by the compilers of *Hymns Ancient and Modern* for their trial book of 1859, and now always appears this way. St. 5 originally was altered at the same time.

The hymn entered the Methodist hymnal in 1905. In line 6 of our last st., some few hymnals have changed Neale's original "prayers" to "praise," as did the 1935 Methodist hymnal. The present hymnal returns to Neale's original.

St. Theodulph

MELCHIOR TESCHNER, 1584-1635

The tune first appeared in *Ein andächtiges Gebet* . . . (Leipzig, 1615), a 12-page tract. Teschner made two 5-voice settings for the hymn "Valet will ich dir geben" by Herberger, of which this is the second. The tune was first set to Theodulph's text with the first 2 musical phrases used as a refrain (see *The Hymnal 1940,* p. 62) by William H. Monk in *Hymns Ancient and Modern* (London, 1861). The original form of the melody was:

This tune is also known as VALET WILL ICH DIR GEBEN.

All Hail the Power of Jesus' Name (71, 72, 73)

EDWARD PERRONET, 1726-1792
Alt. by JOHN RIPPON, 1751-1836

The first st. of this hymn was published with the tune MILES' LANE in Augustus M. Toplady, the *Gospel Magazine,* November, 1779. The entire text, consisting of 8 sts., appeared in the April issue of 1780. The hymn continued to be printed in the original form during the nineteenth century, but editors have always been unhappy with it and keep altering it.

Of the older editors, the most important has been John Rippon who in his *Selection of Hymns from the Best Authors,* 1787, extensively rewrote the hymn. He omitted outright 3 of Perronet's sts.: 2, 3, and 6:

> Let high-born seraphs tune the lyre,
>> And, as they tune it, fall
> Before his face who tunes their choir,
>> And crown him Lord of all.

> Crown him, ye morning stars of light,
>> Who fix'd this floating ball;
> Now hail the strength of Israel's might,
>> And crown him Lord of all.

> Hail him, ye heirs of David's line,
>> Whom David Lord did call;
> The God incarnate, Man divine,
>> And crown him Lord of all.

He added 2 new sts. of his own to fit his unfortunate scheme of affixing titles to the sts.: "Angels," "Martyrs," "Converted Jews," "Believing Gentiles," "Sinners of every Age," "Sinners of every Nation," and "Ourselves." His scheme required him to write 2 original sts., one for "Sinners of every Age" and one for "Ourselves":

> Babes, Men, and Sires, who know his love,
>> Who feel your sin and thrall,
> Now joy with all the hosts above,
>> And crown him Lord of all.

> O that with yonder sacred throng,
>> We at his feet may fall
> We'll join the everlasting song,
>> And crown him Lord of all.

75

The alterations which Rippon made in those lines of Perronet which he retained were likewise mostly because of his titles. Since he entitled st. 5 "Converted Jews," he had to change "Ye seed of Israel's chosen race" to "Ye chosen seed of Israel's race." Since others than Jews were "ransomed of (from) the fall," this line was changed to "A remnant weak and small." To point up the title "Believing Gentiles," "Sinners! whose love can ne'er forget" was changed to "Ye Gentile sinners, ne'er forget." The confused and confusing stanza

> Let every tribe and every tongue,
>   That bound creation's call,
> Now shout, in universal song,
>   The crowned Lord of all

was altered to

> Let every kindred, every tribe
>   On this terrestrial ball,
> To him all majesty ascribe,
>   And crown him Lord of all.

This is certainly an improvement.

Modern hymnals show a great variety of combination of the Perronet and Rippon versions, with sometimes curious alterations of and additions to both.

The first appearance of the hymn in official Methodist hymnals was in the Methodist Protestant of 1837, the Methodist Episcopal, South of 1847, and the Methodist Episcopal of 1849. All print 5 or 6 sts. The earlier hymnals followed the Rippon version rather closely, uniformly omitting his unfortunate titles before sts., yet without noticing that when "Converted Jews" is dropped, "chosen" should revert to its original position before "race."

Since 1905 the Methodist hymnal has printed its first 3 sts. essentially as Perronet wrote them, with the exception of the misplaced "chosen" in st. 2. St. 4 is printed as altered by Rippon, and st. 5 as composed by him.

Coronation (71)

OLIVER HOLDEN, 1765-1844

The tune was composed in 1792 and was first published in *Union Harmony* (Boston, 1793). It was originally in the key of A flat, and the third phrase was a duet. The tune name reflects the repetition of "Crown him."

Diadem (72)

JAMES ELLOR, 1819-1899

This tune was written when the composer was 19. He took it to the hat factory where he worked and where it was enthusiastically sung. Copies were made, and it was sung at the Sunday school anniversary of the Wesleyan chapel, Droylsden, near Manchester, where Ellor directed the music. The tune name comes from the third phrase of st. 1.

Miles' Lane (73)

WILLIAM SHRUBSOLE, 1760-1806

Shrubsole met Perronet when he was a 19-year-old chorister at Canterbury Cathedral. His tune was published anonymously when it appeared with the first st. of Perronet's text in the *Gospel Magazine* in November, 1779. In April, 1780, it appeared with Shrubsole's name when the entire hymn (text and tune) was printed in Stephen Addington, *Collection of Psalm Tunes* (London, 1780), in the key of C for treble, tenor, and bass with the final phrase harmonized in 4 parts.

The tune name is a corruption of "St. Michael's Lane," the site of a London meetinghouse where Addington was minister.

All My Heart This Night Rejoices (379)
Frölich soll mein Herze springen

PAUL GERHARDT, 1607-1676
Trans. by CATHERINE WINKWORTH, 1827-1878

The German text of the hymn first appeared in Johann Crüger, *Frölich soll mein Herze springen*

Catherine Winkworth translated 10 of the 15 sts. and published them in the second series of her *Lyra Germanica*, 1858. In her *Chorale Book for England*, 1863, she omitted sts. 2, 3, and 9, and altered st. 10:1 from "Heedfully my Lord I'll cherish" to "Thee, dear Lord, with heed I'll cherish." St. 10 (Gerhardt's fifteenth) is used by J. S. Bach as a chorale text, No. 33, in *Christmas Oratorio*. It is often printed in modern hymnals as a fourth st.

The hymn entered the Methodist hymnal in 1935. Our 3 sts. are the first 3 as arranged in *Chorale Book for England*.

Warum sollt ich mich denn grämen

JOHANN G. EBELING, 1637-1676

The tune was written in 1666 and was first published in Ebeling's *Das andere Dutzend geistlicher Andachtslieder Herrn Paul Gerhardts mit neuen Melodien* (Berlin, 1666), containing hymns by Gerhardt and new music by Ebeling. Rhythmic variety and use of melodic sequence make it one of the most lighthearted of pre-Bach chorales. It is also known as BONN and EBELING.

All Nature's Works His Praise Declare (343)

HENRY WARE, JR., 1794-1843

In the *Works of Henry Ware, Jr.* (Boston, 1846), edited by Chandler Robbins, the hymn is printed under the title "On Opening our Organ, November 9, 1822." It seems to have been first included in W. Garrett Horder, *Congregational Hymns* (London, 1884).

The last quatrain of the original read:

> O, teach its rich and swelling notes
> To lift our souls on high;
> And while the music round us floats,
> Let earth-born passion die.

As the hymn is now printed, the order of the two couplets is commonly reversed, with "passion" changed to "passions":

> Lord, while the music round us floats,
> May earth-born passions die;
> O grant its rich and swelling notes
> May lift our souls on high!

There is no information when or by whom this alteration took place. The hymn entered the Methodist hymnal in 1935.

Bethlehem

GOTTFRIED W. FINK, 1783-1846

Arthur Sullivan first published the hymn tune form now commonly used in *Church Hymns with Tunes* (London, 1874) set to "While shepherds watched their flocks by night." He called it an "old tune," but it is actually based on Fink's setting for Matthias Claudius' text "War einst ein Riese Goliath." It was composed in 1842 and appeared in Fink's *Musikalischer Hausschatz der Deutschen,* 1843.

In the 1935 Methodist hymnal there were two different melodic forms given for the last line, the setting at 552 being taken from the Presbyterian hymnal of 1933 where the last line was altered by Dr. Clarence Dickinson to give more climax.

All People That on Earth Do Dwell (21)

WILLIAM KETHE, d. 1594

The direct ancestry of the complete English metrical psalter of 150 psalms entitled *The Whole Book of Psalms Collected into English* by T. Sternhold and J. Hopkins, published by John Day (London, 1562) and known as the "Old Version" after the appearance of the "New Version," edited by Tate and Brady, 1696, begins with Sternhold's first printing of 19 psalm renderings printed by Edward Whitchurch, not earlier than 1547, under a title beginning *Certain Psalms.* In the second edition printed in 1549, after Sternhold's death, Hopkins added 18 hitherto unpublished psalms of Sternhold plus 7 of his own and described the collection as containing "Al such Psalmes of Dauid as Thomas Sternhold, late grome of the Kinges maiesties robes, did in his lyfetime drawe into English Metre." Subsequently, however, 3 more psalms of Sternhold were added to these in a rare edition of the growing psalter, printed by John Day, 1561. The full 40 appear in 1562, 1563, and in all later editions.

The next stage in the growth of the psalter took place in Geneva and was the work of William Kethe, probably a Scot, who seems to have gone to Geneva in 1556 to escape from the persecutions of Mary, Queen of England, 1553-58, and who remained there until 1561 to continue work on the "psalmes in meeter." The first edition of the Anglo-Genevan Psalter prepared by the English refugees, 1556, contained "One and Fiftie Psalms," but no version of Psalm 100. Kethe's chief contribution to the continuing psalter consisted of 25 new psalm paraphrases, including Psalm 100, "All people that on earth do dwell," prepared for the 1561 collection called *Fourscore and Seven Psalms of David.* This psalter is extant in 2 printings, a better exemplar probably done in England, and a rather badly printed copy of the same text, probably printed in Geneva later in the same year. A third source for

Kethe's psalm is the so-called "English" psalter of 1561, entitled *Psalms of David in English Meter,* printed by John Day in London and containing 83 psalms.

Only 10 of Kethe's psalms, but not Psalm 100, were adopted for the complete edition of the Sternhold-Hopkins Psalter, *The Whole Book of Psalms.* However, "All people that on earth do dwell" was introduced into the Appendix of the 1564 edition and in the body of the book in 1565. Since then it has appeared in all metrical psalters and in most hymnbooks during 400 years.

Of the three 1561 printings, the best (probably the oldest) exemplar, that in the British Museum, attributes the psalm to Kethe; the corrupt (and probably later) text attributes it to Sternhold; the Day Psalter leaves it anonymous. However, it can now hardly be doubted that as the British Museum copy attests, Kethe is the author of this paraphrase, which has the distinction of being the oldest English metrical psalm in use and the only survivor of the Sternhold-Hopkins Psalter.

The few alterations which have been made in Kethe's text are of some interest. In 1:3 the original read "Him serve with fear." "Fear" is not a correct rendition of Psalm 100:2, which is properly translated "gladness." The Scottish Psalter of 1650 altered "fear" to "mirth." In our hymnals "mirth" was first printed in 1935.

The first line of st. 2 originally read "The Lord, ye know, is God indeed." Here, too, the Scottish Psalter of 1650 altered the text to "Know that the Lord is God indeed," introduced into our hymnal in 1935. Though this rendering is a more accurate translation of the psalm, Kethe's version is frequently retained.

Very early in the transmission of 2:3 "flock" replaced "folk (e)." Though the British Museum exemplar reads "folke," it is spelled "folck" in the Day Psalter of 1561. "Folck" gets altered to "flock (e)." which is the usual text in the Sternhold-Hopkins and Scottish psalters. That Kethe wrote "folke" now seems proved by the text of the British Museum copy referred to above and by the Geneva Bible which in Psalm 100:3 reads "people." "Flock" was printed in our 1878 and 1905 hymnals, but was replaced by "folk" in 1935. Most modern editors prefer "folk."

The Kethe paraphrase first appears in our hymnals in 1878. John Wesley never printed the Kethe version, preferring Isaac Watts's paraphrase of the same psalm, beginning "Before Jehovah's awful throne."

Old 100th

Genevan Psalter, 1551
Attr. to LOUIS BOURGEOIS, c. 1510–c. 1561

Louis Bourgeois, editor of the various editions of the Genevan Psalter from 1542 to 1557, either composed or adapted this melody for Psalm 134 in the 1551 edition. It was set to Kethe's version of Psalm 100 in *Fourscore and Seven Psalms of David* (Geneva, 1561) and in Day's *Psalms of David in English Meter* (London, 1561).

In the original the last phrase started with 3 notes of double length:

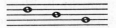

During the last century many books printed the tune with all quarter notes with a fermata at the end of each phrase, a practice which emasculated the strong rhythm of the original. During the eighteenth century the double length notes, which began and ended each phrase, were doubled once again, a practice which also prevented the natural flow of the original.

All Praise to Our Redeeming Lord (301)

CHARLES WESLEY, 1707-1788

The hymn was first published in *Hymns for Those That Seek, and Those That Have, Redemption in the Blood of Jesus Christ,* 1747, entitled "At meeting of Friends." It was printed in 3 sts. of 8 lines each. At least since 1822 in England, 1821 in the United States, the hymn has been printed in six 4-line sts. The original st. 4 was omitted in 1905 and has not since been printed in our hymnals.

The 1964 hymnal is the first to transpose the order of sts. 2 and 3. Traditionally, "He bids us build each other up" is the second st.; "The gift which He on one bestows" is third.

Armenia

SYLVANUS B. POND, 1792-1871
Harm. by A.C.L.

The tune first appeared in *The Musical Miscellany,* which comprised the music published in the *Musical Magazine,* edited by Thomas Hastings (Vol. I, No. 16) and published by Ezra Collier (New York, 1836). It was set there to "Let the sweet hope that thou art mine." It later appeared in Pond's *United States Psalmody* in 1841, the same year that it was printed in Thomas Hastings, *The Manhattan Collection,* published by Daniel Fanshaw in New York.

The tune, little used outside American Methodism, has been re-harmonized.

All Praise to Thee, for Thou, O King Divine (74)

F. BLAND TUCKER, 1895-

The hymn is 1 of 3 hymns by F. Bland Tucker included in the 1964 hymnal, the other 2 being "Alone thou goest forth, O Lord" and "Father, we thank thee who has planted." All were written while he was assisting in the preparation of *The Hymnal 1940* and were first published in that volume.

Based on Philippians 2:5-11, the hymn was written in 1938 with the Ralph Vaughan Williams tune SINE NOMINE in mind. St. 4:2 should read "Art high exalted o'er all creatures now." "High" has been erroneously omitted.

Sine nomine

RALPH VAUGHAN WILLIAMS, 1872-1958

Written for "For all the saints, who from their labors rest," this tune first appeared in *The English Hymnal* (Oxford, 1906), of which Vaughan Williams was musical editor. It was 1 of 3 original tunes which he contributed to the book.

The tune name is a subtle spoof on hymn tune names—"Without a Name."

All Praise to Thee, My God, This Night (493)

THOMAS KEN, 1637-1710

The 3 earliest printed versions of the text can be found in John Julian, *A Dictionary of Hymnology* (Dover, 1957). The first, in 11 sts., is from Henry Playford, *Harmonia Sacra,* Bk. II (London, 1693). The other 2, in 12 sts., printed by Julian in parallel columns, are from the 1695 and 1709 editions of Ken's *Manual of Prayers for the Use of the Scholars of Winchester College.* In the 1674 edition of the *Manual of Prayers,* Ken directs the Winchester scholars, "Be sure to sing the

Morning and Evening Hymn in your Chamber devoutly." It is there-fore to be supposed that Ken's 3 hymns—the morning, evening, and also the midnight hymn—were available at that time. However, they were not included in the *Manual* until the 1695 edition, which de-scribes them as "newly revised." In 1694 Ken seems to have printed the hymns in pamphlet form in protest against pirated printings. The 1709 revision probably was prompted by a spurious publication of his hymns. It doubtless represents the form in which Ken wanted the hymns kept.

All modern printings of the hymn represent various combinations of the 1695 and 1709 versions. English hymnals generally prefer the opening line as in 1695: "Glory to thee, my God, this night"; American hymnals, as in 1693 and 1709: "All praise to thee." Methodist Episco-pal hymnals used "Glory to thee." In the 1935 hymnal in common with the Methodist Episcopal, South hymnals of 1847 and 1889, the 1709 form was adopted.

All modern editors reject Ken's unhappy alteration of 3:3, from "Teach me to die, that so [so that: 1693] I may" (1695), to "To dye, that this vile body may" (1709), but accept the change of "Triumphing rise at the last day" (1695), to "Rise glorious at the awful day" (1709) in 3:4. English hymnals commonly retain "awful," usually spelled "aweful." American hymnals either retain "awful," or substitute "judgment" or omit the entire st. "Judgment Day" appears first in the hymnal of the Methodist Episcopal Church and in all Methodist hymnals since 1905. In 5:3 (the doxology), Ken's 1709 alteration of "y' Angelick Host" to "ye heavenly host" is universally adopted.

The lines of Ken's doxology probably have been sung more often than any other lines ever written. Its structure and meaning are eloquently set forth by James Montgomery in *The Christian Psalmist* (Glasgow, 1825). The passage is quoted in Harry Escott, *Isaac Watts, Hymnographer* (London, 1962).

Tallis' Canon

THOMAS TALLIS, c. 1505-1585

Tallis contributed 9 tunes for *The Whole Psalter* (London, 1561-67), compiled by Matthew Parker, Archbishop of Canterbury. Eight tunes were in the church modes, this being the eighth tune and eighth mode, while the ninth tune was TALLIS' ORDINAL (367).

In the original form each phrase was repeated, making the tune twice as long as now sung. The 4-phrase form was set to "A Psalme before Morning Prayer" in Thomas Ravenscroft, *The Whole Book of Psalms* (London, 1621). It was first wedded to Ken's text in the *Harmonious Companion,* 1732.

It is in the form of a canon, or round, with the following voices entering after the first 4 notes of the tune. It can be done as a 2-, 4-, or 8-part round. It was first set to be sung with Parker's version of Psalm 67.

The tune is also known as BERWICK, BRENTWOOD, CANON, and SUFFOLK.

All the Way My Savior Leads Me (205)

FANNY J. CROSBY, 1820-1915

When the text and tune appeared first in 1875 in a Sunday school collection entitled *Brightest and Best,* Deuteronomy 32:12, "The Lord alone did lead him," was printed above the song.

The text is printed without alteration. This is its first appearance in a Methodist hymnal.

All the Way

ROBERT LOWRY, 1826-1899

Fanny Crosby sent the text to Lowry, who composed the tune. Its first appearance was with the text in *Brightest and Best* (Chicago, 1875), compiled by William H. Doane and Lowry.

All Things Are Thine; No Gift Have We (347)

JOHN GREENLEAF WHITTIER, 1807-1892

The hymn was written in 1872 for the opening of Plymouth Congregational Church, St. Paul, Minn., and was included in Whittier's *Complete Poetical Works,* 1876. It first appeared in a hymnal by W. Garrett Horder, *Congregational Hymns* (London, 1884).

The hymn was originally in 5 sts. Two are omitted here, including the original st. 3, which was appropriate only for the occasion for which the hymn was written.

This is the first appearance of the hymn in a Methodist hymnal.

Herr Jesu Christ, dich zu uns wend

Pensum Sacrum, Görlitz, 1648

Robert G. McCutchan states that this tune "is found as No. 45 in an octavo volume published at Görlitz, Germany: *Pensum Sacrum, Metro-Rhythmicum, CCLXVII Odis . . . denuo expansum expensumque Opera et Studio Tobiae Hauschkonii* (1648). It has an appendix which contains eighty melodies, without texts, suitable for the Latin odes in the volume."

However, two earlier sources are given. The *Orgelbuch zum Gesangbuch der evangelisch-reformierten Kirchen* (Biel, 1953) quotes its source tune as a 1643 manuscript. E. E. Koch in *Geschichte des Kirchenlieds* (Stuttgart, 1866) says that it was already printed in *Cantionale Germanicum* (Dresden, 1628), and Armin Haeussler writes: "Indeed, [Wilhelm] Leitritz tells us that a tradition traces it back to John Huss."

Whatever the original source, it first appeared with the text which gives the tune its name and with its present-day harmonization in *Cantionale Sacrum* (Gotha, 1651).

The version here is the original rhythmic form.

All Things Bright and Beautiful (34)

CECIL FRANCES ALEXANDER, 1818-1895

Concerned with making the Apostles' Creed interesting and intelligible to children, Mrs. Alexander wrote 3 hymns to set forth certain phrases of the creed in simple language. "All things bright and beautiful" spells out the first clause, "Maker of heaven and earth," on the basis of Genesis 1:31. "Once in royal David's city" (see the 1935 Methodist hymnal, No. 442) interprets the second clause, "Born of the Virgin Mary." "There is a green hill far away" (414) is a meditation on "Suffered under Pontius Pilate, was crucified, dead, and buried."

The hymns appeared in her book *Hymns for Little Children,* published in 1848, when she was 30 years old. The innocent childlike quality of her verses has endeared them to young and old alike and has assured them a place in most hymnals.

The hymn entered the Methodist hymnal in 1935, with the first st. printed as a refrain to be sung at the beginning of and after each verse.

The same form has been followed for the present hymnal. Two other sts. have been omitted.

Royal Oak

17th-Century English Melody
Arr. by MARTIN SHAW, 1875-1958
Harm. by V.E.C.

This seventeenth-century melody, called "The Twenty-ninth of May," was a loyal song on the restoration of Charles II, May 29, 1660. Used as a country dance air, it was published in *The Dancing Master,* 1686. It was also known as "The Jovial Crew." For other names and the original see William Chappell, *Old English Popular Music* (the H. E. Wooldridge edition of 1893), II, 52.

Martin Shaw adapted and printed it in sheet form for community singing in *Song Time* in 1915. V. Earle Copes has made a simpler harmonization for the new hymnal.

Part of the charm of the setting arises from the alternation of trochaic and iambic patterns for the refrain, and full trochaic for the sts.

The tune name refers to the tree at Boscobel, Shropshire, England, in which King Charles II hid during his flight following the Battle of Worcester in 1651.

Alone Thou Goest Forth, O Lord (427)
Solus ad victimam procedis, Domine

PETER ABELARD, 1079-1142
Trans. by F. BLAND TUCKER, 1895-

Though Abelard was one of the greatest hymn writers of the Middle Ages, combining in himself personal charm, penetrating intellect, and poetic originality, it appears that only 2 of his some 130 hymns have been translated for English use. The total body of his hymns as known made up a hymnal which he prepared at the request of his wife Heloise after she had become prioress of The Paraclete.

In response to her request for a hymn cycle for a year he wrote hymns for the canonical hours, Matins and Vespers, for the different festivals, for saints' days, and others.

"Alone thou goest forth" is a translation of a hymn for the third nocturnal office on Good Friday. The hymn was prepared in 1938 for

The Hymnal 1940 and is printed without alteration. It is the first Abelard hymn to be printed in a Methodist hymnal.

Bangor
WILLIAM TANS'UR, 1706-1783

Set to Psalm 12 and headed "Bangor Tune," the tune comes from *Complete Melody or Harmony of Zion* by W. Tans'ur (London, Preface dated September 29, 1734), where it was harmonized in 3 parts. Robert Burns refers to this very popular Scottish psalm tune in his poem "The Ordination."

Am I a Soldier of the Cross (239)
ISAAC WATTS, 1674-1748

The hymn is found at the end of Sermon 31, "Holy Fortitude, or Remedies against Fear," on the text I Corinthians 16:13, "Stand fast in the faith, quit you like men, be strong." The date on which the sermon was preached or the hymn written is unknown.

The text appears in our hymnal as Watts wrote it, with the exception of one line. The last line of st. 5 originally read "And seize it with their eye." This line was last printed in a Methodist hymnal in *The Methodist Pocket Hymn Book* (Philadelphia, 1802). When the hymn appears again in Methodist hymnals, beginning in 1831, the line is found altered to its present form, "By faith they bring it nigh." That the original line was thought troublesome elsewhere is evidenced in the Methodist Protestant hymnal of 1837, "The crown enchants their eye," and in the Lutheran hymnal of 1941, "With faith's discerning eye."

The 1849 Methodist Episcopal hymnal changed "sure" in 4:1 to "since," but reverted to "sure" in all later editions. Unhappy with "vile world" (3:3) *The Hymnal 1940* altered it to "vain world."

Arlington
THOMAS A. ARNE, 1710-1778

Arranged as a hymn tune by Ralph Harrison (1748-1810), it appeared in Vol. I of his *Sacred Harmony—A Collection of Psalm-tunes, Ancient and Modern* (2 vols.; London, 1784, 1791), from the minuet in the Overture to *Artaxerxes,* an opera by Arne produced in London in 1762.

It is also called ARTAXERXES and TRIUMPH.

Amazing Grace! How Sweet the Sound (92)

JOHN NEWTON, 1725-1807

The hymn appeared first in *Olney Hymns,* 1779, under I Chronicles, 17:16-17, and entitled "Faith's review and expectation." It is printed without alteration except for Newton's st. 6 which has been omitted.

The text seems to have entered Methodist hymnals through *Zion Songster, A Collection of Hymns and Spiritual Songs Generally Sung at Camp and Prayer Meetings, and in Revivals of Religion,* compiled by Peter D. Myers (New York, 1829). It appears first (in 5 sts.) in Methodist Episcopal, South hymnals of 1847, 1866, 1874; then in the 1878 Methodist Episcopal hymnal in three 8-line sts.; in the 1905 hymnal in six 4-line sts. The 1935 hymnal dropped the last 2 sts.; the 1964 hymnal has restored st. 5.

Since both text and tune of "Amazing grace" are in authentic camp-meeting style, it is not surprising that additional lines have been improvised and added. The best known of these is the st. printed in *The Cokesbury Hymnal,* 1923, and in later editions:

When we've been there ten thousand years,
　Bright shining as the sun,
We've no less days to sing God's praise
　Than when we first begun.

William J. Reynolds traces its probable origin to John P. Rees, who printed the lines as a separate text unrelated to Newton's hymn in the second Appendix of the 1859 edition of *The Sacred Harp.* Then, 51 years later E. O. Excell, *Coronation Hymns* (Chicago, 1910), added the lines as the fourth st. to Newton's hymn. Robert H. Coleman reprinted "Amazing grace" in the Excell form in his *New Evangel* (Dallas, 1911) and in all his subsequent hymnals.

Thus the lines became widely sung as Newton's, and are mistakenly so printed in the *Mennonite Hymnary,* 1940, in *The Baptist Hymnal,* 1956, and in all the Cokesbury hymnals. They probably entered the

Cokesbury hymnals through the popular use of Excell's many song-books and under the influence of Southern Baptist hymnals.

Amazing Grace

Early American Melody
Virginia Harmony, 1831
Harm. by A.C.L.

This popular Southern tune first appeared in *Virginia Harmony* (Lebanon, Va., 1831), compiled by James P. Carrell and David S. Clayton. Robert G. McCutchan suggests that it may be a variant of the old tune LOVING LAMB. Other names found in early American tunebooks are NEW BRITAIN, HARMONY GROVE, SYMPHONY, SOLON, and REDEMPTION.

Ancient of Days, Who Sittest Throned in Glory (459)

WILLIAM C. DOANE, 1832-1913

Picking up the phrase "Ancient of Days" from Daniel 7:9, Bishop Doane wrote a hymn to the Trinity for the bicentenary celebration in 1886 of the granting of the charter to Albany, N. Y., the first chartered city in America. The hymn was first sung in the Episcopal cathedral at Albany and later altered by Bishop Doane for the 1892 Episcopal *Hymnal*.

The Hymnal 1940 altered "still prevails" to "shall prevail" in 3:2, an important shift in meaning, necessitating also altering "gales" to "gale." In 4:3, the text is strengthened by changing "pleasant" to "mighty." Line 4 is altered from "Our plenty, wealth, prosperity, and peace" to "Our faith and hope, our fellowship and peace."

The hymn entered the Methodist hymnal of 1905 in the original form. The 1964 hymnal follows *The Hymnal 1940* in accepting "mighty" and "Our faith and hope, our fellowship and peace," but retains the original "still prevails."

Ancient of Days

J. ALBERT JEFFERY, 1855-1929
Harm. by V.E.C.

The tune was written in 1886 at the request of Bishop Doane, under whom Jeffery served as organist at All Saints' Cathedral in

Albany. It was first printed in 1894 in C. L. Hutchins' musical edition of the 1892 Episcopal *Hymnal,* called ANCIENT OF DAYS. In J. I. Tucker and W. W. Rousseau's music edition of the same hymnal it appeared as ALBANY, a name which is continued in *The Hymnal 1940.* It was originally written for 4 voices and an organ accompaniment.

And Are We Yet Alive (336)

CHARLES WESLEY, 1707-1788

More than 2 centuries of tradition have endeared this hymn to Methodists, who through the years have sung it around the world as the opening hymn for Annual Conference sessions. John Wesley himself initiated the tradition.

The hymn first appeared in *Hymns and Sacred Poems,* 1749, in the section on "Hymns for Christian Friends." John Wesley placed it first in Part V, Section I, of his 1780 *Collection of Hymns for the Use of the People Called Methodists,* "For the Society . . . at meeting."

The hymn was originally in 4 sts. of 8 lines, but st. 4 seems never to have been printed after John omitted it in the 1780 *Collection.*

The 1780 *Collection* altered "glory and thanks" (1:3) to "glory and praise"; "almighty grace" (1:4) to "redeeming grace"; "What mighty conflicts past" (2:2) to "What conflicts have we past"; the 1831 printing changed "yet" (3:1) to "but"; "hide" (3:4) to "hides." These alterations have all been retained to this day by *The Methodist Hymn-Book,* London. They were retained in American Methodist hymnals until 1964; the original Wesley text has been restored except for the retention of "hides" in 3:4.

The 1935 hymnal reduced the hymn to 4 sts. of 4 lines each, omitting 2 other quatrains. The 1964 hymnal has restored the quatrain beginning with "Let us take up the cross," to make 5 sts. of 4 lines.

Dennis

JOHANN G. NÄGELI, 1768-1836
Arr. by LOWELL MASON, 1792-1872

From one of his European trips Mason brought home a manuscript by Nägeli, the Swiss publisher, from which the hymn tune arrangement was made. It was first published in *The Psaltery,* 1845, edited by Mason and George J. Webb and set to "How gentle God's commands."

Leonard Ellinwood suggests that a melody for "O Selig, selig, wer vor dir" in the *Christliches Gesangbuch,* 1828, may be the source for Mason's arrangement.

The tune is also known as RIPON.

And Can It Be That I Should Gain (527)

CHARLES WESLEY, 1707-1788

The hymn was written in London, May, 1738, and published the same year in John Wesley, *A Collection of Psalms and Hymns,* and the next year in *Hymns and Sacred Poems* with the title "Free grace." Under date of May 23, Charles wrote in his Journal: "At nine I began a hymn on my conversion but was persuaded to break off for fear of pride. . . . I prayed Christ to stand by me and finished the hymn." It has not been established whether this is the hymn referred to, or whether it was "Where shall my wondering soul begin?" At least one of these was written in the 2-day period between Charles's conversion and John's coming to faith, after which at 10 o'clock that very evening John with several friends went to Charles's room and "sang the hymn with great joy, and parted with prayer." In any case both hymns were written about the same time, and both are typical and powerful statements of the Wesleyan conversion experience.

"And can it be" was originally in 6 sts. St. 5, dropped by John Wesley's 1780 *Collection,* seems not to have been printed again.

The hymn has been included as a 5-st. hymn in almost all Methodist hymnals, both in England and America, and essentially in its original form. There has been variation in only 2 words. In the last line of st. 1, Wesley wrote "God," not "Lord." To this day English reprints retain the original, not shying away from the paradox, "That thou, my God, shouldst die for me." Since the early years of the nineteenth century American imprints have substituted "Lord" for "God," apparently reluctant to run the risk of using the strange but powerful language of paradox that *God* in Christ had died, language which both Watts and Wesley could use without fear of its being misunderstood.

Until 1935, when the sts. were reduced to 3, Methodist hymnals always printed 5 sts. The 1964 hymnal has restored Wesley's st. 2, " 'Tis mystery all! th'Immortal dies."

In a perceptive analysis, T. B. Shepherd, in an article in *London*

Quarterly and Holborn Review, October, 1945, observes that the 3 main characteristics of Charles Wesley as a poet are his stress on free and unlimited grace, his constant use of quotations from the Bible or poets, and his employment of words expressing space when describing God. These characteristics are clearly illustrated in "And can it be." God's grace is "immense" and free. It cannot be measured; it is illimitable, infinite, beyond depth, height, and width. In describing his conversion, Wesley does not luxuriate in his own feelings; rather, he celebrates God's mercy, God's grace, God's love and light, his redemptive work. The metaphors are bold: darkness—light, life—death, slavery—freedom. With subtle artistry, the hymn alternates heavy phrases with short crisp staccato words, as phrase falls over phrase in a tumultuous rush to the grandeur and repose of the final rapture.

Fillmore

Attributed to JEREMIAH INGALLS, 1764-1828
Harm. by A.C.L.

Robert G. McCutchan states: " 'Fillmore' was doubtless composed by Jeremiah Ingalls, although in tune books of the middle of the last century it is said to be 'An old melody.' It is not found in *The Christian Harmony,* a book published by Mr. Ingalls in 1805, now seldom seen."

The first actual source found so far is in *Joyful Songs Nos. 1–3 Combined,* compiled by William G. Fischer and published by the Methodist Episcopal Book Rooms (Philadelphia, 1869). It is there listed as arranged by William G. Fischer as sung by Chaplain C. C. McCabe.

McCutchan has suggested that the tune was named for President Millard Fillmore.

And Have the Bright Immensities (456)

HOWARD CHANDLER ROBBINS, 1876-1952

The poem was first printed in *Living Church,* April 3, 1931, and then published by the author in his *Way of Light,* 1933. H. Augustine Smith was the first editor to include it in a hymnal, *New Church Hymnal,* 1937. *The Hymnal 1940* also printed it.

Erik Routley in *Hymns Today and Tomorrow* has described the hymn as a brave but unsuccessful attempt to remythologize the Ascension. As impressive as st. 1 is, he suggests, the second runs to romanticism and offers images which are neither clear nor biblical. Yet the very juxtaposition of the "bright immensities" and the "altar candle" is moving, and perhaps one does not need to worry too much about the literal sense of "standing with unhurrying feet."

Halifax
GEORGE FREDERICK HANDEL, 1685-1759
Harm. by A.C.L.

The tune is taken from Handel's opera, *Susanna*, 1748, from the aria "Ask if yon damask rose be sweet." It was first arranged as a hymn tune in Thomas Butts, *Harmonia Sacra* (London, c. 1756), and set to the text "Indulgent Father! how divine." This collection was very popular with early Methodists and served as the source for several tunes still in use despite some reservations John Wesley had of the entire collection. The present version is an abbreviation of Butts's version.

Halifax is in Yorkshire, England, but no logical connection between the tune and name has yet been established.

Angel Voices, Ever Singing (2)
FRANCIS POTT, 1832-1909

Francis Pott, a member of the original committee responsible for the preparation of *Hymns Ancient and Modern,* 1861, wrote the hymn for the dedication of the new organ in the Church of St. John the Evangelist at Wingate, England, where it was first sung February 10, 1861. It was then published by Pott in the second edition of his *Hymns Fitted to the Order of Common Prayer,* 1866.

The hymn entered the Methodist Protestant hymnal in 1901, and the Methodist hymnal in 1905, the latter omitting st. 3. The 1935 and 1964 hymnals print the entire hymn of 5 sts. without alteration.

Angel Voices
ARTHUR S. SULLIVAN, 1842-1900
Adapt. by A.C.L.

This tune was written and published in 1872. The rhythm has been altered from 6/8 to 2/2 for the new hymnal.

93

Angels, from the Realms of Glory (382)

JAMES MONTGOMERY, 1771-1854

The hymn was first printed under the title "Nativity" in the Christmas Eve, 1816, edition of the *Sheffield Iris,* a newspaper on which James Montgomery was employed as an editor. Its first inclusion in a hymnal was in the eighth edition of Thomas Cotterill, *A Selection of Psalms and Hymns for Public and Private Use,* 1819, where its 5 sts. were repeated without alteration. No alterations were made until Montgomery himself prepared the hymn for publication in his *Christian Psalmist,* 1825, when he changed "flock" to "flocks" (2:2), "waiting" to "watching" (4:2), and "repeals" to "revokes" (5:3). Since Montgomery retained these changes in his *Original Hymns,* 1853, they have become standard.

The hymn entered the Methodist Protestant hymnal in 1837 and the Methodist Episcopal hymnal in 1849, with all 5 sts., and remained intact until the 1935 hymnal dropped the final st.

Regent Square

HENRY SMART, 1813-1879

Written for *Psalms and Hymns for Divine Worship* (London, 1867) for use among English Presbyterians, the tune appeared 11 years later in the Methodist Episcopal hymnal of 1878, and in the *Hymn and Tune Book* of the Methodist Episcopal Church, South in 1889.

It was written for Horatius Bonar's "Glory be to God the Father" and was named after Regent Square Presbyterian Church in London, whose minister, James Hamilton, was editor of the collection in which it first appeared.

Angels We Have Heard on High (374)
Les anges dans nos campagnes

Traditional French Carol

The French original was first published in the *Nouveau recueil de cantiques,* 1855. The origin of the carol is unknown, but it is believed to have come from the eighteenth century. The evidence for this is presented in Jan R. H. de Smidt, *Les Noëls et la tradition populaire,* 1932.

The carol entered the Methodist hymnal in 1935, with the translation

94

"Hearken all! what holy singing," which had appeared in 1922 in *The Nativity,* a mystery play whose author is unknown. The 1964 hymnal prefers "Angels we have heard on high," a translation first printed in *Crown of Jesus,* 1862. Some alterations of the 1862 form may be noted:

1:4 originally read "Echo still their joyous strains."
2:2 originally read "Why your rapturous strain prolong?"
2:3 originally read "Say what may the tidings be?"
3:1 originally read "Come to Bethlehem, come and see"
3:4 originally read "The Infant Christ, the new-born King."
4 "See within a manger laid,
  Jesus, Lord of heaven and earth!
Mary, Joseph, lend your aid
To celebrate our Saviour's birth."

Gloria

Traditional French Carol
Harm. by A.C.L.

This tune, set to the old French carol "Les anges dans nos campagnes," was first published in *Nouveau recueil de cantiques,* 1855. Smidt has suggested that the tune also dates from the eighteenth century. Its first appearance with an English text was in R. R. Chope, *Carols for Use in Church,* 1875.

In England the tune is called IRIS.

Are Ye Able, Said the Master (413)

EARL MARLATT, 1892-

The hymn was written to be sung at a consecration service in the Boston University School of Religious Education, 1926. Under the title "Challenge" it was copyrighted and printed as a broadsheet by Dr. Marlatt the same year. Its first inclusion in a hymnal was in the *American Student Hymnal,* edited by H. Augustine Smith, 1928, of which Marlatt was associate editor. The hymn was originally in 6 sts.; sts. 2 and 3 are now commonly omitted.

Dr. Marlatt's own account of the chain of occasions which prompted the making of the various sts. can be read in Robert G. McCutchan, *Our Hymnody,* pp. 306-7, or in E. K. Emurian, *Sing the Wondrous Story* (Natick, Mass., 1963).

Beacon Hill

HARRY S. MASON, 1881-1964

William J. Reynolds quotes the following from a letter by Earl Marlatt, dated July 21, 1962:

The tune BEACON HILL was composed by Harry S. Mason in April, 1924, while he was a graduate student at Boston University School of Religious Education. It was written as a musical setting for Harry Wright's entry into a school song contest. Mr. Wright half read and half sang the text of the song to broken phrases of a tune he had remembered from his school days. Mr. Mason took the basic theme as it was hummed by Mr. Wright, supplied the missing measures and elaborated the whole into stirring music for Mr. Wright's text. The song was then submitted for the contest, but surprisingly to many who had heard and admired it did not rate with the judges. Among those especially disappointed in this result was Professor Earl Marlatt, at that time head resident of the men's dormitory, called "The Hermitage"; he had overheard the song-making in the music room and remembered the arresting tune. Consequently, when he was asked the following spring to write a hymn for the consecration of the officers of the Student Association at the School of Religious Education, he found that the expression, "Are ye able," from a sermon he had preached the preceding Sunday, sang exactly to the first measure of Harry Wright's text and the tune Harry Mason had arranged for it. After that the music miraculously seemed to suggest the words until the whole hymn was finished in a single evening.

Beacon Hill is a famous section in Boston, the earlier location of Boston University School of Theology.

Arise, My Soul, Arise (122)

CHARLES WESLEY, 1707-1788

This hymn, printed only in Methodist hymnals and written now in language strange to Methodists too, may almost be regarded as a compendium of Wesleyan theology. It has been included in virtually all Methodist hymnals since it originally appeared in *Hymns and Sacred Poems,* 1742, under the title "Behold the Man."

For more than 2 centuries the hymn has been printed unaltered, with the exception of one word. In 3:4, Wesley wrote "speak" instead of "plead." "Plead" appears first in the 1849 Methodist Episcopal hymnal. Although "plead" has never displaced "speak" in English Methodist

96

hymnbooks, its presence in the 1849 and 1878 Methodist Episcopal hymnals has made for its continuance in all subsequent Methodist hymnals in America.

Lenox

LEWIS EDSON, SR., 1748-1820

This tune, sometimes called TRUMPET, first appeared in Simeon Jocelyn, *The Chorister's Companion* (New Haven, Conn., 1782 or 1783). It appeared there as a fuguing tune: i.e., the last section is made up of a series of entries by various voice parts, starting with the bass. The form was very popular in singing schools and is related to the Scottish practice of "psalms in report."

Art Thou Weary, Art Thou Languid (99)
κόπον τε καὶ κάματον

Trans. by JOHN M. NEALE, 1818-1866

The hymn appeared first in 1862, in Neale's *Hymns of the Eastern Church,* as a translation or paraphrase of a lyric by St. Stephen the Sabaite, c. 725-94, and under the Greek words κόπον τε καὶ κάματον, which, it was supposed, was the first line of the Greek hymn which prompted Neale's poem. Neale stated that he copied the original from an undated Constantinopolitan book. However, in the second and third editions of the book (1863, 1866) he omitted the detail about copying the Greek text, and in the third edition stated that the hymn "contains so little that is from the Greek that it ought not to have been included in this collection," and insisted that in any future edition it should appear as an appendix. The fourth edition so prints it, but still under the Greek superscription. John Julian's suggestion is that the hymn was really composed by Neale himself, but may have been based on these 4 Greek words which Neale came across in his extensive reading of Greek sacred poets, but which have not yet been identified.

The hymn entered Methodist hymnals with the 1901 edition of the Methodist Protestant hymnal, and then in the 1905 Methodist hymnal. With 2 exceptions the hymn is printed without alteration. Neale began st. 3, "Is there diadem?" This was altered to "Hath he diadem?" in the 1935 hymnal, following some but not all modern editors.

In 7:3, the original read "Angels, martyrs, prophets, virgins." Its

97

alteration to "Saints, apostles, prophets, martyrs" by E. H. Bickersteth, *The Hymnal Companion to the Book of Common Prayer* (London, 1870), has been accepted by most editors.

Since the word "languid" (1:1) has assumed new connotations since Neale wrote the hymn, editors have been reluctant to let it stand. The 1935 hymnal altered it to "troubled"; a more popular variation is "heavy-laden" after Matthew 11:28; yet another is "art thou laden." The 1964 hymnal has returned to the original word, "languid."

Stephanos

HENRY W. BAKER, 1821-1877
Harm. by W. H. MONK, 1823-1889

With its melody by Baker and harmonization by W. H. Monk, the tune first appeared with this text in the Appendix to *Hymns Ancient and Modern* (London, 1868). It is named for the Greek word for "diadem" (see st. 3).

As Men of Old Their First Fruits Brought (511)

FRANK VON CHRISTIERSON, 1900-

On the invitation of the Department of Stewardship and Benevolence of the National Council of Churches of Christ in the U.S.A. and in cooperation with that organization, the Hymn Society of America sought new hymns on stewardship for use at the fortieth anniversary celebration of the department held in Toronto, December 12-16, 1960. "As men of old" was 1 of 10 hymns chosen by the committee for publication in booklet form published by the Hymn Society and copyrighted in 1961.

A third st. has been omitted. In 2:5, "calling" has been altered to "stirring."

High Popples

SAMUEL WALTER, 1916-

The tune was written in 1962 for this hymnal and this text. It is named for High Popples Road where the composer lives during the summer. High popples are the stones washed high on the coast in a heavy storm.

As Pants the Hart for Cooling Streams (255)

Psalm 42 *New Version*
TATE and BRADY, 1696
Alt. by HENRY F. LYTE, 1793-1847

"As pants the hart for cooling streams," "O Lord, our fathers oft have told" (Psalm 44, 5), and "Through all the changing scenes of life" (Psalm 34, 56) are the only metrical psalms in Tate and Brady's *New Version of the Psalms of David* (London, 1696) to survive. The original paraphrase of Psalm 42 was in 6 sts. of 8 lines. H. F. Lyte, *The Spirit of the Psalms*, 1834, selected the first, second, fourth, and twelfth quatrains, thus making the psalm available for common use. Sts. 1 and 2 are unaltered Tate and Brady (after "a" in the first line had been changed to "the"); likewise st. 4, with the exception of the last line. In the first edition of the *New Version*, the last line was "Thy health and safety's spring." This was altered in later editions to "Thy health's eternal spring," which seems to be retained in all hymnals except American Methodist, which from the beginning (1849) have regularly printed "Thy Savior, and thy King."

St. 3 appears in the Lyte paraphrase with "wert" in line 2 altered to "wast," and "And none so blest as I" in line 4 altered to "And none more blest than I." These changes are attested at least as early as 1849.

Ayrshire

KENNETH G. FINLAY, 1882-

The tune was first printed in the Supplement, 1936, to the *Irish Church Hymnal* (Belfast) and set to "Prayer is the soul's sincere desire." Erik Routley in *Companion to Congregational Praise* states, "Like many of this composer's tunes, it is written on the pentatonic [5 notes only] scale and it has a sombre Celtic dignity all its own."

Ayrshire is a county in southwest Scotland.

As with Gladness Men of Old (397)

WILLIAM C. DIX, 1837-1898

Though secondary sources agree that the hymn was written while the author was recovering from an illness, and perhaps on Epiphany, after having read the Gospel lesson, the year in which it was written is variously given from 1858 to 1860. In any case, the hymn seems to have been first printed in the trial edition of *Hymns Ancient and Modern,* 1859; then in A. H. Ward, *Hymns for Public Worship and Private Devotion,* for use at St. Raphael's Church, Bristol, 1860; then in the author's *Hymns of Love and Joy,* 1861; and finally in the first edition of *Hymns Ancient and Modern,* 1861.

The hymn entered Methodist hymnals in 1878, was dropped in the 1905 hymnal, but restored in 1935. Methodist hymnals have always omitted the original st. 5.

The text used in the 1964 hymnal is identical with that of *Hymns Ancient and Modern,* 1861, except for the alteration of "joyful" (2:1) to "joyous," beginning with the 1935 edition. Most hymnals, however, retain "joyful."

Dix

Abridg. from **CONRAD KOCHER, 1786-1872**
by **W. H. MONK, 1823-1889**

The original source was from *Stimmen aus dem Reiche Gottes* (Stuttgart, 1838), a collection of old and new German hymns, set to the text "Treuer Heiland! wir sind hier."

Robert G. McCutchan in *Our Hymnody,* p. 41, gives the original form of the melody, which Monk adapted by shortening it from 7 to 6 lines and setting it to Dix's "As with gladness men of old" for *Hymns Ancient and Modern* (London, 1861).

The tune was named for the author of the text.

Ask Ye What Great Thing I Know (124)

Wollt ihr wissen, was mein Preis?

JOHANN C. SCHWEDLER, 1672-1730
Trans. by **BENJAMIN H. KENNEDY, 1804-1889**

The hymn is based on I Corinthians 2:2 and Galatians 6:14. It was first published in the *Hirschberger Gesangbuch,* 1741, 11 years after the author's death. It was written in six 4-line sts., with refrain.

The most commonly used English translation is that by Benjamin Kennedy, in 6 sts., first published in his collection of 1863, *Hymnologia Christiana.* The hymn was printed first in America in *Hymns of the Church,* the Reformed Church in America, 1869, in 5 sts.

The text entered the Methodist hymnal in 1935 with 4 sts. The original second and third sts. have been omitted.

Hendon

H. A. CÉSAR MALAN, 1787-1864
Arr. by LOWELL MASON, 1792-1872

Malan published several collections of his own texts and tunes in France. The first appeared in 1823, but most sources quote 1827 as the first appearance of this tune. Lowell Mason brought back the tune, arranged it, and published it in his *Carmina Sacra,* 1841.

Hendon is a village in Middlesex, England, where Malan may have visited.

At Even, ere the Sun Was Set (501)

HENRY TWELLS, 1823-1900

Duncan Campbell, *Hymns and Hymn Makers* (London, 1899), quotes an undated letter from Canon Twells about the writing of the hymn:

It was written in 1868, at the request of Sir Henry Baker, who said a new evening hymn was wanted for the first [sic] edition of *Hymns Ancient and Modern,* and being at that time headmaster of a large grammar school—the Godolphin School, Hammersmith—I wrote it one afternoon while the boys were under examination (paper work), and I suppose to be seeing "all fair." I am afraid I could not have been very energetic or lynx-eyed in my duties that day, but I little anticipated the popularity the hymn would attain. I have been asked for leave to insert it in 147 different hymnals in all parts of the English-speaking world, and many more have taken it without leave. Copies have been kindly sent me in Greek, Latin, German, French, Welsh, and Irish.

It is supposed that this letter was written shortly before the publication of *Hymns and Hymn Makers,* 30 years after the writing of the hymn and when Canon Twells was about 75 years old. Thus he might be excused for not remembering that the first edition of *Hymns Ancient and Modern,* words only, was in 1860, and the first full music edition, 1861.

Though the 1868 edition of *Hymns Ancient and Modern* prints the hymn in seven 4-line sts., John Julian states that the hymn originally appeared in 8 sts. But where the 8-st. form was first published is a problem. *The Lutheran Hymnal,* 1941, prints 8 sts. but erroneously seems to attribute all to *Hymns Ancient and Modern,* 1868. John Julian further states that st. 8 (the original fourth, but not the fourth in *Hymns Ancient and Modern*, 1868) was reinstated in *Church Hymns*, 1871, and in Godfrey Thring's *Church of England Hymn Book*, 1882, but there is no firm documentation of the first printing of this st.

The hymn entered the Methodist hymnal in 1905, with 6 sts. In addition to the st. discussed above, the fourth st. in *Hymns Ancient and Modern*, 1868, is also omitted.

Hymn editors have been unhappy with Twells's original first line. Thring objected to "ere" as ignorant of the Jewish law forbidding the carrying of the sick before the setting of the sun, and though Twells agreed to altering "ere" to "when," he maintained there was really no discrepancy between Mark 1:32-33, Luke 4:40, and "At even, ere the sun was set." Nevertheless, Thring's alteration persisted, and in most hymnals "when" replaces "ere." Though Thring preferred "At even, when the sun did set," most hymnals read "At even, when the sun was set." The Methodist hymnal has always printed Twells's original line: "At even, ere the sun was set." For Twells's defense of his original line, see the *Literary Churchman*, June 9 and 23, 1882.

Apart from the omitted sts., the hymn is printed as Twells wrote it.

Abends

HERBERT S. OAKELEY, 1830-1903

The tune was originally written for "Sun of my soul" for the *Irish Church Hymnal* (Belfast, 1874), and Oakeley later reworked the harmony for *The Church Hymnary* (Edinburgh and Oxford, 1898). He wrote the tune because of his aversion to the tune HURSLEY. ABENDS is an appropriate name since it is the German word for evening.

At Length There Dawns the Glorious Day (189)

OZORA S. DAVIS, 1866-1931

The hymn was written in the summer of 1909 while Dr. Davis was on vacation at his summer home on the shore of Lake Sunapee, N.H. Written to be sung in Minneapolis at the autumn meeting of the National Congregational Brotherhood, it was first printed in a pamphlet with other hymns for use at the convention. Its theme of brotherhood is characteristic of much twentieth-century American hymn writing.

It entered the Methodist hymnal in 1935 and is printed without alteration.

Clonmel

Traditional Irish Melody
Harm. by A.C.L.

Known as "The Flight of the Earls," the tune first appeared as a hymn tune in the *Church and School Hymnal* (London, 1926). Eric Thiman gave the tune its present name in *Congregational Praise* (London, 1951). Clonmel is a small town in Ireland.

The melodic line at the beginning of the second and last phrase has been slightly altered.

At the Name of Jesus Every Knee Shall Bow (76)

CAROLINE M. NOEL, 1817-1877

The hymn originally appeared in 7 sts. in the enlarged edition of Miss Noel's book *The Name of Jesus and Other Verses for the Sick and Lonely,* 1870. It was written as a processional hymn for Ascension Day and is based on Philippians 2:5-11.

The hymn entered the Methodist hymnal in 1964, with 4 sts. Three sts. have been omitted.

King's Weston

RALPH VAUGHAN WILLIAMS, 1872-1958

The tune was composed for this text for *Songs of Praise* (Oxford, 1925), a book which broke ground in unusual texts and tunes. *Songs of Praise Discussed* states: "It is a solid tune, in triple time, with a strongly stressed rhythm, and a characteristic exchange of accent in the last two lines; it is a dignified, but not a solemn tune, and must not be sung too slowly."

The tune is named for a country house on the River Avon, near Bristol, England, noted for its beautiful park.

At Thy Feet, Our God and Father (498)

JAMES D. BURNS, 1823-1864

The hymn first appeared in periodical form in the *Family Treasury* (London, 1861) and then in *Psalms and Hymns for Divine Worship* (London, 1867), an English Presbyterian collection. It was originally a New Year's hymn. St. 1:4 read "To begin the year with praise."

"Year" was changed to "day" by American editors in order to make the hymn more generally useful. Otherwise, the hymn is printed as it was written.

The hymn entered the Methodist hymnal in 1935.

St. Asaph

WILLIAM S. BAMBRIDGE, 1842-1923

Upon the recovery of Edward, Prince of Wales (later Edward VII), from typhoid fever, this was one of several tunes written in celebration and thanksgiving in 1872. It was first published in Arthur Sullivan, *Church Hymns with Tunes* (London, 1874).

Author of Faith, Eternal Word (139)

CHARLES WESLEY, 1707-1788

In *Hymns and Sacred Poems* (London, 1740), compiled by John and Charles Wesley, an 85-st. paraphrase of Hebrews 11 was published under the title "The Life of Faith, Exemplified in the Eleventh Chapter of St. Paul's Epistle to the Hebrews." In his 1780 *Collection of Hymns for the Use of the People Called Methodists,* John selected the first 6 sts. as the opening hymn of Section II, "Describing inward Religion." He made only one change in the text: in 4:4, "happiness" was changed to "holiness."

The alteration is interesting since one of John's favorite formulas is "holiness is happiness." Both before and after his conversion Wesley maintained that his aim in life was to become as happy as possible, which required being as holy as possible. As early as July 19, 1731, he wrote, "My present sense is this—I was made to be happy: to be happy I must love God; in proportion to my love of whom my happiness must increase. To love God I must be like Him, holy as He is holy" (*Letters,* I, 92).

The hymn has been printed in virtually all Methodist hymnals, both in England and America, except in the 1935 hymnal. It is now appropriately restored.

Mainzer

JOSEPH MAINZER, 1801-1851
Alt. and harm. by A.C.L.

The tune was set to a version of Psalm 107 in Mainzer's *Choruses* (London, 1841) and to Psalm 102 in his *Standard Psalmody of Scot-*

104

land, 1845. The rhythm has been altered to avoid the monotony caused by the even note values of the original.

Author of Life Divine (315)

CHARLES WESLEY, 1707-1788

The text was first published in *Hymns on the Lord's Supper* by John and Charles Wesley, 1745. There is no decisive evidence to show which of the 2 brothers wrote it. Though *Hymns Ancient and Modern* persists in ascribing the hymn to John and *Songs of Praise* names both "J. and C. Wesley," the assumption of most editors that Charles wrote the hymn is probably correct.

Perhaps because John did not include the hymn either in his *Hymns and Spiritual Songs,* 1753, or in his *Collection of Hymns for the Use of the People Called Methodists,* 1780, it was not reprinted in any Methodist hymnal either in England or America until 1933 in England and 1964 in America.

A treasure indeed, the hymn is printed without alteration.

Author of Life

ROBERT J. POWELL, 1932-

The tune was written in March, 1962, for this text and this hymnal.

Awake, Awake to Love and Work (190)

G. A. STUDDERT-KENNEDY, 1883-1929

The poem, entitled "At a Harvest Festival," was first published in *The Sorrows of God and Other Poems* (London, 1921) and then in Kennedy's collected poetry, *The Unutterable Beauty,* 1927.

The first 3 sts. read:

Not here for high and holy things
  We render thanks to Thee,
But for the common things of earth,
  The purple pageantry
Of dawning and of dying days,
  The splendour of the sea:

The royal robes of autumn moors,
  The golden gates of spring,
The velvet of soft summer nights,
  The silver glistering
Of all the million million stars,
  The silent song they sing,

    Of Faith and Hope and Love undimmed,
    Undying still through death,

The Resurrection of the world,
What time there comes the breath
Of dawn that rustles through the trees,
And that clear voice that saith:

Then follow the 3 sts. of the hymn, the words spoken by "that clear voice."

The hymn entered the Methodist hymnal in 1935.

Morning Song

JOHN WYETH, *A Repository of
Sacred Music, Part II*, 1813
Harm. by A.C.L.

Wyeth's *Repository* (Harrisburg, Pa., 1813) seems to be the original source of many folk tunes and hymns which other editors borrowed freely. Often called CONSOLATION in other books, the tune has been attributed to "Dean," but without documentation. Annabel Morris Buchanan has pointed out the resemblance of this tune to English ballads and carols.

Awake, My Soul, and with the Sun (180)

THOMAS KEN, 1637-1710

See "All praise to thee, my God, this night," pp. 82-83.

John Julian in *A Dictionary of Hymnology* (Dover, 1957) prints the original 14 sts. of the 1695 and 1709 editions in parallel columns. Our hymnal prints the first and last 3 sts. exactly as revised by Ken for his 1709 printing. Though Wesley seems never to have included the hymn in his collections, it was assured a prominent place in English church use by being included in the Supplement to the Tate and Brady Psalter as early as 1782.

The hymn has been included in all official American Methodist hymnals in a 4- or 5-st. form, with or without the familiar doxology, which is retained in the present hymnal, though the sts. selected vary.

Tallis' Canon

See "All Praise to Thee, My God, This Night," pp. 82-84.

Awake, My Soul, Stretch Every Nerve (249)

PHILLIP DODDRIDGE, 1702-1751

The hymn was first printed in Doddridge's *Hymns Founded on Various Texts in the Holy Scriptures,* published from the author's manuscripts by Job Orton (London, 1755). The subject heading was "Messengers, Embassadors"; the title: "Pressing on in the Christian Race"; the text: Philippians 3:12-14.

Though not included in English Methodist hymnals, American Methodist hymnals at least since 1847 have regularly printed the hymn usually, though not always, with the full 5 sts. The 1905 hymnal was the last to print the original st. 4.

The text is printed without other alteration, except the change of "mine" to "my" in the last line.

Christmas

JAMES HEWITT, *Harmonia Sacra,* 1812
Arr. from GEORGE FREDERICK HANDEL, 1685-1759

An adaptation of the soprano aria "Non vi piacque ingiusti Dei" in Act II of the opera *Siroe,* 1728, the hymn tune version first appeared in James Hewitt, *Harmonia Sacra,* 1812, then David Weyman, *Melodia Sacra,* 1815, set to Psalm 132. Lowell Mason included it in the Boston *Handel and Haydn Society Collection of Church Music,* 1821. The tune INNOCENTS possibly has the same ancestor; see p. 268. The tune name comes from frequent association of the tune with "While shepherds watched their flocks by night." Other tune names: LUNENBERG, SANDFORD, and HARLEIGH.

Away in a Manger (384)

ANONYMOUS

All that can be said confidently about the origin of this carol is that Martin Luther himself had nothing to do with it. The evidence suggests that it is wholly an American product. The original 2-st. form probably originated among German Lutherans in Pennsylvania about 1885. The earliest extant printing of this form derives from Philadelphia in 1885. St. 3 appears first in 1892 in a Louisville, Ky., imprint and may have been contributed by an editor or publisher who thought the 2 narrative sts. needed to be supplemented by a prayer.

Richard S. Hill, in a painstaking and brilliant article in Music Library Association *Notes* (December, 1945), conjectures that the association of the carol with Luther is the product of a series of illicit inferences. The decisive one was the association of the carol with the glorification of Luther's family life as depicted in a series of sentimental engravings done in the early nineteenth century by G. F. L. König, beloved by Lutherans everywhere and reproduced in Philadelphia in 1855, with the picture portraying Luther with his family on Christmas Eve as frontispiece. In 1872, the author of the 1855 publication, T. B. Stork, in a book called *Luther at Home* (sponsored by the Lutheran Board of Publication, Philadelphia), in commenting on this picture, states that "Luther's carol for Christmas, written for his own child Hans, is still sung," etc. Since Stork does not name the carol, opportunity to supply the deficiency was wide open. Either "Away in a manger" was written to fill the gap, or, as a popular anonymous carol, was associated with the picture and the cherished concept of Luther as a kindly family man in such a way that, for example, James R. Murray, in *Dainty Songs for Little Lads and Lasses*, 1887, could easily call the hymn "Luther's Cradle Hymn, composed by Martin Luther for his children, and still sung by German mothers to their little ones." But unfortunately for this latter statement, no German original can be found in Luther's writings.

At present, the most that can be said is that the first 2 sts. were written before 1884-85, the third before 1892; but who wrote either is unknown.

The earliest extant printed text has "his" bed, 1885; "a" bed appears in 1887. "The poor baby wakes" becomes "the baby awakes" in 1895. "In the hay," 1885, becomes "on the hay," 1887. The original last line of st. 2, "And stay by my crib watching my lullaby," 1885, became "And stay by my cradle to watch lullaby," 1887, and settled down to "And stay by my cradle till morning is nigh" in 1895. St. 3 seems never to have been altered since its first printing.

The carol entered the Methodist hymnal in 1935 and is retained in identical form.

Away in a Manger

JAMES R. MURRAY, 1841-1905

This tune has been wrongly ascribed to Martin Luther and to an elusive "Carl Mueller."

The first error was caused by Murray himself when he first published the tune, attributing it to Luther, in *Dainty Songs for Little Lads and Lasses,* published by the John Church Company (Cincinnati; registered for copyright May 7, 1887). (See comments on the text.)

The name "Mueller" comes from the incorrect ascription of the tune to a "Carl Mueller" in *Worship and Song,* published by Pilgrim Press (Boston and Chicago, 1921) and edited by Benjamin S. Winchester and Grace Wilbur Conant.

In 1888 the tune appeared in a new collection, *Royal Praise for the Sunday School* by John Murray, published by the John Church Company (Cincinnati, April 25), with the music slightly altered, put in the key of G, and with the heading "Music by J.R.M." Murray published a third collection in 1892 with the tune back in the original key of F.

Be Known to Us in Breaking Bread (313)

JAMES MONTGOMERY, 1771-1854

The hymn was first published in Montgomery's *Christian Psalmist* (Glasgow, 1825) and reprinted in the same form in his *Original Hymns,* 1853, under the title "The Family Table." Written with the Emmaus story, Luke 24:30-31, in mind, for use as a table grace, it is more frequently used as a Communion hymn.

The hymn entered the Methodist hymnal in 1935 and is printed without alteration.

St. Flavian

Adapt. from *The Whole Book of Psalms,* 1562

In the collection printed by John Day, *The Whole Book of Psalms Collected into English* by T. Sternhold and J. Hopkins (London, 1562), this tune was set to Psalm 132. This psalter, sometimes called Day's Psalter, is better known as the "Old Version" or "Sternhold and Hopkins," the complete English psalter patterned after the style of the Genevan Psalter. The present version of the tune is only the first half as printed by Day. Other famous tunes found in this collection are OLD 100TH, OLD 113TH, and ST. MICHAEL (OLD 134TH). The tune is sometimes called OLD 132ND.

St. Flavian was an early bishop of Constantinople.

Be Not Dismayed Whate'er Betide (207)

CIVILLA D. MARTIN, 1869-1948

The text was written in 1904, in Lestershire, N.Y., when Mrs. Martin was ill. The text and tune were first printed together in a songbook her husband was compiling for a Bible school in Lestershire. The hymn was copyrighted in 1905 by John A. Davis, president of the school, but the identity of the book in which it was first published is not known.

This is the first appearance of the hymn in the Methodist hymnal.

Martin

W. STILLMAN MARTIN, 1862-1935

Mrs. Martin writes that she wrote the text of "God will take care of you" one Sunday afternoon while her husband went to a preaching appointment. "When he returned I gave the words to him. He immediately sat down to his little Bilhorn organ and wrote the music. That evening he and two of the teachers sang the completed song."

The tune is sometimes called GOD CARES.

Be Present at Our Table, Lord (518)

JOHN CENNICK, 1718-1755

The two metrical graces which have been most widely enjoyed in English-speaking lands, commonly called the Wesley graces, derive from John Cennick, *Sacred Hymns for the Children of God in the Days of Their Pilgrimage* (London, 1741). Our st. 1 is his grace "Before Meat" in unaltered form. Our st. 3 is Cennick's grace "After Meat," essentially as altered by Edward Bickersteth in his *Christian Psalmody, A Collection of Above 700 Psalms, Hymns, and Spiritual Songs,* 1833. Cennick's original lines were:

We bless Thee, Lord, for this our Food,
But more for Jesu's Flesh and Blood;
The Manna to our Spirits giv'n,
The Living Bread sent down from Heav'n;
Praise shall our Grateful Lips employ,
While Life and Plenty we enjoy;
'Till worthy, we adore thy Name,
While banqueting with Christ, the Lamb.

110

Bickersteth dropped the second quatrain and altered the first 4 lines to read:

> We thank thee Lord for this our food,
> But bless thee more for Jesus' blood;
> May manna to our souls be given,
> The bread of life sent down from heav'n.

Bickersteth's lines 1, 3, and 4 have been adopted for all subsequent printings of the grace, except that our line 3 has substituted "let" for "may." Our 3:2 is similar to but not identical with either Bickersteth or Cennick.

It is Cennick's line 2 which has been the problem, the solution of which has produced a third st., our second. Unhappy with the words "Jesu's Flesh and Blood," in 1833 Bickersteth dropped "flesh and" and inserted "bless thee" to make up the meter. But by 1874 he also dropped "Jesu's Blood." Abandoning Cennick's entire line 2, he substituted for it a slightly altered line from a third grace, printed anonymously in his *Christian Psalmody,* immediately following the Cennick graces, but *not* Cennick: "For life and health, and every good."

Though Bickersteth integrated this new line into Cennick's grace after meat (our st. 3), a later compiler, whose identity is not known, fashioned a new grace beginning with Cennick's line 1, but obtained both phrases and ideas from the anonymous grace printed by Bickersteth in 1833. It is this new grace which, taken from the 1957 *Hymnal* of the Reorganized Church of Jesus Christ of Latter Day Saints, has become our st. 2, but which cannot be accurately attributed either to Cennick or Bickersteth, though partaking of both.

Sts. 1 and 3 entered the Methodist hymnal in 1935, and in their present form.

Old 100th

See **"All People That on Earth Do Dwell,"** pp. 79-81.

Be Still, My Soul: The Lord Is on Thy Side (209)
Stille, mein Wille, dein Jesus hilft siegen

KATHARINA VON SCHLEGEL, b. 1697
Trans. by JANE BORTHWICK, 1813-1897

The hymn first appeared in *Neue Sammlung geistlicher Lieder* (Wernigerode, 1752) in 6 sts. It was reprinted in Albert Knapp,

111

Evangelischer Liederschatz für Kirche und Haus, 1837. In 1855 Miss Borthwick published her translation of 5 of the 6 sts., omitting st. 3, in her *Hymns from the Land of Luther,* second series.

Apparently the first inclusion of Miss Borthwick's translation in a North American hymnal was in 1881 in the hymnal of the Presbyterian Church in Canada, with 4 sts. Most hymnals now print only 3, omitting the translator's third and fifth.

The hymn entered the Methodist hymnal in 1935.

Finlandia

JEAN SIBELIUS, 1865-1957

The tune is an arrangement of a part of the 1899 symphonic poem *Finlandia,* made in 1932 for the hymnal of the Presbyterian Church, U.S.A. The essentially instrumental nature of the music does not lend itself too well to a vocal setting.

Be Thou My Vision, O Lord of My Heart (256)

Ancient Irish
Trans. by MARY E. BYRNE, 1880-1931
Versed by ELEANOR H. HULL, 1860-1935

The original hymn probably was eighth-century Irish, author unknown. Mary Byrne translated it into English prose in 1905 and published it in the Irish journal, *Erin,* Vol. II. Then Eleanor Hull versed Miss Byrne's prose translation, reduced the 16 prose couplets to 12 rhymed ones, and published them in her *Poem Book of the Gael,* 1912.

Miss Hull's 12 couplets are never all printed in hymnals, and the 10 that are printed most frequently are arranged in 4-line sts. Our hymnal prints 8 couplets in 4 sts., omitting couplets 5, 6, 9, and 10. The sts. have never been printed exactly as she wrote them. Various hymnals offer a great variety of alterations. This is the hymn's first appearance in the Methodist hymnal.

Slane

Traditional Irish Melody
Harm. by C.R.Y.

The melody is found in Patrick W. Joyce, *Old Irish Folk Music and Songs,* 1909, set to "With my love on the road." It was harmonized by

David Evans and set to this text in the revised *Church Hymnary* (Edinburgh, 1927); since then it has become widely known and deservedly popular. It has a typical Irish pattern of ABCD, i.e., all 4 lines of the melody are different. The harmonization in the present hymnal is adapted from the one appearing in *Congregational Praise*, 1951.

Slane is a hill some 10 miles from Tara in County Meath where St. Patrick (c. 389-461) lit the Paschal fire on Easter eve in defiance of the Druid priests' edict that no bonfire be lighted before theirs. This show of strength caused King Leoghaire to give protection to St. Patrick.

Before Jehovah's Awful Throne (22)

ISAAC WATTS, 1674-1748
Altered by JOHN WESLEY, 1703-1791

In *Horae Lyricae*, 1706, Watts published a 5-st. metrical paraphrase of Psalm 100, beginning "Sing to the Lord with Joyful Voice" and entitled "Praise to the Lord from All Nations." The psalm was transferred in identical form to Bk. I of his *Hymns and Spiritual Songs*, 1707. It appeared again, radically altered, in *The Psalms of David, Imitated in the Language of the New Testament*, 1719. Though the first and last sts. of the 1706 form remained unchanged, Watts added a new st. 4, which is still widely printed. Of the other 3 sts., only a single line remained unaltered.

As the psalm is sung today, 3 of the 6 sts. of 1719 are used exactly as Watts left them, except for the substitution of "shall" for "must" in the next to the last line of the hymn. This last alteration seems first attested to in the "Additional Hymns," No. 528, in the 1796 edition of John Wesley, *A Collection of Hymns for the Use of the People Called Methodists*, and is still widely printed. The Methodist Episcopal hymnal of 1878 and the 1905 and 1935 hymnals carried it.

The most important subsequent changes of the psalm text are the work of John Wesley. For use in his 1737 Charleston *Collection of Psalms and Hymns*, he dropped Watts's st. 1 and altered the second from

Nations attend before his throne
With solemn fear, with sacred joy

113

to the now established couplet,

> Before Jehovah's awful throne
> Ye nations bow with sacred joy,

and omitted Watts's new st. 4. Thus Wesley set up the 4-st. psalm in the form in which it has been used in almost all Methodist hymnals from the beginning.

It is of interest to note that such treatment of the psalms was sufficient to bring Wesley before the grand jury in Savannah, charged with "making alterations in the metrical Psalms" and "introducing into the Church and Service at the altar compositions of psalms and hymns not inspected or authorized by any proper judicature."

Old 100th

See **"All People That on Earth Do Dwell,"** pp. 79-81.

Behold the Savior of Mankind (428)

SAMUEL WESLEY, 1662-1735

This rather massive hymn of Samuel Wesley, Sr., barely survived the Epworth Rectory fire of 1709. It was found by him afterwards in the garden on a partly charred sheet of paper. The hymn was in 6 sts., 2 of which, though extant, have never been included in any Methodist collection of hymns.

John first printed his father's hymn in the 1737 Charleston *Collection of Psalms and Hymns,* then in the 1739 *Hymns and Sacred Poems.* The same 4 sts. have been included in virtually every Methodist collection since, without alteration.

Windsor

WILLIAM DAMON, *Former Book of Music*, 1591

First appearing in Damon's 1591 *Former Book of Music* and in 1592 in Thomas Est, *The Whole Book of Psalms* with a harmonization by George Kirbye, the tune is quite similar to the tune Christopher Tye used for the third chapter in his metrical version of *The Acts of the Apostles,* 1553, a collection which was also the source of the tune WINCHESTER OLD.

COLESHILL is a modalised form of WINDSOR, and the tune was called DUNDIE in the Scottish Psalter of 1615. It appeared in the Ainsworth Psalter, 1612, used by the Pilgrims.

Behold Us, Lord, a Little Space (549)

JOHN ELLERTON, 1826-1893

The hymn was written in 1870 for a midday service in a city church. Its first inclusion was in *Church Hymns,* 1871. Ellerton was one of the editors.

The original 6 sts. were first printed in the Methodist Episcopal hymnal of 1878 and have been printed since, without alteration.

Dunfermline

Scottish Psalter, 1615

The tune is taken from Andro Hart, *The One Hundred Fifty Psalms of David* (Edinburgh, 1615), where it was one of the "common tunes" (86.86.). Ravenscroft used it for Psalms 36 and 89 and gave it the name DUNFERMLING in his *Whole Book of Psalms* (London, 1621). It is notable for its small compass and economy of material.

James T. Lightwood gives what may be a clue to the tune name when he says, "It is said to have been the composition of a certain Dean John Angus, who was connected with the 'Abbacie of Dumfermling' at the time of the Reformation, when he joined the Protestants, and was appointed to one of the livings attached to the Chapel Royal at Stirling." Dunfermline has been a royal burgh since early in the twelfth century.

Beneath the Cross of Jesus (417)

ELIZABETH C. CLEPHANE, 1830-1869

The 3 sts. usually printed are a part of a poem published in 1872 in the *Family Treasury.* Since Miss Clephane died in 1869, the hymn was at least 3 years old when published.

The hymn entered the Methodist hymnal in 1935, in the same form.

St. Christopher

FREDERICK C. MAKER, 1844-1927

Composed for this text, the tune first appeared in the Supplement to *The Bristol Tune Book* (Bristol, 1881), edited by Alfred Stone. It is named for the legendary Christian martyr.

Beneath the Forms of Outward Rite (321)

JAMES A. BLAISDELL, 1867-1957

Information about the date or circumstances of the composition of the text is lacking. The earliest hymnal inclusion mentioned in Katharine Smith Diehl, *Hymns and Tunes,* is in H. Augustine Smith, *American Student Hymnal,* 1928.

This is the first appearance of the hymn in a Methodist hymnal.

Perry

LEO SOWERBY, 1895-1968

The tune was written in July, 1962, for this text and for this hymnal. Concerning the tune name, Dr. Sowerby writes, "Written at Put-in-Bay, Ohio, the site of the International Peace Monument. It was from this bay that Comm. Perry went forth to his naval victory in Lake Erie in the War of 1812."

Blessed Assurance, Jesus Is Mine (224)

FANNY J. CROSBY, 1820-1915

After hearing the tune played once or twice by the composer, her friend Mrs. Knapp, and on being asked, "What does that melody say to you?" Fanny Crosby replied with the precise words of st. 1 of the hymn. So wrote Fanny Crosby in her *Memories of Eighty Years,* 1906.

The first official Methodist printing of the hymn was in the Methodist Episcopal, South hymnal of 1889. The hymn has been retained unaltered in Methodist hymnals since.

Assurance

PHOEBE P. KNAPP, 1839-1908

The tune was composed in 1873 and with the text appeared the same year in John R. Sweney, *Gems of Praise,* Philadelphia. It was later included in the series of *Gospel Hymns.*

Blessed Jesus, at Thy Word (257)
Liebster Jesu, wir sind hier

TOBIAS CLAUSNITZER, 1619-1684
Trans. by CATHERINE WINKWORTH, 1827-1878

The German text seems to have been first published anonymously in the *Altdorffisches Gesangbüchlein,* 1663. Clausnitzer's name appeared in the 1671 edition. The 3 sts. were intended to be sung at Sunday service, before the sermon.

Miss Winkworth's translation was included in the second series of her *Lyra Germanica,* 1858, and was reprinted without change in her *Chorale Book for England,* 1863.

The hymn entered the Methodist hymnal in 1935 without alteration.

Liebster Jesu

JOHANN R. AHLE, 1625-1673

The tune was written in 1664 for an Advent hymn by Franz Joachim Bormeister entitled "Ja er ist's, das Heil der Welt" and was published in *Neue geistliche auf die Sontage . . .* (Mülhausen, 1664). It has been wedded to the present text since its appearance in *Altdorffisches Gesangbüchlein,* 1671. The original form of the melody may be seen in *Songs of Praise Discussed,* p. 246.

It is also known as NUREMBERG and DESSAU.

Blest Are the Pure in Heart (276)

JOHN KEBLE, 1792-1866

This is 1 of 3 hymns from Keble's *Christian Year* (London, 1827) in our hymnal (see **499, 502**).

The poem was entitled "The Purification," with Matthew 5:3 as superscription, and was written October 10, 1819, for the Feast of the Purification of the Virgin Mary. Sts. 1 and 3 only are from Keble; they are the first and the last of his original 17 sts.

Alterations seem to have begun with st. 3 when in the *New Mitre-Hymnal,* 1836, the editors, W. J. Hall and E. Osler, added 2 sts. of their own and a doxology. Removing Keble's seventeenth and last st.

117

to third place suggested that they should move "still" to line 2, making the first couplet read:

> He to the lowly soul
> Doth still Himself impart.

Though most hymnals including our own have reverted to Keble's original form, the change has been retained by *The Hymnal 1940* and the Presbyterian *Hymnbook,* 1955.

Unhappy with line 3, "And for his cradle and his throne," Hall altered "cradle" to "dwelling." "Dwelling" is now used in all hymnals, though Methodist hymnals printed "temple" during the years 1849-1935. In line 4, Methodist hymnals—from 1849 to date—have substituted "selects" for Keble's "chooseth."

Most hymnals print the Hall-Osler sts.—our 2 and 3—without change. However, our hymnal has altered "heavens" to "throne" (2:1), and since 1878 "Give us" to "O give" (4:3). St. 2 was not included in a Methodist hymnal until 1964.

The hymn entered American Methodist hymnals in 1849 with 2 Keble sts. only; in 1878 one of Hall's sts. was added; in 1964, another, giving us the 4 sts. now printed in all hymnals.

Franconia

JOHANN B. KÖNIG, 1691-1758
Arr. by WILLIAM HAVERGAL, 1793-1870

The original form of the tune appeared in König's *Harmonischer Liederschatz* (Frankfort, 1738) :

It was radically altered by Havergal for *Old Church Psalmody* (London, 1847) .

Blest Be the Dear Uniting Love (338)

CHARLES WESLEY, 1707-1788

"At Parting" follows immediately its correlative, "At the Meeting of Christian Friends," in John and Charles Wesley, *Hymns and Sacred Poems,* 1742. The text was originally in 8 sts., but John reduced it to 6 in his 1780 *Collection of Hymns for the Use of the People Called Methodists.* In reprinting it, he made 3 alterations which measurably improved Charles's text. In 1:4 he altered "joined" to "one"; he replaced "And do his work below" with "And show his praise below" (2:4); and "O let" with "O may" (3:1). In the case of the latter 2, the 1905 and 1935 hymnals reverted to Charles, who yielded to John in 1964.

The hymn has been printed in Methodist hymnals since 1780.

Evan

**Arr. from WILLIAM HAVERGAL, 1793-1870
by LOWELL MASON, 1792-1872**

The extent to which Mason adapted melodies can be seen by comparing the hymnal version of this tune with the original:

The original was published in 1847 for Robert Burns's poem "O Thou dread power, who reign'st above."

Mason used only lines 1, 2, 7, and 8 and changed the rhythm to

3/2. He called the tune EVA and published it in *New Carmina Sacra,* 1850. Mr. Havergal did not approve of the arrangement, calling it "a sad estrangement," and reconstructed the tune himself. Mason changed the name to EVAN less than a month later when it was included in *Cantica Laudis,* 1850. Havergal stated that he did not know why it was called EVAN.

Blest Be the Tie That Binds (306)

JOHN FAWCETT, 1740-1817

The hymn first appeared in Fawcett's *Hymns Adapted to the Circumstances of Public Worship and Private Devotion* (Leeds, 1782), with the title "Brotherly Love." Since 1935, our hymnal has dropped the original sts. 5 and 6.

As beloved as the hymn is, the language particularly of sts. 3 and 4 worries editors. In 3:1 "mutual" has caused concern and since the 1935 hymnal has been altered to "each other's." The first couplet of st. 4 too easily provokes a smile; therefore the st. is rather frequently omitted or else reconstructed. The 1935 hymnal altered 4:1 to "When we are called to part." The present hymnal returns to the original.

Though not included in most English Methodist collections, the hymn is found in all American Methodist hymnals, at least since 1822.

Dennis

See **"And Are We Yet Alive,"** pp. 90-91.

Blow Ye the Trumpet, Blow (100)

CHARLES WESLEY, 1707-1788

The hymn was first published in *Hymns for New-Year's Day* (London, 1750) and was entitled "The Year of Jubilee," with the text Leviticus 25:9. It was very popular in the eighteenth and nineteenth centuries and was frequently printed, abbreviated, and altered.

Not in the 1780 *Collection of Hymns for the Use of the People Called Methodists,* nor yet in *The Methodist Hymn-Book* (London, 1933), the hymn appears in virtually all American Methodist hymnals.

In the 1964 hymnal, sts. 2 and 3 of the original have been omitted.

The only alteration is the last line of st. 4, for which Wesley wrote "Return to your eternal home."

Lenox

See **"Arise, My Soul, Arise,"** pp. 96-97.

Book of Books, Our People's Strength (370)

PERCY DEARMER, 1867-1936

According to the author, the text was written "in order to express the modern appreciation of the Bible." The hymn first appeared in *Songs of Praise,* 1925, of which Canon Dearmer was editor of texts. The first printing in an American hymnal was in H. Augustine Smith, *American Student Hymnal,* 1928.

The hymn entered the Methodist hymnal in 1935.

Liebster Jesu

See **"Blessed Jesus, at Thy Word,"** p. 117.

Bread of the World in Mercy Broken (320, 322, 323)

REGINALD HEBER, 1783-1826

The hymn, entitled "Before the Sacrament," was first published a year after the author's death in his *Hymns Written and Adapted to the Weekly Service of the Church Year,* 1827.

It entered the Methodist hymnal in 1905 unaltered.

Eucharistic Hymn (320)

JOHN S. B. HODGES, 1830-1915

The tune was composed for this text in 1868 while Hodges was rector of Grace Episcopal Church, Newark, N.J. It first appeared in *Book of Common Praise,* 1869. "Eucharist" is one of the names given to Holy Communion, denoting a feast of joy and gladness.

121

Rendez à Dieu (323)

Attr. to LOUIS BOURGEOIS, c. 1510–c. 1561

The tune was composed or adapted by Bourgeois for the French Psalter, 1542, set to Psalm 118, "O give thanks unto the Lord." Measures 4, 5, and 6 were revised by Bourgeois in 1551. Calling the tune NAVARRE, William Mercer wedded it to Heber's text in *Church Psalter and Hymn Book,* 1854.

Sri Lampang (322)

Thailand Folk Melody

This tune is drawn from the 1953 revision of *Hymns for Thai Worship,* Bangkok. The book was produced for The Church of Christ in Thailand, an ecumenical group but composed chiefly of U.S.A. Presbyterians. The rhythm has been altered in lines 2 and 4.

"Sri" means "to the glory of," and "Lampang" can refer either to the name of a city or to a culture in northern Thailand.

Break Forth, O Beauteous Heavenly Light (373)
Ermuntre dich, mein schwacher Geist

JOHANN RIST, 1607-1667
Trans. by JOHN TROUTBECK, 1833-1889

By Johann Rist, the hymn appeared first in his *Himmlische Lieder* (Leipzig, 1641). Bach used st. 9 in his *Christmas Oratorio.* Our English text is taken from the Novello Company edition of the oratorio, 188?, with "The English Translation and Adaptation by the Rev. J. Troutbeck."

This is the first appearance of the hymn in a Methodist hymnal.

Ermuntre dich

JOHANN SCHOP, c. 1590-1664
Harm. by J. S. BACH, 1685-1750

The melody, originally in triple time, appeared with the text in *Himmlische Lieder,* 1641, for which Schop was music editor. J. S. Bach arranged the chorale for his *Christmas Oratorio,* from which this simplified version is drawn. Another tune by Schop, WERDE MUNTER, became the famous tune to "Jesu, joy of man's desiring," also arranged by Bach.

122

Break Forth, O Living Light of God (356)

FRANK VON CHRISTIERSON, 1900-

The hymn was first published in "Ten New Hymns on the Bible," a booklet sponsored by the Hymn Society of America. It was written for the celebration of the publication of the Revised Standard Version of the Bible, 1952.

This is the first inclusion of the hymn in a hymnal.

St. Stephen

WILLIAM JONES, 1726-1800

Set to Sternhold's version of Psalm 23, the tune appears at the end of *Ten Church Pieces for the Organ* (London, 1789) called "St. Stephen's Tune." It was named after the composer's favorite saint, the first Christian martyr. It is also called NAYLAND, NAYLOR, and NEWINGTON.

Break Thou the Bread of Life (369)

MARY A. LATHBURY, 1841-1913

John H. Vincent, the founder and longtime manager of the Chautauqua Institution in N.Y., requested Miss Lathbury to write a hymn for use in meetings of the Chautauqua Literary and Scientific Circle and for groups devoted to Bible study. The 2-st. hymn was written in the summer of 1877, 3 years after the formal dedication of the assembly grounds. The singing of the hymn at Sunday evening Vespers is now traditional.

In the September 13, 1913, issue of the *Wesleyan Methodist Magazine,* London, Alexander Groves published 2 additional sts., which have found some favor in England and which are included in *The Baptist Hymnal* (Nashville, 1956).

The hymn has been in the Methodist hymnal since 1905.

Bread of Life

WILLIAM F. SHERWIN, 1826-1888

Written in 1877 for this text at Lake Chautauqua, N.Y., the tune was included with the text in the Chautauqua Literary and Scientific Circle publications. The first hymnal to include it was *The Calvary*

Selection of Spiritual Songs, edited by Charles S. Robinson and Robert S. MacArthur (New York, 1878).

Breathe on Me, Breath of God (133)

EDWIN HATCH, 1835-1889

The hymn was first published privately in the pamphlet *Between Doubt and Prayer,* 1878; then in Henry Allon, *The Congregational Psalmist,* 1886; and then in 1890 in a posthumous collection of Hatch's poems, *Towards Fields of Light.*

In Allon's hymnal, the original line 2 of st. *3,* "Blend all my soul with thine," was changed to "Till I am wholly thine," which has become the permanent text.

The hymn entered the Methodist hymnal in 1905.

Trentham

ROBERT JACKSON, 1842-1914

Written for Henry W. Baker, "O perfect life of love," it first appeared in *Fifty Sacred Leaflets,* 1888.

Trentham is a village in the county of Staffordshire, England.

Brightest and Best of the Sons of the Morning (400)

REGINALD HEBER, 1783-1826

The hymn was one of a series published in the *Christian Observer,* 1811, appropriate to Sundays and principal holy days of the year, and designed to be sung between the creed and the sermon. It was designated "Epiphany," both in the serial and in the posthumous edition of Bishop Heber's *Hymns Written and Adapted to the Weekly Service of the Church Year,* 1827. In 5 sts., the last a repetition of the first, the hymn has never been altered; the last, however, has been omitted in a few cases.

It has been in American Methodist hymnals at least since 1847.

Morning Star

JAMES P. HARDING, 1850-1911

The tune was originally part of an anthem composed in June, 1892, to be sung at Gifford Hall Mission in Islington, in London's slum district. *The Church Hymnal,* 1894, the music edition of the Protestant

Episcopal *Hymnal,* 1892, was the first book to include the tune in America; its first appearance in a Methodist book was in the 1905 hymnal.

Brightly Beams Our Father's Mercy (148)

PHILIP P. BLISS, 1838-1876

The hymn was first published in *The Charm,* a collection of Sunday school music, edited by the author of both text and tune, 1871. Printed above the music in the words of D. L. Moody is the story which inspired the writing of the hymn:

On a dark, stormy night, when the waves rolled like mountains, and not a star was to be seen, a boat, rocking and plunging, neared the Cleveland harbor. "Are you sure this is Cleveland?" asked the captain, seeing only one light from the light-house. "Quite sure, sir," replied the pilot. "Where are the lower lights?" "Gone out, sir." "Can you make the harbor?" "We *must,* or perish, sir!" And with a strong hand and a brave heart, the old pilot turned the wheel. But alas, in the darkness he missed the channel, and with a crash upon the rocks the boat was shivered, and many a life lost in a watery grave. Brethren, the Master will take care of the great light-house: *let us keep the lower lights burning!*

In 3:2 Bliss wrote "Some poor sailor." Apparently when the hymn entered the Methodist hymnal in 1935, "sailor" was changed to "seaman."

Lower Lights

PHILIP P. BLISS, 1838-1876

The tune was written by Bliss at the same time as the text, first appearing in *The Charm* (Cincinnati, 1871).

By Thy Birth and by Thy Tears (113)

ROBERT GRANT, 1779-1838
Alt. by THOMAS COTTERILL, 1779-1823, and others

Though this hymn had wide vogue in the nineteenth century, the history of its transmission is somewhat baffling. First printed in the *Christian Observer,* 1815, in 5 sts., the hymn was called "Litany." Its first line was "Savior, when in dust to thee," and the last line of each st. was "Hear our solemn litany." The popularity of the hymn was probably because of the fact that as a metrical litany, of which there were few, it seemed unusually valuable for the Lenten meditation on the sufferings of Jesus. But from the beginning, it was subject to alterations. Thomas Cotterill's *Selection of Psalms and Hymns for Public and Private Use,* 1819, apparently the first hymnal inclusion, dropped st. 1, altered the first line of the next from "By thy helpless infant years" to "By thy birth and early years," and in fact left only 5 unaltered lines (not counting the final line common to all sts.) in the 4 sts.

In 1835, H. V. Elliott, *Psalms and Hymns,* attempted to restore integrity to the hymn by reprinting Grant's original text without alteration except "troubled" for "anguish'd" (3:5). When Grant's 12 hymns were collected by his brother, Lord Glenelg, *Sacred Poems,* 1839, "anguish'd" was restored, but "permitted" (2:5) was changed to "mysterious," and "pitying" (2:7) to "favoring," Glenelg claiming his text to be a "a more correct and authentic version."

The hymn seems to have entered the Methodist Episcopal hymnal in 1849, and in 2 forms, both ascribed to Glenelg. Yet neither is a very close replica either of Grant (Glenelg) or Cotterill. Number 564, "Savior, when in dust to thee," omits 2 sts. of Glenelg, and Number 395, "By thy birth and by thy tears," while seeming to follow Cotterill, reduces the 8-line sts. to 6 lines each, alters the first line from "By thy birth and early years," and offers continual inner variations from both Glenelg and Cotterill. Moreover, in both forms the original last line, "Hear our solemn litany," has been replaced with variations on "Hear us when to thee we cry" or with "Savior, help me, or I die."

The 1878 and 1905 hymnals continued to print both forms. "By thy birth and by thy tears" was printed exactly as in 1849; "Savior, when in dust to thee" reverted to the 5-st. Glenelg text. Finally, in 1935 the Glenelg text—"Savior, when in dust to thee"—was dropped, as well as the second of the 4 so-called Cotterill sts. The 3 sts. retained in 1935 and 1964 are identical with those in the 1849 hymnal.

Redhead 76

RICHARD REDHEAD, 1820-1901

The tune is from Redhead's *Church Hymn Tunes, Ancient and Modern* (London, 1853). No tune names were given, only a number.

Hymns Ancient and Modern, 1861, set the tune to "Rock of ages, cleft for me," a pairing still popular in England. Other tune names are AJALON, GETHSEMANE, and PETRA.

Captain of Israel's Host, and Guide (46)

CHARLES WESLEY, 1707-1788

From Charles's *Short Hymns on Select Passages of Holy Scripture,* 1762, the hymn is a commentary on Exodus 13:21. John Wesley included it in his 1780 *Collection of Hymns for the Use of the People Called Methodists.*

For the most part, it was omitted from nineteenth-century American Methodist hymnals, but has been reintroduced in the present hymnal. It has been retained in all English Methodist hymnbooks.

Eisenach

JOHANN H. SCHEIN, 1586-1630
Harm. by J. S. BACH, 1685-1750

The tune was first printed on a single sheet in 1628 for use with Schein's *Cantional oder Gesangbuch Augsburgischer Konfession* (Leipzig, 1627) in the following rhythm:

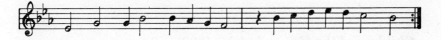

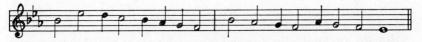

It was printed in the second edition of the Lutheran *Cantional* in 1645, which contained 79 tunes by its editor, Schein. Bach harmonized it, smoothed the rhythm, and it appears in his *St. John Passion* and *Vierstimmige Choralgesänge.* It was written for the text "Mach's mit mir, Gott," which is also used as a tune name.

Named BEER-SHEBA, it appeared in Lowell Mason, *Modern Psalmist,* 1839. Other tune names are LEIPSIG, SCHEIN, and STUTTGART.

Eisenach was the birthplace of J. S. Bach.

Children of the Heavenly Father (521)

CAROLINE V. SANDELL BERG, 1832-1903
Trans. by ERNST W. OLSON, 1870-1958

Lina Sandell, known as the Fanny Crosby of Sweden, began to write hymns as a result of family tragedy, the sudden drowning of her father in 1858. Her first 14 hymns were published that year. Among these was "Children of the heavenly Father." Dr. Olson, the translator, prepared this English text for the *Augustana Hymnal,* 1925.

Tryggare kan ingen vara

Swedish Melody

The tune was first printed anonymously in *Song Book for Sunday Schools* (Stockholm, 1871) in a 4-part arrangement by Theodore Söderberg. While all books credit the tune as Swedish, Gerald Göransson, director of the Royal School of Music in Stockholm, thinks it may be of English origin, and that it came to Sweden in the pietistic revivalism which flourished during the second half of the nineteenth century and brought many English gospel song tunes to Sweden.

The first American appearance of the tune seems to have been in the Augustana Lutheran Synod's edition of *Hemlandssånger,* 1890. The tune name is the opening of the original text which means, "No one can be safer."

Children of the Heavenly King (300)

JOHN CENNICK, 1718-1755

Originally from Cennick's *Sacred Hymns for the Children of God in the Days of Their Pilgrimage,* 1742, the hymn has been included in virtually all Methodist hymnals since the early nineteenth century. Of the original 12 sts., the present hymnal prints 1, 2, 7, 8, 6.

The first couplet originally read:

> Children of the heavenly King,
> As *ye* journey *sweetly* sing.

At least since 1822 American Methodist hymnals have printed "As *we* journey *let us* sing."

Pleyel's Hymn

IGNACE J. PLEYEL, 1757-1831

The first appearance of the tune was as a Long Meter tune in *Arnold and Calcott's Psalms* (London, 1791) set to Joseph Addison, "The spacious firmament on high." The melody is the theme for a set of variations from Pleyel's Quartet, Op. 7, No. 4 (c. 1782). Benjamin Carr set it to Cennick's hymn, using the variations, in his *Masses, Vespers, Litanies, Hymns . . .* (Baltimore, 1805), and it has been in most hymnals since.

Its theme is so short that it becomes monotonously repetitious with its AABA form.

The tune has also been called GERMAN HYMN.

Christ for the World We Sing (292)

SAMUEL WOLCOTT, 1813-1886

At the time the hymn was written, the author was pastor of the Plymouth Congregational Church, Cleveland, Ohio. On seeing the motto "Christ for the world, and the world for Christ" at a gathering of the Y.M.C.A., the hymn was formed in his mind as he returned home that evening, February 7, 1869.

It seems to have been first published in W. H. Doane, *Songs of Devotion for Christian Associations,* 1870. The hymn has been in the Methodist hymnal since 1905.

Italian Hymn

FELICE DE GIARDINI, 1716-1796
Harm. by V.E.C.

Composed for this text, the tune first appeared in *A Collection of Psalm and Hymn Tunes Sung at the Chapel of the Lock Hospital* (1st ed.; London, 1769), edited by the Reverend Martin Madan, chaplain of the hospital, with the heading "Hymn to the Trinity, set by F.G." Measure 13 in the original was as follows:

This collection went through many editions, including one published in Boston in 1809.

129

The tune name is derived from the nationality of the composer. Robert G. McCutchan lists other names: TRINITY, MOSCOW, FAIRFORD, FLORENCE, HERMON, and GIARDINI'S.

Christ, from Whom All Blessings Flow (530)

CHARLES WESLEY, 1707-1788

In 1740 in *Hymns and Sacred Poems,* John and Charles published a poem entitled "The Communion of Saints," 39 sts. in 4 parts. Our hymn is taken from the 10 sts. making up Part IV. With only slight alteration, John reprinted the entire 10 in the 1780 *Collection of Hymns for the Use of the People Called Methodists.* American collections first reduced the hymn to 6 sts. generally agreeing on 1, 2, 5, 6, 7, with the final st. composed of 9a and 10b:

> Many are we now, and one,
> We who have put Jesus on:
> Names, and sects, and parties fall;
> Thou, O Christ, art ALL IN ALL!

The hymn was sung by American Methodists in this fashion until 1905 when it was dropped, not to be rediscovered until 1964. The new printing has dropped st. 6:

> Never from our office move,
> Needful to the others prove,
> Use the grace on each bestowed,
> Tempered by the art of God.

It has replaced the st. composed of 9a and 10b with the full st. 10.

Canterbury

Adapt. from ORLANDO GIBBONS, 1583-1625

For George Wither, *The Hymns and Songs of the Church* (London, 1623), one of the few non-psalter collections between 1551-1700, Orlando Gibbons contributed 16 hymn tunes in 2 parts for soprano and bass. These are his only hymn tunes. This tune was set to the thirteenth song, a paraphrase of part of the Song of Solomon, in 6-line sts., beginning "Oh my love, how comely now" (based on the first chapter of the Song of Solomon). The last 2 lines were repeated with

130

a final embellishment in the last phrase; these are omitted for a 77.77. text.

Canterbury was the place of Gibbons' death. Other tune names: SONG 13, SIMPLICITY, NORWICH, and ST. IRENAEUS.

Christ Is Made the Sure Foundation
Urbs beata Hierusalem

Latin, c. 7th Century
Trans. by JOHN M. NEALE, 1818-1866

Neale's translation of the ancient Latin hymn, variously dated from the sixth to the ninth century, was first published in his *Mediaeval Hymns and Sequences,* 1851, in 9 sts., the first line being "Blessed city, heavenly Salem." For *The Hymnal Noted,* 1851, it was revised and divided into 2 parts, the second beginning with st. 5: "Christ is made the sure foundation." The hymn was subjected to a variety of alterations. The most lasting is the one by the compilers of *Hymns Ancient and Modern,* 1961.

In the original translation, lines 1–3 of the doxology read "Laud and honour"; line 5: "Consubstantial, Co-eternal." The compilers of *Hymns Ancient and Modern* altered these to "Praise and honour" and "One in might, and one in glory." Though these alterations were maintained for a couple of decades in both English and American printings of *Hymns Ancient and Modern,* since the 1880's Anglican printings have generally reverted to Neale's original language.

The Latin hymn occurs in the oldest extant hymnals and in many medieval breviaries was widely used for the dedication of a church. In a 3-st. form, without the doxology, the hymn was in the Methodist Episcopal hymnal of 1878, the Methodist Episcopal, South hymnal of 1889, and the Methodist hymnal of 1905. It was restored with the doxology in 1964 after having been dropped in 1935.

Regent Square

See "Angels, from the Realms of Glory," p. 94.

Christ Is the World's True Light (408)

GEORGE W. BRIGGS, 1875-1959

"The Light of the World," as Briggs entitled the hymn, was first published in *Songs of Praise,* 1931. It was included in his *Songs of*

Faith, 1945. It was intended to be a missionary hymn, but both its language and its content make it suitable for Epiphany season.

Surette

KATHERINE K. DAVIS, 1892-

Composed in 1962, this is 1 of 3 new tunes submitted by Katherine Davis and included in the new hymnal. It is named for Thomas Whitney Surette, who first aroused her enthusiasm for choral music. She attended his summer school of music for 6 years.

Christ Jesus Lay in Death's Strong Bands (438)
Christ lag in Todesbanden

MARTIN LUTHER, 1483-1546
Trans. by RICHARD MASSIE, 1800-1887

The German text, in 7 sts. of 7 lines each, appeared in the Erfurt *Enchiridion* and the Wittenberg *Geistliches Gesangbüchlein* in 1524. Inspired by earlier German and Latin hymns, the chorale has become yet more widely known because Bach used it as the text of his Easter cantata, No. 4.

Richard Massie's translation of the full 7 sts. was published in his *Martin Luther's Spiritual Songs,* 1854. These 7 were reduced to 4 in *Church Hymns,* 1871. The opening line was altered from "Christ lay awhile in Death's strong bands" to its present form, and a second st. was made up of the first 4 lines of Massie's fourth, and the last 3 of his third st. In his 1882 edition of *The Church of England Hymn Book,* Godfrey Thring printed this short form with only one slight change: in 2:6 "shape" became "form."

The hymn entered the Methodist hymnal in 1964 exactly as in Thring's collection.

Christ lag in Todesbanden

JOHANN WALTHER, 1496-1570

The tune is taken from *Geistliches Gesangbüchlein* (Wittenberg, 1524), edited by Walther and containing 32 hymns. It is based on the plainsong sequence for Easter, "Victimae Paschali," as well as on the twelfth-century melody "Christ ist erstanden."

Christ the Lord Is Risen Today (439)

CHARLES WESLEY, 1707-1788, and others

Wesley's magnificent "Hymn for Easterday," in eleven 4-line sts., was first published in *Hymns and Sacred Poems,* 1739. In 1760, Martin Madan, *A Collection of Psalms and Hymns,* reduced the hymn to 8 sts., omitting sts. 7-9, which seem never to have been reprinted in any hymnal. In st. 4 (our second) Madan made his only textual change: "Dying once he all doth save" became "Once he died our souls to save." Though this violates Wesley's intent, it has been accepted by most hymnals including almost all Methodist.

Since John did not include the hymn in any form in the 1780 *Collection of Hymns for the Use of the People Called Methodists,* it did not appear in Wesleyan collections until the Supplement of 1831, when 6 sts. were printed, the first 5 and the eleventh. Madan's alteration of st. 4 (our 2:3) is retained, and in addition the original text of st. 4 (our 2:4), "Where thy victory, O grave?" appears for the first time in a Methodist collection as "Where's thy victory, boasting grave?" This alteration, accepted by virtually all subsequent Methodist hymnals, including our own, may have derived from John Rippon, *A Selection of Hymns from the Best Authors,* 1787. Most other hymnals, however, retain the original Wesley line.

Only one other text change is to be noted: in our 3:3 Wesley wrote "*his* rise." "His" was retained in Methodist hymnals until 1935 when it was altered to "him."

Since 1935, Wesley's st. 4 has been made our second, and his second our third. This third st. is now made up of the first couplet of Wesley's second and the second couplet of his third. The omitted couplets are:

> Lo! our sun's eclipse is o'er,
> Lo! he sets in blood no more,

and

> Vain the stone, the watch, the seal,
> Christ has burst the gates of hell!

Easter Hymn

Lyra Davidica, London, 1708

This anonymous tune first appeared in *Lyra Davidica* (London, 1708) set to "Jesus Christ is risen today." The original form was:

It took its present form in John Arnold, *The Complete Psalmodist* (London, 1741), and was published in John Wesley, *Foundery Collection* (London, 1742) called SALISBURY TUNE. Thomas Butts named the tune CHRISTMAS DAY and set it to "Hark, how all the welkin rings," Charles Wesley's hymn which was later altered to "Hark, the herald angels sing," in *Harmonia Sacra* (London, c. 1756). The tune is suggested for the Christmas hymn in American usage as early as the 1793 edition of *A Pocket Hymn-Book*, Philadelphia.

Other names for the tune are WORGAN and EASTER MORN.

Christ, Whose Glory Fills the Skies (401)

CHARLES WESLEY, 1707-1788

For so perfect a lyric, the hymn has had an undeserved history. And as John Ellerton says, this is due to the "strange perversity" of John, who, though coeditor with Charles of the collection in which the hymn first appeared, *Hymns and Sacred Poems*, 1740, yet in 1780 radically altered the text by substituting for st. 1 the second of a hymn beginning "Lord, how long, how long shall I," also in the 1740 collection:

O disclose thy lovely face,
Quicken all my drooping powers!

134

Gasps my fainting soul for grace,
As a thirsty land for showers:
Haste, my Lord, no longer stay,
Come, my Jesus, come away!

It was not until 1878 that the hymn was restored to its original form in American Methodist hymnals, and not until the twentieth century in English Methodist use.

In 1935, in the last line of st. 2 our hymnal substituted "cheer" for "glad" (used as a verb).

Ratisbon

J. G. WERNER'S *Choralbuch*, Berlin, 1815
Arr. by W. H. MONK, 1823-1889

Monk made a harmonization for *Hymns Ancient and Modern* (London, 1861) of a chorale in Werner's book, *Choralbuch zu den neuen protestantischen Gesangbüchern*. The chorale in turn was an adaptation of the older chorale "Jesus meine Zuversicht" which appeared in C. Runge, *Geistliche Lieder und Psalmen* (Berlin, 1653). A still different form appeared anonymously in Johann Crüger, *Praxis Pietatis Melica* (5th ed.; Berlin, 1653); the Peter Sohren 1668 edition of Crüger's work attaches the initials "J.C." to the tune.

Ratisbon is the name of a famous city, now called Regensburg, in Germany, with historic interest since the first century.

Christian, Dost Thou See Them (238)

οὐ γὰρ Βλέπεις τοὺς ταράττοντας

Attr. to ANDREW OF CRETE, c. 660–c. 740
Trans. by JOHN M. NEALE, 1818-1866

The hymn was first printed in Neale's *Hymns of the Eastern Church*, 1862, under the heading "Stichera for the Second Week of the Great Fast." In the Eastern Church a "sticheron" is a short liturgical hymn attached to a verse ("stichos") of a psalm or other passage of scripture and developing its principal idea.

Though Neale offered a Greek line purporting to be that of a Greek hymn, no such original has been found. Therefore most scholars regard the hymn as Neale's own work, and in some hymnals the hymn is directly ascribed to him.

COMPANION TO THE HYMNAL

Though widely printed, the hymn has never been accepted without some alteration. Our hymnal accepts the earlier alterations, the chief of which are the rewriting of

    1:3-4: How the troops of Midian
               Prowl and prowl around.
    1:7-8: Smite them by the merit
               Of the Holy Cross!
    2:7-8: Smite them by the virtue
               Of the Lenten Fast!

The hymn entered the Methodist Episcopal hymnal in 1878 in its present form.

Walda

LLOYD A. PFAUTSCH, 1921-

Dr. Pfautsch writes, "Walda was written following a discussion in hymnology class [at Southern Methodist University] concerning the poor tunes which had been associated with many of the early Christian hymns." It was written in 1960-61 and appears as a hymn tune for the first time in this book. It has also been published in hymn anthem form with accompaniment for 3 trumpets and 2 trombones. The tune name is a combination of Pfautsch's parents' names: *Wal*ter and Oui*da*.

Come, Christians, Join to Sing (77)

CHRISTIAN HENRY BATEMAN, 1813-1889

First published in the author's *Sacred Melodies for Children,* 1843, the hymn was intended for children. The text was originally in 5 sts., but Bateman reduced it to 3 in his new and enlarged edition called *Sacred Melodies for Sabbath Schools and Families,* 1854. These 3 make up the hymn in our hymnal. Following recent precedent, the original line 1, "Come, children, join to sing," has been altered to make the hymn available to all age groups.

This is its first inclusion in a Methodist hymnal.

Spanish Hymn

Arr. by BENJAMIN CARR, 1768-1831
Harm. by A.C.L.

In 1825 Carr copyrighted variations for pianoforte of a popular parlor piece of the period. In 1826 it was published with the title *Spanish Hymn Arranged and Composed for the Concerts of the Musical Fund Society of Philadelphia by Benjamin Carr, The Air From an Ancient Spanish Melody* (Philadelphia, 1826), arranged for solo, quartet, and full chorus. The flyleaf indicates that its first performance was on December 29, 1824. Montague Burgoyne published it in *A Collection of Metrical Versions* (London, 1827), which indicates that the tune was rather generally known.

Other tune names are MADRID and SPANISH CHANT.

Come Down, O Love Divine (466)
Discendi, amor santo

BIANCO DA SIENA, d. c. 1434
Trans. by RICHARD F. LITTLEDALE, 1833-1890

Littledale translated 4 of the 8 sts. of Bianco's hymn from the *Laudi Spirituali,* as edited by T. Bini, 1851, for his *People's Hymnal,* 1867. The original third translated st. has been omitted.

This is the first appearance of the hymn in the Methodist hymnal.

Down Ampney

RALPH VAUGHAN WILLIAMS, 1872-1958

Written for this text, the tune first appeared in the *The English Hymnal* (Oxford, 1906). Its quietly rising and falling pattern fits both the unusual meter (66.11.D.) and the introspective nature of the text. Erik Routley in *Companion to Congregational Praise* states, "It is perhaps the most beautiful hymn-tune composed since the *Old Hundredth.*"

It is named after the village near Cirencester, Gloustershire, where the composer was born.

Come, Every Soul by Sin Oppressed (101)

JOHN H. STOCKTON, 1813-1877

The hymn appeared first in the author's *Salvation Melodies No. 1,* 1874, in 5 sts. The omitted st.,

O Jesus, blessed Jesus, dear,
I'm coming now to thee:
Since thou hast made the way so clear
And full salvation free,

must have been dropped very early, since Ira D. Sankey, *Sacred Songs and Solos* (London, n.d., but dated 1874 by Benson), has only the usual 4 sts. Likewise, only these 4 appear in Bliss and Sankey's *Gospel Hymns and Sacred Songs*, copyright 1875. Sankey affirms that he had the hymn in his scrapbook on the way to England with D. L. Moody, 1873, and that seeing how hackneyed the familiar chorus,

Come to Jesus,
Come to Jesus,
Come to Jesus just now,

was, he decided to change it to "Only trust him." In this form it was first published in *Sacred Songs and Solos*.

The hymn entered the Methodist hymnal in 1905 in its traditional form.

Stockton

JOHN H. STOCKTON, 1813-1877

The first appearance of the tune seems to be in *Joyful Songs Nos. 1-3 Combined,* published by the Methodist Episcopal Book Rooms (Philadelphia, 1869) where the music is marked "Arr. by W. G. Fischer" and "By permission." It later appeared in Stockton's own *Salvation Melodies No. 1* (Philadelphia, 1874).

Come, Father, Son, and Holy Ghost (344)

CHARLES WESLEY, 1707-1788

First published in Wesley's *Hymns for Children,* 1763, a collection of 100 hymns with some divided into parts, making the whole 105, the hymn was written to be sung "At the opening of a school in Kingswood." The entire 6 sts. were printed in early American collections, to be reduced to 4 in 1847, then dropped entirely from the Methodist Episcopal hymnal in 1878. Though the 1889 hymnal of the Methodist

Episcopal Church, South printed 3 sts., all subsequent Methodist hymnals until 1964 omitted the hymn.

The present hymnal prints sts. 1, 3, 5, and 6 of the original hymn. It should be noted that our third st. contains the following oft-quoted lines:

> Unite the pair so long disjoined,
> Knowledge and vital piety.

St. Catherine

HENRI F. HEMY, 1818-1888
Adapt. by JAMES G. WALTON, 1821-1905

The tune, set to "Sweet Saint Catherine, maid most pure," with melody and organ part, first appeared in Part II of *Crown of Jesus Music* (London, 1864) edited by Hemy. The tune was originally in 10 lines, but only the first 16 measures were taken by Walton, who then added 8 measures of his own for use in *Plain Song Music for the Holy Communion Office,* 1874.

Catherine of Alexandria was a fourth-century Christian martyr. Other names for the tune are TYNEMOUTH, PRINCE, and FINBAR.

Come, Holy Ghost, Our Hearts Inspire (131)

CHARLES WESLEY, 1707-1788

The hymn was first published in *Hymns and Sacred Poems,* 1740, as the third of 3 hymns to be sung "Before Reading the Scriptures." Only 2 alterations have ever been made: "thy" (1:2) has been changed to "thine," and "prolific" (3:1) to "celestial." Both changes were made by John in 1780.

This strong hymn has been included in every Methodist hymnal since 1780.

Winchester Old

THOMAS EST, *The Whole Book of Psalms,* 1592
Tune arrang. attr. to GEORGE KIRBYE, c. 1560-1634

This tune arrangement is attributed to George Kirbye in Est's Psalter published in London, 1592, and set to a version of Psalm 84. Its original source may be from the setting of chapter 8 of *The Acts of the Apostles* (London, 1553) with music by Christopher Tye, the first 4 phrases being:

Hymns Ancient and Modern (London, 1861) set it to "While shepherds watched their flocks by night" and gave us our present form.

Come, Holy Ghost, Our Souls Inspire (467)
Veni, Creator Spiritus

Attr. to RHABANUS MAURUS, c. 776-856
Trans. by JOHN COSIN, 1594-1672

The Latin original dates from the ninth or tenth century. Though most hymnals refuse to name an author, the chief contender appears to be Rhabanus Maurus, abbot of the Benedictine monastery of Fulda, Germany. For a thousand years the hymn has been in continual use. Set in a variety of services, it was appointed especially for morning prayer on Pentecost Sunday. We know it best in our ordination services, a purpose for which it was used as early as the eleventh century.

Among some 60 translations, Cosin's is the most widely known. It was composed by Bishop Cosin for the coronation of Charles I, 1625, for which Cosin was master of ceremonies for Archbishop Laud. First published in Cosin's *Collection of Private Devotions,* 1627, a book dedicated to Queen Henrietta, it was set as the proper hymn for the "Praiers for the Third Hour" (Terce or 9 A.M.). Since he was one of the revisers of the 1662 *Book of Common Prayer,* Cosin included his translation unaltered alongside the older version "Come, Holy Ghost, eternal God," which already had a place in the 1549 book. Though

Cosin's translation condensed the original 24 lines into 18, its simplicity and restraint together with its secure position in the liturgy have enabled it to subordinate other, perhaps better, translations to itself.

The hymn was first included in a Methodist hymnal in 1878, was dropped in 1905 and restored in 1935.

Veni Creator
Plainsong, *Vesperale Romanam*, Mechlin, 1848

The Mechlin (Belgium) collection *Vesperale Romanum,* 1848, was an attempt to bring back to the French Roman Catholic churches the plainsong idiom which had fallen into disuse. The melodies were simplified to make them more usable by singers not accustomed to the more melismatic and florid style. This melody was first associated with the Ambrosian Easter hymn "Hic est dies verus Dei":

Come, Holy Spirit, Heavenly Dove (134)
ISAAC WATTS, 1674-1748

The hymn first appeared in the author's *Hymns and Spiritual Songs,* Bk. II, "Composed on Divine Subjects," 1707, with the heading "Breathing after the Holy Spirit: or, Fervency of Devotion desir'd." The hymn was incorrectly indexed in 1707 as "Come, Sacred Spirit," but this was corrected in the 1709 edition.

Sts. 1, 3, and 5 have never been altered, but Watts himself in the second edition made some alterations in sts. 2 and 4. An interesting alteration in 4:1 is that "Dear Lord" was changed to "Father." This latter change, it is urged, was made by John Wesley, who never used "Dear" of deity, objecting to such familiar language. In any case, in his *Select Hymns,* 1765, Wesley prints 4:1 as "Father, shall we then ever live." In early American hymnals published by Methodists "Father" was retained until 1847 in the Methodist Episcopal, South hymnals and until 1905 in the Methodist hymnal.

Gräfenberg

JOHANN CRÜGER, 1598-1662

The tune first appeared in the second edition of *Praxis Pietatis Melica* (Berlin, 1647) anonymously, set to Paul Gerhardt, "Nun danket all' und bringet Ehr." In the 1656 edition it is marked "J.C." The first 6 measures seem to have been taken from the 1562 Genevan Psalter setting for Psalm 89, and the last 6 notes are similar to the last part of Psalm 75. There is also a relationship to RENDEZ À DIEU, Psalm 118. Walter E. Buszin has pointed out that "a significant influence was exerted on Crüger by Claude Goudimel," which may account for the melodic borrowing.

The rhythmic pattern differs from the 1935 hymnal version and returns to the original form.

Come, Let Us Join Our Friends Above (302)

CHARLES WESLEY, 1707-1788

The hymn was No. 1 in the second series of *Funeral Hymns,* 1759. Originally in 5 sts. of 8 lines each, since 1935 it has been reduced to five 4-line sts. in the Methodist hymnal. Our hymnal prints the first 2 original 8-line sts. and the second half of the fourth.

Major alterations are in 2:1, which originally read "Let all the saints terrestrial sing." In 5:3, "blood-besprinkled bands" became "blood-redeemed" in 1935.

The hymn has been included in American Methodist hymnals since 1847.

Pisgah

J. C. LOWRY in *Kentucky Harmony,* 1817
Harm. by A.C.L.

Ananias Davisson, editor of *Kentucky Harmony,* c. 1815, credits this tune to "J. C. Lowry," but Alexander Johnson in his *Tennessee Harmony,* c. 1819, credits it to "Johnson." The tune is sometimes called

COVENANTERS, but there is no basis for associating the tune with the Covenanters in Scotland.

The tune (sometimes called MT. PISGAH or CHRISTIAN TRIUMPH) is a typical Southern pentatonic folk hymn of the early nineteenth century, and in the original repeats the tune almost verbatim as a refrain with the words "O Lord, remember me."

Come, Let Us Rise with Christ Our Head (457)

CHARLES WESLEY, 1707-1788

The 3 sts. which make up this hymn are among Wesley's *Short Hymns on Select Passages of Holy Scripture*. Though not found under Colossians 3:1, 2 in either the 1762 or 1794-96 editions, they are printed in George Osborn, *The Poetical Works of John and Charles Wesley*, 1870 (XIII, 85-86), in the exact form in which they appear in our hymnal.

This seems to be the first inclusion of this hymn in a hymnal.

St. Matthew

Probably by WILLIAM CROFT, 1678-1727

Set to Psalm 33 and marked as a new tune, this appeared in *A Supplement to the New Version of Psalms by Dr. Brady and Mr. Tate* (6th ed.; London, 1708). All tunes were anonymous, but Croft was the editor of the Supplement, which is also the source for HANOVER and ST. ANNE.

Come, Let Us Tune Our Loftiest Song (231)

ROBERT A. WEST, 1809-1865

The hymn first appeared in the 1849 hymnal of the Methodist Episcopal Church and has been retained unaltered in all subsequent Methodist hymnals. Its author was 1 of 7 appointed by the General Conference of 1848 to prepare a standard hymnal for the church.

Duke Street

JOHN HATTON, d. 1793

Henry Boyd, a teacher of psalmody, included this tune anonymously in his *Select Collection of Psalms and Hymn Tunes* (Glasgow, 1793), marked to be sung to Joseph Addison, "The spacious firmament on high." William Dixon attributed it to Hatton in his *Euphonia* (Liverpool, 1805). It was called NEWRY in *The Methodist Harmonist*, 1821, the first official tunebook of American Methodism. Other names used have been WINDLE and ST. HELEN'S.

Hatton lived on Duke Street in St. Helen's, England.

Come, Let Us Use the Grace Divine (507, 508)

CHARLES WESLEY, 1707-1788

The hymn was first published in Wesley's *Short Hymns on Select Passages of Holy Scripture*, 1762, under the text of Jeremiah 50:5, "Come, and let us join ourselves to the Lord in a perpetual covenant that shall not be forgotten." It came to be used as the hymn for the service of "The Renewal of the Covenant," observed by Methodists on the first Sunday of every year. In England, however, after 1830, the hymn "O God, how often hath thine ear," by W. M. Bunting, displaced the Wesley covenant hymn in this use. American Methodist hymnals, except for the 1849 hymnal which printed 2 of Bunting's 5 sts., have never adopted Bunting's hymn, but from the beginning have printed "Come, let us use the grace divine," with the minor alterations made by John for his 1780 *Collection of Hymns for the Use of the People Called Methodists*. The original 6 sts. were retained until 1935 when the last 2 were dropped as in the present hymnal.

Covenant Hymn (508)

THOMAS CANNING, 1911-

The tune was composed in 1961 as the basis for a setting of John Wesley's Covenant Service, commissioned by the Board of Education of The Methodist Church for first performance at the Seventh Quadrennial Conference of Methodist Youth at the University of Illinois, August, 1961. All other music for the service is developed from motifs from this tune.

St. Martin's (507)

WILLIAM TANS'UR, 1706-1783

First published in *The Royal Melody Complete, or the New Harmony of Zion* (2nd ed.; London, 1740), the tune was marked "Composed in four parts: W.T." Tans'ur was the compiler of the book. It is typical of the florid early eighteenth-century style which was popular with the Wesleyans. It entered into American use through its introduction into early New England singing school collections.

Come, Let Us, Who in Christ Believe (111)

CHARLES WESLEY, 1707-1788

The hymn was first published as No. 8 in *Hymns on God's Everlasting Love,* 1741, in 14 sts. The 4 sts. which have been printed unaltered in every official Methodist hymnal except the Methodist Protestant hymnals of 1871 and 1909 and the 1935 Methodist hymnal were selected by John for his 1780 *Collection of Hymns for the Use of the People Called Methodists.* Nevertheless they hardly do justice to the main intent of the hymn which was to insist that God's grace is free and unbounded:

> He died for all, he none *pass'd by* . . .
> For me, for us, for all mankind . . .
> All nations now in Christ are blest . . .

And, indeed,

> Unless thy grace is free,
> O bleeding Lamb, take back thy love
> O Saviour, pass by *me.*

Campmeeting

Early American Melody
Harm. by ROBERT G. McCUTCHAN, 1877-1958

In *Our Hymnody,* Robert G. McCutchan states that this "was an old camp-meeting chorus of the early days, usually sung to the words

> I will believe, I do believe
> That Jesus died for me, etc.

or, earlier,

> I do believe, I now believe,
> I can hold out no more;

145

I sing by dying love compelled,
And own Thee conqueror.

This early nineteenth-century tune was given its name by Dr. McCutchan for the 1935 Methodist hymnal.

Come, My Soul, Thou Must Be Waking (258)
Seele, du musst munter werden

FRIEDRICH R. L. VON CANITZ, 1654-1699
Trans. by HENRY J. BUCKOLL, 1803-1871

The German text, in 14 sts., was first published anonymously a year after the author's death in Joachim Lange, *Nebenstunden unterschiedener Gedichte,* 1700. Its first hymnal inclusion was in Freylinghausen, *Neues geistreiches Gesangbuch,* 1714. Its first English translation, also published anonymously, appeared in the July issue of the *British Magazine,* 1838, edited by Thomas Arnold of Rugby, and again in Arnold's book of sermons *The Christian Life: Its Course, Its Hindrances, and Its Helps,* 1841, in a footnote. Arnold's 2 printings have 11 sts. each, basically in the same meter; otherwise the language suggests 2 translators. Only the first 3 lines of both hymns are identical. The 1838 form is better read than sung: its accents are often awkward and its syllables carelessly counted.

In Arnold's footnote to the 1841 printing, he writes, speaking of Baron von Canitz, "He was the author of several hymns, one of which is of remarkable beauty, as may be seen in the following translation, for the greatest part of which I am indebted to the kindness of a friend." One is tempted to suppose that Arnold himself made the 1838 translation, that in the meantime Henry J. Buckoll, assistant headmaster of Rugby, known to be a translator of German hymns, had made his own translation, beginning with Arnold's first 3 lines. However, being a better poet than Arnold, he discarded most of Arnold's lines and wrote the sts. which we accept today. These Arnold printed in 1841, acknowledging that "the greatest part" he owed "to the kindness of a friend," but reluctant either to relinquish title to authorship or to name Buckoll as chief contributor.

In 1842, Buckoll himself published a collection of 72 *Hymns, Translated from the German,* taken from *Versuch eines allgemeinen evangelischen Gesang- und Gebetsbuchs,* compiled by "His Excellency the Chevalier Bunsen," 1833. He is careful to state in the preface that "some of the stanzas" in "Come, my soul" as printed in his collection are not his own: "they will be found in the notes to Dr. Arnold's Sermons on the Christian Life." Since 9 of the sts. in Arnold's 1841 and Buckoll's 1842 printings are identical, it seems impossible to deduce from the generous but imprecise comments of each author regarding the other who wrote what.

Of the 4 sts. which entered the Methodist hymnal in 1935, the first 3 are identical with both the 1841 and 1842 printings, except that in 2:1, "Thou too hail the light returning" has become "Gladly hail the sun returning." The first 3 lines of st. 4 are from Arnold's 1841 form, slightly altered; the last 3 lines, though not in any of the original printings, have recently found much favor.

Haydn

Arr. from Franz Joseph Haydn, 1732-1809
Harm. by A.C.L.

The tune is arranged from Haydn's Symphony No. 93 in D major (Salomon Set No. 2), one of the London symphonies. It is from the first movement and has been slightly reharmonized for the new hymnal.

Come, O Thou God of Grace (352)

WILLIAM E. EVANS, 1851-1915

The hymn was written for the dedication of the Park Place Methodist Episcopal Church, South, Richmond, Va., in 1886. The author was pastor of the church at the time. It has been in the Methodist hymnal in this form since 1905.

Italian Hymn

See "Christ for the World We Sing," pp. 129-30.

Come, O Thou Traveler Unknown (529)

CHARLES WESLEY, 1707-1788

Charles Wesley's greatest poem, "Wrestling Jacob," an interpretation of Genesis 32:22-30, a text on which he often thought and spoke, was first published in 14 sts. in *Hymns and Sacred Poems,* 1742. In omitting sts. 5 and 7 in his 1780 *Collection of Hymns for the Use of the People Called Methodists,* John established the form of the hymn for all later Methodist hymnals down to 1905 when for the first time only 7 sts. were printed; in 1935 these were further reduced to the 4 of the present hymnal. In England, the 12 continue to be printed. American Methodist nineteenth-century hymnals retained all 12 sts., but divided them into 2, 3, or 4 parts or hymns.

The omitted sts., including the 2 John omitted, are in the original numbering:

> 3. In vain thou strugglest to get free,
>   I never will unloose my hold:
> Art thou the Man that died for me?
>   The secret of Thy love unfold;
> Wrestling I will not let Thee go,
> Till I Thy Name, Thy Nature know.

> 4. Wilt Thou not yet to me reveal
>   Thy new, unutterable Name?
> Tell me, I still beseech Thee, tell,
>   To know it now resolved I am;
> Wrestling I will not let Thee go,
> Till I Thy Name, Thy Nature know.

> 5. 'Tis all in vain to hold Thy tongue,
>   Or touch the hollow of my thigh:
> Though every sinew be unstrung,
>   Out of my arms Thou shalt not fly;
> Wrestling I will not let Thee go,
> Till I Thy Name, Thy Nature know.

> 6. What tho' my shrinking flesh complain,
>   And murmur to contend so long,
> I rise superior to my pain,
>   When I am weak then I am strong,
> And when my all of strength shall fail,
> I shall with the God-man prevail.

> 7. My strength is gone, my nature dies,
>   I sink beneath Thy weighty hand,

Faint to revive, and fall to rise;
    I fall, and yet by faith I stand,
I stand, and will not let Thee go,
Till I Thy Name, Thy Nature know.

10. My prayer hath power with God; the grace
    Unspeakable I now receive,
Through faith I see Thee face to face,
    I see Thee face to face, and live:
In vain I have not wept, and strove,
Thy Nature, and Thy Name is Love.

11. I know Thee, Saviour, who Thou art.
    Jesus the feeble sinner's friend;
Nor wilt Thou with the night depart,
    But stay, and love me to the end;
Thy mercies never shall remove,
Thy Nature, and Thy Name is Love.

12. The Sun of Righteousness on me
    Hath rose with healing in his wings,
Withered my Nature's strength: from Thee
    My soul its life and succour brings;
My help is all laid up above;
Thy Nature, and Thy Name is Love.

13. Contented now upon my thigh
    I halt, till life's short journey end;
All helplessness, all weakness I,
    On Thee alone for strength depend,
Nor have I power, from Thee, to move;
Thy Nature, and Thy Name is Love.

14. Lame as I am, I take the prey,
    Hell, earth, and sin with ease o'ercome:
I leap for joy, pursue my way,
    And as a bounding hart fly home,
Thro' all eternity to prove
Thy Nature, and Thy Name is Love.

149

The construction of the poem is as clear as its language is crisp, compact, intense, and powerful. The first 8 sts. set forth with mounting pathos the anguished cry of man—not "Who am I?" but "Who art *Thou?*" The last 6 with glad assurance provide the full answer, each ending with the line *Thy nature and thy name is love.*

It is no wonder that Charles Wesley's brief obituary in the *Minutes of the Methodist Conferences,* 1788, should quote Isaac Watts as having said that this single poem was worth all the verses he himself had written, or that James Montgomery should have commented on its "consummate art," or that Dean Stanley should have described it as "not only a hymn but a philosophical poem filled with depth and pathos."

Unforgettable is the picture of John Wesley when 2 weeks after Charles's death, he gave out this hymn before a sermon; and when he reached the lines

> My company before is gone,
> And I am left alone with thee,

he burst into tears, covered his face with his hands, while the whole congregation wept with him. The same verse was used by Dean Stanley at the unveiling of the memorial to the Wesleys in Westminster Abbey, 1876, shortly after the death of his wife.

Candler

Traditional Scottish Melody
Harm. by C.R.Y.

This is an adaptation of the old Scottish tune "Ye Banks and Braes o' Bonnie Doon." Robert Burns wrote to a friend in 1794:

There is an air called "The Caledonian Hunt's delight," to which I wrote a song that you will find in Johnson. "Ye Banks and Braes o' bonnie Doon." ... Do you know the history of the air? It is curious enough. A good many years ago Mr. James Miller ... was in company with our friend Clarke; and talking of Scottish music, Miller expressed an ardent desire to be able to compose a Scots' air. Mr. Clarke, probably by way of joke, told him to keep to the black keys of the harpsichord, and preserve some kind of rhythm, and he would infallibly compose a Scots' air. Certain it is that in a few days Mr. Miller produced the rudiments of an air, which Mr. Clarke, with some touches and corrections fashioned into the tune in question. . . . Now, to show you how difficult it is to trace the origin of airs, I have heard it repeatedly asserted that this was an Irish air; nay, I have met with an Irish gentleman who affirmed that he had heard it in Ireland among the old women, while, on the other hand, a countess informed me that the first person who introduced the air into this country was a baronet's lady of her acquaintance, who took down the notes from an itinerant piper in the Isle of Man. How difficult then to ascertain the truth respecting our poesy and music!

Whether this pentatonic melody be composed or folk, it was used widely in early American hymnals which leaned heavily on folk material. *The Christian Lyre,* 1830, quotes the melody and calls it STAR OF BETHLEHEM. William Hauser also included it in *The Hesperian Harp,* 1848.

The tune was named for Bishop Candler of Atlanta, Ga., who was instrumental in keeping the tune and text in the 1935 book.

Come, Sinners, to the Gospel Feast (102)

CHARLES WESLEY, 1707-1788

"The Great Supper," a metrical paraphrase of Luke 14:16-24, first appeared in *Hymns for Those That Seek, and Those That Have, Redemption in the Blood of Jesus Christ,* 1747. In 24 sts., it is an impassioned invitation to commitment: "This is the time, no more delay." The historic importance of the hymn in the Methodist societies is shown by the fact that after "O for a thousand tongues," it was placed second by John in the 1780 *Collection of Hymns for the Use of the People Called Methodists,* and remained second or third in all Methodist collections until about 1850.

John, by reducing the 24 sts. to 9 and with minor alterations of text, determined the sts. from which all later selections were made. The sts. which he omitted are those which most closely paraphrase the Lukan passage.

American Methodist hymnals reduced the 9 to 7 in 1822 and to 5 in 1847, 1849. The 5 have always included our present 4 (1, 2, 12, 20 of the original). Beginning with the 1905 hymnal, Wesley's twenty-fourth and last st. has become our fifth.

151

Winchester New

Musikalisches Handbuch, Hamburg, 1690
Arr. by WILLIAM HAVERGAL, 1793-1870

The tune was first published in the Hamburg collection in the meter of 98.98.88. Freylinghausen in *Geistreiches Gesangbuch* (Halle, 1704) expanded it to 9 10. 9 10. 10 10. Because of the need for more Long Meter tunes caused by the large number of hymns by Watts and Wesley in the meter, Thomas Moore put it in Long Meter and triple time in *Psalm-Singer's Delightful Pocket-Companion* (Glasgow, 1762). William H. Havergal made the final alteration of common time in *Old Church Psalmody* (London, 1847).

John Wesley published it in his *Foundery Collection* (London, 1742) under the name SWIFT GERMAN TUNE. Other names are FRANK-FORT, WINCHESTER TUNE, BARRE, and CRASSELIUS (the name given by Havergal).

Winchester is an ancient city in Hampshire, England.

Come, Sound His Praise Abroad (24)

ISAAC WATTS, 1674-1748

The 4 sts. which make up this hymn have been included in American Methodist hymnals since 1847 and 1849 in the exact form in which Watts printed them in *The Psalms of David, Imitated in the Language of the New Testament*, 1719. Sts. 5 and 6 have always been omitted.

Cambridge

Arr. from RALPH HARRISON, 1748-1810
by SAMUEL S. WESLEY, 1810-1876

The original source of the tune is *Sacred Harmony—A Collection of Psalm-tunes, Ancient and Modern* (2 vols.; London, 1784, 1791). Samuel Wesley included it in his *European Psalmist* (London, 1872).

The tune is named for an east English city, the seat of the famous university. It is also called CAMBERWELL.

Come, Thou Almighty King (3)

ANONYMOUS

This anonymous "Hymn to the Trinity" was found together with 6 sts. of Charles Wesley's "Jesus, let thy pitying eye" in a 4-page tract bound in the British Museum's copies of the 1757, 1759, and 1760 editions of George Whitefield's *Collection of Hymns for Social Worship*. For this reason it was long attributed to Wesley and was so described in the Methodist hymnals of 1878, 1889, and even in 1905, if with a question mark. However, Wesley never printed the hymn or wrote in this meter. To this day, English Methodist hymnals have never printed it. Martin Madan included it in the Appendix to his 1763 *Collection of Psalms and Hymns,* and therefore on occasion it has erroneously been attributed to him. Perhaps since the hymn was so obviously an imitation of "God save the King," the author chose to remain anonymous. This is the oldest English hymn in this meter.

Since "God save the King" appeared about 1743 and "Jesus, let thy pitying eye" in 1749, and since Whitefield's *Collection* was first published in 1753, without including "Come, thou almighty King," the hymn was probably written a year or two prior to 1757.

The text is here printed in its 1757 form except for the alteration in 4:1 of "the" to "thee" (first in the Methodist hymnal of 1878) and the omission of the original second st.

A favorite hymn among Methodists, it was No. 1 in the 1889 hymnal and No. 2 in 1905 and 1935.

Italian Hymn

See **"Christ for the World We Sing,"** pp. 129-30.

Come, Thou Fount of Every Blessing (93)

ROBERT ROBINSON, 1735-1790

According to John Julian, a church book kept by Robert Robinson contains an entry in his own handwriting to the effect that "Mr. Wheatley of Norwich published a hymn beginning, 'Come, thou fount of every blessing' (1758)." In any case the earliest extant printing of the hymn is in *A Collection of Hymns, Used by the Church of Christ in Angel-Alley* (Bishopsgate, 1759). St. 4 seems never to have been reprinted after Martin Madan dropped it in 1760.

Madan's text has been most generally followed by later hymnals in spite of some variety of alterations attested to in nineteenth-century printings. Since Wesley never printed the hymn, it did not appear in English Methodist hymnals until the last quarter of the nineteenth century. It is found in American Methodist hymnals as early as 1822 and has always been printed as in 1964 except that prior to 1847 the original last line, "Seal it *from* thy courts above," was used. "For" was occasionally substituted for "from" in the late eighteenth century but was not well established until the nineteenth. *The Methodist Hymn-Book* (London, 1933) still prints "from."

Nettleton

Early American Folk Hymn
JOHN WYETH, *A Repository of Sacred Music, Part II,* **1813**

The tune was called HALLELUJAH in John Wyeth's famous collection which seems to be one of the earliest and most complete collections of American folk hymnody. The collection was published in Harrisburg, Pa., in 1813, and Wyeth indicates in the index that this tune was new; however, Wyeth was not a composer and could not have written the tune. The tune name he gives is drawn from the chorus: "Hallelujah! Hallelujah! We are on our journey home." The tune is printed, most awkwardly, in 4/4 time.

The tune name of NETTLETON refers to a well-known evangelist of the early nineteenth century who compiled *Village Hymns for Social Worship.* It is highly unlikely that he composed the tune, but is possible that he made use of it in revival meetings since the text is quite typical of other camp-meeting songs. In some books the tune is called GOOD SHEPHERD.

Come, Thou Long-Expected Jesus (360)

CHARLES WESLEY, 1707-1788

The hymn was first published in a collection of 18 *Hymns for the Nativity of Our Lord,* 1744, in two 8-line sts. It is printed today as Wesley wrote it, with the change of only one word: in 1:3 Wesley wrote "relieve." By mid-eighteenth century "release" appeared as an acceptable substitute.

Since the hymn was not included by John in his 1780 *Collection of Hymns for the Use of the People Called Methodists,* it disappeared from English Wesleyan use until 1875. It entered the hymnal of the

Methodist Episcopal Church, South in 1847, but did not appear in the hymnal of the Methodist Episcopal Church until 1875. It has been included in all later Methodist hymnals.

Hyfrydol

ROWLAND H. PRICHARD, 1811-1887

Written about 1830 when the composer was about 20, the tune was first published in *Cyfaill y Cantorion,* 1844. With the exception of one note (D) in the last phrase, the range of the melody is only 5 notes, from F to C.

The tune name means "Good Cheer."

Come, Ye Disconsolate, Where'er Ye Languish (103)

THOMAS MOORE, 1779-1852
Alt. by THOMAS HASTINGS, 1784-1872

The poem first appeared in Thomas Moore's *Sacred Songs,* 1816, and in slightly different form in an 1824 edition. In the 1816 printing 1:2 read "Come, at God's altar fervently kneel"; in the 1824, "Come, at the shrine of God." Both forms continued to be printed in Moore's *Collected Works,* though the 1816 form is more frequently found.

Thomas Hastings is responsible for turning the poem into a hymn. Including it in his *Spiritual Songs for Social Worship,* 1832, he gave 1:2 its permanent hymn form: "Come to the mercy seat." In 2:2 he altered "Hope, when all others die" to "Hope of the penitent." In 2:3 "in mercy saying" replaced "in God's name saying," which in turn gave way to "tenderly saying." But more radically Hastings omitted Moore's st. 3 and in its stead composed a st. of his own which won the field and is now always printed—our third st.

The 1847 and 1889 hymnals of the Methodist Episcopal Church, South were generally faithful to Moore's unaltered text. The hymn entered the Methodist Episcopal hymnal in 1849 in the Hastings form, which has been retained to this day.

Consolator

A Collection of Motets and Antiphons, London, 1792
Arr. from **SAMUEL WEBBE, SR., 1740-1816**

The tune was originally for solo voice, published by the Roman Catholic organist Webbe, and set to the text "Alma redemptoris mater." Thomas Moore in his *Sacred Songs*, 1816, states that the music is "a German air" which inspired him to write the text. It is not clear whether it is a German air which Webbe arranged or whether Webbe is the composer. Thomas Hastings and Lowell Mason arranged it for solo and duet in *Spiritual Songs for Social Worship*, 1831.

It was called CONSOLATION (WEBBE) in the 1935 hymnal, but the name has been changed to CONSOLATOR, as used by other American hymnals, to avoid confusion with the tune CONSOLATION by Mendelssohn. Other tune names are ALMA, ALMA REDEMPTORIS, and COME, YE DISCONSOLATE.

Come, Ye Faithful, Raise the Strain (446, 448)

Ἄισωμεν πάντες λαοί

JOHN OF DAMASCUS, c. 675–c. 749
Trans. by JOHN M. NEALE, 1818-1866

The finest hymns of John of Damascus, the most important of the Greek hymnodists, are the 8 odes or hymns which make up the "Golden Canon," the series of hymns written on the Song of Moses, Exodus 15, the lesson for the First Sunday after Easter. J. M. Neale translated the first 4 of these, the first of which is "Come, ye faithful, raise the strain." It was published first in the *Christian Remembrancer*, April, 1859, and then in Neale's *Hymns of the Eastern Church*, 1862.

The first 4 sts. in our hymnal are printed without alteration. St. 5 is the doxology which the editors of *Hymns Ancient and Modern* composed for the Appendix later added to the 1861 edition as a substitute for Neale's st. 4.

The hymn entered the Methodist hymnal in 1905 with 4 sts., which were reduced to 3 in 1935 and enlarged to 5 in 1964.

Ave virgo virginum (448)

Traditional German Melody
JOHANN LEISENTRITT, *Gesangbuch*, 1584

This fourteenth- or fifteenth-century tune first appeared as a hymn tune in *Ein Gesangbuch der Brüder in Böhmen und Mähren* (Nuremburg, 1544) with the heading "Gaudeamus pariter omnes" and set to the fifteenth-century Bohemian Advent hymn "Nun lasst uns zu dieser Frist." Our present version comes from Leisentritt, *Catholicum Hymnologium Germanicum*, 1584, where a note indicates that the tune is for "Ave virgo virginum," a *Marienlied. The English Hymnal* (Oxford, 1906) was the first hymnal to set the tune to this text.

It is also called GAUDEAMUS PARITER.

St. Kevin (446)

ARTHUR S. SULLIVAN, 1842-1900

Written for this text, the tune first appeared without a tune name in *The Hymnary* (London, 1872), edited by Sullivan. It was given a name in Sullivan's *Church Hymns with Tunes* (3rd rev. ed.; London, 1903).

St. Kevin (Coemgen), whose name means "fair begotten," was a hermit in the Vale of Glendalough (Valley of the Two Lakes), Ireland, where he is credited with establishing a monastery. He died about 618 at the age of 120 years.

Come, Ye Sinners, Poor and Needy (104)

JOSEPH HART, 1712-1768

The hymn first appeared in the author's *Hymns Composed on Various Subjects,* 1759. Though it lacks poetic graces, it is a straightforward proclamation of salvation by grace alone; it was therefore very popular in eighteenth- and nineteenth-century evangelical circles. Though John Wesley never included it in any of his hymnals, the full 7 sts. are found in American Methodist hymnals at least as early as 1822. As a favorite invitation hymn, it stood as No. 2 in our hymnals until 1849.

Hart entitled the hymn "Come, and welcome, to Jesus Christ." The first st. originally began "Come, ye sinners, poor and wretched." Our hymnals have always substituted "needy" for "wretched." The 1905 hymnal dropped the last 3 of the 7 sts. There are only slight alterations in the 4 that are retained.

Pleading Savior

The Christian Lyre, **1830**

The tune is a pentatonic folklike melody from *The Christian Lyre* (New York, 1830), a collection of popular and familiar melodies, edited by Joshua Leavitt and published by Jonathan Leavitt. The name comes from the hymn by John Leland (1754-1841), "Now the Saviour stands a-pleading," to which the tune is set in the collection.

Come, Ye Thankful People, Come (522)

HENRY ALFORD, 1810-1871

A paraphrase of Mark 4:26-29 and Matthew 13:36-43, this popular harvest hymn appeared first in the author's collection of *Psalms and Hymns,* 1844. It was included in identical form in *The Poetical Works of Henry Alford,* 1853, but revised (only slightly) for the edition of 1865, with footnote attached: "This hymn having been in various collections much disfigured by alterations made without the author's consent, he gives notice that he is responsible for this form of it only." The "disfigured" text referred to was that of *Hymns Ancient and Modern,* 1861, still printed in *Hymns Ancient and Modern,* 1950. In spite of Alford's insistence that the 1865 edition was the only authorized form of the hymn, he revised it again, and even more extensively, for his 1867 hymnal *The Year of Praise,* altering 2:1 and 4:1, 2, 3, 5, 6 to their present form.

The hymn has been printed in all Methodist hymnals since 1878 and always in its 1867 form.

St. George's Windsor

GEORGE J. ELVEY, 1816-1893

Composed for James Montgomery's "Hark, the song of jubilee" the tune first appeared in E. H. Thorne, *A Selection of Psalm and Hymn Tunes* (London, 1858). *Hymns Ancient and Modern,* 1861, first wedded it to this text. It was named for St. George's Chapel at Windsor, where Elvey was organist for 47 years.

Come, Ye That Love the Lord (5)

ISAAC WATTS, 1674-1748

The hymn was first published in Watts's *Hymns and Spiritual Songs,* Bk. II, "Composed on Divine Subjects," 1707, in 10 sts., and entitled "Heavenly Joy on Earth." Its first line read "Come, *we* that love the Lord." "We" was altered to "ye" by John Wesley for his

1737 *Collection of Psalms and Hymns* and has been retained in all Methodist hymnals, both in England and America, except the Methodist hymnal of 1935.

In the second edition of *Hymns and Spiritual Songs,* 1709, Watts himself made some important revisions. He altered the original repetitious and clumsy lines of 8:2-3 (our st. 3) to the form in which they now always appear. Wesley, however, in 1780 dropped the "s" from "fruits," a reading accepted in all Methodist hymnals. Likewise in 1709 Watts altered the last line of the hymn from "To a more joyful sky" to its present form.

In 1737 Wesley dropped Watts's sts. 2 and 9. These have never been included in any later Methodist hymnal, though st. 9 is widely known:

> The hill of Zion yields
> A thousand sacred sweets,
> Before we reach the heavenly fields,
> Or walk the golden streets.

Given the grimness of much eighteenth-century nonconformist piety, it is a delight to read in the original st. 2:

> Religion never was designed
> To make our pleasure less.

In his 1737 *Collection,* Wesley changed the title to read "Heaven begun on Earth," and in the 1780 *Collection of Hymns for the Use of the People Called Methodists* to "Describing the Pleasantness of Religion."

One other interesting alteration is in our 2:3. Watts wrote "favorites." In 1737 Wesley substituted "servants," an emendation which was retained in American Methodist hymnals until 1935, when it was replaced by "children," a wording attested to as early as the mid-eighteenth century.

The 8 sts. Wesley selected in 1737 made up the hymn in all Methodist hymnals until 1935 when the number was reduced to the present 4.

St. Thomas

AARON WILLIAMS, *The New Universal Psalmodist,* **1770**

In *The Universal Psalmodist* (1st ed.; London, 1763), the tune as we know it appears as the second quarter of a 16-line quadruple

Short Meter tune called HOLBURN. In Isaac Smith, *A Collection of Psalm Tunes,* 1770, and in *The New Universal Psalmodist,* 1770 (where it is set to "Great is the Lord our God," a version of Psalm 48), the shorter fragment appears by itself, called ST. THOMAS. In the original the second phrase begins:

and the third phrase ends:

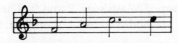

It has appeared in all American Methodist tunebooks, beginning with *The Methodist Harmonist,* 1821, where it is incorrectly attributed to Handel. The tune is also called WILLIAM'S.

It was probably named for Thomas the apostle.

Creator of the Stars of Night (78)
Conditor alme siderum

ANONYMOUS, Latin, 9th Century
Adapt. from JOHN M. NEALE, 1818-1866
in *The Hymnal 1940*

The Latin original is first found in a ninth-century manuscript in Bern. It was variously appointed to be sung on certain days during Advent according to the rite. Neale, using the Sarum Breviary text, translated the 6 sts. for his *Hymnal Noted,* 1851. Neale's translation, no longer printed unaltered, may be found in his *Collected Poems,* 1914. Though many translations of the hymn have been made, most editors follow Neale but with substantial alterations. Our hymnal uses the version of *The Hymnal 1940,* but omits the second and third of the 6 sts., thereby omitting the Advent motif.

The concluding doxology is noteworthy as being the first extant appearance of this Christian praise formula to conclude a hymn. Used in the *Gloria Patri* form to conclude psalms and antiphons since about A.D. 400, it is most familiar to us in the form of Thomas Ken's "Praise God from whom all blessings flow."

This is the first appearance of the hymn in a Methodist hymnal.

Conditor alme

Sarum Plainsong, Mode IV
Arr. by C. WINFRED DOUGLAS, 1867-1944

With only one note per syllable, this syllabic chant has always traditionally been associated with this text. The version used is the arrangement by Canon Winfred Douglas for *The Hymnal 1940.*

The tune was adapted for Lutheran use with Michael Weisse, "Kehrt euch zu mir, ihr liebe Leut" and later "Lob sei dem allmächtigen Gott." In other rhythmic guise it became the setting to Bèze's version of Psalm 141 in the 1562 Genevan Psalter. Lowell Mason and George Webb included a setting in 4/2 called AMBROSE in *The National Psalmist* (Boston, 1848) to Charles Wesley, "My soul, inspired with sacred love." It is one of the simplest of all hymn melodies.

Cross of Jesus, Cross of Sorrow (426)

WILLIAM J. SPARROW-SIMPSON, 1859-1952

Originally in 10 sts., the first and last being identical, the text was part of the libretto written by Sparrow-Simpson for John Stainer's cantata *The Crucifixion,* 1887. Our hymnal prints sts. 1-3 and 10. In 1:3 (also 4:3) "did suffer" has replaced the original "was tortured."

The hymn entered the Methodist hymnal in the present hymnal.

Charlestown

AMOS PILSBURY, *The United States
Sacred Harmony,* 1799
Harm. by C.R.Y.

The tune has recently been traced to Amos Pilsbury, *The United States Sacred Harmony* (Boston, 1799), where it is called CHARLESTON for Pilsbury's home in South Carolina. The last phrase begins:

In *The American Compiler of Sacred Harmony No. 1,* compiled by Stephen Jenks and Elijah Griswold (Northampton, Mass., 1803), it is called DETROIT, while in *The Christian Lyre,* 1830, it is called BARTIMAEUS and is set to "Mercy, O thou Son of David," the cry of the blind Bartimaeus.

A popular tune in the nineteenth century, it appears for the first time in any modern hymnal with a harmonization by Carlton R. Young.

Crown Him with Many Crowns (455)

MATTHEW BRIDGES, 1800-1894 and
GODFREY THRING, 1823-1903

This noble and majestic coronation hymn, though widely printed, is seldom found twice in the same form. In *Hymns of the Heart*, 1851, Matthew Bridges first wrote a 6-st. poem, each st. beginning "Crown him," to illustrate the text "And on his head were many crowns." Then in 1874 Godrey Thring, unhappy with some of Bridges' lines, wrote a new hymn, also in 6 sts., but with a different set of crowns. Present-day hymnals present a combination of the 2 hymns. Thring himself, editing *A Church of England Hymn Book,* 1880 (revised in 1882 as *The Church of England Hymn Book*), made up the hymn out of Bridges' st. 1 plus 4 of his own.

The hymn entered the Methodist hymnal in 1905, composed of sts. 1 and 3–5 of Bridges' lyric, with slight alteration. In 1935 Thring's st. 4, "Crown him the Lord of life," replaced Bridges' fifth, "Crown him the Lord of years." And in 1964, the st. beginning "Crown him the Lord of love" was altered by substituting, with slight alteration, the second half of Bridges' st. 6 for the original second quatrain.

Diademata

GEORGE J. ELVEY, 1816-1893

The tune was written for this text and included in the Appendix to *Hymns Ancient and Modern,* 1868. The tune name is the Greek word used in Revelation 19:12 for "crowns."

Day Is Dying in the West (503)

MARY A. LATHBURY, 1841-1913

The hymn was written at the request of Dr. J. H. Vincent, founder of the Chautauqua Institution, for the Sunday evening Vesper services on the assembly grounds. It continues to be sung every Sunday during the 8-week season both at the 5 o'clock service and at the evening sacred song service in the amphitheater.

The first 2 sts. were copyrighted in 1877 by Bishop Vincent. Its first hymnal inclusion was in *The Calvary Selection of Spiritual Songs,* edited by Charles S. Robinson and Robert S. MacArthur (New York, 1878). Miss Lathbury added sts. 3 and 4 in 1890.

The hymn entered the Methodist hymnal in 1905 with 2 sts. Sts. 3 and 4 have been added in the present hymnal.

Chautauqua

WILLIAM F. SHERWIN, 1826-1888

Sherwin, whom Dr. Vincent had chosen to be music director at the assembly, wrote the tune in 1877; it was first included with the text in *The Calvary Selection of Spiritual Songs.* It is also called EVENING PRAISE.

Dear Lord and Father of Mankind (235)

JOHN GREENLEAF WHITTIER, 1807-1892

The hymn is taken from Whittier's 17-st. poem "The Brewing of Soma," first published in the *Atlantic Monthly,* April, 1872. The poet had read in a Hindu scripture about how the priests of Indra had brewed from honey and milk a "drink of the gods" which when drunk by the worshipers produced a frenzy, a sacred madness, an ecstatic storm of drunken joy, the beginning of a "new, glad life." Offended by the noisy and hysterical camp meetings and neighborhood revivals, Whittier recalled how age

> after age has striven
> By music, incense, vigils drear,
> And trance, to bring the skies more near
> Or lift men up to heaven.

He then concludes the poem with 6 sts. of Christian prayer, beginning "Dear Lord and Father of mankind."

The credit for discovering a 5- or 6-st. hymn in the poem apparently belongs to the English Baptist hymnal editor W. Garrett Horder, who selected sts. 12 and 14–17 for use in his *Worship Song,* 1884. Unfortunately, Horder made some textual changes which later caused confusion. He is responsible for changing "foolish" to "feverish" (1:2), a reading which got into the 1905 Methodist hymnal. The

163

1935 hymnal returned to the original. Horder further altered "heats of our desire" (5:1) to "pulses of desire" to avoid the repetition of "heats" again introduced in his unhappy substitution of "its heats expire" for "let flesh retire" (5:3). "Pulses" is the only alteration made by Horder that is retained in our hymnal.

The hymn entered the Methodist hymnal in 1905.

Rest

FREDERICK C. MAKER, 1844-1927

The tune was composed for this text for inclusion in G. S. Barrett's popular *Congregational Church Hymnal* (London, 1887). It is also called ELTON.

Dear Master, in Whose Life I See (254)

JOHN HUNTER, 1848-1917

The hymn first appeared in the *Monthly Calendar* of Trinity Congregational Church, Glasgow, during the early years of the author's pastorate there, 1887-1901. Its first hymnal inclusion was in his *Hymns of Faith and Life,* 1889.

The text entered the Methodist hymnal in 1935 in its original and present form.

Hursley

Adapt. from *Katholisches Gesangbuch*, Vienna, 1774(?)

An undated Catholic *Gesangbuch* published in Vienna is the source of this tune which was published with the text "Grosser Gott, wir loben dich," a German paraphrase of the *Te Deum.* The first Protestant appearance was in J. G. Schicht, *Allgemeines Choralbuch* (Leipzig, 1819).

The tune name comes from the parish where John Keble was vicar. The tune was his choice for his hymn "Sun of my soul, thou Savior dear." Other tune names are PASCAL, PARIS, STILLORGAN, and FRAMINGHAM.

See also GROSSER GOTT (8), the original tune from which HURSLEY is taken.

Deck Thyself, My Soul, with Gladness (318)
Schmücke dich, o liebe Seele

JOHANN FRANCK, 1618-1677
Trans. by CATHERINE WINKWORTH, 1827-1878

The first st. of Franck's fine Communion hymn appeared in Johann Crüger, *Geistliche Kirchen-Melodien* (Berlin, 1649). The 9-st. form was first published in the 1653 edition of the same hymnal.

Catherine Winkworth's first translation, omitting sts. 3, 5, and 7 of the German, was made for the second series of her *Lyra Germanica,* 1858. She revised this translation for her *Chorale Book for England,* 1863. Our hymnal prints sts. 1, 5, and 6 from the 1863 revision.

The hymn entered the Methodist hymnal in 1964.

Schmücke dich

JOHANN CRÜGER, 1598-1662

The tune first appeared in Crüger's *Geistliche Kirchen-Melodien.* The change in rhythm in the middle section is the original form and is related to the rhythmic designs of the Genevan Psalter (i.e. the half note pulse remains constant). Thus the middle section is a form of mild syncopation rather than triple time.

It is sometimes called BERLIN.

Depth of Mercy! Can There Be (94)

CHARLES WESLEY, 1707-1788

The hymn was first published in *Hymns and Sacred Poems* by John and Charles Wesley, 1740, in thirteen 4-line sts. Included in virtually all Methodist hymnals, it was gradually reduced to 5 sts. in 1849, then to 4 in 1935. The 1964 hymnal substitutes Wesley's st. 3 (our second) for the original second, printed in 1935:

> I have long withstood his grace,
> Long provoked him to his face,
> Would not hearken to his calls,
> Grieved him by a thousand falls.

Our 4 sts. are 1, 3, 13, and 9 of the original.

At least as early as 1849 "Fall" (3:2) was altered to "sins." The 1935 hymnal altered 4:2 from "Shows his wounds and spreads his hands" to its present form. Otherwise the sts. are as Wesley wrote them.

Seymour

CARL MARIA VON WEBER, 1786-1826
Arr. by HENRY W. GREATOREX, 1813-1858
Harm. by V.E.C.

The tune was drawn from the opening chorus of *Oberon,* Weber's last opera, composed during 1825-26 and first performed in Covent Garden, London, April 12, 1826. Greatorex arranged it for his *Collection of Psalm and Hymn Tunes,* 1851, set to "Jesus, Lover of my soul." Though the tune was the one most suggested in answer to an advertisement, William H. Monk refused to use it in *Hymns Ancient and Modern.*

The tune has been reharmonized to rid it of some of its excess chromaticism. It is also called WEBER.

Draw Thou My Soul, O Christ (188)

LUCY LARCOM, 1826-1893

The hymn was first published in Miss Larcom's collection of her own poems *At the Beautiful Gate and Other Songs of Faith,* 1892. It entered the Methodist hymnal in 1935 with st. 4. omitted.

St. Edmund

ARTHUR S. SULLIVAN, 1842-1900

First appearance of the tune was in *The Hymnary* (London, 1872), a collection edited by Sullivan, set to Thomas R. Taylor's hymn "We are but strangers here."

It is also called FATHERLAND.

Earth Has Many a Noble City (405)
O sola magnarum urbium

AURELIUS CLEMENS PRUDENTIUS, 348–c. 413
Trans. by EDWARD CASWALL, 1814-1878

The hymn is made up of a selection of verses from the Epiphany section of *Liber Cathemerinon,* the 52-st. poem of Prudentius. When

Pope Pius V revised the Roman Breviary, 1568, he introduced 4 centos from this hymn into the divine office, of which *O sola magnarum urbium* was one. In the 1570 breviary it was appointed to be sung at daybreak (Lauds) on the Feast of Epiphany and during the 8 days following.

Of the many English translations available, Caswall's is the favorite, either in its original form as printed in his *Lyra Catholica*, 1849, beginning "Bethlehem, of noblest cities," or as altered by the compilers of *Hymns Ancient and Modern*, 1861. This latter form is used in our hymnal.

The hymn entered the Methodist hymnal in 1964.

Stuttgart

Psalmodia Sacra, **Gotha, 1715**
Adapt. by HENRY J. GAUNTLETT, 1805-1876

The tune first appeared in *Psalmodia Sacra* (Gotha, 1715), edited by A. C. Ludwig and C. F. Witt as follows:

The tune, apparently composed or arranged by Witt, was adapted by Henry J. Gauntlett for *Hymns Ancient and Modern*, 1861, for this text.

Eternal Father, Strong to Save (538)

WILLIAM WHITING, 1825-1878

Written in 1860, the hymn has been variously revised, by its first publishers, the compilers of *Hymns Ancient and Modern*, 1861, by the author himself in the Appendix to *Psalms and Hymns for Public Worship*, 1869, and by others.

The hymn originally began "O thou who bidd'st the ocean deep." The compilers of *Hymns Ancient and Modern*, 1861, substituted our familiar first line "Eternal Father, strong to save." This alteration was accepted by Whiting for his 1869 revision and is now always printed. In 1874/75 Whiting seems to have made a third version which did not differ too much from *Hymns Ancient and Modern.*

The 2 versions most frequently printed are Whiting's 1869 version and the 1875 *Hymns Ancient and Modern* version.

Though of English origin, this hymn is commonly known to Americans as the "Navy Hymn." At Annapolis it is sung in the 1869 version.

The hymn entered the Methodist Episcopal hymnal in 1878, in the 1875 *Hymns Ancient and Modern* form, except for 3 small details which agree with the Whiting 1869 version. It was dropped from the 1905 hymnal, was picked up again in 1935 and altered to agree fully with the 1875 *Hymns Ancient and Modern* form.

Biblical echoes are many: Job 28:10-11, Mark 4:35-41 and parallels, and Psalm 107:23-31.

Melita

JOHN B. DYKES, 1823-1876

The tune was written for this text and included in *Hymns Ancient and Modern,* 1861, for which Dykes composed 7 original tunes. "Melita" is the ancient name for the isle of Malta, where Paul the apostle landed after a storm at sea (see Acts 28:1).

Eternal God and Sovereign Lord (351)

COSTEN J. HARRELL, 1885-

In 1940 Bishop Harrell wrote a 5-st. hymn beginning:

> Eternal God and sovereign Lord,
> By men and heavenly hosts adored,

for use on the occasion of the opening for worship of the West End Methodist Church, Nashville, Tenn., of which he was then pastor. Later, taking the same first 2 lines, he wrote a second hymn in 4 sts. for the service of consecration of Bishops Hall for Theological Studies, Candler School of Theology, Emory University, September 20, 1957. The hymn was later used at the dedication of buildings at Oxford College, Oxford, Ga., and also at the Interdenominational Theological Center, Atlanta.

The text of this second hymn is identical with that found in our hymnal, except that 3:3, 4,

> As shepherds of the surging crowd,
> And spokesmen of the living God,

has been altered to its present form.

Its first hymnal inclusion is in our present hymnal.

Germany

WILLIAM GARDINER, *Sacred Melodies*, 1815

Gardiner attributed the tune to Beethoven in his collection (vol. II, 1815), but stated later in his *Music and Friends,* 1838, that the tune is "somewhere in the works of Beethoven, but I cannot point it out." The source is something of an enigma. Leonard Ellinwood suggests that the opening and closing lines are similar to the *Allegretto ma non troppo* of Beethoven's Piano Trio, Op. 70, No. 2, 1809. Robert G. McCutchan quotes James Love's observation that the first phrase is quite similar to the air "Possenti Numi" from Mozart's *Magic Flute,* but this accounts for only the first phrase. Since Gardiner says, "Subject from Beethoven," perhaps it is best to ascribe the tune to Gardiner.

Other names are FULDA, WALTON, BEETHOVEN, and MELCHIZEDEC.

Eternal God, Whose Power Upholds (476)

HENRY H. TWEEDY, 1868-1953

The hymn, written in 1929, was submitted to the Hymn Society of America's 1928-29 competition on the missionary theme. It was awarded first place among over 1,000 hymns and first sung at the Presbyterian Church in Riverdale, N.Y., May 30, 1930.

The hymn entered the Methodist hymnal in 1935 in its original form.

Halifax

See "And Have the Bright Immensities," pp. 92-93.

Eternal Son, Eternal Love (471)

CHARLES WESLEY, 1707-1788

The hymn was first published in *Hymns and Sacred Poems,* 1742, in 9 sts. of 8 lines each under the heading "The Lord's Prayer Paraphras'd." St. 1 began:

> Father of all, whose powerful voice
> Called forth this universal frame.

In John's *Collection of Hymns for the Use of the People Called Methodists,* 1780, the 9 sts. were divided into 3 parts, printed as 3 hymns. The hymn was so printed both in English and American Methodist hymnals until 1849 when the hymnal of the Methodist Episcopal Church printed only the first 2 sts. In 1878 the ninth st. was added to make a 3-st. hymn. In 1905 the entire hymn was dropped from American Methodist hymnals, not to be rediscovered until 1964.

The Methodist Hymn-Book (London, 1933) prints sts. 4, 5, and 9, dividing each 8-line st. into two 4-line sts. The first line of st. 4 has been altered from "Son of thy Sire's, eternal love" to "Eternal Son, eternal love." In line 3, "bleeding grace" was changed to "saving grace."

Our hymnal follows the London hymnal in making use of the original fourth and fifth sts., retaining the alterations noted above, and making 4 sts. out of the 2, but omitting st. 9.

The hymn has commonly been ascribed to John, probably because he printed it at the end of a sermon on the Sermon on the Mount. It is still designated as John's in *The Methodist Hymn-Book,* though there seems to be no authority for this. Since the 2 brothers agreed not to distinguish their hymns and since Charles wrote by far the greater number, Wesleyan hymns are probably to be ascribed to Charles unless there is specific evidence to the contrary. We may suppose, therefore, that Charles wrote this hymn.

Hebron

LOWELL MASON, 1792-1872

This tune is found in the Boston *Handel and Haydn Society Collection of Church Music* (9th ed., 1830), edited by Lowell Mason. It was written in 1830 in a rhythmic pattern which was a favorite with Mason; AZMON in Common Meter is similar. It was published 3 years later in *Spiritual Songs for Social Worship* (Utica, 1832) edited by Thomas Hastings and Mason.

Fairest Lord Jesus, Ruler of All Nature (79)
Schönster Herr Jesu

ANONYMOUS in *Münster Gesangbuch,* 1677
Trans. ANONYMOUS

The original hymn in 6 sts. was first published in the Roman Catholic *Münster Gesangbuch,* 1677. The text is known to have been written at least 15 years earlier since it has been found in a Münster manuscript dated 1662. The hymn first came to be widely used when A. H. Hoffman von Fallersleben, author of *Deutschland über alles,* and E. F. Richter, director of the choir school at St. Thomas' Church in Leipzig, found a new tune for it in Glaz, Silesia, and included the hymn, greatly altered, in their compilation *Schlesische Volkslieder* (Leipzig, 1842), a collection of Silesian folk songs.

The text was printed under the caption "Jesus über Alles." St. 6 was omitted. The second st., "Fair are the meadows," was practically new, and other verses were much changed.

The popularity of the hymn in English translation dates from its publication in Richard Storrs Willis, *Church Chorals and Choir Studies* (New York, 1850). Willis printed the 3 familiar sts. in the identical form in which we know them under the erroneous caption "Crusader's Hymn," and with a footnote recounting the tradition, quite certainly unfounded, that it was "wont to be sung by the German knights on their way to Jerusalem." Willis seems not to have known who made the translation.

Two other translations of the hymn are in use: Lutheran hymnals print a 4-st. translation beginning "Beautiful Savior" by J. A. Seiss, published in *The Sunday School Book* of the American Lutheran General Council (Philadelphia, 1873). Recent British hymnals prefer a 6-st. translation by Lilian Stevenson, published in the World Student Christian Federation hymnal *Cantate Domino,* c. 1925.

The hymn has been included in the Methodist hymnal since 1905, in identical form.

St. Elizabeth

Silesian Folk Song
Schlesische Volkslieder, Leipzig, 1842
Arr. by RICHARD STORRS WILLIS, 1819-1900

The tune first appeared with the text in Fallersleben and Richter's *Schlesische Volkslieder.* Fallersleben stated that he heard it sung among the haymakers in the district of Glaz in the summer of 1836.

In England it was used by Henry Allon and Henry J. Gauntlett in *The Congregational Psalmist* (London, 1861), while in America it was introduced in Willis' *Church Chorals and Choir Studies* with his 4-part harmonization.

The tune name comes from the use of the tune by Franz Liszt as part of the Crusader's March in his oratorio *The Legend of St. Elizabeth*, 1857-62. However, the tune has no connection with the crusades, even though another tune name often used is CRUSADER'S HYMN (see comments on the text, above). Another name, SCHÖNSTER HERR JESU, is confusing since there is another German tune by this name. It is also called ASCALON.

Faith of Our Fathers! Living Still (151)

FREDERICK W. FABER, 1814-1863

Shortly after Faber followed J. H. Newman out of the Church of England into the Roman Catholic Church, he published a collection of hymns, *Jesus and Mary—Catholic Hymns for Singing and Reading*, 1849. "Faith of our fathers" appeared in 4 sts., the first and fourth (our third) being identical with the text as always printed in Methodist hymnals, beginning with the 1878 hymnal of the Methodist Episcopal Church. Very early the hymn was published in 2 forms, one for Ireland and one for England.

The original second st., now frequently omitted, was printed in our 1878 and 1905 hymnals, but was dropped in 1935. Its fervent longing for martyrdom seems to us somewhat extravagant:

> Our Fathers, chained in prisons dark,
>   Were still in heart and conscience free:
> How sweet would be their children's fate,
>   If they, like them, could die for thee!

The third st., introduced in altered form as the second in our 1935 hymnal, has always been unacceptable to Protestants and early met with alteration. The original read:

> Faith of our Fathers! Mary's prayers
>   Shall win our country back to thee;
> And through the truth that comes from God
>   England shall then indeed be free.

Various alterations have been offered. Its present form in our hymnals was set with the 1935 hymnal.

St. Catherine

See "Come, Father, Son, and Holy Ghost," pp. 138-39.

Father Eternal, Ruler of Creation (469)

LAURENCE HOUSMAN, 1865-1959

The hymn was written by Housman in 1919 at the request of H. R. L. (Dick) Sheppard, then rector of St. Martin's in the Fields. It was written for the Life and Liberty Movement, a group formed after World War I to promote international peace. Its first hymnal inclusion was in *Songs of Praise,* 1925.

Our hymnal omits the original st. 4.

Geneva 124

Genevan Psalter, 1551

Composed or adapted by Louis Bourgeois for the Genevan Psalter, 1551, the tune was taken over into the various English and Scottish psalters. In the 1612 Ainsworth Psalter used by the Pilgrims it was assigned to 8 psalms. A shortened form called TOULON is found in some hymnals. It is also called OLD 124TH since it was set to Psalm 124.

Since John Calvin insisted that all congregational singing be in unison and that no accompaniment be used, the unifying force is the rhythmic design in which there is a steady half note pulse.

Father, I Stretch My Hands to Thee (140)

CHARLES WESLEY, 1707-1788

The hymn first appeared in Wesley's *Collection of Psalms and Hymns,* 1741, under the title "A Prayer for Faith," and in six 4-line sts. Though earlier Methodist hymnals retained all 6 sts., our 1905 hymnal dropped the third and the sixth sts., printing 1, 2, 5, and 4 in that order.

Doubt has been expressed about authorship, but the hymn is probably correctly ascribed to Charles Wesley.

173

Naomi

JOHANN G. NÄGELI, 1768-1836
Arr. by LOWELL MASON, 1792-1872
Harm. by C.R.Y.

This is one of the tunes brought back to America by Lowell Mason from a European trip and first published here in *Occasional Psalm and Hymn Tunes,* 1836, and set to "Father, whate'er of earthly bliss."

"Naomi" is a Hebrew word meaning "pleasant"; she was the wife of Elimelech, mother of Mahlon and Chilion, and mother-in-law of Ruth the Moabitess. Mason composed or arranged so many tunes that he turned to the Bible for a sufficient supply of names.

Father, in Whom We Live (465)

CHARLES WESLEY, 1707-1788

The hymn, entitled "To the Trinity," was first published in *Hymns for Those That Seek, and Those That Have, Redemption in the Blood of Jesus Christ,* 1747. The original four 8-line sts. have always been included in all English Methodist hymnbooks. The 1849 hymnal of the Methodist Episcopal Church retained only the first 2 sts. of the hymn, dividing them into four 4-line sts., as had previously been done in England. The entire hymn was omitted from the 1905 and 1935 hymnals, to be restored in 1964 in a form which prints the first quatrain of each of the 4 original 8-line sts.

St. Bride

SAMUEL HOWARD, c. 1710-1782

Called ST. BRIDGET'S TUNE, this first appeared in William Riley, *Parochial Psalmody* (London, 1762) to the Tate-Brady version of Psalm 130, "From lowest depths of woe."

The tune is named for the church St. Bride (a contraction of St. Bridget) in Fleet Street where Mr. Howard was organist. The church was destroyed in an air raid on London, December 29, 1940. It is also called ALL SAINTS' in Edward Miller, *The Psalms of David,* 1790.

Father of Mercies, in Thy Word (367)

ANNE STEELE, 1716-1778

The hymn was first published in Anne Steele, *Hymns on Subjects Chiefly Devotional* (London, 1760) in 12 sts. of 4 lines each, under the title "The Excellency of the Holy Scriptures." In 1763, 6 sts. (1, 3, 4, 9, 11, and 12) were selected for inclusion in *A Collection of Hymns Adapted to Public Worship,* a Bristol Baptist collection edited by John Ash and Caleb Evans.

As a rule, modern printings of the hymn use 3 or 4 or all of these same 6. The Methodist hymnal printed all 6 down to 1878, dropped the entire hymn in 1905, restored it again as a 3-st. (1, 11, 12) hymn in 1935, and with the present hymnal added as its second st. the seventh st. of the original.

Tallis' Ordinal

See "According to Thy Gracious Word," p. 69.

Father, We Praise Thee, Now the Night Is Over (504)
Nocte surgentes vigilemus omnes

Attr. to GREGORY THE GREAT, 540-604
Trans. by PERCY DEARMER, 1867-1936

In its Latin form the hymn is found in at least one tenth-century manuscript, in Bern, in a number of eleventh-century hymnaries of the English church, and in the Roman, Sarum, York, and other breviaries. It is generally assigned to Sunday Matins (the night office, originally conducted at midnight) or Nocturnes, from Trinity Sunday to Advent. *Nocte surgentes* means literally "rising at night," not "now the night is over."

The hymn is traditionally ascribed to Gregory the Great, sixth century, but without satisfactory evidence. Since the meter is a classical form, the Sapphic, 11 11 11.5, and since the poets of the Carolingian Renaissance were experimenting with such meters in the ninth and tenth centuries, it is tempting to suppose that the hymn dates from that time. A. S. Walpole, *Early Latin Hymns* (Cambridge, England, 1922), suggests Alcuin of York, 735-804, as author.

Some 20 English translations have been made. The most widely used form is that in our hymnal, prepared by Percy Dearmer for *The English Hymnal* (Oxford, 1906).

The hymn entered the Methodist hymnal in 1964.

Christe sanctorum

French Church Melody
FRANÇOIS DE LA FEILLÉE, *Nouvelle Méthode de plain-chant,* 1782

In the transition from plainsong to measured hymn tunes in continental Roman Catholic hymnody, many plainsong melodies were transformed into material more acceptable for congregational use. Nearly all examples are either Long Meter in triple time or, as in this tune, in the Sapphic meter. In the transition, modal melodies were altered into the more common major and minor tonality, and the rhythm regularized. The original source of this tune was the Paris Antiphoner, 1681, where it is set to "Ceteri numquam nisi vagiendo." The form commonly used is taken from La Feillée's *Nouvelle Méthode de plain-chant* (5th ed.; Paris, 1782).

Father, We Thank Thee Who Hast Planted (307)

Didache, c. 110
Trans. by F. BLAND TUCKER, 1895-

The *Teaching of the Twelve Apostles,* commonly called the Didache, was discovered in Constantinople in 1875 and first published in 1883. It contains the earliest of the "Church Orders." Now generally held to be composite, it is made up of a version of a moral catechism (chapters 1-5) and of a primitive manual of Church Order (6-15). These 2 documents may have been edited and combined by some scribe in Alexandria about A.D. 150. The second section, giving rules for baptism, fasting, prayer, visiting teachers and prophets, and the Lord's Supper, and containing the fine prayers which F. Bland Tucker has effectively paraphrased, appears to reflect the practices of the rural churches of Syria toward the end of the first century.

The 4 sts. of the hymn are a close paraphrase of prayers in chapters 9 and 10.

A careful introduction to and translation of the Didache may be found in Cyril C. Richardson, *Early Christian Fathers* (Philadelphia, 1953), pp. 161-79. Tucker's translation was made in 1939 and was first published in *The Hymnal 1940.*

This is the first appearance of the hymn in the Methodist hymnal.

Commandments

Genevan Psalter, 1547
Attr. to LOUIS BOURGEOIS, c. 1510-c. 1561

The melody was composed or adapted by Louis Bourgeois and set to Clément Marot's version of the Ten Commandments and to Psalm 140. The first line is similar to a secular chanson, but the rest is probably the work of Bourgeois. The third line is essentially the first line inverted, and the second and fourth lines are identical except for the cadences. The half note pulse is constant, creating a pleasant syncopation in the second measure, which should not be rushed and should not be sung as triple time.

The tune is also called LES COMMANDEMENS DE DIEU.

Fight the Good Fight with All Thy Might (240, 241)

JOHN S. B. MONSELL, 1811-1875

The hymn first appeared in *Hymns of Love and Praise for the Church Year* by John S. B. Monsell, 1863, under the caption "Nineteenth Sunday after Trinity" and with the text "Fight the good fight of faith, lay hold on eternal life" (I Timothy 6:12).

The first 2 sts. are printed without alteration. St. 3 has been radically altered, and since 1935 our hymnal has changed 4:1*b* from "his arms are near" to "for he is near."

The hymn first entered the Methodist hymnal in 1905.

Grace Church, Gananoque (240)

GRAHAM GEORGE, 1912·

The composer writes, "Tune developed about 1950 as an attempt to replace the singable but reiterative 'Pentecost' and the better but irrelevant-sounding (because of its association with 'Jesus shall reign') 'Duke Street.'" It was revised in 1962 and submitted to the hymnal committee. The sturdy, angular melody adds strength to a text which fails to gain strength in a triple-time setting.

The tune is named for the church in which the composer serves. It is located on the St. Lawrence Seaway and is a tourist resort near which the composer's summer island retreat lies.

Pentecost (241)

WILLIAM BOYD, 1847-1928

The tune was composed about 1864 at the request of S. Baring-Gould for "Come, Holy Ghost, our souls inspire" and first sung at a mass meeting of Yorkshire colliers on Whitsunday, 1864. It was published in *Thirty-Two Hymn Tunes* (Oxford, 1868). Robert G. McCutchan writes: "Boyd was asked how it came to be associated with 'Fight the good fight' ":

> Ah, that is a funny thing. One day as I was walking along Regent Street I felt a slap on my back and turning round saw my dear friend Arthur Sullivan. "My dear Billy," he said, "I've seen a tune of yours which I must have." [He was then editing *Church Hymns*, 1874.] "All right; send me a cheque and I agree." No copy of the book, much less a proof, was sent me, and when I saw the tune I was horrified to find that Sullivan had assigned it to "Fight the good fight." We had a regular fisticuffs about it, but judging from the favor with which the tune has been received, I feel that Sullivan was right in so mating words and music.

Boyd is correct; there is no real "fight" in PENTECOST, and as the tune name suggests, it would be more appropriate for a hymn about the Holy Spirit.

For All the Blessings of the Year (525)

ALBERT H. HUTCHINSON

For use in the 1935 hymnal, this hymn was taken from *Hymns for the Widening Kingdom,* No. 97, which in turn derived it from *Songs of Worship* (Canada, n.d.). *The Beacon Hymnal,* 1924, gives 1909 as the date of composition. No other information about the origin seems available.

Childhood

HENRY WALFORD DAVIES, 1869-1941

The preface to *A Students' Hymnal,* 1923, states, "Some of the tunes in this book whose authorship is collectively marked 'University of Wales' have been composed by a small community of minds. In two cases no less than five melodists took an essential part in a four-line tune." The collection was produced by students at the University of Wales, Aberystwyth, under the direction of Walford Davies, professor of music. It was written by him for "It fell upon a summer's day," a hymn for children.

The last phrase has been slightly altered to fit the meter of the new text.

For All the Saints, Who from Their Labors Rest (536, 537)

WILLIAM W. HOW, 1823-1897

The hymn, in 11 sts., was first published in Earl Nelson's collection, *Hymns for Saints' Days, and Other Hymns,* 1864, under the title "Saints'-Day Hymn" and with the text "A cloud of witnesses" (Hebrews 12:1). The original first phrase read "For all thy saints." "Thy" was changed to "the" with the author's sanction.

Majestic in language and emotionally powerful, the hymn gloriously unites the church militant and the church triumphant in a paean of endless praise.

The hymn entered the Methodist hymnal in 1905 with 8 sts.; these were reduced to 6 in 1935.

Sarum (537)

JOSEPH BARNBY, 1838-1896

The tune was written in 1868 for the *Sarum Hymnal* (London, 1869) for this text. It is also called ST. PHILIP and FOR ALL THE SAINTS. It is gradually disappearing from most English hymnals.

Sine nomine (536)

See **"All Praise to Thee, for Thou, O King Divine,"** p. 82.

For the Beauty of the Earth (35)

FOLLIOT S. PIERPOINT, 1835-1917

Originally in 8 sts., the hymn was first published in Orby Shipley, *Lyra Eucharistica* (2nd ed., 1864). Entitled "The Sacrifice of Praise," it was intended to show forth Holy Communion as a joyful as well as a holy feast. The references to Communion are clear in the original form of the refrain:

Christ our God, to thee we raise
This our sacrifice of praise,

in the original st. 6 (altered as our fifth) :

For thy Bride that evermore
Lifteth holy hands above,
Offering up on every shore
This pure sacrifice of love,

and in the original st. 8.

However, the hymn has been variously altered to make it available for other occasions. This was easily done by altering the second line of the refrain to "This our hymn of grateful praise," by altering "This" to "its" or "her" (5:4), and by omitting entirely the eighth and last st. with its refrain.

The hymn entered the Methodist hymnal in 1905 with sts. 1, 2, 3, 4, 6 (and minor alterations in 6), and 5, radically altered from:

For each perfect gift of thine
To our race so freely given,
Graces human and divine,
Flowers of earth and buds of Heaven,

to our present st. 6.

Though the original first line of the refrain, "Christ our God, to thee we raise," is retained in some important recent hymnals, it more frequently appears as in our hymnal: "Lord of all, to thee we raise." Other current restatements are "Gracious God, to thee," "Father, unto thee," and "Christ, our Lord, to thee."

Dix

See "As with Gladness Men of Old," pp. 99-100.

For the Bread, Which Thou Hast Broken (314)

LOUIS F. BENSON, 1855-1930

The hymn was first published in the author's private collection *Hymns, Original and Translated,* 1925. It was intended as a post-Communion hymn. The first draft seems to have been made November 21, 1924. When Benson showed the hymn to Henry Sloane Coffin, the latter suggested an additional st. relating the sacrament to service. Within a day or so our st. 4 was added.

The hymn entered the Methodist hymnal in 1935, unaltered.

Kingdom

V. EARLE COPES, 1921-

The tune was written in 1959 for this text for use at the National Convocation of Methodist Youth, 1960. While it has been published in anthem form, this is its first appearance in a hymnal. The tune with its subtle touches of anapestic movement softens the trochaic pattern of the text.

The tune name comes from the last line of the hymn.

For the Might of Thine Arm We Bless Thee (534)

CHARLES SILVESTER HORNE, 1865-1914

The hymn was written to be sung at Whitefield's Tabernacle, London. It was first published in *The Fellowship Hymn-Book,* 1909, and was suggested by Mrs. Hemans' "Hymn of the Vaudois Mountaineers in Times of Persecution," beginning, "For the strength of the hills we bless Thee." Three of Horne's 4 sts. follow Mrs. Hemans' poem rather closely.

The hymn entered the Methodist hymnal in 1935, with st. 4 omitted. In 1964, sts. 2 and 3 were dropped and st. 4 added.

Cormac

Traditional Irish Melody
Harm. by A.C.L.

This is the tune for "Down by the salley gardens" in *Feis Ceoil Collection of Irish Music.* It has a typical ABBA form of many Irish melodies and ends with 3 repeated tonic notes (see also SLANE, 256).

Cor-mac means "son of a chariot" and was the name given to a prince of Leinster who was born in a chariot while his mother was making a journey.

Forth in Thy Name, O Lord, I Go (152)

CHARLES WESLEY, 1707-1788

The text first appeared in *Hymns and Sacred Poems*, 1749, under the title "Before Work" and in 6 sts. John included it in his *Collection of Hymns for the Use of the People Called Methodists*, 1780, but strangely omitted st. 3:

> Preserve me from my calling's snare,
>   And hide my simple heart above,
> Above the thorns of choking care,
>   The gilded baits of worldly love.

As a result this good st. has been omitted in all subsequent Methodist hymnals. *The English Hymnal* (Oxford, 1906) seems to be the only hymnal which prints all 6.

The text has been included in all American Methodist hymnals. Since the Methodist Episcopal hymnal of 1849, only 4 sts. have been printed. Since 1905 these have been 1, 2, 5, and 6 of the original. In the Methodist Episcopal hymnal of 1878 st. 2 replaced the fourth.

Keble

JOHN B. DYKES, 1823-1876
Harm. by A.C.L.

The tune was written for "Sun of my soul" by John Keble; hence the name. It first appeared in the revised edition of *Hymns Ancient and Modern* (London, 1875).

From All That Dwell Below the Skies (14)

Stanzas 1, 2, ISAAC WATTS, 1674-1748
Stanzas 3, 4, ANONYMOUS

In his *Psalms of David, Imitated in the Language of the New Testament*, 1719, Watts printed 3 paraphrases of Psalm 117 under the title "Praise to God from all Nations," in Common Meter, Long Meter,

182

and Short Meter, respectively. Our first 2 sts. are the Long Meter form, printed without alteration.

Sts. 3 and 4 appeared first in *A Pocket Hymn-Book, Designed as a Constant Companion for the Pious. Collected from Various Authors,* edited by Robert Spence, c. 1781, a class leader and bookseller residing in York, England. John Wesley retained these 2 in his own *Pocket Hymn-Book for the Use of Christians of All Denominations,* 1787. Sometimes John or Charles is credited with the sts., but there is no evidence for this. Spence himself may or may not have written them.

Methodist hymnals have generally followed Welsey's lead and printed all 4 sts. The 1935 hymnal rearranged the sts. in the order of 1, 4, 3, 2. Our 1964 hymnal, however, has returned to the traditional 1, 2, 3, 4 form.

Duke Street

See **"Come, Let Us Tune Our Loftiest Song,"** pp. 143-44.

From Every Stormy Wind That Blows (232)

HUGH STOWELL, 1799-1865

The hymn in 6 sts. was first published with the title "Peace at the Mercy-Seat" in the initial volume of *Winter's Wreath, a Collection of Original Compositions in Prose and Verse,* an illustrated annual which ran in London 1828-32. The hymn was rewritten in 1831 for the author's *Selection of Psalms and Hymns Suited to the Services of the Church of England* and was reprinted in identical form in his *Pleasures of Religion, with Other Poems,* 1832.

The hymn entered the Methodist Episcopal hymnal in 1849 with 5 sts. St. 6 has never been printed in our hymnals. The first 5 sts. were printed down to 1935, when the original fourth was deleted. In our hymnals the following alterations are to be noted:

2:4: "blood-bought" for "blood-stained," 1849
3:1: "scene" for "spot," 1849
4:1: "Ah! there" for "There, there," 1935
4:1: "eagles' wings" (1849), "eagle wings" (1878) for "eagle-wing"
4:2: "And sin and sense molest no more" for "And time and sense seem all no more," 1849

Retreat

THOMAS HASTINGS, 1784-1872

The tune was composed in 1840 for this text and first appeared in Hastings' *Sacred Songs for Family and Social Worship,* 1842.

From Thee All Skill and Science Flow (485)

CHARLES KINGSLEY, 1819-1875

In *Charles Kingsley: His Letters and Memories of His Life,* edited by his wife (2nd ed., 1877), the statement appears that at the laying of the foundation stone of the workingmen's block of Queen's Hospital in Birmingham, a hymn which Kingsley had been requested to compose for the occasion was sung by a choir of 1,000 voices. The hymn was originally in 6 quatrains, beginning:

> Accept this building, gracious Lord,
>   No temple though it be;
> We raised it for our suffering kin,
>   And so, Good Lord, for Thee.

In the collected edition of Kingsley's *Poems,* 1880, additional information is given to the effect that the choir was composed of "School Children," and the hymn is dated 1871. However, in the 1884 edition of the *Poems,* there is no mention of the laying of the foundation stone. Rather, the occasion is described as the "Opening of the New Wing of the Children's Hospital, Birmingham." Furthermore, the hymn is dated Eversley, 1870. It is not clear how these data are to be reconciled.

As sung today, only the last 4 quatrains are used. The hymn entered the Methodist hymnal in 1935, without alteration.

Massachusetts

KATHERINE K. DAVIS, 1892-

The tune was written in 1962 for this text at the request of the hymnal committee. It is named for the state where the composer resides.

Gentle Mary Laid Her Child (395)

JOSEPH S. COOK, 1859-1933

The carol was written in 1919 for a carol competition sponsored by the *Christian Guardian* and was first published in the Christmas issue of the magazine by the Methodist Publishing House, Toronto. Its first hymnal inclusion was in the *Hymnary of the United Church of Canada* (Toronto, 1930).

It entered the Methodist hymnal in 1935.

Tempus adest floridum

Piae Cantiones, 1582
Harm. by ERNEST MACMILLAN, 1893-

The collection from which this tune is taken was compiled by Theodoricus Petrus of Nyland, Finland, in 1582. There it is set to a spring carol (see "Spring has now unwrapped the flowers," 442). John Mason Neale started the tune's association with Christmas when he wrote his legend of Good King Wenceslas in 1853 for use with the tune. Sir Ernest MacMillan harmonized it for the *Hymnary of the United Church of Canada* where the present text and tune were first combined.

Give Me the Wings of Faith (533)

ISAAC WATTS, 1674-1748

The hymn in 5 sts. was first published in Bk. II of *Hymns and Spiritual Songs* (2nd ed., 1709), under the title "The Examples of Christ and the Saints." The entire 5 sts. were published in Methodist hymnals until 1935 when the original st. 2 was dropped.

Sims

WILLIAM J. REYNOLDS, 1920-

The tune was written early in 1965. It was first published in *Songs of Salvation, No. 3,* compiled by Reynolds and published by Broadman Press. It is named for W. Hines Sims, secretary of the Church Music Department for Southern Baptists.

Give to the Winds Thy Fears (51)
Befiehl du deine Wege

PAUL GERHARDT, 1607-1676
Trans. by JOHN WESLEY, 1703-1791

Wesley's translation of Gerhardt's hymn appeared first in *Hymns and Sacred Poems*, 1739, in 16 sts. of 4 lines each, and under the title "Trust in Providence. From the German." Gerhardt's hymn was first published in Johann Crüger's important hymnal *Praxis Pietatis Melica* (5th ed.; Berlin, 1653) as an acrostic on Luther's version of Psalm 37:5, each word of the psalm verse being the first word of a st. Wesley's free paraphrase made Gerhardt's 12 sts. of 8 lines each into 16 sts. of 4 lines, omitting Gerhardt's sts. 5, 9, 10, and 11.

Though a number of English translations have been made, Wesley's remains the most popular. Because of its length of 14 sts., however, it has commonly been divided at st. 9 into 2 hymns, with centos made from each half. American Methodist hymnals until 1935, when the entire hymn was dropped, printed 2 hymns, usually of 6 sts. each, beginning with Wesley's first, "Commit thou all thy griefs," and "Give to the winds thy fears," Wesley's st. 9. Wesley's sts. 6, 8, 15, and 16 were left unprinted until the 1964 hymnal made the sixteenth the last of its 4 sts., the others being 9, 10, and 13, a cento peculiar to this hymnal.

St. Bride

See "Father, in Whom We Live," p. 174.

Glorious Things of Thee Are Spoken (293)

JOHN NEWTON, 1725-1807

The hymn first appeared in the first edition of *Olney Hymns*, 1779, edited by William Cowper and John Newton. Its title was "Zion, or the City of God" (Isaiah 33:27, 28), though its reflections of Psalm 87:3 and Exodus 13:22 are equally clear. Since the original 5 sts. are of unequal worth, no hymnal prints them all, nor is there much agreement as to which ones to omit.

All hymnals print the first 2, virtually without alteration. Our 1964 hymnal makes its st. 3 by printing the first 4 lines of Newton's third, but since 1905 has replaced the second 4 lines with a repetition of 1:1-4. American Methodist hymnals have always omitted sts. 4 and 5.

Austria

FRANZ JOSEPH HAYDN, 1732-1809

To honor the emperor's birthday, February 12, 1797, Haydn wrote this tune for Lorenz Hauschka's national anthem "Gott erhalte Franz den Kaiser." Haydn had been impressed with the British national anthem during his visit to England in 1794 and wished to compose a national song for Austria. The tune may be based on the Croatian folk song "Vjatvo rano se ja vstanem." Haydn used the tune later as the theme for variations in the slow movement of his String Quartet in C, Op. 76, No. 3, which is known as the "Emperor Quartet."

Edward Miller first published it as a hymn tune in *Sacred Music* (London, 1802), but his adaptation of the melody to fit 77.77.D. was not entirely successful; the use of the tune in 87.87.D. in *The Foundling Hospital Collection,* 1796, set to "Praise the Lord, ye heavens adore him" proved to be more successful and made the tune popular.

The tune is also called AUSTRIAN HYMN.

Go, Make of All Disciples (342)

LEON M. ADKINS, 1896-

The hymn was written in the summer of 1955 in preparation for Christian Education Week, September 25–October 2, the theme of which was "Go—Make Disciples of All." It was first sung September 25 at a commissioning service of church school officers and teachers at the University Methodist Church, Syracuse, of which the author was pastor. The first public printing of the hymn was in the *Church School,* February, 1956.

In somewhat altered form, the hymn entered the Methodist hymnal with the present edition, its first hymnal inclusion.

Lancashire

HENRY SMART, 1813-1879

To commemorate the three hundredth anniversary of the Reformation in England, the tune was composed for a music festival at Blackburn, England, October 4, 1835. First printed on leaflets, it first appeared in a hymnal in Smart's *Psalms and Hymns for Divine Worship* (London, 1867) set to "From Greenland's icy mountains."

The 1905 Methodist hymnal was the first to use the tune with Ernest Shurtleff's "Lead on, O King eternal."

Blackburn is located in the county Lancashire. The tune is also called GREENLAND because of the text to which the tune was first sung.

Go, Tell It on the Mountain (404)

American Folk Hymn
Adapt. by JOHN W. WORK, 1901-1967

The text of the sts. is that found in *American Negro Songs and Spirituals,* 1940, by John W. Work, who attributes the words to Frederick J. Work. Since the words are not in character with typical spiritual texts, the spiritual has become a Christmas carol. The usual traditional sts. read:

When I was a seeker
I sought both night and day,
I asked the Lord to help me,
And he showed me the way.

He made me a watchman
Upon a city wall,
And if I am a Christian,
I am the least of all.

Go, Tell It on the Mountain

American Folk Hymn
Arr. by JOHN W. WORK, 1901-1967

In *American Negro Songs and Spirituals* (New York, 1940) John W. Work of Fisk University discusses the origins of the folk song of American Negroes. Since no attempts were made before 1840 to collect their songs, it is difficult to determine what or how they first sang. Several points, however, are clear. (1) The slaves brought with them an inherent musicality, both melodic and rhythmic. (2) The African song form of "call and response chant," using a melodic fragment with an answering chorus, was brought to America and survived with new texts. (3) The interchange of slaves among colonies, uniformity of social conditions, and influences of Christianity as practiced in Baptist and Methodist churches welded the Negroes into a somewhat homogeneous group. (4) The slaves made obvious and conscious attempts to reproduce—not to imitate—the songs they heard sung, especially religious songs.

George Pullen Jackson states that all the spirituals had their antecedents in the camp-meeting and gospel songs, which in turn had their antecedents in the folk music of the British Isles. Yet E. M. von Hornbostel, Henry F. Krehbiel, Charles S. Johnson, Thomas E. Jones, and Gunther Schuller present strong evidence to show that many American Negro "call and response chants" have been found and heard in African usage.

The present interest in and knowledge of these spirituals grew out of the development of the Fisk University Jubilee Singers who toured America and Europe, 1871-78. John W. Work recounts the story in chapter 2 of his book. Since then many spirituals have been composed by singers and preachers. Some survived; others did not. In the oral passing many alterations were made, so that melodic patterns and texts often vary from place to place.

The text of "Go, tell it on the mountain" was created by Frederick J. Work, who taught it to the Fisk Singers for campus carolling early in this century. Of the tune, John Work states, "He may have composed it. I know he composed the verses."

Jackson in *White and Negro Spirituals* points out a similarity of the verse melody to the tune "We'll March Around Jerusalem," found in the *New York Revivalist,* 1868; he also notes that William Arms Fisher in *Seventy Negro Spirituals* called attention to the similarity of the chorus to George F. Root's Civil War song "Tramp, tramp, tramp, the boys are marching." It is possible, however, that the pentatonic nature of the scale which was often used in the spirituals (with no fourth or seventh steps) could create a type of melody which would sound similar to many other such pentatonic tunes.

Go to Dark Gethsemane (434)

JAMES MONTGOMERY, 1771-1854

There are 3 early versions of the hymn as published: one in Thomas Cotterill, *A Selection of Psalms and Hymns for Public and Private Use* (9th ed.; London, 1820); another in E. Parsons and others, *Selection of Hymns, Compiled and Original* (Leeds, 1822); and the third in Montgomery's *Christian Psalmist* (Glasgow, 1825).

The author himself seems to have been responsible for the alterations in the 1822 and 1825 printings. Only st. 1 of the original 4 has remained unaltered. The 1822 version radically altered sts. 2 and 3 and omitted st. 4.

The 1825 version retained all the alterations made for the Parsons 1822 collection, except 3:5, which returned to the 1820 form: " 'It is finished,' hear him cry." St. 4 was printed as it appears in our hymnal, except that in line 6 "how" replaced the "so" of 1820.

The hymn entered the Methodist Episcopal hymnal in 1878 in its 1825 form, except for the "so" (4:6) of 1820 restored. Dropped in 1905 and 1935, the hymn was restored in the present hymnal. The first and second sts. are from Cotterill, 1820; the third and fourth from the 1825 version, with the original "so" retained in the last line.

Redhead 76

See **"By Thy Birth and by Thy Tears,"** pp. 125-27.

God Be with You Till We Meet Again (539, 540)

JEREMIAH E. RANKIN, 1828-1904

From information in a Rankin letter, giving an account of the writing of the hymn as a "Christian Good-bye," 1882 has been widely accepted as the year of composition. However, this is now known to be an incorrect date. The hymn was published as early as 1880 in *Gospel Bells,* a Chicago collection edited by J. W. Bischoff, Otis F. Presbrey, and Rankin.

The hymn was first sung at a gospel meeting in the First Congregational Church, Washington, D.C., where Rankin was pastor. Methodists popularized the hymn at Ocean Grove Campmeeting Association in New Jersey; Dwight L. Moody and Ira D. Sankey carried it around the world. Many a missionary returning home has heard the hymn sung as his ship sailed from the pier.

The hymn entered the Methodist hymnal in 1905 with the familiar refrain which is dropped in the present hymnal.

God Be with You (539)

WILLIAM G. TOMER, 1833-1896

The tune was first published with the text in *Gospel Bells.* The author sent the text to 2 musicians and chose the music of W. G.

Tomer, teacher in the public schools in New Jersey. The music was revised by Dr. J. W. Bischoff, the organist of the First Congregational Church in Washington, where it was first sung.

Randolph (540)

RALPH VAUGHAN WILLIAMS, 1872-1958

Composed for the text for inclusion in *The English Hymnal* (Oxford, 1906), this tune is one of the composer's most felicitous melodies. The first and last lines are identical, while the middle 2 phrases are balanced, one rising and one falling.

God Calling Yet! Shall I Not Hear (105)

Gott rufet noch; sollt ich nicht endlich hören.

GERHARDT TERSTEEGEN, 1697-1769
Trans. by SARAH FINDLATER, 1823-1907

Tersteegen's hymn was first published in the second edition of his *Geistliches Blumengärtlein inniger Seelen,* 1735, in 8 sts. of 4 lines each. The Borthwick translation first appeared in the second series of *Hymns from the Land of Luther,* 1855, for which both sisters, Jane and Sarah (Mrs. Findlater), made translations. The translation in this collection was done in 6 sts. and in the original meter (11. 11. 11. 11.), the first line being "God calling yet!—and shall I never hearken."

Edward A. Park, editor of *The Sabbath Hymn Book* (Andover, 1858), radically altered the Borthwick translation for use in his collection, shortening it to 5 sts. and turning it into Long Meter.

Though the hymn is frequently ascribed to Jane, she informed John Julian that it was one of Sarah's 53 translations. Jane was responsible for 61. Most handbooks follow Julian in ascribing the translation to Sarah, Mrs. Findlater.

The hymn entered the Methodist Episcopal hymnal in 1878 in the 5 sts. as altered for *The Sabbath Hymn Book.*

Federal Street

HENRY K. OLIVER, 1800-1885

The tune was composed in 1832 and published by Lowell Mason in the *Boston Academy Collection of Church Music,* 1836, set to a

191

text by Anne Steele on the death of a child. Oliver in reading Theodore Hook's novel, *Passion and Principle,* had been upset by the serious nature of the book and in recalling Anne Steele's line "So fades the lovely blooming flower" jotted down the melody. He took the composition to a music class conducted by Lowell Mason in Salem, Mass., in 1834.

The tune is named for the street in Salem where Oliver lived or for the street in Boston on which the church of his childhood days was located.

God Hath Spoken by His Prophets (460)
GEORGE W. BRIGGS, 1875-1959

The hymn is one of "Ten New Hymns on the Bible," written for the celebration of the publication of the Revised Standard Version of the Bible, 1952, sponsored by the Hymn Society of America.

The present hymnal seems to be the first American hymnal to include this text.

Ebenezer
THOMAS J. WILLIAMS, 1869-1944

Set to a Welsh hymn by William Williams of Pantycelyn, this first appeared as a hymn tune in *Llawlyfr Moliant,* published in 1890 when the composer was only 21. Originally it was part of an anthem called "Goleu yn y Glyn" (Light in the valley) by T. J. Williams. W. Gwenlyn Evans, who heard the tune in Manchester, copied it down and copyrighted it even though the composer was still living. The tune was very popular in Wales, and a false legend grew up about the tune being picked up by a peasant on the coast of the Lleyn Peninsula in a sealed bottle which washed ashore. For many years it has been called TONY-BOTEL (tune in the bottle). The tune name was given to it by Evans. It has also been called ASSURANCE.

God Is Love, by Him Upholden (62)
JOHN S. B. MONSELL, 1811-1875

In his *Spiritual Songs for the Sundays and Holy Days,* 1856, the author published a hymn in 6 sts. for the First Sunday after Trinity, beginning:

192

God is love! that anthem olden
Sing the glorious orbs of light.

Monsell printed the hymn in the same form in his *Parish Hymnal,*
1873. It was similarly printed by Godfrey Thring in his *Church of
England Hymn Book,* 1880. The first lines, however, appeared troublesome. In an 1857 edition of *Spiritual Songs* and reprinted in Francis
Pott, *Hymns Fitted to the Order of Common Prayer,* 1861, a second
version appeared beginning:

God is love: the heavens tell it
Through their glorious orbs of light.

Monsell's final edition, which is now generally used, first appeared in
2 1875 editions of *Spiritual Songs.*
This is the first appearance of the hymn in a Methodist hymnal.
Monsell's sts. 2 and 3 are omitted. Our text differs from Monsell's
1875 texts only in replacing "death" with "earth" (3:4).

Wylde Green

PETER CUTTS, 1937-

Written 1955-56, the tune was sung at the 1960 conference of the
Hymn Society of Great Britain and Ireland meeting at Cambridge. It
was later published in a small booklet of hymns, *New Songs,* printed
by the Congregational Church, Redhill, Surrey, and edited by Bernard
Massey in 1962.
The name is that of the composer's home church, near Birmingham.

God Is Love; His Mercy Brightens (63)

JOHN BOWRING, 1792-1872

The hymn first appeared in the author's *Hymns,* 1825, in 5 sts. of
4 lines each, the first being repeated as the fifth. *The Leeds Hymn
Book,* 1853, omitted the repetition, a practice now commonly followed.
Only one word in the text has been altered: "Mist" (3:3) was
changed to "gloom" in Godfrey Thring, *The Church of England
Hymn Book,* 1882.

The hymn entered the Methodist hymnal in 1878 and has been retained unaltered.

Stuttgart

See "Earth Has Many a Noble City," pp. 166-67.

God Is My Strong Salvation (211)

JAMES MONTGOMERY, 1771-1854

The hymn in 2 sts. of 8 lines each was first published in the author's *Songs of Zion, Being Imitations of Psalms,* 1882. It entered the Methodist hymnal in 1849, the only alteration being "thy" for "thine" (2:5).

Wedlock

American Folk Hymn
Harm. by A.C.L.

This appears in George Pullen Jackson, *Down-East Spirituals,* No. 56, and he credits it to Cecil J. Sharp and Maud Karpeles in *English Folk-Songs from the Southern Appalachians* (London, 1932), II, 272. They recorded the tune in North Carolina in 1918 sung to the text "When Adam was created," a text about the responsibility of woman to be subservient to man in marriage. The text has its roots in Chaucer's *Canterbury Tales.* There is a musical variant in the 1844 edition of *The Sacred Harp.* Jackson suggests a relation to the Irish chantey "The Banks of Newfoundland."

God Moves in a Mysterious Way (215)

WILLIAM COWPER, 1731-1800

The hymn was first published in *Twenty-six Letters on Religious Subjects, to which are added Hymns, by Omicron* (John Newton), 1774, and in July of the same year in the *Gospel Magazine.* Reprinted in *Olney Hymns,* 1779, the hymn was properly identified as Cowper's. In these printings the hymn was entitled "Light shining out of Darkness."

Evidence is insufficient to determine the exact date of writing. The stories which try to connect the hymn with one or another of Cowper's periods of melancholy or attempts at suicide are probably legends. It is true that Cowper suffered attacks of suicidal mania followed by periods of melancholy, and the hymn can hardly be unrelated to one or more of them. The probable date is 1773 or 1774.

The hymn has been included in virtually all Methodist hymnals. The full 6 sts. were printed unaltered until the 1935 hymnal dropped the second. The 1964 hymnal has retrieved the second but has dropped the fifth.

Dundee (French)
Scottish Psalter, 1615

Called FRENCH TUNE, this is 1 of the 12 "common" tunes in *The One Hundred Fifty Psalms of David,* edited by Andro Hart (Edinburgh, 1615). Thomas Ravenscroft called it DUNDY in his *Whole Book of Psalms* (London, 1621). The name suggests that the tune may be related to some of the basic melodic materials of the Genevan Psalter, but the compressed meter is typical of the Scottish tunes.

"Common" refers to a tune which will fit many texts, while other "proper" meters are for particular hymns.

God of All Power and Truth and Grace (281)
CHARLES WESLEY, 1707-1788

The hymn was first published in *Hymns and Sacred Poems,* 1742, under the title "Pleading the Promise of Sanctification, Ezek. xxxvi, 23, etc." John printed the entire 28 sts. at the end of his sermon on "Christian Perfection" but abridged the hymn to 13 sts. for his 1780 *Collection of Hymns for the Use of the People Called Methodists.* He divided them into 2 hymns with 9 sts. in Part I and 4 in Part II, the latter beginning with st. 23, "Holy, and true, and righteous Lord."

Though the entire 28 sts. never appear in any Methodist hymnal, 1, 2, 3, or 4 centos, variously made up from 18 of the sts., have been included in all our hymnals except 1935. The opening lines of these centos read: "God of all power and truth and love" (st. 1); "Give me a new, a perfect heart" (st. 8); "Father, supply my every need" (st. 19); "Holy, and true, and righteous Lord" (st. 23).

The sts. used in our 1964 hymnal are 1, 2, 7, 8, and 14, a combination never before printed in an American Methodist hymnal, but identical with that used in *The Methodist Hymn-Book* (London, 1933).

Vom Himmel hoch

Geistliche Lieder, Leipzig, 1539
Attr. to MARTIN LUTHER, 1483-1546

The first appearance of the tune was in Valten Schumann, *Geistliche Lieder* (Leipzig, 1539), set to Luther's Christmas carol "From heaven high to earth I come." Its melodic material is similar to many other German chorales of the period; e.g. compare the last phrase with the last phrase of EIN' FESTE BURG.

The tune is sometimes called ERFURT.

God of Grace and God of Glory (470)

HARRY EMERSON FOSDICK, 1878-1969

The hymn was written at the author's summer home, Boothbay Harbor, Me., for use on the occasion of the opening of Riverside Church, New York, October 5, 1930. It was also sung at the dedication service, February 8, 1931.

Its first hymnal inclusion was in *Praise and Service,* 1932, where it was set to the tune REGENT SQUARE. The hymn entered the Methodist hymnal in 1935 and is retained without alteration.

Cwm Rhondda

JOHN HUGHES, 1873-1932

This tune was composed in 1907 for the annual Baptist Cymanfâu Ganu (Singing Festival) at Capel Rhondda, Pontypridd, Wales. Hughes's widow says it was written on a Sunday morning at Salem Chapel, a country church in Wales. It first appeared in the revised *Fellowship Hymn-Book* (London, 1933) and *The Methodist Hymn-Book* (London, 1933). Two years later it was published in the 1935 Methodist hymnal, where it was first wedded to "God of grace and God of glory."

The tune is named for a valley in the industrial district of south Wales.

God of Love and God of Power (153)

GERALD H. KENNEDY, 1907-

The hymn was written during the author's first Methodist appointment at Calvary Methodist Church, San Jose, Calif., 1936-39. This is its first inclusion in a hymnal.

Unser Herrscher

JOACHIM NEANDER, 1650-1680

The tune is taken from *Glaub- und Liebes- übung* (Bremen, 1680), where lines 5 and 6 in the original are in triple time. The present form dates from the seventeenth century. Other names are NE-ANDER, MAGDEBURG, and EPHESUS.

God of Our Fathers, Whose Almighty Hand (552)

DANIEL C. ROBERTS, 1841-1907

The hymn was written for a Fourth of July celebration in Brandon, Vt., in 1876. The author was at the time rector of St. Thomas' Episcopal Church in Brandon. Published first in various papers, the text was first included in the hymnal of the Protestant Episcopal Church, 1892. It entered the Methodist hymnal in 1905.

National Hymn

GEORGE W. WARREN, 1828-1902

This text was first sung to the tune RUSSIAN HYMN. After it had been accepted for inclusion in the revised Protestant Episcopal *Hymnal*, 1892, Warren composed a tune which first appeared in J. I. Tucker and W. W. Rousseau's 1894 musical edition of the 1892 Protestant Episcopal *Hymnal*.

God of Our Life, Through All the Circling Years (47)

HUGH T. KERR, 1872-1950

The hymn was written for the fiftieth anniversary of Shadyside Presbyterian Church, Pittsburgh, Pa., in 1916, while the author was pastor. This is its first appearance in the Methodist hymnal.

Sandon
CHARLES H. PURDAY, 1799-1885

The tune was first published in Purday's *Church and Home Metrical Psalter and Hymnal* (London, 1860), set to "Lead, kindly light." The tune was originally called LANDON, and the change from "L" to "S" may have been a typographical error, though there is an old English residence named Sandon.

God of the Ages, by Whose Hand (206)
ELISABETH BURROWES, 1885-

In cooperation with the Department of International Affairs of the National Council of Churches of Christ in the U.S.A., the Hymn Society of America obtained and published "Twelve New World Order Hymns" in 1958 for use in the Fifth World Order Study Conference in November of that year. Mrs. Burrowes' hymn, written in 1956, was one of these. This is its first inclusion in a hymnal.

Rockingham (Mason)
LOWELL MASON, 1792-1872
Harm. by A.C.L.

Sometimes called ROCKINGHAM (NEW), the tune was written in 1830 and published in *The Choir* (Boston, 1832). The rhythmic pattern was a favorite of Mason.

The tune is sometimes called GRAVITY in southern shaped-note songbooks.

God of the Earth, the Sky, the Sea (36)
SAMUEL LONGFELLOW, 1819-1892

The hymn in 5 sts. first appeared in Samuel Longfellow and S. Johnson, *Hymns of the Spirit*, 1864. St. 2 is commonly omitted.

This is the first appearance of the hymn in the Methodist hymnal.

Germany

See **"Eternal God and Sovereign Lord,"** pp. 168-69.

God Rest You Merry, Gentlemen (378)

18th-Century Traditional English Carol

Described as "the most popular of Christmas carols," the text has come down to us in 2 versions, both of which have somewhat faulty texts. The carol is first found in the British Museum collection *Roxburghe Ballads,* c. 1770. This text as edited in William Sandys, *A Selection of Christmas Carols with Tunes,* 1833, is the better known. Our 5 of the 7 original sts. are taken from this version.

The second version, which may be as old or older, is conveniently to be found in *The Oxford Book of Carols* (rev. ed., 1964). It adds the familiar lines:

> God bless the ruler of this house,
> And send him long to reign,
> And many a merry Christmas
> May live to see again.
> Among your friends and kindred,
> That live both far and near,
> And God send you a happy New Year.

"All other (s) doth deface" (5:6) is obscure. Some hymnals substitute "All anger should efface" or "Doth bring redeeming grace."

This is the first appearance of the carol in the Methodist hymnal.

God Rest You Merry

Traditional English Melody

The tune is taken from *Christmas Carols New and Old* (London, 1871), edited by H. R. Bramley and Stainer. Its opening phrase is similar to that of the "Wassail Song," "Somerset Wassail," and "While shepherds watched" (see *The Oxford Book of Carols,* Nos. 15, 32, and 33). *The Oxford Book of Carols* gives this as the version "as sung in London."

God Send Us Men, Whose Aim 'twill Be (191)

FREDERICK J. GILLMAN, 1866-1949

The hymn was first published in *The Fellowship Hymn-Book* (London, 1909), of which Gillman was one of the editors.

As printed in America, the text has 2 alterations: in 1:2 "ancient" replaces "worn-out"; 3:1 substitutes "God send us men of steadfast will" for the double "God send us men! God send us men!" This is its first appearance in the Methodist hymnal.

Kedron

American Folk Hymn
AMOS PILSBURY, *The United States Sacred Harmony,* 1799

The tune first appeared in Amos Pilsbury, *The United States Sacred Harmony* (Boston, 1799). Kedron (or Kidron) is the river into which King Josiah threw the materials of Baal worship. It runs through the valley between Jerusalem and the Mount of Olives, emptying into the Dead Sea.

God, That Madest Earth and Heaven (497)

REGINALD HEBER, 1783-1826
FREDERICK LUCIAN HOSMER, 1840-1929

Originally the hymn appeared in one st. only, our first, in Heber's posthumous *Hymns Written and Adapted to the Weekly Service of the Church Year,* 1827. Additions have been made by 3 hymn writers. The most commonly accepted supplemental st. is one by Archbishop Whately:

> Guard us waking, guard us sleeping;
> And, when we die,
> May we, in Thy mighty keeping,
> All peaceful lie.
> When the last dread trump shall wake us,
> Do not Thou, our Lord, forsake us,
> But to reign in glory take us
> With Thee on high.

This st. first appeared in *Sacred Poetry Adapted to the Understanding of Children and Youth* (Dublin, 1836), then in T. Darling, *Hymns for the Church of England,* 1855, and as an appendix to Whately's *Lectures on Prayer,* 1860.

The hymn was further expanded by William Mercer for his *Church Psalter and Hymn Book,* 1864 edition. Mercer added 2 sts. of his own to Heber and Whately.

Hosmer's st., which forms our second, was written in 1912 for the *Hymn and Tune Book,* 1914, an American Unitarian hymnal. It represents an important shift of perspective from Whately's "last dread trump" to the daily "tasks that call us."

The hymn entered the Methodist hymnal in 1935, in its present form.

Ar hyd y nos

Traditional Welsh Melody
Harm. by L. O. EMERSON, 1820-1915

Best known to the secular song "All through the night," the tune is a traditional Welsh melody found in Edward Jones, *Musical Relics of the Welsh Bards* (Dublin, 1784). Robert G. McCutchan writes, "Bishop Heber heard a Welsh harper playing this tune in the hall of a house where he was visiting. Retiring to a quiet corner, he wrote the stanza to fit it. The Bishop's sister, Mary, included the stanza and tune in the choir book in use at the church at Hodnet."

The tune was used in *The Christian Lyre,* 1830, to "There's a friend above all others." The first major hymnal to include it was *The English Hymnal* (Oxford, 1906).

God the Omnipotent! King, Who Ordainest (544)

HENRY F. CHORLEY, 1808-1872
JOHN ELLERTON, 1826-1893

The hymn is composite, including sts. from 2 sources. In John Hullah, *Part Music,* 1844, Chorley's hymn, written to supply a text for the music of the "Russian Hymn," was published in 4 sts. It began "God the all-terrible! King who ordainest." In 1870, during the Franco-Prussian War, Ellerton wrote a similar hymn in imitation of Chorley. It began "God the almighty, in wisdom ordaining." Ellerton's 4 sts. were printed in Robert Brown-Borthwick, *Select Hymns for Church and Home,* 1871.

From these 2 hymns a combined version appeared in *Church Hymns,* 1871, the first 3 sts. taken from Chorley, the last 3 from Ellerton. Most subsequent printings of the hymn are made up of sts. from the 2 hymns, usually with some textual alterations.

"God the Omnipotent," originally written for Chorley's st. 2, first replaced "God the all-terrible" in *Hymns of the Spirit,* 1864, and has since become popular. Our 1878 and 1905 hymnals printed the original Chorley hymn with slight alterations. The 1935 and 1964 hymnals have selected 3 sts. from Chorley and 1 (our third) from Ellerton, but substituted "God the Omnipotent" for "God the all-terrible" (1:1).

Russian Hymn

ALEXIS F. LVOV, 1799-1870

The music was composed in 1833 at the command of Czar Nicholas I to provide a national song for Russia, to replace "God save the King" (AMERICA) which had been used with Russian words as a national anthem. It was first printed with the text "God the Omnipotent" as an English hymn tune in Hullah's *Part Music.* It is also called REPHIDIM.

God, Who Touchest Earth with Beauty (273)

MARY S. EDGAR, 1889-

The hymn was a prize hymn in a contest conducted by the American Camping Association, 1926. Translated into many languages, the hymn has proved very popular with youth around the world.

This is its first appearance in the Methodist hymnal.

Bullinger

ETHELBERT W. BULLINGER, 1837-1913

Composed in 1874 while Bullinger was curate at Walthamstow, Essex, England, it was set to "Jesu, refuge of the weary." Its first hymnal appearance was in John Wesley's *Collection of Hymns for the Use of the People Called Methodists . . . with a New Supplement,* 1877.

God, Whose Farm Is All Creation (514)

JOHN ARLOTT, 1914-

The hymn was commissioned in 1950 for inclusion in the *BBC Hymn Book.* This is its first inclusion in an American hymnal.

HYMNS

Sankey

IRA D. SANKEY, 1840-1908
Harm. by A.C.L.

This folklike melody was first published in *Gospel Hymns No. 5,* 1887, set to "Glory ever be to Jesus." It appears there with a refrain, which is omitted in the present form.

Good Christian Men, Rejoice and Sing (449)

CYRIL A. ALINGTON, 1872-1955

The hymn was written for the Vulpius tune, for inclusion in *Songs of Praise* (Oxford, 1925). The author was headmaster of Eton at the time.

Gelobt sei Gott

MELCHIOR VULPIUS, c. 1560-1616

First appearance of the tune was in *Ein schönes geistliches Gesangbuch* (Jena, 1609), edited by Vulpius. It is probably of folk origin. It was introduced into English hymnody in *Songs of Praise,* 1925. The tune is sometimes called VULPIUS.

Good Christian Men, Rejoice, with Heart (391)
In dulci jubilo
Nu singet und seyt fro!

Latin, 14th Century
Trans. by **JOHN M. NEALE, 1818-1866**

The original carol, in alternating Latin and German lines, is mentioned as early as the fourteenth century by a writer who states that the words were first sung by angels to the mystic Heinrich Suso (d. 1366) who was thereby caught up in a celestial dance. The earliest version, found in the Leipzig University manuscript 1305 and dated c. 1400, was published at least as early as the second edition of Joseph Klug, *Geistliche Lieder,* 1533. Its first appearance in England was in *Lyra Davidica,* 1708. Of the many paraphrases, Neale's is the one most commonly sung. It appeared first in his *Carols for Christmas-tide,* 1853.

Neale's original version included a short line 4 in each st.: "News!

203

News!" "Joy! Joy!" "Peace! Peace!" These words are now usually omitted since there is really no music for them.

The hymn came into the Methodist hymnal in 1935.

In dulci jubilo
14th-Century German Melody
Harm. by V.E.C.

The carol melody was found with the text in a Leipzig University manuscript. The first printed appearance was in Klug's *Geistliche Lieder* (see above).

A harmonization of lighter texture in keeping with the character of the tune has been made by V. Earle Copes for the new hymnal.

Great God, Attend, While Zion Sings (25)
ISAAC WATTS, 1674-1748

The hymn first appeared in Watts's *Psalms of David, Imitated in the Language of the New Testament,* 1719, as Psalm 84, Second Part, Long Meter, entitled "God and his church"; or, "Grace and glory." The hymn has been included in all American Methodist hymnals at least since the 1847 Methodist Episcopal, South hymnal and the 1849 Methodist Episcopal hymnal, in the original 5 sts. These were reduced to 4 in 1905, when the fourth was omitted. Dropped from the 1935 hymnal, the psalm was reinstated in 1964.

Park Street
FRÉDÉRIC M. A. VENUA, 1786-1872

William Gardiner included the tune in *Sacred Melodies* (1st ed.; London, 1812) with the text "Thee will I love, O Lord my strength," arranged for strings, organ, harp, and voices. Later it was published in the Boston *Handel and Haydn Society Collection of Church Music* in the 1822 edition for which Lowell Mason was editor. There it was set to "Hark! how the choral song of Heaven."

Great God, We Sing That Mighty Hand (509)
PHILIP DODDRIDGE, 1702-1751

The hymn was first published in Job Orton's posthumous edition of Doddridge's *Hymns Founded on Various Texts in the Holy Scrip-*

tures, 1755. It appeared in 5 sts. under the title "Help obtained of God. Acts 26:22. For New-Year's-Day." Like all Doddridge's hymns it was first sung from a flyleaf by his congregation following a sermon.

The hymn entered the Methodist hymnal in 1935 in 4 sts. with the fifth omitted, which was restored in the present hymnal. The text is printed exactly as in the 1755 Orton edition.

Wareham

WILLIAM KNAPP, 1698-1768

From *A Set of New Psalm Tunes and Anthems* (London, 1738), the tune was set to Psalm 36:8-10, headed "For the Holy Sacrament." In Knapp's *New Church Melody* it appeared in Common Meter and was called BLANDFORD TUNE. The melody is completely stepwise except for one skip.

The tune name is that of the composer's birthplace.

Guide Me, O Thou Great Jehovah (271)
Arglwydd arwain trwy'r Anialwch

WILLIAM WILLIAMS, 1717-1791
Stanza 1, trans. from the Welsh by PETER WILLIAMS, 1722-1796
Stanzas 2, 3, probably trans. by the author

The Welsh text in 5 sts., entitled "Strength to pass through the Wilderness," first appeared in William Williams' first collection of his Welsh hymns, *Alleluia,* 1745. Peter Williams translated sts. 1, 3 and 5 into English for his *Hymns on Various Subjects,* 1771. A year later, the original author—or his son John—made another version, retaining Peter Williams' first st., then translating anew 3 and 4 of the original and adding a new fourth. This 4-st. hymn was printed in 1772 as a leaflet, with the heading: "A Favourite hymn sung by Lady Huntingdon's young Collegians. Printed by the desire of many Christian friends. Lord, give it thy blessing." The hymn was then included in the Lady Huntingdon and other early collections. It is this 1772 version which has been most frequently printed, with st. 4 usually omitted.

The hymn seems to have entered Methodist hymnals with the Methodist Episcopal, South hymnal of 1847 and the Methodist Episcopal hymnal of 1849 in 3 sts., the only alteration being the replacement of "Death of deaths, and hell's destruction" with "Bear me through the swelling current" (3:3), a change already made in the late

COMPANION TO THE HYMNAL

eighteenth century. This alteration was retained until 1935 when the original form of 3:3 was restored, but "deaths" was made "death."

Cwm Rhondda

See "God of Grace and God of Glory," p. 196.

Hail, Thou Once Despised Jesus (454)

Probably by JOHN BAKEWELL, 1721-1819
Probably alt. by MARTIN MADAN, 1726-1790

The hymn first appeared in 2 sts. in *A Collection of Hymns Addressed to the Holy, Holy, Holy, Triune God, in the Person of Christ Jesus, Our Mediator and Advocate*, 1757. It has always been supposed that John Bakewell, one of Wesley's lay preachers, made the collection and wrote the hymn, though there is no supporting evidence. When the hymn next appeared, in Madan's *Collection of Psalms and Hymns*, 1760, it was expanded to 4 sts. St. 1 was retained without alteration. A new st. 2 beginning "Paschal Lamb by God appointed" appeared. The 1757 second st. was split, each half becoming the first quatrain of sts. 3 and 4 respectively, and 2 new quatrains were introduced to complete sts. 3 and 4. There is no evidence to show whether Bakewell rewrote his hymn for Madan, or whether Madan himself or in collaboration with Bakewell contributed the added lines.

The next important changes in the hymn were made by Augustus M. Toplady, in his *Psalms and Hymns for Public and Private Worship*, 1776, to reflect his Calvinistic views. Though John Julian says that Toplady omitted st. 2 entirely on doctrinal grounds, the st. is retained in the 1776 edition of Toplady in the library of Princeton Theological Seminary, with the alteration of "appointed" (2:3) to "anointed," a reading which has henceforth been retained. Several other alterations were made by Toplady. Also a fifth st. was added, now known to be from a 1757 collection and no longer printed.

The hymn has been included in American Methodist hymnals virtually from the beginning. The 4 sts. followed the Toplady text until the present hymnal which has returned to the Madan text with the exception of one line and some few other minor alterations for the most part made by Toplady.

In Babilone

Traditional Dutch Melody
Arr. by JULIUS RÖNTGEN, 1855-1932

Found in the *Oude en nieuwe Hollantse Boerenlities en Contra-danseu,* c. 1710, a collection of about 1,000 old and new Dutch peasant songs and country dances, the tune is similar to the tune VRUECHTEN in *The Oxford Book of Carols.* Ralph Vaughan Williams found it in some arrangements by Julius Röntgen and included it in *The English Hymnal* (Oxford, 1906).

Hail to the Lord's Anointed (359)

JAMES MONTGOMERY, 1771-1854

The hymn was written to be sung at a Moravian convocation in Yorkshire, Christmas Day, 1821. On April 4, 1822, its author recited it at the close of his address at a missionary meeting in Pitt Street Wesleyan Chapel, with Adam Clarke presiding. Clarke was so impressed with the excellence of the paraphrase of Psalm 72 that he asked Montgomery for the manuscript. He printed the entire 8 sts. in his *Commentary on the Bible,* 1822, at the end of his exposition of the psalm.

A part of the hymn had already been printed in the May issue of the *Evangelical Magazine* the same year, and a second completed version in Montgomery's *Songs of Zion, Being Imitations of Psalms,* 1822.

The hymn entered American Methodist hymnals as early as the Methodist Episcopal, South hymnal of 1847. Usually the identical 4 sts. now in use have been used. These are 1, 2, 4, and a final st. composed of the first half of 7 and the last half of 8. Clarke's text varies only slightly from Montgomery's text in *Songs of Zion.* Our text shows only other slight alterations.

Ellacombe

Gesangbuch der H. W. K. Hofkapelle, 1784

The tune first appeared among German-speaking Roman Catholics in the *Gesangbuch der herzoglichen würtembergischen katholischen Hofkapelle,* listed as "Melodie No. 16." The tune came into English usage from an 1833 collection edited by Xavier Ludwig Hartig who

207

dated the tune 1700 but gave no source or proof. Ellacombe is a village in Devonshire, England.

The harmonization is fundamentally that of William H. Monk in the Appendix to *Hymns Ancient and Modern,* 1868.

Happy the Home When God Is There (516)

HENRY WARE, JR. 1794-1843

The hymn first appeared in *A Selection of Hymns and Poetry for Use of Infants and Juvenile Schools and Families* (3rd ed.; Boston, 1846), compiled by Mrs. Herbert Mayo. It was signed "Mrs. W," and the authorship remained obscure for some time. The hymn was included in the 1878 Methodist Episcopal hymnal, the author designated as "Unknown."

Omitted in 1905, the hymn was reinstated in the 1935 and 1964 hymnals, properly ascribed to Henry Ware, Jr.

The original line 4 of st. 3 was "And live but for the skies."

St. Agnes

JOHN B. DYKES, 1823-1876

The tune was written for "Jesus, the very thought of thee" and first appeared in *A Hymnal for Use in the English Church* (London, 1866), edited by John Grey. In England it is known as ST. AGNES, DURHAM to differentiate it from another tune with the same name by James Langran.

St. Agnes was a young Roman Christian girl, martyred at the age of 13 on January 21, 304, for refusing to marry a young nobleman. She is the patron saint of young girls.

Happy the Souls to Jesus Joined (535)

CHARLES WESLEY, 1707-1788

The hymn was first published in *Hymns on the Lord's Supper,* 1745, in 4 sts. John included the hymn in his 1780 *Collection of Hymns for the Use of the People Called Methodists,* with slight alterations: in 1:3, 4, "we" and "our" become "they" and "their"; in 4:2 "hence" was made "thence." As altered by John, the 4 sts. have been included in every American Methodist hymnal until 1905. Omitted in 1905 and 1935, the hymn was reinstated in 1964 with the first 3 sts.

Ballerma

From a melody by
FRANÇOIS H. BARTHÉLÉMON, 1741-1808
Adapt. by ROBERT SIMPSON, 1790-1832

The hymn tune adaptation was made by Robert Simpson who led the psalmody in the East Parish Church in Greenock, Scotland. The manuscript was found among his effects when he died in 1832. John Turnbull printed it in *Stevens' Selection of Sacred Music*, Vol. II, 1833, and from this source it passed into usage as a "Scottish psalm-tune." Actually it is a secular air by Barthélémon called "Belerma and Durandarte," set to a poem in Matthew Gregory Lewis' novel *The Monk*, 1795. Called "A Spanish Ballad," it was printed by Benjamin Carr in his *Musical Journal*, Vol. III, No. 63 (Philadelphia, 1801-02) from whence it passed into American usage.

BALLERMA's original source and form can be seen in the tune AUTUMN set to "Jesus spreads his banner o'er us" (331).

Hark! the Herald Angels Sing (387, 388)

CHARLES WESLEY, 1707-1788
Alt. by GEORGE WHITEFIELD, 1714-1770

The hymn was first published in *Hymns and Sacred Poems*, 1739, in ten 4-line sts. The original first 2 lines began:

> Hark how all the welkin rings,
> Glory to the King of kings.

In 1743, in the fourth edition of the collection, Wesley altered "heaven born" to "heavenly" (our 3:1), and "men" to "man" (our 3:6). The most notable changes, however, appeared in George Whitefield's *Collection of Hymns for Social Worship*, 1753. Among a number of alterations, the most important is the replacement of the first 2 lines with the present form. Whitefield also restored the original "heaven-born" (our 3:1) and changed "a" virgin to "the" virgin (our 2:4). Martin Madan, *A Collection of Psalms and Hymns*, 1760, also made alterations which have survived until this day, notably our 1:7-8 to its present form.

When the hymn was added to the 1782 edition of Tate and Brady's *New Version of the Psalms of David*, Whitefield's new opening lines were used with Madan's alteration (our 1:7-8) and in this way came to be commonly accepted, though some hymnals preferring the original texts printed the hymn in 2 forms. It was this printing which first doubled the sts. and employed the opening lines as a refrain.

Hymns Ancient and Modern, 1861, also made some lasting improvements, one of which has been adopted for our 1935 and 1964 hymnals —our 2:7-8 to its present form.

John Julian is doubtless correct in saying that this hymn "is found in a greater number of hymn books, both old and new, than any other of C. Wesley's compositions." It has been included as a matter of course in all American Methodist hymnals, though there has been much variation in the sts. and texts printed. For the most part, the text as it entered *The Book of Common Prayer* from the Tate and Brady Psalter has been used. In 1935, for theological reasons, a radical alteration of 2:3-4 was introduced.
For

> Late in time behold him come
> Offspring of a Virgin's womb,

there was substituted

> Long desired, behold him come
> Finding here his humble home.

Our 1964 hymnal has here returned to the original Wesley. Most of our earlier hymnals either omitted this st. entirely or retained Wesley's "a" virgin's womb. Not until 1964 did our hymnal return to Whitefield's "the" virgin's womb. Current hymnals are divided in their preference, with perhaps more of them remaining with Wesley.

Easter Hymn (387)

See **"Christ the Lord Is Risen Today,"** pp. 133-34.

Mendelssohn (388)

FELIX MENDELSSOHN, 1809-1847
Adapt. by WILLIAM H. CUMMINGS, 1831-1915

The melody is taken from *Festgesang*, Op. 68, No. 7, first performed in Leipzig in 1840 to celebrate the anniversary of the invention of printing. Written for male voices and brass, the second chorus, "Vaterland in deinen Gauen," was adapted in 1855 by William Cummings, organist at Waltham Abbey, and published in London in 1857 in R. R. Chope, *Congregational Hymn and Tune Book,* where it was called ST. VINCENT. Other names are JESU REDEMPTOR, BETHLEHEM, BERLIN, FESTGESANG, and NATIVITY.

Mendelssohn did not like the English translation of the original text made by W. Bartholomew of the second chorus and wrote:

If the right [words] are hit at, I am sure that piece will be liked very much by the singers and the hearers, but it will *never* do to sacred words. There must be a national and merry subject found out, something to which the soldierlike and buxom motion of the piece has some relation, and the words must express something gay and popular, as the music tries to do it.

Have Faith in God, My Heart (141)

BRYN AUSTIN REES, 1911-

The hymn was accepted in manuscript form by the editorial committee responsible for *Congregational Praise,* 1951, and was first printed in that hymnal. It enters our hymnal without alteration.

Franconia

See **"Blest Are the Pure in Heart,"** pp. 117-18.

Have Thine Own Way, Lord (154)

ADELAIDE A. POLLARD, 1862-1934

Not much is known about the origin of this hymn. It seems to have issued out of a time of despair when "wounded and weary," the author sought refreshment in complete abandonment of self and submission to God's will.

The year of its composition is unknown. Its first hymnal inclusions may have been in the 1907 publications: Stebbins' *Northfield Hymnal with Alexander's Supplement;* Ira D. Sankey, *Hallowed Hymns New and Old;* and Sankey and John H. Clements, *Best Endeavor Hymns.*

Adelaide

GEORGE C. STEBBINS, 1846-1945

Written for this text, the tune appeared in 1907 in the Stebbins, Sankey, and Clements hymnbooks, all published by Biglow and Main (see above). *The Baptist Hymnal* (Nashville, 1956) calls the tune POLLARD.

He Leadeth Me: O Blessed Thought (217)

JOSEPH H. GILMORE, 1834-1918

Following a midweek service in the First Baptist Church, Philadelphia in 1862, in which he had lectured on Psalm 23 and while in conversation at the home of his host, Dr. Gilmore was suddenly moved to write the hymn, and in the exact form in which it stands today. Without his knowing about it, his wife sent the lyric to the *Watchman and Reflector,* a Boston magazine which published it December 4, 1862. Its first hymnal inclusion was in W. B. Bradbury, *The Golden Censer* (New York, 1864).

The hymn entered the Methodist hymnal in 1878. Though most hymnals print the hymn exactly as Gilmore wrote it, our 1935 and 1964 hymnals have altered 3:1 from "clasp thy hand in mine" to "place my hand in thine."

He Leadeth Me

WILLIAM B. BRADBURY, 1816-1868

The tune first appeared with the text in *The Golden Censer.* Finding the text in the *Watchman and Reflector,* Bradbury used the first 4 lines of each st. The fifth and sixth lines were the same and became the first 2 lines of the refrain. Apparently Bradbury added the third line, which was not in the original. The final line of the refrain is an alteration of the final line of each st. of the original. Thus the musical ideas of the refrain led to the textual alteration.

He Who Would Valiant Be (155)

JOHN BUNYAN, 1628-1688
Adapt. by PERCY DEARMER, 1867-1936

In its original form, beginning "Who would true valor see," the lyric is found in Part II of *Pilgrim's Progress,* 1684, in the chapter entitled "Mr. Valiant for Truth." Since it was not intended by Bunyan to be sung as a hymn, this seems not to have occurred to editors (except Paxton Hood, *Our Hymn Book,* 1873) until the editors of *The English Hymnal* (Oxford, 1906) seriously made the venture. Convinced that neither Bunyan nor today's churchgoers would sanction the hymn unaltered, the editors of *The English Hymnal* promptly proceeded to remove the lions, hobgoblins, and foul fiends, and introduce other more churchly words. The result is the hymn as it appears in our 1935 and 1964 hymnals. Most American hymnals print this altered text.

Though this form of the lyric has been popularized by *The English Hymnal* and *Songs of Praise,* English hymnals generally favor Bunyan's original text on the ground that it is so infinitely superior to any modern version that in spite of its ruggedness and occasional quaintness of expression it should be sung exactly as Bunyan wrote. Louis F. Benson, too, queries: "When you have stripped it of its rude vigor and quaint charm, was the dare worth while?"

Interpreters have noted with some perplexity the resemblance of the lyric to Shakespeare's "Under the greenwood tree" in *As You Like It.* It is not thought likely that Bunyan had read Shakespeare.

Bunyan's 1:5-8 and 2:1-4 remain unaltered. The original words of the altered lines read:

    1:1-4: Who would true Valour see
                 Let him come hither;
                 One here will constant be,
                 Come wind, come weather.
    2:5-8: No lion can him fright,
                 He'l with a giant fight,
                 But he will have a right,
                 To be a pilgrim.
    3:1-8: Hobgoblin, nor foul fiend,
                 Can daunt his spirit:
                 He knows, he at the end,
                 Shall life inherit.
                 Then fancies fly away,
                 He'l fear not what men say,
                 He'l labour night and day,
                 To be a pilgrim.

St. Dunstan's

C. WINFRED DOUGLAS, 1867-1944

The tune was composed December 15, 1917, on the train from New York to the composer's home, St. Dunstan's Cottage, Peekskill, N.Y. It was first published in *New Hymnal,* 1918.

The tune captures the dactyllic rhythm of the first 2 lines, then moves easily into the iambic flow of the last 2.

Heavenly Father, Bless Me Now (95)

ALEXANDER CLARK, 1834-1879

The hymn was first published in *The Voice of Praise,* 1872, prepared for the use of the Methodist Protestant Church. The author was a member of the commission responsible for the collection. The original 6 sts. were retained in the Methodist Protestant hymnals of 1882 and 1901. The hymn was introduced into the Methodist hymnal in 1935, with 4 sts., 2 omitted.

Aus der Tiefe

Attr. to MARTIN HERBST, 1654-1681

With the initials "M. H.," the tune appeared in *Nürnbergisches Gesangbuch* (Nuremberg, 1676-77). It was Johannes Zahn's conjecture that Herbst was the composer. The tune is sometimes incorrectly called HEINLEIN, from a discredited conjecture that Paul Heinlein (1626-86) was the composer.

Heralds of Christ, Who Bear the King's Commands (406)

LAURA S. COPENHAVER, 1868-1940

The hymn was written in 1894 in 4 sts., but was first published in 1915 as a poem called "The King's Highway." Its first hymnal inclusion seems to have been in *Hymns for the Living Age,* 1923. It entered the Methodist hymnal in 1935 in 3 sts., 1 omitted.

National Hymn

See "God of Our Fathers, Whose Almighty Hand," p. 197.

Here, O My Lord, I See Thee Face to Face (326, 327)

HORATIUS BONAR, 1808-1899

At a request of his elder brother, J. J. Bonar, minister of St. Andrew's Free Church, Greenock, Scotland, the author wrote the hymn in 10 sts. for distribution in leaflet form among the members of the congregation, after the Communion service of the first Sunday in October, 1855. The hymn was then revised for publication in the first series of Bonar's *Hymns of Faith and Hope,* 1857.

Though as many as 7 sts. are included in some hymnals, most reduce it to 3, 4, 5, or 6 sts. Our 1905 hymnal printed 6. These were reduced to 4 in 1935, to which has been added a fifth in 1964, the new st. beginning "This is the hour of banquet and of song." In this st. (2:4), "hallowed hour" has replaced the original "brief, bright hour."

Adoro te (326)

Benedictine Plainsong, Mode V, 13th Century

Mode V is closely related to the tonality of our major scale with its strong major triad as the intonation. The plainsong version in modern use is based on the French church melody version, to which it has been traced by C. E. Pocknee in the *Paris Processionale,* 1697.

Penitentia (327)

EDWARD DEARLE, 1806-1891

Taken from *Church Hymns with Tunes* (London, 1874), edited by Arthur Sullivan, the tune was originally written for Samuel J. Stone's "Weary of earth, and laden with my sin."

Holy Ghost, Dispel Our Sadness (132)
O du allersüsste Freude

PAUL GERHARDT, 1607-1676
Trans. by JOHN C. JACOBI, 1670-1750

The hymn was first published in Johann Crüger, *Praxis Pietatis Melica* (3rd ed., 1648) in ten 8-line sts. The first English translation was made by J. C. Jacobi for his *Psalmodia Germanica,* c. 1722. Augustus M. Toplady recast the hymn in 6 sts. and published it in the *Gospel Magazine,* June, 1776.

It has been included in all Methodist hymnals since the Methodist Episcopal hymnal of 1849 except 1935, and with its present text.

Hyfrydol

See "Come, Thou Long-Expected Jesus," pp. 154-55.

Holy God, We Praise Thy Name (8)
Grosser Gott, wir loben dich!

Attr. to IGNAZ FRANZ, 1719-1790
Trans. by CLARENCE WALWORTH, 1820-1900

The hymn is a metrical paraphrase of the *Te Deum*. It appeared first in Maria Theresia, *Katholishes Gesangbuch* (Vienna, c. 1774). Four years later it was included in altered form in Ignaz Franz, *Gesangbuch*. It is often attributed to Franz, but actually its author is unknown.

The Walworth paraphrase is dated 1853 in the *Evangelical Hymnal*, 1880. It appeared in the *Catholic Psalmist* (Dublin, 1858). It first entered the Methodist hymnal in 1964.

Grosser Gott

Katholisches Gesangbuch, Vienna, c. 1774

The full history of this tune may be found in Wilhelm Bäumker, *Katholische deutsche Kirchenlied,* III, 285-87. The present form of the melody was developed in J. G. Schicht, *Allgemeines Choralbuch* (Leipzig, 1819). In other guise the tune appears as HURSLEY (see comments on "Dear Master, in whose life I see," p. 164), and it was probably the ancestor of the tune FRAMINGHAM which appeared in the 1830 Boston *Handel and Haydn Society Collection of Church Music. The Hymnal 1940* calls the tune TE DEUM since the German hymn for which the tune is named is a version of the *Te Deum*.

Holy, Holy, Holy! Lord God Almighty (26)

REGINALD HEBER, 1783-1826

This superb hymn, included in all English language hymnals and translated into many other languages, was written to be sung on

Trinity Sunday between the Nicene Creed and the sermon. Though the hymn was written while Heber was vicar at Hodnet, Shropshire, 1807-23, it was first published after his death in *A Selection of Psalms and Hymns for the Parish Church of Banbury* (3rd ed., 1826) and then in *Hymns Written and Adapted to the Weekly Service of the Church Year,* 1827, to which Heber contributed 57 hymns.

The hymn unaltered has been included in all Methodist hymnals beginning with the 1878 Methodist Episcopal hymnal.

Nicaea

JOHN B. DYKES, 1823-1876

This is 1 of 7 tunes written by Dykes for *Hymns Ancient and Modern* (London, 1861). The tune is based on the major triad, and it is possible that Dykes was unconsciously imitating the tune WACHET AUF (366) which had been made popular in England through Mendelssohn's use in his *Lobgesang.* Certainly Dykes never created any other tune of this character or nobility. The tune name refers to the place where the Nicene Creed established the doctrine of the Trinity at the Council of Nicaea, Asia Minor, A.D. 325.

Holy Spirit, Faithful Guide (106)

MARCUS M. WELLS, 1815-1895

Both hymn and tune were rather quickly written by Wells the Sunday following an inspiration which came to him the preceding Saturday while working in a cornfield.

The hymn first appeared in the November, 1858, issue of the *New York Musical Pioneer,* a monthly edited by Isaac B. Woodbury, then in *The Sacred Lute,* edited by T. F. Perkins, 1864.

Faithful Guide

MARCUS M. WELLS, 1815-1895

See comments on the text, above.

Holy Spirit, Truth Divine (135)

SAMUEL LONGFELLOW, 1819-1892

The hymn was first published in *Hymns of the Spirit,* 1864, edited by the author and Samuel Johnson. It was in 6 sts. and entitled "Prayer for Inspiration."

It entered the Methodist Episcopal hymnal in 1878 with the first 4 sts., and with the exception of the 1905 hymnal has remained in the same form in our later hymnals.

Canterbury

See "Christ, from Whom All Blessings Flow," pp. 130-31.

Hope of the World (161)

GEORGIA HARKNESS, 1891-

The hymn was written for and selected as the winning hymn by the Hymn Society of America from among nearly 500 hymns submitted for use at the Second Assembly of the World Council of Churches, meeting at Evanston, 1954. It was first published in the July issue of the *Hymn* and in "Eleven Ecumenical Hymns," 1954.

It is printed unaltered in our hymnal.

Vicar

V. EARLE COPES, 1921-

Written expressly for the text for this hymnal in 1963, the tune is named for Copes's father, and also stands for a priestly order in the Church of England.

Hosanna, Loud Hosanna (423)

JEANNETTE THRELFALL, 1821-1880

Miss Threlfall's hymns were written at "idle moments" and sent anonymously to various periodicals. Thirty-five of these poems were first collected in a small volume, *Woodsorrel, or Leaves from a Retired Home*, 1856. Years later she selected 15 of these and added 55 others for a volume called *Sunshine and Shadow*, 1873. "Hosanna, loud hosanna" is taken from the 1873 volume.

The hymn entered the Methodist hymnal in 1935 in 3 sts., with 1 omitted.

Ellacombe

See "Hail to the Lord's Anointed," pp. 207-8.

How Are Thy Servants Blest, O Lord (52)

JOSEPH ADDISON, 1672-1719

The hymn was first published in the *Spectator,* September 20, 1712, at the conclusion of an essay which reflects on how the ocean, "this prodigious bulk of waters," affects the imagination. "Such an object naturally raises in my thoughts the idea of an Almighty Being, and convinces me of his existence as much as a metaphysical demonstration." The concluding poem Addison called a "divine ode, made by a gentleman upon the conclusion of his travels." It is, of course, his own lyrical recollection of a storm at sea, some 10 years before. It is almost a paraphrase of Psalm 107:23-32.

All 10 sts. seem never to have been included in a hymnal. The hymn entered the Methodist Episcopal, South hymnal of 1847 and the Methodist Episcopal hymnal of 1849 with 6 sts., the original 3, 4, 5, and 6 omitted. The 1935 hymnal reclaimed st. 6 (our 2) but dropped 2, 7, and 8, retaining the original 1, 6, 9, and 10.

In 2 ways the poem as now used in the hymnal has been radically altered. First, the reference to the storm at sea has entirely disappeared. Second, all first-person singular pronouns have been made plural, with other text changes.

Caithness

Scottish Psalter, 1635

The tune is taken from Andro Hart, *The One Hundred Fifty Psalms of David* (Edinburgh, 1635), the first Scottish Psalter to print "proper" tunes to the psalms in 4 parts. It is 1 of 31 "common tunes," which would fit any psalm in the book in Common Meter. The handbook to *Songs of Praise* calls it "a smooth tune, with an elegant contour."

Caithness is a county in northeast Scotland.

How Beauteous Were the Marks Divine (80)

A. CLEVELAND COXE, 1818-1896

The poem entitled "Hymn to the Redeemer" was written in 1840 and published that year in the author's collection *Christian Ballads.*

It was variously printed, and Coxe gave it its final form in 1869 for Philip Schaff's *Christ in Song,* where it appears in 6 sts. of 8 lines.

The poem began:

> When o'er Judea's vales and hills,
> Or by her olive-shaded rills,
> Thy weary footsteps went of old,
> Or walked the lulling waters bold.

Then follows our first 3 sts. Three 8-line sts. intervene between our third and fourth sts. Our fourth is composed of lines 1-2 and 5-6 of the original last st. of the poem.

The hymn entered the Methodist Episcopal hymnal in 1878 with 5 sts. These were reduced to 4 in 1935.

Windham

ordinary **DANIEL READ, 1757-1836**

The tune comes from *The American Singing Book,* 1785. It was a popular early American hymn tune.

How Blessed Is This Place (350)

ERNEST E. RYDEN, 1886-

The hymn was written for the *Augustana Hymnal* of the Augustana Lutheran Church, 1925, to provide a hymn suitable for the dedication of an altar. Though the author had Genesis 28:17 and 35:1-7 in mind, the hymn has found broad use in worship generally.

Kent

JOHN F. LAMPE, 1703-1751

Called INVITATION by the composer, the tune comes from Lampe's *Hymns on the Great Festivals and Other Occasions* (London, 1746), set to Charles Wesley's "Sinners, obey the Gospel Word." The composer's style was ornate and florid, the original form being liberally embellished with grace notes and passing notes. It is a typical eighteenth-century Methodist hymn tune.

Other names are DEVONSHIRE, GUILDFORD, ST. PAUL'S ROCHESTER, WILTON, and ST. LUKE.

How Can a Sinner Know (114)

CHARLES WESLEY, 1707-1788

The hymn first appeared in *Hymns and Sacred Poems,* 1749, in eight 8-line sts., beginning a series under the title "The Marks of Faith." The first quatrain in each st. was in Short Meter, the second in Common Meter. When John printed the hymn in his 1780 *Collection of Hymns for the Use of the People Called Methodists,* he omitted the original sts. 4 and 5, and removed 2 syllables from each fifth line, thus reducing the entire hymn to Short Meter.

The hymn has been included in all Methodist hymnals with the original first three 8-line sts. sung as six 4-line sts. and in the text of the 1780 *Collection.* Beginning with the 1889 hymnal of the Methodist Episcopal Church, South, our hymnals have reduced the sts. to the original first two 8-line sts. Since 1935, the second quatrain of st. 2 has been replaced by the first 4 lines of st. 6.

St. Michael

Genevan Psalter, 1551
Adapt. by WILLIAM CROTCH, 1775-1847

The tune, sometimes called OLD 134TH, was adapted from the Genevan Psalter, 1551, where it was set to Clément Marot's version of Psalm 101. In the Anglo-Genevan Psalter, 1561, it was set to Psalm 134. Crotch abbreviated the tune, changed the last phrase, called it ST. MICHAEL, and revived it to popular usage in his *Psalm Tunes* (London, 1836).

How Firm a Foundation (48)

"K" in JOHN RIPPON, *A Selection of Hymns,* 1787

The hymn in 7 sts. first appeared in John Rippon, *A Selection of Hymns from the Best Authors,* 1787, under the title "Exceeding Great and Precious Promises." Authorship was ascribed to "K." As early as 1822, "K" was spelled out as Richard Keen, precentor in the London Baptist church where Rippon was minister. John Julian regards this guess as probable, though evidence is scant and Keen is scarcely a known person.

The hymn has been included in all Methodist hymnals since the 1847 Methodist Episcopal, South and the Methodist Episcopal of 1878, with 6 or 7 sts. until 1935 when sts. 2 and 6 were omitted.

Foundation

Early American Melody
Harm. by C.R.Y.

The tune is not by Anne Steele. Because of a poor page layout in the Methodist Episcopal, South *Hymn and Tune Book*, 1889, it appeared that Anne Steele was the composer, and the error was picked up in many other collections. Actually it is a pentatonic (five-note gapped scale) tune typical of many of the folk hymns of the South.

It seems that the first printed version is in William Walker, *Southern Harmony*, 1835, called THE CHRISTIAN'S FAREWELL. It appeared in 1844 in *The Sacred Harp*, called BELLEVUE and credited to "Z. Chambless."

The new harmonization by Carlton R. Young is in the tradition of "dispersed harmony" of early American hymnals, with open fourths and fifths.

How Gentle God's Commands (53)

PHILIP DODDRIDGE, 1702-1751

The hymn first appeared in Job Orton's posthumous edition of Doddridge's *Hymns Founded on Various Texts in the Holy Scriptures* (London, 1755). In 2:1-2, Doddridge wrote:

> While Providence supports,
> Let Saints securely dwell,

and in 4:2: "Down to the present day." When the hymn entered the Methodist Episcopal hymnal in 1878, these alterations had already been made. Otherwise the text is unchanged.

Dennis

See "And Are We Yet Alive," pp. 90-91.

How Happy Are Thy Servants, Lord (328)

CHARLES WESLEY, 1707-1788

The hymn was first published in *Hymns on the Lord's Supper*, 1745. Perhaps because John did not include it in his 1780 *Collection of Hymns for the Use of the People Called Methodists,* it has not been widely printed. It is not in *The Methodist Hymn-Book* (London, 1933), nor has it been included in any American Methodist hymnal until 1964. The 4 sts. appear here without alteration.

Martyrdom

See "Alas, and Did My Savior Bleed," pp. 70-71.

How Happy Every Child of Grace (115)

CHARLES WESLEY, 1707-1788

The hymn was first printed in *Funeral Hymns,* second series, 1759, in eight 8-line sts. It has been included in every American Methodist hymnal, usually in 3 sts., until these were reduced to our present 2 in 1935.

Cleansing Fountain

American Folk Melody

The melody is in typical camp-meeting style, with much repetition of material. Its rousing quality is more suited to this text than to "There is a fountain," to which it is more familiarly used. Asa Hull in his *Pilgrims' Harp,* 1869, called it a "Western Melody," as did other early nineteenth-century tunebooks. Lowell Mason's tune COWPER, written in 1830, has some similarity (see *The Sabbath Hymn and Tune Book,* 1859, p. 96), and Robert G. McCutchan has suggested that Mason may have heard CLEANSING FOUNTAIN before composing COWPER.

How Lovely Is Thy Dwelling Place (295)

Scottish Psalter, 1650

This metrical psalm came into use through the Scottish Psalter. The 1635 edition had 14 quatrains. These were later reduced to the 11 now printed in the 1929 Scottish Psalter, with the text much altered.

Our earlier hymnals, beginning with the 1847 hymnal of the Methodist Episcopal Church, South, used other paraphrases of Psalm 84: Charles Wesley's "How lovely are thy tents, O Lord"; Isaac

Watts's "Lord of the worlds above," or more commonly, his "How pleasant, how divinely fair"; or John Milton's "How lovely are thy dwellings, Lord." Our 1935 hymnal first substituted the text of the Scottish Psalter for other paraphrases of the psalm, using the first 5 quatrains.

Salzburg

JOHANN MICHAEL HAYDN, 1737-1806
Harm. by V.E.C.

The tune is an adaptation of an air from one of Haydn's masses "for the use of country choirs." Christian Ignatius Latrobe included it in *Selection of Sacred Music* (6 vols.; London, 1806-25) in 6/8 time in F major. Haydn lived in Salzburg the last part of his life.

This tune should not be confused with another tune of the same name which is actually ALLE MENSCHEN MÜSSEN STERBEN.

How Sweet the Name of Jesus Sounds (81)

JOHN NEWTON, 1725-1807

The hymn was first published in *Olney Hymns,* 1779, in 7 sts., with the title of "The Name of Jesus." John Wesley printed the entire hymn without alteration in the *Arminian Magazine,* December, 1781. The original st. 4 seems never to have been reprinted.

The only troublesome line has been our 3:1. The original read "Jesus, my Shepherd, Husband, Friend." Though the author had the images of the Song of Solomon in mind, "husband" has been embarrassing to many editors, and various emendations have been made. "Shepherd, brother, friend" and "Shepherd, guardian, friend" are the most frequently printed forms.

The hymn has been included in all Methodist hymnals since 1849, usually in 5 sts. Until 1935, Newton's st. 3 was printed in our hymnals.

St. Peter

ALEXANDER R. REINAGLE, 1799-1877

The tune is taken from Reinagle's *Psalm-Tunes for the Voice and Pianoforte* (Oxford, 1830), where it was set to Psalm 118. The tune is named for St. Peter's Church in East, Oxford, where the composer was organist.

I Am Coming to the Cross (116)

WILLIAM McDONALD, 1820-1901

The text and tune were written in 1870 in Brooklyn. The hymn was first sung at a national camp meeting, Hamilton, Mass., June 22 of the same year. Its earliest printings were in *The Baptist Praise Book,* 1871; Joseph Hillman, *The Revivalist,* 1872; and in a pamphlet for camp meetings published by the *Advocate of Christian Holiness* the same year.

The hymn entered Methodist hymnals with the Methodist Protestant in 1882 and the Methodist Episcopal, South in 1889 with the original 5 sts. and refrain, the only alteration being the omission of the special refrain for the last st., beginning "Still I'm trusting, Lord, in thee." Our 1935 hymnal dropped the original st. 4. The present hymnal has discontinued the refrain but inserted it as st. 4.

Coming to the Cross

WILLIAM G. FISCHER, 1835-1912

(See comments on text, above.) The tune is also called TRUSTING.

I Am Thine, O Lord (159)

FANNY J. CROSBY, 1820-1915

The text and tune first appeared in a Sunday school collection, *Brightest and Best* (Chicago, 1875), edited by Robert Lowry and W. H. Doane. It entered the Methodist hymnal unaltered with the hymnal of the Methodist Episcopal Church, South in 1889.

I Am Thine

WILLIAM H. DOANE, 1832-1915

See comments on text, above.

I Heard the Voice of Jesus Say (117)

HORATIUS BONAR, 1808-1889

The text was written while the author was pastor at Kelso, Scotland, perhaps some years before its publication in his *Hymns, Original and Selected,* 1846, with the title "The Voice from Galilee." It was reprinted in Bonar's *Hymns of Faith and Hope,* 1857.

The hymn entered the Methodist hymnal with the Methodist Episcopal hymnal of 1878 in its original form. It has been retained unaltered.

Vox dilecti

JOHN B. DYKES, 1823-1876

Written for this text, the tune first appeared in the Appendix to *Hymns Ancient and Modern* (London, 1868). Dykes wrote the tune because he felt that there was no appropriate setting available for this particular text. The first half in minor and the second half in major are designed to set forth the invitation and acceptance of the text, a device rarely found in hymn tunes.

I Know Not How That Bethlehem's Babe (123)

HARRY WEBB FARRINGTON, 1879-1931

As a first-year graduate student at Harvard, the author entered the hymn in the competition for the prize Christmas hymn, 1910. Awarded first place, it was printed with an account of its origin in Farrington's *Rough and Brown,* 1921. Its first hymnal inclusion was in *The Abingdon Hymnal,* 1928. It entered the Methodist hymnal in 1935.

Shirleyn

EARL E. HARPER, 1895-1967
Harm. by A.C.L.

The author requested the composer to make a simple tune with a flowing melody for the text, for he thought other tunes used were too complicated or dissonant. The tune was written during the summer of 1927 at a summer school of church music at Attleboro Springs, Mass., and tried out on the class in hymnology. It was included in *The Abingdon Hymnal,* 1928.

The climax of the tune comes in the fourth phrase, where Farrington felt it should be. The harmonization has been slightly altered for the new hymnal.

I Know Not What the Future Hath (290)

JOHN GREENLEAF WHITTIER, 1807-1892

The sts. are taken from Whittier's "Eternal Goodness," written in 1865 and first published in his *Tent on the Beach and Other Poems,* 1867, in 22 sts. A 4-st. cento was included in the Methodist Protestant hymnal of 1901. Our current 5 sts., introduced into the 1935 hymnal, are 16, 17, 22, 19, and 20 of the original.

Cooling

ALONZO J. ABBEY, 1825-1887

First published in *The American Choir,* 1858, the tune has been seldom included in other than Methodist hymnals.

I Know That My Redeemer Lives (445)

SAMUEL MEDLEY, 1738-1799

The text first appeared in George Whitefield, *Psalms and Hymns, Extracted from Different Authors,* 1775, and in Richard De Courcy's collection (4th ed., 1793), but both times without signature. Authorship was clarified in the posthumous collection of Medley's hymns entitled *Hymns: The Public Worship and Private Devotions of True Christians, Assisted in Some Thoughts in Verse: Principally Drawn from Select Passages of the Word of God* (London, 1800).

In 9 sts., the hymn originally began:

> I know that my Redeemer lives.
> What comfort this sweet passage gives!

It entered the Methodist Episcopal hymnal in 1849 in altered form with sts. 1, 3, 8, and 9. The hymn has remained unchanged in our hymnals since that date. Thirty-two of the original 36 lines begin with "He lives."

Truro

ANONYMOUS in THOMAS WILLIAMS, *Psalmodia Evangelica,* 1789

The tune first appeared in *Psalmodia Evangelica: A Collection of Psalms and Hymns in Three Parts for Public Worship,* 2 volumes edited by Williams, set to "Now to the Lord a noble song." The setting gives interesting emphasis to the words "He lives."

227

I Look to Thee in Every Need (219)

SAMUEL LONGFELLOW, 1819-1892

The text was first published in *Hymns of the Spirit,* 1864, edited by the author and Samuel Johnson.

It has been included in the Methodist hymnal since 1905.

O Jesu

Hirschberger Gesangbuch, 1741
Altered by A.C.L.

The melody, set to "O Jesu, warum legst du mir," and with a half note at the beginning and end of each line, appeared in J. B. Reimann, *Sammlung alter und neuer Melodien evangel. Lieder,* 1747, a tunebook for the *Hirschberger Gesangbuch.* It is possibly by Reimann.

The last phrase has been altered from the 1935 hymnal version:

I Love Thy Kingdom, Lord (294)

TIMOTHY DWIGHT, 1752-1817

Intended to be a paraphrase of the third part of Psalm 137, though actually suggested by verses 5-6, the text was first published in Dwight's 1801 revision of Isaac Watts, *The Psalms of David.*

The text was originally in 8 sts. The first 6 in order were used in the Methodist Episcopal, South hymnals of 1847 and 1889. The 1849 Methodist Episcopal hymnal printed 1, 2, 5, 6, and 8, a cento now generally used.

The hymn is perhaps the oldest hymn written by an American which has remained in continuous use. It is the only 1 of Dwight's 33 to survive.

St. Thomas

See "Come, Ye That Love the Lord," pp. 158-60.

I Love to Tell the Story (149)

KATHERINE HANKEY, 1834-1911

Miss Hankey wrote a long poem on the life of Jesus entitled "The Old, Old Story," the date of which is uncertain. The 2 printings most readily available are both undated and of different lengths. That in the Benson Collection at Princeton Theological Seminary has 55 quatrains; the one in Union Theological Seminary, New York, prints "with additions" under the title and has 74 quatrains. The section beginning "I love to tell the story," which concludes both imprints, contains only 7 quatrains: neither edition includes the eighth quatrain necessary to make up the four 8-line sts. always printed in our hymnals. The missing quatrain is the second half of our st. 2.

Apparently these lines were added when the hymn was detached from the long poem for use in the author's collection *Heart to Heart*, published in a number of editions. Several theories have been offered for the original date of this collection and the added quatrain. A clue is that at the end of the list of hymns in *Heart to Heart* is the statement that they are "arranged according to date of writing, 1859-1869." "I love to tell the story" is placed nineteenth in the list of 32 hymns. This could mean that the long poem including 7 of the quatrains making up our hymn is to be dated in the early 1860's, and the complete hymn dated 1866-68.

The hymn, long a favorite of Methodists, has been included in all our hymnals since the Methodist Episcopal of 1878. The refrain was probably added by the composer Fischer, when the entire hymn was first printed in *Joyful Songs Nos. 1–3 Combined,* 1869.

Hankey

WILLIAM G. FISCHER, 1835-1912

Fischer's tune was first published with the text in *Joyful Songs Nos. 1-3 Combined* (Philadelphia, 1869) . It is 1 of 24 tunes by Fischer out of the total of 41. It quickly became popular and appeared in Philip Bliss's *Gospel Songs* (Cincinnati, 1874) and in Bliss and Ira D. Sankey's *Gospel Hymns and Sacred Songs,* 1875.

I Need Thee Every Hour (265)

ANNIE S. HAWKS, 1835-1918

The hymn was first published in a small collection composed for use by the National Baptist Sunday School Association Convention, Cincinnati, in November, 1872. With the refrain and tune provided by Robert Lowry, Mrs. Hawks's pastor, it was then included in *Royal*

Diadem for the Sunday School (New York, 1873), edited by Lowry and W. H. Doane. The hymn was made popular by the Moody-Sankey revival meetings.

It entered the Methodist Episcopal, South hymnal in 1875 with the full 5 sts. Our 1935 hymnal dropped st. 5, which has been reclaimed in the present hymnal.

Need

ROBERT LOWRY, 1826-1899

See comments on text, above.

I Sing the Almighty Power of God (37)

ISAAC WATTS, 1674-1748

The sts. of this cento are 1, 3, and 5 of the 8 sts. of No. 2, entitled "Praise for Creation and Providence" in Watts's *Divine Songs Attempted in Easy Language, for the Use of Children,* 1715. This collection of 8 hymns is the first hymnal written exclusively for children.

In the preface, Watts states that "the greatest part of this little book was composed several years ago. . . . The children of high and low degree, of the Church of England, or dissenters, baptized in infancy, or not, may all join together in these songs. And as I have endeavoured to sink the language to the level of a child's understanding, and yet to keep it, if possible, above contempt; so I have designed to profit all, if possible, and offend none."

The hymn was included in the Methodist Protestant hymnals of 1837 and 1901, then in the present hymnal of 1964.

Forest Green

See "All Beautiful the March of Days," p. 72.

I Sought the Lord, and Afterward I Knew (96)

ANONYMOUS
The Pilgrim Hymnal, 1904

The text first appeared in *Holy Songs, Carols, and Sacred Ballads* (Boston, 1880). It was printed under the verse "He first loved us."

The hymn has been dated as early as 1878, but there seems to be no documentation either for this or for its authorship. *The Pilgrim Hymnal,* 1904, seems to be the first American hymnal to include it. It entered the Methodist hymnal in 1935.

Minor alterations have been made in 1:2 and 2:3-4.

Wachusett

KATHERINE K. DAVIS, 1892-

The tune was written at the invitation of the tunes subcommittee of the hymnal committee to secure a setting which would better solve the accent and punctuation problems of the text. It was written in 1963. Miss Davis writes, "Wachusett is the mountain nearest my home, and the sight of it lifts the thoughts as well as the eyes."

I Want a Principle Within (279, 280)

CHARLES WESLEY, 1707-1788

The text was first published in the 1749 edition of *Hymns and Sacred Poems* in 5 sts. of 8 lines each, under the title "For a Tender Conscience." St. 1 began "Almighty God of truth and love." For his 1780 *Collection of Hymns for the Use of the People Called Methodists,* John Wesley shortened the hymn to five 4-line sts., beginning with "I want a principle within."

Though the hymn has been included in all American Methodist hymnals, John's 4-line st. form has been rejected in favor of the original 8-line form. Up until the present hymnal, three 8-line sts. were printed. The present hymnal, by adding the entire original st. 4, is the first of our hymnals to print four 8-line sts.

Euclid (280)

LLOYD A. PFAUTSCH, 1921-

The tune was written in 1963, according to the composer, "to provide a new tune for the strong Wesley text. . . . It seemed to me that this text needed to be given new life instead of being weakened by continued association with GERALD." It is named for the street in Dallas, Tex., where the composer lives and where the hymn tune was written.

Gerald (279)

Adapt. from LOUIS SPOHR, 1784-1859

The tune is adapted from a solo, with chorus, in Spohr's oratorio written in 1834, called *Das Heiland's letzte Stunden* (The Last Hours of the Savior) and first performed at Cassell, Germany, on Good Friday, 1835. The solo given to Mary, "Though all thy friends prove faithless," was adapted to "As pants the hart," by J. Stimpson and published as an anthem which became popular.

The tune was originally called SPOHR, but another tune by this name created confusion. The name GERALD was chosen by the 1935 hymnal editorial committee to include parts of the name of Dr. Fitzgerald Sale Parker, a member of the 1905 as well as the 1935 hymnal committees, and Miss Geraldine Reid Sherrill, secretary to the editor.

I Would Be True (156)

HOWARD A. WALTER, 1883-1918

The poem "My Creed" was written January 1, 1907, while the author was teaching in Waseda University in Tokyo. He sent the 2 sts. to his mother, who promptly sent them to *Harper's Bazaar,* where it was published in the May issue of the same year. In November, 1909, it was reprinted in *Current Literature,* introduced by the line "Here is something that is neat and sweet."

Walter later added a third st., which is sometimes printed, but omitted here. The hymn entered the Methodist hymnal with the present hymnal.

Peek

JOSEPH Y. PEEK, 1843-1911

The tune was composed with the assistance of Grant C. Tullar, organist and composer. Peek met H. A. Walter in the summer of 1909 and was given a copy of "My Creed." The melody which occurred to him was whistled for Tullar who wrote it down and harmonized it.

If, on a Quiet Sea (147)

AUGUSTUS M. TOPLADY, 1740-1778

The text was first published in the *Gospel Magazine,* February, 1772, in eight 8-line sts., later printed in 16 sts. The title was "Weak Believers encouraged." The opening quatrain ran:

Your harps, ye trembling saints,
Down from the willows take:
Loud, to the praise of love divine,
Bid ev'ry string awake.

The hymn entered the Methodist Episcopal hymnal in 1849 in the same radically altered form in which it appears in 1964. No one of the sts. has escaped alteration. Our sts. are the fourth, fifth, eighth, and tenth of Toplady's 16.

Venice

WILLIAM AMPS, 1824-1910

The tune was first published in E. H. Thorne, *A Selection of Church Music* (London, 1853). The opening notes have been altered from passing eights to quarters. Note the imitation of the first line melody in the second line tenor part.

If Thou But Suffer God to Guide Thee (210)
Wer nur den lieben Gott lässt walten

GEORG NEUMARK, 1621-1681
Trans. by CATHERINE WINKWORTH, 1827-1878

The German text was written in 1640 or 1641 after Neumark had had the bitter experience of being robbed by highwaymen of all but a prayer book and a few coins, and was long without work and almost destitute, when unexpectedly he was employed as a tutor in the home of a wealthy judge in Kiel. Then and there, he wrote this hymn based on Psalm 55:22 and entitled it "A Song of Comfort: God will care for and help everyone in His own time."

The hymn was first published in Neumark's *Fortgepflanzter musikalisch-poetischer Lustwald* (Jena, 1657), in 7 sts.

Catherine Winkworth made 2 translations of the hymn, 1 in the first series of her *Lyra Germanica*, 1855, beginning "Leave God to order all thy ways," and 1 in her *Chorale Book for England* (London, 1863), beginning "If thou but suffer God to guide thee." Both translations were in 7 sts.

The hymn entered the Methodist hymnal in 1905 with a cento made up of 1, 3, 4, and 7 from *Lyra Germanica*, slightly altered. In our 1935 hymnal st. 1 is from the *Chorale Book;* the second, a conflation of the 2 versions; and the third from *Lyra Germanica.* Our 1964 hymnal prints 1, 3, and 7 of the *Chorale Book,* without alteration.

Wer nur den lieben Gott

GEORG NEUMARK, 1621-1681

The melody, restored from 4/4 time to the original triple time, is taken from Neumark's *Lustwald* (see above). It is also called BREMEN, NEUMARK, and AUGSBERG.

I'll Praise My Maker While I've Breath (9)

ISAAC WATTS, 1674-1748
Alt. by JOHN WESLEY, 1703-1791

In his *Psalms of David, Imitated in the Language of the New Testament,* 1719, Watts published 2 versions of Psalm 146, with much the same words but in different meters. Both were entitled "Praise to God for his Goodness and Truth." John Wesley chose the second version for use in his 1737 Charleston *Collection of Psalms and Hymns,* in his 1741 London *Collection of Psalms and Hymns,* and in his 1780 *Collection of Hymns for the Use of the People Called Methodists.* By altering "with my breath" (1:1) to "while I've breath," and "The Lord hath eyes to give the blind" (3:1) to "The Lord pours eyesight on the blind," and by omitting Watts's sts. 2 and 5, Welsey gave the hymn the form in which it has always been used.

It was a favorite of John, and he announced it at his last service at City Road, February 22, 1791, sang parts of it during the morning of March 1, and died March 2 with "I'll praise; I'll praise" on his lips.

In identical form the hymn has been included in all Methodist hymnals.

Old 113th

Strassburger Kirchenamt, 1525
Probably by MATTHÄUS GREITER, c. 1490-1552
Harm. by V.E.C.

This is 1 of 7 melodies contributed by Greiter to the *Strassburger Kirchenamt,* 1525, set to Psalm 36 in John Calvin's first psalter, *Aulcuns Pseaumes et cantiques mys en chant* (Strassburg, 1539). It is found in both German and Genevan books, and in Germany is usually set to "O Mensch, bewein' dien' Sünde gross." It has carried both meditative and forceful texts.

The form was altered in the Anglo-Genevan Psalter, 1561, and the tune set to Psalm 113. During the eighteenth century the tune was shortened from the original.

The tune is also known as LUCERNE.

Immortal, Invisible, God Only Wise (27)

WALTER CHALMERS SMITH, 1824-1908

The text was first published in the author's *Hymns of Christ and the Christian Life,* 1867, in 6 sts. with I Timothy 1:17 as the biblical text. At the suggestion of W. Garrett Horder, who introduced the hymn into English hymnody in his *Congregational Hymns,* 1884, Smith made a number of changes in the words, thereby improving the text considerably.

The hymn entered the Methodist hymnal in 1935, with sts. 1, 2, and 3, and a st. composed of 5a and 6a.

St. Denio

Welsh Melody
JOHN ROBERTS, *Caniadau y Cyssegr,* 1839

The tune is drawn from Roberts' *Caniadau y Cyssegr* (Sacred Songs), published in Wales in 1839, called PALESTINA. It is founded on the folk song "Can Mlynedd i 'nawr'" (A Hundred Years from Now), popular in the early nineteenth century. Gustav Holst introduced it into English hymnody with this text in *The English Hymnal* (Oxford, 1905).

The tune is also called JOANNA.

Immortal Love, Forever Full (157, 158)

JOHN GREENLEAF WHITTIER, 1807-1892

Whittier's 38-st. poem called "Our Master" was first published in his *Tent on the Beach and Other Poems,* 1867. A cento made up of sts. 5, 13, 14, 15, and 16, beginning "We may not climb the heavenly steeps," was introduced into our 1878 Methodist Episcopal hymnal.

It was reprinted without change until the 1964 hymnal put Whittier's opening st. at the head of the hymn, and for the first time printed 6 sts.

Ayrshire (157)

See "As Pants the Hart for Cooling Streams," p. 99.

Serenity (158)

Arr. from **WILLIAM V. WALLACE, 1814-1865**
by **UZZIAH C. BURNAP, 1834-1900**

The original tune was a love song, "Ye winds that waft my sighs to thee." The adaptation was made by Burnap for 3 hymns, 1 of which was "The Lord's my Shepherd, I'll not want." It assumed its present rhythmic pattern in the 1878 Methodist Episcopal hymnal.

In Bethlehem Neath Starlit Skies (377)

GRACE M. STUTSMAN, 1886-

Both text and tune were printed by the author on a Christmas greeting card, 1927. The carol entered the Methodist hymnal in 1935.

Waits' Carol

GRACE M. STUTSMAN, 1886-

A special arrangement of the music was made for the 1935 hymnal by the composer.

In Christ There Is No East or West (192)

JOHN OXENHAM, 1852-1941

The author was invited by the London Missionary Society to write a libretto for *The Pageant of Darkness and Light,* for a missionary exhibition in London, 1908. The theme was "The Orient in London." The text was written for this occasion.

It was first published in the author's *Bees in Amber,* 1913, and then in his *Selected Poems,* 1924. Its first American hymnal inclusion was in *Hymns for the Living Age,* 1923. It entered the Methodist hymnal in 1935.

St. Peter

See "How Sweet the Name of Jesus Sounds," p. 224.

In Heavenly Love Abiding (230)

ANNA L. WARING, 1823-1910

The text was first published in the author's *Hymns and Meditations by A. L. W.*, 1850, under the biblical text "I will fear no evil, for thou art with me" (Psalm 23:4). Originally 3:4 read "Where the dark clouds have been."

It entered the Methodist Episcopal hymnal in 1878 in its present form.

Nyland

Traditional Finnish Melody
Harm. by DAVID EVANS, 1874-1948

A recent revision of the Finnish *Koraalikirja* (chorale book) states that the tune was first sung near Kuortane, a small village in Etalapohjanmaa (South Ostrobothnia). David Evans apparently discovered the tune in a collection (in 2 booklets of 40 tunes each) issued in 1908 by Pastor Immanuel Colliander and others who were trying to introduce Finnish folk melodies into their hymnody. In 1909 NYLAND was 1 of 29 such tunes adopted by the state church, appearing in the Appendix to the 1909 edition of the *Suomen Evankelis Luterilaisen Kirken Koraalikirja* (the chorale book of Finland's Evangelical Lutheran Church).

The tune name stands for a province in Finland. It was given the name by Evans who harmonized the tune for the revised *Church Hymnary* (Edinburgh, 1927).

In Memory of the Savior's Love (319)

THOMAS COTTERILL, 1779-1823
Stanza 2, ANONYMOUS

The text, entitled "For the Sacrament," first appeared in *A Selection of Psalms and Hymns for Public and Private Use,* 1805, edited by Jonathan Stubbs, assisted by Cotterill and others. In 6 sts., it began "Bless'd with the presence of their God." Cotterill published his own form of the collection in 1810, the eighth edition (1819) of which was the most important, for it was the cause of a lawsuit against Cotterill for using hymns in public worship. This proved to be the last legal action taken against the use of hymns in church. Cotterill withdrew the book, but in 1820 published a revised smaller one which did not contain this hymn.

In later printings the text has been altered almost beyond recognition. Richard Whittingham, *A Selection of Psalms and Hymns,* 1835, abstracted sts. 3, 5, and 6 to form the hymn as commonly used. The omission of the first 2 sts. required changing the first line from "In memory of his dying love" to "In memory of the Savior's love."

In 1964 an additional st. has been added to our hymnal as the second st., not by Cotterill, but taken from the Evangelical United Brethren hymnal with 1 alteration: 2:3 has been altered from "Brethren we are" to "as brethren all."

The authorship of this st. has not been established. It does not appear in any edition of Cotterill's *Selection of Psalms and Hymns* and can hardly have been written by him. It has been in constant use in the hymnals of the Church of the Brethren since 1852, and the text sounds as if written by someone in the Church of the Brethren.

The hymn has been included in our 1878 Methodist Episcopal hymnal and in the 1935 hymnal in 3 sts., and in 1964, in 4.

Salzburg

See **"How Lovely Is Thy Dwelling Place,"** pp. 223-24.

In the Bleak Midwinter (376)

CHRISTINA G. ROSSETTI, 1830-1894

The text was first published in *Scribner's Monthly,* January, 1872, then in an 1875 collection, *Christina Rossetti's Poems,* and also in *The Poetical Works of Christina Georgina Rossetti,* 1904. Its first hymnal inclusion was in *The English Hymnal* (Oxford, 1906).

The hymn entered the Methodist hymnal in 1935 in 4 sts. The original st. 3 is omitted.

Cranham

GUSTAV HOLST, 1874-1934

The English Hymnal (Oxford, 1906) was the first hymnal to include this melody. In contrast to other hymn tunes of Holst, which are austere, the tune is simple and naïve.

In the Cross of Christ I Glory (416)

JOHN BOWRING, 1792-1872

The text, entitled "The Cross of Christ," appeared first in the author's *Hymns,* 1825. The theme was suggested by Galatians 6:14.

It entered the Methodist Episcopal hymnal in 1878, unaltered.

Rathbun

ITHAMAR CONKEY, 1815-1867

Conkey composed the hymn tune in 1849 while he was organist at the Central Baptist Church in Norwich, Conn. It was first published in Henry W. Greatorex's *Collection of Psalm and Hymn Tunes,* 1851, set to "Savior, who thy flock art feeding." It was named for Mrs. Beriah S. Rathbun, the church's leading soprano.

In the Hour of Trial (237)

JAMES MONTGOMERY, 1771-1854
Alt. by FRANCES A. HUTTON, 1811-1877

The original manuscript of the hymn, entitled "In Trial and Temptation," is dated October 13, 1834. Yet it was not published until 1853 when it appeared in the author's *Original Hymns,* slightly altered, and under the title "Prayers on Pilgrimage." This text was reprinted in William Mercer, *Church Psalter and Hymn Book,* 1854, and in this form came into common use. However, the text was significantly revised by Mrs. Frances A. Hutton for use in *Supplement and Litanies,* edited by H. W. Hutton of Lincoln, undated. The Hutton text was modified further in Godfrey Thring, *A Church of England Hymn Book,* 1880.

Our sts. 1 and 2 are by Montgomery, with minor alterations by Thring. Our 3 and 4 are Mrs. Hutton's substitutes for Montgomery's original sts.

The hymn entered the Methodist Protestant hymnal in 1901 and the Methodist hymnal in 1905.

Penitence

SPENCER LANE, 1843-1903

Lane composed this tune one Sunday noon in 1875 as a substitute tune for the evening service at St. James's Episcopal Church, Woonsocket, R.I., to replace the rector's choice which he did not like.

It was first published in Charles L. Hutchins, *The Church Hymnal*, 1879, as the third tune for this text.

Infant Holy, Infant Lowly (396)

Polish Carol
Paraphrase by E. M. C. REED, 1885-1933

The English paraphrase of the carol was first published in *Music and Youth,* a monthly of which Reed was editor, 1923-26. The first hymnal inclusion was in *School Worship,* edited by George Thalben-Ball and published by the Congregational Union of England and Wales, 1926.

The carol entered the Methodist hymnal in 1935.

W zlobie lezy

Polish Carol
Arr. by E. M. C. REED, 1885-1933
Harm. by A.C.L.

(See comments on text, above.) The music has been slightly altered and reharmonized for this hymnal. The rhythm comes from a typical Polish dance form.

It Came upon the Midnight Clear (390)

EDMUND H. SEARS, 1810-1876

The text in 5 sts. was written in 1849 in Wayland, Mass., the author being at the time minister of the Unitarian church there. It was first published in the *Christian Register,* December 29, the same year. One of the first carol-like hymns composed in America, it was introduced to English hymnals by E. H. Bickersteth, *The Hymnal Companion to the Book of Common Prayer,* 1870.

The hymn entered the Methodist Episcopal hymnal in 1878 with 5 sts., reduced to 4 in 1935, to 3 in 1964.

Carol

RICHARD STORRS WILLIS, 1819-1900

Originally set to "See Israel's gentle Shepherd stand," the tune is arranged from the twenty-third study in Willis' *Church Chorals and*

Choir Studies (New York, 1850). The arrangement, consisting of a new third phrase and the repetition of the second as the closing phrase, was made by Willis himself. A letter by him dated "Detroit, 25 Oct. '87," states:

Study No. 23 has undergone various vicissitudes. I expanded it first into a "Christmas Carol" while a vestryman in the "Church of the Transfiguration," N.Y. [The Little Church around the Corner] adapted it to the words, "While shepherds watched their flocks by night." Later Dr. (now Bishop) Potter requested a copy of the manuscript for Grace Church, which I gave him. On my return from Europe in '76, I found that it had been incorporated into various church collections.

I've Found a Friend (163)

JAMES G. SMALL, 1817-1888

Entitled "Jesus, the Friend," the text was first published in *The Revival Hymn Book,* second series, 1863, and then in Small's *Poems and Sacred Songs* (Scotland, 1866).

The hymn entered the Methodist Protestant hymnal in 1901 and the Methodist hymnal in 1935 in 3 sts., with 1 st. omitted.

Friend

GEORGE C. STEBBINS, 1846-1945

The tune was composed in January, 1878, while Stebbins was assisting George F. Pentecost in a revival meeting in the Music Hall, Providence, R.I. It was first published in *Gospel Hymns No. 3,* 1878. The dotted rhythm of the original has been removed.

Jerusalem the Golden (303)
Urbs Sion aurea

BERNARD OF CLUNY, 12th Century
Trans. by JOHN M. NEALE, 1818-1866

Bernard of Cluny's poem *De Contemptu Mundi,* "On the Contemptibleness of the World," is a bitter satire of 2,966 lines lamenting the moral corruption of the twelfth century while painting its dark colors of despair on a gold background showing forth the glories of heaven. The familiar opening line, "Hora novissima, tempora pessima sunt,

241

vigilemus," shows how exquisitely the poet has caught the lilt of the meter known as dactylic hexameter, and how by the successful use of a complicated rhyme scheme he has created a poem of rare beauty. In Neale's judgment these verses of Bernard are the "most lovely" as the *Dies Irae* is the "most sublime," and the *Stabat Mater*, the "most pathetic" of medieval poems.

Though the poem was not written as a hymn, at least 8 centos have been drawn for hymn use. Four of these were included in the Methodist Episcopal hymnal of 1878: "Jerusalem the golden," "For thee, O dear, dear country," "Brief life is here our portion," and "The world is very evil." The Methodist Protestant hymnal of 1882, the Methodist Episcopal, South hymnal of 1889, and the 1905 hymnal printed only the first 2 of these. In 1935 "Jerusalem the golden" alone was retained.

Neale's first translations, published in his *Mediaeval Hymns and Sequences*, 1851, began with line 167, "Hic breve vivitur" ("Brief life is here our portion"), following the cento of 95 lines made by Archbishop Trench in his *Sacred Latin Poetry*, 1849. Though Neale describes this cento as a "mere patchwork—much being transposed as well as cancelled," yet he translated the larger part of it, claiming his work to be no more than a close imitation. Of the 4 hymns named, only "The world is very evil" is missing.

The popularity of the 1851 translation led Neale to consider a fuller extract from the Latin and a further translation into English. In 1858 he translated 218 lines which he published as *The Rhythm of Bernard de Morlaix*. It was this translation which he included in the second edition of *Mediaeval Hymns and Sequences*, 1863, under the title *Hora novissima*. Beginning "The world is very evil," the new translation began with the first 6 Latin lines and then jumped to 106.

As "Jerusalem the golden" appears in our hymnal, the first 2 sts. are only slightly altered from Neale's own 1863 slightly revised form of his 1851 text. Two minor alterations, together with the writing of the entire st. 4, which has no equivalent in the Latin text, are the work of the editors of *Hymns Ancient and Modern*, 1861. Our st. 3 is composed of 2 quatrains not joined together by Neale or *Hymns Ancient and Modern*, but now finding favor in some hymnals. This is the first appearance of this st. in a Methodist hymnal.

Ewing

ALEXANDER EWING, 1830-1895

The tune was composed in 1853 and published in leaflet form that year in 3/2 time and set to "For thee, O dear, dear country." It is the only tune Ewing ever wrote. It was first published in *A Manual of Psalm and Hymn Tunes* (London, 1857), edited by John Grey, and called ST. BEDE's. William H. Monk altered the time signature to 4/4 in *Hymns Ancient and Modern,* 1861, a change which Ewing disapproved. He said: "In my opinion the alteration of the rhythm has very much vulgarized my little tune. It now seems to me a good deal like a polka. I hate to hear it." The original form may be seen in Robert G. McCutchan, *Our Hymnody,* p. 513.

Jesus Calls Us o'er the Tumult (107)

CECIL FRANCES ALEXANDER, 1818-1895

The first text of the hymn was published under the direction of the Tract Committee of the Society for Promoting Christian Knowledge in *Hymns for Public Worship,* 1852, and entitled "St. Andrew's Day." Hence the appropriateness of the original lines of 2:1: "As of old Saint Andrew heard it."

In order to make the hymn generally suitable, some hymnals, including ours, substitute "apostles" or "th'apostles" for "Saint Andrew," in 2:1. The only other alteration is the substitution of "Jesus'" for "His dear" in 2:4.

The hymn entered the Methodist hymnal in 1935 with 4 sts. The original st. 2 was added in 1964.

Galilee

WILLIAM H. JUDE, 1851-1922

Composed in 1874 for this text, the tune first appeared in *Congregational Church Hymnal* (London, 1887), edited by G. S. Barrett and E. J. Hopkins.

COMPANION TO THE HYMNAL

Jesus Christ Is Risen Today (443)
Surrexit Christus hodie

Latin, 14th Century
Trans. in *Lyra Davidica*, 1708
Stanza 2, JOHN ARNOLD, *The Complete Psalmodist*, 1749
Stanza 3, CHARLES WESLEY, 1707-1788

The first st. of the hymn is a translation of the first of 5 sts. of a Latin Easter carol which appeared first in German and Bohemian manuscripts of the fourteenth century. Though anonymously translated into English in *Lyra Davidica* (London, 1708), the hymn took its present form by way of John Arnold's 1749 edition of *The Complete Psalmodist,* in which only the first of the *Lyra Davidica* sts. was retained, and entirely new second and third sts., unrelated to the Latin, were substituted. Arnold's st. 3 is omitted here. These 3 sts. were printed in the Supplement to the Tate and Brady Psalter, c. 1816.

Since at least the middle of the nineteenth century, Charles Wesley's one-st. "Hymn to the Trinity" in the 1740 edition of *Hymns and Sacred Poems* has frequently been appended as a concluding doxology.

The hymn entered the Methodist hymnal in 1935.

Llanfair

ROBERT WILLIAMS, c. 1781-1821
Harm. by DAVID EVANS, 1874-1945

The tune is taken from the blind composer's manuscript book and is dated July 14, 1817, called BETHEL. Joseph Parry included it in *Peroriaeth Hyfryd,* 1837, with a harmonization by John Roberts of Henllan. James T. Lightwood has questioned whether Williams wrote the tune or merely noted it.

The melody lacks the variety of treatment of its more famous Easter partner, EASTER HYMN. The harmonization in use today is by David Evans.

Llanfair is a shortened form of Llanfairynghornwy, the composer's home locality in Anglesey.

Jesus, I My Cross Have Taken (251)

HENRY F. LYTE, 1793-1847

The text first appeared in the third edition of the author's *Sacred Poetry,* 1824, in 6 sts. of 8 lines each, under Mark 10:28 and signed

"G." In his *Poems, Chiefly Religious*, 1833, Lyte claimed authorship. It entered the Methodist Episcopal hymnal in 1878 with 6 sts., 2 of which were dropped in 1905. A few slight alterations have been made.

Ellesdie

The Christian Lyre, 1830
Harm. by A.C.L.

Named DISCIPLE, the melody appears in *The Christian Lyre*, 1830, with air and bass only. Hubert P. Main arranged it in *Winnowed Hymns*, 1873, compiled by C. C. McCabe and D. T. MacFarlan, where it is headed "Air, Mozart." However, no Mozart source has ever been located.

The tune name, according to Robert G. McCutchan, is a "made name," from the initials "L. S. D." of some person unknown.

The tune is also known by several other names.

Jesus Is All the World to Me (97)

WILL L. THOMPSON, 1847-1909

Both text and tune were written by Thompson and first published in the *New Century Hymnal* (Liverpool, Ohio, 1904), and copyrighted that year.

This is the first appearance of the hymn in the Methodist hymnal.

Elizabeth

WILL L. THOMPSON, 1847-1909

(See comments on the text, above.) The tune is named for Elizabeth Johnson, whom Thompson married in 1891.

Jesus Is Tenderly Calling (110)

FANNY J. CROSBY, 1820-1915

The hymn first appeared in *Gospel Hymns No. 4*, 1883. This is its first appearance in the Methodist hymnal.

Jesus Is Calling

GEORGE C. STEBBINS, 1846-1945

Written for this text, the tune first appeared with the text in *Gospel Hymns No. 4*, 1883. In his *Memoirs and Reminiscences*

245

COMPANION TO THE HYMNAL

Stebbins wrote there was "no incident that occasioned the setting made to Fanny Crosby's words, 'Jesus Is Tenderly Calling,' nor did either the words nor the music impress me as possessing more than ordinary merit, even for evangelistic work. The music was written with the view of making the song available as an invitation hymn; but that it would meet with instant favor, and in a few years would become generally known, did not enter my mind."

The tune is also called CALLING TODAY.

Jesus, Keep Me Near the Cross (433)

FANNY J. CROSBY, 1820-1915

The author wrote the text to fit the tune. Both appeared together in *Bright Jewels*, a compilation edited by W. B. Bradbury, W. H. Doane, W. F. Sherwin, and Chester G. Allen, 1869.

The hymn entered the Methodist Protestant hymnal in 1882 and the Methodist Episcopal, South hymnal of 1889. After having been dropped in 1905, it was picked up again in 1935.

Near the Cross

WILLIAM H. DOANE, 1832-1915

Doane wrote the tune and gave it to Fanny Crosby, who then provided the text to fit the music, the reverse of the usual procedure.

Jesus, Lord, We Look to Thee (309)

CHARLES WESLEY, 1707-1788

The text appeared first in the 1749 edition of *Hymns and Sacred Poems* under the heading "For a Family." The 6 sts. were included in John Wesley's *Collection of Hymns for the Use of the People Called Methodists*, 1780, with only 1 alteration: in 5:4 "height" was made "heights," a reading retained in all subsequent printings.

The entire hymn was included in all American Methodist hymnals until 1901 and 1905, when it was dropped only to be reclaimed in 1964.

Savannah

Foundery Collection, 1742

The tune name indicates a relationship to John Wesley's trip to Georgia, and possibly he heard it sung by the Moravians. In compiling his famous *Foundery Collection*, 1742, Wesley borrowed from many sources. SAVANNAH is actually a tune from the manuscript *Choralbuch*, c. 1740, compiled by Tobias Friedrich, the first organist at Herrnhut. The tune is sometimes called HERRNHUT, and sometimes IRENE for the ship on which the Moravians sailed from London to America in 1742.

Jesus, Lover of My Soul (125, 126)

CHARLES WESLEY, 1707-1788

Written in 1738 shortly after Wesley's conversion, the text was first published in the 1740 edition of *Hymns and Sacred Poems*, under the heading "In Temptation," and in five 8-line sts. Its distinguishing first line, which caused our fathers some embarrassment, has its biblical ground in the Wisdom of Solomon 11:26: "O Lord, thou lover of souls." Though the hymn was included in the important Wesleyan collection of 1753, *Hymns and Spiritual Songs*, in later editions of the same work, and in the 1765 *Select Hymns*, John omitted it from his standard 1780 *Collection of Hymns for the Use of the People Called Methodists*, in which it was not included until the Supplement of 1797.

The text in 4 sts. has been included in every Methodist collection beginning with *The Methodist Pocket Hymn Book* (Philadelphia, 1802), and without alteration. The original st. 3 which we have always omitted was omitted by Welsey himself in the 1753 *Hymns and Spiritual Songs* and in later printings.

Editorial alterations, or better, mutilations, inflicted on the hymn through the years have been collected in the *Proceedings of the Wesley Historical Society*, 1889, pp. 15-17, and in the *Choir*, November, 1918, pp. 206-8.

Aberystwyth (125)

JOSEPH PARRY, 1841-1903

The tune was first published in E. Stephen and Joseph David Jones's *Ail Llyfr Tonau ac Emynau* (Wales, 1879) set to "Beth sydd i mi yn y byd." Later Parry used the tune to this text in his cantata *Ceridwen*.

The name comes from the town where Parry was professor of music at the Welsh University College when he wrote the tune.

Martyn (126)

SIMEON B. MARSH, 1798-1875

On his way from Amsterdam to Johnstown, N.Y., in the fall of 1834 to conduct a singing school, Marsh stopped his horse, dismounted, and sketched the tune. It was first published in Thomas Hastings, the *Musical Miscellany*, Vol. I, 1836, set to John Newton, "Mary, at her Saviour's tomb." In *Sacred Songs for Family and Social Worship*, edited by Thomas Hastings, 1842, the tune appears with the Newton text at No. 34 and with "Jesus, lover of my soul" at No. 35.

In spite of rhythmic dullness, the hymn has continued to be popular in many places.

Jesus, My Strength, My Hope (253)

CHARLES WESLEY, 1707-1788

The text appeared in the 1742 edition of *Hymns and Sacred Poems* in seven 8-line sts. under the title "A Poor Sinner." Since John omitted st. 7 in his *Collection of Hymns for the Use of the People Called Methodists*, 1780, it has never been reprinted. John also rearranged the order of the sts., putting st. 2 in sixth place.

The text has been included in virtually all American Methodist hymnals since 1802, first with the 6 sts. as John had arranged them, then with 3 sts. in 1847 and 1849, and finally with the 4 we have in 1935 and 1964. These 4 are the first 3 and the fifth as arranged in the 1780 *Collection*.

Ich halte treulich still

Probably by J. S. BACH, 1685-1750

The tune is taken from Georg Christian Schemelli, *Musikalisches Gesangbuch* (Leipzig, 1736). It is thought to be by its editor, J. S. Bach.

Jesus, Priceless Treasure (220)

Jesu, meine Freude

JOHANN FRANCK, 1618-1677
Trans. by CATHERINE WINKWORTH, 1827-1878

The text, patterned after a love song by Heinrich Alberti, "Flora, meine Freude, meiner Seele Weide," 1641, was first published in

Johann Crüger, *Praxis Pietatis Melica* (5th ed.; Berlin, 1653).

Catherine Winkworth made 2 translations of the hymn, 1 in her *Chorale Book for England* (London, 1863), in 5 sts.; 1 in *Christian Singers of Germany,* 1869, in 6 sts.

The hymn entered the Methodist hymnal in 1964 with 3 sts. from the latter translation. Our text substitutes "God dispels our fear" for "Jesus calms my fear" (2:6) and makes the personal pronouns plural in 2:8, 9 and 3:7.

Jesu, meine Freude

Traditional German Melody
Adapt. by JOHANN CRÜGER, 1598-1662

Marked as a "traditional melody," the tune comes from *Praxis Pietatis Melica* and was arranged by Crüger, who may have borrowed a phrase from "Kyrie, Gott Vater in Ewigkeit," itself an adaptation of the plainsong "Kyrie, fons bonitatis." The first 2 measures of the tune by Crüger are almost identical.

Jesus, Savior, Pilot Me (247)

EDWARD HOPPER, 1816-1888

The text in 6 sts. was first published anonymously in the *Sailor's Magazine,* March 3, 1871. *The Baptist Praise Book* of the same year reduced it to 4 sts. Hopper became known as author following the appearance of the hymn in *Spiritual Songs,* 1875. Quite appropriately he was pastor of the Church of the Sea and Land in New York City.

The hymn entered the Methodist Protestant hymnal in 1901, the Methodist hymnal in 1905, with the usual 3 sts.

Pilot

JOHN E. GOULD, 1822-1875

The tune was composed for this text in 1871. The first appearance was in *The Baptist Praise Book,* 1871.

Jesus Shall Reign (472)

ISAAC WATTS, 1674-1748

The text was first published in Watts's *Psalms of David, Imitated in the Language of the New Testament,* 1719, in 8 sts. as a paraphrase of the second part of Psalm 72, entitled "Christ's Kingdom among the Gentiles." Though it has been described as the earliest of the great hymns on missions, it rarely was included in eighteenth-century hymnals. The church had not yet been awakened to the cause of world evangelization.

In his preface, Watts set forth his principle for interpreting the psalms: "Where the original runs in the form of prophecy concerning Christ and his salvation, I have given an historical turn to the sense; there is no necessity that we should always sing in the obscure and doubtful style of prediction, when the things foretold are brought into the open light by a full accomplishment."

Though John Wesley seems never to have printed this psalm, it has been included in all American Methodist hymnals, and though it appeared in the 1847 hymnal of the Methodist Episcopal Church, South, in 7 sts., the more usual number has been 4. Until 1905 our hymnals have used a cento of 4 sts. made up of 1, 2a, 3b, 4, and 5.

Watts's st. 8 was reintroduced into our 1905 hymnal and has been retained as our last st. The 1964 hymnal also reintroduced Watts's sixth, our st. 5.

Duke Street

See "Come, Let Us Tune Our Loftiest Song," pp. 143-44.

Jesus Spreads His Banner o'er Us (331)

ROSWELL PARK, 1807-1869

The hymn was first published in the author's *Selection of Juvenile and Miscellaneous Poems* (Philadelphia, 1836). In 6 sts. of 8 lines, it was entitled "The Communion," with an Isaac Watts quatrain under the title:

> Why was I made to hear thy voice,
> And enter while there's room,
> While thousands make a wretched choice,
> And rather starve than come.

Intended to be sung while noncommunicating members of the congregation were leaving, it began:

> While the sons of earth, retiring,
> From the sacred temple roam;
> Lord, thy light and love desiring,
> To thine altar fain we come.
> Children of a Heavenly Father,
> Friends and brethren would we be;
> While we round thy table gather,
> May our hearts be one in thee.

The hymn has been in Methodist hymnals since the Methodist Episcopal hymnal of 1849, with the same 2 sts. unchanged.

Autumn

Arr. from FRANÇOIS H. BARTHÉLÉMON, 1741-1808

Set to words taken from the novel *The Monk* by Matthew Gregory Lewis, this tune was published sometime after 1796 as a song with harp accompaniment and ascribed to Barthélémon, the eminent violinist. Benjamin Carr published an American edition entitled "Belerma and Durandarte," a Spanish ballad, in his *Musical Journal*, Vol. III, No. 63 (Philadelphia, 1801-2). The hymn tune BALLERMA (535, p. 209), arranged by Robert Simpson, was probably taken from this tune.

Jesus! the Name High over All (341)

CHARLES WESLEY, 1707-1788

The hymn was first printed in the 1749 edition of *Hymns and Sacred Poems* in twenty-two 4-line sts. under the title "After Preaching (in a Church)."

It began:

> Jesu, accept the grateful song,
> My wisdom and my might,
> 'Tis thou hast loosed the stammering tongue,
> And taught my hands to fight.

John Wesley reduced the hymn to 7 sts. for his *Collection of Hymns for the Use of the People Called Methodists*, 1780, omitting sts. 1-8, 11, 15-17, and 19-21. Of his 7, the fifth (the original fourteenth) has never been reprinted. The other 6 sts. have been included in virtually all American Methodist hymnals from at least 1821 until 1905, when the third st. was dropped. This st. has now been replaced by the original st. 8, a st. omitted by John and beginning "Thee I shall constantly proclaim."

Gräfenberg

See "Come, Holy Spirit, Heavenly Dove," pp. 141-42.

Jesus, the Sinner's Friend, to Thee (118)

CHARLES WESLEY, 1707-1788

The hymn first appeared in the 1739 edition of *Hymns and Sacred Poems,* under the biblical text Galatians 3:22: "The scripture hath concluded all under sin, that the promise by faith of Jesus Christ might be given to them that believe."

John Welsey reduced the thirteen 4-line sts. to 6 for his *Collection of Hymns for the Use of the People Called Methodists,* 1780. These 6 entered American Methodist hymnals in 1821 with only 2 major changes: in the hymnals of 1847 and 1849, sts. 3 and 4 (numbered 5 and 6 in 1739) were dropped.

Federal Street

See "God Calling Yet! Shall I Not Hear," pp. 191-92.

Jesus, the Very Thought of Thee (82)
Dulcis Jesu Memoria

Attr. to BERNARD OF CLAIRVAUX, 1091-1153
Trans. by EDWARD CASWALL, 1814-1878

The "Jubilus rithmicus de amore Jesu," inspired by the Song of Solomon, is a song of joy repeating continually the name of Jesus. It is of an uncertain twelfth-century date. Being the chief and characteristic item in an office for the celebration of the name of Jesus, the poem was widely copied. Though originally in 42 strophes, in the course of time from 1 to 13 strophes were added, as well as doublets, differing doxologies, and textual variations. Manuscripts were found in England, France, Italy, and Germany.

The authorship of the poem remains in dispute. Though commonly attributed to Bernard of Clairvaux, it remained anonymous for 2 centuries. The chief support of the tradition ascribing the poem to Bernard is its place in the great devotional movement of the Middle Ages in which mystical piety centers in personal devotion to Jesus, who is addressed not as the Lord Jesus Christ, but with the tenderness, even effusiveness, with which men address men. The first-person singular is used, and emotions are given free rein. Thus, though there is nothing in the manuscript tradition either to prove or disprove Bernard's authorship, it is imbued with the spirit of his prose writings.

Since the earliest and best texts were copied in England and were most purely maintained in English manuscripts to the end of the Middle Ages, F. J. E. Raby in the *Bulletin* of the Hymn Society of Great Britain and Ireland, October, 1945, came to the conclusion that the poem "is the work of an Englishman and was written about the end of the twelfth century."

Edward Caswall translated "St. Bernard's Hymn; or the Loving Soul's Jubilation" in fifty 4-line sts. published in *The Masque of Mary and Other Poems* (London, 1858). As the hymn is commonly printed, in 5 sts., it accords with the text in Caswall's *Lyra Catholica* (London, 1849). Only st. 5 varies from *The Masque of Mary* text, and this with only minor alterations.

The hymn entered the Methodist Episcopal hymnal in 1878 with minor variations from Caswall's 1849 text. Our cento, selected by Caswall himself for *Lyra Catholica,* is made up of 1–4 and 40 of *The Masque of Mary* 50-st. translation.

St. Agnes

See **"Happy the Home When God Is There,"** p. 208.

Jesus, Thine All-Victorious Love (278)

CHARLES WESLEY, 1707-1788

The hymn was first published in the 1740 edition of *Hymns and Sacred Poems* in twelve 4-line sts., under the title "Against Hope, believing in Hope." St. 1 read:

My God! I know, I feel Thee mine,
And will not quit my claim,
Till all I have be lost in Thine,
And all renewed I am.

John Welsey included the entire 12 sts. with only minor alterations in his 1780 *Collection of Hymns for the Use of the People Called Methodists,* and the hymn has been included in virtually every American Methodist hymnal from the beginning, first in 8 sts., later in 4, 5, and 6. The present 4 are 4, 9, 11, and 12 of the original hymn.

Azmon

CARL G. GLÄSER, 1784-1829
Arr. by LOWELL MASON, 1792-1872

The tune, listed as anonymous in Mason's *Modern Psalmist* (Boston, 1839), was one of many picked up on one of his European tours. It was also included in the *Seraph,* June, 1839, a monthly publication of church music "consisting of Psalm and Hymn Tunes, Chants, Anthems, etc., Original and Selected by Lowell Mason," published in Boston by Stephen Jenks and Palmer. Here it was in 4/4 time. Two years later it appeared in *Carmina Sacra,* 1841, with the same words but in 3/2.

In *The Sabbath Hymn and Tune Book,* 1859, Mason called the tune DENFIELD and credited it to "C. G." It has appeared in 4/4, 6/8, 3/4 and 3/2. It is also called GASTON.

Jesus, Thou Joy of Loving Hearts (329)
Jesu, dulcedo cordium

Attr. to BERNARD OF CLAIRVAUX, 1091-1153
Trans. by RAY PALMER, 1808-1887

This hymn is the second cento in our hymnal from the "Jubilus" attributed to Bernard of Clairvaux, discussed above under "Jesus, the very thought of thee" (pp. 252-53.) Our 5 sts. are 4, 3, 20, 28, and 10 of the Latin. Palmer translated these for *The Sabbath Hymn Book* (Andover, 1858), edited by Edward A. Park, Austin Phelps, and Lowell Mason. Here, the hymn was entitled "Delight in Christ"; in the complete edition of Palmer's *Poetical Works,* 1876, the title was "Jesus the Beloved."

The hymn entered the Methodist Episcopal hymnal in 1878 in its present and unaltered form.

Rockingham (Mason)

See "God of the Ages, by Whose Hand," p. 198.

Jesus, Thy Blood and Righteousness (127)
Christi Blut und Gerechtigkeit

NICOLAUS VON ZINZENDORF, 1700-1760
Trans. by JOHN WESLEY, 1703-1791

Count von Zinzendorf's text in 33 sts. was available to Wesley in Appendix viii of *Herrnhut Gesangbuch,* 1735. Wesley's selective translation reduced the hymn to 24 sts. It was first published in the 1740 edition of *Hymns and Sacred Poems* under the title "The Believer's Triumph. From the German." For his *Collection of Hymns for the Use of the People Called Methodists,* 1780, the translation was reduced to 11 sts.

Included in every American Methodist hymnal, already by 1821 the hymn had been reduced to 5 sts. which continued to be printed until the 1901 Methodist Protestant hymnal and the 1935 hymnal, when the original sixth st. was dropped. For his 1780 *Collection,* Wesley altered our 4:3-4 to its present form from:

> For all thou hast the ransom given,
> Purchas'd for all, peace, life, and heaven.

Herr Jesu Christ, mein's Lebens Licht

As Hymnodus Sacer, Leipzig, 1625

The melody emerged from a folk song, "Ich fahr dahin," in the *Lochheimer Gesangbuch,* c. 1452, and is 1 of 8 tunes with 12 texts in *As Hymnodus Sacer.* The tune also appeared in a Königsberg 1602 manuscript. Mendelssohn used it in his oratorio *St. Paul,* and his arrangement, called BRESLAU, is found in some hymnals. In the Swiss Evangelical hymnal, it is set to "Ach bleib bei uns."

Jesus, Thy Boundless Love to Me (259)
O Jesu Christ, mein schönstes Licht

PAUL GERHARDT, 1607-1676
Trans. by JOHN WESLEY, 1703-1791

The text first appeared in Johann Crüger, *Praxis Pietatis Melica* (5th ed., 1653). Wesley seems to have found the hymn, with 32 others which he translated from German into English while in Georgia, in the *Herrnhut Gesangbuch*, 1735. His translation in 16 sts. was first published in the 1739 edition of *Hymns and Sacred Poems* under the title "Living by Christ." In his *Plain Account of Christian Perfection*, he quotes the second st. with the comments: "In the beginning of the year 1738, as I was returning from thence [Georgia], the cry of my heart was,

> O grant that nothing in my soul
> May dwell, but thy pure love alone!
> O may thy love possess me whole,
> My joy, my treasure, and my crown;
> Strange flames far from my heart remove;
> My every act, word, thought, be love.

"I never heard that anyone objected to this. And indeed who can object? Is not this the language, not only of every believer, but of every one that is truly awakened? But what have I wrote, to this day, which is either stronger or plainer?"

For his 1780 *Collection of Hymns for the Use of the People Called Methodists,* Wesley reduced his hymn to 9 sts. These 9 sts. were printed in our hymnals as 2 hymns until 1847 and 1849 when the hymn was reduced to 4 sts., including dropping the st. printed above which Wesley prized and quoted in *Plain Account*. In 1935 st. 4 was dropped.

St. Catherine

See "Come, Father, Son, and Holy Ghost," pp. 138-39.

Jesus, United by Thy Grace (193)

CHARLES WESLEY, 1707-1788

The text was first published in the 1742 edition of *Hymns and Sacred Poems*. Entitled "A Prayer for Persons joined in Fellowship" and beginning "Try us, O God, and search the ground/Of every sinful heart," it consisted of twenty-nine 4-line sts. divided into 4 parts. In his *Collection of Hymns for the Use of the People Called Methodists,* 1780, John Wesley printed the 6 sts. of Part I, altering only "sinless" in 5:4 (our st. 3) to "spotless." He omitted Parts II and III, 14 sts. in all, but printed all 9 sts. of Part IV, beginning "Jesu, united by thy grace."

A cento or centos from the hymn have been included in all American Methodist hymnals from the beginning. Our earlier hymnals printed both Parts I and IV as John had transmitted them, but abridgments began to take place as early as the Methodist Episcopal hymnal of 1849. Our 1905 hymnal was the last to print 2 separate hymns from the original 4-part hymn. The 1935 hymnal was the first to combine sts. from I and IV, making 1 instead of 2 hymns. The hymn was made up of IV, 1; I, 3 and 5; and IV, 4, in that order. The 1964 hymnal has added 2 sts.: IV, 5 and 6.

St. Agnes

See "Happy the Home When God Is There," p. 208.

Jesus, We Look to Thee (310)

CHARLES WESLEY, 1707-1788

The hymn first appeared in the 1749 edition of *Hymns and Sacred Poems* in four 8-line sts. In his *Collection of Hymns for the Use of the People Called Methodists,* 1780, John Wesley omitted st. 4 and halved the first 3, making six 4-line sts. These 6, usually printed as three 8-line sts., were included in all American Methodist hymnals until the Methodist Protestant of 1901 and the Methodist hymnal of 1905, when the entire hymn was dropped. The 1935 hymnal reclaimed 4 quatrains, omitting the third and sixth. The 1964 hymnal has added the sixth and rejected the minor alterations made by John in favor of Charles's original text.

Mornington

Arr. from a chant by GARRET WELLESLEY, 1735-1781

Arranged from a chant written by the Earl of Mornington, c. 1760, the tune appeared as a psalm tune in Short Meter in W. E. Miller,

David's Harp, 1805, in which ADESTE FIDELIS was also introduced into English Methodist hymnody.

Jesus, We Want to Meet (487)

A. T. OLAJIDE OLUDE, 1908-
Trans. by BIODUN ADEBESIN, 1928-
Versed by A. C. L.

While Adebesin was serving at the United Nations, he and his family became members of Christ Methodist Church in New York City. The 1964 hymnal committee was meeting at the church the day Adebesin joined, in January of 1962, and Austin C. Lovelace, then minister of music at Christ Church, and Carlton R. Young, editor of the hymnal, spent the evening with Adebesin when he translated the Nigerian hymn that he had learned during the 1950's. It was his suggestion that the drumbeat be added for optional use.

Nigeria

A. T. OLAJIDE OLUDE, 1908-
Harm. by M. O. AJOSE, 1912-

The words and music were written in 1949 for a musical monthly service at Abeokuta to popularize Yoruba music in Christian worship. Inspired by the use of indigenous music with native drums accompaniment in Lagos and Ibadan, Mr. Olude has written well over 300 texts and tunes since his first compositions during theological training in 1925 at Wesley College, Ibadan.

The tune is also called JESU A FE PADE, which means "Worship or Praise" or "Opening of Sunday Worship."

Jesus, Where'er Thy People Meet (98)

WILLIAM COWPER, 1731-1800

A new prayer meeting place, an old mansion in Olney, was the occasion for the writing and first use of this hymn in 1769. As first printed in *Olney Hymns,* 1779, there were 6 sts. The hymn entered the Methodist Protestant hymnal in 1837 with the first 3 sts. St. 4 was added in the 1878 Methodist Episcopal hymnal.

Our text shows 2 alterations. In 2:2 Cowper wrote "Inhabitest the humble mind," but since 1849 that line has been changed to the present version. Since 1837 "Dear Shepherd" has been replaced by "Great Shepherd" (3:1).

Malvern

LOWELL MASON, 1792-1872

Once a very popular tune, but less so now, it first appeared in *The Psaltery,* edited by Mason and George J. Webb (Boston, 1845).

Jesus, with Thy Church Abide (311)

THOMAS B. POLLOCK, 1836-1896

This "Litany of the Church" was first published in the author's 1871 Appendix to *Metrical Litanies for Special Services and General Use,* in 18 sts. It was radically rewritten for the 1875 revised edition of *Hymns Ancient and Modern:* 7 sts. were dropped and 9 new ones written.

The hymn entered the Methodist hymnal in 1935 with 6 sts., 3 of which were among the original 18, the other 3 new sts. from the 1875 *Hymns Ancient and Modern.* One was dropped in 1964.

Canterbury

See **"Christ, from Whom All Blessings Flow,"** pp. 130-31.

Joy to the World! the Lord Is Come (392)

ISAAC WATTS, 1674-1748

The hymn, first published in *The Psalms of David, Imitated in the Language of the New Testament,* 1719, is a paraphrase of the second half of Psalm 98 entitled "The Messiah's Coming and Kingdom." In 2:1 Watts wrote "Joy to the earth." Though "earth" was retained in our 1847, 1889, and 1901 hymnals, the hymn entered the Methodist Episcopal hymnal of 1878 with "world," which has prevailed. Watts also wrote "sins and sorrows" (3:1); yet, some of our earlier hymnals —1882, 1878, and 1905—printed the singular, "sin and sorrow." Otherwise the hymn has been printed unaltered since the 1847 hymnal of the Methodist Episcopal Church, South, and the 1878 Methodist Episcopal hymnal.

Antioch

Arr. from GEORGE FREDERICK HANDEL, 1685-1759
by LOWELL MASON, 1792-1872

Louis F. Benson lists 1836 as the date of composition or first appearance of the tune, but the first publication is in Mason's *Modern Psalmist* (Boston, 1839) with the notation "from Handel." Here it is listed among other works which have "either been arranged, adapted, or composed for this work, or taken from other recent works of the Editor." The opening phrase is similar to Handel's chorus "Lift up your heads," and there are suggestions of the introduction to "Comfort ye."

Other names are COMFORT, HOLY TRIUMPH, MESSIAH, and MEDIA.

Joyful, Joyful, We Adore Thee (38)

HENRY VAN DYKE, 1852-1933

According to Tertius Van Dyke, the author's son, the text was written in 1907 while his father was on a preaching visit at Williams College. At breakfast he put a manuscript on the table before President Garfield, with the words: "Here is a hymn for you. Your mountains [the Berkshires] were my inspiration. It must be sung to the music of Beethoven's 'Hymn to Joy.'" Included in the third edition of Van Dyke's *Poems*, 1911, it is there dated 1908.

The hymn entered the Methodist hymnal in 1935, with minor alterations.

Hymn to Joy

Arr. from LUDWIG VAN BEETHOVEN, 1770-1827
by EDWARD HODGES, 1796-1867

The hymn tune arrangement by Hodges, while organist at Trinity Church, New York, was drawn from the last movement of Beethoven's *Ninth* (Choral) *Symphony,* composed 1817-23 and published in 1826. The tune, evolved through some 200 sketches by Beethoven, was the inspiration for Van Dyke's poem. The theme was first used in *The Mozart Collection* (New York, 1846), edited by Elam Ives, Jr., where there were 3 arrangements of it, all called BONN. Hodges' arrangement was published in S. P. Tuckerman, *Trinity Collection of Church Music,* 1864, but when the tune was first wedded to Van Dyke's text in the *Presbyterian Hymnal* in 1911, it was to an adaptation of the Ives's version. Walford Davies included the tune in *The Fellowship Hymn-Book,* 1933, but usage has been mostly American.

It is also called BONN and JOY.

Judge Eternal, Throned in Splendor (546)

HENRY S. HOLLAND, 1847-1918

The hymn was first published in 1902 in the *Commonwealth,* the official monthly journal of the Christian Social Union. Holland was editor of the periodical from 1895 to 1912. Its first hymnal inclusion was in *The English Hymnal* (Oxford, 1906), with 3 sts.

The hymn entered the Methodist hymnal with the present hymnal, omitting 2 of the 4 original sts. and with the alteration of "realm" (1:4) to "land." In American printings, "nation" replaces "empire" in 2:5.

Tantum ergo

SAMUEL WEBBE, SR., 1740-1816

The tune was first published anonymously in Part II of Webbe's *Essay on the Church Plain Chant* (London, 1782). The name is taken from the text of the 2 concluding sts. of Thomas Aquinas' "Pange lingua," a part of the service of Benediction.

The tune is sometimes called CORINTH, CARMEN, WEBBE, WALPOLE, BENEDICTION, and ORIEL.

Just as I Am, Thine Own to Be (169)

MARIANNE HEARN, 1834-1909

The hymn first appeared in *Voice of Praise,* 1887, a publication of the National Sunday School Union, London. It was obviously suggested by the familiar "Just as I am, without one plea." Two sts. have been omitted.

It entered the Methodist hymnal in 1964.

Just as I Am

JOSEPH BARNBY, 1838-1896

Written for Charlotte Elliott's "Just as I am, without one plea," this is 1 of 246 tunes composed by Barnby. It first appeared in *Home and School Hymnal* (London, 1892).

It is also called BARNBY, CREWDSON, and DUNSTAN.

Just as I Am, Without One Plea (119)

CHARLOTTE ELLIOTT, 1789-1871

According to the stories, while Miss Elliott was living in Westfield Lodge, Brighton, England, in 1834, her brother was engaged in preparing for a bazaar to raise money for building a college where daughters of poor clergymen might be educated at low expense. She was a complete invalid, and her apparent uselessness precipitated a spiritual conflict in which she questioned the reality of her whole spiritual life. Resolution of her anguish came when she restated for herself the essentials of her faith in the text of this hymn. First published in a leaflet in 1835, it was included in Miss Elliott's *Hours of Sorrow, Cheered and Comforted (or Thoughts in Verse)*, 1836, with a seventh st. added. This st., never printed in our hymnals, is often used as the last st., particularly in England:

> Just as I am—of that free love,
> "The breadth, length, depth, and height" to prove,
> Here for a season, then above—
> O Lamb of God, I come!

The first hymnal inclusion seems to have been in *The Invalid's Hymn Book* (2nd rev. ed., 1841).

The hymn entered the Methodist Episcopal hymnal in 1878 with the 6 original sts. The only alteration was made in 1935 when in 3:3 "Fightings within, and fears without" was rearranged to become "Fightings and fears within, without."

Woodworth

WILLIAM B. BRADBURY, 1816-1868

The tune was first published in the 1849 *Third Book of Psalmody,* better known as the *Mendelssohn Collection,* by Thomas Hastings and Bradbury. It is a transitional type of hymn tune between Lowell Mason and the gospel songs. Originally in the key of C, it was sung to "The God of love will sure indulge."

The correct meter of the text is 888.6., but since WOODWORTH is a Long Meter tune, the needless repetition of "I come" is required to fill out the music.

Lamp of Our Feet (368)

BERNARD BARTON, 1784-1849

The hymn in 11 sts. first appeared in *The Reliquary,* 1836, 1 of 8 volumes of poetry published by Barton. The hymn entered the Methodist Protestant hymnal in 1901 with 6 sts. (1-3, 9-11) and the Methodist hymnal in 1905 with 4 sts. (1, 2, 9, and 11). Our st. 4 has been slightly altered.

Evan

See "Blest Be the Dear Uniting Love," pp. 119-20.

Lead, Kindly Light, Amid the Encircling Gloom (272)

JOHN HENRY NEWMAN, 1801-1890

Newman wrote the text during a period of mental and spiritual anguish compounded by bodily illness. While writing his work on the Arians, he became aware of the difference between the "fresh, vigorous power" of the church of the first centuries and the "do-nothing perplexity" of the Church of England of his time.

When his work on the Arians was completed, and at the impairment of his health, Newman set out for southern Europe in December, 1832. Alone in Sicily in May, 1833, "ill of a fever," aching to get to England, kept in Palermo 3 weeks for want of a vessel, he at last got aboard an orange boat bound for Marseilles. "Then it was that I wrote the lines, 'Lead, kindly Light,' which has since become well known. We were becalmed a whole week in the Strait of Bonifacio. I was writing verses the whole time of my passage."

The date given for the writing of the text is June 16, 1833. It was published in the *British Magazine,* February, 1834, under the title "Faith" and in *Lyra Apostolica,* 1836. Its first American inclusion was in *A Book of Hymns for Public and Private Devotions,* edited by S. Longfellow and S. Johnson, 1846.

The hymn entered the Methodist Episcopal hymnal in 1878.

Lux benigna

JOHN B. DYKES, 1823-1876

The tune was composed on August 29, 1865, while Dykes was walking through the Strand in London. Its first appearance was in

D. T. Barry, *Psalms and Hymns for the Church School and Home* (London, 1867), where it was called ST. OSWALD after Dykes's parish in Durham. Originally in the key of G, it was transposed up to A flat and the name changed in the Appendix to *Hymns Ancient and Modern,* 1868.

The tune name means "kindly light."

Lead On, O King Eternal (478)

ERNEST W. SHURTLEFF, 1862-1917

The hymn was written to be sung at Andover Theological Seminary at the commencement exercises of the class of 1887, of which the author was a member. It was published the same year in Shurtleff's *Hymns of the Faith.*

The hymn entered the Methodist Protestant hymnal in 1901 and the Methodist hymnal in 1905 in its present form.

Lancashire

See **"Go, Make of All Disciples,"** pp. 187-88.

Lead Us, O Father, in the Paths of Peace (269)

WILLIAM H. BURLEIGH, 1812-1871

Written before 1859, the hymn appeared in *The New Congregational Hymn-Book* of that date. It was also included in C. D. Cleveland, *Lyra Sacra Americana,* an English collection of 1868, which is often given as its source.

The hymn entered the Methodist hymnal in 1905, the only alteration being the substitution of "darksome" for "moral" in 3:3. In 1935, "faith *or* hope" replaced "faith *and* hope" (2:4). The 1964 text is identical with that of 1935.

Langran

JAMES LANGRAN, 1835-1909

Set to "Abide with me," the tune appeared in leaflet form in 1861. Later it was included in John Foster, *Psalms and Hymns Adapted to the Services of the Church of England,* 1863. In England the tune is called ST. AGNES.

Let All Mortal Flesh Keep Silence (324)

Σιγησάτο πᾶσα σάρξ

Liturgy of St. James
Trans. by GERARD MOULTRIE, 1829-1885

In the Liturgy of St. James of Jerusalem—the Syrian rite—while the Communion elements are being brought into the sanctuary at the beginning of the Liturgy of the Faithful, the readers sing "the thrice-holy hymn to the quickening Trinity," and the priest chants the prayer: "Let all mortal flesh keep silence, and stand with fear and trembling . . . for the King of Kings, and Lord of Lords, Christ our God, comes forward to be sacrificed and to be given for food to the faithful." This use may be dated as far back as the fifth century.

A prose translation of the entire rite was made for John Mason Neale and Richard F. Littledale, *A Translation of the Primitive Liturgies*, 1868-69, which is similar to Gerard Moultrie's metrical translation, made for Orby Shipley, *Lyra Eucharistica* (2nd ed., 1864).

The first st. of the hymn entered the Methodist hymnal in 1935 as a Call to Worship; the 4-st. hymn was first included in 1964.

Picardy

Traditional French Tune

The tune is probably from the seventeenth century. It is found in volume 4 of *Chansons populaires des provinces de France* (Paris, 1860), as having been sung by Mme. Pierre Dupont to "Jesus Christ s'habille en pauvre," a folk song she remembered from her childhood in Picardy. *The English Hymnal* (Oxford, 1906) first adapted it to this text. In mood it is very different from most French carols.

Let All on Earth Their Voices Raise (39)

ISAAC WATTS, 1674-1748

From *The Psalms of David, Imitated in the Language of the New Testament*, 1719, the psalm is entitled "The God of the Gentiles." The original st. 2 has been omitted.

Many of the alterations of the original text are due to turning it into 886.D. meter. But "heathens" (1:4) and "barbarous nations" (3:3) have yielded to gentler words.

The hymn entered the Methodist Episcopal hymnal in 1849 with the same 3 sts. Only in 1935 did "heathens" give way to "people." Methodist Protestant and Methodist Episcopal, South hymnals never printed the hymn.

Old 113th

See **"I'll Praise My Maker While I've Breath,"** pp. 234-35.

Let All the World in Every Corner Sing (10)
GEORGE HERBERT, 1593-1633

John Wesley's affection for George Herbert's poetry is well known. In the Charleston *Collection of Psalms and Hymns,* 1737, there were 6 from Herbert's collection *The Temple.* In the 1739 *Hymns and Sacred Poems,* there were over 40, which Wesley altered to meter suitable for singing.

"Let all the world" was published in 1633. Herbert called it "Antiphon," intending for a chorus to sing the refrain and a single voice the sts. The first inclusion in a Methodist hymnal was in 1935.

All the World
ROBERT G. McCUTCHAN, 1877-1958

Written under the pen name of "John Porter," the tune first appeared in the 1935 hymnal, for which it was written. The composer had antiphonal treatment in mind, with the first and last phrases being the antiphon sung by the congregation. The original version had a pianistic accompaniment, which has been reduced for organ in the new hymnal.

Let All Together Praise Our God (389)
Lobt Gott ihr Christen allzugleich

NICOLAUS HERMANN, c. 1490-1561
Trans. by ARTHUR TOZER RUSSELL, 1806-1874

The German text in eight 4-line sts. was first published in the author's collection *Die Sonntags-Evangelia . . . in Gesänge verfasset* (Wittenberg, 1560). Russell's English translation of sts. 1, 3, 6, and 8

266

appeared in his *Psalms and Hymns, Partly Original, Partly Selected, for the Use of the Church of England,* 1851.

This is the first inclusion of the hymn in a Methodist hymnal. Only slight alterations have been made.

Lobt Gott, ihr Christen

NICOLAUS HERMANN, c. 1490-1561
Harm. by A.C.L.

The tune first appeared in *Ein christlicher Abendreihen* . . . (Leipzig, 1554), set to "Kommt her, ihr lieben Schwesterlein," one of Hermann's hymns for children. It appeared with the text in his collection *Die Sonntags Evangelia.*

Much of the tune's charm lies in the rising scale which leads into the refrainlike last phrase. It is also known as NICOLAUS, HERMANN, BRAY, and ST. GEORGE.

Let Us Break Bread Together (330)

American Folk Hymn

Miles Mark Fisher, *Negro Slave Songs in the United States,* 1953, suggests that though this spiritual was sung as a Communion hymn after the Civil War, it may be derived from a song used to convene a secret meeting of Negroes after the colony of Virginia took the lead in prohibiting the assemblage of Negroes by drumbeat. St. 3 and the refrain hardly relate to Holy Communion, which does not necessarily require early morning administration or facing the east. This sounds rather like an eighteenth-century signal song summoning a protest group.

The 1964 hymnal is our first to include Afro-American songs.

Let Us Break Bread

American Folk Hymn
Harm. by C.R.Y.

(For general remarks about spirituals, see "Go, tell it on the mountain," pp. 188-89.)

John W. Work writes: "I believe it was first published by William Lawrence about 1928. It was sung pretty generally in the churches of

267

Charleston, South Carolina, Lawrence's home. Noah Ryder's later choral arrangement of the song popularized it."

Let Us with a Gladsome Mind (61)

JOHN MILTON, 1608-1674

Milton was a 15-year-old boy in St. Paul's School, London, when he made this psalm paraphrase in 1623. It was first published in *Poems of Mr. John Milton, Both English and Latin, Compos'd at Several Times,* 1645. The hymn was in 24 sts., and centos of various lengths get printed. Six sts. appeared in the 1837 Methodist Protestant hymnal, 4 in the 1847 Methodist Episcopal, South hymnal, and three 8-line sts. in the 1878 Methodist Episcopal hymnal.

The text was dropped in 1905, but a 3-st. cento made up of Milton's first, seventh, and twenty-second sts. was reintroduced in 1935. Our 1964 hymnal has added as st. 4 a repeated first st., slightly altered. Only slight changes have been made in the Milton text.

Two pleasant couplets, frequently printed, follow the original seventh st.:

> And caused the golden-tressed sun,
> All the day long his course to run,
> The horned moon to shine by night,
> Amongst her spangled sisters bright.

Innocents

From the *Parish Choir*, London, 1850
Arr. by W. H. MONK, 1823-1889

This slight tune is taken from the November, 1850, issue of the *Parish Choir,* an Anglican, high church publication of the Society for Promoting Church Music. While the possible source has been given as an air from Handel's opera *Siroe,* beginning "Non vi piacque," an 1838 "Venetian air" by Samuel Webbe the Younger, and an unpublished song by Joseph Smith entitled "The Sun," there is not enough thematic material to warrant any musicological research. To Monk must go the credit for the tune as it appears.

The tune is also called DURHAM, ALL SAINTS, and AN ANCIENT LITURGY.

Let Zion's Watchmen All Awake (335)

PHILIP DODDRIDGE, 1702-1751

The hymn, in 5 sts., was written "For the Ordination of a Minister," probably at Floor, Northamptonshire, England, where it was dated October 21, 1736. It was first printed in Doddridge's *Hymns Founded on Various Texts in the Holy Scriptures* (London, 1755), entitled "Watching for Souls in the View of the great Account. Heb. 13:17."

Though apparently never printed by John Wesley, it has been included in all American Methodist hymnals from the very beginning. All 5 sts. were printed until 1847 and 1849, when st. 5 was permanently dropped. Alterations have been slight.

Arlington

See **"Am I a Soldier of the Cross,"** pp. 87-88.

Lift Up Our Hearts, O King of Kings (194)

JOHN H. B. MASTERMAN, 1867-1933

The hymn first appeared in *A Missionary Hymn Book* (London, 1922). It entered the Methodist hymnal in 1964 with 3 of its 4 sts. arranged in the order of 2, 3, 1.

Deus tuorum militum

Grenoble *Antiphoner*, 1753

The French church melodies mark the transition from plainsong to measured hymn tunes in continental Roman Catholic hymnody during the sixteenth and seventeenth centuries. Nearly all are in the Sapphic form, 11 11 11.5., or Long Meter in triple time. This tune is one of the least related to plainsong, with its chordally structured first measure. Some of the tunes were based on plainsong, others on secular songs.

The English Hymnal (Oxford, 1906) introduced the tune to contemporary usage, taking this tune from the Grenoble Antiphoner, 1753. The name means "the God of your soldiers."

Lift Up Your Heads, Ye Mighty Gates (363)
Macht hoch die Tür die Tor' macht weit

GEORG WEISSEL, 1590-1635
Trans. by CATHERINE WINKWORTH, 1827-1878

The German text first appeared in *Preussische Festlieder,* 1642, in five 8-line sts. Catherine Winkworth's translation, also in 5 sts., was first published in the first series of her *Lyra Germanica,* 1855, and designated for use on the Fourth Sunday in Advent. The hymn entered the Methodist hymnal in 1935, with three 4-line sts. composed of the first 4 lines of sts. 1, 4, and 5. The only alterations are those consequent to substituting the plural for the singular pronouns in our st. 3.

Truro

See "I Know That My Redeemer Lives," p. 227.

Light of the World, We Hail Thee (398)

JOHN S. B. MONSELL, 1811-1875

The hymn was first published in the author's *Hymns of Love and Praise for the Church Year,* 1863, and appointed for the Sixth Sunday after Epiphany, with John 9:5 as text.

It entered our 1935 hymnal with 3 sts., omitting Monsell's third. Our present hymnal has altered "flushing" to "flooding" (1:2).

Complainer

WILLIAM WALKER, 1809-1875
Harm. by C.R.Y.

The tune is probably by Walker, though the source, *Southern Harmony* (New Haven, 1835), contains many spiritual folk songs collected by Walker in the South. The tune has been reharmonized, and the rhythm has been altered to fit the many misplaced accents of the text.

Lo, He Comes with Clouds Descending (364)

CHARLES WESLEY, 1707-1788

Wesley was moved by John Cennick's strong, yet coarse if not grotesque, hymn in 6 sts., sung in the Moravian chapel, Dublin,

270

April 20, 1750, and published in Cennick's *Collection of Sacred Hymns* (5th ed., 1752). Wesley took up the same theme, and in the same meter created a hymn which has become a classic.

Wesley's 4 sts. have been included in every American Methodist hymnal from the beginning except the 1935 hymnal, and as Wesley published them in 1758 in his *Hymns of Intercession for All Mankind.* Some of our earlier hymnals altered "The dear tokens" to "All the tokens" (3:1), and "Jah! Jehovah" for "Hallelujah" (4:5).

Cennick's hymn began:

> Lo! he cometh, countless trumpets
> Blow before his bloody sign!
> Midst ten thousand saints and angels,
> See the Crucified shine.
> Allelujah!
> Welcome, welcome bleeding Lamb!

Half of Cennick's sts. did not survive the cento of Wesley and Cennick made by Martin Madan, *A Collection of Psalms and Hymns,* 1760, who used Wesley's first and second sts. unaltered, and his fourth, with only the last 2 lines altered to:

> O come quickly
> Hallelujah! Come Lord, come.

Since Madan's mixture was the form most generally known, 3 of Cennick's sts., usually in altered form, continued to be sung. Our Methodist hymnals, however, have never published either Cennick's or Madan's form of the hymn.

Bryn Calfaria

WILLIAM OWEN, 1814-1893
Harm. by C.R.Y.

Prysgol (Owen's Welsh name) wrote the melody for an evangelistic hymn, "Gwaed y groes sy'n codi fynny." It was first published in Vol. II of *Y Perl Cerddorol* (The Pearl of Music), a collection of anthems and hymn tunes by Owen. *The English Hymnal* (Oxford, 1906) was the first to use it in the present arrangement.

The tune name means "Mount Calvary."

271

Look, Ye Saints! The Sight Is Glorious (453)
THOMAS KELLY, 1769-1854

The hymn was first published in Kelly's *Hymns on Various Passages of Scriptures* (3rd ed., 1809). In 4 sts., it was printed under the biblical text "And he shall reign for ever and ever" (Revelation 11:15). The hymn entered the Methodist Episcopal hymnal in 1878.

Bryn Calfaria

See "**Lo, He Comes with Clouds Descending,**" pp. 270-71.

Lord Christ, When First Thou Cam'st (355)
WALTER RUSSELL BOWIE, 1882-1969

The text was written by request of one of the editors of *Songs of Praise* (rev. ed., 1931), who was searching for a modern equivalent of the medieval *Dies Irae*. The text suggests that every advent is both a first and second advent. Christ always comes both in love and with judgment.

It entered the Methodist hymnal in 1964.

Kirken den er et gammelt Hus
LUDWIG M. LINDEMAN, 1812-1887

Written for Nikolai Grundtvig's hymn "Built on the rock," this was the composer's first hymn tune and one of the most popular in the Norwegian Lutheran tradition. It was first published in W. A. Wexel, *Christelige Psalmer,* 1840.

The tune name means "The Church that is an old house."

Lord, Dismiss Us with Thy Blessing (165)
JOHN FAWCETT, 1739/40-1817

The hymn in 3 sts. appeared anonymously in the *Supplement to the Shawbury Hymn Book* (Shrewsbury, 1773) and was circulated without signature in various collections. The first suggestion of authorship came 13 years after the hymn's first appearance, in the York *Selection of Hymns for Social Worship,* where it is signed "F." In J. Harris, *A Collection of Psalms and Hymns* (7th ed., 1791), and in an 1800 Dublin *Collection of Hymns for Christian Worship,* it is signed "Fawcett." In spite of the uncertain evidence, John Julian thinks Fawcett is "very probably" the author.

R. Conyers, *A Collection of Psalms and Hymns from Various Authors* (3rd ed., 1774), is responsible for changing 1:6 from "In this dry and barren place" to its present form.

The hymn entered Methodist hymnals with 3 sts. in 1837, attributed to "Wes.Col"; in 1849, attributed to George Burder; in 1878 and 1882, attributed to Walter Shirley. Our 1905 hymnal is the first to attribute the hymn to Fawcett and the last to print st. 3.

Our 1935 and 1964 hymnals print the first 2 sts. as they appear in Conyers' 1774 *Collection.*

Sicilian Mariners

W. D. TATTERSALL, *Improved Psalmody,* 1794

The tune is typical of the late eighteenth-century Roman Catholic hymnody against which La Feillée and Samuel Webbe stood strongly. Tattersall probably picked up the tune from some Catholic source and included it in his *Improved Psalmody,* 1794. Four years later it appeared in William Smith and William Little's *Easy Instructor,* a 1798 American shaped-note book, set to "Lord, dismiss us."

According to Wilhelm Bäumker, *Katholische deutsche Kirchenlied* (4 vols.; Freiburg, 1886-1911), and Johann von der Heydt, *Geschicte der Evangelischen Kirchenmusik,* 1926, the German poet Johann Gottfried von Herder brought the tune from Italy to Germany in 1788 or 1789 and published it in *Stimmen der Völker in Liedern,* 1807. It appeared in Ralph Shaw, *The Gentleman's Amusement* (Philadelphia, 1794-95). No connection has ever been proved with Sicily, but the tune has gained popularity in Catholic circles set to "O sanctissima, O piissima." Even Beethoven made an arrangement of the tune.

The tune is also known as DISMISSAL.

Lord, Guard and Guide the Men Who Fly (541)

MARY C. D. HAMILTON

The text is dated 1915 in *The Armed Forces Hymnal.* It was published in *A Book of Verse of the Great War,* edited by William R. Wheeler (Yale, 1917).

Hesperus

HENRY BAKER, 1835-1910

Written by Baker as a student in 1854, the tune first appeared anonymously with the text "Sun of my soul," by John Keble in John Grey, *A Hymnal for Use in the English Church* (London, 1866). Apparently the tune was submitted to a contest by the London *Penny Post* for a new setting of Keble's hymn without the knowledge of Baker. After E. H. Bickersteth included it in a compilation in 1871, Baker acknowledged his authorship.

It is also called QUEBEC, WHITBURN, and ELIM.

Lord, I Want to Be a Christian (286)

American Folk Hymn

According to eighteenth-century records, in 1756 a slave in Hanover, Va., went to the Presbyterian minister William Davies with the request: "I come to you, sir, that you may tell me some good things concerning Jesus Christ and my duty to God, for I am resolved not to live any more as I have done." That is, "Lord [sir], I want to be a Christian." Miles Mark Fisher, *Negro Slave Songs in the United States,* conjectures that this spiritual well fits the Virginia ministry of Davies between 1748 and 1759 and, being in accord with the slave's request at Hanover in 1756, probably originated there.

A third traditional st. is here omitted: "I don't want to be like Judas, in my heart."

This is the first appearance of the hymn in a Methodist hymnal.

I Want to Be a Christian

American Folk Hymn

(For general remarks about spirituals, see "Go, tell it on the mountain," pp. 188-89.)

The tune and text first appeared in Frederick J. Work, *Folk Songs of the American Negro* (Nashville, 1907). This is definitely a "call and response chant" type.

Lord, in the Strength of Grace (182)

CHARLES WESLEY, 1707-1788

The hymn was first published as an 8-line st. in *Short Hymns on Select Passages of Holy Scripture,* 1762, under the text "Who is willing

274

to consecrate his service this day unto the Lord?" (I Chronicles 29:5). In *A Collection of Hymns for the Use of the People Called Methodists*, 1780, it was printed in 2 halved sts., the form which it has retained ever since.

The hymn has been included in virtually every American Methodist hymnal and in unaltered form.

Franconia

See "Blest Are the Pure in Heart," pp. 117-18.

Lord, It Belongs Not to My Care (218)

RICHARD BAXTER, 1615-1691

The poem was first published in the author's *Poetical Fragments* (London, 1681).

Beginning:

> My whole, though broken heart, O Lord:
> From henceforth shall be thine,

the text was dated "London, at the Door of Eternity, August 7, 1681," and was entitled "The Covenant and Confidence of Faith." Since his wife had died June 14 of that year, Baxter added, "This covenant, my dear wife, in her former sickness, subscribed with a cheerful will."

In eight 8-line sts., 1-3 and 5-6 seem never to have been used in a hymn. The cento begins st. 4 with "Lord, it belongs" for "Now, it belongs."

The hymn entered the Methodist Episcopal hymnal in 1878 with six 4-line sts. In 1905 it was reduced to the 5 sts. now printed. In our hymnals 2:4 has always been altered from "That shall have the same pay" to its present form.

Horsley

WILLIAM HORSLEY, 1774-1858

This is the third of Horsley's *Twenty-Four Psalm Tunes* (London, 1844). Since no tune names were given, it was named for the composer.

275

Lord Jesus, I Love Thee (166)
WILLIAM R. FEATHERSTONE, 1846-1873

Adequate information about the date of origin of the text is lacking. A. J. Gordon found it in *The London Hymn Book,* 1864, and wrote the tune GORDON which has made it popular. Widely familiar because of its inclusion in all gospel songbooks, it entered the Methodist Protestant hymnal in 1901 in 4 sts. The 1935 Methodist hymnal printed the hymn, omitting st. 3.

The hymn originally began: "My Jesus, I love thee."

Gordon
ADONIRAM J. GORDON, 1836-1895

(See comments on the text, above.) The tune first appeared in the 1876 edition of *The Service of Song for Baptist Churches,* compiled by Gordon and S. L. Caldwell and published in Boston.

Lord Jesus, Think on Me (284)
Μνώεο Χριστέ
SYNESIUS OF CYRENE, c. 375-430
Trans. by ALLEN W. CHATFIELD, 1808-1896

The Greek hymn by the Bishop of Cyrene is the epilogue to a series of 9 hymns setting forth the great themes of Christian doctrine in terms of neoplatonic philosophy, with the prayer "Remember, Lord, your servant who composed these hymns." Chatfield, who translated the entire 10 hymns, published a 5-st. English version in his *Songs and Hymns of the Earliest Greek Christian Poets,* 1876. When he revised his text for inclusion in his *Collected Psalms and Hymns,* the same year, he added 4 new sts.

The hymn entered the Methodist hymnal in 1964, with only slight alterations.

Southwell
WILLIAM DAMON, *The Psalms of David in English Meter,* London, 1579

This is one of the earliest Short Meter tunes, appearing in Damon's collections of 1579 and 1591 as well as in Thomas Ravenscroft, *The Whole Book of Psalms* (London, 1621). In all these editions the fourth and fifth notes of line 3 are raised, making the tune Dorian (a natural minor scale with a raised sixth step).

In Ravenscroft's Psalter it was called a "Northerne Tune" and was harmonized by Martin Peirson. Lowell Mason introduced the tune to America in *The National Psalmist* (Boston, 1848), using William Havergal's version with an opening long note for each line, as found in his *Old Church Psalmody* (London, 1847).

Lord of All Being, Throned Afar (64)

OLIVER W. HOLMES, 1809-1894

The text was first published in the December, 1859, issue of the *Atlantic Monthly,* at the end of the last essay in the series *The Professor at the Breakfast Table.* Surveying his year's record, the "Professor" extended "Peace to all such as may have been vexed in spirit by any utterance these pages have repeated" and gently urged his readers to "forget for the moment the difference in the hues of truth we look at through our human prisms, and join in singing (inwardly) this hymn to the Source of the light we all need to lead us, and the warmth which alone can make us all brothers." Then followed: "A Sun-day Hymn."

The hymn has been in the Methodist Episcopal hymnal since 1878, without alteration.

Louvan

VIRGIL C. TAYLOR, 1817-1891

Set to Thomas Moore, "There's nothing bright above, below," the tune was first published in *The Sacred Minstrel,* 1846. The rhythm has been altered to avoid false accents with the text.

Lord of Life and King of Glory (517)

CHRISTIAN BURKE, 1857-1944

The text was written in December of 1903 and first published in the *Treasury,* a religious periodical, February, 1904. It was the prize-winning entry in a competition for hymns for mothers' meetings. Its first hymnal inclusion appears to have been in *The English Hymnal* (Oxford, 1906).

It entered the Methodist hymnal in 1935.

Sicilian Mariners

See "Lord, Dismiss Us with Thy Blessing," pp. 272-73.

Lord of the Harvest, Hear (339)

CHARLES WESLEY, 1707-1788

The text was published in the 1742 *Hymns and Sacred Poems* and was entitled "A Prayer for Laborers." The hymn has been used in virtually all American Methodist hymnals except those of 1905 and 1935.

Only the Methodist Protestant hymnal of 1837 printed all 6 sts. All other printings excluded the sixth. The first 5 sts. were included until 1847 and 1849, when st. 4 was dropped.

St. Bride

See "Father, in Whom We Live," p. 174.

Lord, Speak to Me, That I May Speak (195)

FRANCES R. HAVERGAL, 1836-1879

The text was written April 28, 1872, at Winterdyne, Bewdley, England. First printed the same year in a leaflet, it was included in the author's collection *Under the Surface,* 1874, with the heading "A Worker's Prayer. None of us liveth unto himself, Romans 14:7."

The hymn originally had 7 sts. It entered Methodist hymnals in 1901 and 1905 with 5 and 6 sts. Our 1935 hymnal omitted Havergal's second, third, and fifth sts. The third st. has been reclaimed for the present hymnal.

Canonbury

ROBERT SCHUMANN, 1810-1856

The adaptation of "Nachtstücke," Op. 23, No. 4, composed in 1839, is first found in J. Ireland Tucker, *Hymnal with Tunes, Old and New,* 1872. During the latter part of the nineteenth century it was popular and fashionable to arrange hymn tunes from classical piano pieces, despite the fact that most sources used were not conceived for vocal performance.

Lord, While for All Mankind We Pray (551)

JOHN R. WREFORD, 1800-1881

Written in 1837 as a "Prayer for our country," the text in 6 sts. was first published in *Lays of Loyalty* and then included in J. R. Beard, *A Collection of Hymns for Public and Private Worship* (London, 1837).

The hymn entered Methodist hymnals in 1847 and 1849 with 4 sts. Methodist Episcopal hymnals always used 1, 3, 4, and 6 of the original; Methodist Episcopal, South, 1, 3, 5, and 6; the 1901 Methodist Protestant printed 1, 3, 4, 5, and 6. Our hymnals have always omitted st. 2.

St. 5 referred originally to England. It has either been omitted, as in the present hymnal, or altered for American usage.

Harlech

Traditional Welsh Melody

The tune, called "March of the Men of Harlech," is taken from the body of Welsh harp music "Gorhoffed Gwŷr Harlech." The music was composed and sung by professional bards and harpers who sang and played in the important houses and inns.

Lord, Whose Love Through Humble Service (479)

ALBERT F. BAYLY, 1901-

The hymn was written in June, 1961, in response to an invitation by the Hymn Society of America to submit hymns on social welfare. After revision by the Hymn Society, it was chosen as Conference Hymn for the second National Conference on the Churches and Social Welfare, October, 1961.

This is its first inclusion in a hymnal.

Beecher

JOHN ZUNDEL, 1815-1882

The tune is included in Zundel's *Christian Heart Songs* (New York, 1870). It was composed for the words "Love divine, all loves excelling," and the tempo listed by the composer calls for 65 seconds per st.! The tune is also called LOVE DIVINE and ZUNDEL, but the more familiar name refers to Henry Ward Beecher with whom Zundel was associated for 28 years.

Love Came Down at Christmas (375)

CHRISTINA G. ROSSETTI, 1830-1894

The poem was first published in the author's *Time Flies; a Reading Diary*, 1885. The original last line, "Love, the universal sign," was later revised by the author herself to its present form.

The hymn entered the Methodist hymnal in 1935.

Garton

Traditional Irish Melody
Harm. by A.C.L.

The tune is found in C. V. Stanford, *A Complete Collection of Irish Music as Noted by George Petrie*, 1902, and is said to be a favorite in County Donegal. It has been reharmonized for the present hymnal.

The name is taken from Lough Gartan, a small lake in Donegal, Ireland.

Love Divine, All Loves Excelling (283)

CHARLES WESLEY, 1707-1788

The hymn in 4 sts. was first printed in *Hymns for Those That Seek, and Those That Have, Redemption in the Blood of Jesus Christ*, 1747. Already in 1761, 2:5 ("Take away our *power* of sinning") caused sufficient concern to permit the whole st. to be dropped from a new Wesley collection, *Hymns for Those to Whom Christ Is All in All*. Charles had italicized "power" in 1747, probably anticipating criticism. But John Fletcher asked, "Is not this expression too strong? Would it not be better to soften it by saying, 'Take away the love of sinning'? (or the bent of the mind towards sin). Can God take away from us our *power of sinning* without taking away our power of free obedience?" John Wesley also objected to this extreme view of Christian perfection and omitted the st. from *A Collection of Hymns for the Use of the People Called Methodists*, 1780. However, the st. continued to be printed in a variety of hymnals. In Augustus M. Toplady, *Psalms and Hymns for Public and Private Worship*, 1776, and in the Countess of Huntingdon's *A Select Collection of Hymns to be Universally Sung in the Countess of Huntingdon's Chapel*, 1786, "love" replaced "power." It was included in the 1787 edition of *A Pocket Hymn-Book*, where "bent of" appeared (changed to "bent to" by

1829). Coke and Asbury retained "bent" when they adapted the York book for Methodists in America, with the result that it has since been printed in all our hymnals.

Several other important alterations have been made. In 1760, Martin Madan, *A Collection of Psalms and Hymns,* altered "second rest" (2:4) to "promised rest." This emendation was adopted by Toplady, the Countess of Huntingdon, and R. Conyers, *A Collection of Psalms and Hymns from Various Authors* (1st ed.; London, 1767). Only the Methodist Protestant hymnal of 1901 and the 1935 hymnal adopted "promised." Madan also printed "love" instead of "loves" in st. 1, a change which was followed by several eighteenth- and nineteenth-century editors. The singular appeared in our 1849, 1878, and all 3 Methodist Protestant hymnals. "Loves" was restored in 1905. The line is obviously modeled on Dryden's "Fairest Isle, all isles excelling."

In 1:2, John Wesley inserted a comma after "heaven," making "to earth come down" a prayer instead of a declaration of faith. Our hymnals have printed the comma since 1849. "Life" (3:2) was altered to "grace" by John in 1780. "Grace" continues to be printed in English Methodist hymnals as it was in our hymnals of 1905 and 1935. The present hymnal returns to the original.

"Sinless" (4:2) has been altered variously to "unspotted" and "holy." John adopted "spotless" in 1780, the word which has been printed in American Methodist hymnals from the beginning.

Beecher

See **"Lord, Whose Love Through Humble Service,"** p. 279.

Low in the Grave He Lay (444)

ROBERT LOWRY, 1826-1899

The text and tune (CHRIST AROSE) were written in 1874 when Lowry was pastor of a Baptist church in Brooklyn. It was first published in *Brightest and Best* (Chicago, 1875), a collection edited by Lowry and William H. Doane. Widely printed in gospel songbooks, it makes its first appearance here in an official Methodist hymnal.

Christ Arose

ROBERT LOWRY, 1826-1899

See comments on text, above.

Majestic Sweetness Sits Enthroned (83)

SAMUEL STENNETT, 1727-1795

The text first appeared in 1787 in John Rippon, *A Selection of Hymns from the Best Authors, Intended to Be an Appendix to Dr. Watts's Psalms and Hymns.* In 9 sts., based on the Song of Solomon 5:10-16, it was entitled "Chief among ten thousand; or the Excellencies of Christ." The opening st. read:

> To Christ, the Lord, let every Tongue
> Its noblest Tribute bring:
> When he's the Subject of the Song
> Who can refuse to sing?

The hymn entered Methodist hymnals in 1847 with 4 sts. (3, 5, 8, 9) and 1878 with 6 (3, 4, 5, 7, 8, 9). In 1905, st. 4 was dropped; in 1935, st. 4 replaced 5, and 9 was dropped; in 1964, sts. 8 and 4 have been replaced by 5 and 9. Sts. 1, 2, and 6 have never been used. Centos used have always begun with st. 3: "Majestic sweetness sits enthroned." Our 1964 hymnal uses 3, 5, 7, and 9.

There is only one notable change in the text. Our first st. originally had for its second line: "Upon his awful Brow."

Ortonville

THOMAS HASTINGS, 1784-1872

Written in the key of C, the tune first appeared in Hastings' *Manhattan Collection* (New York, 1837) with this text for which it was written.

Make Me a Captive, Lord (184)

GEORGE MATHESON, 1842-1906

The hymn was written in 1890 at Row, Dumbartonshire, Scotland, and published the same year in the author's *Sacred Songs.* It was entitled "Christian Freedom" and printed under the biblical text "Paul, the prisoner of Jesus Christ" (Ephesians 3:1). The 4 sts. entered the Methodist hymnal in 1935.

Diademata

See "Crown Him with Many Crowns," p. 162.

Many and Great, O God (40)

American Folk Hymn
Paraphrase by PHILIP FRAZIER, 1892-1964

The hymn is taken from *Dakota Odowan* (the Dakota Hymn Book), first published in 1879. A joint product of the early missionaries A. L. Riggs, John P. Williamson, and J. R. Murray, the hymnal was published by the American Missionary Association and the Presbyterian Board of Foreign Missions. Having been revised 5 times, the book is still being used by the Dakota Congregational and Presbyterian churches. The base of the hymn is Jeremiah 10:12-13.

Since the hymn was becoming popular with Y.W.C.A. groups, but with Indian words, the chairman of the music committee of the national Y.W.C.A. in 1929 requested Frazier to make an English version. Mr. Frazier paraphrased the first and last sts., and he and Mrs. Frazier presented the paraphrase at the national convention of the Y.W.C.A. in Detroit in 1930. The hymn in this form now appears in all the *Young Camp* songbooks and also in *Hymns of the Rural Spirit.*

Its appearance in our 1964 hymnal is its first inclusion in a major hymnal.

Lacquiparle

American Folk Hymn

(See comments on text, above.)

The tune first appeared with a typical nineteenth-century harmonization by J. R. Murray, but has been simply reharmonized for the 1964 hymnal.

It is the tune the Dakota Indians sang as they followed their dead to the final resting place. The tune name in French means "lake that speaks."

March On, O Soul, with Strength (243)

GEORGE T. COSTER, 1835-1912

Written in Bedford Park, London, August 3, 1897, the text first appeared in the February, 1898, issue of the *Evangelical Magazine,*

London. Its first hymnal inclusion was in *Hessle Hymns*, 1901. The author was at the time minister of Trinity Church, Hessle.

Entitled "Battle Song," it was introduced by the text "O my soul, march on with strength" (Judges 5:21). The hymn was originally in 6 sts. and in 66.66.86. meter. In addition to the omission of the original sts. 3 and 4, and the alteration of the metrical scheme, a few words have been changed.

With sts. 1, 2, 5, and 6, the hymn entered the Methodist hymnal in 1935.

Arthur's Seat

Arr. from **JOHN GOSS**, 1800-1880
by **UZZIAH C. BURNAP**, 1834-1900

The tune first appeared in *Hymns and Songs of Praise* (New York, 1874), whose musical editors were Burnap and John K. Paine. The tune name is taken from a hill 823 feet high overlooking Edinburgh, named for Arthur, the British prince who defeated the Saxons in that region.

Master, Speak! Thy Servant Heareth (274)

FRANCES R. HAVERGAL, 1836-1879

The hymn in 9 sts. was written on Sunday evening, May 19, 1867, at Weston super Mare, a seaside resort in England. It was first published in the author's *Ministry of Song*, 1869, with the title "Master, Say On!" Its biblical base is the conversation between Eli and Samuel (I Samuel 3:1-10).

The hymn entered the Methodist hymnal in 1935 with sts. 1, 5, 8, and 9.

Amen, Jesus han skal raade

ANTON P. BERGGREEN, 1801-1880

The tune was written in 1849 and published in 1853 in Berggreen's *Psalm Tunes*. The name means "Amen, Jesus, he shall reign."

May the Grace of Christ Our Savior (334)

JOHN NEWTON, 1725-1807

A metrical paraphrase of II Corinthians 13:14, the hymn was written to be sung after the sermon. Its first appearance was in *Olney Hymns*,

1779. Originally a single st. of 8 lines, it was so used in our 1847, 1849, and 1899 hymnals. Halved in 1878, it has since been sung in 2 sts.

Stuttgart

See "Earth Has Many a Noble City," pp. 166-67.

Men and Children Everywhere (11)

JOHN J. MOMENT, 1875-1959

The hymn is taken from *The Hymnal* of the Presbyterian Church, U.S.A., edited by Clarence Dickinson in 1933. It is dated 1930.

This is its first inclusion in a Methodist hymnal.

Rock of Ages

Traditional Hebrew Melody

This is the well-known MOOZ TSUR, first sung in the home at the kindling of the Hanukkah lights. Later the tune was introduced into the synagogue.

A. Z. Idelsohn points out the similarity of measures 1-4 to the German tune NUN FREUT EUCH and the last 2 measures to the popular German battlesong "Benzenauer," composed in 1504. Thus the tune has typical German characteristics which make it a part of the songs of Ashkenazim, Jews living in western, central, and eastern Europe and their descendants in America, Africa, Asia, and Australia. Originally it meant only the German Jews.

Idelsohn gives measures 13-16 thus:

Mid All the Traffic of the Ways (225)

JOHN OXENHAM, 1852-1941

Written during World War I, the poem was published in the author's collection *The Vision Splendid,* 1917. It is entitled "Sanctuary" and has 7 sts.

The hymn entered the Methodist hymnal in 1935 with sts. 1, 2, 3, and 6.

Horsley

See "Lord, It Belongs Not to My Care," p. 275.

Mine Eyes Have Seen the Glory (545)

Stanzas 1–4, JULIA WARD HOWE, 1819-1910
Stanza 5, ANONYMOUS

In December, 1861, Mrs. Howe and her husband journeyed to Washington in the company of Governor Andrew of Massachusetts and his wife. Troops were encamped around the city. According to Mrs. Howe's own account, "The gallop of horsemen, the tramp of foot-soldiers, the noise of drum, fife, and bugle were heard continually." One day, with friends, including her pastor James Freeman Clarke, she went several miles outside the city to watch a review of federal troops. The maneuvers were, however, interrupted by a sudden attack of the enemy, and in the confusion Mrs. Howe and her party attempted to return to the city on a road congested by troops. To while away the time, they began to sing army songs. After they sang "John Brown's body lies a-mouldering in the grave," someone remarked on the excellence of the tune. Mrs. Howe said she had often wished to write some words which might be sung to it, and before dawn the next morning she found herself weaving together line after line and st. after st. Groping for paper and pen, she wrote them down. A day or so later she repeated the lines to Dr. Clarke, who expressed delight in them. On her return to Boston, she carried the work to James T. Field, editor of the *Atlantic Monthly,* who proposed the title "Battle Hymn of the Republic" and published the poem in the February, 1862, issue of the magazine.

The song soon attracted the attention of a Methodist chaplain, C. C. McCabe, later to become a bishop, who taught it to the 122nd Ohio volunteers to which he was attached, then to other troops, and also to prisoners in Libby prison where he was a prisoner of war.

The hymn entered the Methodist hymnal in 1964, with the omission of the original st. 3:

I have read a fiery gospel writ in burnished rows of steel:
"As ye deal with my contemners, so with you my grace shall deal;

Let the Hero, born of woman, crush the serpent with his heel,
Since God is marching on."

Our st. 5 was not written by Mrs. Howe. It is frequently made a part of the hymn in British hymnals and may have originated in England. It remains anonymous.

Battle Hymn of the Republic
American Camp-meeting Tune

Though the tune has been attributed to William Steffe, there is no proof of his authorship. It is a variant of an old camp-meeting tune, "Say, brothers, will you meet us." William J. Reynolds suggests that the tune apparently originated in South Carolina. It was well known before the Civil War.

More Love to Thee, O Christ (185)
ELIZABETH P. PRENTISS, 1818-1878

Though the text was written probably as early as 1856, Mrs. Prentiss did not make its existence known for many years. It was first printed in a leaflet in 1869. Its first hymnal inclusion was with the tune in William H. Doane, *Songs of Devotion for Christian Associations,* 1870.

St. 3, though sometimes omitted as in the 1878 Methodist Episcopal, the 1901 Methodist Protestant, and the 1935 Methodist hymnals, discloses the physical suffering and mental anguish from which Mrs. Prentiss wrote. The hymn has been included in all our hymnals since the Methodist Episcopal of 1878.

More Love to Thee
WILLIAM H. DOANE, 1832-1915

Written for this text, the tune first appeared in Doane's *Songs of Devotion for Christian Associations* (New York, 1870).

Must Jesus Bear the Cross Alone (183)
THOMAS SHEPHERD, 1665-1739, and others

The origin and transmission of the text are obscure. St. 1 is said to be an altered form of a quatrain which originally appeared in Shepherd's *Penitential Cries,* dated 1693 by John Julian. Its original form was:

> Shall Simon bear the cross alone,
> And other saints be free?
> Each saint of thine shall find his own
> And there is one for me.

While no hymnal printing this form has been available to us, *The American Church Harp,* edited by W. R. Rhinehart (Dayton, Ohio, 1856), prints our current first st., but with the original "Simon" instead of "Jesus." This 1856 imprint contains 4 sts. in a somewhat irregular meter: 14.14.16.13., with the last phrase of 6 syllables repeated. The 3 sts. of the hymn as we know it are the first half of each of sts. 1–3 in the 1856 book.

Our st. 2, according to Julian, is first found in a missionary collection published at Norwich, England, c. 1810, author unknown. However, both our sts. 2 and 3 were taken from *The Oberlin Social and Sabbath School Hymn Book,* compiled by George N. Allen, variously dated 1844 and 1849. The edition available to us is dated 1846.

The Oberlin printing of the first 2 lines of the third st. reads:

> I'll bear the consecrated cross,
> Till from the cross I'm free.

The 1856 Dayton hymnal alters "I'll" to "We'll." The first printing of the hymn exactly as it appeared in Methodist hymnals since 1878 appears to be that of H. W. Beecher, *Plymouth Collection of Hymns,* 1855. Apparently it was Beecher who altered 3:1-2 to its present form.

Beecher credited the hymn to Allen, the editor of the Oberlin collection. *Plymouth Collection* added 3 sts. of unknown origin, but ascribed to the editor's brother, C. Beecher. The third of these, altered slightly, is printed in some hymnals as a fourth st.:

> O precious cross! O glorious crown!
> O resurrection day!
> Ye angels! from the stars flash down,
> And bear my soul away.

Maitland

GEORGE N. ALLEN, 1812-1877

Allen composed the tune for this text for inclusion in his *Oberlin Social and Sabbath School Hymn Book,* 1846. In Beecher's *Plymouth Collection,* 1855, it was incorrectly called a "Western Melody." It is also known as CROSS AND CROWN.

My Country, 'Tis of Thee (547)

SAMUEL F. SMITH, 1808-1895

Traditional accounts of the origin of "America" are based on the author's recollections, often retold with variations, and as we have them, written several years after the event. Henry S. Burrage's account in his *Baptist Hymn Writers and Their Hymns,* 1888, is most frequently quoted. In J. T. Howard, *Our American Music,* 1965 edition, one of Smith's own statements is printed. According to this story, in 1831 William C. Woodbridge returned from Europe bringing a number of German music books which he gave to Lowell Mason. Mason brought the books to Smith, then a theological student at Andover Theological Seminary, saying, "Here, I can't read these, but they contain good music, which I should be glad to use. Turn over the leaves, and if you find anything particularly good, give me a translation or imitation of it, or write a wholly original song—anything, so I can use it." Sometime later, Smith, in looking over the books, was struck with the tune of "God save the King." "I think I instantly felt the impulse to write a patriotic hymn of my own adapted to the tune. Picking up a scrap of waste paper which lay near me, I wrote at once, probably within half an hour, the hymn 'America' as it is now known everywhere." When asked to date the writing, Smith is reported to have said that it was first written at Andover, Mass., February, 1832. "The first time it was sung publicly was at a children's celebration of American independence, at the Park Street Church, Boston, I think, July 4, 1832."

It now appears, however, that Smith recalled 2 of his dates incorrectly. Woodbridge returned from Europe in 1829, not in 1831. And the program of the Boston Sabbath School Union at Park Street Church, 2 copies of which exist, definitely dates the celebration in

1831. An account of the affair was printed in *Christian Watchman,* July 8, 1831.

The first collection to include the hymn was Mason's *Choir, or Union Collection of Church Music,* 1832.

The Park Street Church program prints 5 sts., the third of which seems never again to have been printed.

The hymn entered the Methodist Episcopal hymnal in 1878.

America

ANONYMOUS in *Thesaurus Musicus,* 1744

According to F. Chrysander in Vol. I of *Jahrbücher für musikalische Wissenschaft,* the tune first appeared in 1744 in *Thesaurus Musicus.* In the style of a galliard, it seems to have both German and English ancestry. Since at least the 1740's it has been used with the text "God save the King." Though Smith's impetus for writing the text came from the tune he found in a German collection, the tune had already appeared by that time in *The Christian Lyre,* Vol. I, 1830, set to 2 texts and called CREATION. This collection contained the most familiar tunes of the time, indicating that the tune was well known to many singers.

My Faith Looks Up to Thee (143)

RAY PALMER, 1808-1887

On graduating from Yale in 1830, the author went to New York to teach for a year in a "select school for young ladies" which was patronized by "the best class of families" and was in a section "occupied by genteel residences." Palmer resided in the family of the lady who kept the school, and it was there that the hymn was written. According to the account in Palmer's *Poetical Works,* 1876, the 6 sts. of the hymn were unprompted by any external occasion whatever. They "were composed and imperfectly written, first on a loose sheet, and then accurately copied into a small morocco-covered book. . . . This first complete copy is still—1875—preserved."

Then a year or 2 after the hymn was written, Lowell Mason met the author on the street, requested some hymns for a hymn and tune book that he and Thomas Hastings were about to publish. Palmer got out the little book, gave a copy of the hymn to Mason who promptly sat down and wrote the tune OLIVET. The combination first circulated in the Hastings-Mason collection *Spiritual Songs for Social Worship*. The date of this imprint is variously given as 1831, 1832, and 1833.

Confusion here may be because the 1832 imprint of *Spiritual Songs for Social Worship* is copyrighted 1831 but has a preface dated 1832.

No more than our 4 sts. seem ever to have been printed. The hymn entered the Methodist Episcopal hymnal in 1849 and has been included in all later Methodist hymnals unaltered.

Olivet

LOWELL MASON, 1792-1872

See comments on text, above.

My God, I Thank Thee (50)

ADELAIDE A. PROCTER, 1825-1864

The hymn was first published in the author's *Legends and Lyrics*, 1858, in 6 sts. It entered the Methodist hymnal in 1905 with 5 sts., omitting the original fourth. The 1935 hymnal dropped 3, 6, and 7; the 1964 hymnal has reclaimed st. 3.

Wentworth

FREDERICK C. MAKER, 1844-1927

The first appearance of the tune was in the second series of *The Bristol Tune Book*, 1876. It was edited in the 1935 Methodist hymnal with ties and slurs to avoid poor accentuations in the text.

My Hope Is Built on Nothing Less (222)

EDWARD MOTE, 1797-1874

The text appeared in Rees's collection, 1836, but is best known as printed in *Hymns of Praise, A New Selection of Gospel Hymns,* by Mote, published the same year. In 6 sts., it was entitled "The immutable Basis of a Sinner's hope." It began: "Nor earth, nor hell, my soul can move."

The hymn entered the Methodist Episcopal hymnal in 1878 with 3 sts., to which a fourth was added in 1905. Already the first 2 original sts. had been recombined to make a new first st. out of 2*a* and 1*b*. Our sts. 2, 3, and 4 are 3, 4, and 6 of the original. All received early alterations. Mote wrote:

2:2 I rest upon unchanging grace
  3 In every rough and stormy gale.
3:2 Supports me in the sinking flood
4:1 When I shall launch in worlds unseen
  2 O may I then be found in him.

The original st. 5 has never been used in our hymnals.

The Solid Rock

WILLIAM B. BRADBURY, 1816-1868

The tune was composed for this text in 1863 and published in Bradbury's *Devotional Hymn and Tune Book* (Philadelphia, 1864).

My Jesus, As Thou Wilt (167)
Mein Jesu, wie du willt

BENJAMIN SCHMOLCK, 1672-1737
Trans. by JANE BORTHWICK, 1813-1897

Based on Mark 14:36, "Abba, Father, all things are possible unto thee; take away this cup from me: nevertheless not what I will, but what thou wilt," the text in 11 sts. was first published in Schmolck's *Heilige Flammen der himmlisch gesinnten Seele,* 1704. Jane Borthwick translated 7 sts., omitting sts. 2, 6, 7, and 9 of the original, for her *Hymns from the Land of Luther,* 1854.

The hymn entered the Methodist Episcopal hymnal in 1878 with sts. 1, 4, and 7. These 3 have been retained in all our hymnals since. The 1889 Methodist Episcopal, South, the 1901 Methodist Protestant, and the 1905 Methodist hymnals added Borthwick's second st. to make a 4-st. hymn:

> My Jesus, as Thou wilt!
>   If needy here and poor,
> Give me Thy people's bread,
>   Their portion rich and sure.
> The manna of Thy word
>   Let my soul feed upon;
> And if all else should fail—
> My Lord, Thy will be done!

Munich

Neuvermehrtes Gesangbuch, Meiningen, 1693
Harm. by **FELIX MENDELSSOHN, 1809-1847**

The tune is based on a melody from the third edition of the Meiningen *Gesangbuch*, set to "O Gott, du frommer Gott." Mendelssohn adapted it for "Cast thy burden upon the Lord" in *Elijah*, 1847, and it is his form and harmonization which have been adopted by hymnal editors. For this text the meter has been altered to fit 66.66.D.

It is also called KÖNIGSBERG.

My Soul, Be on Thy Guard (246)

GEORGE HEATH, 1750-1822

The hymn first appeared in Heath's *Hymns and Poetic Essays Sacred to the Public and Private Worship of the Deity* (Bristol, 1781). Alterations have been made in every st. except the second. The original read:

1:3 An host of sins are pressing hard.
3:2 Nor once at ease sit down
  3 Thy arduous work will not be done
  4 Till thy hast got thy crown.
4:2 God will the work applaud
  3 Reveal his love at thy last breath
  4 And take to his abode.

Most of the alterations had taken place before the hymn entered our hymnals in 1837 with the Methodist Protestant and the 1849 Methodist Episcopal.

Laban

LOWELL MASON, 1792-1872

Called CONFLICT, the tune was composed in 1830 and published in Mason's *Spiritual Songs for Social Worship* (Utica, 1832), where it was marked "Arr. for Air and 2^d Treble. Allegro. Staccato." Mason used a fermata on the last note of the third phrase in the first 2 editions, but in later books he used the dull rhythmic form which is found in the 1935 hymnal. The tune is published in cut time, which adds vigor to the setting.

Nearer, My God, to Thee (263)

SARAH F. ADAMS, 1805-1848

The text is 1 of 13 texts submitted by Mrs. Adams to William J. Fox for use in his *Hymns and Anthems,* 1841, a collection prepared for the use of his congregation at the Unitarian South Place Chapel, Finsbury, England. Its first American inclusion was in J. F. Clarke, *The Disciples' Hymn Book* (Boston, 1844).

The hymn has been included in its original form in all our hymnals since the 1878 Methodist Episcopal hymnal.

Bethany

LOWELL MASON, 1792-1872

The tune was composed in 1856 at the request of Edward A. Park and Austin Phelps for the *Sabbath Hymn and Tune Book* (Andover, 1859). Mason wrote to a friend in 1868:

They applied to me for a musical setting for the hymn, "Nearer, My God, to Thee." The metre was irregular. But one night some time after, lying awake in the dark, eyes wide open, through the stillness of the house the melody came to me, and the next morning I wrote down the notes of BETHANY.

Robert G. McCutchan suggests that the tune was prompted by the air "Oft in the stilly night."

Mason chose biblical names for many of his tunes without any specific reason or appropriateness.

Ne'er Forget God's Daily Care (519)

CHAO TZU-CH'EN, 1888-
Trans. by BLISS WIANT, 1895-

The hymn is taken from the author's compilation *Hymns for the People,* 1931. Bliss Wiant translated the text for use in lecturing on Chinese hymns when on furlough in America in 1946. It was first published in pamphlet form by Lynn Rohrbough's Cooperative Recreation Service. Its first hymnal inclusion is in our 1964 hymnal.

Wiant

Chinese Melody
Arr. by BLISS WIANT, 1895-

The tune was collected in 1929 by Bliss Wiant from his students at Yenching University, Peking, and was first used with the text in

Hymns for the People (Peking, 1931), which contained 50 Chinese tunes and 50 original hymn texts written by Chao Tzu-ch'en.

Never Further Than Thy Cross (430)

ELIZABETH R. CHARLES, 1828-1896

The text was first published in the *Family Treasury* (London, 1860), and then in the author's *Poems,* 1867.

It entered the Methodist Episcopal hymnal in 1878, with the original fourth st. omitted. Originally 2:1 read "Gazing thus." It was altered to "Here, O Christ" in 1935. In 4:2, "shall" was changed to "must" in 1878.

Canterbury

See **"Christ, from Whom All Blessings Flow,"** pp. 130-31.

New Every Morning Is the Love (499)

JOHN KEBLE, 1792-1866

Entitled "Morning" and prefaced by "His compassions fail not. They are new every morning" (Lamentations 3:22b-23a), and beginning "Hues of the rich unfolding morn," Keble's 16-st. poem was written in 1822. In 1827 it was first published in *The Christian Year,* a collection of meditations on the themes of the liturgical year.

The hymn entered the Methodist Episcopal hymnal of 1878 with a cento of 5 sts.: 6, 7, 8, 14, and 16. In 1935, st. 8 was dropped and the ninth added:

> If in our daily course our mind
> Be set to hallow all we find,
> New treasures still, of countless price,
> God will provide for sacrifice.
>
> Old friends, old scenes, will lovelier be,
> As more of heaven in each we see:
> Some softening gleam of love and prayer
> Shall dawn on every cross and care.

295

The hymn has been reduced to 4 sts. for the 1964 hymnal. Sts. 9, 8*b*, and 14*b* were dropped, and a new st. (our third) was recomposed from 14*a* and 8*a*.

Melcombe

SAMUEL WEBBE, SR., 1740-1816
Rhythm altered by A.C.L.

The tune is taken from *An Essay on the Church Plain Chant* (London, 1782), where it was set to "O Salutaris." It was given its present name in Ralph Harrison, *Sacred Harmony—A Collection of Psalm-tunes, Ancient and Modern* (2nd vol., 1791), and its harmonization by William H. Monk in *Hymns Ancient and Modern*, 1861, where it was wedded to this text. The rhythm has been altered in the present hymnal to avoid the monotony of all quarter notes and to allow more time for breath at phrase endings.

It is also called NAZARETH.

Not Alone for Mighty Empire (548)

WILLIAM P. MERRILL, 1867-1954

The text was probably written in 1909, when Dr. Merrill was pastor of Sixth Avenue Presbyterian Church in Chicago. According to the author's own account, while attending a union Thanksgiving service, he was much moved by a prayer offered by Jenkin Lloyd Jones which spoke meaningfully of the spiritual blessings and assets of our country. "I went home and wrote a rather diffusive hymn about it and later made it over into the present one."

It was first printed in the *Continent*, 1911, a Presbyterian paper formerly published in Chicago. The hymn entered the Methodist hymnal in 1935.

Hyfrydol

See **"Come, Thou Long-Expected Jesus,"** pp. 154-55.

Now, on Land and Sea Descending (505)

SAMUEL LONGFELLOW, 1819-1892

The text in two 8-line sts. first appeared in *Vespers,* 1859, a collection of hymns for use in the Second Unitarian Church, Brooklyn, where

Longfellow was then pastor. It was later included in *Hymns of the Spirit,* edited by Longfellow and Samuel Johnson, 1864. It has been in the Methodist hymnal since 1935.

Vesper Hymn

Russian Air
A Selection of Popular National Airs, 1818

Sir John Stevenson included the tune as a glee for 4 voices in *A Selection of Popular National Airs* (London, 1818), calling it a "Russian Air" and adding a last line of his own composition. Though it has been often credited to Dimitri Bortniansky, no proof has yet been found.

Joshua Leavitt included the tune in *The Christian Lyre,* 1830, giving it an early start in American hymnody.

Now Praise We Great and Famous Men (532)

WILLIAM G. TARRANT, 1853-1928

This metrical paraphrase of Ecclesiasticus 44:1-15 was first published in the author's *Songs of the Devout,* 1912. The original last st. is omitted:

> So praise we great and famous men,
> The fathers named in story;
> And praise the Lord, who now as then
> Reveals in man his glory.

Ach Gott und Herr

As Hymnodus Sacer, **Leipzig, 1625**

The hymn tune has undergone many changes. It was originally in minor, but Christoph Peter put it in major in *Andachts-Zymbeln* (Freiberg, 1655). Johann Crüger modified the second half in 1640, and Bach regularized the rhythm in his *Vierstimmige Choralgesänge* (Leipzig, 1769). The original form was:

Now Thank We All Our God (49)
Nun danket alle Gott

MARTIN RINKART, 1586-1649
Trans. by CATHERINE WINKWORTH, 1827-1878

Known as the German *Te Deum,* the hymn is the most celebrated hymn of the second period of German hymn writing, 1570-1648. It probably appeared first in Rinkart's *Jesu Herz-Büchlein,* 1636, though no copy of this book survives. It does appear in the 1663 edition. It was set in Johann Crüger, *Praxis Pietatis Melica,* 1647 (see comments on tune, below). Though the hymn has been associated with important public events such as the Peace of Westphalia at the close of the Thirty Years' War, or the centenary of the Augsburg Confession, its origin seems to be more modest. The first 2 sts. are a *Tischlied,* grace before meat, to which a metrical version of the *Gloria Patri* has been added as a third.

The English translation is that in the second series of Catherine Winkworth's *Lyra Germanica,* 1858.

The hymn entered the Methodist Protestant hymnals of 1882 and 1901 in the 3 sts. unaltered. In the 1905 Methodist hymnal it appeared with the first 2 sts. only, to which the third was added in 1935.

Nun danket

JOHANN CRÜGER, 1598-1662
Harm. by FELIX MENDELSSOHN, 1809-1847

The original form of the tune appeared anonymously in Crüger's *Praxis Pietatis Melica* (4th ed.; Berlin, 1647). Mendelssohn altered the melody and harmonized it in 6 parts for his *Lobgesang* (Hymn of Praise), 1840. It is his version, reduced to 4 voices, which appears in all modern hymnals.

Now the Day Is Over (495)

SABINE BARING-GOULD, 1834-1924

The text in 8 sts. with the biblical inspiration of Proverbs 3:24 was written for the children of Horbury Bridge, near Wakefield, England, while the author was curate there. It was first published in the *Church Times,* February 16, 1867, and then included in the Appendix to *Hymns Ancient and Modern,* 1868. The hymn entered the Methodist hymnal in 1905 with 6 sts.

Merrial

JOSEPH BARNBY, 1838-1896

Composed in 1868, the tune was first published in Barnby's *Original Hymn Tunes*, 1869, with no tune name. Charles S. Robinson introduced the tune to America in *Spiritual Songs*, calling it EMMELAR, a name made from his daughter's initials, M. L. R. Later he changed it to MERRIAL, for his daughter's name, Mary L. The tune is much more popular in the United States than in Britain.

Now the Green Blade Riseth (441)

J. M. C. CRUM, 1872-1958

"Love is come again" was written for the old French tune associated with the carol "Noël nouvelet." It is taken from *The Oxford Book of Carols* (London, 1928), edited by Percy Dearmer, R. Vaughan Williams, and Martin Shaw. This is its first printing in a Methodist hymnal.

French Carol

Traditional French Carol
Harm. by MARTIN SHAW, 1875-1958

(See comments on text, above.) The tune was included in *The Oxford Book of Carols* in a harmonization by Martin Shaw to carry a new Easter text by Crum. It is in the Dorian mode, with a raised sixth step. The melody is the basis for Marcel Dupré's famous *Variations on a Noel*.

O Beautiful for Spacious Skies (543)

KATHARINE LEE BATES, 1859-1929

The original version of the poem was written in the summer of 1893. At the end of a summer school in Colorado Springs, where she had lectured on English religious drama, Miss Bates with other instructors celebrated the close of the session by making an expedition to the top of Pike's Peak. Because of the discomfort caused by the rarefied air, the party remained only long enough for "one ecstatic gaze." "It was then and there," she wrote in 1918, "as I was looking out over the sea-like expanse of fertile country spreading away so far under those ample skies, that the opening lines of the hymn floated into my mind. When we left Colorado Springs the four stanzas were pencilled in my note-book." The lines were neglected until 2 summers later when Miss Bates copied them out and sent them to the *Congregationalist,* where they first appeared in print, July 4, 1895.

This 1895 version was much inferior to the text as finally copyrighted by the author. Original lines read:

1:1   O beautiful for halcyon skies
  4   Above the enameled plain
7-8   Till souls wax fair as earth and air
       And music-hearted sea!

2:7-8 Till paths be wrought through wilds of thought
         By pilgrim foot and knee!

3:1   O beautiful for glory-tale,
  3   When once and twice, for man's avail,
  4   Men lavished precious life!
7-8   Till selfish gain no longer stain
       The banner of the free!

4:7-8 Till nobler men keep once again
         Thy whiter jubilee!

In 1904 Miss Bates rewrote the hymn making the phraseology more simple and direct. In this form it was first published in the *Evening Transcript* of Boston, November 19, 1904. Sts. 1, 2, and 4 appeared exactly then as they are used today. While lines 5-8 of the difficult third st. were revised to their present form, the first 4 lines still limped. It was only "after the lapse of a few years, during which the hymn had run the gauntlet of criticism, I changed the wording of the opening quatrain of the third stanza." The 1904 version read:

> O beautiful for glory-tale
> Of liberating strife,
> When valiantly for man's avail,
> Men lavished precious life!

The final copyrighted form of the text, as printed in our hymnal, dates at least from 1918, the year in which Miss Bates wrote a history of the hymn for the library of the Boston Athenaeum.

The imagery of the fourth st., the "alabaster cities," and "whiter jubilee" of the first version were inspired by the "White City" of the Columbian World's Exposition at Chicago, which Miss Bates visited on the way west.

The hymn entered our hymnal in 1935.

Materna
SAMUEL A. WARD, 1847-1903

The tune was composed for the hymn "O mother dear, Jerusalem" —hence the tune name meaning "motherly." There are 2 conflicting stories about its composition. One is that Ward jotted down the tune on his cuff while crossing New York harbor to Coney Island in 1882, and that it was first sung by a choir of 200 men and boys at Grace Episcopal Church, Newark, N.J., where Ward was organist. The other story is that the tune was composed in memory of his eldest daughter, Clara, who died in 1885. This version is given by Ward's son-in-law, Henry W. Armstrong.

It was first published in the *Parish Choir*, July 12, 1888, and then included in Charles L. Hutchins, *The Church Hymnal*, 1894. In 1912 it was wedded to this text when the president of Massachusetts Agricultural College asked permission of Mrs. Ward to set the tune to Miss Bates's text.

O Brother Man, Fold to Thy Heart Thy Brother (199)
JOHN GREENLEAF WHITTIER, 1807-1892

Whittier's 15-st. poem "Worship" was written in 1848 and published in his *Labor and Other Poems*, 1850, prefaced by James 1:27. The poem expresses contempt for pagan forms of worship: "red altars . . . smoked with warm blood . . . dismal moaning of dirge-like music and sepulchral prayer; pale wizard priests . . . the pomp of rituals . . . the savor of gums and spices . . . the poor flattery of the organ keys." Rather, "the benignant Father" requires only the simple duty of man to man. Then follow the sts. from which our cento is made.

The hymn entered the Methodist hymnal in 1935 with sts. 13, 11, and 14. A fourth st., Whittier's fifteenth and last, was appropriately added in 1964.

Welwyn

ALFRED SCOTT-GATTY, 1847-1918

The tune is from *Arundel Hymns* (London, 1902), a Roman Catholic collection. It came into wide Protestant usage through inclusion in the revised *Church Hymnary* (Edinburgh, 1927).

O Come, All Ye Faithful (386)
Adeste, fideles

ANONYMOUS, Latin, 18th Century
Trans. by FREDERICK OAKELEY, 1802-1880,
and others

Seven manuscripts containing the Latin hymn are known; they are dated 1743-61. All appear to have been written, signed, and dated by John Francis Wade, an Englishman who made his living by copying and selling plainchant and other music, and who carried on his business at the great French Catholic center, Douay. Dom John Stéphan in his extensive study of the manuscripts, *The Adeste Fideles: A Study on Its Origin and Development*, 1947, concludes that the 1743 manuscript is the *first* and *original* version of the hymn, and that Wade composed the words and music sometime between 1740 and 1743.

With the 4 original sts. the hymn circulated widely in Winchester, Dublin, Portugal, Edinburgh, Paris, and apparently throughout Europe. Three additional sts. were added to the Latin hymn early in the nineteenth century, probably by Abbé Etienne Jean François Borderies, sometime after his return to France in 1794, after exile in England where he heard the hymn. These 3 sts. together with the first st. are extant in an 1822 imprint and make up the usual French form of the hymn. The 7 were reproduced with an English translation in London, 1847. These 7 may be found in Latin and English parallel columns in *Historical Companion to Hymns Ancient & Modern*, 1962, pp. 146-47.

The Oakeley translation was made in 1841 for use in his chapel in London—now known as All Saints', Margaret Street—and from the original 4-st. Latin text used in England. His original translation began "Ye faithful, approach ye." The first line was changed to the familiar form when first printed in F. H. Murray, *A Hymnal for Use in the English Church* (London, 1852).

The hymn entered the Methodist hymnal in 1905 with 4 sts. in the less-popular Edward Caswall translation, made in 1849 for *Lyra Catholica*. Our 1935 hymnal exchanged Caswall for the Oakeley, but omitted Oakeley's st. 2, a nonsingable restatement of the *Te Deum*:

> God of God,
> Light of Light,
> Lo, He abhors not the Virgin's womb;
> Very God,
> Begotten, not created;

Because of some awkwardness in most of the sts., alterations are continually being made in the text.

Adeste fideles

JOHN F. WADE, c. 1710-1786

Dom John Stéphan has concluded that Wade was the author of the tune as well as the text (see comments on text, above). Originally the tune was in triple time and was first arranged in 4/4 by Samuel Webbe, Sr., in his *Essay on the Church Plain Chant* (London, 1782). It has been incorrectly called PORTUGUESE HYMN.

O Come, and Dwell in Me (277)

CHARLES WESLEY, 1707-1788

John Wesley made up the hymn for his 1780 *Collection of Hymns for the Use of the People Called Methodists* from 3 separate one-st. lyrics of 8 lines each, published in Charles Wesley, *Short Hymns on Select Passages of Holy Scripture*, 1762, and originally printed under the texts II Corinthians 3:17, II Corinthians 5:17, and Hebrews 11:5, respectively. John's alterations were few but meaningful. In 1:1 he changed "Come then" to "O come." "Mind" was changed to "will" (our 3:3), "seek" to "ask" (4:1), and "thine" to "my" (4:4).

Included in all American Methodist hymnals from the beginning,

303

the 8-line sts. have always been halved. The second quatrain of the original st. 2 has never been used:

> The original offence
> Out of my heart [John: *soul*] erase
> Enter thyself, and drive it hence,
> And take up all the place.

Until 1905, the second half of st. 1 was always included as the second st.:

> The seed of sin's disease
> Spirit of health remove,
> Spirit of finished holiness,
> Spirit of perfect love.

Until the Methodist Episcopal hymnal of 1849, its first line was given as "This inward, dire disease." The 1849 hymnal restored the original Wesley form as given above. This st. was first dropped in 1905.

John's alterations have all been retained in our 1964 hymnal except in 3:3 in which the original "mind" has been restored. Further, in printing "done" instead of "past" (2:3), our hymnals have here always diverged from both Charles and John.

St. Michael

See **"How Can a Sinner Know,"** p. 221.

O Come, O Come, Emmanuel (354)
Veni, veni, Emmanuel

Latin, 12th Century
Stanzas 1, 4, trans. by JOHN M. NEALE, 1818-1866
Stanzas 2, 3, trans. by HENRY S. COFFIN, 1877-1954

From very early times, perhaps the sixth or seventh century, the 7 "Greater Antiphons" or "Great O's," short anthem-verses, were sung at Vespers in Advent, one being sung each evening from December 17 to Christmas Eve and either before or after Mary's song, the *Magnificat*. An English prose translation of the 7 is included in the 1964

O Could I Speak the Matchless Worth (168)

SAMUEL MEDLEY, 1738-1799

The hymn first appeared in 8 sts. in the author's *Hymns: The Public Worship and Private Devotions of True Christians, Assisted in Some Thoughts in Verse: Principally Drawn from Select Passages of the Word of God* (3rd ed., 1789).

It entered our hymnals in 1878 with sts. 2, 5, 6, and 8. The omitted first st. reads:

> Not of terrestrial mortal themes,
> Not of the world's delusive dreams
> My soul attempts to sing:
> But of that theme divinely true,
> Ever delightful, ever new,
> My Jesus and my King.

Our 1935 hymnal dropped 5a, and by adding 5b to 6a made our st. 2.

Ariel

Arr. by LOWELL MASON, 1792-1872

Henry L. Mason in *Hymn Tunes of Lowell Mason* lists Mozart as the source of the tune, but no proof has been found. In the *Boston Academy Collection of Church Music,* 1836, the tune is credited to Lowell Mason with the footnote: "This tune is taken from *Occasional Psalm and Hymn Tunes,* 1836, by permission of the proprietor of that work." With 4 diverse and unrelated musical ideas, the tune has little to commend it. Mozart could hardly have written so poor a tune.

O Day of God, Draw Nigh (477)

ROBERT B. Y. SCOTT, 1899-

The hymn was written in 1937 for use by the Fellowship for a Christian Social Order. Its first hymnal inclusion was in *Hymns for Worship,* 1939. Our st. 4 is Dr. Scott's own rewriting of his original text, which read:

> O Day of God, bring nigh
> Thy bright and shining light

To rise resplendent on the world
And drive away the night.

St. Michael

See **"How Can a Sinner Know,"** p. 221.

O Day of Rest and Gladness (488)

CHRISTOPHER WORDSWORTH, 1807-1885

Entitled "Sunday," the text was first published as No. 1 in the author's *Holy Year, or Hymns for Sundays and Holydays* (New ed., 1862), a collection of 117 original poems.

The hymn in 4 sts. has been in Methodist hymnals since 1878. Two sts. have been omitted.

Mendebras

Arr. by LOWELL MASON, 1792-1872

The tune is one of the anonymous German melodies brought back from Europe and arranged by Mason. It first appeared in his *Modern Psalmist* (Boston, 1839), set to "I love thy kingdom, Lord." According to Louis F. Benson, Charles S. Robinson was the first to wed the tune to this text in *Songs for the Sanctuary,* 1865.

O For a Closer Walk with God (268)

WILLIAM COWPER, 1731-1800

Entitled "Walking with God"—a reference to Genesis 5:24, "Enoch walked with God"—the text first appeared in Richard Conyers, *A Collection of Psalms and Hymns from Various Authors* (2nd ed., 1772). It was written December 9, 1769, during the serious illness of a friend, Mrs. Mary Unwin. In a letter written the next day Cowper wrote, "I began to compose the verses yesterday morning before daybreak but fell asleep at the end of the first two lines: when I waked again, the third and fourth were whispered to my heart in a way which I have often experienced."

Cowper made a few alterations in the text for *Olney Hymns,* 1779. It is this form of the text which has been printed unaltered in all American Methodist hymnals from the beginning.

307

Naomi

See "Father, I Stretch My Hands to Thee," pp. 173-74.

O For a Faith That Will Not Shrink (142)
WILLIAM H. BATHURST, 1796-1877

The hymn was first published in the author's *Psalms and Hymns for Public and Private Use,* 1831, under the title "The Power of Faith," Luke 17:5. It entered the Methodist Episcopal hymnal in 1849 with all 6 sts. The fourth and fifth sts. were dropped in 1935.

Some minor alterations retained in our present version had already been made by 1849.

Pisgah

See "Come, Let Us Join Our Friends Above," pp. 142-43.

O For a Heart to Praise My God (282)
CHARLES WESLEY, 1707-1788

The text was first published in *Hymns and Sacred Poems,* 1742, in 8 sts. headed Psalm 51:10: "Make me a clean Heart, O God." Martin Madan, in reprinting the hymn in his *Collection of Psalms and Hymns,* 1763 edition, made one alteration which John Wesley adapted in his 1780 *Collection of Hymns for the Use of the People Called Methodists:* in the first line of the last st., "gracious" was substituted for "dearest." John changed "dear" to "great" (2:2) and "An humble lowly" to "O for a lowly" (3:1). This latter reading was retained in our hymnals until 1905 when the original reading was restored.

Included in all Methodist hymnals, the 8 sts. were printed as in the 1780 *Collection* until our 1849 Methodist Episcopal hymnal dropped 5, 6, and 7. These have never been readmitted.

Since 1905 "shed" has replaced "spilt" in 1:4, a reading which seems to have appeared first in Richard Conyers, *A Collection of Psalms and Hymns from Various Authors,* 1767 edition; then, in H. V. Elliott, *Psalms and Hymns* (London, 1835); in *Hymns Ancient and Modern,* 1889; and now generally.

308

Irish

A Collection of Hymns and Sacred Poems, 1749
Probably arr. by JOHN F. LAMPE, 1703-1751

This typically eighteenth-century triple-time tune first appeared in *A Collection of Hymns and Sacred Poems* (Dublin, 1749), among a few tunes at the end of the book. It was set to "Hymn CXCI: Time, what an empty vapour 'tis."

One conjecture is that it may have been the work of John Lampe, who with John Wesley was in Dublin in 1749. Another possibility is that it was a folk song. The Scottish poet James Hogg in *Jacobite Relics of Scotland* says the melody was associated in Galloway with a poem called "The Cameronian Cat."

Caleb Ashworth of Rossendale included the tune in his *Collection of Tunes,* c. 1760, and gave the tune its name. It has also been called DUBLIN and IRISH TUNE.

O For a Thousand Tongues to Sing (1)

CHARLES WESLEY, 1707-1788

Under the heading "For the Anniversary Day of One's Conversion," the 18-st. hymn beginning "Glory to God, and praise, and love" was first published in *Hymns and Sacred Poems,* 1740. Since Wesley dated his conversion May 21, 1738, the hymn was probably written in 1739, about a year later. The famous first line of st. 1 (Wesley's seventh) was based on a statement by Peter Böhler to Wesley, "Had I a thousand tongues, I would praise him with them all."

Richard Conyers in *A Collection of Psalms and Hymns from Various Authors,* 1767 edition, seems to have first made a cento beginning with Wesley's st. 7, "O for a thousand tongues to sing," and continuing with sts. 9, 10, 11, and 12. For his 1780 *Collection of Hymns for the Use of the People Called Methodists,* John Wesley followed Conyers' lead, beginning with the seventh st. He omitted sts. 11, 15, and 16 of the ensuing sts. to make a 9-st. hymn. It was also John Wesley who in his 1780 *Collection* first established the practice, since observed in all our Methodist hymnals except 1935, of making this hymn No. 1 in our hymnals.

Though John unfortunately omitted the strong eleventh st., "He speaks, and listening to his voice," our hymnals quickly remedied the omission. Thus, our 1836, 1837, 1847, and 1882 hymnals printed John's

9 plus the original eleventh in 2 parts, Part I being the 6 sts. which have made up the hymn in all later printings. Part II (sts. 13-14, 17-18) was finally dropped in 1849, 1889, and 1901.

The first 6 sts. of the original hymn are too intimately related to Charles Wesley's conversion to be suitable for common worship, but the opening sts. deserve to be known:

> Glory to God, and praise, and love
> Be ever, ever given;
> By saints below, and saints above,
> The Church in earth and heaven.
> On this glad day the glorious Sun
> Of Righteousness arose,
> On my benighted soul he shone,
> And filled it with repose.

Azmon

See "Jesus, Thine All-Victorious Love," pp. 253-54.

O God, Before Whose Altar (486)

P. H. B. LYON, 1893-

Hymns Ancient and Modern, 1950, found the text in the *Rugby School Hymn Book*, 1932. This is its first use in a Methodist hymnal.

Llangloffan

Traditional Welsh Melody
Hymnau a Thonau, 1865

Taken from Daniel Evans' *Hymnau a Thonau er Gwasanaeth yr Eglwys yng Nghymru* (Hymns and Tunes), 1865, this is a typical Welsh tune. There is an English folk song called "The Painful Plough" which is a variant.

O God, Beneath Thy Guiding Hand (550)

LEONARD BACON, 1802-1881

In celebration of the bicentennial of the founding of New Haven, Conn., April 25, 1838, a worship service was held in the Center Congregational Church of that city, which was also celebrating its two hundredth anniversary. Leonard Bacon, the minister, both gave the oration and wrote the text.

A revised version was later published in *Psalms and Hymns for Christian Use and Worship,* 1845, of which Bacon was an editor. The original hymn began "The Sabbath morn was bright and calm." One st. of the 1845 revision has been omitted.

Duke Street

See "Come, Let Us Tune Our Loftiest Song," pp. 143-44.

O God of Earth and Altar (484)

GILBERT K. CHESTERTON, 1874-1936

The text was first printed in the *Commonwealth,* a periodical of the Christian Social Union edited by Henry S. Holland. Its first hymnal inclusion was in *The English Hymnal* (Oxford, 1906). This is its first use in a Methodist hymnal.

King's Lynn

Traditional English Melody
Arr. by RALPH VAUGHAN WILLIAMS, 1872-1958

The tune is one of the English folk tunes which Vaughan Williams arranged for *The English Hymnal* in 1906. It is named for the town in Norfolk where Charles Burney was organist of St. Margaret's Church, 1752-59.

O God of Light, Thy Word, a Lamp Unfailing (371)

SARAH E. TAYLOR, 1883-1954

The hymn is one of "Ten New Hymns on the Bible," written for the celebration of the publication of the Revised Standard Version of the Bible, 1952. The celebration was sponsored by the Hymn Society of America.

Welwyn

See "O Brother Man, Fold to Thy Heart Thy Brother," pp. 301-2.

O God, Our Help in Ages Past (28)

ISAAC WATTS, 1674-1748
Alt. by JOHN WESLEY, 1703-1791

In his *Psalms of David, Imitated in the Language of the New Testament*, 1719, Watts made 3 metrical paraphrases of portions of Psalm 90. The first in Long Meter was entitled "Man Mortal, and God Eternal, a mournfull Song at a Funeral." It began:

> Through every age, eternal God,
> Thou art our rest, our safe abode.

The second of the 3, "Our God, our help in ages past," in Common Meter, is a paraphrase of verses 1-5. It was entitled "Man Frail and God Eternal." The third hymn in the same meter covers verses 8, 11, 9, 10, and 12, and is headed "Infirmities and Mortality the Effect of Sin; or, Life, old Age and Preparation for Death."

"Our God, our help in ages past"—as Watts wrote the first line—was done in 9 sts. Two of these, the original fourth and eighth, have never been included in our hymnals. John Wesley omitted them when he first published the hymn in *A Collection of Psalms and Hymns* (London, 1738) and likewise when he included it in his *Collection of Hymns for the Use of the People Called Methodists,* 1780.

Of historical importance also are the alterations which John made in sts. 1, 2, and 9. Though Watts's first words in the first and last sts., "Our God," are reminiscent of "Our Father" in the Lord's Prayer, Wesley altered "Our" to "O." All our hymnals and many others have accepted this change. He likewise altered "Thy saints have dwelt secure" (2:2) and "Be thou our guide while troubles last" (6:3) to their present forms. Only one of John's alterations was later rejected. In the last line he changed "eternal" to "perpetual." This change survived in our hymnals until 1905 when "eternal" was restored.

Our hymnals generally printed John's 7 until the 1935 hymnal dropped

> The busy tribes of flesh and blood
> With all their lives and cares
> Are carried downwards by thy flood,
> And lost in following years,

and the st. beginning "Time, like an ever-rolling stream," which has been restored in 1964 as our st. 5.

St. Anne
Probably by WILLIAM CROFT, 1678-1727

The tune first appeared in *A Supplement to the New Version of Psalms by Dr. Brady and Mr. Tate* (6th ed.; London, 1708), set to Psalm 42 and written in the key of D. Written with soprano and bass only, each phrase began and ended with a note of double length. There was also a passing tone between the second and third notes of the last phrase. Croft is listed as composer of the tune in Philip Hart, *Collection* (London, 1720).

The opening 4 notes are common to many compositions: 3 of Henry Lawes's psalm tunes, 1638; Handel's sixth Chandos Anthem, 1734; and Bach's triple fugue in E flat, called "St. Anne."

O God, Thou Giver of All Good (515)
SAMUEL LONGFELLOW, 1819-1892

The hymn was first published in Longfellow and Samuel Johnson's *Hymns of the Spirit*, 1864, headed "Give us this day our daily bread." This is the first inclusion of the hymn in a Methodist hymnal.

The 2 omitted sts. are worth printing:

> Thy name be hallowed evermore;
> O God! Thy kingdom come with power;
> Thy will be done, and day by day
> Give us our daily bread, we pray.

> Lord! evermore to us be given
> The living bread which comes from heaven;
> Eternal life on us bestow;
> Thou art the Gift, the Giver Thou.

Puer nobis nascitur
Adapt. by MICHAEL PRAETORIUS, 1571-1621
Harm. by GEORGE R. WOODWARD, 1848-1934

The fifteenth-century carol "Puer nobis" (Unto us a boy is born) is probably the ancestor of the tune adapted by Praetorius in his *Musae*

Sioniae, Vol. VI, 1609. Another altered form had been previously published by Cyriak Spangenberg in his *Christliches Gesangbüchlein* (Eisleben, 1568). The triple time movement is indicative of the carol ancestry. It is also called SPLENDOUR.

O God, Whose Will Is Life and Good (411)

HARDWICKE D. RAWNSLEY, 1851-1920

A prayer for physicians and those who care for the sick, the hymn first appeared in *A Missionary Hymn Book* (London, 1922). It entered our hymnal in 1935. The hymn originally began "Father, whose will."

Tallis' Ordinal

See "According to Thy Gracious Word," p. 69.

O Gracious Father of Mankind (260)

HENRY H. TWEEDY, 1868-1953

Written in 1925, the text was first published in *Christian Song*, edited by Louis F. Benson, 1926. It was prompted by a discussion in a class on public worship relative to the dearth of contemporary hymns. Moved by this need, the author wrote this his first hymn, submitted it to the *Homiletic Review* for a hymn-writing contest, and was awarded the prize by a committee whose chairman was Edwin Markham.

The hymn entered the Methodist hymnal in 1935.

Llangloffan

See "O God, Before Whose Altar," p. 310.

O Guide to Every Child of Thine (84)

Στόμιον πώλων ἀδαῶν

CLEMENT OF ALEXANDRIA, c. 160-215
Trans. by KENDRICK GROBEL, 1908-1965

The translation of the text was made in 1962, particularly for the 1964 Methodist hymnal. Carlton Young, editor of the hymnal, in conversation with Dr. Grobel about inadequate Victorian translations, invited him to prepare one on the Clement text. After a very careful study of the original text of Clement, Grobel's conclusions were:

It is definitely by Clement himself. . . . It is now clear to me that it was Clement's hymnic conclusion to his *Paidagogos*: practically every figure of speech in the hymn, even the most extreme, occurs in the prose body of the book, and the hymn really pulls the whole book together.

It is not a hymn of, by, or for children! *Paidagogos* itself means, etymologically, "child-guide." Throughout the book Clement means by that term Christ or the Logos—the spirit of Christ speaking in the Old Testament, the Christ of the New Testament, and the exalted Christ who governs the Church since the resurrection (or the ascension). But Clement's compilation makes his book into a Guide-book in Christian Manners and Morals—not children's, not even *young* Christians', but *Christians*' morals. . . .

I am not at all sure that Clement's Greek hymn is a great one, or even a very good one. But it is a great milestone, as the earliest complete Christian hymn that has come down to us . . . and perhaps deserves to be kept alive among us.

Analyzing his own paraphrase, Grobel wrote:

The first line of my paraphrase is not from Clement's hymn—it is the upshot of the whole book, furnishes the point of view for all that follows, and softens the shock of so unaccustomed an address as "O Bridle-bit of untrained colts." Stanzas I and II stay reasonably close to the Greek. The first four lines of Stanza III are a faint echo of the naïve and extreme lines 42-51. The remaining lines are derived from lines 57-63.

Another paraphrase of the text appears at 86, "Shepherd of eager youth."

Nun freut euch

JOSEPH KLUG, *Geistliche Lieder,* **Wittenberg, 1535**

It is possible that the tune in Klug's *Geistliche Lieder* (Wittenberg, 1535 edition) was in the first edition, published in 1529, but no copy is extant. Though it was originally set to "Nun freut euch, lieben Christen g'mein," it was later set to the German *Dies Irae*, "Es ist gewisslich an der Zeit." It appeared in *The Christian Lyre*, 1830, set to "Great God, what do I see and hear," following the connection with the Last Judgment. However, its essential character is joyous rather than somber.

The tune is also called LUTHER, ES IST GEWISSLICH AN DER ZEIT, ALTDORF, MONMOUTH, and LUTHER'S HYMN.

O Happy Day, That Fixed My Choice (128)

PHILIP DODDRIDGE, 1702-1751

The text was first published in Job Orton's edition of Doddridge's *Hymns Founded on Various Texts in the Holy Scriptures* (London, 1755) and again in altered form in an edition published by Doddridge's great-grandson, John Doddridge Humphreys, 1839. Entitled "Rejoicing in our Covenant Engagements to God," in the 1755 printing the text is erroneously designated as I Chronicles 15:15; it should be II Chronicles 15:15.

Where the 2 versions differ, it seems impossible to determine which text, if either, is original. Orton admitted to tampering with the text; Humphreys claimed to print the accurate text. The problem is 4:3-4. The 1755 text reads:

> With ashes who would grudge to part
> When called on angels' bread to feast?

The 1839 version reads:

> O who with earth would grudge to part,
> When called with angels to be blessed.

John Julian leaves the question open, suggesting that the 1755 text is more in harmony with Doddridge's style, but that the weight of the evidence favors 1839.

The text entered our hymnals in 1837 with the Methodist Protestant hymnal. The Methodist Episcopal, South hymnal of 1847 and the 1905 Methodist hymnal followed Orton. Our 1837, 1849, and 1878 hymnals printed the 2 problem lines:

> Nor ever from thy Lord depart
> With him of every good possessed.

The 1935 hymnal introduced the text as printed in the 1964 hymnal.

The refrain, not an original part of the hymn, was added when the Edward F. Rimbault tune HAPPY DAY was adapted to revivalist use. It entered our hymnals in 1882 with the Methodist Protestant hymnal and was retained until the present hymnal dropped the tune and the refrain with it.

Hebron

See "Eternal Son, Eternal Love," pp. 169-70.

O Holy City, Seen of John (481)

WALTER RUSSELL BOWIE, 1882-1969

The text was written in 1909 at the request of Henry Sloane Coffin who was collecting material for *Hymns of the Kingdom of God,* the hymnal edited by him and A. W. Vernon, published in 1910. According to Bowie's statement, Dr. Coffin "wanted some new hymns that would express the convictions that our hope of the Kingdom of God is not alone some far-off eschatological possibility but in the beginnings, at least, may be prepared for here on our actual earth. It is in this sense that it would differ from the mood of 'O mother dear, Jerusalem.' "

The hymn entered the Methodist hymnal in 1935.

Morning Song

See "Awake, Awake, to Love and Work," pp. 105-6.

O Holy Savior, Friend Unseen (144)

CHARLOTTE ELLIOTT, 1789-1871

The text in 9 sts. was written in 1834, soon after the death of the author's father. It was printed the same year in the first edition of her *Invalid's Hymn Book,* under the title "Clinging to Christ," and in a group of hymns in the category "In severe suffering, mental or bodily." The text was published again with considerable variation in Miss Elliott's *Hours of Sorrow, Cheered and Comforted (or Thoughts in Verse)*, 1836.

317

It entered the Methodist Protestant hymnal in 1901 with 5 sts. (1, 5, 6, 7, 9), printed exactly as in *The Invalid's Hymn Book;* and in the 1905 Methodist hymnal with the 4 sts. as they appear in our 1964 hymnal (1, 5, 6, 7), but with quite a few alterations, some of which are attested to as early as the 1860's.

Flemming

FRIEDRICH F. FLEMMING, 1778-1813

Written in 1811 for male voices to the ode of Horace's "Integer vitae," the tune was once a favorite of college men's glee clubs.

O How Glorious, Full of Wonder (41)

CURTIS BEACH, 1914-

This paraphrase of Psalm 8 was contributed to *The Pilgrim Hymnal,* 1958. Hymn 44 in our 1964 hymnal offers an older paraphrase of the same psalm as printed in the 1912 Psalter of the United Presbyterian Church.

Hymn to Joy

See "Joyful, Joyful, We Adore Thee," pp. 260-61

O How Happy Are They (227)

CHARLES WESLEY, 1707-1788

The text in 16 sts. and in 2 parts, 7 and 9 sts. each, was first published in *Hymns and Sacred Poems,* 1749. It was included in the section on "Hymns for one fallen from grace." In the American *Methodist Pocket Hymn Book* (Philadelphia, 1802), it was 1 of 5 hymns classified under "Convinced of Backsliding."

The meter of the 1749 printing was somewhat irregular, in fact careless, the first st. being 569.D.; the second, 569.669.; the third, 658.569., etc. In the 1787 and 1802 *Pocket Hymn Book,* the lines all appear 669.D., as in our present hymnal.

Both parts of the hymn were printed in full in our early hymnals. Only the full first part, 7 sts., was kept in the 1847, 1889, and 1882 hymnals. Our 1849 Methodist Episcopal hymnal reduced the hymn to 5 sts.

In the 1849 hymnal, the hymn is classified under the general subject "Justification by faith" and is entitled "Joy of the young convert."

Our 1964 hymnal has added as a sixth st. the last verse of "Away with my fears," also from *Hymns and Sacred Poems*, 1749, and entitled "On his Birthday." This hymn, altered to "Away with *our* fears," by John for his 1780 *Collection of Hymns for the Use of the People Called Methodists,* was included in our hymnals until it was dropped in 1849. This st. as Wesley wrote it reads:

> My remnant of days
> I spend in his praise
> Who die the whole world to redeem:
> Be they many or few,
> My days are his due,
> And they all are devoted to him!

True Happiness

Southern Harmony, 1835
Harm. by A.C.L.

The melody was either composed or harmonized by William Walker, the editor of *Southern Harmony*, 1835. The collection contains many American folk hymns, and it is impossible to determine authorship in most cases.

The tune is also called CONVERT in other collections.

O Jesus, I Have Promised (164)

JOHN E. BODE, 1816-1874

Written c. 1866 to be used as the confirmation hymn for a daughter and 2 sons, the text began "O Jesus, we have promised." It was first published in leaflet form in 1868; then in the Appendix to *Psalms and Hymns for Public Worship,* published by the Society for Promoting Christian Knowledge in 1869. It was printed under the title "A Hymn for the Newly Confirmed," with the text of Luke 9:57, "Lord, I will follow thee whithersoever thou goest," and in the familiar first-person singular form.

The hymn entered the Methodist Protestant hymnal in 1901 and the Methodist hymnal in 1905 with 3 sts.: 1, 2, and 5. The third st. was added in 1935.

Angel's Story

ARTHUR H. MANN, 1850-1929

The tune was written for Mrs. Emily H. Miller's hymn "I love to hear the story which angel voices tell" and first appeared in *The Methodist Sunday School Tune-Book* (London, 1881).

O Jesus, Thou Art Standing (108)

WILLIAM W. HOW, 1823-1897

The text was first published in the Supplement to the 1867 edition of *Psalms and Hymns,* edited by How and T. B. Morrell. It was based on Revelation 3:20 and was prompted by a reading of Jean Ingelow's poem "Brothers, and a Sermon," notably similar to Holman Hunt's painting "The Light of the World."

The text entered the Methodist Protestant hymnal in 1901 and the Methodist hymnal in 1905 in the 3 sts. now used.

St. Hilda

Based on JUSTIN H. KNECHT, 1752-1817
by EDWARD HUSBAND, 1843-1908

The original form of the tune was taken from *Vollständige Sammlung . . . Choralmelodien* (Stuttgart, 1799), edited by Johann F. Christmann and Knecht, who contributed 97 tunes. Husband took the first 2 lines of the tune called KNECHT and added the last 2 lines of his own composition in 1871.

St. Hilda was a seventh-century English woman influential in religion and politics. The tune is also called ST. EDITH and BARTON.

O Little Town of Bethlehem (381)

PHILLIPS BROOKS, 1835-1893

The handbooks seem to disagree both on the year when Bishop Brooks, then rector of Holy Trinity Church in Philadelphia, journeyed by horseback from Jerusalem to Bethlehem, during Christmas week, and when he wrote this much-loved carol. Since his biographer, A. V. G. Allen, states that he returned home from his year abroad in September, 1866, the Bethlehem visit must have been in 1865. It was in 1868 that the carol was first sung at a Sunday school Christmas service in his church. It may have been written for this occasion.

Its first hymnal inclusion was in *The Church Porch, A Service Book and Hymnal for Sunday Schools,* edited by William R. Huntington (New York, 1874). The original fourth st. has been omitted.

The hymn entered our hymnals with 4 sts. in 1901 and 1905.

St. Louis

LEWIS H. REDNER, 1830-1908

Redner was the organist and Sunday school superintendent at Holy Trinity Church in Philadelphia when he was requested by the pastor-author, Phillips Brooks, to make a musical setting for the text. The inspiration finally came on Christmas Eve. The tune was jotted down during the night and the harmonization completed the next morning. It was first sung December 27, 1868, and first published with the text in Huntington's *Church Porch,* a service book and hymnal for Sunday schools for the Protestant Episcopal Church (see comments on text, above).

The tune name ST. LOUIS was apparently first given by Huntington in his 1874 collection. There is no connection with any real saint, the French king, or with the city in Missouri.

O Living Christ, Chief Cornerstone (349)

MAUD M. CUNINGGIM, 1874-1965

The text was written in 1926 for the occasion of the cornerstone laying of the Belle H. Bennett Memorial, including Wightman Chapel, at Scarritt College for Christian Workers in Nashville, Tenn. It entered the Methodist hymnal in 1935.

St. Peter

See "How Sweet the Name of Jesus Sounds," p. 224.

O Lord, May Church and Home Combine (520)

CARLTON C. BUCK, 1907-

The text was first published by the Hymn Society of America in 1961 in "Thirteen New Marriage and Family Life Hymns," obtained by the society in cooperation with the Department of Family Life of the National Council of the Churches of Christ in the U.S.A. and the Canadian Council of Churches for the North American Conference on Church and Family, April 20–May 5, 1961.

The text was originally written in three 8-line sts.; the first st. has been omitted, the other 2 halved, with the first line altered from "May church and Christian home combine."

St. Peter

See "How Sweet the Name of Jesus Sounds," p. 224.

O Lord My God! When I in Awesome Wonder (17)
O store Gud

CARL BOBERG, 1859-1940
Trans. by STUART K. HINE, 1899-

According to the translator, Stuart K. Hine, the poem was written in the summer of 1885 and first published in *Mönsterås Tidningen* on March 13, 1886. The original was in 9 sts. with refrain. After appearing in several Swedish periodicals the poem was apparently forgotten. Then after a couple of years, the author, while visiting in the province of Värmland, was surprised to hear his poem sung to an old Swedish melody. When in 1890 he became editor of the *Sanningsvittnet,* he published both text and tune on April 16, 1891.

The first English translation seems to have been made in 1925 by E. Gustav Johnson, in America. Sts. 1, 2, 7–9 were translated under the title "O mighty God." The hymn was not to become popular, however, until after it had made a pilgrimage through Germany and Russia. In 1907 it was translated into German, "Wie gross bist Du," by Manfred von Glehn, in Estonia. From German it was translated into Russian in 1927 by I. S. Prokhanoff, the most prolific translator in Russia, and published the same year in Moscow in a Russian hymnal.

As the text is known today, it is the work of Hine, who settled in Western Ukraine in 1923. Though Hine learned the Russian "How great thou art" as soon as it was published in 1927, it did not occur to him to translate it into English until he went to Subcarpathian Russia. It was "amid unforgettable experiences" in the Carpathian mountains that the thoughts in the first 3 sts. of the English text were born.

"There is no mention of mountains at all in the Swedish, German or Russian." A mountain thunderstorm, the "woods and forest glades," and singing birds in Romania inspired the first 2 sts. The third was prompted by the cries of repentant sinners on reading the story of the Crucifixion.

In 1939 the war compelled Hine to return to England, where he used the 3 sts. in his gospel campaigns. The fourth st. was not completed until 1938. It was suggested by Polish refugees in Britain asking, "When are we going home?" In 1949 Hine published the Russian and English words together in his Russian gospel magazine *Grace and Peace*, distributing it to refugees in 15 countries, including North and South America. In the 1950's the hymn became known throughout the world and popular in many languages.

In 1958 Hine added 2 optional sts.:

> Oh, when I see ungrateful man defiling
> This bounteous earth, God's gifts so good and great;
> In foolish pride God's holy name reviling
> And yet, in grace, His wrath and judgment wait:
>
> When burdens press, and seem beyond endurance,
> Bowed down with grief, to Him I lift my face;
> And then in love He brings me sweet assurance:
> "My child! For thee sufficient is My grace."

In the pamphlet "The Story of 'How Great Thou Art,'" 1958, **Hine** prints "a fairly literal rendering" of Boberg's 9 Swedish verses. The differences between the hymn as now sung and the Boberg poem are so great that only a few phrases are rightly to be attributed to the Swedish original. Boberg, is, however, to be credited with providing the inspiration for Hine's hymn, particularly by means of the exclamation "O (Thou) great God!"

O store Gud

Swedish Folk Melody
Arr. by Manna Music, Inc.

The old Swedish melody, to which Boberg's text was first sung, was included by him in *Sanningsvittnet*, 1891, set in 3/4 time for piano and guitar by Ad. Edgren. In 1894 it was included in the hymnbook of the Swedish Missionary Alliance set in 4/4, much as it is sung now.

O Lord of Heaven and Earth and Sea (523)

CHRISTOPHER WORDSWORTH, 1807-1885

The text entitled "Charitable Collections" was first published in the third edition of the author's collection *The Holy Year, or Hymns for Sundays and Holydays* (3rd ed., 1863). All 9 sts. of the original hymn were printed in our 1905 hymnal. In 1935 these were reduced to sts. 1, 2, 3, 6, 9. The omission of sts. 7 and 8 removes the "Charitable Collections" note from the hymn but makes it an excellent hymn for Harvest and Thanksgiving:

> We lose what on ourselves we spend,
> We have as treasure without end
> Whatever, Lord, to Thee we lend,
> Who givest all.
>
> Whatever, Lord, we lend to Thee,
> Repaid a thousandfold will be;
> Then gladly will we give to Thee,
> Giver of all.

Oldbridge

ROBERT N. QUAILE, 1867-1927

The tune was composed in 1903 for "The radiant morn hath passed away" and first published in *The English Hymnal* (Oxford, 1906).

O Lord, Our Fathers Oft Have Told (54)

Psalm 44 *New Version*
TATE and BRADY, 1696

The original version of this psalm as printed in Tate and Brady's *New Version of the Psalms of David*, 1696, includes a paraphrase of all 26 verses of the psalm. Since the psalm equates the enemies of the nation with the enemies of God, it could easily be applied to any national conquest. Some verses from the 1696 text make this clear:

> How Thou, to plant them here, didst drive
> the Heathen from this land,
> Dispeopled by repeated Strokes
> of thy avenging Hand.

For not their courage, nor their Sword
  to them Possession gave;
Nor Strength, that, from unequal Force,
  their fainting Troops could save;

Thro' thy victorious Name, our Arms
  the proudest Foes shall quell;
And crush them with repeated Strokes,
  as oft as they rebel.

The history of the transmission of the text for use in psalter or hymnals shows a progressive abandonment of the more crass military language.

A cento of 4 sts. (1, *3a*, *3b*, 4) was included in the 1847 Methodist Episcopal, South hymnal. The text was essentially that of the 1709 edition of Tate and Brady, but the most offensive lines were omitted, and "possession" (2:2) was replaced with "salvation." Beginning with our 1849 Methodist Episcopal hymnal, the eighth verse of the psalm was added, and substantial alterations were made in most of the verses, giving us the 5-st. hymn we now have.

Winchester Old

See "Come, Holy Ghost, Our Hearts Inspire," pp. 139-40.

O Lord, Our Lord, in All the Earth (44)

The Psalter, 1912

The text is a paraphrase of Psalm 8 as found in the 1912 Psalter of the United Presbyterian Church. Two sts. are omitted. This is its first inclusion in a Methodist hymnal.

Christus, der ist mein Leben

Ein schönes geistliches Gesangbuch, Jena, 1609
MELCHIOR VULPIUS, 1560-1616

In 1662 the melody was altered to its present form in Johann Crüger, *Praxis Pietatis Melica,* from which Bach took the melody and harmonized it in his *Vierstimmige Choralgesänge,* 1769. It was called BREMEN in the 1935 Methodist hymnal, and is also known as VULPIUS and MEIN LEBEN. The original form of the melody may be seen in Robert G. McCutchan, *Our Hymnody,* p. 516.

O Love Divine, How Sweet Thou Art (285)

CHARLES WESLEY, 1707-1788

The text was first printed in *Hymns on the Great Festivals and Other Occasions,* 1746, headed "Desiring to Love." It was then included in *Hymns and Sacred Poems,* 1749. John Wesley used predominantly the 1749 text for his 1780 *Collection of Hymns for the Use of the People Called Methodists,* making only a few stylistic changes. He strengthened 1:4 by altering "I thirst, and faint, and die to prove" to its present form. More important, he shortened the hymn by omitting sts. 5 and 7:

O that with humbled Peter I
Could weep, believe, and thrice reply
  My faithfulness to prove,
Thou knowst (for All to Thee is known)
Thou knowst, O Lord, and Thou alone,
  Thou knowst that Thee I love.

Thy only Love do I require,
Nothing in Earth beneath desire,
  Nothing in Heaven above;
Let Earth, and Heaven, and all Things go,
Give me thy only Love to know,
  Give me thy only Love.

The full 7 sts. were printed in the Methodist Episcopal, South hymnals of 1847 and 1889. John's 5 sts. have been included in virtually all our Methodist hymnals until the 1901 Methodist Protestant hymnal and the 1935 Methodist hymnal dropped the last 2 sts.

To the first 3 sts., always printed, our 1964 hymnal has added Charles's seventh st. (our st. 4), its only use in an American Methodist hymnal except those of 1847 and 1889. The only recent alteration in the text is in 3:4, which originally read "For love I sigh, for love I pine." The change to the present form was made for the 1935 hymnal.

Allgütiger, mein Preisgesang

GEORG PETER WEIMAR, 1734-1800

The tune is taken from Weimar's *Choral-Melodienbuch*, published in Erfurt in 1803. It is also known by the name of ERFURT.

O Love Divine, That Stooped to Share (270)

OLIVER W. HOLMES, 1809-1894

The text was written in 1849 and published first in the *Atlantic Monthly*, November, 1859, in *The Professor at the Breakfast Table*. It was entitled "Hymn of Trust."

The hymn entered the Methodist Episcopal hymnal in 1878.

Hesperus

See "Lord, Guard and Guide the Men Who Fly," pp. 273-74.

O Love Divine, What Hast Thou Done (420)

CHARLES WESLEY, 1707-1788

The text was first published in *Hymns and Sacred Poems*, 1742, in 4 sts. The refrain is a quotation from Ignatius' Letter to the Romans: *amor meus crucifixus est*, "My love is crucified." John Wesley reprinted it in *A Collection of Hymns for the Use of the People Called Methodists*, 1780, with only one alteration: in 2:2 "back to God" replaced "near to God." "Back" was retained until the 1964 hymnal restored the original.

The hymn has been included in all American Methodist hymnals except the Methodist Protestant hymnal of 1837 in 4 sts., until the 1935 hymnal dropped st. 4. Two other sts., however, met with some alterations: 1:2 and 1:5 originally read "The immortal God hath died for me" or "for me hath died." Though this form was printed in various hymnals, the generally preferred alterations have been "The incarnate God" (1:2) and "The Son of God" (1:5), which have been printed in 1849, 1878, 1905, and later hymnals.

Wesley wrote "Come see, ye worms, your Maker die" (our 3:3). "Worms" was retained in various hymnals until the Methodist Episcopal hymnal of 1878 replaced it with "Sinners," which continues to be printed. "Maker" was replaced by "Savior" in 1802, though "Maker" was retained in 1836, 1847, and 1889. The Methodist Episcopal hymnal of 1849 picked up "Savior," which has been accepted by all later hymnals.

Our 1935 hymnal was the first to reverse the order of sts. 2 and 3.

Selena

ISAAC B. WOODBURY, 1819-1858

The tune first appeared in Woodbury's first book, *The Anthem Dulcimer,* 1850, set to "Asleep in Jesus." Because of its extreme monotony of rhythm it has been dropped from most hymnals.

O Love That Wilt Not Let Me Go (234)

GEORGE MATHESON, 1842-1906

The handbooks differ about the date of composition of the text. The author himself said that it was written on June 6, 1882. Yet this must be an incorrect date since the hymn was published in the Church of Scotland monthly *Life and Work,* January, 1882. Its first hymnal inclusion was in *The Scottish Hymnal,* 1884.

The hymn entered the Methodist hymnal in 1905.

St. Margaret

ALBERT L. PEACE, 1844-1912

Composed for this text, the tune first appeared with the text in *The Scottish Hymnal* (Edinburgh, 1884). Peace wrote that the tune was composed

during the time the music of *The Scottish Hymnal,* of which I was the musical editor, was in preparation. I wrote it at Brodick Manse, where I was on a visit to my old friend, Mr. M'Lean. There was no tune of that particular metre available at that time, so I was requested by the Hymnal Committee to write one especially for Dr. Matheson's hymn. After reading it over carefully, I wrote the music straight off, and may say that the ink of the first note was hardly dry when I had finished the tune.

The name "Margaret" is greatly revered in Scotland.

O Master, Let Me Walk with Thee (170)

WASHINGTON GLADDEN, 1836-1918

The text was written in 1879 for the magazine *Sunday Afternoon,* edited by the author. Entitled "Walking with God," it was included in "The Still Hour," a column designed for devotional reading. The text was in three 8-line sts., but the second was dropped with Gladden's consent when it was first published in the hymnal *Christian Praise,* 1880, compiled by C. H. Edwards.

The hymn entered our hymnal in 1901.

Maryton

H. PERCY SMITH, 1825-1898

Written for "Sun of my soul," the tune was first published in *Church Hymns with Tunes* (London, 1874). It was the choice of Gladden for his hymn. It is named for a manor.

O Master of the Waking World (407)

FRANK MASON NORTH, 1850-1935

According to Dr. North's own account:

In 1927 Dr. Henry H. Meyer was moved to give emphasis to "World Service" in the first issue of *The Church School Journal* for 1928. He asked me to write a hymn. My unrelenting interest in the Missionary Movement refused to let me excuse myself. I was in constant touch with men and women who were giving their lives to the "work of missions,"—who was I, that I should not at least try to put into verse what was in their hearts, and mine, and, if the verse could be sung, so much the better. The task was not simple; this hymn was the result. It was first published in *The Church School Journal,* January, 1928.

The hymn entered the Methodist hymnal in 1935 in 4 sts., with 1 st. omitted. One notable alteration is that in our 2:8, "The world is" has replaced "The isles are."

Melita

See "Eternal Father, Strong to Save," pp. 167-68.

O Master Workman of the Race (171)
JAY T. STOCKING, 1870-1936

The text was written at the request of the editors of *The Pilgrim Hymnal,* 1912, who wanted a hymn celebrating the dignity of labor. While the author was watching some carpenters at work in a camp in the Adirondacks, the image of Jesus as carpenter flashed before him. He wrote the hymn then in almost the exact form in which it now appears.

It entered the Methodist hymnal in 1935.

St. Michel's
WILLIAM GAWLER, *The Hymns and Psalms,* c. 1788

The tune is drawn from Gawler's collection "used at the Asylum or House of Refuge for Female Orphans," published in London, 1785-88, where it was set as a Long Meter tune to "Creator Spirit, by whose aid." The anonymous setting is also called GOSHEN, HINTON, PALESTINE, ST. MARIA, BEULAH, WOOLRICH COMMON, and ST. MICHEL.

O Morning Star, How Fair and Bright (399)
Wie schön leuchtet der Morgenstern
PHILIPP NICOLAI, 1556-1608
Trans. by CATHERINE WINKWORTH, 1827-1878

Sometimes known as the "Queen of the Chorales," with "Wake, awake, for night is flying" as "King," the hymn was first published in Nicolai's *Freuden-Spiegel* (Frankfort, 1599). The first line originally read "Wie herrlich strahlt der Morgenstern." The title was "A Spiritual bridal song of the believing soul, concerning her Heavenly Bridegroom, founded in the 45th Psalm of the Prophet David."

In 1768 J. A. Schlegel radically rewrote the text, providing the new first line "Wie schön leuchtet." The English translations are commonly made from Schlegel's revision. Catherine Winkworth made several translations which vary considerably from each other. In her *Christian Singers of Germany,* 1869, there were 7 sts.; in her *Chorale Book for England,* 1863, there were 4. No one translation is wholly satisfactory; therefore hymnals show a great variety of alterations.

The hymn entered the Methodist hymnal in 1964, with the first 2 sts. of the translation as found in the *Chorale Book for England,* with only a few changes. In 1:5 "Bridegroom" is replaced by "Master"; in 1:7 "Holy art Thou" becomes "Thou art holy"; in 2:9 "Here in sadness" replaces "For thy gladness"; and in 2:10 "pine in sadness" becomes "long for thy gladness."

Wie schön leuchtet der Morgenstern

PHILIPP NICOLAI, 1556-1608
Harm. by J. S. BACH, 1685-1750

The chorale was first published in the Appendix to Nicolai's *Freuden-Spiegel des ewigen Lebens* (see comments on text, above), a volume of meditations during the Black Plague which devastated his home city. The present form and harmony are taken from Bach's Cantata 1, composed in 1740.

The tune is also called FRANKFORT.

O My Soul, Bless God the Father (65)

The Book of Psalms, 1871

This metrical version of Psalm 103 appeared anonymously in *The Book of Psalms* of the United Presbyterian Church, 1871. The original 16 sts. paraphrased verses 1-2, 3-4, 12-13, 17-18, and 21-22 of the psalm. It entered the Methodist hymnal in 1935, with 6 sts., a cento made up of sts. 1, 2, 8, 11, 12, and 16.

The only alterations in text are the substitutions of "God the Father" for "thou Jehovah" (1:1) and "the Father," for "Jehovah" (6:4).

Stuttgart

See "Earth Has Many a Noble City," pp. 166-67.

O Perfect Love (333)

DOROTHY B. GURNEY, 1858-1932

The text was written in 1883 at Pull Wike, Ambleside, England, for the marriage of Mrs. Gurney's sister. It was written to be sung with John B. Dykes's tune STRENGTH AND STAY. Its place in wedding ceremonies was secured when Joseph Barnby set it to the familiar tune

PERFECT LOVE, written for the wedding of Princess Louise of Wales and the Duke of Fife, 1889 (see comments on tune, below).

The text was first included in a hymnal in the Supplement to *Hymns Ancient and Modern*, 1889. The three sts. were printed under the text "The Lord do so to me and more also, if ought but death part me and thee."

Perfect Love

Arr. from JOSEPH BARNBY, 1838-1896

The hymn version was arranged from an anthem composed for the marriage of the Duke and Duchess of Fife, July 27, 1889. It first appeared in John Stainer, *The Church Hymnary*, 1898.

O Sacred Head, Now Wounded (418)

Salve caput cruentatum
O Haupt voll Blut und Wunden

ANONYMOUS Latin
Trans. by PAUL GERHARDT, 1607-1676
Trans. by JAMES W. ALEXANDER, 1804-1859

The Latin poem, beginning *Salve mundi salutare,* in 7 parts, has been variously ascribed to Bernard of Clairvaux, 1091-1153, or to Arnulf of Louvain, 1200-1251, with the weight of opinion now falling to the side of Arnulf. Manuscripts containing it are not found earlier than the fourteenth century and show a considerable variety of texts. The poem in 7 parts may not be a unity: the last sections may not have belonged to the original poem.

The hymn belongs to the class of hymns known as "crucifix hymns." By the thirteenth century, in the Latin church verses came to be addressed to the limbs of Christ as he hangs on the cross: to the feet, the knees, the hands, the sides, the breast, the heart, the face, or head. One part was to be used for each of the 7 days of the week. It was part 7, *salve caput,* which Gerhardt translated in his "O Haupt voll Blut und Wunden," which in turn became "O sacred head, now wounded" in Alexander's translation.

Gerhardt's translation in 10 sts. first appeared in Johann Crüger, *Praxis Pietatis Melica* (Berlin, 1656 ed.). It was this translation which brought the hymn into general Christian use.

The Alexander translation in 8 sts., made from the German text, first appeared in *The Christian Lyre,* compiled by Joshua Leavitt, 1830. This translation has always been used in our hymnals. It was first included in the Methodist Episcopal hymnal of 1878 with 4 sts. Since then it has been included in a variety of Methodist hymnals in 3 or 4 sts. The 1935 and 1964 hymnals have selected sts. 1, 3, and 6 of the original. Since 1935 our st. 1 has been made up of the original 1*a* plus 2*b.*

Passion Chorale

HANS L. HASSLER, 1564-1612
Harm. by J. S. BACH, 1685-1750

The tune first appeared in Hassler's *Lustgarten neuer Deutscher Gesang* (Nuremberg, 1601), set to a love song, "Mein G'muth ist mir verwirret von einer Jungfrau zart" (My heart is distracted by a gentle maid). It first appeared as a hymn tune in *Harmoniae Sacrae* (3rd ed.; Görlitz, 1613), set to "Herzlich thut mich verlangen." In Johann Crüger's *Praxis Pietatis Melica* it was set to Gerhardt's "O Haupt voll Blut und Wunden," with which it has been associated ever since (see comments on text, above). Bach used the tune 5 times in his *St. Matthew Passion.*

O Shepherd of the Nameless Fold (304)

MARY A. LATHBURY, 1841-1913

Written in 1881 and entitled "The Nameless Fold," the hymn was "Chautauqua Hymn for 1881." It first appeared in the *Assembly Hymnal,* published the same year by Biglow and Main.

This is the first inclusion of the hymn in a Methodist hymnal. The original second st. has been omitted.

Norse Air

Norse Folk Melody
Arr. by WILLIAM J. KIRKPATRICK, 1838-1921

The original melody is "The Hardy Norseman's House of Yore." R. L. de Pearsall wrote, "This melody was given to me by the late Joseph Ponny of Vienna, who heard it at a family festival in the interior of Norway and noted it on the spot. It was there described to him as a very ancient popular song, referable to the times of the Kempions or sea-kings, and as being always sung with the greatest enthusiasm."

The arrangement was made by William J. Kirkpatrick, editor of many gospel song collections.

O Sometimes the Shadows Are Deep (245)

ERASTUS JOHNSON, 1826-1909

The text was written in 1873 and first published that year in John R. Sweney, *Gems of Praise* (Philadelphia, 1873). The story is that while the author was attending a convention of the Y.M.C.A. at Carlisle, Pa., telegrams came in announcing bank failures and a general panic, "throwing a pall of gloom over the convention." Johnson wrote the hymn against this background.

It entered our hymnals with the 1889 Methodist Episcopal, South hymnal.

The Rock of Refuge

WILLIAM G. FISCHER, 1835-1912

The tune was written at the same time as the text and first published with the text in *Gems of Praise*.

O Son of God Incarnate (85)

WILBUR FISK TILLETT, 1854-1936

The author wrote:

I felt that a new hymn on the Incarnation was needed. . . . Christ is designated by St. John as the "Logos," the *Word* of God. A word is a thought-bearer, a love-bearer, and a will-bearer from one person to another. . . . Christ is the personal "Word of God," and as such is the most effective bearer of the thought and love and will of God to the human race.

The hymn first appeared on the front page of the *Christian Advocate,* October 28, 1921. It entered the Methodist hymnal in 1935.

Far-Off Lands

Melody of the Bohemian Brethren
Arr. by C. WINFRED DOUGLAS, 1867-1944

The Bohemian Brethren tune, published in the Swedish *Hemmets Koralbok*, 1921, was set to the text "Hur Ljuvt det är att komma." It was arranged by Canon Douglas for *The Hymnal 1940*.

O Son of Man, Thou Madest Known (197)

MILTON S. LITTLEFIELD, 1864-1934

The text, written in 1916, was first published in *The School Hymnal*, edited by Milton S. Littlefield with the collaboration of Luella Gardner Littlefield, 1920. It entered the Methodist hymnal in 1935.

Canonbury

See "Lord, Speak to Me That I May Speak," p. 278.

O Sons and Daughters, Let Us Sing (451)
O filii et filiae

JEAN TISSERAND, d. 1494
Trans. by JOHN M. NEALE, 1818-1866

The text, originally in 9 sts., *L'aleluya du jour de Pasques*, was probably written by Jean Tisserand, a Franciscan friar who died in Paris in 1494. It is found in an untitled booklet printed between 1518 and 1536. Three sts. were later added to the poem. Neale translated all 12 for his *Mediaeval Hymns and Sequences*, 1851, admitting that "here and there" he borrowed a line from preceding translations. In his second printing of the text in *The Hymnal Noted*, 1856, he omitted sts. 3 and 5, and made a number of alterations in the verses. *Hymns Ancient and Modern*, 1861, reduced the hymn to 9 sts., altered the first line from "Ye sons and daughters of the King" to "O sons and daughters, let us sing," and radically rewrote the hymn, leaving only one of Neale's sts. unaltered. *Hymns Ancient and Modern*, 1950, shows other alterations, the most important one for us being the replacement of "Sunday" with "Easter" in 2:1.

The hymn entered the Methodist hymnal in 1964 with a cento made up of sts. 1, 2, 4, 10, and 11. The text was that of *Hymns Ancient and Modern,* 1950, except for 5:2-3, which since 1856 had read:

> To God your hearts and voices raise
> In laud and jubilee and praise.

O filii et filiae

French Carol, c. 15th Century

The first known appearance of the tune is in *Airs sur les hymnes sacrez, odes et noëls* (Paris, 1623). There it is an arrangement of a traditional French tune which may go back to the fifteenth century. Like all folk music, the melody has many variants.

O Spirit of the Living God (136)

HENRY H. TWEEDY, 1868-1953

The hymn was written to interpret the story of Pentecost in Acts so that it might speak meaningfully to men today. Halford E. Luccock asked for the hymn for inclusion in the Methodist hymnal of 1935. This was its first appearance in any hymnal.

Llanfyllin

Traditional Welsh Melody

This is the familiar nineteenth-century Welsh tune LLANGLOFFAN in the major mode, as it was published in the Canadian *Book of Common Praise,* 1938. The tune is equally effective in major or minor.

O Splendor of God's Glory Bright (29)
Splendor paternae gloriae

AMBROSE OF MILAN, 340-397
Trans. by ROBERT S. BRIDGES, 1844-1930

The text was probably written by Ambrose. Early illustration of this is in a letter of Fulgentius XIV.10 (d. 533) and in later writers—Bede in the eighth century and Hincmar in the ninth. There is also close similarity in thought and expression to passages in Ambrose's unquestioned writings. Indeed, in his *De Fide,* 4:9, he explains how the

Son is rightly called "Splendor." The use of the hymn for Lauds, the early morning prayers, on Monday in the ancient cycles of Hymns for the Week, is prescribed as early as in the rule of Aurelian of Arles (d. 555). The earliest manuscript containing the hymn is c. 890. The Latin is in 8 sts.

The hymn entered the Methodist hymnal in 1935 in 2 translations. No. 38 used the translation of John Chandler made from seventeenth- and eighteenth-century Latin texts, and published in his *Hymns of the Primitive Church*, 1837, as re-edited by Louis F. Benson.

No. 638 used the first 4 sts. of Robert Bridges' translation as made for his 1899 *Yattendon Hymnal*. This latter translation only appears in our 1964 hymnal.

Wareham

See **"Great God, We Sing That Mighty Hand,"** pp. 204-5.

O the Depth of Love Divine (332)

CHARLES WESLEY, 1707-1788

The text first appeared in *Hymns on the Lord's Supper*, 1745, by John and Charles Wesley. Though one of the richest and most moving hymns on the Lord's Supper ever written, it has been strangely overlooked, even by Methodists. Since John did not include it in his *Collection of Hymns for the Use of the People Called Methodists*, 1780, and since it was not in the American *Methodist Pocket Hymn Book* (Philadelphia, 1802), it has been lost to our hymnals, never having been printed in any American Methodist hymnal until 1964. It is not even included in *The Methodist Hymn-Book* (London, 1933).

It is printed here exactly as Charles wrote it.

Barnabas

Adapt. from French Psalter, 1561

The original form of the melody was a setting of Psalm 75. The rhythm was straightened out using quarter notes, and the tune included in *Tunes New and Old* (London, 1864), edited by Henry J. Gauntlett, and in *The Wesleyan Tune-Book* (London, 1876).

O Thou Eternal Christ of God (482)

CALVIN W. LAUFER, 1874-1938

The text was written on Palm Sunday, 1933. It entered our hymnal in 1935. This appears to be its first hymnal inclusion.

Llangloffan

See "O God, Before Whose Altar," p. 310.

O Thou in All Thy Might So Far (12)

FREDERICK LUCIAN HOSMER, 1840-1929

The hymn called "The Mystery of God" was written in 1876 and was first printed in the New York *Inquirer*. The author included it in his *Thought of God in Hymns and Poems*, 1885. Its first hymnal inclusion seems to have been in *The Harvard University Hymn Book* of 1895.

It entered the Methodist hymnal in 1905 with the full 5 sts. The hymn was omitted from our 1935 hymnal but has been reclaimed in 1964, with the omission of 1 st., the original fourth.

Richmond

THOMAS HAWEIS, 1733-1820

Haweis wrote the tune to go with his own text "O Thou, from whom all goodness flows" in *Carmina Christo*, c. 1792. Samuel Webbe, Jr., omitted 4 measures, reducing the tune to its present length. It was named for the composer's friend Leigh Richmond, rector at Turvey, Bedfordshire.

The tune is also called HAWEIS and SPA FIELDS CHAPEL.

O Thou, in Whose Presence (129)

JOSEPH SWAIN, 1761-1796

The text was originally entitled "A Description of Christ by His Graces and Power" and is a paraphrase of portions of the Song of Solomon. It appeared in nine 8-line sts. in Swain's *Experimental Essays on Divine Subjects in Verse* (London, 1791). John Julian says it is included also in the author's *Redemption, A Poem in Five Books*, also dated 1791. However, we have been unable to find the hymn in

338

Redemption, either in the British Museum copy or the Union Theological Seminary (New York) 1811 copy, or in the poem by the same name but in 8 books (2nd ed., 1797), or in Swain's *Walworth Hymns,* 1792.

The 2 earliest American printings available to us are in Joshua Leavitt, *The Christian Lyre* (New York, 1830), and *The American Church Harp,* edited by W. R. Rhinehart (Dayton, 1856). The former prints eight 4-line sts. *The American Church Harp* prints ten 4-line sts.

The hymn entered the Methodist Episcopal hymnal in 1878, with six 4-line sts., the first 4 of which are Swain's first 4 quatrains, the fifth, his 5*b.* The sixth is not in Swain:

> Dear Shepherd I hear, and will follow thy call;
>   I know the sweet sound of thy voice;
> Restore and defend me, for thou art my all,
>   And in thee I will ever rejoice.

This last quatrain, of undetermined authorship, was never printed again in a Methodist hymnal. However, a new st., beginning "Restore, my dear Savior, the light of thy face," was added in its place in the 1889 Methodist Episcopal, South hymnal and has been retained as st. 4 in all our later hymnals. This st. is not in our copy of Swain, and we are unable to determine either its author or date.

Davis

JOHN WYETH, *A Repository of Sacred Music, Part II,* 1813
Harm. by A.C.L.

Called BELOVED in the 1935 hymnal, the tune has been credited to Freeman Lewis and was supposedly published in *The Beauties of Harmony,* 1813. However, it is almost certainly an American folk hymn. It was called MEDITATION in the 1905 hymnal, and is also called DULCIMER and MY BELOVED.

O Thou, to Whose All-Searching Sight (213)
Seelen-Bräutigam, O du Gottes-Lamm

NICOLAUS VON ZINZENDORF, 1700-1760
Trans. by JOHN WESLEY, 1703-1791

The German text appeared in the *Sammlung Geistlicher und Lieblicher Lieder,* 1725. It was available to Wesley in the *Hernnhut*

Gesangbuch, 1735. Of the 11 sts., Wesley omitted sts. 3-9 and inserted as a fourth a translation of J. A. Freylinghausen's "Wer ist wohl, wie du," making a 6-st. hymn.

Wesley's translation was first published in *A Collection of Psalms and Hymns* (London, 1738) and then in *Hymns and Sacred Poems,* 1739. For his 1780 *Collection of Hymns for the Use of the People Called Methodists,* he changed 2 words: in 1:4 "bands" became "bonds"; in 4:1 (our third) "head" was altered to "soul."

The entire hymn was included in virtually all American Methodist hymnals until the 1905 hymnal dropped the second st. Our 1935 hymnal reduced the hymn to 4 sts. These 4 sts. are printed in our 1964 hymnal exactly as Wesley printed them in 1780, except that "yearns" has replaced "pants" in 1:3 since 1935.

Rockingham (Mason)

See **"God of the Ages, by Whose Hand,"** p. 198.

O Thou Who Art the Shepherd (201)

JOHN W. SHACKFORD, 1878-

At the request of the Department of Social Welfare of the National Conference on the Churches and Social Welfare, the Hymn Society of America was asked to solicit hymn texts on the theme "The interrelationship of worship and service of love as expressions of our abiding faith in God." The hymns were to be sung at the second conference in Cleveland, Ohio, October, 1961. Of the 7 hymns chosen out of more than 200 submitted texts, "O thou who art the shepherd" was one. The text was first published by the Hymn Society in the pamphlet "Social Welfare Hymns."

This is the first inclusion of the hymn in a hymnal.

Munich

See **"My Jesus, As Thou Wilt,"** pp. 292-93.

O Thou Who Camest from Above (172)

CHARLES WESLEY, 1707-1788

The text in two 8-line sts. was first published in *Short Hymns on Select Passages of Holy Scripture,* 1762. It was based on Leviticus

6:13: "The fire shall ever be burning upon the altar; it shall never go out."

For the 1780 *Collection of Hymns for the Use of the People Called Methodists,* John made 2 alterations in the text. In 2:4 he altered "prayer" to "love," and in 4:4 *"my* sacrifice" to *"the* sacrifice." In American Methodist hymnals from the beginning "love" was printed until the 1878 Methodist Episcopal hymnal returned to the original "prayer." The Methodist Episcopal, South hymnals of 1847 and 1889 printed "love," which was retained in 1905, to be again displaced by "prayer" in 1935 and the present hymnal. All our hymnals followed John's shift from "my" to "the" until 1964 restored the hymn to the exact form in which Charles wrote it.

Robert Bridges, who included the hymn in his *Yattendon Hymnal,* 1899, gave expression to a frequently held objection to the 6-syllable word "inextinguishable" (2:2):

This fine hymn has been kept out of use by the second line of the second stanza, *with inextinguishable blaze.* This cannot be sung. . . . The objection to such a long word is not exactly that "a whole congregation is poised on it," but that the accents of a melody have too much meaning to allow of such a distribution over one word, the parts of which are not in English of sufficient importance so that the expression of the musical phrase is ridiculously superabundant.

Bridges' judgment is not to be contested on his own ground; nevertheless, there is something grandly extravagant about the polysyllable here which makes its point by its very awkwardness. Bridges' "with everbright, undying blaze" seems weak in comparison.

Eisenach

See **"Captain of Israel's Host, and Guide,"** p. 127.

O Where Are Kings and Empires Now (308)

A. CLEVELAND COXE, 1818-1896

The text is a cento taken from a ballad in ten 8-line sts., called "Chelsea" and beginning:

> When old Canute the Dane
> Was merry England's king;

> A thousand years agone, and more,
>   As ancient rymours sing;
> His boat was rowing down the Cam,
>   At eve, one summer day,
> Where Ely's tall cathedral peered
>   Above the glassy way.

The poem was written while the author was a student at General Theological Seminary in New York. Chelsea is the quarter in which the seminary is located. The ballad appeared first in the *Churchman*, 1839, and then in Coxe's *Christian Ballads*, 1840.

The 4 quatrains which have made up the hymn in our hymnals since 1878 are sts. 6*a*, 8*b*, 7*a*, and 7*b*. Several alterations have been made.

St. Anne

See "O God, Our Help in Ages Past," pp. 312-13.

O Word of God Incarnate (372)

WILLIAM W. HOW, 1823-1897

The text is based on Psalm 119:105. It was headed by Proverbs 6:23, "For the commandment is a lamp; and the law is light; and reproofs of instruction are the way of life," when it first appeared in the 1867 Supplement to *Psalms and Hymns*, edited by How and T. B. Morrell in 1854.

It entered our hymnals in 1901 and 1905.

Munich

See "My Jesus, As Thou Wilt," pp. 292-93.

O Worship the King (473)

ROBERT GRANT, 1779-1838

The text in 6 sts. was first published in *Christian Psalmody, a Collection of Above 700 Psalms, Hymns, and Spiritual Songs*, selected and edited by Edward Bickersteth (London, 1833). It is a resetting of William Kethe's paraphrase of Psalm 104 as printed in the Anglo-Genevan Psalter, 1561. Kethe's first st. ran:

Methodist *Book of Worship,* p. 70. Sometime during the twelfth or thirteenth century they were made into a metrical hymn, though this cannot be traced earlier than the appendix to the *Psalteriolum Cantionum Catholicarum* (Cologne, 1710). Neale published a nineteenth-century Latin version in his *Hymni Ecclesiae e Breviariis,* 1851, retaining only 5 of the "Veni's." These he translated for his *Mediaeval Hymns and Sequences,* 1851. In his *Hymnal Noted* (London, 1851), he printed a radically revised form of his earlier translation and in addition a prose version of 8, including an additional "Virgin of Virgins, how shall this be?" which was introduced for December 23 since in English usage Advent Vespers began December 16.

The hymn entered the Methodist hymnal in 1935 with 3 sts., only the first of which was by Neale as altered for *Hymns Ancient and Modern,* 1861. Sts. 2 and 3 were Henry Sloane Coffin's paraphrases of the first and sixth antiphons: *O Sapientia* and *O Rex gentium, et desideratus earum,* neither of which had been translated by Neale. Translated by Coffin in 1916, these sts. were first printed in Coffin's *Hymns of the Kingdom of God,* 1923 edition. In 1964, a fourth st. was added, Neale's third as altered for *Hymns Ancient and Modern,* 1861.

Veni Emmanuel

Adapt. from Plainsong, Mode I
by **THOMAS HELMORE, 1811-1890**

Helmore included the arrangement in *The Hymnal Noted,* Part II (London, 1854), stating that the melody was "from a French Missal in the National Library, Lisbon." Later, in an article on plainsong in *Dictionary of Musical Terms,* 1881, Helmore wrote that the tune was "copied by the late J. M. Neale from a French Missal." In the *Musical Times,* September, 1966, Mother Thomas More, a canoness of St. Augustine, wrote that she had found the manuscript in the National Library of Paris, where the tune was set to a "Libera" trope, a devotional hymn for the dead, with the text "Bone Jesu dulcis cunctis." It is a fifteenth-century processional belonging to the Franciscan nuns and appears with notes for "Rejoice" the same length as the other notes of the tune, rather than longer note values. On the opposite page a second melody was given for the same text.

My soul praise the Lord, speake good of his name,
O Lord our great God how doest thou appear,
So passing in glorie, that great is thy fame,
Honour and maiestie in thee shine most clear.

Though John Julian states that Bickersteth's text was not authorized and was altered from a source unknown to us, it is the text that was printed not only in *Christian Psalmody,* 1833, but also in Grant's *Sacred Poems* (new ed., 1839), collected by Lord Glenelg as "a more correct and authentic version." This text appeared also in H. V. Elliott, *Psalms and Hymns for Public, Private, and Social Worship,* 1835, and in Roundell Palmer, *A Hymnal Chiefly from "the Book of Praise,"* set to music by John Hullah (London, 1868) and, generally, with only the most minor changes.

The text entered the Methodist Episcopal, South hymnal in 1847 with the 6 sts. and the 1878 Methodist Episcopal hymnal with 4 sts.— 1, 2, 4, and 5. Our 1901 Methodist Protestant and 1905 Methodist hymnals also used 1, 2, 4, and 5. The 1935 hymnal dropped st. 2 and added st. 3. The 1964 hymnal has retained st. 2, making 5 in all, and omitting only Grant's sixth.

Lyons

Arr. from JOHANN MICHAEL HAYDN, 1737-1806

The arrangement first appeared in William Gardiner's Volume II of *Sacred Melodies from Haydn, Mozart, and Beethoven* (London, 1815), set for mixed voices and orchestra to "O praise ye the Lord, prepare a new song." Though the melody has been attributed to Haydn, the source has not yet been identified.

Oliver Shaw introduced the tune to America in his *Sacred Melodies* (Providence, 1818), and his student, Lowell Mason, used it in the 1822 Boston *Handel and Haydn Society Collection of Church Music.*

O Young and Fearless Prophet (173)

S. RALPH HARLOW, 1885-

The text was written during the depression years in 1931. While the author was driving with his family from Poughkeepsie, N.Y., to Northampton, Mass., the words of the hymn came to him. Stopping at Pittsfield for lunch, he wrote the words on the back of a menu card, almost in their final form. The hymn was first used in student conferences. Its first inclusion in a church hymnal was in the 1935 Methodist hymnal.

The original fifth st. has always been omitted. It read:

Stir up in us a protest against unearned wealth,
While men go starved and hungry, who plead for work and health;
Where homes with little children cry out for lack of bread;
Who live their years o'erweighted beneath a gloomy dread.

Dr. Harlow writes that in rejecting this st., "The chairman of the committee told me that 'the church is not ready to sing that yet.' I told him that it was not as radical as the *Magnificat* in Luke 1:46-55. . . . Later I changed this verse from 'unearned wealth' to 'the greed of wealth.' "

In 4:2 "race" was altered to "station" with the author's reluctant consent. St. 3 originally read as in our 1935 hymnal:

O help us stand unswerving against war's bloody way,
Where hate and lust and falsehood hold back Christ's
     holy sway;
Forbid false love of country, that blinds us to His call
Who lifts above the nation the brotherhood of all.

Dr. Harlow prefers the form as it appears in our 1964 hymnal.

Blairgowrie

JOHN B. DYKES, 1823-1876

The tune was written in February, 1872, for "The Voice that breathed o'er Eden" for the wedding of a friend. Blairgowrie is Gaelic for "plain of the wild goats" and is a small inland town northwest of Dundee, Scotland.

O Zion, Haste (299)

MARY A. THOMSON, 1834-1923

According to the author's account, the greater part of the hymn was written in 1868. Intending it to be sung to the tune PILGRIMS but not satisfied with any refrain she could write, she left the hymn unfinished. About 3 years later she wrote the refrain, completing the hymn. Its first hymnal inclusion was in the 1894 hymnal of the Protestant Episcopal Church (see comments on tune, below).

The 6 original sts. entered the Methodist hymnal in 1905. These were reduced to 4 in 1935.

Tidings

JAMES WALCH, 1837-1901

The tune was written in 1875 for "Hark, hark, my soul!" because Walch did not like the tunes written by Henry Smart and John B. Dykes for that text. It was first published in *The Hymnal Companion to the Book of Common Prayer* (2nd ed.; London, 1877). Charles L. Hutchins introduced it into American usage in *The Church Hymnal* (New York, 1894) to this text.

Of the Father's Love Begotten (357)
Corde natus ex Parentis

AURELIUS CLEMENS PRUDENTIUS, 348-c. 413
Trans. by JOHN M. NEALE, 1818-1866 and
HENRY W. BAKER, 1821-1877

The text is taken from the *Hymnus omnis horae,* beginning "Da puer plectrum," No. 9 in the *Liber Cathemerinon* of the Spanish poet Prudentius, the first great poet of the Latin church. The *Cathemerinon* was a collection of 12 hymns for the daily hours ranging in length from 80 to 220 lines. It was Prudentius' interest that every hour of the day the believer should be mindful of Christ as the Alpha and the Omega, the beginning and the end.

Various centos were used in different rites. Neale's translation in *The Hymnal Noted,* 1851, was in 6 sts. He scheduled it as the evening hymn from the Nativity until Epiphany and printed Revelation 1:8 as the superscription.

The version now commonly used is the revision made by Baker for use in the preliminary edition of *Hymns Ancient and Modern,* 1859. Baker's hymn was in 8 sts. plus the doxology which, like the "Evermore and evermore" refrain, is a liturgical addition to the hymn.

The hymn entered the Methodist hymnal in 1964 with sts. 1, 6, and 9 of the *Hymns Ancient and Modern* text.

Divinum mysterium

13th Century Plainsong, Mode V
Arr. by C. WINFRED DOUGLAS, 1867-1944

The original was a medieval *Sanctus* trope—a musical interpolation, probably of Byzantine origin. A trope was a vocalization on a syllable, such as the last vowel of "Alleluia." To aid the memory, special texts were written to accompany these ornamented passages.

Thomas Helmore found the tune in *Piae Cantiones* (Nyland, 1582) and made a version which because of its lack of fidelity to the original has disappeared from use. Like all plainsong, it should ideally be sung in unison without accompaniment; it is also suitable for antiphonal singing.

The tune is also called CORDE NATUS.

On a Hill Far Away (228)

GEORGE BENNARD, 1873-1958

The hymn was written in 1913 after repeated but unsuccessful attempts to compose a hymn which might set forth the full meaning of the cross. After a series of successful evangelistic meetings in New York state, the author returned to Michigan, his home state, and "was enabled to complete the poem with facility and dispatch." After securing the help of a friend to put both text and tune in manuscript, he sent it to Charles S. Gabriel, who, recognizing its potential popularity, had it published at once.

This is the first appearance of the hymn in a Methodist hymnal.

The Old Rugged Cross

GEORGE BENNARD, 1873-1958

See comments on text, above.

On Jordan's Stormy Banks I Stand (291)

SAMUEL STENNETT, 1727-1795

The text was first published in John Rippon, *A Selection of Hymns from the Best Authors,* 1787, in eight 4-line sts., entitled "The Promised Land."

It entered our hymnals with the Supplement to *The Methodist Pocket Hymn Book,* 1808, and has been in every Methodist hymnal since. All 8 sts. were retained until the 1847, 1849, and 1882 hymnals omitted st. 8. The hymn was further reduced to the 6 quatrains printed beginning with the 1878 Methodist Episcopal and 1901 Methodist Protestant hymnals and in all our hymnals since 1905.

Though some minor changes have been made in the text of our st. 2, the alterations in st. 3 (originally 6 and 7) are important. These sts. originally read:

346

> When shall I reach that happy Place,
>   And be for ever blest?
> When shall I see my Father's Face,
>   And in his Bosom rest?
>
> Filled with Delight, my raptured Soul
>   Can here no longer stay:
> Tho' Jordan's waves around me roll,
>   Fearless I'd launch away.

Promised Land

American Folk Melody

The tune is found in William Walker, *Southern Harmony,* 1835, attributed to "Miss M. Durham," who may have sung the version noted by Walker. It is there found in the minor mode.

Altering the tune to the major mode was the work of Rigdon M. McIntosh, 1836-1899, for many years music editor of the publishing house of the Methodist Episcopal Church, South. The alteration seems to have appeared first in *The Gospel Light* (Atlanta, 1895), edited by H. R. Christie.

On This Stone Now Laid with Prayer (348)

JOHN PIERPONT, 1785-1866

The text was written for the laying of the cornerstone of the Suffolk Street Chapel, Boston, for the ministry to the poor, May 23, 1839. The original text had been considerably altered by 1849 when it entered our hymnals. In 1935 it was reduced to the present 4 sts.

Pleyel's Hymn

See "Children of the Heavenly King," pp. 128-29.

Once to Every Man and Nation (242)

JAMES RUSSELL LOWELL, 1819-1891

W. Garrett Horder, an English hymnodist, was the first to see the possibility of finding a hymn in Lowell's "Present Crisis." It was a poem of eighteen 5-line sts. written as a protest against the Mexican

War which Lowell repudiated since the annexation of the new Southwest Territory would enlarge the area of the slaveholding states.

The poem was first printed in the Boston *Courier*, December 11, 1845, on the day, whether by accident or design, when the House committee reported favorably on the resolution to admit Texas to the Union, and a similiar bill was introduced into the Senate.

From the 90 lines, Horder selected 32, rearranging them and making a few alterations, to make four 8-line sts. His first st. is Lowell's fifth, with 1 line omitted: "Parts the goats upon the left hand, and the sheep upon the right." The second st. is Lowell's eleventh, with the fourth line omitted: "Doubting in his abject spirit, till his Son is crucified." St. 3 is the first 2 lines of Lowell's thirteenth with "heretics" changed to "martyrs," and "Christ's bleeding feet I track" altered to "Christ, thy bleeding feet we track," to which are added the first 2 lines of st. 18. The fourth st. is composed of the third line of Lowell's sixth and lines 3-5 of Lowell's eighth.

Horder first published the hymn in his *Hymns, Supplemental to Existing Collections*, 1896, and then in the 1905 edition of *Worship Song*. He entitled it "Manliness" and printed "The time of thy visitation" (Luke 19:44) above it.

The hymn entered the Methodist hymnal in 1905.

Ebenezer

See **"God Hath Spoken by His Prophets,"** p. 192.

One Holy Church of God Appears (296)

SAMUEL LONGFELLOW, 1819-1892

The text was first published in *Hymns of the Spirit* edited by Longfellow and Samuel Johnson, 1864. It was entitled "The Church Universal." This is its first inclusion in a Methodist hymnal. The omitted st. 3 reads:

> Her priests are all God's faithful sons,
> To serve the world raised up;
> The pure in heart her baptized ones,
> Love, her communion-cup.

St. Stephen

See "Break Forth, O Living Light of God," p. 123.

Onward, Christian Soldiers (305)

SABINE BARING-GOULD, 1834-1924

The text, in 6 sts., was written for a children's festival at Horbury Bridge, near Wakefield, to be sung in procession with a cross and banners as the children marched from one village to another. The original fourth is no longer printed.

The hymn was first printed in the *Church Times,* October 15, 1864, then in the 1868 Supplement to *Hymns Ancient and Modern.* In 2:5 "We are not divided" was altered to "Though divisions harass" by *Hymns Ancient and Modern.*

The hymn entered our hymnals with the Methodist Episcopal hymnal of 1878 in 5 sts.; the Methodist Episcopal, South hymnal of 1889 with 3 sts.; and the 1901 Methodist Protestant hymnal with 4 sts. The 1935 and 1964 hymnals dropped the second st. which had been included in the 1878 and 1905 hymnals:

> At the sign of triumph
> Satan's host doth flee,
> On, then, Christian soldiers,
> On to victory!
> Hell's foundations quiver
> At the shout of praise;
> Brothers, lift your voices
> Loud your anthems raise.

St. Gertrude

ARTHUR S. SULLIVAN, 1842-1900

The first appearance of the tune was in the *Musical Times,* December, 1871, but it was originally written for *The Hymnary* (London, 1872), edited by Sullivan. It was composed during one of his visits to the home of Mrs. Gertrude Clay-Ker-Seymer in Dorsetshire. Sullivan complimented his hostess by naming the tune for her and sainting her at the same time.

The tune was introduced to America in John R. Sweney, *Gems of Praise* (Philadelphia, 1873).

Open My Eyes, That I May See (267)

CLARA H. SCOTT, 1841-1897

The hymn first appeared in *Best Hymns No. 2*, compiled by E. A. Hoffman and H. F. Sayles (Chicago, 1895). This is its first appearance in an official Methodist hymnal.

Open My Eyes

CLARA H. SCOTT, 1841-1897

(See comments on text, above.) *The Baptist Hymnal*, 1956, calls the tune SCOTT.

Open Now Thy Gates of Beauty (13)
Tut mir auf die schöne Pforte

BENJAMIN SCHMOLCK, 1672-1737
Trans. by CATHERINE WINKWORTH, 1827-1878

The German text was first published in Schmolck's *Kirchen-Gefährte*, 1732, in 7 sts. Catherine Winkworth translated 5 of them for her *Chorale Book for England* (London, 1863).

This is the first inclusion of the hymn in our hymnals. Our 2 sts. are the first 2 of the longer hymn.

In 2:1-2, Miss Winkworth wrote:

> *Yes my* God, I come before Thee,
> Come thou also *down* to me.

Unser Herrscher

See "God of Love and God of Power," p. 197.

Out of the Depths I Cry to Thee (526)
Aus tiefer Not schrei ich zu dir

MARTIN LUTHER, 1483-1546
Trans. by CATHERINE WINKWORTH, 1827-1878

Toward the end of 1523, Luther, desiring to have more hymns sung in the church service, wrote to his friend the court chaplain George Spalatin, to solicit his help:

Everywhere we are looking for poets. Now since you are so skillful and eloquent in German, I would ask you to work with us in this and to turn a

Psalm into a hymn as in the enclosed sample of my own work. But I would like you to avoid new-fangled, fancied words and to use expressions simple and common enough for the people to understand, yet pure and fitting. The meaning should also be clear and as close as possible to the Psalm. Irrespective of the exact wording, one must freely render the sense by suitable words. I myself am not sufficiently gifted to do these things as I would.

Then suggesting to Spalatin Psalm 6 or 143, he continued, "I have already translated the *De profundis* [130]."

The "sample" Luther mentioned was probably his paraphrase of Psalm 130, "Out of the depths." Then this hymn would be dated in the latter part of 1523. A broadsheet of the hymn was known in Magdeburg as early as May 6, 1524.

In 4 sts., the text was first published in *Etlicher christlicher Lieder Lobgesänge* (Nuremberg, 1523-24) and then in the Erfurt *Enchiridion geistlicher Gesänge und Psalmen für die Laien,* 1524. A revised and better-known text in 5 sts. appeared in Johann Walther, *Geistliches Gesangbüchlein* (Wittenberg, 1524). In 1525, a doxology was added as a sixth st., but this was not by Luther.

During the Diet of Augsburg, 1530, when Luther was confined in the castle of Coburg, he said to his servant in an hour of great anxiety, "Come, let us defy the devil, and praise God by singing the hymn 'Aus tiefer Not schrei ich zu dir.' " In 1546 the hymn was sung at Halle while Luther's body was being brought from Eisleben to Wittenberg for burial.

Catherine Winkworth made her translation from the Wittenberg hymnal. Her first translation appeared in the first series of her *Lyra Germanica,* 1855, appointed for the Fifth Sunday in Lent; her second in the *Chorale Book for England,* 1863. Both were in 5 sts.

This is the first inclusion of the hymn in a Methodist hymnal. Our version is nearest to that of the *Chorale Book for England;* however, the second st. is considerably altered.

Aus tiefer Not

Attr. to MARTIN LUTHER, 1483-1546
JOHANN WALTHER, *Geistliches Gesangbüchlein*, Wittenberg, 1524
Harm. by A.C.L.

The melody may be by Martin Luther or Johann Walther. It was published with the text in the Erfurt *Enchiridion* the same time as in

Walther's Wittenberg collection, 1524 (see comments on text, above). The tune is in the Phrygian mode, the scale of E minor, without any sharps. It is also called COBERG, after the German castle (see comments on text, above).

Pass Me Not, O Gentle Savior (145)

FANNY J. CROSBY, 1820-1915

Written in 1868, the hymn was first published in *Songs of Devotion for Christian Associations,* compiled by W. H. Doane, 1870. It was the first hymn of Fanny Crosby to win worldwide attention.

The hymn entered the Methodist Episcopal, South hymnal in 1889, the Methodist Protestant hymnal in 1901, and the Methodist hymnal in 1905, always in 4 sts. Minor alterations have been made through the years. The ones that have been retained in the present 1964 hymnal are "smiling" altered to "calling" (1:3); "merits" altered to "merit" (3:1).

Pass Me Not

WILLIAM H. DOANE, 1832-1915

The tune was written for the text, and both were published together in Doane's *Songs of Devotion for Christian Associations* (New York, 1870).

Peace, Perfect Peace (229)

EDWARD HENRY BICKERSTETH, 1825-1906

The text was written during the summer of 1875 while the author was spending a holiday in Harrogate in the north of England. One Sunday morning the vicar preached a sermon on Isaiah 26:3 and called attention to the fact that in Hebrew the words translated "perfect peace" are "peace, peace." That afternoon he visited an aged and dying relative, Archdeacon Hill of Liverpool. With the sermon text in his mind, he took up a sheet of paper, then and there wrote down the hymn exactly as it stands, and read it to his dying friend.

The hymn was published the same year in *Songs in the House of Pilgrimage,* a tract of 5 hymns. Its first hymnal inclusion was in

Bickersteth's *Hymnal Companion to the Book of Common Prayer,* 1876 edition.

The hymn entered our hymnal in 1905 with all 7 sts. Sts. 6 and 7 were dropped in 1935. They read:

> Peace, perfect peace, death shadowing us and ours?
> Jesus has vanquished death and all its powers.

> It is enough: earth's struggles soon shall cease,
> And Jesus call us to heaven's perfect peace.

Song 46

ORLANDO GIBBONS, 1583-1625

The present version consists of the first 2 lines of a 9-line tune set to 1 of George Wither's songs in *The Hymns and Songs of the Church* (London, 1623), a collection of texts by Wither and tunes by Gibbons. Because of an error in Edward F. Farr's reprint of the songs in 1856, the number is incorrect. The tune fits Song 47 for Christmas Day, "A song of joy unto the Lord we sing." *The English Hymnal* (Oxford, 1906) was the first to wed the tune to this text.

Pour Out Thy Spirit from on High (337)

JAMES MONTGOMERY, 1771-1854

The hymn, entitled "For a Meeting of Ministers," was written January 23, 1833. It was published the same year in J. Birchall, *A Selection of Hymns,* and Edward Bickersteth, *Christian Psalmody.* It is also found in Montgomery's *Original Hymns,* 1853.

The hymn entered the Methodist hymnal in 1964 with the text as printed in *Hymns of Worship and Service,* 1916. A few alterations may be noted: the pronouns were originally first person, not third; in 1:2 "Ordained" has replaced "assembled"; in 1:4 "Thy priests" is changed to "them"; and in 2:4 "the angels" is now "Thy servants."

Herr Jesu Christ, mein's Lebens Licht

See **"Jesus, Thy Blood and Righteousness,"** p. 255.

Praise, My Soul, the King of Heaven (66)

HENRY F. LYTE, 1793-1847

The text was first published in Lyte's *Spirit of the Psalms,* 1834, a collection of over 280 free paraphrases of individual psalms. This is the second of 3 versions of Psalm 103. The hymns were written for the author's congregation at the small fishing village at Lower Brixham, Devonshire, where he was curate from 1823 until his death.

The hymn was originally in 5 sts., the fourth of which is now generally omitted. The original fifth line of each st. read "Praise Him! praise Him!" The first 3 sts. were included in the Methodist Episcopal hymnal of 1878 and the 1901 Methodist Protestant hymnal. The entire hymn dropped out of our 1905 hymnal, but 4 sts. were printed in 1935 as in 1964. As in most hymnals now, our text is the altered form as found in *Hymns Ancient and Modern,* 1861.

Regent Square

See "Angels, from the Realms of Glory," p. 94.

Praise the Lord Who Reigns Above (15)

CHARLES WESLEY, 1707-1788

The text first appeared in *A Collection of Psalms and Hymns,* 1743, (2nd ed. of 1741), published by John and Charles Wesley. The text was originally in four 8-line sts. Two quatrains, 2b and 3a, were dropped in *A Collection of Psalms and Hymns for the Lord's Day,* 1784, and a new 2b st. was made up of 2a and 3b. In our hymnal 3a appears as 2a.

Though John did not include the hymn in his *Collection of Hymns for the Use of the People Called Methodists,* 1780, he did include it in its 1784 form of 3 sts. in the *Sunday Services,* which he prepared for the American colonies, 1788. Nevertheless, the hymn has not been included in any American Methodist hymnal until 1964, where sts. 1, 3, and 4 of the original hymn have been retained.

Amsterdam

Foundery Collection, London, 1742

The source of the tune is J. A. Freylinghausen, *Geistreiches Gesangbuch* (Halle, 1704), from which John Wesley adapted 6 tunes. In the 1742 book, Wesley's first tunebook, he falsely attributed it to James

Nares, an eighteenth-century English composer. The meter, 76.76.77.76., with its interplay of trochaic and iambic, came to be known as the Wesleyan meter because of Charles Wesley's fondness for it.

Praise the Lord! Ye Heavens Adore Him (42)

The Foundling Hospital Collection, 1796

In 1774 a collection of 16 hymns was published under the title *Psalms and Hymns and Anthems of the Foundling Hospital,* for use in the hospital chapel. The collection was enlarged in 1796 to 22 hymns with music. A pamphlet containing the 2 sts. making up our hymn was found pasted in some copies of this latter edition and also again at the end of the edition of 1801 of words only. When or by whom the hymn was written or the pamphlet printed is not known. It could have been after 1801 if the insert was made in the 1796 and 1801 collections at the same time.

The hymn entered our hymnals in 1837, 1878, and 1889. Dropped in 1905, it was restored in 1935. A third st. by Edward Osler, first published in 1836, was included in the 1901 Methodist Protestant hymnal and is frequently printed.

Austria

See "Glorious Things of Thee Are Spoken," pp. 186-87.

Praise to the Living God (30)

(*The God of Abraham Praise*)

Based on the Yigdal of DANIEL BEN JUDAH, 14th Century
Trans. by NEWTON MANN, 1836-1926
and MAX LANDSBERG, 1845-1928

The great Jewish scholar Maimonides, 1130-1205, codified the 13 articles of the Jewish creed. Daniel ben Judah, fourteenth century, made them into a Yigdal or doxology. The first English paraphrase in 12 sts. was made about 1770 by Thomas Olivers, a Welsh Wesleyan preacher. Olivers stated that he rendered it from the Hebrew, "giving it as far as I could a Christian character." This hymn began "The God of Abraham praise." It was this text which was used in all our Methodist hymnals 1785-1935. The 1837 Methodist Protestant hymnal printed all 12 of Olivers' sts. All our other hymnals between 1802 and

1889 used the first 4 sts. only. The 1901 Methodist Protestant hymnal included 1, 2, 4, 10, and 12; the 1905 Methodist hymnal, 1, 2, 4, 6, 9, and 12.

Then c. 1885, the Unitarian minister Newton Mann in cooperation with Max Landsberg, a Jewish rabbi, both in Rochester, N.Y., made a new metrical version of the Yigdal, but in another meter. Later Mann's successor, W. C. Gannett, rewrote this version to fit the tune, and the hymn found its way into the *Union Hymnal* for Jewish worship. This hymn in 5 sts. began "Praise to the living God."

Our 1935 hymnal jettisoned the Olivers translation for sts. 1, 2, and 5 of the Mann-Landsberg, but retained Olivers' first line, beginning the hymn "The God of Abraham praise." Our 1964 text has given up Olivers entirely.

In 1935, "for aye" (1:4 and 3:8) was changed to "and still," and "Eternal life hath He" (3:1) was altered to its present form.

Leoni

Arr. from a Hebrew Melody
by MEYER LYON (LEONI), 1751-1797

The tune is named after Meyer Lyon (Meier Leon), precentor at Duke Place Synagogue in London, where Thomas Olivers heard him sing the 13 articles of the Jewish creed antiphonally with the congregation at the end of the sabbath eve service. It was first printed on a leaflet in 1772, which went through 8 editions in less than 2 years and 30 editions by 1799. The tune was included in John Wesley, *Sacred Harmony*, 1780.

It may be an old synagogue melody, and it is based on an old folk motif common to Jewish, Spanish, Basque, and Russian music.

It is likely that Joseph Rhodes, precentor at the Foundery, who went with Olivers to the service at the synagogue, harmonized the tune. It is also called YIGDAL, JUDEA, and JERUSALEM.

Praise to the Lord, the Almighty (55)
Lobe den Herren

JOACHIM NEANDER, 1650-1680
Trans. by CATHERINE WINKWORTH, 1827-1878

The German text was first published in Neander's *Glaub- und Liebes-übung* (Bremen, 1680). Catherine Winkworth's translation, in 4 sts., appeared in her *Chorale Book for England*, 1863.

The hymn entered the Methodist hymnal in 1935 with the first 3 sts. St. 4 was added in 1964. Two slight changes have been made in the text: in 2:4 "e'er" has been added after "desires"; in 4:5 "ever" replaces "aye."

Lobe den Herren

Stralsund Gesangbuch, 1665
Harm. from *Chorale Book for England,* 1863

The original tune set to "Hast du denn, Liebster" is found in the second edition of *Ander thiel des erneuerten Gesangbuch* (Stralsund, 1665). It was set to LOBE DEN HERREN in Neander's *Glaubens- und Liebesübung* and appeared with Miss Winkworth's translation in her *Chorale Book for England,* as harmonized by Sterndale Bennett.

There are many slight variants of the melody, which Johannes Zahn thinks is based on an old secular air.

Prayer Is the Soul's Sincere Desire (252)

JAMES MONTGOMERY, 1771-1854

The text was written in 1818 at the request of Edward Bickersteth for his *Treatise on Prayer,* 1819. First printed in pamphlet form in 1818 together with 3 other hymns by Montgomery, for use in the nonconformist Sunday schools in Sheffield, it was then included in the Bickersteth volume and again in 1819 in the famous eighth edition of Thomas Cotterill, *A Selection of Psalms and Hymns for Public and Private Use,* 1819, as four 8-line sts. In Montgomery's *Christian Psalmist* (Glasgow, 1825) and *Original Hymns,* 1853, the hymn is printed in eight 4-line sts. with only slight variations from the Cotterill text, doubtless made by Montgomery himself.

The hymn has been included in all Methodist hymnals beginning with the 1837 Methodist Protestant, which printed all 8 sts. Since 1847 and 1849 we have used sts. 1-5 and 8. In 1878 the order has been shifted to 1-3, 5, 4, and 8.

Shaddick

BATES G. BURT, 1878-1948

The tune was composed in 1941 for "City of God, how broad and far." *The Hymnal 1940* included it with this text. The name is in honor of Charles J. Shaddick, for many years organist and choirmaster at St. Paul's in Marquette, Mich.

Rejoice, the Lord Is King (483)

CHARLES WESLEY, 1707-1788

The text appeared in 6 sts. in Charles Wesley's *Hymns for Our Lord's Resurrection*, 1746. Though John Wesley did not include it in his 1780 *Collection of Hymns for the Use of the People Called Methodists*, it has been in every American Methodist collection since *The Methodist Pocket Hymn Book* of 1802, except the Methodist Protestant hymnal of 1882. All 6 sts. were printed until the 1889 Methodist Episcopal, South hymnal omitted st. 5, and the 1901 Methodist Protestant omitted sts. 5 and 6. Our 1905 Methodist hymnal was the last to print 6 sts. without alteration.

The 1935 hymnal printed only sts. 1-3. In 1935 the original "Mortals, give thanks" (1:3) was changed to its present form. When our 1964 hymnal restored st. 6, it altered "Jesus the judge" (our 4:2) to "Our Lord the judge." The original last 2 lines read:

> We soon shall hear the Archangel's voice,
> The trump of God shall sound, rejoice.

Darwall's 148th

JOHN DARWALL, 1731-1789

The tune was composed for Psalm 148, "Ye boundless realms of joy," in Aaron Williams, *The New Universal Psalmodist* (5th ed.; London, 1770). The initial note was A. The meter, 66.66.88., or H.M., was called the "Hallelujah Meter" in early American hymnals because of its exuberance and joyfulness.

Rejoice, Ye Pure in Heart (233)

EDWARD H. PLUMPTRE, 1821-1891

The text was written for the May, 1865, choir festival at Peterborough Cathedral. According to most sources, after its printing for festival use, it was first published in Plumptre's *Lazarus and Other*

Poems (2nd ed., 1865). However, we could not find this hymn in the copy of the 1865 imprint at the Speer Memorial Library at Princeton, and we are tempted to regard as more probable *The Hymnal 1940 Companion* derivation of the hymn from the third edition of *Lazarus,* 1868. In any case, the first hymnal inclusion was in the Appendix to the 1868 edition of *Hymns Ancient and Modern.*

The hymn first entered the Methodist hymnal in 1905, with 7 of the original 11 sts., omitting 3, 6, 10, and 11. The 1935 hymnal dropped 4, 5, and 9. The 1964 hymnal has added the original st. 6 (our st. 3) for the first time.

Some minor alterations have been made. In 1905 "festal banner" was altered to "glorious banner" (1:3). In 1935 "meek" was replaced with "fair" (2:2) and "praises speak" with "praise declare" (2:4). These alterations remain in the 1964 book.

Marion

ARTHUR H. MESSITER, 1834-1916

Written for this text, the tune was included in *Hymnal with Music,* 1889, edited by Messiter, as the "preliminary report of the committee on the Hymnal appointed by the General Convention of 1886, modified with music as used in Trinity Church, New York."

The tune, written in 1883, was named for the composer's mother.

Rescue the Perishing (175)

FANNY J. CROSBY, 1820-1915

According to Fanny Crosby's own account, the hymn was written in 1869, after an evening meeting in a New York mission. Some days previously William H. Doane had sent her the subject "Rescue the perishing." During that evening she could think of nothing else. After returning home she went to work on the hymn and finished it before retiring. It was first published in Doane's *Songs of Devotion for Christian Associations,* 1870.

The hymn entered our hymnals with the 1901 Methodist Protestant and 1905 Methodist hymnals.

Rescue

WILLIAM H. DOANE, 1832-1915

The tune was first published with the text in Doane's *Songs of Devotion for Christian Associations* (New York, 1870). After Fanny Crosby wrote the words, she gave them to Doane who then wrote the tune.

Ride On, Ride On in Majesty (425)

HENRY H. MILMAN, 1791-1868

The text was probably written before 1823, the year in which Reginald Heber was consecrated bishop in Calcutta, and to whom it was sent for inclusion in the collection Heber was making. It was published in Heber's posthumous hymnal *Hymns Written and Adapted to the Weekly Service of the Church Year*, 1827, and designated for "The Sixth Sunday in Lent."

The hymn entered our hymnals in 1901 with 4 sts. (1, 2, 4, 5) and in 1905 in complete form. The fourth st. was dropped in 1935:

> Ride on! ride on in majesty!
> Thy last and fiercest strife is nigh;
> The Father on his sapphire throne
> Expects His own anointed Son!

The original text of 1:3, "Thine humble heart pursues its road," was altered to the form which appears in all our hymnals by F. H. Murray, *A Hymnal for Use in the English Church*, 1852 edition. Otherwise, the hymn is printed unaltered.

The King's Majesty

GRAHAM GEORGE, 1912-

The tune was composed in 1939 as a substitute for WINCHESTER NEW and was first published in *The Hymnal 1940*. It is an excellent example of a modern unison tune using free rhythm and free harmonies. *The Guide to the Pilgrim Hymnal*, p. 141, quotes a letter from the composer giving further details.

Rise, My Soul (474)

ROBERT SEAGRAVE, 1693–c. 1759

Robert Seagrave, an Anglican clergyman who was a supporter of the Wesleyan movement, published a collection of *Hymns for Christian Worship: Partly Composed and Partly Collected from Various Authors,* "for the purpose of enlivening the services of his congregation." The first edition (London, 1742) was in 82 pages. The second, third, and fourth editions (1742, 1744, and 1748) had increased respectively to 90, 112, and 156 pages. According to Daniel Sedgwick, in his 1860 edition of Seagrave's *Hymns,* "the successive and endless editions of this collection contain not only additional hymns, but present those already published in a considerably altered form." "Rise, my soul" appears to have entered the Seagrave collection in the second of the 2 1742 editions.

The text was originally in 4 sts. The original st. 3 has generally been omitted. St. 2:5 originally read "So my soul derived from God." George Whitefield in 1753 altered the line to read "So a soul that's born of God"—the form which was found in all Methodist Episcopal and Methodist Episcopal, South hymnals since 1847.

In 2:6, Seagrave wrote *"Pants* to view his glorious face." Our 1935 hymnal altered "pants" to "longs." The 1849 and 1878 Methodist Episcopal hymnals replaced the original of our 3:5-8 with a text printed also in Henry Ward Beecher, *Plymouth Collection,* 1855, where the hymn is mistakenly attributed to John Cennick. Seagrave's original quatrain, "Yet a season and you know," as now printed, was restored in 1905.

Amsterdam

See **"Praise the Lord, Who Reigns Above,"** pp. 354-55.

Rise to Greet the Sun (490)

CHAO TZU-CH'EN, 1888-
Trans. by MILDRED A. WIANT, 1898-
and BLISS WIANT, 1895-

The text was translated by Bliss and Mildred Wiant in 1946 for use in lecturing in the United States on Chinese music. It has been put into circulation in a collection of Chinese hymns and folk songs called

The Pagoda, published by the Cooperative Recreation Service, Delaware, Ohio. This is its first appearance in an American hymnal.

Le p'ing

HU TE-AI, c. 1900
Harm. by BLISS WIANT, 1895-

The tune was arranged by Bliss Wiant and first published with the text in *Hymns of Universal Praise*, 1936. The tune name means "joyous peace."

Rise Up, O Men of God (174)

WILLIAM P. MERRILL, 1867-1954

The hymn was prompted by a suggestion of Nolan R. Best, editor of the *Continent*, that a brotherhood hymn was needed by the Presbyterian Brotherhood Movement. About that time Merrill saw an article by S. Lee entitled "The Church of the Strong Men," which furnished the inspiration for the hymn. While on a steamer on Lake Michigan, returning to Chicago for a Sunday at his own church, he suddenly thought of the words. The text was first published in the February 16, 1911, issue of the *Continent* and then with the music in *The Pilgrim Hymnal*, 1912.

It entered the Methodist hymnal in 1935.

Festal Song

WILLIAM H. WALTER, 1825-1893

Set to "Awake and sing the song," c. 1745, of William Hammond, the tune first appeared in J. I. Tucker and W. W. Rousseau's Protestant Episcopal *Hymnal Revised and Enlarged*, 1894. It was first wedded to "Rise up" in the 1912 *Pilgrim Hymnal*.

Rock of Ages, Cleft for Me (120)

AUGUSTUS M. TOPLADY, 1740-1778

A single st. of the text, composed of the first 2 lines of st. 1 and the last 2 lines of st. 3, appeared first in the October, 1775, issue of the *Gospel Magazine*. It was embedded in an article signed "Minimus," but written by Toplady, the editor of the magazine. Entitled "Life a Journey," the article contained a message of hope for those who had fallen into sin: "Yet, if you fall, be humbled; but do not despair. Pray afresh to God." This seems to have been the genesis of the full 6-line hymn in 4 sts. which appeared in the March, 1776, issue of the same magazine at the end of an article called "A remarkable calculation Introduced here for the sake of the Spiritual Improvements subjoined. Questions and answers relating to the National Debt."

Pointing out that the English national debt was so large that it could never be paid, Toplady calculated that every man's debt to God is likewise so great that it can be paid, but only for the elect few and only by the blood of the crucifixion:

Our dreadful account stands as follows: At ten years old each of us is chargeable with 315 millions and 360,000 sins. At twenty, with 630 millions and 720,000. At thirty, with 946 millions and 80,000. . . . At eighty, with 2,522 millions and 880,000.

The Rock of Ages metaphor appears to have come from the marginal rendering of Isaiah 26:4: "In the Lord Jehovah is the rock of ages"; perhaps also from Exodus 33:22: "I will put thee in a clift of the rock"; and I Corinthians: "and that Rock was Christ." However, the direct inspiration for the hymn may have come from some lines of a sermon by Dr. Daniel Brevint, "The Christian Sacrament and Sacrifice," as quoted in Charles Wesley, *Hymns on the Lord's Supper*, 1745:

O Rock of Israel, Rock of Salvation, Rock struck and cleft for me, let those two streams of Blood and Water, which once gushed out of Thy side, bring down pardon and holiness into my soul. And let me thirst after them now, as if I stood upon the mountain whence sprung this Water; and near the cleft of that Rock, the wounds of my Lord, whence gushed this sacred Blood. All the distance of time and countries between Adam and me doth not keep his sin and punishment from reaching me, any more than if I had been born in his house. Adam descended from above, let Thy Blood reach as far, and come as freely to save and sanctify me as the blood of my first father did both to destroy and to defile me. Blessed Jesu, strengthen my faith, prepare my heart, and then bless Thine Ordinance.

Though Toplady included the hymn in his *Psalms and Hymns for*

Public and Private Worship, 1776, it did not become popular until Thomas Cotterill printed it in his *Selection of Psalms and Hymns,* 1815, in a revised and condensed version in 3 sts. Cotterill further revised it in 1819 and then altered line 2 in our third st., "When my eye-strings break in death," to "When mine eyelids close in death," and again in 1830 to the present form, which has been printed in all our hymnals since 1837. It was Cotterill's 1830 revision which entered the 1831 Supplement of the Wesleyan hymnbook *A Collection of Hymns for the Use of the People Called Methodists* and which has appeared in all subsequent American Methodist hymnals without change.

Toplady

THOMAS HASTINGS, 1784-1872

The tune was written in 1830 in the key of D for "Air, 2nd Treble and bass," and was first published in *Spiritual Songs for Social Worship,* 1832, edited by Hastings and Lowell Mason.

The tune is also called DEVOTION and ROCK OF AGES.

Safely Through Another Week (489)

JOHN NEWTON, 1725-1807

The text in five 6-line sts. was first published in Richard Conyers, *A Collection of Psalms and Hymns* (3rd ed., 1774), and then 5 years later in *Olney Hymns,* by Newton and William Cowper. The few alterations made in the second printing have established themselves: 2:2 originally read "in," not "through"; 4:4, "our wants," not "complaints"; 4:5, "let," not "may." However, since the hymn was originally written for Saturday evening, some important modifications had to be made to fit it to Sunday: 1:4 read "On the approaching sabbath day"; 2:6, "night," not "day"; 3:1, "When the morn shall bid us rise"; 3:5, "there," not "here."

The original st. 2, now rarely printed, has never been included in our hymnals.

The hymn entered the Methodist Protestant hymnal in 1837, the Methodist Episcopal, South in 1847, and the Methodist Episcopal in 1878. It has been in all our later hymnals, in the same 4 sts.

Sabbath

Arr. by LOWELL MASON, 1792-1872

In Mason's *Hallelujah*, 1824, the tune was named OLEAN and called a German tune. It is also known as WORSHIP and SABBATH MORN.

Savior, Again to Thy Dear Name We Raise (236)

JOHN ELLERTON, 1826-1893

The hymn in 6 sts. was written in 1866 for a choir festival of the Middlewich and Nantwich Choral Association. The author revised it and reduced it to 4 sts. for the 1868 Appendix to the first edition of *Hymns Ancient and Modern.*

The hymn entered our hymnals in 1878 with the 4 sts. of *Hymns Ancient and Modern*. Our 1935 hymnal altered 1:4 to read: "And still our hearts to wait thy word of peace." The original text has been restored in the present hymnal.

Ellers

EDWARD J. HOPKINS, 1818-1901

Hopkins composed a unison setting with varied harmony for each st. for Robert Brown-Borthwick, *Supplemental Hymn and Tune Book* (3rd ed., 1869). Samuel Smith, editor of the Appendix to *The Bradford Tune Book,* 1872, requested the composer to make the 4-part setting which is currently sung.

Savior, Breathe an Evening Blessing (496)

JAMES EDMESTON, 1791-1867

The text in two 8-line sts. was first published in the author's *Sacred Lyrics*, 1820. It was headed by a quotation from Henry Salt's *Voyage to Abyssinia* . . . (London, 1814) : "At night their short evening hymn, 'Jesu Mahaxaroo,'—'Jesus forgive us,' stole through the camp." This line prompted the writing of the lyric. Edward Bickersteth in *Christian Psalmody,* 1833, was one of the first to use it as a hymn.

It has been included in all American Methodist hymnals since 1849, in the original text until the present hymnal adopted the last quatrain of the hymn in the *Hymnary of the United Church of Canada,* 1930, in place of the original last 4 lines:

> Be thou nigh, should death o'ertake us;
> Jesus, then our refuge be,
> And in paradise awake us,
> There to rest in peace with thee.

Stuttgart

See **"Earth Has Many a Noble City,"** pp. 166-67.

Savior, Like a Shepherd Lead Us (121)

Hymns for the Young, 1836
Attr. to DOROTHY A. THRUPP, 1779-1847

The hymn appeared anonymously in *Hymns for the Young* (4th ed., 1836), compiled by Dorothy Thrupp. It appeared again in W. Carus Wilson, *Children's Friend,* June, 1838, signed "Lyte." In the same year it appeared again in Mrs. Herbert Mayo's *Selection of Hymns and Poetry for Use of Infants and Juvenile Schools and Families,* but without the mention of Thrupp. John Julian thinks the evidence is against Thrupp, and uncertain with regard to Henry Lyte. Some handbooks favor Lyte.

Bradbury

WILLIAM B. BRADBURY, 1816-1868
Harm. by V.E.C.

The tune was composed for these words for Bradbury's *Oriola,* 1859, a Sunday school collection. A repetitive tune, it has been shortened by omitting the third line.

Savior, More Than Life to Me (226)

FANNY J. CROSBY, 1820-1915

The text was written in 1874 and first published in *Brightest and Best,* a Sunday school collection compiled by Robert Lowry and William H. Doane (Chicago, 1875). It was entitled "Every Day and Hour," with Psalm 51:2 underneath: "Cleanse me from my sin." The hymn entered our hymnals in 1889.

Every Day and Hour

WILLIAM H. DOANE, 1832-1915

Doane wrote the tune in 1874 and sent it to Fanny Crosby, requesting her to write a hymn entitled "Every Day and Hour." It was published in *Brightest and Best*, 1875 (see comments on text, above).

Savior, Teach Me, Day by Day (162)

JANE E. LEESON, 1809-1881

The hymn in four 8-line sts. first appeared in the author's *Hymns and Scenes of Childhood, or A Sponsor's Gift*, 1842, and under the title "Obedience."

The hymn entered Methodist hymnals in 1882 (2 quatrains) and 1901 (4 quatrains). The 1905 hymnal continued with the same 4 made up of 1:1-4, 2:1-4, 3:5-8 with our st. 4 composed of the original 2:8-9 and 4:8-9.

Originally 1:2 read "Love's sweet lesson"; 1:3, "Sweeter lesson." These have been altered to the present form in 1964, following the text of *The Hymnal 1940*.

Orientis partibus

Melody from the Office of PIERRE DE CORBEIL, d. 1222
Harm. by RICHARD REDHEAD, 1820-1901

The medieval melody was sung at the Feast of the Ass, January 14, a church festival commemorating the flight into Egypt. Combining medieval Latin and old French, it began "Orientis partibus adventavis asinus" (from the Eastern regions the Ass is now come). M. Felix Clément has traced the melody to a manuscript in the library of Sens and attributes it to the work of Corbeil, archbishop of Sens. A Beauvais manuscript in the British Museum gives a melodic form much like that sung today in the arrangement by Richard Redhead, but there is reason to believe that triple time is closer to the spirit of the original than the straight common time adopted by Redhead. Redhead's version was published in *Church Hymn Tunes, Ancient and Modern* (London, 1853).

The tune has also been called CORTON.

367

Savior, Thy Dying Love (177)

SYLVANUS D. PHELPS, 1816-1895

The text was written in 1862 and was first published unsigned in the Boston *Watchman and Reflector*, March 17, 1864, but in a text so different from the familiar one as to be scarcely recognizable. The author apparently rewrote the hymn when Lowry requested its use for a collection which he and W. H. Doane were to publish, *Pure Gold*. It was given the title "Something for Jesus," with Acts 9:6 printed underneath.

The hymn entered the Methodist hymnal in 1901, in its present form.

Something for Jesus

ROBERT LOWRY, 1826-1899

The tune was written for *Pure Gold for the Sunday School* (New York, 1871), a collection that sold more than one million copies (see comments, above).

See How Great a Flame Aspires (464)

CHARLES WESLEY, 1707-1788

The hymn was probably written for the coal miners in Staffordshire, perhaps in 1743 or 1744. It may have been suggested by the glow of the colliery fires. It appeared in *Hymns and Sacred Poems*, 1749, the last of 4 hymns with the title "After Preaching to the Newcastle Colliers."

John Wesley included the hymn in his *Collection of Hymns for the Use of the People Called Methodists*, 1780, with 2 slight alterations which have since been retained: in 4:2 "an" gives place to "a"; in 4:7, "shall" to "will."

The hymn has been in all American Methodist collections since 1822 and in the form as printed in 1780. The third st. was dropped in 1905 and 1935, to be restored in 1964.

Arfon (Major)

Welsh Hymn Melody
Harm. by C.R.Y.

This is the traditional Welsh melody ARFON, put into the major mode, just as LLANFYLLIN is the major form of LLANGLOFFAN. For information about ARFON, see pp. 374-75.

See Israel's Gentle Shepherd Stand (312)

PHILIP DODDRIDGE, 1702-1751

The text in 5 sts. was first published in Job Orton's posthumous edition of Doddridge's *Hymns Founded on Various Texts in the Holy Scriptures* (London, 1755). Its title was "Christ's Condescending Regard to Little Children. Mark 10:14."

The first 3 sts. of the hymn entered our hymnals in 1837 and have been included in all our hymnals since.

Meditation (Gower)

JOHN H. GOWER, 1855-1922

The tune was written for "There is a land of pure delight" and published in Gower's *Original Tunes* (Denver, 1890).

See the Morning Sun Ascending (7)

CHARLES PARKIN, 1894-

The text was written for the May, 1953, session of the Maine Annual Conference. It was suggested by Revelation 5:11-14, 7:11-12.

Unser Herrscher

See **"God of Love and God of Power,"** p. 197.

Servant of All, to Toil for Man (186)

CHARLES WESLEY, 1707-1788

The text was first published in *Hymns and Sacred Poems,* 1739, headed "To be sung at Work." In 5 sts., it began "Son of the carpenter, receive this humble work of mine." In editing the hymn for his *Collection of Hymns for the Use of the People Called Methodists,* John Wesley omitted the first and last sts., beginning the hymn "Servant of all." Until 1964 the hymn was included in only 1 American Methodist hymnal, 1878, when the full 5 sts. were printed as Charles wrote them. The hymn in our 1964 hymnal includes as its third st. the second st. of "another" hymn to be sung at work, which immediately follows "Son of the Carpenter." The 4 sts. from the first hymn are given in the order 2, 1, 4, and 5.

Shaddick

See "Prayer Is the Soul's Sincere Desire," pp. 357-58.

Servant of God, Well Done (288)

CHARLES WESLEY, 1707-1788

The text in four 8-line sts. was published at the end of the funeral sermon which John Wesley preached at the death of George Whitefield. The sermon was preached at Whitefield's Tabernacle, London, Sunday, November 18, 1770.

The hymn has been included in all our American Methodist hymnals since 1847 in six 4-line sts. until 1935 when 2 more quatrains were dropped. The two 8-line sts. in the present hymnal represent a recombination of the original 1a, 3a and 3b, 4a.

Diademata

See "Crown Him with Many Crowns," p. 162.

Shepherd of Eager Youth (86)

CLEMENT OF ALEXANDRIA, c. 160-215
Trans. by HENRY M. DEXTER, 1821-1890

For an account of Clement's original hymn, see comments on "O Guide to every child," pp. 314-15.

This English translation was made in 1846 for use in connection with a sermon on the text Deuteronomy 32:7, "Remember the days of old," the theme being "Some prominent characteristics of the early Christians." It was first sung from manuscript by the choir of the church in Manchester, N.H., in which Dexter was ordained into the Congregational ministry. "I first translated it literally into prose," the author wrote, "and then transfused as much of its language and spirit as I could into the hymn."

It first appeared in the *Congregationalist,* December 21, 1849. Its first hymnal inclusion was in F. H. Hedge and F. D. Huntingdon, *Hymns for the Church of Christ,* 1853.

The text entered our hymnals in 1878, with all 5 sts. These were printed until the present hymnal omitted the original st. 2.

Some minor alterations had already been made by 1878. In 1964 the original first line was altered from "Shepherd of *tender* youth"; "make our faith strong" to "our faith make strong" (3:7); and "Infants, and the glad throng" to "let all the holy throng" (4:4).

Hinman

AUSTIN C. LOVELACE, 1919-

The tune was composed in 1953 at the request of James R. Sydnor for the Presbyterian U. S. *Hymnbook* (Philadelphia, 1955), in which it first appeared. It was named for the street on which the First Methodist Church is located in Evanston, Ill.

Silent Night, Holy Night (393)
Stille Nacht, heilige Nacht!

JOSEPH MOHR, 1792-1848
Stanzas 1-3, trans. by JOHN F. YOUNG, 1820-1885
Stanza 4, ANONYMOUS

The text in 6 sts. was written in 1818 for a Christmas Eve service in St. Nicholas' Church, Oberndorf, Upper Austria. Joseph Mohr, who was assistant priest, asked Franz Gruber, the acting organist, to set this text for their 2 voices, choir, and guitar, probably to help out in a situation caused by an organ breakdown. During the next few years the hymn spread through the Tyrol and was variously put in manuscript form. The earliest manuscript in the composer's hand is dated 1833, and is scored for chorus, organ, and orchestra. It was first published in the collection known as the *Leipziger Gesangbuch,* 1838, and then in a Dresden collection of "four genuine Tyrolean songs" (see comments on tune, below).

The English translation by John F. Young was first published in John C. Hollister, *The Sunday School Service and Tune Book,* 1863, and again in Charles L. Hutchins, ed., *The Sunday School Hymnal and Service Book,* 1871. The hymn entered the Methodist hymnal in 1905 with the 3 sts. of Young as published in these 1863 and 1871 collections. Our 1935 hymnal replaced Young's second st. beginning "Shepherds quake at the sight," with the st.:

> Silent night, holy night,
> Darkness flies, all is light;
> Shepherds hear the angels sing,

371

"Alleluia! hail the King!
Christ the Savior is born,
Christ the Savior is born."

and added as a fourth, the st. beginning "Wondrous star, lend thy light." The origin of these 2 sts. seems to be undetermined.

Our 1964 hymnal has replaced the st. beginning "Darkness flies" with Young's original st. 2, "Shepherds quake," but the anonymous st. beginning "Wondrous star" has been retained.

Stille Nacht

FRANZ GRUBER, 1787-1863

(See comments on text, above.) The tune was composed for 2 voices and guitar (Zupfgeige), and was first sung with Mohr on tenor lead with Gruber singing bass and playing the guitar. The organ repairman, Karl Mauracher of Zillerthal, secured a copy and spread it about the Tyrol, calling it a "Tiroler Volkslied." The Strasser family of Zillerthal sang it at the Leipzig fair in 1831, and a Dresden musician named Friese in the audience jotted down a copy.

The manuscript dated 1833, scored for chorus, organ, and orchestra, is obviously more complex than the first version. It was published in the *Leipziger Gesangbuch,* 1838, and in America it was first included in the Methodist collection *The Devotional Harmonist,* 1849, with a free paraphrase by J. W. Warner.

Sing Praise to God Who Reigns Above (4)
Sei Lob und Ehr dem höchsten Gut

JOHANN J. SCHÜTZ, 1640-1690
Trans. by FRANCES E. COX, 1812-1897

The German text in 9 sts., based on Deuteronomy 32:3, was first published in the author's *Christliches Gedenckbüchlein,* 1675. Miss Cox offered her translation of 8 sts. in *Lyra Eucharistica* (2nd ed., 1864) and also included it in the 1864 *Hymns from the German,* a collection which printed both German and English texts in parallel columns.

The hymn entered the Methodist hymnal in 1935 with sts. 1, 3, 5, and 7. The eighth st. was added in 1964. Two alterations may be noted: "throughout" was changed to "but through" (3:2) and *"Then, all my gladsome"* to *"Thus,* all my *toilsome"* (4:1).

Mit Freuden zart

Bohemian Brethren's *Kirchengesänge* . . . , 1566

The original form of the melody went thus:

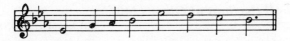

Its melodic motives relate it to many other tunes, such as LASST UNS ERFREUEN, OLD 113TH, and the Psalm 138 melody of the Genevan Psalter. It is probably older than the 1566 collection.

Pierre Pidoux in *Le Psautier Huguenot,* 1962, quotes a secular chanson published in 1529-30 by Pierre Attaignant which has an opening phrase that is practically identical.

Sing Them Over Again to Me (109)

PHILIP P. BLISS, 1838-1876

The text and tune, both written by Bliss, first appeared in *Words of Life,* 1874, a Sunday school paper published by Fleming H. Revell. Its first hymnal inclusion was in *Gospel Hymns No. 3,* 1878. It entered our hymnals in 1901, and now in 1964.

The hymn was often sung by the author composer and his wife as a duet.

Words of Life

PHILIP P. BLISS, 1838-1876

See comments on text, above.

Sing to the Great Jehovah's Praise (510)

CHARLES WESLEY, 1707-1788

The text was originally published anonymously in a penny tract of 7 pieces called *Hymns for New-Year's Day,* 1750. Originally in three 8-line sts., the hymn was so printed in our hymnals until the 1837 and 1849 hymnals halved the sts. The only one of our hymnals to omit the hymn entirely was the 1882 Methodist Protestant hymnal. The 1901 and 1935 hymnals omitted 2 quatrains. All our other hymnals have printed the entire hymn.

Minor alterations have been made in the text of 3 of the sts.

Lobt Gott, ihr Christen

See "Let All Together Praise Our God," pp. 266-67.

Sing with All the Sons of Glory (440)

WILLIAM J. IRONS, 1812-1883

The text is taken from the author's *Psalms and Hymns for the Church,* 1873, where it is printed under the text "Now is Christ risen from the dead" (I Corinthians 15:20). It entered our hymnals in 1878. The original lines of 1:4-8 were:

> Even now the dawn is breaking,
> Soon the night of time shall cease,
> And in God's own likeness, waking,
> Man shall know eternal peace.

In 1878 they were already altered to the form in which they now appear. Otherwise the hymn is as the author wrote it.

Hymn to Joy

See "Joyful, Joyful, We Adore Thee," pp. 260-61.

Sinners, Turn: Why Will You Die (112)

CHARLES WESLEY, 1707-1788

The text was first published in *Hymns on God's Everlasting Love,* 1741. Headed by "Why will ye die, O House of Israel" (Ezekiel 18: 31), it was in sixteen 8-line sts. John Wesley reduced the hymn to its first 4 sts., omitting 5-16.

The hymn, first in John Wesley's 4 sts., then in 3, has been included in all American Methodist collections since 1802.

Arfon

Welsh Hymn Melody

The tune is found in G. Legeay, *Noëls Anciens,* 1875, set to the Christmas carol "Un nouveau présent des Cieux" and in R. Guilmant, *Noëls,* 1885, set to "Joseph est bien marié." It was first called ARFON in *Caniadau y Cyssegr,* 1878. It is not clear whether the Welsh or the French form is the original, for the melody has characteristics of both types of music.

The tune in 87.87.D. is known as MERIBAH.

So Lowly Doth the Savior Ride (422)

ALMER M. PENNEWELL, 1876-

The text is taken from a collection of the author's poems *Sing, Parson, Sing,* published in 1949 by the Pinecrest Press, Chicago. This seems to be its first inclusion in a hymnal.

"Dear Messiah" has been changed to *"great* Messiah" (3:1).

Epworth Church

V. EARLE COPES, 1921-

The tune was written in 1962 for another Common Meter text being considered for the 1964 hymnal. It is named for the church in Norfolk, Va., where the composer attended as a boy and had his first organ lesson.

Softly Now the Light of Day (494)

GEORGE W. DOANE, 1799-1859

The text in two 8-line sts. was first published in the author's *Songs by the Way, Chiefly Devotional: with Translations and Imitations,* 1824. Entitled "Evening," with the biblical text "Let my prayer be—as the evening sacrifice" (Psalm 141:2), it was immediately followed by a "midnight" hymn, with the text "God my Maker, who giveth songs in the night."

Early divided into 4 sts., it entered our hymnals in 1849 with the omission of 2 and 4. The only one of our hymnals ever to include st. 4 is the 1901 Methodist Protestant hymnal.

Though the 1882 hymnal printed only sts. 1 and 3, all other hymnals since 1878 have included the first 3 sts.

The only alterations made in the original text are the change of "I" and "me" to "we" and "us." These appeared in our hymnals beginning with 1849.

375

Mercy

Arr. from **LOUIS M. GOTTSCHALK, 1829-1869**
by **EDWIN P. PARKER, 1836-1925**

Parker, a Congregational minister at Hartford, Conn., made the arrangement from Gottschalk's piano piece *The Last Hope,* 1854. It first appeared in one of Charles S. Robinson's collections. It has been reharmonized to omit much of the objectionable chromaticism.

The tune is also called GOTTSCHALK and LAST HOPE.

Soldiers of Christ, Arise (250)

CHARLES WESLEY, 1707-1788

Quoting Frank Baker in *Representative Verse of Charles Wesley,*

It is uncertain whether this stirring poem first appeared at the end of the first and second editions of John Wesley's *Character of a Methodist,* both issued in 1742 (it was omitted from the third and later editions), or in an undated broadside, of which there is a copy in the British Museum, placed c. 1740-9 in a magnificent collection of broadsides. There is only one significant difference between the two versions, however, the use of "Table" for Altar in the broadside version of stanza 13.

Its first appearance in a Wesley collection was in *Hymns and Sacred Poems,* 1749. In sixteen 8-line sts., it was entitled "The Whole Armour of God, Ephesians vi." In his 1780 *Collection of Hymns for the Use of the People Called Methodists,* John Wesley printed 12 of the sts. as 3 separate hymns, omitting sts. 5, 6, 9, and 10, but otherwise without alteration.

The hymn has been in every American Methodist collection. *The Methodist Pocket Hymn Book* (Philadelphia, 1802) printed the first of the 3 centos in the 1780 *Collection.* The last hymnals to print the 12 sts. selected by John were the 1836 Methodist Episcopal and the 1837 Methodist Protestant. In 1847 and 1849, the hymn was reduced to 3 sts. Our 1964 cento, composed of sts. 1, 2, and 16, first appeared in the Methodist Episcopal, South hymnals of 1847 and 1889, and then regularly since the 1905 Methodist hymnal. The 1935 hymnal altered the last 2 lines to read "Till Christ the Lord who reigns on high/shall take the conquerors home." The present hymnal returns to the original Wesley.

Percy Dearmer comments: "The mastered simplicity of this, its faultless technique, its sagacity in the use of imperfect rhymes, are signs of high accomplishment."

Diademata

See **"Crown Him with Many Crowns,"** p. 162.

Sometimes a Light Surprises (231)

WILLIAM COWPER, 1731-1800

The hymn in 4 sts. first appeared in *Olney Hymns,* 1779, entitled "Joy and peace in believing." The biblical references were Matthew 6:34 and Habakkuk 3:17-18. Erik Routley has described the hymn as "Cowper's happiest hymn, and his greatest."

It entered the Methodist Episcopal hymnal in 1878.

Llanfyllin

See **"O Spirit of the Living God,"** p. 336.

Spirit Divine, Attend Our Prayers (461)

ANDREW REED, 1787-1862

On February 10, 1829, the Board of Congregational Ministers resident in and about London urged the appointment of a special day of humiliation and prayer with a view to promoting a revival of religion in British churches. Good Friday was the day set. This hymn was prepared by the author for that occasion. It was first published in the *Evangelical Magazine,* June, 1829; then republished in the author's *Hymn Book,* 1842. Samuel Longfellow somewhat radically revised the hymn for *Hymns of the Spirit,* 1864, reducing it to 6 sts.

The hymn entered our Methodist hymnals with sts. 1, 2, 3, 6, and 7 in 1878; 1, 2, 3, 6, and 5 in 1889 and 1905; and 1, 2, 3, and 5 in 1901. The hymn was omitted entirely in 1935, but sts. 1, 3, 5, and 7 were reclaimed in 1964. Our 1964 printing reproduces the original Reed with only one change: in 4:2 "make a lost world thy home" is replaced by "and make this world thy home." Our earlier printings followed Longfellow in st. 1 with a few other changes of unknown origin.

377

Ballerma

See "Happy the Souls to Jesus Joined," pp. 208-9.

Spirit of Faith, Come Down (137)

CHARLES WESLEY, 1707-1788

The text was first published in John and Charles Wesley, *Hymns of Petition and Thanksgiving for the Promise of the Father*, 1746, a collection of 32 hymns. The text was originally in 5 sts.; John omitted the third in his 1780 *Collection of Hymns for the Use of the People Called Methodists.*

John Wesley changed "My dear atoning Lamb" (our 3:2) to its present form. The hymn has been included in either the 3- or 4-st. form in virtually all Methodist hymnals.

Bealoth

TIMOTHY B. MASON, *The Sacred Harp*, 1840
Harm. by A.C.L.

Henry L. Mason in *Hymn Tunes of Lowell Mason—A Bibliography* lists BEALOTH as an original tune by Lowell Mason, date of composition unknown. Yet Robert G. McCutchan quotes from a letter from Henry L. Mason: "There is a characteristic quality to the tunes Mason wrote. . . . I do not believe my grandfather wrote this tune; I should be surprised if any conclusive evidence is brought to bear showing that he did."

The tune first appeared in *The Sacred Harp, or Beauties of Church Music*, Vol. II (Boston, 1840), collected by Timothy B. Mason. Apparently it was previously published in the *Seraph*, a monthly publication of new church music. There it opens with a rising sixth, which has been omitted to avoid a false accent on the second syllable of "Spirit."

Bealoth is the Hebrew for "citizens" and is the name of a city in southeast Judah, near Salem, now called Kurnub. The tune is also known as PHILLPUT.

Spirit of God, Descend upon My Heart (138)

GEORGE CROLY, 1780-1860

Most handbooks mistakenly assert that the source of the hymn was Croly's *Psalms and Hymns for Public Worship*, 1854. However, the hymn cannot be found in this collection or in any of Croly's published works. Its first appearance seems to be in Charles Rogers, *Lyra Britannica,* 1867, where it is ascribed to Croly.

It entered the Methodist Protestant hymnal in 1901 in 4 sts., with the third omitted. The full 5 sts. have been in our hymnals since 1905.

Morecambe

FREDERICK C. ATKINSON, 1841-1897

Called HELLESPONT, the tune was written in 1870 for "Abide with me" and published in leaflet form for use at the church in Manningham, England, where Atkinson was organist. It was first included in G. S. Barrett and E. J. Hopkins, *Congregational Church Hymnal* (London, 1887).

Morecambe is a well-known coastal town on Morecambe Bay in west England, near Lancaster.

Spirit of Life, in This New Dawn (462)

EARL MARLATT, 1892-

The text was written late in 1923 from a poem entitled "Cosmology," later "Creation," and finally "May Morning"—a poem for which Dr. Marlatt was awarded "The Golden Flower" at the May Day Poetry Tournament in Boston. The initial inspiration came from Michelangelo's "Creation of Adam" in the Sistine Chapel, which the author had seen the preceding spring. "Touch thou our dust" in st. 2 recalls the painting.

The hymn was made from the poem in answer to an announcement of a prize hymn contest by the *Pulpit,* and was first published in that magazine. "I didn't realize it until I had written it and read it over," wrote Dr. Marlatt, "that it traced the day from 'dawn' to 'evening time,' and between them revealed the Trinity: Creative Father, redeeming Son, consoling Holy Spirit."

Its first hymnal inclusion was in *American Sacred Hymns,* 1928. It entered the Methodist hymnal in 1935.

Maryton

See "**O Master, Let Me Walk with Thee,**" p. 329.

Spring Has Now Unwrapped the Flowers (442)
Tempus adest floridum

The Oxford Book of Carols, 1928

The spring carol *Tempus adest floridum* first appeared in *Piae Cantiones* (Nyland, 1582). This translation was first published in *The Oxford Book of Carols,* 1928.

The carol here enters our hymnal for the first time, with sts. 1, 3, and 5. The omitted sts. are also in character:

> Herb and plant that, winter long,
> Slumbered at their leisure.
> Now bestirring, green and strong,
> Find in growth their pleasure:
> All the world with beauty fills,
> Gold the green enhancing;
> Flowers make glee among the hills,
> And set the meadows dancing.

> Earth puts on her dress of glee;
> Flowers and grasses hide her;
> We go forth in charity—
> Brothers all beside her;
> For, as man this glory sees
> In the awakening season,
> Reason learns the heart's decrees,
> And hearts are led by reason.

Tempus adest floridum

See "**Gentle Mary Laid Her Child,**" p. 185.

Stand Up and Bless the Lord (16)

JAMES MONTGOMERY, 1771-1854

The text based on Nehemiah 9:5 was written for the Red Hill Wesleyan Sunday School anniversary, Sheffield, March 15, 1824. The second line originally read "Ye *children* of his choice." "Children" was changed to "people" for the author's *Christian Psalmist* (Glasgow, 1825).

Our 1837, 1847, and 1889 hymnals printed all 6 sts. St. 4 was dropped in 1878 and 1901, and the entire hymn dropped in 1882 and 1905. Our 5-st. form was reclaimed in 1935.

St. Michael

See **"How Can a Sinner Know,"** p. 221.

Stand Up, Stand Up for Jesus (248)

GEORGE DUFFIELD, Jr., 1818-1888

According to the author's own account, dated May 29, 1883, the hymn was inspired by the words of Dudley A. Tyng's last sermon. This sermon was preached the Sunday before his death to the ministers gathered for a noonday prayer meeting in the Y.M.C.A. in Philadelphia, during the great revival of 1858. His cry to the 5,000 men present was "Stand up for Jesus." The following Wednesday, leaving his study for a moment, Tyng went to the barn where a mule was at work on a horsepower, shelling corn. As Tyng patted the mule's neck, the sleeve of his silk study gown caught in the cogs of the wheel, and his arm was torn out by the roots. He died within a few hours.

The next Sunday George Duffield, Jr., preached from Ephesians 6:14 and concluded his exhortation with the hymn "Stand up, stand up for Jesus," which he had written for this purpose. The hymn in 6 sts. was first published on a flyleaf, then in the Presbyterian *Church Psalmist,* 1859, and with increasing frequency in a number of hymnals.

It is conjectured that since Tyng had been persecuted for his stand against slavery, he probably meant to say, "Stand up for Jesus in the person of the downtrodden slave."

Our present cento is made up of sts. 1, 3, 4, and 6. In this form it entered our hymnals in 1878, though later hymnals used various centos.

Webb

GEORGE J. WEBB, 1803-1887

Webb wrote the tune in 1830 while on shipboard bound for America. He set it to "'Tis dawn, the lark is singing," and it was first published in *The Odeon* (Boston, 1837), a collection of secular melodies edited by Webb and Lowell Mason.

Set to "The morning light is breaking," it appeared in Moses L. Scudder, *The Wesleyan Psalmist,* 1842. According to Samuel W. Duffield in his *English Hymns,* William B. Bradbury was the first to wed the text and tune as they are used here.

The tune is also called GOODWIN, MORNING LIGHT, and MILLENNIAL DAWN.

Standing on the Promises (221)

R. KELSO CARTER, 1849-1926

The text and tune were first published in *Songs of Perfect Love,* compiled by John R. Sweney and Carter (Philadelphia, 1886). The original st. 3 has been omitted.

This is the first inclusion of the hymn in an official Methodist hymnal.

Promises

R. KELSO CARTER, 1849-1926

See comments on text, above.

Still, Still with Thee (264)

HARRIET B. STOWE, 1812-1896

"I *do* have hopes of inexpressible beauty and sweetness," Mrs. Stowe wrote, "and of late they come oftener and oftener,—They come between dawn and daylight when I seem to be asleep and am not, but am conscious as near to God—*almost* as I would ask." Often she arose in the morning at 4:30 and went out to enjoy the birds and the dawn. On one such occasion, "in that rare, sweet atmosphere" she wrote the words of this hymn.

Though written in 1853, reflecting the words "When I awake I am still with thee" (Psalm 139:18), the hymn was not published until 1855 in *Plymouth Collection of Hymns,* the collection made by her brother H. W. Beecher.

The hymn entered our hymnal in 1905 with all 6 sts. The 1935 hymnal omitted st. 3.

Consolation

Arr. from FELIX MENDELSSOHN, 1809-1847

The setting, called "Consolation" in some editions, was marked simply "Adagio non troppo" by Mendelssohn in his *Songs Without Words,* Op. 30, No. 3 in Bk. II. In W. Mercer, *The Church Psalter and Hymn Book,* 1864, the first half of the setting, harmonized by John Goss, was set to "Abide with me." In E. J. Hopkins, *The Temple Church Hymn Book,* 1869, it was called EPIPHANY and was arranged by Adolphus Levy to fit the text "Brightest and best." Charles S. Robinson used it in *Spiritual Songs,* 1875, and in Charles L. Hutchins' 1894 musical edition of the Protestant Episcopal hymnal the tune was called BRIGHTEST AND BEST, and the index credits the arrangement to A. Levy, 1880.

Other tune names are REYNOLDS and BERLIN.

Strong Son of God, Immortal Love (146)

ALFRED TENNYSON, 1809-1892

In Memoriam, Tennyson's renowned lament over the sudden and tragic death in 1833 of his dear friend and prospective brother-in-law Arthur Henry Hallam, is composed of a series of elegiac poems. The poems were written between 1833 and 1850 when the collection was first published.

The prologue, in 11 sts., is dated 1849. As an invocation, the prologue views the poem as complete and gathers into itself the essential concerns of the whole. It was not intended to be sung; yet a cento is included in many hymnals.

Our 1905 hymnal includes sts. 1, 3-5. A fifth st. has been added in 1964, the original seventh.

Keble

See **"Forth in Thy Name, O Lord, I Go,"** p. 182.

Sun of My Soul, Thou Savior Dear (502)

JOHN KEBLE, 1792-1866

The text in 14 sts. was written November 25, 1820, and was first published in the author's *Christian Year* (London, 1827). Luke 24:29 was printed underneath the title "Evening." The first st. ran:

'Tis gone, that bright and orbed blaze,
Fast fading from our wistful gaze;
Yon mantling cloud has hid from sight
The last faint pulse of quivering light.

Our 6 sts. are 3, 7-8, 12-14 of the original, printed without alteration. The hymn in this form entered our hymnals in 1878.

Hursley

See **"Dear Master, in Whose Life I See,"** p. 164.

Sweet Hour of Prayer (275)

Attr. to W. W. WALFORD, 1772-1850

According to Thomas Salmon's account in the *New York Observer,* September 13, 1845, which accompanied the first printing of the 4 sts. of this hymn, the hymn was written by a blind preacher named W. W. Walford. Salmon was pastor of a Congregational church at Coleshill, Warwickshire, 1838-42. On one occasion, when Salmon was paying Walford a visit, the latter dictated the hymn to him. In 1842 Salmon came to the United States. Three years later the *Observer* published the hymn, previously submitted by Salmon, together with the above account of its origin.

Since no person as W. W. Walford has been identified, the accuracy of Salmon's statement has been questioned. Most frequently this W. W. Walford has been identified with William Walford, 1772-1850. However, there is no direct evidence that William Walford wrote the hymn.

For further discussion of the problem, see William J. Reynolds, *Hymns of Our Faith,* pp. 186-88.

The hymn entered our hymnals in 1878, 1882, and 1889 with sts. 1, 3, and 4. In 1935, the fourth st. was dropped and the second restored to its place.

Sweet Hour

WILLIAM B. BRADBURY, 1816-1868

Composed by Bradbury for this text, the tune appeared in *The Golden Chain* (New York, 1861). According to Robert G. McCutchan, Bradbury stated in his *Anthem Book,* 1860, that the tune was taken from *Musical Tracts.* Since compilers like Bradbury used successful material in many other collections, it is difficult to determine where a tune was first published.

The tune is also called CONSOLATION and WALFORD.

Take My Life, and Let It Be Consecrated (187)

FRANCES R. HAVERGAL, 1836-1879

The text in six 4-line sts. was written in December, 1873, and first published in *Songs of Grace and Glory,* 1874, edited by Charles B. Shepp and Havergal. It entered our Methodist Protestant hymnal in 1901 with 5 quatrains. Since 1905 the entire hymn has been included, printed in 3 sts. of 8 lines each.

Messiah

LOUIS J. F. HÉROLD, 1791-1833
Arr. by GEORGE KINGSLEY, 1811-1884

The tune first appeared in *The Sacred Choir,* 1839, set to "Rock of Ages, cleft for me."

Take the Name of Jesus with You (87)

LYDIA BAXTER, 1809-1874

Written in 1870, the text was first published in *Pure Gold for the Sunday School,* edited by Robert Lowry and William H. Doane, 1871. The hymn has been included in every Methodist hymnal since 1878 except the 1901 Methodist Protestant hymnal.

Precious Name

WILLIAM H. DOANE, 1832-1915

The tune was first published in *Pure Gold,* 1871, edited by Doane (see comments on text, above).

Take Time to Be Holy (266)

WILLIAM D. LONGSTAFF, 1822-1894

The origin of the hymn is disputed. Ira D. Sankey in his autobiography writes that Longstaff wrote the text after hearing a sermon in New Brighton on I Peter 1:10, and that it was first published in Sankey's *Gospel Hymns No. 6* and *Sacred Songs and Solos* 1874. However, George Stebbins, the composer of the tune HOLINESS, says that the words "Take time to be holy" were spoken by Griffith John, a missionary to China, at a conference in that country. They were quoted at a meeting in Keswick, England, which Longstaff attended and which inspired Longstaff to compose the hymn that very night. According to Robert G. McCutchan, the hymn first appeared in an English publication about 1882 and later in *Hymns of Consecration,* used at Keswick.

The hymn entered the Methodist Protestant hymnal in 1901 and then in 1935.

Holiness

GEORGE C. STEBBINS, 1846-1945

The tune was written in 1890 while Stebbins was on a trip to India. It was mailed to Ira D. Sankey in New York, who published it in his *Winnowed Songs for Sunday School* (New York, 1890) and the following year in *Gospel Songs No. 6.*

Take Up Thy Cross (160)

CHARLES W. EVEREST, 1814-1877

The text in 5 sts. was first published in the author's *Visions of Death and Other Poems,* 1833. Everest's original text seems to have been considerably altered in Earl Nelson, *The Salisbury Hymn-Book,* 1857, with a sixth st., a doxology, added. *Hymns Ancient and Modern,* 1861, printed the text as found in *The Salisbury Hymn-Book,* making only one change: in 4:1 "follow *me*" was altered to "follow *Christ.*"

The hymn entered our hymnals in 1878 with sts. 1-5. The fourth st. was dropped in 1889 and 1905. These printings have all used the text as printed in the 1861 *Hymns Ancient and Modern.*

Germany

See "Eternal God and Sovereign Lord," pp. 168-69.

Talk with Us, Lord (262)

CHARLES WESLEY, 1707-1788

The text in 6 sts. was first published in *Hymns and Sacred Poems*, 1740. Entitled "On a Journey," it began:

> Savior, who ready art to hear,
> (Readier than I to pray)
> Answer my scarcely utter'd Prayer,
> And meet me on the way.

John Wesley omitted this first st. in his 1780 *Collection of Hymns for the Use of the People Called Methodists* and altered "me," "I," "my," "it," "heart," in the next 2 sts. to "us," "we," "our," and "hearts." In st. 3:2 (the original fourth) he changed "make" to "bid." The first-person singular is retained in the last 3 sts.

Editors note that in 2:2 Wesley probably unconsciously quotes from Milton's *Paradise Lost*, Bk. IV, lines 639-40, where Eve, speaking to Adam, says:

> With Thee conversing, I forget all time,
> All seasons and their change; all please alike.

The hymn in 5 sts. as altered by John has been included in all American Methodist hymnals except the 1901 Methodist Protestant.

Gräfenberg

See "Come, Holy Spirit, Heavenly Dove," pp. 141-42.

Tell Me the Stories of Jesus (88)

WILLIAM H. PARKER, 1845-1929

The text in 6 sts. was written for the Sunday school anniversary of the Chelsea Street Baptist Church, New Basford, Nottingham, 1885.

Its first hymnal inclusion was in the *Sunday School Hymnary* published in 1905.

The hymn entered the Methodist hymnal in 1935 with 3 sts.: 1, 2, and 5.

Stories of Jesus

FREDERIC A. CHALLINOR, 1866-1952

Written for these words, the tune was the prizewinning tune in a competition sponsored by the National Sunday School Union, London, in its centennial year, 1903. Frederick Bridge, organist at Westminster Abbey and judge of the contest, acclaimed, "This is the best. A fine hymn, too. In a few years both will be sung all over the kingdom."

The *Sunday School Hymnary*, 1905, was the first hymnal to include it.

Thanks to God Whose Word Was Spoken (18)

R. T. BROOKS, 1918-

The hymn was written in 1954 for the Triple Jubilee of the British and Foreign Bible Society.

Lauda anima

JOHN GOSS, 1800-1880

Written for "Praise, my soul, the King of heaven," the tune first appeared in Robert Brown-Borthwick, *Supplemental Hymn and Tune Book* (3rd ed.; London, 1869) in the key of D for unison and organ, and in E for 4 parts. It is also called PRAISE, MY SOUL, the translation of the Latin title, and BENEDIC ANIMA MEA.

The Bread of Life, for All Men Broken (317)

TIMOTHY TINGFANG LEW, 1891-1947
Trans. by WALTER REGINALD OXENHAM TAYLOR, 1889-

The hymn is 1 of 50 original Chinese hymns included in the Chinese Union hymnbook, commonly called *Hymns of Universal Praise*. The translation into English was made in 1943 for the *BBC Hymn Book*, published in 1951. The English text attempts to preserve the original meter of the Chinese.

Sheng En

SU YIN-LAN, 1915-1937
Arr. by BLISS WIANT, 1895-

The tune was composed in 1934, and it was arranged by Su Yin-lan's teacher Bliss Wiant and first published in *Hymns of Universal Praise*, 1936. The name means "holy grace."

The Church's One Foundation (297)

SAMUEL J. STONE, 1839-1900

In 1866 the author published 12 hymns on the 12 articles of the Apostles' Creed. Stone was moved by the rigorous defense by Bishop Robert Gray of Capetown in behalf of the traditional method of biblical interpretation, as opposed to Bishop Colenso's advocacy of the application of source-criticism to the Pentateuch. The collection was called *Lyra Fidelium*. This hymn is headed "Article IX. The Holy Catholic Church; the Communion of Saints. He is the Head of the Body, the Church."

In *Lyra Fidelium*, the hymn is in 7 sts. of 8 lines. A revised form in 5 sts. was made in 1868 for the Appendix to *Hymns Ancient and Modern*. This is the form that is in general use. In 1885 an expanded version of 10 sts. was made for processional use in Salisbury Cathedral. The doctrinal debate is reflected in the original st. 4, included in *Hymns Ancient and Modern* and in most English hymnals:

> Though with a scornful wonder
>   Men see her sore opprest,
> By schisms rent asunder,
>   By heresies distrest;
> Yet saints their watch are keeping,
>   Their cry goes up, "How long?"
> And soon the night of weeping
>   Shall be the morn of song.

The hymn entered our hymnals with the Methodist Protestant of 1901 and the Methodist hymnal of 1905 using sts. 1, 2, 5, and the first 4 lines each of 6 and 7.

Aurelia

SAMUEL S. WESLEY, 1810-1876

The tune was written in 1864 for "The voice that breathed o'er Eden" by John Keble, but before it came off the press Wesley was invited to serve with Charles Kemble as an editor for *A Selection of Psalms and Hymns* (London, 1864). In this book Wesley's tune was set to "Jerusalem the golden." Its inclusion in the Appendix to *Hymns Ancient and Modern*, 1868, set to "The Church's one foundation," boosted its popularity.

Wesley's wife suggested the tune name, taken from "aureus," the Latin word for golden.

The Day Is Past and Over (491)

Τὴν ἡμέραν διελθών

ANONYMOUS Greek, probably 6th Century
Trans. by JOHN M. NEALE, 1818-1866

The text in 5 sts. is taken from 2 parts of the late evening service of the Greek Orthodox Church. The first 3 sts. form a separate supplication. Between the third and fourth sts. a series of liturgical acts take place including the *Gloria Patri,* the Creed, versicles, the Lord's Prayer, and other items. The author of the sts. has not been identified, but they probably date from the sixth or seventh century.

Neale first published his translation in *The Ecclesiastic and Theologian,* 1853, and then in his *Hymns of the Greek Church* the same year. A revised edition appeared in *Hymns of the Eastern Church,* 1862.

The hymn entered our hymnal in 1935, omitting st. 9. The most important alterations in our version have been the changes from the singular pronouns to the plural. Also "hours of sin" or "fear" have been changed to "dark," and "save" (1:6 and 2:6) has been changed to "guard," making all last lines begin uniformly.

Du Friedensfürst, Herr Jesu Christ

BARTHÖLOMÄUS GESIUS, 1555–c. 1613
Harm. by J. S. BACH, 1685-1750

The tune is taken from *Geistliche deutsche Lieder* (Frankfort, 1601).

The Day Is Slowly Wending (506)

MAY ROWLAND, 1870-1959

The text was written in 1920 to be used at the close of an evening service. It was first published in our 1935 hymnal.

Vesper Hymn (Rendle)

LILY RENDLE, 1875-1964

The tune was written in 1930 for this text and submitted to the 1935 hymnal committee. Its first appearance was in the 1935 hymnal, and it has not been published in any other hymnal.

The Day of Resurrection (437)

'Αναστάσεως ἡμέρα

JOHN OF DAMASCUS, c. 657–c. 749
Trans. by JOHN M. NEALE, 1818-1866

Among the hymns of John of Damascus, the canon for Easter Day, called the "Golden Canon" or the "Queen of Canons," holds the most prominent place. In the introduction to his translation, Neale in *Hymns of the Eastern Church,* 1862, recounts how a modern writer describes the way the hymn is used at Athens. At 12:00 midnight on Easter Eve a cannon shot announces that Easter Day has begun. At that moment the Archbishop, elevating the cross, cries out, "Christ is risen." Instantly the vast multitude, waiting in long silence, bursts forth in a shout of indescribable joy, "Christ is risen! Christ is risen!" Then the oppressive darkness is succeeded by a blaze of light from a thousand tapers. Bands of music strike up their gayest strains. Everywhere men clasp each other's hands and embrace with countenances beaming with delight. And above the mingling of many sounds the priests can be heard chanting, "The day of resurrection/Earth, tell it out abroad."

The hymn entered our hymnals in 1878 in Neale's translation, with 1 slight alteration: excision of " 'Tis," the first word, already altered in *The Parish Hymn Book,* 1863. St. 3:5-6 originally read "Invisible and visible/Their notes let all things blend." In 1935 these lines were altered to their present form.

Lancashire

See "Go, Make of All Disciples," pp. 187-88.

The Day Thou Gavest, Lord, Is Ended (500)

JOHN ELLERTON, 1826-1893

Written in 1870 for *A Liturgy for Missionary Meetings,* the hymn was revised for publication in *Church Hymns* the next year. It entered our hymnal in 1905, with the omission of st. 4.

Minor alterations in the text may be noted. In Ellerton's *Hymns, Original and Translated,* 1888, 1:4 reads "Thy praise shall sanctify our rest." The reading of *Church Hymns,* giving "Hallow now" instead of "Sanctify," is usually printed. St. 3:4 is altered in our hymnals from "nor dies the strain" to "nor die the strains"; and 4:3 in *Church Hymns,* "But stand, and rule, and grow for ever," appears in Ellerton's *Hymns,* 1888, as "thy kingdom stands, and grows for ever."

Commandments

See **"Father, We Thank Thee Who Hast Planted,"** pp. 176-77.

The First Noel (383)

Traditional English Carol

Though the carol may be of seventeenth-century origin, the text in 9 sts. is first found in Davies Gilbert, *Some Ancient Christmas Carols,* 1823, and again somewhat altered in William Sandys, *Christmas Carols, Ancient and Modern* (London, 1833). The carol entered our hymnal in 1935 with sts. 1, 2, 3, 4, and 6 of the Sandys text, except "certain" for "three" in st. 1.

Since in the New Testament it was the "wise men" of Matthew who saw the star, not the shepherds of Luke, some editions correct the text to fit the scriptures. The carol is more suitable for Epiphany than for Christmas.

The First Noel

Traditional English Melody

(See comments on text, above.) Millar Patrick in the *Handbook to the Church Hymnary Supplement,* 1935, states that there is belief that the tune originally was a descant to a tune of Jeremiah Clark, "An Hymn for Christmas Day," an elaborated form of ST. MAGNUS (see p. 393). Erik Routley in *The English Carol* also points out that the tune fits as a descant to the carol "Rejoice and be merry." The repetitive nature of the tune and its unusual range, lying mostly between the third of the scale and the upper octave, lend support to the descant theory.

The harmonization is from H. R. Bramley and John Stainer, *Christmas Carols New and Old*, 1871.

The Head That Once Was Crowned with Thorns (458)

THOMAS KELLY, 1769-1854

The text in 6 sts. was first published in the author's *Hymns on Various Passages of Scripture* (5th ed., 1820), under the text "Perfect through sufferings" (Hebrews 2:10). It entered our hymnals in 1849 in 5 sts. Sts. 4 and 5 were omitted, and the sixth st. was added in 1935. The 1964 hymnal has restored the entire 6 sts.

Two lines have called for alteration: 2:2 originally read "Is his, is his by right." This was altered to "Is to our Jesus given," which in turn resulted in the alteration of 2:4 to "He reigns o'er earth and heaven" in 1849 and 1878; then in 1889 and 1901 2:2 was changed to "Is his by sovereign right" and 2:4 to "He reigns in glory bright." Finally in 1935, 2:2 and 2:4 were altered to their present forms.

St. Magnus

JEREMIAH CLARK, c. 1670-1707

The melody first appeared anonymously in Henry Playford, *The Divine Companion or David's Harp New Tun'd* (2nd ed.; London, 1707). In the collection there is the note, "The three following psalms set by Jeremiah Clark." Since ST. MAGNUS is the fourth tune, there has been some doubt as to Clark's authorship. However, its closeness in style to the other tunes is good evidence.

The tune name, given by William Riley in *Psalms and Hymns*, 1762, refers to a church built by Christopher Wren in 1676 on Lower Thames Street near London Bridge. It is also called NOTTINGHAM.

The Heavens Declare Thy Glory, Lord (365)

ISAAC WATTS, 1674-1748

This paraphrase of Psalm 19, headed by "The Books of Nature and of Scripture Compared; or, The Glory and Success of the Gospel," first appeared in the author's *Psalms of David, Imitated in the Language of the New Testament,* 1719. Watts's way of Christianizing the psalms is explained in a note which follows st. 6:

Tho' the plain design of the Psalmist is to shew the Excellency of the Book of Scripture above the Book of Nature, in order to convert and save a Sinner, yet the Apostle Paul in Rom. 10. 18. applies or accommodates the 4th v. to the spreading of the Gospel over the Roman Empire, which is called the whole World in the New Testament; and in this Version I have endeavoured to imitate him.

The hymn entered our hymnals in 1837. It has been included in all our hymnals except the 1882 Methodist Protestant hymnal and the 1935 hymnal.

Hebron

See **"Eternal Son, Eternal Love,"** pp. 169-70.

The King of Heaven His Table Spreads (325)

PHILIP DODDRIDGE, 1702-1751

The hymn in 6 sts. first appeared in Doddridge's *Hymns Founded on Various Texts in the Holy Scriptures,* the posthumous edition by Job Orton (London, 1755). It was entitled "Room at the Gospel-Feast, Luke 24:22." A few changes in text had already been made by the time it entered our Methodist Protestant hymnal in 1837: in 1:2 "dainties" was altered to "blessings"; in 2:3 *"and* the rich blood" to "*through* the rich blood." In 1935 "crowd" was altered to "come" (4:3).

It entered our 1837 hymnal in 5 sts. It has been included in all later Methodist hymnals except the 1901, and always in 4 sts., with the original third and fifth omitted.

Dundee (French)

See **"God Moves in a Mysterious Way,"** pp. 194-95.

The King of Love My Shepherd Is (67)

HENRY W. BAKER, 1821-1877

This paraphrase of Psalm 23 was first published in the 1868 Appendix to *Hymns Ancient and Modern*. It entered our hymnals in 1901 with all 6 sts. The 1905 and 1935 hymnals omitted st. 5, which has been restored in the present hymnal.

In part, the hymn is a recasting of George Herbert's

> The God of love my shepherd is
> And he that doth me feed;
> While he is mine, and I am his,
> What can I want or need?

Dominus regit me

JOHN B. DYKES, 1823-1876

The tune was composed for this text and included in the Appendix to *Hymns Ancient and Modern,* 1868. The name is the Vulgate Latin for Psalm 23.

The King Shall Come (353)

ANONYMOUS Greek
Trans. by JOHN BROWNLIE, 1857-1925

The text in 7 sts. first appeared in Brownlie's *Hymns from the East, Being Centos and Suggestions from the Service Books of the Holy Eastern Church,* 1907. No indication of the source for the translation is known.

This is the first inclusion of the hymn in a Methodist hymnal. The cento is made up of sts. 1, 2, 3, 4, and 7.

St. Stephen

See "Break Forth, O Living Light of God," p. 123.

The Lord Jehovah Reigns (31)

ISAAC WATTS, 1674-1748

This paraphrase of Psalm 148 in 4 sts. first appeared in *Hymns and Spiritual Songs,* 1707. Since the Methodist Protestant hymnal of 1837, it has been included in all our hymnals except 1889 and 1901. The first 2 sts. have always been printed without alteration. However, the first lines of st. 3 have been variously changed. Watts wrote:

> Through all his ancient works
> Surprising wisdom shines,
> Confounds the powers of hell,
> And breaks their curst designs.

Augustus M. Toplady in *Psalms and Hymns for Public and Private Worship,* 1776, changed "surprising" to "unbounded," and lines 3-4 to "He breaks the powers of hell/and blasts their vain designs." More generally, and in all our hymnals "ancient" has given place to "mighty" and "surprising" to "amazing." Line 3 was not altered in our hymnals until the 1935 hymnal altered 3-4 to the present form.

Millennium

Plymouth Collection, 1855

A camp-meeting tune, popular in the South, the tune was included in Henry Ward Beecher, *Plymouth Collection of Hymns,* 1855. It also appeared in *The Wesleyan Tune-Book* (London, 1876).

The Lord Our God Alone Is Strong (346)

CALEB T. WINCHESTER, 1847-1920

The text was written in 1871 for the dedication of a hall of science at Wesleyan University in Connecticut. In 5 sts., it entered our hymnals in 1878. The 1935 hymnal dropped the original third st.

Truro

See "I Know That My Redeemer Lives," p. 227.

The Lord Our God Is Clothed with Might (32)

H. KIRKE WHITE, 1785-1806

The hymn was first published in William Collyer, *Hymns Partly Collected and Partly Original,* 1812. It has been included in virtually all American Methodist hymnals since the Methodist Protestant hymnal of 1837. The rather fierce original first line of st. 3, "Howl, winds of night, your force, combine," retained in several of our hymnals, had already been altered in the Methodist Episcopal hymnal of 1848 to its present milder form.

Detroit

Supplement to Kentucky Harmony, 1820
Harm. by A.C.L.

The tune appeared anonymously in the 1820 book. Both *Virginia Harmony,* 1831, and *Southern Harmony,* 1835, credit the tune to "Bradshaw." There is some similarity to "The wife of Usher's well," an English folk song collected by Cecil Sharp in the Appalachian mountains.

The Lord Will Come and Not Be Slow (468)

JOHN MILTON, 1608-1674

In April, 1648, Milton, moved by the stress of Civil War, made metrical paraphrases of psalms 80-88. To reassure readers of the authentic character of his versions, he put Hebrew words in the margin and printed every English word not in the Hebrew text in italics.

The psalm entered our hymnals in 1878 with 5 quatrains made up in the order of psalms 85:13*b* and 13*a,* 85:10, 86:9, 85:11, and 86:12. In this form the psalm was reprinted in 1905, dropped in 1935, but readmitted in 1964 with some variations. It is now in 3 sts. of 8 lines, and 85:10 and 86:12 have given place to 85:9 and 86:10, and an additional quatrain, 82:8, has been added to make the present text. Milton's lines are printed without alteration, except for the change necessitated by inverting the order of 85:13*a* and *b,* to make the beginning "The Lord will come."

Old 107th

French Psalter, 1542
Harm. adapt. from CLAUDE GOUDIMEL, c. 1505-1572

This rough-hewn Dorian melody, published in the French Psalter (Paris, 1542), was altered rhythmically in the Scottish Psalter, with masculine cadences replacing feminine cadences. In the 1564 Scottish book it was set to William Kethe's version of Psalm 107.

The Lord's My Shepherd, I'll Not Want (68)
Scottish Psalter, 1650

The Scottish Psalter of 1650, from which this metrical paraphrase of Psalm 23 is taken, has been called the "Prince of Versions" because it is said to contain the cream of all the best psalters in existence at the time it was made. Millar Patrick in *Four Centuries of Scottish Psalmody,* 1949, in analyzing the text of this version, noted that at least 7 different psalters, beginning with the Old Version of 1564, have contributed phrases or lines to the 1650 text.

The psalm entered our hymnals in 1901. It was restored in 1935. It has always been printed essentially in original form.

Evan

See "Blest Be the Dear Uniting Love," pp. 119-20.

The Man Who Once Has Found Abode (216)
The Book of Psalms, 1871

This metrical version of Psalm 91 by an unknown writer is taken from *The Book of Psalms* of the United Presbyterian Church, 1871. Six of the original 11 sts. entered our hymnal in 1935.

Tallis' Canon

See "All Praise to Thee, My God, This Night," pp. 82-84.

The People That in Darkness Sat (361)
JOHN MORISON, 1749-1798
Scottish *Translations and Paraphrases,* 1781

This paraphrase of Isaiah 9:2-8 first appeared in *Translations and Paraphrases in Verse, of General Passages of Sacred Scripture, Collected and Prepared by a Committee of the General Assembly of the*

Church of Scotland, in Order to Be Sung in Churches (Edinburgh, 1781). The book was intended to provide a supplement to the psalter while still retaining a scriptural basis for congregational song. The text was probably by John Morison, a member of the committee who prepared the book, which was a revision of a 1745 collection.

The hymn was originally in 6 sts. *Hymns Ancient and Modern,* 1861, radically altered the 1781 version and added a seventh st., which has not been printed in any of our hymnals. The text entered our hymnal in 1964 with sts. 1, 4, 5, and 6 of the *Hymns Ancient and Modern* text.

Caithness

See "How Are Thy Servants Blest, O Lord," p. 219.

The Righteous Ones Shall Be Forever Blest (214)

Unknown Thailand Christian
Trans. by VIDA RUMBAUGH, 1927-

The original text, based on Psalm 1, in the Thai language, has appeared in several Thailand hymnals. The author and date of its first publication are not known. Miss Rumbaugh translated the hymn into English in 1963 for our 1964 hymnal.

Sri Lampang

See "Bread of the World in Mercy Broken," pp. 121-22.

The Son of God Goes Forth to War (419)

REGINALD HEBER, 1783-1826

The text in eight 4-line sts. was first published posthumously in the collection which Heber had long projected, *Hymns Written and Adapted to the Weekly Service of the Church Year,* 1827. It was written for St. Stephen's Day, the day following Christmas.

Our 1901 Methodist Protestant hymnal printed the entire hymn in four 8-line sts.; in 1905, 2 quatrains were omitted, and the fifth and eighth sts. were combined to make our third.

All Saints New

HENRY S. CUTLER, 1824-1902

Written for this text, the tune first appeared in *Hymnal with Tunes, Old and New,* 1872, edited by J. Ireland Tucker. "New" was added to the tune name to avoid confusion with another tune called ALL SAINTS. In the 1905 Methodist hymnal it was called CUTLER.

The Spacious Firmament on High (43)

JOSEPH ADDISON, 1672-1719

The text appeared first in the *Spectator,* August 23, 1712, as a paraphrase of Psalm 19:1-6 and at the end of a discourse on the proper means of strengthening and confirming faith. "The Supreme Being has made the best arguments for his own existence, in the formation of the heavens and the earth; and these are arguments which a man of sense cannot forbear attending to, who is out of the noise and hurry of human affairs." Then quoting Psalm 19:1-4, Addison continued, "As such a bold and sublime manner of thinking furnishes very noble matter for an ode, the reader may see it brought into the following one." Then followed our 3-st. hymn.

The hymn entered our hymnals with the Methodist Protestant hymnal of 1837.

Creation

FRANZ JOSEPH HAYDN, 1732-1809

Called HAYDN and in Long Meter, the tune in 6 lines, set to "Awake, my soul, and with the sun," appeared in *The Sacred Choir* (New York, 1838), edited by George Kingsley. It is an adaptation from the chorus "The heavens are telling" from the oratorio *The Creation,* 1798. The adapter is unknown, but Isaac B. Woodbury has been suggested. However, the tune had been adapted by William Gardiner in *Sacred Melodies from Haydn, Mozart, and Beethoven* (London, 1812), and Lowell Mason in *The Choir, or Union Collection of Church Music,* 1832, in anthem form, using only the first portion of the music. In 1848, *The National Psalmist,* edited by Lowell Mason and George J. Webb, combined the Addison text and Haydn tune in a form which is only slightly different in rhythm and harmony from the present version.

400

The original text of the chorus is anapestic, while the hymn text is iambic; as a result the hymn version suffers musically from the alteration of rhythm.

The Strife Is O'er, the Battle Done (447)
Finita jam sunt praelia (or *proelia*)

ANONYMOUS Latin
Trans. by FRANCIS POTT, 1832-1909

The anonymous Latin hymn has been attributed to the seventeenth or even the twelfth century. John M. Neale translated it in 1851 and published it in his *Mediaeval Hymns and Sequences* as "Finished is the battle now." It is not known where he obtained his Latin text.

The hymn was introduced into our hymnals in 1935 as translated by Francis Pott and printed in his *Hymns Fitted to the Order of Common Prayer,* 1861, with the omission of Pott's st. 4.

Victory

Arr. from GIOVANNI P. DA PALESTRINA, 1525-1594
by W. H. MONK, 1823-1889

The basic material for the tune is taken from the *Gloria Patri* in Palestrina's *Magnificat Tertii Toni,* published in 1591 in a different tonality from the hymn tune version. Monk made an arrangement for the *Parish Choir,* c. 1850, set to John Cosin, "Come, Holy Ghost." The result was a dull, square anthem with block harmony. His second arrangement was made for *Hymns Ancient and Modern,* 1861, using only the first 2 phrases of Palestrina and adding "Alleluias" before and after the tune. The result is a fairly effective hymn tune, but with little of Palestrina's tune and none of his modality. The opening "Alleluias" have been omitted.

The Voice of God Is Calling (200)

JOHN HAYNES HOLMES, 1879-1964

In 1913, before departing for a summer holiday in Europe, Holmes had been invited by the Young People's Religious Union (Unitarian) to write a hymn for the annual conference that fall. On the voyage home at the end of the summer, on board the *S. S. Laconia,* he wrote the hymn one afternoon at a single sitting.

Based on Isaiah 6:8, it was first published in the *Christian Register*. Its first hymnal inclusion was in *The New Hymn and Tune Book*, 1914.

The hymn entered the Methodist hymnal in 1935.

Meirionydd

WILLIAM LLOYD, 1786-1852

The tune was composed or arranged by Lloyd, in whose book it was found in manuscript form, called BERTH. It was first published in *Caniadau Seion*, 1840, edited by R. Mills. The present name comes from the county lying immediately south of Caernarvon, the composer's home.

There Is a Balm in Gilead (212)

American Folk Hymn

The medicinal ointment mentioned in Jeremiah 8:22 and 46:11 is not easily identifiable botanically, nor is it certain that the tree grew in Gilead in Transjordan. However, caravans from the East passed through Gilead, and this in itself could be enough to fix the association of balm with Gilead.

The answer which Jeremiah expected to his question "Is there no balm in Gilead?" is "No." The spiritual, however, turns the negation into affirmation, hopelessness into hope.

As is usually the case, no information of the origin of the words is available.

Balm in Gilead

American Folk Hymn
Arr. by DANIEL L. RIDOUT, 1899-

(For general remarks about spirituals, see "Go, tell it on the mountain," pp. 188-89.)

The hymn first appeared in Frederick J. Work, *Folk Songs of the American Negro* (Nashville, 1907).

There Is a Fountain Filled with Blood (421)

WILLIAM COWPER, 1731-1800

The hymn in 7 sts., probably written in 1771, was first published in R. Conyers, *A Collection of Psalms and Hymns from Various Authors*, (2nd ed., 1772), and then reprinted in *Olney Hymns*, 1779, with the heading "Praise for the fountain opened—Zech. 13:1." The hymn entered our Methodist Episcopal hymnal in 1849 with the first 5 sts. and has been included in every Methodist hymnal since. Sts. 6 and 7 have been printed in only one of our hymnals—the Methodist Episcopal of 1878:

> Lord, I believe thou hast prepar'd
> (Unworthy tho' I be)
> For me a blood-bought free reward,
> A golden harp for me.

> 'Tis strung and tun'd for endless years,
> And form'd by pow'r divine,
> To sound in God the Father's ears
> No other name but thine.

Of the first 5 sts., only 2:3-4 have called for alteration. Cowper wrote:

> And there *have* I, *as* vile as he,
> *Washed* all my sins away.

By 1849 these lines had already been altered to the form in which we sing them.

Cleansing Fountain

See **"How Happy Every Child of Grace,"** p. 223.

There Is a Green Hill Far Away (414)

CECIL FRANCES ALEXANDER, 1818-1895

The hymn in 5 sts. was written in 1847 and was first published in the author's *Hymns for Little Children*, 1848. The hymns were designed to make the articles of the Apostles' Creed meaningful for Sunday school.

COMPANION TO THE HYMNAL

Mrs. Alexander originally wrote *"Without* a city wall"* (1:2). When a child asked what was meant by a green hill not having a city wall, she substituted "outside" for "without." It has further been objected that the Gospels do not say it was a "hill" but a "skull" (Luke 23:33) ; and Judean hills are seldom green. Nevertheless, the hymn as written has its own simple childlike charm, and is plain and moving.

It entered our hymnals in 1901 and in 1935 with sts. 1, 2, 3, and 5. The fourth st. was added in 1964. The 1901 hymnal repeated the first st. at the end of the hymn in order to make three 8-line sts.

Windsor

See **"Behold the Savior of Mankind,"** p. 114.

There's a Song in the Air (380)

JOSIAH G. HOLLAND, 1819-1881

The text first appeared in W. T. Giffe, *The Brilliant,* 1874, and then in the author's *Complete Poetical Writings,* 1879. Its first hymnal inclusion was in our 1905 hymnal.

Christmas Song

KARL P. HARRINGTON, 1861-1953

The tune was composed during a vacation, July, 1904, at North Woodstock, N. H. It was chosen for inclusion in the 1905 Methodist hymnal. Harrington was a member of the 1905 hymnal commission.

There's a Voice in the Wilderness Crying (362)

JAMES L. MILLIGAN, 1876-1961

The hymn was introduced into the Methodist hymnal in 1935 from the *Hymnary of the United Church of Canada,* 1930. It was written on the occasion of the consummation of the union of the Canadian churches.

Hereford

FRANCIS D. HEINS, 1878-1949

The tune was written for this text for the *Hymnary,* 1930 (see comments on text, above). It is named for the composer's birthplace.

404

There's a Wideness in God's Mercy (69)

FREDERICK W. FABER, 1814-1863

The text is part of a poem of thirteen 4-line sts. Called "Come to Jesus," beginning "Souls of men, why will ye scatter/Like a crowd of frightened sheep?" Faber published it first in his *Oratory Hymns,* 1854. It was again published in the posthumous collection *Hymns Selected from F. W. Faber.*

The hymn, made up of quatrains 4, 6, 8, and 13, has been included in our hymnals since 1878, except the 1882 and the 1901 Methodist Protestant hymnals, which used respectively 4, 6, 12, and 13 and 2, 3, 4, 6, 10, and 13. The 1889 Methodist Episcopal, South hymnal altered the original 2:2 to read "There are blessings for the good," and 4:1 to "If our *faith* were but more simple."

In Babilone

See "Hail, Thou Once Despised Jesus," pp. 206-7.

These Things Shall Be (198)

J. ADDINGTON SYMONDS, 1840-1893

The hymn is taken from a 15-st. poem called "A Vista," published in the author's *New and Old: A Volume of Verse,* 1880. The poem began:

> Sad heart, what will the future bring
> To happier men when we are gone?
> What golden days shall dawn for them,
> Transcending all we gaze upon?

W. Garrett Horder had already included a cento from the poem in his *Congregational Hymns,* 1884. *The Methodist Hymn-Book* (London, 1904) was the first denominational hymnal to use it. It came into our hymnals in 1935 with the present sts.: 4, 6, 7, and 13.

Truro

See "I Know That My Redeemer Lives," p. 227.

Thine Is the Glory (450)
À toi la gloire

EDMOND L. BUDRY, 1854-1932
Trans. by R. BIRCH HOYLE, 1875-1939

The hymn is taken from *Cantate Domino*, the hymnal of the World Student Christian Federation, first published about 1925. The French text is attributed to Edmond Budry and is dated 1884. Hoyle's translation is dated 1923.

This is the first inclusion of the hymn in a Methodist hymnal.

Judas Maccabeus

GEORGE FREDERICK HANDEL, 1685-1759

The tune is arranged from the chorus "See, the conquering hero comes" from *Judas Maccabaeus*, an oratorio composed at the suggestion of Frederic, Prince of Wales, to celebrate the victory of his brother, Duke of Cumberland, at the battle of Culloden, 1745. The chorus from which the tune is taken did not appear in the original 1746 work, but was transferred in 1751 from *Joshua* (written in 1748) to *Judas Maccabaeus*.

MACCABEUS is another name for the tune.

This Is My Father's World (45)

MALTBIE D. BABCOCK, 1858-1901

The poem "My Father's World," in sixteen 4-line sts., was first published in the author's *Thoughts for Every-Day Living*, 1901. A cento of 6 quatrains in three 8-line sts., made up of 2-3, 4-5, 14 and 16, entered the Methodist hymnal in 1935.

Two changes have been made in the text: 1:2 reads "And to" for "E'en yet to"; 3:6 reads "Why should my heart be sad" for "Should my heart ever be sad?"

Terra Beata

FRANKLIN L. SHEPPARD, 1852-1930

The tune was composed by Sheppard, a friend of Babcock. It was included in the composer's Sunday school songbook *Alleluia*, 1915. Many editors have insisted that the tune is an original composition by Sheppard, but he insisted that it was an English folk tune he remembered from his childhood. Robert G. McCutchan in *Hymn Tune Names* calls the tune a traditional English melody. It was called RUSPER when it first appeared in *The English Hymnal* (Oxford, 1906), a collection which used many English folk songs. This name came from a parish near Horsham, Sussex, England. McCutchan felt that RUSPER was the original of TERRA BEATA.

Sheppard named the tune for "beautiful earth." A later arrangement or harmonization by Edward Shippen Barnes was called TERRA PATRIS, "Father's world."

This Is My Song (542)

LLOYD STONE, 1912-
Stanza 3, GEORGIA HARKNESS, 1891-

The first 2 sts. of the hymn, written by Lloyd Stone, were published first by the Lorenz Publishing Company in a popular collection called *Sing a Tune,* copyrighted in 1934. Miss Harkness wrote st. 3 at the request of Miss Marion Norris, then executive secretary of the Wesleyan Service Guild, who desired to supplement Stone's patriotic song with a more distinctly Christian emphasis. This additional st. was written within the years 1937-39 and was copyrighted by Lorenz in 1964.

This is the first appearance of the hymn in a Methodist hymnal.

Finlandia

See "Be Still, My Soul," pp. 111-12.

Thou Art the Way: To Thee Alone (75)

GEORGE W. DOANE, 1799-1859

The hymn in 4 sts. appeared first in the author's *Songs by the Way, Chiefly Devotional: with Translations and Imitations,* 1824, under the text "I am the Way, and the Truth and the Life" (John 14:6). The hymn was included in English hymnals as early as 1833 and 1836. It was the only American hymn in the original edition of *Hymns Ancient and Modern,* 1861, and has been retained in all revisions.

The hymn entered American Methodist hymnals in 1837 and has had a place in all our hymnals except the Methodist Episcopal, South of 1847 and the Methodist Protestant of 1882.

St. Bernard

Tochter Zion, Cologne, 1741
Arr. by JOHN RICHARDSON, 1816-1879

The original tune was one of the *Marienlieder* (hymns praising Mary) first published in *Neues Gott und dem Lamm geheiligtes Kirchen- und Haus-Gesangbuch der . . . Tochter Zion,* 1741, edited by H. Lindenborn. It underwent several changes until its present form in *Easy Hymn Tunes Adapted for Catholic Schools,* 1851, edited by John Richardson. It was set there to Bernard of Clairvaux's hymn "Jesus, the very thought of thee."

Thou Hidden Love of God, Whose Height (531)
Verborgne Gottesliebe du

GERHARDT TERSTEEGEN, 1697-1769
Trans. by JOHN WESLEY, 1703-1791

Tersteegen's poem in 10 sts. on "The Longing of the soul quietly to maintain the secret drawings of the love of God," based on Galatians 2:20, was first published in his *Geistliches Blumengärtlein inniger Seelen,* 1729. Wesley made the translation in eight 6-line sts. while in Savannah, Ga., in 1736, probably from the *Herrnhut Gesangbuch* which had omitted sts. 4 and 5 of the original text. The hymn was not published until after Wesley's return to England, when it appeared in *A Collection of Psalms and Hymns,* 1738. It has been pointed out that there is no equivalent of 1:5-6 in the German text. Wesley derived the lines from the well-known passage in Augustine's *Confessions:* "Thou hast made us for thyself, and our hearts are restless until they rest in Thee."

John Wesley reprinted the entire 8 sts. in his *Collection of Hymns for the Use of the People Called Methodists,* 1780, but modified 2 small but important words. In 2:4 (not printed in our hymnal) he changed "but though my will *be* fixed" to "seem," and in 8:6 (our 4:6) changed "is" to "be," making the line a prayer, not a statement of fact.

The hymn in 5, 8, or 4 sts. has been included in all American Methodist hymnals since 1802, except the 3 Methodist Protestant hymnals. Since 1905 the cento in our hymnals has been made up of sts. 1, 4, 6, and 8.

Vater unser

Geistliche Lieder, Leipzig, 1539

In its earliest source the tune was set to Martin Luther's version of the Lord's Prayer, from which it derived its name. In the 1561 Anglo-Genevan Psalter it was set to Psalm 112—hence its alternate name of OLD 112TH. The tune was a favorite of John Wesley and was included by him in the *Foundery Collection,* 1742, set to this text.

In the original German version each phrase began and ended with a note of double length. Wesley retained this pattern for all except the last phrase where a pause would have stopped the flow of thought.

Thou Hidden Source of Calm Repose (89)

CHARLES WESLEY, 1707-1788

The text first appeared in *Hymns and Sacred Poems,* 1749. John Wesley reprinted it without alteration in his *Collection of Hymns for the Use of the People Called Methodists,* 1780. The 1808 Supplement to *The Methodist Pocket Hymn Book* altered the final phrase of the hymn from "my heaven in hell" to "my all in all." This reading remained in all American Methodist hymnals until the original text was restored with the present hymnal. The only other alteration made in our hymnals is the replacement of "med'cine" (3:3) with "healing," in the 1935 and 1964 hymnals.

St. Petersburg

DIMITRI S. BORTNIANSKY, 1751-1825

The tune first appeared in Johann Heinrich Tscherlitzky, *Choralbuch* (Moscow, 1825) set to a st. by Gerhardt Tersteegen, "Ich bete an die macht der Liebe." The source there listed is a mass by Bortniansky written in 1822, but this has not been found. Tscherlitzky was organist at St. Petersburg and later in Berlin.

In the collection of Bortniansky's sacred works, compiled by Peter Tschaikowsky in 1884, the tune is set to a Russian hymn. James T. Lightwood states that the melody is not used in Russian churches, but only on semireligious occasions such as the "blessing of the waters" at St. Petersburg on January 6.

The first appearance in English hymnals was in Montague Burgoyne, *A Collection of Metrical Versions,* 1827, as a Long Meter tune without the first 2 lines repeated.

The tune is also called WELLS, WELLSPRING, and SHANGANA.

Thou My Everlasting Portion (176)

FANNY J. CROSBY, 1820-1915

Written in 1874, the hymn was first published in the same year in *Songs of Grace and Glory,* edited by William F. Sherwin and Silas J. Vail, and set to the Vail tune which suggested the text. In 1875 it was included in *Brightest and Best,* compiled by Robert Lowry and W. H. Doane, and again a year later in *Gospel Hymns No. 2.*

It entered our hymnals in 1889. The refrain has been dropped with the present hymnal.

Close to Thee

SILAS J. VAIL, 1818-1884

Vail took his tune to Fanny Crosby and asked her to write a text for it. The refrain suggested the words "Close to thee." It was first published in *Songs of Grace and Glory* (New York, 1874).

The tune name comes from the first line of the refrain, a practice common to gospel songs.

Thou, Whose Almighty Word (480)

JOHN MARRIOTT, 1780-1825

According to a statement in a volume of the author's sermons published by his sons in 1838, the hymn was written c. 1813. It began "Thou, whose eternal word." First printed anonymously in the *Evangelical Mazagine,* June 1825, it was probably copied by the *Friendly Visitor* in July of the same year and printed unsigned with the title "Missionary Hymn."

The hymn has been variously altered by different editors. It entered our hymnals in 1849 with the first 3 sts. The fourth was added in 1878. The 2 lines which have been changed in our hymnals are 4:1 and 4:3. St. 4:1 originally began "Blessed and Holy" or "Blessed and Holy Three." The 1905 hymnal altered this to "Holy and Blessed Three," following the precedent of Thomas Raffles, *Supplement to Dr. Watts' Psalms and Hymns*, 1853, and *Hymns Ancient and Modern*, 1861. Our 1935 hymnal altered 4:3 from "Wisdom, love and might" to "Grace, love, and might," following *The Salisbury Hymn-Book*, 1857, and *Hymns Ancient and Modern*, 1861.

Dort

LOWELL MASON, 1792-1872

The tune was written in 1832 for a patriotic hymn. It was first published in *The Choir, or Union Collection of Church Music,* in a form slightly different from that published later in the *American Tune Book*, 1869.

Thou, Whose Unmeasured Temple Stands (345)

WILLIAM C. BRYANT, 1794-1878

The text was written in 1835 for the dedication of a chapel on Prince Street in New York City. It was first printed in a collection of 19 hymns privately published by the author, first in 1864 and then again in 1869. The first line is sometimes printed in an altered form: "O Thou, whose own vast temple stands."

The hymn entered our hymnals in 1905. St. 2 read:

> Lord, from thine inmost glory send,
> Within these courts to bide,
> The peace that dwelleth without end
> Serenely by thy side!

And 3:1-2:

> May erring minds that worship here
> Be taught the better way;

These have been thought to be the original form of the text before Bryant printed them.

Since 1935 our hymnals have printed the text as it appeared in the 1864 and 1869 editions of Bryant's *Hymns*.

Dundee (French)

See "God Moves in a Mysterious Way," pp. 194-95.

Through All the Changing Scenes of Life (56)

New Version
TATE and BRADY, 1696

The paraphrase of Psalm 34 is taken from Tate and Brady's *New Version of the Psalms of David*, 1696, but was radically revised in 1698. The 22 verses of the psalm are written in 18 quatrains, divided into 2 parts: 1-10 and 11-22. Our cento is made up of sts. 1, 3, 7, 8, and 18. These reproduce the 1698 text unaltered.

Included in 6 sts. in the 1849 and 1889 Methodist Episcopal, South hymnals, the psalm appears elsewhere in our hymnals only in 1935 and the present hymnal.

Irish

See "O For a Heart to Praise My God," pp. 308-9.

'Tis Finished! The Messiah Dies (429)

CHARLES WESLEY, 1707-1788

In *Short Hymns on Select Passages of Holy Scripture*, 1762, Charles Wesley wrote two 8-line sts. on the text "It is finished" (John 19:30). He was not satisfied with these sts., however, and at his death left in manuscript another hymn on the same text in eight 4-line sts., of which 1 and 8 are 1:1-4 and 2:5-8 of the 1762 text, slightly altered; sts. 2-7 are new. This 8-st. hymn was given in the 1830 Supplement to the *Wesley Hymn Book*, London.

The hymn as found in Methodist hymnals is taken from the 1830 printing. The Methodist Episcopal, South hymnals of 1847 and 1889 printed 6 and 5 sts. respectively; the Methodist Episcopal of 1849 and 1878, sts. 1-4 and 8. The Methodist Protestant hymnals of 1882 and 1901, 1-4, 8, and 1-4 respectively. The hymn was omitted in 1905 and 1935. A cento made up of sts. 1, 3, and 5 has been restored in 1964.

Winchester New

See "Come, Sinners, to the Gospel Feast," pp. 151-52.

'Tis Midnight, and on Olive's Brow (431)

WILLIAM B. TAPPAN, 1794-1849

The text was first published in the author's *Poems,* 1822. It entered our hymnals in 1878. In 2:2 Tappan wrote "Immanuel Wrestles," and in 4:1 "from ether plains." Beginning with 1878, most of our hymnals altered "Immanuel" to "The Savior" and *"ether* plains" to *"heavenly* plains."

Olive's Brow

WILLIAM B. BRADBURY, 1816-1868

The tune was written for this text and first published in *The Shawm* (New York, 1853), compiled by Bradbury and George F. Root. The book was a "Library of Church Music, embracing about one thousand pieces, consisting of psalm and hymn tunes adapted to every meter in use." It included a special index for "all the Peculiar Metres of the Methodist hymnbooks as used in the North, these hymns being differently marked from those of the other religious denominations." PM stood for "Peculiar Meter" or "Particular Meter," and the book listed 33, being marked "1st P.M.," "2nd P.M.," etc.

'Tis So Sweet to Trust in Jesus (208)

LOUISA M. R. STEAD, c. 1850-1917

Both text and tune were copyrighted and first published in *Songs of Triumph,* compiled by J. R. Sweney and W. J. Kirkpatrick (Philadelphia, 1882). There is no evidence to show when the text was written or for what occasion. Since Mrs. Stead was widowed about 1880, it has been conjectured that she wrote the hymn out of the experience of sorrow occasioned by the loss of her husband.

The hymn entered the Methodist hymnal with the present 1964 hymnal.

Trust in Jesus

WILLIAM J. KIRKPATRICK, 1838-1921

See comments on text, above.

413

To Bless the Earth, God Sendeth (512)

The Psalter, 1912

This paraphrase of Psalm 65:9-13 is taken from the 1912 Psalter of the United Presbyterian Church, from the paraphrase beginning "Thy might sets fast the mountains/Strength girds thee evermore." Our cento omits the first st., and alters references to God in the second person to the third person in sts. 2 and 3. Thus:

> To bless the earth *Thou* sendest
> From *Thy* abundant store

becomes

> To bless the earth *God* sendeth
> From *His* abundant store,

and so forth.

This is the first appearance of this paraphrase in a Methodist hymnal.

Far-Off Lands

See "O Son of God, Incarnate," pp. 334-35.

To Thee, O Lord, Our Hearts We Raise (524)

WILLIAM C. DIX, 1837-1898

The text in 4 sts. was first printed in *Hymns for the Service of the Church* (Bristol, 1864). It enters the Methodist hymnal here for the first time. One st. has been omitted.

Norse Air

See "O Shepherd of the Nameless Fold," pp. 333-34.

Truehearted, Wholehearted (179)

FRANCES R. HAVERGAL, 1836-1879

The text was written in September, 1874, at Ormont Dessous, Switzerland, while the author was traveling with friends. It was first published in her *Loyal Responses, or Daily Melodies for the King's Minstrels,* 1878. Its first American hymnal inclusion seems to have been in *Gospel Hymns No. 6,* 1891, where the third and last 6 sts. were omitted. In our hymnals, the first 4 sts. appeared in the 1901 Methodist Protestant hymnal as Havergal wrote them. The third st. has not since been included in our hymnals. Our 1905 hymnal has established the text for our later hymnals, printing sts. 1, 2, and 4, and altering 4:1 from "Whole-hearted! Savior, beloved and glorious" to its present form. Sts. 5, 6, and 7 begin "Half-hearted!"

The tenth st., altered, became the refrain.

Truehearted
GEORGE C. STEBBINS, 1846-1945

Composed in the spring of 1878 during a revival meeting in New Haven, Conn., the tune first appeared as a 4-part song for male voices in *The Male Chorus* (New York and Chicago, 1888), compiled by Stebbins and Ira D. Sankey. Stebbins rearranged it for mixed voices in *Winnowed Songs for Sunday School,* 1890.

Turn Back, O Man (475)
CLIFFORD BAX, 1886-1962

At Gustav Holst's request, the poem was written to fit the tune GENEVA 124 of which Holst made a special arrangement for this text, using chorus and orchestra, in 1919. When Bax published the poem in his *Farewell, My Muse,* 1932, he dated it 1916.

This is its first use in a Methodist hymnal.

Geneva 124

See "Father Eternal, Ruler of Creation," p. 173.

Unto the Hills I Lift Mine Eyes (57)
The Psalter, 1912

This paraphrase of Psalm 121 is taken from the 1912 Psalter of the United Presbyterian Church. The first line originally read "I to the hills will lift my eyes." No other changes have been made.

This is the first inclusion of the hymn in a Methodist hymnal.

Dunfermline

See "Behold Us, Lord, a Little Space," p. 115.

Wake, Awake, for Night Is Flying (366)
Wachet auf! ruft uns die Stimme

PHILIPP NICOLAI, 1556-1608
Trans. by CATHERINE WINKWORTH, 1827-1878

Sometimes called the "King of Chorales," the German hymn was first published in the Appendix to Nicolai's *Freuden-Spiegel des ewigen Lebens,* "The Mirror of the Joy of Eternal Life" (Frankfort, 1599). The volume contained Nicolai's meditations on death and eternal life in the midst of the pestilence in Westphalia in which over 1,300 people died between July, 1597, and January, 1598. It was in this appendix also that another great chorale of Nicolai appeared, "O Morning Star, how fair and bright." The text was based on Matthew 25:1-13, the Gospel for the Twenty-seventh Sunday after Trinity, the Sunday for which Bach composed his Cantata 140.

A bit amusing is the way in which Nicolai honored a friend and old pupil, Count Wilhelm Ernst, by making the lyric a reversed acrostic. W (*achet*) ; st. 2, Z (*ion hoert*) ; st. 3, E (*hr und Preis*), that is Ernst zu Wallenstein.

The hymn enters our hymnal for the first time in 1964 in the translation made by Catherine Winkworth for the second series of her *Lyra Germanica,* 1858. Apart from substituting "Alleluia" for "Hallelujah," the only alterations are in 2:7-8. These originally read:

Ah come, Thou blessed Lord,
O Jesus, Son of God.

Wachet auf

PHILIPP NICOLAI, 1556-1608

The original version with free rhythm has been used here rather than the Bach harmonization which straightens the rhythm and adds passing tones.

416

Walk in the Light (403)

BERNARD BARTON, 1784-1849

The text in six 4-line sts., based on I John 1:7, first appeared in the author's *Devotional Verses, Founded on Select Texts of Scripture,* 1826. It entered our Methodist Episcopal hymnal in 1849, omitting st. 2:

> Walk in the light, and sin, abhorred,
>   Shall ne'er defile again;
> The blood of Jesus Christ thy Lord
>   Shall cleanse from every stain.

Five sts. were printed until the 1935 hymnal omitted the fourth (the original fifth):

> Walk in the light! and e'en the tomb
>   No fearful shade shall wear;
> Glory shall chase away its gloom,
>   For Christ hath conquered there.

Manoah

HENRY W. GREATOREX, *Collection of Psalm and Hymn Tunes,* 1851

No source for the tune is given in Greatorex's book, published in 1851. It may be his composition or arrangement. Manoah was Samson's father.

Watchman, Tell Us of the Night (358)

JOHN BOWRING, 1792-1872

The text first appeared in Bowring's *Hymns,* 1825. Its popularity is because of its skill in re-creating in dialogue form the longings expressed in Isaiah 21:11-12 and its question and answer form, which makes it useful for antiphonal singing.

It has been in all of our hymnals since the Methodist Episcopal of 1849.

Aberystwyth

See "Jesus, Lover of My Soul," pp. 247-48.

Shepherds' Pipes

ANNABETH McCLELLAND GAY, 1925-

Mrs. Gay writes:

Every Christmas since we've been married, my husband and I have written a Christmas song as our greeting to our friends. He writes the words and I write the music. In 1952 it was my turn to write the tune first and this melody came very easily one evening. When I played it for him, he said, "I wonder if Palestinian shepherds played on pipes because that's what it sounds like to me."

The tune was first published in *The Pilgrim Hymnal* (Boston, 1958) set to "The Lord is rich and merciful" by Thomas T. Lynch.

We Believe in One True God (463)

TOBIAS CLAUSNITZER, 1619-1684
Trans. by CATHERINE WINKWORTH, 1827-1878

The German text of this metrical version of the Apostles' Creed first appeared in the Culmbach-Bayreuth *Gesangbuch,* 1668. The hymn was included in our 1878 Methodist Episcopal hymnal as Catherine Winkworth translated it in her *Chorale Book for England* (London, 1863). Not in our hymnals again until 1964, it now follows the Winkworth translation as altered for use in *The Lutheran Hymnal,* except for the change of meter from 87.77.77. to 77.77.77., and in 2:6 "all" has been replaced by "sin's."

Ratisbon

See **"Christ, Whose Glory Fills the Skies,"** pp. 134-35.

We Come unto Our Fathers' God (58)

THOMAS H. GILL, 1819-1906

The author describes the day on which the hymn was written, November 22, 1868, as "almost the most delightful day of my life. Its production employed the whole day and was a prolonged rapture."

In 7 sts., it was first published in Gill's *Golden Chain of Praise Hymns,* 1869.

The hymn entered the Methodist hymnal in 1935 with sts. 1, 3, 6, and 7.

Nun freut euch

See "O Guide to Every Child of Thine," pp. 314-15.

We Gather Together (59)
Wilt heden nu treden voor God den Heere

Netherlands Folk Hymn
Trans. by THEODORE BAKER, 1851-1934

Written by an unknown author at the end of the sixteenth century, to celebrate Dutch freedom from Spanish rule, the hymn was first published in the 1626 edition of Adrian Valerius' *Nederlandtsch Gedenckclanck*. From this collection it was popularized by Edward Kremser (see comments on tune, below).

Baker's English translation first appeared in Coenraad V. Bos, *Dutch Folk-songs,* 1917. It entered the Methodist hymnal in 1935.

Kremser

Nederlandtsch Gedenckclanck, 1626
Arr. by EDWARD KREMSER, 1838-1914

(See comments on text, above.) Kremser, director of a male choral society in Vienna, published 6 tunes from Valerius' collection in his *Sechs altniederländische Volkslieder* (Leipzig, 1877). This was 1 of the 6 tunes, and it was set to a German translation of this text.

We Give Thee But Thine Own (181)

WILLIAM W. HOW, 1823-1897

The text in 6 sts. was written in 1858 and first published in *Psalms and Hymns,* edited by T. B. Morrell and How, 1864 edition. It was printed under the text "He that hath pity upon the poor lendeth unto the Lord" (Proverbs 19:17).

The hymn entered our Methodist Episcopal hymnal in 1878 with 6 sts. and the 1901 Methodist Protestant with 4 sts. Sts. 3 and 5 were dropped in 1935.

Schumann

Cantica Laudis, 1850

The arrangement is found at No. 176 in *Cantica Laudis,* 1850, issued by Lowell Mason and George J. Webb. It was called WHITE and said to be arranged from Robert Schumann. Clara Schumann informed James Love, the Scottish hymnologist, that she could not identify it as one of her husband's works. It is also called HEATH.

We Lift Our Hearts to Thee (492)

JOHN WESLEY, 1703-1791

"A Morning Hymn" first appeared in John Wesley's *Collection of Psalms and Hymns*, 1741, in 6 sts. All sts. were included in our American Methodist hymnal until the 1849 Methodist Episcopal hymnal dropped st. 4:

> O may no gloomy crime
> Pollute the rising day!
> Or Jesu's blood, like evening dew,
> Wash all the stains away.

Of the later hymnals, only the Methodist Episcopal, South of 1889 retained this st.

St. Thomas

See "Come, Ye That Love the Lord," pp. 158-60.

We Plow the Fields (513)
Wir pflügen und wir streuen

MATTHIAS CLAUDIUS, 1740-1815
Trans. by JANE M. CAMPBELL, 1817-1878

The German text was first published in 1782 in a sketch called "Paul Erdmann's Fest," a peasant song in seventeen 4-line sts. with refrain. The poem began "Im Anfang war's auf Erden." It is a romantic picture, charming in its simplicity and piety, of a North German harvest festival in the farmhouse of Paul Erdmann.

Miss Campbell's translation, an adaptation of sts. 3, 5, 7, 9, 10, and 13, was first published in C. S. Bere, *Garland of Song*, 1861. It admirably reproduces the folk spirit and picturesque quality of the song.

The hymn entered the Methodist hymnal in 1878. Sts. 3:5 and 3:7 had already been altered from "no gifts have we to offer" and "But that which thou desirest" to their present forms.

Wir pflügen

JOHANN A. P. SCHULZ, 1747-1800

Also called DRESDEN and CLAUDIUS, this tune first appeared anonymously in A. L. Hoppenstadt, *Lieder für Volkschulen* (Hanover, 1800). It is credited to Schulz in Lindner's *Jugendfreund*, 1812.

We Thank Thee, Lord (203)

CALVIN W. LAUFER, 1874-1938

The text was written in 1919. Its intent is to emphasize the truth that communion with God and compassion for one's fellows are inseparable. It was first published in *The Century Hymnal*, 1921.

The hymn entered the Methodist hymnal in 1935.

Field

CALVIN W. LAUFER, 1874-1938

The text was written at a luncheon with Hubert H. Field, who was a close friend of Laufer. Following another luncheon with Field in the fall of 1919, the tune was written at the close of the same day. It was first sung in Dr. Field's church in September, 1919, and included in *The Century Hymnal*, 1921, and later in the same year in Carl F. Price, *Songs of Life*.

We Three Kings of Orient Are (402)

JOHN H. HOPKINS, JR., 1820-1891

The carol was written in 1857 and first published in the author's *Carols, Hymns and Songs*, 1863. The biblical text is Matthew 2:1-11. It entered the Methodist hymnal in 1935.

Kings of Orient

JOHN H. HOPKINS, JR., 1820-1891

See comments on text, above.

We, Thy People, Praise Thee (6)

KATE STEARNS PAGE, 1873-1963

The author, a teacher in the Diller-Quaile School of Music, New York City, wrote the words for the school song. The hymn was first published with the Haydn tune by E. C. Schirmer, Boston, in a small booklet called *Selected Hymns for Use in School or Home,* 1922. Reprinted in Edith Lovell Thomas, *Singing Worship,* 1935, the hymn became widely known in church schools.

This is the first appearance of the hymn in a Methodist hymnal.

St. Anthony's Chorale

FRANZ JOSEPH HAYDN, 1732-1809
Arr. by EDITH LOVELL THOMAS, 1878-

The tune is taken from the second movement of *Divertimento* in B flat for wind instruments. It was labelled "Chorale St. Antoni" (a misspelling of Antonii). It was found in unpublished music unearthed by C. F. Pohl, the biographer of Haydn, and is called "Feldpartiten" Octet for 2 oboes, 2 horns, 3 bassoons, and serpent. It was written c. 1780 and has been made famous by the Brahms variations on the theme for orchestra.

We Would See Jesus (90)

J. EDGAR PARK, 1879-1956

The hymn was written for *Worship and Song,* edited by B. S. Winchester and Grace W. Conant, 1913. Having recently written 2 books on the Sermon on the Mount, the author wrote the hymn "for youth and promise and sunshine . . . and an inner glimpse of the Young Man of Nazareth living and moving among us."

Cushman

HERBERT B. TURNER, 1852-1927

The tune was written for Anna B. Warner's hymn "We would see Jesus, for the shadows lengthen," while Turner was editing *Hymns and Tunes for Schools,* 1907, at Hampton Normal and Agricultural Institute, Hampton, Va.

Welcome, Happy Morning (452)
Salve festa dies

VENANTIUS FORTUNATUS, c. 530–c. 609
Trans. by JOHN ELLERTON, 1826-1893

Our cento is taken from a poem of 110 lines on the Resurrection. The complete poem radiantly portrays the coming of spring as a symbol of the new life which sprang forth in the world with Christ's rising from the tomb and as the tribute of nature to her triumphant Lord. *Salve festa dies* begins line 39.

Ellerton's translation first appeared in Robert Brown-Borthwick, *Supplemental Hymn and Tune Book*, 1868, and then in Ellerton's own collection, *Hymns, Original and Translated*, 1888.

The text was originally in 6 sts. Five of them were included in our 1878 Methodist Episcopal hymnal: 1-2 and 4-6. The 1935 hymnal used only the first 2 sts., adding a third from another source. Our 1964 hymnal prints 1-2 and 5, and repeats the first as a fourth.

Hermas

FRANCES R. HAVERGAL, 1836-1879

The tune was written for Miss Havergal's children's hymn "Golden harps are sounding," a children's processional for the festival of the Ascension. It was first published in her *Psalmody* (London 1871). It is named for Paul's friend listed in Romans 16:14.

Were You There (436)

American Folk Hymn

Though precise origin and transmission of spirituals can rarely be traced, the life situation in which they came to expression is clear enough. The poignancy of this spiritual is most deeply felt when one remembers that the Negro, having seen lynched bodies on the "tree," easily identified himself with his crucified Lord. The spirituals generally interpret the biblical stories rather than recount them. The singer stands in the midst of the event and so makes the past present, telling the story in the "I-form." The narrator finds himself at the foot of the cross.

This is the first inclusion of the hymn in a Methodist hymnal.

Were You There

American Folk Hymn

(For general remarks about spirituals, see "Go, tell it on the mountain," pp. 188-89.)

The folk hymn first appeared in its present form in Frederick J.

424

Work, *Folk Songs of the American Negro* (Nashville, 1907). It is another example of the "slow, sustained long-phrase melody." An earlier form with a variant first phrase is in William C. Barton, *Old Plantation Songs*, 1899, and other variants are in Charles L. Edwards, *Bahama Songs and Stories* (Boston, 1895).

George Pullen Jackson quotes a similar version sung by Miss Gracie Whitaker who had "heard it from her mother and others" and recorded by J. A. Rickard in Cookeville, Tenn., who stated "the song is well known in the upper (practically negro-less) Cumberland region of Tennessee." Jackson classifies it in *White and Negro Spirituals*, in the "Fainne Geal" or "Roll Jordan" pattern, suggesting that the tune has British antecedents.

We've a Story to Tell to the Nations (410)

H. ERNEST NICHOL, 1862-1926

Nichol wrote both words and music in 1896, using the pseudonym "Colin Sterne" (his name with the letters rearranged). It appeared the same year in the *Sunday School Hymnary*, published in London.

The hymn entered our hymnal in 1935.

Message

H. ERNEST NICHOL, 1862-1926

See comments on text, above.

What a Friend We Have in Jesus (261)

JOSEPH M. SCRIVEN, 1819-1886

The text was written near Port Hope, Ontario, about 1855. Written to comfort the author's mother, it was not intended for wider use. It seems to have been first published in Horace L. Hastings, *Social Hymns, Original and Selected*, 1865, where it is listed as anonymous. In Philip P. Bliss and Ira D. Sankey, *Gospel Hymns and Sacred Songs*, 1875, the lyric is credited to Horatius Bonar. Not until the 1887 edition of *Gospel Hymns No. 5* is Scriven recognized as author.

The hymn entered the Methodist Episcopal hymnal in 1878.

Converse

CHARLES C. CONVERSE, 1832-1918

The tune was composed in 1868 and published in *Silver Wings* (Boston, 1870), compiled by "Karl Reden," Converse's pseudonym. It was credited there to "Reden." Ira D. Sankey discovered the tune in a paper-covered pamphlet of Sunday school hymns as he was compiling *Gospel Hymns No. 1* and dropped one of the items so Converse's hymn could be included.

It has also been called ERIE and WHAT A FRIEND.

What Child Is This (385)

WILLIAM C. DIX, 1837-1898

These 3 sts. are taken from a longer poem, *The Manger Throne*, written c. 1865 on Epiphany Day, after the author had read the Gospel for the day, Matthew 2:1-12.

The carol entered the Methodist hymnal in 1935.

Greensleeves

16th-Century Old English Melody

The tune is taken from a wait's carol published in *New Christmas Carols*, 1642, with words of a New Year carol, "The old year now away is fled." However, it predates this collection. In the registers of the Stationers' Company, September, 1580, Richard Jones had licensed to himself "A new Northern Dittye of the *Lady Greene Sleeves*." Twelve days later, the ballad was converted to religious use, *"Green Sleeves moralised to the Scripture, declaring the manifold benefits and blessings of God bestowed on sinful man."* Shakespeare mentions the tune in *The Merry Wives of Windsor*.

The harmonization is chiefly that of John Stainer.

What Grace, O Lord, and Beauty Shone (178)

JOHN S. B. MONSELL, 1811-1875

The text in 5 sts. was first published in *Hymns and Poems*, edited by Edward Denny, 1839. It was entitled "The Forgiving One," and under the text was printed "Grace is poured into my lips" (Psalm

45:2). The hymn entered our hymnals in 1878 and 1889 with all 5 sts. The second st. has been omitted in the present hymnal.

Christus, der ist mein Leben

See "O Lord, Our Lord, in All the Earth," pp. 325-26.

What Shall I Do My God to Love (130)

CHARLES WESLEY, 1707-1788

The text was first published in *Hymns and Sacred Poems,* 1749, 1 of 8 hymns under the title "After a Recovery." In eighteen 4-line sts., it began:

> O what an evil heart have I,
> So cold, and hard, and blind,
> With sin so ready to comply,
> And cast my God behind!

John Wesley reduced the hymn to 9 sts. for his *Collection of Hymns for the Use of the People Called Methodists,* 1780, beginning with st. 9 and continuing from the eleventh to the eighteenth. Our earlier hymnals, beginning with 1802 and through 1847, began the hymn with st. 9 as John did:

> Infinite, unexhausted love!
> Jesus and love are one:
> If still to me thy bowels move,
> They are restrained to none.

Since 1849, our printings have always begun with st. 11, "What shall I do my God to love," and have included 4 or 5 sts. selected from sts. 12, 13, 14, and 15. The entire hymn was omitted in 1905 and 1935. Our 1964 hymnal has happily restored it, replacing sts. 14 and 15 with 17 and 18, thereby improving the hymn.

Richmond

See "O Thou in All Thy Might So Far," pp. 338.

427

What Shall I Render to My God (196)

CHARLES WESLEY, 1707-1788

The hymn is taken from *Select Psalms* (Psalm 116) as printed in Osborn, *The Poetical Works of John and Charles Wesley*, 1870. In eleven 8-line sts., the psalm begins, "The Lord who saved me by his grace."

According to the preface in Vol. VIII of *The Poetical Works*, it is 1 of 16 psalms not hitherto published. Only twice has a cento from this psalm been included in our hymnals: the 1878 hymnal printed 5 quatrains: 7*a*, 8*a*, 9*a*, 10*a*, and 11*b*. Our 1964 hymnal uses 7*a*, 7*b*, 8*a*, 10*a*, and 11*b*, making a very fine hymn indeed.

Armenia

See **"All Praise to Our Redeeming Lord,"** pp. 81-82.

What Wondrous Love Is This (432)

American Folk Hymn

William Hauser, *The Hesperian Harp*, 1848, attributes the original form of this song to the Reverend Alexander Means, a Methodist minister of Oxford, Ga.

An older text as printed in George Pullen Jackson, *Spiritual Folk-Songs of Early America*, runs:

> When I was sinking down, sinking down, sinking down;
> When I was sinking down, sinking down;
> When I was sinking down beneath God's righteous frown,
> Christ laid aside his crown for my soul, for my soul;
> Christ laid aside his crown for my soul.
>
> To God and to the Lamb I will sing, I will sing;
> To God and to the Lamb I will sing;
> To God and to the Lamb who is the great I AM,
> While millions join the theme, I will sing, I will sing;
>
> While millions join the theme I will sing.
> And when from death I'm free I'll sing on, I'll sing on;
> And when from death I'm free I'll sing on.
> And when from death I'm free I'll sing and joyful be,

> And through eternity I'll sing on, I'll sing on,
> And through eternity I'll sing on.

This is the first inclusion of this hymn in a Methodist hymnal.

Wondrous Love

Southern Harmony, 1835
Harm. by C.R.Y.

The first known appearance as a hymn tune is in William Walker, *Southern Harmony,* in the Appendix to the second edition, 1835. There it is credited to "Christopher," who is unknown. George Pullen Jackson in *The Story of the Sacred Harp, 1844–1944* (Nashville, 1944) says of the tune:

Its tune and its stanzaic structure were borrowed from the worldly song about the famous pirate, Captain Kidd. The link between the two songs may be clearly seen if one sings the "Wondrous Love" tune to the following words:

> My name was Robert Kidd, when I sailed, when I sailed,
> My name was Robert Kidd, when I sailed;
> My name was Robert Kidd, God's laws I did forbid,
> So wickedly I did when I sailed, when I sailed,
> So wickedly I did when I sailed.

The "Captain Kidd" tune was already a very old and widely sung melody when it was picked up nearly 250 years ago and associated with the tale of the wild pirate who was executed in England in 1701.

When All Thy Mercies, O My God (70)

JOSEPH ADDISON, 1672-1719

In the *Spectator,* August 9, 1712, Addison wrote a brief essay on gratitude:

There is not a more pleasing exercise of the mind than gratitude. It is accompanied with such an inward satisfaction, that the duty is sufficiently rewarded by the performance. It is not like the practice of many other virtues, difficult and painful, but attended with so much pleasure, that were there no positive command which enjoined it, nor any recompense laid up for it hereafter, a generous mind would indulge in it, for the natural gratification that accompanies it.

If gratitude is due from man to man, how much more from man to his Maker.

And then, after expressing appreciation for pagan poets and Hebrew psalmists, Addison offers for the consideration of his gentle readers this hymn of 13 sts.

The hymn has been included in virtually all American Methodist collections beginning in 1802. Only once have all 13 sts. been included, in the 1847 Methodist Episcopal, South hymnal. The number of sts. has varied from 10, 8, 7, and 6, to 4. Since 1935 sts. 1, 5, 6, and 11 have made up the hymn.

Winchester Old

See "Come, Holy Ghost, Our Hearts Inspire," pp. 139-40.

When I Survey the Wondrous Cross (435)

ISAAC WATTS, 1674-1748

The text in 5 sts. first appeared in the author's *Hymns and Spiritual Songs,* 1707, Bk. III, the section for the Lord's Supper. The second line in the 1707 edition reads "Where the young Prince of Glory died." "We can only suppose that some one who had no feeling for poetry persuaded the young author to change it, for he did so in the enlarged second edition of 1709," writes Percy Dearmer. In the second edition Watts bracketed the fourth st. for optional use. Since George White-field in his 1757 Supplement to *Collection of Hymns for Social Worship* omitted the fourth st., it has rarely been printed. The omitted st. reads:

> His dying Crimson like a Robe
> Spreads o'er his Body on the Tree,
> Then am I dead to all the Globe,
> And all the Globe is dead to me.

The hymn in 4 sts. entered our hymnals in 1847. In 4:2 Watts wrote "present," which was retained in all our hymnals until 1935, when it was altered to "offering," a change which seems to have been made first in England in 1831 by Hugh Stowell in his *Selection of Psalms and Hymns Suited to the Services of the Church of England.*

Hamburg

LOWELL MASON, 1792-1872

The tune was written in 1824 in Savannah, Ga., where Mason was a bank clerk. It was first sung in the First Presbyterian Church there. In the Boston *Handel and Haydn Society Collection of Church Music* (3rd ed., 1825), Mason indicates that it was arranged from a Gregorian chant. A similar musical example can be seen in the setting of the Lord's Prayer **(826)**, which is a setting of Tone I, Ending 1.

When Morning Gilds the Skies (91)
Beim frühen Morgenlicht

ANONYMOUS, German, 19th Century
Stanzas 1, 2, 4, trans. by EDWARD CASWALL, 1814-1878
Stanza 3, trans. by ROBERT BRIDGES, 1844-1920

The German hymn, probably nineteenth century, is of unknown authorship. Various versions are found as in the *Katholisches Gesangbuch* (Würzburg, 1828), in fourteen 4-line sts., or *Frankische Volkslieder* (Leipzig, 1855). Caswall's translation was probably made from a third version. His translation first appeared in 6 sts. in Henry Formby, *Catholic Hymns,* 1854. Then, in his *Masque of Mary,* 1858, the other 8 sts. of the original were added. Various centos have been made from the longer hymn for hymnal use.

The hymn first entered our hymnals in 1901 with four 6-line sts.; then in 1905, with 8; in 1935, with 6. Beginning with 1935 a st. from Robert Bridges' *Yattendon Hymnal,* 1899, has been incorporated with the Caswall translation, the st. beginning "Ye nations of mankind." The 1964 hymnal reduces the hymn to 4 sts., which are sts. 1-2, 20, 22, 27-28 of the original 2-line sts. with our third st., the st. by Robert Bridges.

Laudes Domini

JOSEPH BARNBY, 1838-1896

The tune was written for this text and published in the Appendix to *Hymns Ancient and Modern* (London, 1868). Barnby included it in his *Original Hymn Tunes,* 1869, with a different ending, but this version has not gained favor. The tune should be kept moving briskly, with no ritard.

When the Storms of Life Are Raging (244)

CHARLES A. TINDLEY, 1851-1933

Both text and tune were written by Tindley and copyrighted in 1905. They appeared together in *Songs of Paradise,* a collection which had tunes by Tindley and was arranged by F. A. Clark, a Philadelphia Negro musician, and by Tindley's sons, Frederick J. and Charles Albert, Jr. The first edition of this work was c. 1905.

This is the first inclusion of the hymn in the Methodist hymnal.

Stand by Me

CHARLES A. TINDLEY, 1851-1933
Arr. by DANIEL L. RIDOUT, 1899-

See comments on text, above. Ridout made this arrangement for the 1964 hymnal.

When We Walk with the Lord (223)

JOHN H. SAMMIS, 1846-1919

According to Ira D. Sankey, *The Story of the Gospel Hymns,* 1906, at a meeting in Brockton, Mass., conducted by Dwight L. Moody, a young man arose in the testimony meeting and said, "I am not quite sure—but I am going to trust, and I am going to obey." Daniel B. Towner, musical director of the Moody Bible Institute, who was leading the singing, heard the words, jotted them down, and sent them to Sammis, a Presbyterian minister. He wrote the text, for which Towner supplied the tune. Both text and tune were first printed in *Hymns Old and New* (Chicago, 1887).

This is the first inclusion of the hymn in an official Methodist hymnal. The second st. has been omitted.

Trust and Obey

DANIEL B. TOWNER, 1850-1919

See comments on text, above.

Where Cross the Crowded Ways of Life (204)

FRANK MASON NORTH, 1850-1935

Caleb T. Winchester, one of the editors of the 1905 Methodist hymnal, suggested to Dr. North that a new missionary hymn would be welcome. North's long intimacy with the crowds of New York's teeming streets as well as with the capitals and towns of the world, together with his Christian concern for all men, has come to poignant and powerful expression in this hymn, based on Matthew 22:9, on which he had preached shortly before writing the lines.

It was first printed in the June, 1903, issue of the *Christian City*, of which Dr. North was then editor.

The hymn has been in the Methodist hymnal since 1905.

Germany

See **"Eternal God and Sovereign Lord,"** pp. 168-69.

Where Shall My Wondering Soul Begin (528)

CHARLES WESLEY, 1707-1788

The hymn in 8 sts., entitled "Christ the Friend of Sinners," was first printed in *Hymns and Sacred Poems*, 1742. It is probably this hymn which Charles refers to in his *Journal* for Tuesday, May 23, 1738, as he recounts the "assurance" he had received 2 days before on Pentecost Sunday (see comments on "And can it be that I should gain," pp. 91-92). "I now found myself at peace with God, and rejoiced in hope of loving Christ. . . . I saw that by faith I stood." The day after this event, he wrote, "At nine I began an hymn upon my conversion, but was persuaded to break off, for fear of pride. Mr. Bray coming, encouraged me to proceed in spite of Satan. I prayed Christ to stand by me, and finished the hymn." And when the next evening, May 24, John came to announce that his heart has been "strangely warmed," Charles records, "Towards ten, my brother was brought in triumph by a troop of our friends, and declared, 'I believe.' We sang the hymn with great joy, and parted with prayer."

This hymn, therefore, has been called "the first hymn of the Methodist Revival."

When John included it in his *Collection of Hymns for the Use of the People Called Methodists*, 1780, he omitted the original sixth st.:

> Come all ye Magdalens in Lust,
> Ye Ruffians fell in Murders old;

Repent and live: despair and trust!
Jesus for you to Death was sold;
Tho' Hell protest, and Earth repine,
He died for Crimes like Yours—and Mine.

The hymn was included in our hymnals of 1836, 1837, 1847, and 1849 in 6, 5, or 4 sts. It was omitted from all our hymnals between 1849 and 1964, when it was restored with sts. 1-3, 5, and 7. The omitted fourth and eighth sts. read:

No—tho' the Anxient Dragon rage
And call forth all his Hosts to War,
Tho' Earth's self-righteous Sons engage;
Them, and their God alike I dare:
Jesus the Sinner's Friend proclaim,
Jesus, to Sinners still the same.

For you the purple Current flow'd
In Pardons from his wounded Side:
Languish'd for you th'Eternal God,
For you the Prince of Glory dy'd:
Believe; and all your Guilt's forgiven,
Only Believe—and yours is Heaven.

Fillmore

See **"And Can It Be That I Should Gain,"** pp. 91-92.

While Shepherds Watched Their Flocks (394)

NAHUM TATE, 1652-1715

The text first appeared in *The Supplement to the New Version of Psalms by Dr. Brady and Mr. Tate,* 1700. The Supplement contained 16 hymns and was bound with the *New Version.* It is Tate's only hymn to survive.

The hymn has been in most American Methodist collections since 1802, with all 6 sts. The original of 5:3-4 read:

Of angels praising God, and thus
addressed their joyful song:

For the most part, since 1849, our hymnals have printed the lines as they appear in the 1964 hymnal.

Winchester Old

See "Come, Holy Ghost, Our Hearts Inspire," pp. 139-40.

With Thine Own Pity, Savior (340)

RAY PALMER, 1808-1887

In the author's *Poetical Works,* 1876, is a poem entitled "Consecration and Work." It is printed under the text "Thou knowest that I love thee. . . . Feed my sheep" (John 21:16). There are six 4-line sts. with a 6-line refrain. The poem begins:

Lord, thou hast taught our hearts to glow
With love's undying flame.

This is the first inclusion of the hymn in our hymnals. The cento is made up of sts. 4, 3, 5, and 6 in that order. In 3:2 *"sweet* love" has been altered to *"great* love."

Gräfenberg

See "Come, Holy Spirit, Heavenly Dove," pp. 141-42.

Ye Servants of God (409)

CHARLES WESLEY, 1707-1788

The hymn was first published in *Hymns for Times of Trouble and Persecution,* 1744, a collection which was enlarged in 1745 to include 48 hymns. It was 1 of 4 hymns entitled "Hymns to be sung in a Tumult." The "tumult" referred to was produced by the dynastic quarrels in which England was involved in the 1740's and by the absurd and slanderous accusation that the Wesleys and their followers were ringleaders in the attempt to overthrow the Crown. Though James II had abdicated the throne in 1688, his descendants and adherents, ardent Roman Catholics known as Jacobites, were biding their time, looking for the opportunity to restore the House of Stuart. The 1740's seemed to bring the time. Frederick the Great joined with France to make war on England, and Charles Edward, grandson of James II, invaded the island in 1745. Though this Jacobite rebellion was quickly put down, oddly enough popular fury fell on the Methodists. They were dubbed Papists and Jacobites and were accused of surreptitiously aiding the Pretender. John Wesley himself was even reputed to be the young Pretender in disguise, meetings were broken up, their people mobbed, plundered, and dragged before magistrates.

The hymn was originally in 6 sts., but the second and third sts. have never been included in our hymnals. Sts. 1, 4, 5, and 6 have been included in all our hymnals since 1849. Only 2 alterations have been made in the text: in 3:3 Wesley wrote "Our Jesus's praises." This has been revised to "The praises of Jesus" since at least 1849. In 4:2 *"and* wisdom" was altered to *"all* wisdom," in England in 1831, in America as early as 1878.

Hanover
Probably by WILLIAM CROFT, 1678-1727

The tune first appeared in *The Supplement to the New Version of Psalms by Dr. Brady and Mr. Tate* (6th ed., 1708), as edited by John Playford. It is anonymous with this inscription: "a new tune for the 149th Psalm of the New Version and 104th Psalm of the Old." ST. ANNE (probably by Croft) also appears for the first time in this same collection. In style it marks a transition from the severe and austere style of the older psalter tunes.

It was named HANOVER at a time when Handel was assumed to be the composer of the tune. Handel was appointed court-conductor at Hanover in 1710, where he remained only 1 year before coming to England to live.

Other tune names are BROMSWICK, TALLY'S, ST. GEORGE'S TUNE, LOUTH, and OLD 104TH.

Ye Watchers and Ye Holy Ones (19)
ATHELSTAN RILEY, 1858-1945

The text was written for the tune, to be included in *The English Hymnal* (Oxford, 1906), of which Riley was one of the compilers. It reflects the language of the Greek liturgies. St. 2 is a paraphrase of the Theotokion, "Hymn to the Mother of God," sung at the close of the choir office.

It entered our hymnal in 1935, omitting the third st. which has been added in 1964.

Lasst uns erfreuen

See **"All Creatures of Our God and King,"** pp. 72-73.

COMMENTS ON TEXTS AND TUNES— CANTICLES, SERVICE MUSIC, AND COMMUNION MUSIC

All Things Come of Thee (807, 808)

The text is from I Chronicles 29:14b, KJV.

807

LLOYD MOREY, 1886-1965

Morey wrote this for the select choir of Wesley Foundation, University of Illinois, while he was organist at Trinity Church. It was copyrighted in 1927 by Paul Tincher Smith and published by the Choir Library of West Lafayette, Ind.

808

Attr. to LUDWIG VAN BEETHOVEN, 1770-1827

Though this widely used offertory chant is attributed to Beethoven, its source has never been located. *The Pilgrim Hymnal* lists no source or composer, and some earlier Methodist hymnals list it as "Source Unknown." There is so little musical material in the 2 measures that it is hardly likely that Beethoven would recognize the work as his own.

Amen (816–825)

"Amen" is a Hebrew word meaning "so let it be" or "truly." Though the word is used in scripture and tradition in a variety of ways, its most appropriate liturgical use is as a response of the congregation to prayer: "And all the people shall say, Amen" (Deuteronomy 27:16 ff.).

No. 816 is a simple plagal cadence, while 817 is a perfect cadence Amen.

The Dresden Amen at 818 may have been composed by Johann Gottlieb Naumann (1741-1801) for use at the royal chapel at Dresden. It was later published in the Zittau choir book. Both Mendelssohn and Wagner made extensive use of it.

The Danish Amen, 819, is widely used in Lutheran churches in Denmark, but its source is unknown.

No. 820, Greek, is also from an unknown source, but may be from some Eastern Orthodox usage.

Evan Copley's setting at **821** was submitted for use in this hymnal, and this marks its first publication.

Eric DeLamarter's setting at **822** was published by Clayton F. Summy in a collection of service music in 1930 and was composed for use at the Fourth Presbyterian Church in Chicago.

No. **823**, Canon George Briggs's Amen, is taken from the 1938 revision of the Canadian *Book of Common Praise*.

The setting by Louis Bourgeois, **824**, is taken from the last 2½ measures of the tune NUNC DIMITTIS, often sung to "O gladsome light, O grace." The tune was first published in the Genevan Psalter, 1549, and the arrangement used in our hymnal is by Peggy Hoffmann in *Seventeen Introits and Responses,* published by H. W. Gray, 1960.

The sevenfold Amen, **825**, was composed by John Stainer to be sung after the prayer of consecration at Holy Communion and was first published in his *Choir-Book for the Office of Holy Communion,* 1873.

Blessed Art Thou, O Lord (668)
Benedictus es, Domine

WILLIAM CROTCH, 1775-1847

The Greek Old Testament inserts between Daniel 3:23 and 24 of the Hebrew text a prayer of Azariah and a Song of the Three Young Men, as "with one mouth [they] praised and glorified and blessed God in the furnace." The hymn is similar to psalms 103 and 148. Date, original language, and provenance are undetermined.

Our canticle is verses 29-34. It has of old been used in the Morning Office of the Eastern Church and in the Mozarabic liturgy in Spain. Not in the Church of England *Book of Common Prayer*, it was authorized by the General Convention of the Protestant Episcopal Church in 1919 and was included in the American *Book of Common Prayer* as a short substitute for the *Te Deum* or the *Benedicite* (616), a continuation of the same hymn.

The English version is that of the Great Bible, 1539. The canticle entered our hymnal in 1964.

The musical setting by William Crotch is 1 of 74 chants composed by him. It is an example of double chant, consisting of 4 phrases instead of 2.

Blessed Be the Lord God of Israel (666)
Benedictus

WILLIAM CROTCH, 1775-1847

The 3 canticles of Luke 1–2, the *Benedictus,* the *Magnificat,* and the *Nunc dimittis,* are the first full-length Christian hymns recorded. The *Benedictus* (Luke 1:68-79), assigned by Luke to Zechariah, is a Messianic hymn, made up largely of Old Testament passages. It may have been independently composed in Aramaic or Hebrew, then used with reference to John the Baptist, and then adapted for Christian use.

Its medieval use was as the canticle for Lauds, the service at dawn at which psalms 148–50, in which *laudate* (praise ye) often occurs, were sung. In *The Book of Common Prayer,* 1549, when parts of Lauds and Matins were combined to form the office of Morning Prayer, the *Benedictus* was assigned to a place after the New Testament lesson. The version is that of the Great Bible, 1539.

The canticle has been included in our hymnals since 1878.

For comments on the musical setting by William Crotch, see "Blessed Art Thou, O Lord," p. 442.

Come, and Let Us Sweetly Join (790)

CHARLES WESLEY, 1707-1788

First published in *Hymns and Sacred Poems,* 1740, the hymn was in 5 parts, 4 sts. each, except the fifth which had 6. The first 4 parts were included in John Wesley's 1780 *Collection of Hymns for the Use of the People Called Methodists* and were printed in American Methodist collections at least through 1836. Our hymnals gradually reduced the number of sts. printed until the 1905 hymnal dropped the entire hymn. The quatrain printed here is the first half of st. 1.

Savannah

See "Jesus, Lord, We Look to Thee," pp. 246-47.

Come, Bless the Lord (783)

AUSTIN C. LOVELACE, 1919-

The text is Psalm 134:1*a*, 2, RSV, except that "ye" has replaced "you."

COMPANION TO THE HYMNAL

Lovelace wrote the music in 1955 at Evanston, Ill. It was first published in *Service Music for the Adult Choir* by Westminster Press (Philadelphia, 1956).

Communion Service in E Minor (833–837)

PHILIP R. DIETTERICH, 1931-

See comments under "Glory Be to God on High," (833), pp. 445-46.

Enter into His Gates (785)

ROBERT E. SCOGGIN, 1930-

The text is Psalm 100:4, KJV.

Scoggin writes that the music was composed in the summer of 1958 "as one of several such responses while on vacation traveling with my family. Pat [the composer's wife] was driving, and I was soaking up the inspiration of the moment, sitting in the front seat composing these short Introits." This is its first appearance in a hymnal.

Father, Give Thy Benediction (815)

SAMUEL LONGFELLOW, 1819-1892

The text is made up of the first 2 and last 2 lines of an 8-line "Benediction of Peace." It was first published anonymously in the 1864 edition of *Hymns of the Spirit,* compiled by Longfellow and Samuel Johnson. All 8 lines were printed in our 1935 hymnal.

Alta Trinita beata

Laudi spirituali, 14th Century

The tune is taken from a Proper melody from a fourteenth-century manuscript of the laudi spirituali. The laudi spirituali were popular melodies with sacred macaronic texts—i.e. a combination of ecclesiastical Latin and popular Italian. Some of the English and German carols, such as "In dulci jubilo," are similar.

Charles Burney's notation in his *General History of Music,* 1782, is the source of the modern form, which was simplified and much modified. For the 1964 hymnal, the melody has been further shortened.

CANTICLES, SERVICE MUSIC, AND COMMUNION MUSIC

Glory Be to God (800)
Gloria Deo

JOHN MERBECKE, 1523–c. 1585

The *Gloria Deo* was appointed for responsive use in the opening sentences of the ritual for the Lord's Supper as ordered in the 1935 Methodist hymnal. Our present liturgy makes no provision for its use.

Merbecke's musical setting is a simple harmonization of a single note intonation, such as an organist might provide to support congregational chant.

Glory Be to God on High (830A, 833, 840)
Gloria in excelsis

Known also as the Greater Doxology (see comments on "Glory Be to the Father," pp. 446-47) and the Angelic Hymn, the *Gloria in excelsis* is an expansion of Luke 2:14, originally a Jewish Messianic song (see Psalm 118:26) acclaiming the coming salvation. The second st., addressed to Jesus Christ in his passion and exaltation, is built on the *Kyrie* and *Agnus Dei*.

St. 3 reflects the acclamation in the Eastern liturgies by which the people respond to the celebrant just before Communion, "One holy, One Lord Jesus Christ, to the glory of God the Father."

Used first in the daily offices of the Eastern Church, since at least the fourth century it was introduced into the Roman Mass by Pope Symmachus (498-514) as an extension of the *Kyrie* at the beginning of the service. Archbishop Thomas Cranmer kept the position of the *Gloria* at the beginning of the service in 1549, but in 1552 removed it to its traditional English place as part of the Post-Communion thanksgiving. It remained in this position in our liturgy until our 1964 *Ritual*, following current trends, returned it to its original location in the Roman mass and in the First Prayer Book of Edward VI, 1549, at the beginning of the service.

830A

Old Scottish Chant

The original source of this chant has never been identified, although it has come to be widely used in many denominations. The form is that of Anglican chant, adapted to fit the threefold form of the *Gloria in excelsis*.

445

833

The setting is taken from Dietterich's *Communion Service in E Minor* (833-837). This service was composed specifically for the 1964 hymnal in order that thematic unity might be achieved throughout the Communion service. It is the first complete choral setting of the service to appear in a Methodist hymnal.

840

The *Gloria,* as well as other parts of the service music by Merbecke, is taken from his *Book of Common Prayer Noted,* 1550. He was instructed to use only one note to each syllable; thus he proceeded to use the plainsong melodies in common usage in the cathedrals at that time, more or less stopping the music of the chant when the text was completely set. Therefore, the basis of his setting is an altered and abbreviated plainsong version.

Glory Be to the Father (792, 793, 794)
Gloria Patri

Eric Werner in *The Sacred Bridge* writes:

Through the magnificent variety of the world of Christian prayer, so manifold in all its forms and churches, there runs, like the proverbial red thread, the rigid formula of the Lesser Doxology. It recurs so often in each service, so majestically does it conclude the individual prayer, that this formula is familiar to every Christian, no matter in which ecclesiastic doctrine he is brought up and to what liturgical usage he may be accustomed.

The 2 great doxological prayers of the Western Church as we now know them, the Lesser Doxology (*Gloria Patri*) and the Greater Doxology (*Gloria in excelsis*), were formed in the third and fourth centuries under the pressure of Arianism and other Gnostic sects. The pattern of praise, however, goes far back to Jewish antecedents, as may be seen, for example, in the responses to the 5 books of the psalter: psalms 41:13, 72:18-19, 89:52, 106:48, and 150.

The simpler New Testament antecedents may be seen in Romans

16:27, Ephesians 3:21, II Peter 3:18, Jude 25, and Revelation 5:13. An important stage in the development is illustrated by Matthew 28:19. The Trinitarian doxology first became dominant in the third century. The latest addition to the formula, "As it was in the beginning," is because of the insistence of the orthodox parties in the Arian controversy on the "consubstantiality" of the Son with the Father, that is, that the God of the Old Testament was the same as the God manifested in Christ in the New, and that the unity and equality of the three Persons of the Trinity are eternal.

The most characteristic liturgical use of the *Gloria Patri* has been after the reading of the psalm, to provide a New Testament or Trinitarian ending.

792

HENRY W. GREATOREX, 1813-1858

The musical setting is taken from Greatorex's *Collection of Psalm and Hymn Tunes,* 1851. This is *Gloria Patri* No. 1 in the collection.

793

Mode VIII-1

See **"My Soul Doth Magnify the Lord,"** pp. 454-55.

794

CHRISTOPH MEINEKE, 1782-1850

The music is taken from the "Evening Prayer" in Meineke's *Music for the Church* (Baltimore, 1844), composed for use at St. Paul's Church in Baltimore.

God Be in My Head (813)

HENRY WALFORD DAVIES, 1869-1941

The oldest extant text of the hymn is found on the title page of the Sarum Primer (Book of Hours), 1514. Its first use as a congregational hymn was in *The Oxford Hymn Book,* 1908, from which it has entered many hymnals and books of devotion.

Davies' musical setting was first published in 1910 on a leaflet. It was later included in the 1912 festival service book of the London Church

Choir Association. The rising sixth, which is the basis of the tune, and the rich and thickened harmony of the last line are characteristic of Sir Walford Davies' work.

God Be Merciful unto Us (804)

RONALD A. NELSON, 1927-

The text is Psalm 67:1, KJV.

The music is a portion of the psalm for the introit for Tuesday in Holy Week, as abbreviated by Earle Copes. It first appeared in *Introits and Graduals for the Lutheran Service,* published by Augsburg Publishing House (Minneapolis, 1961). The volume contains original settings by contemporary composers.

God Himself Is with Us (788)
Gott ist gegenwärtig!

GERHARDT TERSTEEGEN, 1697-1769
Trans. COMPOSITE

The text was first published in the author's *Geistliches Blumengärtlein inniger Seelen,* 1729. It was entitled "Remembrance of the Glorious and Delightful Presence of God." It is the most widely used of Tersteegen's hymns. John Wesley translated it with the first line "Lo, God is here! Let us adore," and published it in his *Hymns and Sacred Poems,* 1739.

Our translation is composite and is based on the translation made for the *Moravian Hymn Book* of 1826. The st. used here is the first.

Arnsberg

JOACHIM NEANDER, 1650-1680

The tune, also called WUNDERBARER KÖNIG, GRONINGEN, and GOTT IST GEGENWÄRTIG, is credited to Neander by S. Kümmerle and other authorities. It first appeared in Neander's *Glaub- und Liebes- übung* (Bremen, 1680), set to "Wunderbarer König," probably also by Neander.

Holy, Holy, Holy (830B, 836, 843)
Sanctus

The text of the *Sanctus* is derived from the splendid vision of Isaiah 6:1-3. Widely used in the Jewish synagogue, it was taken over by the Church before the third century. In Archbishop Thomas Cranmer's 1549 service, the *Benedictus qui venit* ("Hosanna in the highest. Blessed is he that cometh in the name of the Lord," Matthew 21:9) was inserted before the final phrase. This was dropped in 1552 and subsequent English prayer books. The English Proposed Liturgy of 1928 and the Scottish, 1929, have restored it for optional use. The Liturgy of the Church of South India, 1950, adds "Blessed be he that hath come and is to come in the name of the Lord, Hosanna in the highest."

830B

JOHN MERBECKE, 1523–c. 1585

See comments under **"Glory Be to God on High" (840)**, pp. 445-46.

836

PHILIP R. DIETTERICH, 1931-

See comments under **"Glory Be to God on High" (833)**, pp. 445-46.

843

ANONYMOUS

Robert G. McCutchan has suggested that "the most effective way to use [this setting] is to have a solo voice, preferably a baritone, sing the Preface, the choir and the congregation joining at the beginning of the Sanctus, according to the early Latin rite." It is more correct to say that the Preface may only be sung by a solo voice as a continuation of the intoning of the entire Preface, meaning either the Proper for the season or the general one beginning "It is very meet, right and our bounden duty," etc. Therefore, only the congregation's part has been included, and this has been placed in a lower key and the rhythm altered to avoid the many false accents in the previous hymnal.

I Was Glad (786)

AUSTIN C. LOVELACE, 1919-

The text is Psalm 122:1, KJV.

Composed in 1955 at Evanston, Ill., the musical setting was first published in *Service Music for the Adult Choir* by Westminster Press (Philadelphia, 1956). It has been altered by the composer for the hymnal version.

It Is a Good Thing to Give Thanks (667)
Bonum est confiteri

RICHARD FARRANT, c. 1530-1581

In Jesus' day, Psalm 92 was appointed for use in the Temple at the morning sacrifice on the sabbath. In the Benedictine Rule, sixth century, verses 1-4 were said at Lauds on Friday. Not in the Church of England *Book of Common Prayer,* these 4 verses were introduced in the American *Book of Common Prayer* in 1789 for use at Evening Prayer when the *Magnificat* was omitted, and for which it is now an option.

The canticle entered our hymnal in 1935.

Farrant's chant in F is not an original chant, but an early arrangement of a psalm tone in G, harmonized to form an Anglican chant.

Jesus, Stand Among Us (791)

WILLIAM PENNEFATHER, 1816-1873

This st. is the first of a 3-st. hymn which seems to have been printed first posthumously in 1873 in the author's *Original Hymns and Thoughts in Verse.* It was probably written for the Mildmay Conferences, sometime after 1864.

All three sts. of the hymn were included in our 1935 hymnal.

Glenfinlas

KENNETH G. FINLAY, 1882-

The pentatonic (5 note) tune first appeared in the 1925 edition of *Songs of Praise.* It was written in 3 parts for children, with the composer later providing the 4-part version.

Lead Me, Lord (802)

SAMUEL S. WESLEY, 1810-1876

The text is from the Great Bible version of Psalm 5:8 and Psalm 4:8, with slight alterations.

Wesley's music is a simplified version of his famous anthem.

Let Thy Word Abide in Us (796)

GEORGE DYSON, 1883-1964

The text is a prayer in the language of the Gospel of John as found in John 5:38.

Dyson's musical setting was first published in *The Call to Worship*.

Lift Up Your Hearts (835, 841, 842)
Sursum Corda

Beginning at least with the third century, in all historic liturgies, East and West, the *Sursum Corda* has introduced the *Sanctus* with Preface, thus opening the Consecration Prayer. Lamentations 3:41 is the biblical basis for the first couplet; the second is derived from the Jewish benediction over the "Cup of Blessing."

835

PHILIP R. DIETTERICH, 1931-

See comments under "Glory Be to God on High" (833), pp. 445-46.

841

JOHN MERBECKE, 1523–c. 1585

See comments under "Glory Be to God on High" (840), pp. 445-46.

842

JOHN CAMIDGE, 1735-1803

The musical setting is taken from Camidge's *Service in E,* written for use at Yorkminster.

Listen to Our Prayer (803)

Text from India
Trans. by LEILA JACKSON BROWN, 1930-

The text was first published in 1956 by the Cooperative Recreation Service, Delaware, Ohio.

Binti Hamari

Melody from India

This folk song was sung to Victor Sherring, director of the India Centenary Choir, by one of the choir members. It was transcribed by Robert Kauffman, a missionary in India at the time, as Mr. Sherring played it on the harmonium. On the repetitions, which are essential in Indian practice, there are always variations, i.e. a solo voice answered by the whole choir, or echo effects.

Lord, Have Mercy upon Us (827)
Kyrie eleison

THOMAS TALLIS, c. 1505-1585

The use of the *Kyrie* in the churches has been both ancient and varied, going back to Semitic and pagan beginnings. As printed here, the text is intended as response after the Ten Commandments.

The custom of singing the *Kyrie* after each commandment was introduced by Calvin in 1540 in his Strassburg liturgy. In the Second Prayer Book of Edward VI, 1552, Archbishop Thomas Cranmer followed Calvin's precedent, and added to "Lord, have mercy" the words "upon us" and "incline our hearts to keep this law (these laws)."

Tallis' harmonization of a plainchant was set to the *Venite* in his *Service, Preces, and Litany in F*. The present form was published by William Boyce in his *Cathedral Music*, Vol. I, 1760. In English usage the first form (using "keep this law") is sung after each of the first 9 commandments, and the second form after the tenth. The text has been edited so that this pattern may be used, but it is also possible to use only one or the other after the complete reading of all the commandments.

Lord, Have Mercy Upon Us (834, 838, 839)
Kyrie eleison

Though no provision is made in our Order for the Administration of the Sacrament of the Lord's Supper for the use of the *Kyrie*, 3 musical settings are given.

One of the oldest forms of prayer and liturgical response in Christian worship, the *Kyrie* entered the Western Church from the East. In the fourth century it became the customary response to the litanies and was so introduced as Preface to the mass at Rome by Pope Gelasius I (492-96). Gregory the Great, c. 540-604, changed the second *Kyrie* to *Christe*. This practice has been continued. Used in threefold or ninefold forms, it is said or sung antiphonally by clergy and people. In the 1549 service, Archbishop Thomas Cranmer used the *Kyrie* at the beginning, after the Prayer for Purity and before the *Gloria in excelsis*. When the Ten Commandments were introduced at the beginning of the service and the *Gloria* placed at the end, the *Kyrie* followed the commandments. However, much variation of position is to be found in the various rites.

834

PHILIP R. DIETTERICH, 1931-

See comments under **"Glory Be to God on High" (833)**, pp. 445-46.

838

JOHN MERBECKE, 1523–c. 1585

See comments under **"Glory Be to God on High" (840)**, pp. 445-46.

839

The musical setting is taken from a Lutheran service of 1526.

Lord Jesus Christ, Be Present Now (784)
Herr Jesu Christ, dich zu uns wend

JOHANN NIEDLING, *Lutherisch Handbüchlein*, 1655
Trans. by CATHERINE WINKWORTH, 1827-1878

Though the text is sometimes attributed to Wilhelm II, Duke of Saxe-Weimar, there is no real evidence to support this claim. The hymn may have been first printed in the second edition, 1651, of Part I of *Cantionale Sacrum* (1st ed.; Gotha, 1646) in four 4-line sts. entitled "To be sung before the Sermon." It next appeared in Johannes Niedling, *Lutherisch Handbüchlein* (4th ed.; Altenburg, 1655). E. E. Koch, *Geschichte des Kirchenlieds,* writes that it was in the first

453

edition, 1638, but this appears to be merely a guess. In any case, the Duke's name does not seem to be attached to the hymnal until the Altdorf *Liederfreund,* 1676.

In 1678 the hymn was formally directed to be sung in all the churches in Saxony on all Sundays and festivals.

The translation is that of Catherine Winkworth in her *Chorale Book for England* (London, 1863).

Herr Jesu Christ, dich zu uns wend

See **"All Things Are Thine,"** pp. 84-85.

Lord, Now Lettest Thou Thy Servant (673)
Nunc dimittis

JOSEPH BARNBY, 1838-1896

Simeon's Song, Luke 2:29-32, is one of the earliest songs from the Bible to be used in the worship of the Church. It has been sung at the evening offices since the fourth century. In the English *Book of Common Prayer* it furnishes the transition between the New Testament lesson and the Creed. Since Calvinists used it at the close of Holy Communion, a metrical version was included with the psalms in the Genevan Psalter.

The song entered the Methodist hymnal in 1905.

Barnby's chant, originally in E, appeared in *The Cathedral Psalter,* 1873, of which Barnby was one of the editors.

My Soul Doth Magnify the Lord (670)
Magnificat

Tone VIII, 1

Mary's Song, Luke 1:46-55 (credited to Elizabeth by some ancient manuscripts and some modern scholars), is modelled on the Song of Hannah, I Samuel 2:1-10, with allusions to other parts of the Old Testament. Because of the influence of the Mary cultus of the Middle Ages, it was the text most frequently set to music, next to the mass. Therefore its very powerful lines became widely known.

In the Eastern Church it was used at early Morning Prayer at least from the fourth century. St. Benedict, sixth century, appointed it for Vespers, probably following Roman usage. This determined its place in *The Book of Common Prayer,* 1549, in the office of Evening Prayer, between the Old and New Testament lessons.

The canticle entered our hymnal in 1905 in its present form, the Great Bible version.

The tonality of the musical setting hovers between the dominant and the tonic above, with the exception of one note above the tonic. Like Tone V (see "O come, let us sing," pp. 455-56) it has the sound of the major mode, but its constant return to the dominant gives it an entirely different quality.

O Be Joyful in the Lord (669)
Jubilate Deo

HENRY ALDRICH, 1647-1710

Psalm 100 was used in both Temple and synagogue services from ancient times, from which it entered Morning Prayer services of the Church. The psalm was introduced into the 1552 *Book of Common Prayer* as an alternative to the *Benedictus.* It has been included in our hymnals since 1878, and according to tradition in the version of the Great Bible, 1539.

Robert G. McCutchan states that while the music is credited to Aldrich, there is some doubt about the composer. The arrangement, which has been simplified by omitting passing tones, comes from *A Collection of Tunes and Chants for Public Worship,* 1848, compiled by William Harrison.

O Come, Let Us Sing (663, 664)
Venite, exultemus

The daily use of Psalm 95 was first prescribed by the Benedictine Rule, sixth century, for the "vigil," the night service which came to be known as Matins, celebrated after midnight. From this use it entered the Roman (1568) and Sarum (pre-Reformation) breviaries. In 1549 it was set in its familiar place in *The Book of Common Prayer* of the Church of England, after the Prayer of Absolution and the Lord's Prayer.

The version used is that of the Great Bible, 1539.

Objections to the last 4 verses of the psalm caused the first American *Book of Common Prayer*, 1789, to substitute Psalm 96:9, 13 for them. Though the Hebrew, Greek, and Latin versions of Psalm 96:13 read "peoples," the Great Bible and KJV reading, "people," prevailed in the texts of the *Venite* until the influence of the English Revised (1885) and American Revised (1901) versions, when the original "peoples" was restored in the American *Book of Common Prayer*, 1928. In Methodist hymnals the canticle was first included in 1878. "People" remained until the 1964 hymnal restored the original "peoples."

For comments on "Glory be to the father," see pp. 446-47.

663

Tone V

Developed from plainsong, the psalm tones were basic tonalities used in the monasteries for chanting the psalms. Each "mode" fitted a particular mood or type of text. All are comfortable in range and may be transposed up or down to fit the available voices. Tone V is easy to learn since it sounds like the tonality of the tonic triad in a major key. For other information concerning parts of a chant, see the Instructions on Chanting (662).

664

WILLIAM BOYCE, 1710-1799

Originally in D (to accommodate the boys' voices in cathedral choirs), the chant is taken from *Divine Harmony, Being a Collection of Two Hundred and Seven Double and Single Chants in Score, Ancient and Modern, Sung at His Majesty's Chapels Royal* (London, 1770), where it is mistakenly credited to a "Mr. Davis." In Vol. I of Ralph Harrison, *Sacred Harmony* (London, 1784), it appears as a chant and a Short Meter tune, both credited to Boyce.

O Lamb of God (830C, 837)
Agnus Dei

The scriptural basis is John 1:29. Though the text of John reads "sin" in the singular, historically the plural "sins" has generally been used in the liturgies, both in the *Gloria in excelsis* and the *Agnus Dei*. Archbishop Thomas Cranmer retained the plural as in the Latin mass (*peccata*) in the 1549 *Book of Common Prayer;* this form has been generally followed though some present-day services have restored the singular form as in John 1:29.

The independent use of the *Agnus Dei* in the Communion Service is ascribed to Pope Sergius I, 687-701, a Syrian who ordered it to be sung at the time of the Fraction. As he introduced it, it seems to have been sung twice, once by the choir and then repeated by the people. In the twelfth century it seems to have been sung 3 times in French churches, with "grant us thy peace" substituted for "have mercy upon us" at the third repetition.

The *Agnus Dei* has been included in the Methodist liturgy since 1934.

830C

JOHN MERBECKE, 1523–c. 1585

See comments under **"Glory Be to God on High"** (840), pp. 445-46.

837

PHILIP R. DIETTERICH, 1931-

See comments under **"Glory Be to God on High"** (833), pp. 445-46.

O Lord, Open Thou Our Eyes (798)

JOHN CAMIDGE, 1735-1803

The versicles are an adaptation for congregational use of Psalm 119:18, "Open thou mine eyes, that I may behold wondrous things out of thy law," KJV.

Camidge's musical setting was composed for use at Yorkminster.

O Send Out Thy Light (797)

AUSTIN C. LOVELACE, 1919-

The text is that of Psalm 43:3*a*.

Lovelace's music was composed in 1959 for use with the Chancel Choir of the First Methodist Church in Evanston, Ill.

Opening Sentences for the Christian Year (773-782)

These opening sentences or Invitatory Antiphons prefaced the *Venite* in Morning Prayer during the Middle Ages to accentuate the festivals of the various seasons. Seven of those printed in our hymnal are taken from the American *Book of Common Prayer,* 1928, which in turn are based on similar antiphons in the Sarum rite. Our hymnal has added texts for the Lenten Season, Palm Sunday, and Kingdomtide.

For comments on the music, see "O Come, Let Us Sing" (663), pp. 455-56.

Our Father Who Art in Heaven

See comments on "The Lord's Prayer," p. 461.

Out of the Deep (671, 672)
De profundis

Psalm 130 is a penitential psalm which issues from a confident trust and joyful assurance of salvation. It is of special interest to Methodists because of its association with John Wesley's search for "justifying, saving faith." On the afternoon of May 24, 1738, he was asked to go to St. Paul's, London, where "the anthem was 'Out of the deep have I called unto Thee, O Lord: Lord, hear my voice. . . . O Israel, trust in the Lord: for with the Lord there is mercy, and with Him is plenteous redemption.'" It was that evening when he went "very unwillingly" to the Aldersgate Street society, where his heart was "strangely warmed."

The psalm as a canticle first entered our hymnal in 1935, KJV. The 1964 hymnal prints the text as Wesley heard it, in the Great Bible version.

671

WILLIAM CROFT, 1678-1727

This is the same chant as found in the middle section of "We Praise Thee, O God" (665).

Sing We to Our God Above (811)

CHARLES WESLEY, 1707-1788

This doxology was first published in *Hymns and Sacred Poems,* 1740. It was the second of 7 "Hymns to the Trinity."

Savannah

See "Jesus, Lord, We Look to Thee," pp. 246-47

Thanks Be to Thee (799)
Gratia tibi

THOMAS TALLIS, c. 1505-1585

As the people's acclamation *before* the reading of the Gospel, the ancient and traditional text was "Glory be to thee, O Lord." This form goes back to Sarum and 1549. In Anglican liturgies the *Laus tibi* (801) is the response used *after* the reading of the Gospel. The Scottish Liturgy of 1637, however, appointed the *Gratia tibi* here, and in its short form, "Thanks be to thee, O Lord." The 1929 Scottish Liturgy added to this "for this thy glorious Gospel."

Our text is that of the Scottish Liturgy with "glorious" altered to "holy" and with alternates: "Christ" is paired with "Gospel," and "Lord" with "Scripture" to permit the chant to be used with any scripture.

Tallis' setting is one of the minor responses of a "full service" composed by him. It was ordered to be sung after the reading of the Gospel in *The Book of Common Prayer,* 1549.

The Lord Is in His Holy Temple (787)

CARLTON R. YOUNG, 1926-

This popular opening sentence from Habakkuk 2:20 comes at the end of a paragraph which pours scorn on the worship of idols: "Woe to him who says to a wooden thing, Awake; to a dumb stone, Arise! Can this give revelation? Behold, it is overlaid with gold and silver, and there is no breath at all in it. But the Lord is in his holy temple; let all the earth keep silence before him" (RSV).

The music was composed in 1963 following a meeting of the subcommittee on service music for the 1964 hymnal, at the Conrad Hilton Hotel, Chicago, Ill.

The Lord's Prayer (826)

Ancient Chant

The Lord's Prayer is given in 2 forms in the New Testament: Matthew 6:9-13 and Luke 11:2-4. Matthew's form is the one universally used in common worship. Its very inception and form are liturgical, intended for "common" worship with its plurals—"our," "us," and "we." Since the doxology is not in the best manuscripts of Matthew, some church liturgies omit "For thine is the kingdom, etc."

The historic English Bible has used "debts" and "debtors" (Matthew) or "sins" and the equivalent of debtors (Luke) in all versions beginning with the Great Bible, 1539. However, Tyndale, 1525, translated Matthew 6:12 "trespasses" and "Trespacers" to accord with 6:14, which is properly translated "trespasses." It was Tyndale's translation which was taken up into the English liturgies, both Protestant and Catholic, when Henry VIII issued the ordinance of 1541: "His Grace perceiving now the great diversity of the translations hath willed them all to be taken up and instead of them hath caused an uniform translation of the said Paternoster . . . to be set forth, willing all his loving subjects to learn and use the same to their parishioners."

Thus, though the Rheims Bible, 1581, and the King James Version, 1611, used "debts" and "debtors" in Matthew 6:12, the Tyndale translation had already been established in the prayer books of 1549 and 1552. It has prevailed until this day in Anglican (hence Methodist), Roman Catholic, and also Lutheran usage.

The concluding doxology first came into common English use with the Scottish *Book of Common Prayer,* 1637, and after the English revision of 1662.

The musical setting is based on the form of Mode I, Ending 1. It is similar to the melodic forms of Lowell Mason's tune HAMBURG.

This Is the Day the Lord Hath Made (789)

ISAAC WATTS, 1674-1748

The hymn in 5 sts. was first published in the author's *Psalms of David, Imitated in the Language of the New Testament,* 1719. It was entitled "Hosanna; the Lord's Day; or, Christ's resurrection and our salvation."

The st. used here is the first and is printed in its original form. It is based on Psalm 118:24. The rest of the hymn only lightly touches the psalm.

Twenty-Fourth

Probably by LUCIUS CHAPIN, 1760-1842

There were no less than 7 Chapins active in the field of church music during the first quarter of the nineteenth century, and this tune has been credited to both Amzi and Lucius Chapin. Charles Hamm in an article in *Journal of Research in Music Education,* Fall, 1960, attributes the tune to Lucius.

It was first published either in John Wyeth, *A Repository of Sacred Music, Part II,* 1813, or in Robert Patterson, *Church Music* (Cincinnati, 1813). Wyeth claims first publication in his index. The melody is a folk hymn, and was included in 6 other important collections from *Kentucky Harmony,* c. 1815, to *The Sacred Harp,* 1844. In some it is called PRIMROSE.

To God the Father (812)

JOHN WESLEY, 1703-1791

This doxology is st. 6 of "A Morning Hymn," published by John Wesley in 1741 in *A Collection of Psalms and Hymns.* The hymn, beginning "We lift our hearts to thee," has been included in all Methodist hymnals, with 5 or 6 sts. (see 492). The doxology has usually been printed with the hymn, but in 1849 and 1878 it was printed separately, with the doxologies at the end of the book.

St. Michael

See **"How Can a Sinner Know,"** p. 221.

To God the Only Wise (810)

ISAAC WATTS, 1674-1748

The text is the first and last sts. of the 5-st. hymn first published in the author's *Hymns and Spiritual Songs,* 1707. It is a paraphrase of Jude 24-25.

St. Michael

See "How Can a Sinner Know," p. 221.

To Thee Before the Close of Day (814)
Te lucis ante terminum

Latin, c. 7th Century
Line 1, trans. by JOHN D. CHAMBERS, 1805-1893
Lines 2-4, trans. by JOHN M. NEALE, 1818-1866

The hymn has been used throughout the Western Church since very ancient times, always in the last service of the day, Compline. Neale's first line was "Before the ending of the day." His translation first appeared in his *Hymnal Noted*, 1851. Our first line is Neale altered by John D. Chambers for his *Psalter, or Seven Ordinary Hours of Sarum*, 1852, and his *Lauda Syon*, 1857.

Jam lucis
Plainsong, Mode VI

The melody is the ferial tune usually sung to the office hymn for Prime. In some books it is printed in the form of Anglican chant because of the repeated notes which begin each line. It is one of the few plainsong melodies which uses only one syllable for each note.

Versicles Before Prayer
Ferial (805)
Festal (806)

THOMAS TALLIS, c. 1505-1585

These versicles are taken from Psalm 85:7 and Psalm 51:10-11. They are related to the Collects for Peace and Grace which follow the Collect for the Day in the Morning Prayer service in *The Book of Common Prayer*. The English *Book of Common Prayer* since 1549 has employed 6 pairs of versicles here. The 1789 American *Book of Common Prayer* reduced the number to these 2.

"Ferial" in ecclesiastical usage means "non-festal," that is, days other than Saturdays and Sunday on which no feast falls.

The musical settings are Tallis' harmonization of John Merbecke's melodies as published in Merbecke's *Book of Common Prayer Noted,* 1550, in turn based on psalm tone formulae. In the festal setting, the melody for the congregation is in the tenor.

We Praise Thee, O God (665)
Te Deum laudamus

EDWIN G. MONK, 1819-1900
WILLIAM CROFT, 1678-1727

The *Te Deum* and the *Gloria in excelsis* are the 2 most notable non-scriptural hymns of the historic Church, East and West. The esteem in which the *Te Deum* has been held finds ample expression in the ninth-century legend which tells that St. Ambrose and St. Augustine sang it antiphonally at Augustine's baptism, 387. The hymn, at least the first 2 parts, is now generally attributed to Bishop Niceta (d. after 414) of Remesiana, in Yugoslavia. The oldest extant manuscript containing it is the late seventh-century *Antiphonary* of Bangor, Ireland. The monastic Rule of St. Caesarius of Arles (c. 470-542) speaks of it as a canticle for Matins. The Benedictine Rule appointed it for Matins on Sunday. Its use is also prescribed by Sarum.

Parts 1 and 2 (1-6, 7-12) of the hymn are built up out of traditional materials, such as parts of the Apostles' Creed, the *Gloria in excelsis,* and the *Sanctus.* Its nucleus seems to have been a second-century Greek hymn in praise of Christ as God. Properly translated it began: "We praise Thee as God; we acknowledge Thee to be the Lord." Later Trinitarian controversies made it fully Trinitarian.

Verse 8 literally translated reads "When thou tookest upon thee (to become) man to deliver him, thou didst not abhor a [or, "the"] Virgin's womb," and continues so to be read in the Church of England *Book of Common Prayer.* The American Church, in 1786, altered the verse to its present form. "Sharpness of death," verse 9, means "sting of death" (I Corinthians 15:56). In verse 12, an original *munerari* (rewarded) was often mistakenly written *numerari* (numbered), which has been retained since the 1491 Roman Breviary.

Part 3, obviously added later, is a Latin fifth-century composition, at first attached to the *Gloria in excelsis* and later shifted to *Te Deum.* It is made up of brief suffrages or prayers from psalms 28:9, 145:2, 123:3, 33:21, 71:1.

The 1549 *Book of Common Prayer* prescribed its use daily at Matins, except in Lent; the 1552 book removed this exception. As an alternate, the *Benedicite* is permitted.

The canticle has been in our hymnals since 1878, always in its present form.

Monk's chant in B flat and Croft's chant in G minor are 2 Anglican chants of contrasting tonality and mood, combined to underscore the sectional nature of the text.

Write These Words (795)

Ancient Chant

The text is a prayer beseeching the Lord to fulfil his promise, Jeremiah 31:33, "I will put my law within them, and I will write it upon their hearts" (RSV).

The musical setting is a modern adaptation of a melodic fragment taken from plainsong.

Part III

BIOGRAPHIES

Abbey, Alonzo Judson (b. Olive, Ulster County, N.Y., 1825; d. Chester, N.J., March 24, 1887) was a writer of voluminous tunes and some texts. *The Triad,* 1866, contains more than 100 tunes with his initials. He compiled or coedited 9 collections.

Composer: COOLING (290, p. 227)

Abelard, Peter (b. Pallet, France, 1097; d. the Priory of St. Martel, April 21, 1142) was born of nobility. He showed a capacity for learning early and forsook the military life of his family. At the age of 22, he was named lecturer at Notre Dame Cathedral and soon attracted students from all over Europe. He has been called the "first of the modernists," for his critical appraisal of scripture and the writings of the Fathers of the Church laid the foundation for scholasticism.

Abelard's famous love affair with Heloise, niece of Canon Fulbert, began at Notre Dame. When the romance was discovered, they fled to Brittany, were married, and had a son. Upon their return to Paris, thugs hired by Canon Fulbert emasculated Abelard. Both Abelard and Heloise entered separate religious orders. She became head of a religious order for women, and he returned to teaching. In time, he was silenced by the verdict of a court established by Bernard of Clairvaux. Abelard appealed his heresy conviction to Rome but died on his way there to plead his case.

Abelard and Heloise are buried in the cemetery of Père-la-Chaise in Paris.

Author: Alone Thou Goest Forth (427)

Adams, Sarah Fuller Flower (b. Harlow, Essex, England, February 22, 1805; d. London, England, August 14, 1848) was the daughter of Benjamin Flower, editor of the *Cambridge Intelligencer* and the *Political Review.* In 1834 she was married to an inventor and civil engineer, William Bridges Adams. As an actress she portrayed Lady Macbeth in the Richmond Theater but later retired from the theater because of ill health and began to write poetry. William Johnson Fox, her minister at the South Place Unitarian Church, Finsbury, London, included her poetry in his journal, the *Monthly Repository,* and later 13 of her hymns in *Hymns and Anthems,* 1840-41, compiled for his congregation's use. Mrs. Adams' sister, Eliza, served as music editor of the collection.

Mrs. Adams' literary achievements include the dramatic poem *Vivia Perpetua*, 1841, a child's catechism, and the collection of hymns *The Flock at the Fountain*, 1845. She collaborated with Vincent Novello in the music edition of *Songs for the Months*.

Author: Nearer, My God, to Thee (263)

Addison, Joseph (b. Milston, Wiltshire, England, May 1, 1672; d. London, England, June 17, 1719) was the son of an African clergyman, Lancelot Addison. He was educated at Charterhouse and at Magdalen College, Oxford (B.A. 1691, M.A. 1693), and later was a fellow of Magdalen, 1698-1711. After traveling for a time, he joined the Whig Party and held several offices of the state, including Chief Secretary for Ireland.

Addison's literary fame rests on his contributions to the *Tatler*, the *Guardian*, the *Freeholder*, and the *Spectator*, the latter founded by him in 1711 and in which appeared all his hymns contained in the present hymnal. Both Isaac Watts and John Wesley greatly respected his work, and the latter included 2 of his hymns in the 1737 Charleston *Collection of Psalms and Hymns*.

Author: How Are Thy Servants Blest, O Lord (52)
The Spacious Firmament on High (43)
When All Thy Mercies, O My God (70)

Adebesin, Biodun Akinremi Olvsoji (b. Lagos, Nigeria, January 1, 1928) began playing piano at the age of 9 and continued studying music in school and college. His education includes a Cambridge certificate, and he is an associate of the Royal College of Music. He has led and played in various jazz, theater, and club bands and orchestras, in-including Bobby Benson's Band, 1949-50, his own "Hot Shots," 1952, and the African Cultural Group Band in New York, 1962-65.

Adebesin has served as a teacher, banker, civil servant, and as a member of the Nigerian Diplomatic Service. He is the author of *Okanlawon* and *Ale Wa Adara*.

Translator: Jesus, We Want to Meet (487)

Adkins, Leon McKinley (b. Ticonderoga, N.Y., July 14, 1896) was educated at Middlebury College (B.A. 1919) and Boston University School of Theology (S.T.B. 1925). He entered the Troy Conference of the Methodist Episcopal Church in 1921 and later became a member of the New England Southern and the Central New York conferences. After serving Methodist pastorates in Delmar, N.Y., 1927-37, Schenectady, 1937-50, and University Methodist Church in Syracuse, 1950-55, he was general secretary, Division of the Local Church, Board of Education of The Methodist Church from 1955 until his retirement in 1966. Middlebury College conferred upon him the D.D. degree in 1945.

Many of Adkins' numerous poems, composed for occasions in the life and work of the church, are published in Methodist church school periodicals. He was a member of the 1964 Methodist hymnal committee, serving on the texts subcommittee.

Author: Go, Make of All Disciples (342)

Ahle, Johann Rudolf (b. Mülhausen, Thuringia, December 24, 1625; d. Mülhausen, July 8, 1673) studied at Göttingen and Erfurt, and was cantor in Erfurt's St. Andreas' Church. In 1649 he became organist of St. Blasius' Church in Mülhausen and in 1661 was elected mayor (Bürgermeister) of the city.

Very active in promoting reform in church music, Ahle wrote 400 "sacred arias" influenced by Italian opera. Some of these arias were later modified into congregational melodies. *Compendium pro tenellis,* a treatise on better choir music, was published in 1648. He also published a number of cantatas, arias, organ music, instrumental music, and 2 volumes of spiritual songs, which included settings by Lutheran pastors Vockered, Starke, Bormeister, Rinkart, Harsdörffer, and Tscherning.

For more information about Ahle, see J. Wolf, "Johann Rudolf Ahle" in *Sammelbände der Internationalen Musik-Gesellschaft,* II (1920), 3.

Composer: LIEBSTER JESU (257, 370, p. 117)

Ajose, Michael Olatunji (b. Lagos, Nigeria, September 16, 1912) was educated at King's School, Enu-owa, and the Methodist Boys' High

School in Lagos. He studied piano and organ with private teachers and for a time was assistant organist at Wesley Church in Olowogbowo, Lagos. In 1957 he was named organist. Since 1963 Ajose has been Official Synod Organist of the Methodist Conference. His musical education has been continued at the local Nigerian centers of Trinity College of Music and the National Academy of Music.

At the time of this writing, Ajose is the General Secretary of the Association of Church Musicians in Nigeria, Lagos branch. In his words, "The aim of that association is to collect, compose, edit, and publish indigenous musical compositions suitable for divine worship." The association was founded in 1960. He is also active in the Yoruba Church Music Association, Ibadan.

Arranger: NIGERIA (**487**, p. 258)

Aldrich, Henry (b. Westminster, England, 1647; d. Oxford, England, December 14, 1710) was educated at Christ Church, Oxford (M.A. 1669), was named dean in 1689, and greatly influenced the musical offerings of that school. He was a man of many distinguished achievements in architecture, theology, language, logic, and music theory.

Composer: O Be Joyful in the Lord (**669**, p. 455)

Alexander, Cecil Frances (b. Redcross, County Wicklow, England, 1818 or 1823; d. Londonderry, Ireland, October 12, 1895) was the daughter of John Humphreys. She was married in 1850 to the Reverend (later bishop) William Alexander, an Irish clergyman. Her hymns number about 400, with most of them written for children. *Hymns for Little Children,* 1848, contains the familiar paraphrases of the articles of the Apostles' Creed.

For more complete information about Mrs. Alexander, see the *Hymn,* V, 37.

Author: All Things Bright and Beautiful (**34**)
     Jesus Calls Us o'er the Tumult (**107**)
     There Is a Green Hill Far Away (**414**)

Alexander, James Waddell (b. Hopewell, Va., March 13, 1804; d. Sweetsprings, Va., July 31, 1859) was educated at the College of New Jersey, now Princeton (B.A. 1820) and licensed to preach by the presbytery of New Brunswick in 1825. He attended Princeton Theological Seminary and was ordained in 1827. Thereafter, he held several positions, including pastor of First Presbyterian Church, Trenton, 1829-32; professor of rhetoric, College of New Jersey, 1832-44; pastor of Duane Street Presbyterian Church in New York City, 1844-49; professor of church history, Princeton Seminary, 1849-51; and pastor of Fifth Avenue Presbyterian Church in New York City from 1851 until his death in 1859.

As an author and contributor to various journals, he maintained an active interest in Latin and German hymnody, with writings and translations appearing in the *New York Observer*, the *Princeton Review*, and *Kirchenfreund*.

Translator: O Sacred Head, Now Wounded (418)

Alford, Henry (b. London, England, October 7, 1810; d. Canterbury, England, January 12, 1871) was educated at Trinity College, Cambridge (B.A. 1832); later he became a fellow. Ordained in 1833, he served with his father at Winkfield, Wiltshire, and at Ampton. He served as vicar of Wymeswold, Leicestershire, 1835-53; minister of Quebec Chapel, London, 1853-57; then as dean of Canterbury. Though a child of a family which had produced 5 consecutive generations of Anglican clergy, he maintained close ties with Evangelicals and Independents.

Alford is best remembered for his 4-volume commentary on the Greek New Testament, the standard commentary of its time. His hymns and translations are contained in *Psalms and Hymns*, 1844, *The Year of Praise*, 1867, and his *Poetical Works* (1st ed., 1853).

Author: Come, Ye Thankful People, Come (522)

Alington, Cyril Argentine (b. Ipswich, England, 1872; d. St. Weonards, Herefordshire, England, May 16, 1955) was the son of H. G. Alington. He was educated at Marlborough and Trinity colleges, Oxford (B.A. 1893, M.A. 1895, D.D. 1917), ordained deacon in 1899 and priest in 1901. His teaching career includes fellow of All Souls', 1896, assistant master at Marlborough College, 1896-99, and at Eaton College, 1899-1908. He was headmaster at Shrewsbury School, 1908-16, and at Eaton College, 1917-33, when he became dean of Durham.

Alington also served as select preacher to Oxford, 1909-10 and 1928-29, and chaplain to the king, beginning in 1921.

In addition to many hymns, he published essays, novels, and theological writings.

Author: Good Christian Men, Rejoice and Sing (449)

Allen, George Nelson (b. Mansfield, Mass., September 7, 1812; d. Cincinnati, Ohio, December 9, 1877) graduated from Oberlin College in 1838 and remained there as a faculty member until 1865. At Oberlin he taught music and geology and established the choral and instrumental program of music education, which later was developed into the Oberlin Conservatory of Music. Allen contributed both hymns and tunes to several collections.

Allen compiled *The Oberlin Social and Sabbath School Hymn Book,* 1846.

Composer: MAITLAND (183, p. 289)

Ambrose of Milan (b. Treves [Germany], c. 337-40; d. Milan, Italy, April 4, 397) was the son of a civil servant in Gaul. Ambrose was educated in Rome in preparation for a civil career which he assumed as governor of northern Italy, with residence in Milan. Upon the death of the Arian bishop, Auxentius, and with no leader acceptable to both factions, Ambrose was elected bishop at the age of 34 even though he was not baptized. He gave his wealth to the poor and the church, and studied theology and began preaching. He became a staunch supporter of the Nicene faith against the Arians. Ambrose was opposed to the resurgence of the Roman state religion and a champion of civil rights.

There is evidence to support the view that Ambrose brought the Eastern (Syrian) custom of hymn-singing to the churches of Milan, especially the practice of antiphonal psalmody. His organization of the Milan liturgy became known as Ambrosian chant, or rite, and was later assimilated into the mainstream of chant during Gregory's reform. It is not clear which specific hymns are by Ambrose, but it is certain that his work marks a departure from nonmetrical to metrical hymns in the West. Ambrosian hymns set a style for simplicity which persisted until the eleventh century. Ruth E. Messenger in *Historical*

Companion to Hymns Ancient and Modern, 1962, has written that "one is impressed by the faithful presentment of scriptural narrative, the expression of the ideal Christian pattern of faith, purity, hope, patience, humility and love, the ethical teachings of Jesus and the examples of the saints. These hymns are objective, simple, easily understood and expressive of the aspiration of a common worship."

Author: O Splendor of God's Glory Bright **(29)**

Amps, William (b. Cambridge, England, December 18, 1824; d. Cambridge, May 20, 1910) was the organist at King's College, Cambridge, 1855-76, and conductor of the Cambridge University Musical Society. He also was organist of St. Peter's Church.

Amps composed several compositions in the shorter musical forms.

Composer: VENICE **(147, p. 233)**

Andrew of Crete (b. Damascus, c. 660; d. Island of Hierissus near Mitylene, c. 740) entered a monastery at Jerusalem. He was sent by Theodore, patriarch of Jerusalem, to the Sixth General Council at Constantinople, 680 and 681, where he was ordained deacon and appointed warden of the orphanage. In 712, he was made archbishop of Crete. As a representative to the Second Trullan Council, Constantinople, 692, which condemned the Sixth Ecumenical Council, he fell from orthodoxy but later acknowledged his error.

Author: Christian, Dost Thou See Them **(238)**

Arlott, John (b. Basingstoke, Hampshire, England, February 25, 1914) has served as a civil servant, police detective, and newspaper columnist. His work with the British Broadcasting Company has included responsibilities as poetry producer and general instructor in the training school. His avocation, and in a sense his present vocation, is in the sports world, in particular as association football correspondent for the *Observer.* He is the author of 30 books about cricket.

Arlott's interest in poetry is marked by collections of his verse: *Of Period and Place, Clausentum,* and 2 anthologies—*Landmarks* and *First Time in America.* His hymns first appeared in the *BBC Hymn Book,* 1951.

Author: God, Whose Farm Is All Creation **(514)**

We Are Climbing Jacob's Ladder (287)

American Folk Hymn

The biblical basis for the folk hymn is Genesis 28:10-17. Though the origin and authorship of this song, like that of all true folk songs, are indeterminate, the Jacob's ladder theme is attested as popular in the spirituals as early as 1824 or 1825. The metaphor of climbing a ladder was sometimes used to denote the climb to freedom, either to a return to Africa or an escape to the North. If these freedoms failed, there was, after all, the ladder to heaven.

This is the first inclusion of this spiritual in one of our official hymnals.

Sometimes 2 other sts. are sung:

Do you think I'd make a soldier?
Soldier of the cross.

Rise, shine, give God glory!
Soldier of the cross.

Jacob's Ladder

American Folk Hymn

(For general remarks about spirituals, see "Go, tell it on the mountain," pp. 188-89.)

The first publication of this tune has not been ascertained. It belongs essentially to the second category of spirituals which John W. Work lists: "the slow, sustained, long-phrase melody." Its harmonic nature, use of the 4-scale step, rising melodic contour with climax in the third phrase, and use of only one phrase or idea in each st. are strongly reminiscent of the camp-meeting songs (e.g. "Give me that old time religion") .

We Bear the Strain of Earthly Care (202)

OZORA S. DAVIS, 1866-1931

The text was written in 1909 at the author's summer house on Lake Sunapee, N. H., in response to a commission to write a hymn for the convention of the National Congregational Brotherhood held at Minneapolis in that year.

Arne, Thomas Augustine (b. London, England, March 12, 1710; d. London, March 5, 1778) was the son of an upholsterer. He chose music over law after studying at Eton, even though he spent 3 years in the solicitor's office. Arne studied music privately and played the violin.

The first of his many dramatic productions was the music written for Joseph Addison's *Rosamund,* March 7, 1733. Other productions of his were performed at the Haymarket Theatre, Drury Lane Theatre, and Covent Garden.

Arne was among the first to introduce female voices into choral writing. A Roman Catholic, he wrote liturgical music and 2 oratorios, but his best-known work is probably the patriotic song "Rule Britannia!"

Oxford conferred on him the Mus.D. degree in 1759. He ranks as England's most famous native composer of the eighteenth century.

Composer: ARLINGTON (239, 335, pp. 87-88)

Arnold, John (b. Great Warley, Essex, England, 1720; buried February 14, 1792) was the son of John Arnold of Great Warley, Essex. He compiled *The Complete Psalmodist* (1st. ed., 1741). In the 1739 preface to the work are his picture and the inscription "Aetatis suae 19," which establishes his birthdate. Arnold's preface to the 1750 edition contains instructions, as was the current English practice, on the articulation of "Trills, Shakes and Slurs."

For a listing of Arnold's publications and an account of *The Complete Psalmodist* see the *Bulletin of the Hymn Society of Great Britain and Ireland,* III (1954), 173.

Source: Jesus Christ Is Risen Today (443)

Atkinson, Frederick Cook (b. Norwich, England, August 21, 1841; d. East Dereham, England, 1897) was a chorister at the Norwich Cathedral under Zechariah Buck, whom he assisted during the years 1849-60 as choirmaster and organist. In 1867 he received the B.M. from Cambridge. He served as organist and choirmaster at St. Luke's Church in Manningham, Bradford; the Cathedral at Norwich, 1881-85, and after that date at St. Mary's Parish Church, Lewisham.

Atkinson composed a number of services, anthems, songs, and piano pieces.

Composer: MORECAMBE (138, p. 379)

Babcock, Maltbie Davenport (b. Syracuse, N.Y., August 3, 1858; d. Naples, Italy, May 18, 1901) was educated at Syracuse University, 1879, and Auburn Theological Seminary, 1882, where he was known as an athlete and musician. After his ordination in 1882 into the Presbyterian ministry, he served until 1887 at Lockport, N.Y., Brown Memorial Church in Baltimore, Md., 1885-99, and Brick Presbyterian Church in New York City, succeeding Henry Van Dyke in 1899.

Babcock was a very gifted preacher whose words communicated to the needs of a broad cross section of the community. He wrote some hymns for *The School Hymnal,* 1899, composing tunes for these texts. Portions of his sermons and poems were issued after his death in *Thoughts for Every-Day Living,* 1901.

His death occurred while he was traveling to the Holy Land.

Author: This Is My Father's World (45)

Bach, Johann Sebastian (b. Eisenach, Thuringia, March 21, 1685; d. Leipzig, July 28, 1750) was born of a distinguished musical family. He was trained at Ohrdruf and Lüneburg and served briefly as organist at Arnstadt and Mülhausen. Biographers usually divide his creative period into 3 parts: Weimar, 1708-17, Cöthen, 1718-23, and Leipzig, 1723-50. Though widely recognized as the greatest organist of his day, Bach lived without hearing many of his compositions performed. Mendelssohn in Germany and England and Samuel Wesley, son of Charles, in England began the task of rediscovering the works of the greatest composer German Protestantism has produced.

In terms of hymnody and congregational song, Bach is represented in contemporary hymnbooks mainly by way of his harmonizations of existing sixteenth- and seventeenth-century chorale melodies. He used these settings in cantatas, motets, and passions, written largely for choirs. Liturgically, his contribution is that though he was profoundly orthodox, his music, particularly the cantata, bridged the gap between the early chorale texts and tunes, and the great mass of pietistic seventeenth-century literature.

The *Bach-Gesellschaft,* some 46 volumes, came into print between 1851 and 1900.

Composer: ICH HALTE TREULICH STILL (253, p. 248)
Arranger: DU FRIEDENSFÜRST, HERR JESU CHRIST (491, p. 390)

EISENACH (46, 172, p. 127)
ERMUNTRE DICH (373, p. 122)
PASSION CHORALE (418, p. 333)
WIE SCHÖN LEUCHTET DER MORGENSTERN (399, p. 331)

Bacon, Leonard (b. Fort Detroit, Mich., February 19, 1802; d. New Haven, Conn., December 23, 1881) was the son of missionaries to the Detroit Indians. He lived with them for about 9 years, at which time he went to live and study at Hartford, the home of his uncle. There he graduated from Yale in 1820, later receiving his theological education at Andover Theological Seminary. Ordained a Congregational minister, he was installed as pastor in Center Church in New Haven in 1825, where he served for 41 years. During this time he was influential in the Yale College community, teaching part time, 1866-71, and helping to found the influential religious journal the *Independent*, 1848.

Bacon was an outspoken absolutionist, a historian, and hymnologist. In 1823, while still a student, he edited the tract *Hymns and Sacred Songs for the Monthly Concert (of Prayers for Missions)*. He was an editor of *Psalms and Hymns for Christian Use and Worship*, 1845. His hymns have found their way into both English and American collections, but only one is in common use today.

Author: O God, Beneath Thy Guiding Hand (550)

Baker, Henry (b. Nuneham, Oxfordshire, England, 1835; d. Wimbledon, England, April 15, 1910) was the son of an Anglican clergyman. He was educated at Winchester and Cooper's Hill, where he studied civil engineering. His profession took him to India to build railroads.

John B. Dykes encouraged Baker to seek musical training, and in 1867 he received the B.M. degree from Exeter College, Oxford. A number of his tunes appear in W. Garrett Horder, *Worship Song*, 1905.

Composer: HESPERUS (270, 541, p. 274)

Baker, Henry Williams (b. Belmont House, Vauxhall, England, June 21, 1821; d. Monkland, England, February 12, 1877) was educated at Trinity College, Cambridge (B.A. 1844, M.A. 1847) and was ordained in 1844. In 1851 he became vicar of Monkland, near Leominster, and remained there until his death. He was knighted in 1859.

Baker served as chairman of the committee which prepared *Hymns Ancient and Modern,* 1861, contributing a number of translations and original hymns to the hymnal. He also became its chief advocate against its critics, some of whom nicknamed the hymnal "Hymns Asked for and Mutilated" in reference to the fact that Baker freely altered texts without permission, though usually improving them. He was responsible not only for the supervision of the editorial task but for engaging the music services of William Henry Monk and F. A. Gore Ouseley, and from the "New Victorian School of Composition" John Dykes, George J. Elvey, John Stainer, and Joseph Barnby. For a concise history of *Hymns Ancient and Modern* and a discussion of its changes, 1860-1950, including the musicians, poets, and other persons responsible for this monument of English hymnody, see *Historical Companion to Hymns Ancient and Modern,* pp. 119-24, and *A Hundred Years of Hymns Ancient and Modern,* 1960. For a comment on the music of the hymnal, see Erik Routley, *The Music of Christian Hymnody,* pp. 116-21.

Author: The King of Love My Shepherd Is (67)
Translator: Of the Father's Love Begotten (357)
Composer: STEPHANOS (99, p. 98)

Baker, Theodore (b. New York, N.Y., June 3, 1851; d. Dresden, Germany, October 13, 1934) was trained for a career in business but turned to music and in 1874 studied in Leipzig (Ph.D. 1882). His thesis was the first serious study of American Indian music. He returned to America in 1891 and in 1892 became literary editor and translator for G. Schirmer. After his retirement in 1926 he returned to Germany.

Baker's publications include *A Dictionary of Musical Terms,* 1895, *A Pronouncing Pocket Manual of Musical Terms,* 1905, and *Baker's Biographical Dictionary of Musicians* (1900; 1905; 1919 by Alfred Remy; 1950 by Carl Engel; 1949 supplement by Nicolaus Slonimsky and a 1958 edition by Slonimsky). An important aspect of this work, under Baker, was the inclusion for the first time of a number of American composers in a standard reference work.

Translator: We Gather Together (59)

Bakewell, John (b. Brailsford, Derbyshire, England, 1721; d. Lewisham, England, March 18, 1819) at the age of 18 read Boston's *Fourfold State* and began to reflect upon religion. He began to preach in his neighborhood in 1744 and became related to the Wesleyan movement in 1749 in London. His life and ministry, stretching from the beginnings of the revival through the post-Wesley era, are of great significance in understanding how the Wesleyan movement became a church. His friends in the mid-eighteenth century included evangelicals such as the Wesleys, Martin Madan, Augustus M. Toplady, and John Fletcher.

Bakewell's ministry was for many years with the Greenwich Royal Park Academy. He introduced Methodism to the city of Greenwich. He is buried near John Wesley at City Road Chapel, where his tombstone contains in part this epitaph:

> He adorned the doctrine of God, our Saviour, eighty years,
> and preached *His* glorious Gospel about seventy years.

Attributed author: Hail, Thou Once Despised Jesus (454)

Bambridge, William Samuel (b. Waimate, New Zealand, January 18, 1842; d. Marlborough, Wiltshire, England, January 10, 1923) was born into a musical family and moved to England with his family at the age of 6. At 10 years of age he was the organist at Clewer Church. He received his B.M. from Oxford in 1872 and did further study at the Royal Academy of Music. He was an associate of the Royal Academy of Music and a fellow of the Royal College of Organists. During the years 1864-1911 he was organist-choirmaster at Marlborough College and conductor of local and school choral groups, as well as Grand Organist of the Freemasons of England.

Taking an active interest in local government, Bambridge served on the town council for 40 years with 2 terms as mayor. His published works include songs, hymns, carols, and some music for choirs.

Composer: ST. ASAPH (498, p. 104)

Baring-Gould, Sabine (b. Exeter, England, January 28, 1834; d. Lew-Trenchard, Devonshire, England, January 2, 1924) was educated at Clare College, Cambridge (B.A. 1854, M.A. 1856). He was the assistant master of the choir school of St. Barnabas' Church in Pimlico, 1857, and the same at Hurstpierpoint College, Sussex, until 1864. In 1864 he was ordained deacon, priest in 1865, and he served curacies at Horbury, Yorkshire, and Dalton, near Thirsk, Yorkshire. He became rector of East Mersea, Essex, in 1871 and Lew-Trenchard in 1881, after having inherited the family estate there in 1872.

Baring-Gould's interests were catholic, including folk music, poetry, fiction, biography, and history. Among the works of this prolific writer are *Lives of the Saints* (15 vols., 1872-77), *Curious Myths of the Middle Ages* (2 series, 1866-68), *The Origin and Development of Religious Belief* (2 vols., 1869-70), and various sermons, hymns, and translations. His *Songs and Ballads of the West,* 1889-91, in collaboration with H. Fleetwood Shepherd, and his own *Garland of Country Song,* 1894, were pioneer editions of English folk music that set the stage for the work of Cecil J. Sharp. Baring-Gould's most famous hymns were written for the children at Horbury Bridge.

> Author: Now the Day Is Over (495)
> Onward, Christian Soldiers (305)

Barnby, Joseph (b. York, England, August 12, 1838; d. London, England, January 28, 1896) was chorister at Yorkminster at the age of 7, played the organ there at 12 years, and was choirmaster at the age of 14. He received additional training at the Royal Academy of Music in 1854 under Cipriani Potter. Positions held in London include organist for St. Michael's, St. James the Less, the Sacred Harmonic Society at St. Andrews', 1863-71, and for St. Anne's, Soho, 1871-76, which was known for its annual presentation of Passion music. From 1875 to 1892 he was precentor and musical advisor to Eaton College and to Novello and Company in 1861-76, where the "Barnby's Choir" was formed. He served as principal of the Guildhall School of Music and was knighted in 1892. Editor of 4 collections, Barnby assisted in the preparation of *The Cathedral Psalter,* 1873.

Barnby conducted various annual festivals and gave the first English performance of Dvořák's *Stabat Mater,* 1883, with the London Music Society. His compositions include the oratorio *Rebekah,* 1870, *Psalm 97,* 1883, services, motets, 45 anthems, and organ and piano pieces. Erik Routley in *The Music of Christian Hymnody* has written of Barnby's hymn tunes, of which there were some 246: "Joseph Barnby

481

leaves us several tunes that exemplify the less enduring aspects of Victorianism." And on the positive side, "Barnby could write a good Anglican chant and a good drawing-room ballad."

Barnby's tunes were not named, and editors and compilers have added the names.

Composer: JUST AS I AM (169, p. 261)
LAUDES DOMINI (91, p. 431)
MERRIAL (495, p. 299)
PERFECT LOVE (333, p. 332)
SARUM (537, p. 179)
Lord, Now Lettest Thou Thy Servant (673, p. 454)

Barthélémon, François Hippolyte (b. Bordeaux, France, July 27, 1741; d. London, England, July 23, 1808) was born of French-Irish parentage. He served for a brief time in the Irish brigade but studied on the continent. In his twenties he was one of the most famous violinists of his day, playing in London theater orchestras, where he met and became a close friend of Haydn during the latter's visit in 1792. He traveled extensively in Ireland and on the continent, 1776-77, and in England conducted the orchestras at Vauxhall and Marylebone Gardens, 1770-76. James T. Lightwood writes that Barthélémon also taught music and composed some tunes for use in the orphan home on Westminster Bridge Road, now near Crydon. He was a member of the Swedenborgian Church.

Barthélémon's compositions include 5 operas, a violin concerto, 6 string quartets, glees, and catches.

For more information, see James T. Lightwood's article in the *Choir*, XXXI (1940), 131-32.

Composer: AUTUMN (331, p. 251)
BALLERMA (461, 535, p. 209)

Barton, Bernard (b. London, England, January 31, 1784; d. Woodbridge, England, February 19, 1849) was known as England's "Quaker Poet." He was educated at Ipswich in the Quaker school and apprenticed at the age of 14 to a shopkeeper at Halstead, Essex, later going into the corn and coal business at Woodbridge, Suffolk. Upon the death of his wife, he tutored at Liverpool for a year, returning to

Woodbridge where he was a bank clerk for about 40 years. His friendships in literary circles included Edward Fitzgerald, Lord Byron, Walter Scott, and Robert Southey.

Barton published several volumes of verse and prose. His poems have become known and used in America through Unitarian collections.

> Author: Lamp of Our Feet (368)
> Walk in the Light (403)

Bateman, Christian Henry (b. Wyke, near Halifax, Scotland, August 9, 1813; d. Carlisle, England, July, 1889) studied for the Moravian ministry and in 1843 became minister of Richmond Place Congregational Church in Edinburgh. After serving various Congregational churches, he was ordained in the Church of England. From 1869 to 1879 he was curate of St. Luke's, Jersey, and military chaplain; vicar of All Saints', Childshill, 1871-75; and curate of St. John's, Penymyndd, 1877-84.

His hymns were contained in 2 widely circulated children's hymnals.

> Author: Come, Christians, Join to Sing (77)

Bates, Katharine Lee (b. Falmouth, Mass., August 12, 1859; d. Wellesley, Mass., March 28, 1929) was the daughter of a Congregational minister. She was educated at Wellesley College (B.A. 1880) and began teaching at Natick High School and the next year at Dana Hall, both in Massachusetts. In 1886 she became an instructor in English at Wellesley and later headed the department. Miss Bates taught, traveled, and did extensive research during her active career. She retired from Wellesley in 1925. Oberlin, Middlebury, and Wellesley conferred upon her honorary doctorates.

She was the author or coauthor of about 20 collections or books, including a textbook, *History of American Literature,* 1908, and a book of poems on the Holy Land, *The Pilgrim Ship,* 1926.

> Author: O Beautiful for Spacious Skies (543)

Bathurst, William Hiley (b. Clevedale, near Bristol, England, August 28, 1796; d. Lydney Park, Gloucestershire, England, November 25, 1877) was educated at Winchester and Christ Church, Oxford (B.A.

1818). After graduating, he took holy orders and assumed the rector-ship of the parish church on his uncle's estate at Barwick in Elmet, and at that time changed his name from Bragg to Bathurst after his uncle. He stayed at Barwick in Elmet until 1852, when he retired to the family estate at Lydney Park. At that time in his career, he took exception to certain doctrinal teachings of the church, in particular baptism and the burial services.

Bathurst's works include *Psalms and Hymns for Public and Private Use,* 1831, *Metrical Musings, or Thoughts on Sacred Subjects in Verse,* 1849, *The Georgics of Virgil,* 1849, and *The Roman Antiquities of Lydney Park,* published posthumously in 1879.

Author: O For a Faith That Will Not Shrink (142)

Bax, Clifford (b. London, England, July 13, 1886; d. London, Novem-ber 18, 1962) was the third son of Alfred Ridley Bax and brother of the composer Arnold Bax. Educated through private tutoring and at Slade School of Art and Heatherley's, he began a career in painting, but turned to literary pursuits and playwriting after travel in Ger-many, Belgium, and Italy.

In addition to plays, some set to music by Frederick Austin, Arm-strong Gibbs, and Martin Shaw, Bax published poems, short stories, monographs, and his memoirs *Inland Far,* 1925, an account of a tour through Spain with the composer Gustav Holst. An anthology of Bax's works was compiled by Meom Stewart in 1953.

For a discussion of Bax's literary and theatrical efforts, see J. C. Trewin, "A Man of Grace" in the *Illustrated London News,* Decem-ber 1, 1962, and the obituary by Ivor Brown in *Drama,* Spring, 1963.

Author: Turn Back, O Man (475)

Baxter, Lydia (b. Petersburg, N.Y., September 8, 1809; d. New York, N.Y., June 22, 1874) was converted under the preaching of the Baptist missionary Eben Tucker. She and her sister formed the Baptist church at Petersburg. She married and moved to New York City, and her home became a center for preachers and evangelists, even though she became an invalid.

A collection of her verse, *Gems by the Wayside,* was published in

1855. Only one hymn, of the many of hers made popular by Sankey and others, is in use today.

Author: Take the Name of Jesus with You (87)

Baxter, Richard (b. Rowton, England, November 12, 1615; d. London, England, December 8, 1691) was educated at Donnington Free School, Wroxeter, and by tutor at Ludlow. After a short experience in court, he lived on his father's estate and studied theology. He was ordained in the Church of England and served at Bridgnorth and Kidderminster. During the Civil War, he attached himself as a chaplain to the Parliamentary army, but opposed Cromwell's rise to supreme power. For a short time during the Restoration, he was the king's chaplain. He took part in the Savoy Conference, 1661, which resulted in his *Reformed Liturgy*, which he characterized by his comment: "I could not have time to make use of any save the Bible and my concordance, comparing all with the Assembly's Directory and the Book of Common Prayer." After declining the bishopric of Hereford and with the advent of the Act of Uniformity in 1662, he was subjected to great trouble, which culminated in his trial before the brutal Jeffreys in 1685. Baxter spent 2 years in prison and died 4 years after his release. His life and work in the midst of turbulent seventeenth-century England have been described in these words: "He grew too Puritan for bishops and too Episcopalian for the Presbyterians."

Baxter has been called the greatest of the Protestant schoolmen. His prolific writings include *The Saints' Everlasting Rest*, 1650, *The Reformed Pastor*, 1656, *The Call to the Unconverted*, 1657, and a narrative of his life and time, *Reliquiae*.

Author: Lord, It Belongs Not to My Care (218)

Bayly, Albert Frederick (b. Bexhill on Sea, Sussex, England, September 6, 1901) was educated at St. Mary Magdalen School, St. Leonards, and Hastings Grammar School. For a short time he trained as a shipwright at the Royal Dockyard School at Portsmouth and then was educated for the ministry at Mansfield College, Oxford, 1925-28. He received the B.A. degree from London University.

Bayly has served as a Congregational minister at Fairway Hall, Monkseaton, Northumberland, 1928-38; Morpeth, Northumberland,

1938-46; Hollingreave, Burnley, Lancashire, 1946-50; Swanland, East Yorks, 1956-62; and Thaxted, Essex, since 1962.

His several published books of verse include *Again I Say Rejoice,* 1967, missionary pageants, and librettos for 3 of W. L. Lloyd Webber's cantatas.

Author: Lord, Whose Love Through Humble Service (479)

Beach, Curtis (b. Cambridge, Mass., February 9, 1914) comes from several generations of ministers. He was educated at Harvard (B.A. 1935), Boston University School of Theology (S.T.B. 1941), and the University of Southern California (Ph.D. 1957). During the years 1943-59 he served as minister of the Neighborhood Church, Pasadena, Calif., and since that date as minister of the Smithfield Congregational Church in Pittsburgh, Pa.

Beach's hymns have been used in American Protestant and Catholic hymnals and in the hymnal of the United Church of Japan. He is also the author of *The Gospel of Mark: Its Making and Meaning,* 1959.

Author: O How Glorious, Full of Wonder (41)

Beethoven, Ludwig van (b. Bonn, December 16, 1770; d. Vienna, March 26, 1827) brought to full maturity the sonata, concerto, string quartet, and symphony. His sacred works include *Mass in C,* 1807, *Mass in D* (*Missa Solemnis*), 1818-23, and the oratorio *Christus am Oelberg* (Christ on the Mount of Olives), about 1803. Several of Beethoven's themes have been adapted as hymn tunes.

For a brief biography and a complete listing of Beethoven's works see *Baker's Biographical Dictionary of Musicians,* pp. 110-18.

Composer: HYMN TO JOY (38, 41, 440, p. 260)
All Things Come of Thee (808, p. 441)

Bennard, George (b. Youngstown, Ohio, February 4, 1873; d. Reed City, Mich., October 10, 1958) was the son of a coal miner. He spent his childhood in Albia and Lucas, Iowa, where he was converted during a Salvation Army meeting. As the sole supporter of his widow mother and 4 sisters, Bennard could not pursue a formal education.

He moved the family to Illinois, became married, and he and his wife became Salvation Army workers. Later he resigned this work and conducted revivals and worked as a Methodist evangelist in the northern Middle West and Canada. In later years he settled in Michigan, and the Annual Conference of The Methodist Church held on the campus of Albion College in Michigan became an occasion for recognizing Bennard and his wife.

Bennard wrote some 300 hymns. Reed City, Mich., and Youngstown, Ohio, have erected wooden crosses as a public recognition of the popularity of the hymn "The Old Rugged Cross."

Author and composer: On a Hill Far Away (THE OLD RUGGED CROSS) (228)

Benson, Louis FitzGerald (b. Philadelphia, Pa., July 22, 1855; d. Philadelphia, October 10, 1930) was educated at the University of Pennsylvania in law and was admitted to the bar in 1877. Seven years later he entered Princeton Theological Seminary, was ordained a Presbyterian minister in 1886, and served as pastor at the Church of the Redeemer in Germantown, Pa., until 1892. From this time on he was engaged in teaching, writing, research, and editing. In the latter capacity the Presbyterian Church U.S.A. engaged his services as editor for a series of hymnals. He also lectured on hymnody and liturgics at Auburn and Princeton seminaries. International recognition of his hymnological research came from John Julian in 1907.

Without a doubt Benson is the finest, most comprehensive, and sensitive hymnological scholar America has produced. His monumental *English Hymn* (1915; reprinted by John Knox Press, 1962) ranks with Julian's *Dictionary of Hymnology*. Benson's work includes the editing of *The Hymnal*, 1895, its revision in 1911, *The Hymnal for Congregational Churches*, *The Chapel Hymnal*, 1898, and *The School Hymnal*, 1899. Benson's *Hymnody of the Christian Church* (1927; reprinted by John Knox Press, 1960) is an important history of Western hymnody. Princeton Seminary houses the extensive hymnological library collected by Benson.

Author: For the Bread, Which Thou Hast Broken (314)

Berg, Caroline V. Sandell (b. Fröderyd, Sweden, October 3, 1832; d. Stockholm [?], Sweden, July 27, 1903) was the daughter of a Lutheran pastor. The death of her father in 1858 caused her to turn to writing poems, some 650 in all. Writings over the initials L.S., Lina Sandell, she, like other women hymn writers of her day, expressed the intense feelings unloosed in the revival which swept northern Europe, England, and America. The foremost Swedish lay preacher of this revival was Carl Olaf Rosenius, a disciple of the British Methodist evangelist George Scott.

The popularity of Miss Sandell's hymns was largely because of the musical settings of Oskar Ahnfelt, the guitar playing, singing associate of Rosenius. Miss Sandell once remarked, "Ahnfelt has sung my songs into the hearts of the people." Jenny Lind, herself much taken by the preaching of Ahnfelt, personally underwrote the expense of the first edition of *Ahnfelt's Sanger,* consisting primarily of Miss Sandell's hymns. Miss Sandell (Mrs. C. O. Berg) has been called the "Fanny Crosby of Sweden."

E. E. Ryden has furnished the biographical information on this poet.

Author: Children of the Heavenly Father (521)

Berggreen, Anton Peter (b. Copenhagen, Denmark, March 2, 1801; d. Copenhagen, November 9, 1880) studied law and music at the university and became a church organist and teacher of singing. In 1859 he became inspector of singing in the Danish public schools and served as organist at Trinity Church in Copenhagen, 1838-80. Later he taught in the Metropolitan School.

His most significant work in church music was the editing of the Danish Church's chorale book in 1853, which remained conservative despite the popular trend towards the light evangelical religious song. His works include a comic opera, *Billedit og Busten,* 1832, 11 volumes of folk music (about 2,000 songs) entitled *Folkesange og Melodien,* 1842, and 14 volumes of songs for use in the schools, 1834-76. One of his pupils was Niels Gade (1817-1890).

Composer: AMEN, JESUS HAN SKAL RAADE (274, p. 284)

Bernard of Clairvaux (b. Castle Fontaines, near Dijon, France, 1090 or 1091; d. Clairvaux, August 20, 1153) was the greatest religious force of his age. He was canonized 21 years after his death and declared a Doctor of the Church in 1830. Bernard was born of nobility. He displayed extraordinary powers of persuasion early when he brought 30 companions with him to enter the monastery of Citeaux, about 1112. In 1115 he founded the Cistercian monastery of Clairvaux where he remained as an abbot until his death.

The qualities of self-giving, monastic self-mortification, consistency of character, and evangelical zeal were combined in Bernard. He was a great preacher, and his travel and correspondence acquainted him with all the problems of his day. His activity included the healing of the papal schism created by the double election of Popes Innocent II and Anacletus II. He was bitterly opposed to the dialectical methods of Abelard and secured Arnold of Brescia's expulsion from France. Bernard also organized and preached the necessity of the ill-fated Second Crusade, 1147.

Attributed author: Jesus, the Very Thought of Thee (82)
Jesus, Thou Joy of Loving Hearts (329)

Bernard of Cluny (twelfth century) is often confused with Bernard of Clairvaux. Nothing is known of this poet, the author of *De Contemptu Mundi*, except that he lived as a monk at Cluny under Peter the Venerable, the abbot during the years 1122-55. The poem is dedicated to Peter.

Author: Jerusalem the Golden (303)

Bianco da Siena (b. Anciolina, in the Val d'Arno, date unknown; d. Venice, Italy, c. 1434) in 1367 entered the order of Jesuates, the unordained men of the St. Augustine discipline. Little more is known of his life. His *Laudi Spirituali* was edited and published in 1851 by Telesforo Bini, at Lucca. These hymns in the vernacular are contemporary with efforts of the *laudisti,* a religious order, active in the fourteenth and fifteenth centuries that specialized in devotional verse.

Author: Come Down, O Love Divine (466)

Bickersteth, Edward Henry (b. Barnsbury Park, Islington, England, January 25, 1825; d. Westbourne Terrace, London, May 16, 1906) was the son of Edward (1801-50), a clergyman and compiler of *Christian Psalmody*, 1833 and 1841. Edward Henry was educated at Trinity College, Cambridge (B.A. 1847, M.A. 1850), and was ordained a priest in 1849. His 30-year ministry at Christ Church, Hampstead, began in 1855. In 1855 he was appointed dean of Gloucester and the same year was consecrated bishop of Exeter.

Bickersteth's publications include *Psalms and Hymns*, 1858, based on his father's collection, and *The Hymnal Companion to the Book of Common Prayer*, 1870 (enlarged in 1876 and 1900), which gained great acceptance in evangelical parishes. John Julian has commented that Bickersteth's best work was not in congregational hymns but those for private use.

Author: Peace, Perfect Peace (**229**)

Blaisdell, James Arnold (b. Beloit, Wisc., December 15, 1867; d. Claremont, Calif., January 29, 1957) was educated at Beloit College (B.A. 1889) and Hartford Theological Seminary (B.D. 1892). He was ordained a Congregational minister in 1892 and served pastorates in Waukesha, Wisc., and Olivet, Mich. As an educator he served as professor of biblical literature at Beloit, 1903-10, and president of Pomona College in Claremont, Calif., 1910-28. Various schools conferred honorary degrees upon him, including Hartford Theological Seminary, Occidental College, and the University of California.

Author: Beneath the Forms of Outward Rite (**321**)

Bliss, Philip Paul (b. Clearfield County, Pa., July 9, 1838; d. Ashtabula, Ohio, December 29, 1876) joined the Baptist Church at the age of 12. He worked as a boy on a farm and in lumbering, gaining some formal grammar school education. After study with J. G. Towner and W. B. Bradbury, he became an itinerant music teacher and continued formal musical education in the summer months at the Normal Academy of Music in Genesco, N.Y. Root and Cady, Chicago music publishers, published his first song, and he joined their staff in 1864, working there until 1868. It was Dwight L. Moody who influenced him to become a singing evangelist. Bliss traveled through the South, Middle West, and East, leading music in various revivals, including those led by Major D. W. Whittle. Bliss and his wife Lucy were among the 100 persons who perished in a train wreck near Ashtabula, Ohio.

Among his many collections, most of them written for the texts of George F. Root, is *Gospel Songs, a Choice Collection of Hymns and Tunes, New and Old, for Gospel Meetings, Sunday School, Etc.,* 1874. This is the beginning of an unfortunate association of both "gospel songs" and "hymns" with the music of revival and the Sunday schools of Reconstruction times. Bliss collaborated with Ira D. Sankey in compiling *Gospel Hymns No. 2,* 1876.

> Author and composer: Brightly Beams Our Father's Mercy (LOWER LIGHTS) **(148)**
> Sing Them Over Again to Me (WORDS OF LIFE) **(109)**

Boberg, Carl (b. Mönsteras, Sweden, August 16, 1859; d. Kalmar, Sweden, January 7, 1940) was the son of a shipyard carpenter. He was converted at the age of 19. He attended a Bible school for 2 years and preached in his hometown. During the years 1890-1916 he edited the weekly *Sanningsvittnet* (Witness of the Truth) and was a member of the Swedish parliament, 1911-24.

> Author: O Lord My God! **(17)**

Bode, John Ernest (b. St. Pancras, England, February 23, 1816; d. Castle Camps, Cambridgeshire, England, October 6, 1874) was educated at Eton, Charterhouse, and Christ Church, Oxford (B.A. 1837, M.A. 1840). He was the first to receive the Hertford Scholarship, 1835, and served for 7 years as tutor, 1837-43. Ordained a priest in 1843, he became rector at Westwell, Oxfordshire, in 1847 and remained there until 1860, after which he was rector at Castle Camps until his death. In 1855 he gave the Bampton Lectures at Oxford.

Included in Bode's poetical output are *Ballads from Herodotus,* 1853, *Short Occasional Poems,* 1858, and *Hymns from the Gospel of the Day, for Each Sunday and the Festivals of Our Lord,* 1860. Bode contested the Oxford chair of professor of poetry in 1857, by defending his *Ballads from Herodotus,* but he lost by one vote to Matthew Arnold.

> Author: O Jesus, I Have Promised **(164)**

491

Bonar, Horatius (b. Edinburgh, Scotland, December 19, 1808; d. Edinburgh, July 31, 1889) was educated at the University of Edinburgh, where Thomas Chalmers was professor of Divinity. Licensed to preach in the Church of Scotland, he served as assistant at Leith and was ordained in 1838 at Kelso, where he was pastor of the North Parish. Later he joined Chalmers and the Free Church of Scotland and served a pastorate at a Free Church in Kelso. A visit to the Holy Land, 1855-56, and a study of Jewish prophecy directed his preaching and writing toward the Second Advent. Bonar was the minister of Chalmers Memorial Free Church, Grange, Edinburgh, 1866-83, and was elected moderator of the General Assembly in 1883. The University of Aberdeen conferred upon him the D.D. degree in 1853.

For many years Bonar edited the *Journal of Prophecy*. He wrote a great number of hymns, some 100 of which are found in English, Scottish, and American collections. His works include *Songs for the Wilderness*, 1843, *The Bible Hymn Book*, 1845, *Hymns, Original and Selected*, 1846, *Hymns of Faith and Hope*, 1857 and 1861, *The Songs of the New Creation*, 1872, *Hymns of the Nativity*, 1879, and *Communion Hymns*, 1881.

> Author: Here, O My Lord, I See Thee Face to Face (**326, 327**)
> I Heard the Voice of Jesus Say (**117**)

Borthwick, Jane Laurie (b. Edinburgh, Scotland, April 9, 1813; d. Edinburgh, September 7, 1897) was the oldest daughter of James Borthwick. After travel on the continent and at the urging of her father, she joined with her sister Sarah Findlater to translate German hymns. She translated 69 of the 122 hymns of *Hymns from the Land of Luther*, 4 series, 1854-62. According to Armin Haeussler, she and her sister rank "next to Catherine Winkworth as writers of excellent hymn translations from German into English." Besides her work in hymnody, Miss Borthwick actively supported missions and social agencies throughout her life.

> Translator: Be Still, My Soul (**209**)
> My Jesus, As Thou Wilt (**167**)

Bortniansky, Dimitri Stepanovitch (b. Glukhov, Ukraine, October 28, 1752; d. St. Petersburg, October 10, 1825) studied under Baldassare

Galuppi, the Italian composer who was maestro to the Russian court, 1766-68. After subsequent study in Bologna, Rome, and Naples, he returned to St. Petersburg in 1779. In 1796 he became director of vocal music at the court chapel.

Bortniansky initiated vocal reforms and composed many works for the imperial chapel choir, including an orthodox mass. Other compositions include an Italian opera, 1776-79, 4 French operas, 1786-87, many sacred concerts, and psalms for 4- and 8-part choir. Tschaikowsky edited and published his choral works in 10 volumes, about 1884.

Composer: ST. PETERSBURG (89, p. 409)

Bourgeois, Louis (b. Paris, France, c. 1510; d. c. 1561) was cantor in 1540 and choirmaster in 1545 at St. Peter's Church in Geneva, where he was given responsibility by John Calvin for the musical editorship of the Genevan Psalter during the years 1542-57. He was a skillful composer and adapter of existing melodies, and though his own compositions are not identified, many are attributed to him. In 1547 he did harmonize and publish 2 sets of psalms in 4-6 parts for nonliturgical use. Harmonized editions of the Genevan Psalter after 1562 are the work of Claude Goudimel. Bourgeois published the theoretical work *Le droict chemin de musique* in 1550.

The Music of the French Psalter of 1562 by W. S. Pratt, 1939, documents Bourgeois' influence upon the music of the completed psalter.

Composer: Amen (824, p. 442)
Attributed composer: COMMANDMENTS (307, 500, p. 177)
OLD 100TH (21, 22, 518, 809, p. 81)
RENDEZ À DIEU (323, p. 122)

Bowie, Walter Russell (b. Richmond, Va., October 8, 1882; d. Alexandria, Va., April 23, 1969) was educated at Harvard (B.A. 1904, M.A. 1905) and Virginia Theological Seminary (B.D. 1909). Ordained priest in 1909, he served as rector of Emmanuel Church, Greenwood, Va., 1908, of St. Paul's, Richmond, 1911, and of Grace Church in New York City, 1923-39. During World War I he was a hospital chaplain in France. He held the positions of dean of students and professor of practical theology, 1939-50, and professor of homiletics,

1950-55, at the Protestant Episcopal Theological Seminary in Virginia (formerly Virginia Theological Seminary). Bowie delivered the Lyman Beecher Lectures, 1934, and the Hale Lectures, 1939. He received the honorary degree of S.T.D. from Syracuse University in 1933.

Bowie's distinguished career includes the editorship of the *Southern Churchman,* and he was a member of the committee which prepared the Revised Standard Version of the Bible. Among his many published works are *The Story of the Bible,* 1951 and 1952, *Lift Up Your Hearts,* 1955, and *The Compassionate Christ,* 1965. His hymns are found in both American and English hymnals.

Author: Lord Christ, When First Thou Cam'st (355)
O Holy City, Seen of John (481)

Bowring, John (b. Exeter, England, October 17, 1792; d. Exeter, November 23, 1872) was born of Puritan parents. He prepared for a mercantile career. Bowring became one of the world's outstanding linguists, claiming to read 200 and speak 100 languages. His early interests resided in social and economic reform, and in 1825 he succeeded Jeremy Bentham as the editor of the radical *Westminster Review.* He entered political life as a member of Parliament in 1835, was appointed consul at Canton in 1849, minister plenipotentiary to China in 1854, and later governor of Hong Kong and chief superintendent of trade with China. Queen Victoria knighted him in 1854.

Bowring's varied writings, including hymns, are contained in 36 volumes. Unitarian hymnbooks in England and America first printed his hymns, but other denominations have brought a number into common use.

Author: God Is Love; His Mercy Brightens (63)
In the Cross of Christ I Glory (416)
Watchman, Tell Us of the Night (358)

Boyce, William (b. London, England, February 7, 1710; d. Kensington, London, February 16, 1779) was a chorister at St. Paul's in London under Charles King. He studied organ with Maurice Greene and served as private tutor and organist at several parishes. In 1758 he was appointed one of the organists of the Chapel Royal, but increasing deafness turned his career away from performance to editing and composing.

Boyce's great work, begun by Greene, is *Cathedral Music* (3 vols., 1760-78; 2nd ed., 1788; reprints and editions, 1844 and 1849) , a collection of services, anthems, and other church music by sixteenth-, seventeenth- and eighteenth-century English composers. His own music includes instrumental, organ, and choral works and incidental music for the theater.

Composer: O Come, Let Us Sing (**664,** p. 456)

Boyd, William (b. Montego Bay, Jamaica, 1847; d. Paddington, England, February 16, 1928) began to compose music at the age of 10. He was educated at Hurstpierpoint, where he was a pupil of Sabine Baring-Gould, and at Worcester College, Oxford. In 1882 he was ordained priest and served as rector of Wigginholt with Greatham, Sussex, 1884-89, and as vicar of All Saints', Norfolk Square, 1893-1918.

Boyd harmonized Baring-Gould's collection of Icelandic folk music, about 1863. While a student at Oxford he was 1 of 14 contributors to *Thirty-Two Hymn Tunes,* composed by members of Oxford University, 1868.

Composer: PENTECOST (**241,** p. 178)

Bradbury, William Batchelder (b. York, Me., October 6, 1816; d. Montclair, N.J., January 7, 1868) was born of a musical family and as a young man moved to Boston to study harmony with Sumner Hill. Later he entered the Boston Academy of Music and sang in Lowell Mason's choir at Bowdoin Street Church. When he moved to Brooklyn and later to New York City, he played the organ and organized singing classes in the manner of Mason and George J. Webb. In 1847 he traveled to England and Germany and studied with Moritz Hauptmann and Ignaz Moscheles in Leipzig. Returning to New York City in 1849, he devoted his time to teaching, conducting musical conventions and normal institutes, composing, and editing. It is said that during the years 1841-67 he produced more than 2 music collections a year. His collection *The Jubilee,* 1858, sold a quarter of a million copies. With his brother he established the Bradbury Piano Company, which later became a part of the Knabe Piano Company.

Composer: BRADBURY (**121,** p. 366)

HE LEADETH ME (**217**, p. 212)
OLIVE'S BROW (**431**, p. 413)
SWEET HOUR (**275**, p. 385)
THE SOLID ROCK (**292**, p. 292)
WOODWORTH (**119**, p. 262)

Brady, Nicolaus (b. Bandon, County Cork, Ireland, 1659; d. Richmond, Surrey, England, 1726) was a clergyman. He was educated at Westminster, Christ Church, Oxford, and Trinity College, Dublin. He served as chaplain to William III. His longest term of service was at Richmond, 1696-1726.

Many of Brady's sermons were published. He wrote one tragedy, *The Rape, or the Innocent Impostors,* 1692, and a partial translation of Virgil's *Aeneid,* 1726. He and Nahum Tate collaborated to produce the *New Version* of the Psalter in 1696.

Source: As Pants the Hart for Cooling Streams (**255**)
O Lord, Our Fathers Oft Have Told (**54**)
Through All the Changing Scenes of Life (**56**)

Bridges, Matthew (b. Malden, Essex, England, July 14, 1800; d. Sidmouth, Devonshire, England, October 6, 1894) grew up in the Church of England, but under the influence of the Oxford Movement and despite his early writings against the Roman Catholic Church, he became a Roman Catholic in 1848. He spent the latter part of his life in Quebec, Canada.

Bridges' literary output includes *The Roman Empire Under Constantine the Great,* 1828, *Hymns of the Heart,* 1847 and 1851, and *The Passion of Jesus,* 1852. His poems were introduced in America through Henry Ward Beecher's *Plymouth Collection,* 1855.

Author: Crown Him with Many Crowns (**455**)

Bridges, Robert Seymour (b. Walmer, Kent, England, October 23, 1844; d. Boar's Hill, Abingdon, Berkshire, England, April 21, 1930), the English poet laureate, was a scholar, musician, and physician. He was educated at Eton and Corpus Christi College, Oxford, and at St. Bartholomew's Hospital in London, but gave up medical practice in 1881 because of ill health and took up residence in Yattendon, Berkshire, in order to devote himself to literature and hymnody.

His many works include *Shorter Poems,* 1873, *Yattendon Hymnal,*

1895-99, and *Testament of Beauty,* 1929. His intense interest in the music of hymnody is reflected in *A Practical Discourse on Some Principles of Hymn-Singing,* 1899, and *About Hymns,* 1911. The *Collected Essays* were published 1927-36, the *Poetical Works,* 1929-30.

During 1924 he was a guest of the University of Michigan for 3 months where he received the honorary LL.D. degree. He was awarded the Order of Merit in 1929.

> Translator: Ah, Holy Jesus (412)
> O Splendor of God's Glory Bright (29)
> When Morning Gilds the Skies (91)

Briggs, George Wallace (b. Kirkby, Nottingham County, England, December 15, 1875; d. Hindhead, Surrey, England, December 30, 1959) was educated at Emmanuel College, Cambridge, where he took a first class in classical studies in 1897. After a brief appointment in Wakefield, Yorkshire, he became chaplain in the Royal navy, 1902-9. During the years 1909-18 he was vicar of St. Andrew's, Norwich, rector of Loughborough, 1918-27, canon of Leicester, 1927-34, and canon of Worcester until his retirement in 1956.

Mrs. Briggs characterizes her husband's work in this way: "All his life he was writing hymns, never dating them, and several published at much later dates." She has furnished the following list of his collected works: contributor to *Songs of Praise,* 1925, *Prayers and Hymns for Use in Schools,* 1927, *Little Bible,* 1931, *Prayers and Hymns for Junior Schools,* 1933, *Daily Service,* 1936, *Daily Reading,* 1939, *Daily Prayer* (with Eric Milnerwhite), 1941, and *Songs of Faith,* 1945, which had no music edition and had little use outside of Worcester Cathedral. Erik Routley in the preface to *Hymns for Church and Schools* calls Briggs the "most prolific of the century's successful hymn writers."

Briggs was one of the founders of the Hymn Society of Great Britain and Ireland. For 3 months in 1950 he visited the United States, lecturing at Berkeley and New Haven and before the American Hymn Society in New York City. One of his prayers was used at the meeting of Franklin D. Roosevelt and Winston Churchill aboard the *Prince of Wales* on August 10, 1941, when they jointly authored the Atlantic Charter:

> Stablish our hearts, O God, and strengthen our resolve,
> that we fight not in enmity against men, but against

672

Ancient Chant
Arr. by JAMES R. HOUGHTON, 1899-

The tune is taken from a collection of *Antiphons and Chants* (c. 1848) sung at the Church of the Advent in Boston, Mass. The melodic form would indicate a type of psalm tone. However, the arrangement emphasizes the harmony and takes the form of a double chant as sung by the Boston University School of Theology Seminary Singers under Dr. Houghton. The most recent source of the chant is in the *Hymn and Tune Book,* 1914, published by the American Unitarian Association.

Praise Be to Thee (801)
Laus tibi

JOHN MERBECKE, 1523–c. 1585

The phrase is appointed to be said or sung after the reading of the Gospel. The *Laus tibi* has not had so early or invariable a tradition as the *Gloria tibi*. It does not occur in the Sarum rite or in the 1549 Church of England *Book of Common Prayer*. This form is taken from the Roman Missal, through the American *Book of Common Prayer* of 1928.

Merbecke's setting is a simple harmonization of a single note intonation, such as an organist might provide to support congregational chant.

Praise God, from Whom All Blessings Flow (809)

THOMAS KEN, 1637-1710

The text is Bishop Ken's metrical version of the Lesser Doxology (*Gloria Patri*). He wrote it as the last st. for his morning, evening, and midnight hymns (see comments on "All praise to thee, my God, this night," pp. 82-83).

Old 100th

See "All People That on Earth Do Dwell," pp. 79-81.

459

the powers of darkness enslaving the souls of men; till all enmity and oppression be done away, and the peoples of the world be set free from fear, to serve one another; as children of one father, who is above all, and through all, and in all.

Composer: Amen (823, p. 442)
Author: Christ Is the World's True Light (408)
God Hath Spoken by His Prophets (460)

Brooks, Phillips (b. Boston, Mass., December 13, 1835; d. Boston, January 23, 1893) was educated at Boston Latin School, Harvard University (B.A. 1855), and Virginia Theological Seminary. After his ordination in 1859 he served as rector of the Church of the Advent in Philadelphia; in 1862 as rector of Holy Trinity Church, Philadelphia; and rector of Trinity Church in Boston, 1868-91. He became bishop of Massachusetts in 1891, serving until his untimely death.

Brooks stands as one of America's greatest preachers. Many of his sermons have been published. In 1877 he gave the Lyman Beecher Lectures at Yale. He traveled to the Holy Land in 1866 and later preached to Queen Victoria and at Westminster Abbey and St. Paul's Cathedral, London. In 1885 Oxford conferred upon him the D.D. degree.

Author: O Little Town of Bethlehem (381)

Brooks, Reginald Thomas (b. London, England, June 30, 1918) was educated at the London School of Economics and St. Catherine's and Mansfield colleges, Oxford. He is the producer of the Religious Broadcasting Department of the British Broadcasting Company Television. Formerly he served as Congregational minister in Skipton and Bradford.

Author: Thanks to God Whose Word Was Spoken (18)

Brown, Leila Jackson (b. Grand Rapids, Mich., May 31, 1930) was educated at Albion College (B.A. 1952) and the American Conservatory of Music in Chicago. During the years 1952-55, she served as a Methodist missionary in Lucknow, U.P., India, where she taught in the secondary school and directed the Central Methodist Church choir. In 1956-59 she served in Ipoh, Perak, Malaysia, and 1961-65 she served in Petaling Jaya, Selangor, Malaysia.

Mrs. Jackson represents the new generation of missionaries who has taken a renewed interest in the indigenous folk hymnody and folk music of Asia and Africa. A basic problem which she and others like her have met and solved to a remarkable degree is the difference in rhythmic and melodic notation between Western music and the music of Africa and Asia, the resolution of which is necessary if Western churches are to make intelligent rendering of this music. She has been instrumental in several collections of indigenous folk music: *Jai Ho, the Centenary Sangeet*, 1955, *Joyful Songs of India*, 1956, *Hamare Git*, 1961, and *Malaya Sings*, with Don Smith, 1956 and 1967.

The publications of the Cooperative Recreation Service, Delaware, Ohio, are helpful in exploring further the vast amount of folk hymnody uncovered and edited by this group of talented missionaries.

Translator: Listen to Our Prayer (**803**, p. 451)

Brownlie, John (b. Glasgow, Scotland, August 3, 1857; d. Crieff, Perthshire, November 18, 1925) was educated at the University of Glasgow and at the Free Church College in Glasgow. During the years 1885-90 he served as junior minister at the Free Church, Portpatrick, Wigtownshire, and became minister in charge in 1890. He was made a member of the school board in 1888, became a governor of the Stranrear High School in 1897, and in 1901 was chairman of the governors.

Brownlie's hymns and translations from the Latin and Greek are contained in *Hymns of Our Pilgrimage*, 1889, *Zionward* and *Hymns of the Pilgrim Life*, 1890, *Pilgrim Songs*, 1892, *Hymns from East and West*, 1898, *Hymns of the Greek Church*, published in 4 series, 1900-1906, and *Hymns from the East*, 1907. He wrote a handbook to the 1898 edition of *Church Hymnary*, entitled *Hymns and Hymn-Writers of the Church Hymnary*, 1899.

John Julian has paid tribute to Brownlie in these words: "Mr. Brownlie's translations have all the beauty, simplicity, earnestness, and elevation of thought and feeling which characterize the originals."

Translator: The King Shall Come (**353**)

Bryant, William Cullen (b. Cummington, Mass., November 3, 1794; d. Long Island, N.Y., July 12, 1878) was educated at Williams College in Massachusetts. He studied law and was admitted to the bar in 1815.

After 10 years of practice his interests turned to literary activity, and he became an editor of the *New York Evening Post* in 1826 and later its owner. He was a leading abolitionist.

His 100 poems for the most part deal with the realm of nature, and he is best remembered for his poem *Thanatopsis,* written when he was 18. As a hymn writer Bryant is a disciple of the work of Isaac Watts, composing about 20 hymns in the Watts style. A religious eclectic, he moved from being a Congregationalist in his youth to Unitarian, Episcopalian, Presbyterian, and finally Baptist.

Author: Thou, Whose Unmeasured Temple Stands (345)

Buck, Carlton C. (b. Salina, Kan., August 31, 1907) was educated at Biola Institute, Whittier College, Los Angeles Bible Seminary (B.S.M. 1946), and San Gabriel College (M.A. 1950). After an early career in church music, he was ordained in 1934 into the Christian Church, serving First Christian Church in Arlington, Calif., 1934-39, and Christian churches in Holtville, Orange, and Fullerton, Calif., 1939-60. Since then he has been minister at the First Christian Church in Eugene, Ore.

He is the author of numerous hymns, poems, meditations, librettos, and 3 books: *At the Lord's Table,* 1956, *At the Lord's Treasury,* 1959, and *Quiet Time Verse,* 1965.

Author: O Lord, May Church and Home Combine (520)

Buckoll, Henry James (b. Siddington, near Cirencester, Gloucester, England, September 9, 1803; d. Rugby, England, June 6, 1871) was the son of a clergyman. He was educated at Rugby and Queen's College, Oxford (B.A. 1826, M.A. 1829). In 1827 he was ordained into the ministry but sought a career in education and for 45 years was assistant master at Rugby.

His interest in translating was expressed in his several translations from German hymnbooks, but Armin Haeussler notes that Buckoll's translations never became popular because of his insistence that the original meters be retained. Buckoll probably edited the first edition of the Rugby school collection *Psalms and Hymns for the Use of Rugby School Chapel.* He edited *Collection of Hymns,* used by the Rugby parish church, 1839. With Dean Goulburn he revised the school collection, 1850, which included 14 of his translations, and

Hymns, Translated from the German, 1842, with 67 translations. For the most part his own work found use in public school music books, rather than church hymnbooks.

Translator: Come, My Soul, Thou Must Be Waking (258)

Budry, Edmond L. (b. August 30, 1854; d. November 12, 1932) was for 35 years pastor of the Free Church in Vevey, Switzerland. He studied theology on the "Faculté libre" at Lausanne. In 1881 he became pastor at Cully and remained there until 1889 when he went to Vevey. He retired in 1923.

Budry wrote the text of over 60 chorales, of which "Thine is the glory" is the best known and most often sung. He freely translated and adopted German, English, and Latin hymns, and wrote poetry well into his old age. At the age of 70 he wrote his famous *Veni creator spiritus.* His chorales appear in a number of French church hymnals.

Author: Thine Is the Glory (450)

Bullinger, Ethelbert William (b. Canterbury, England, December 15, 1837; d. London, England, June 6, 1913) began his musical education as a choirboy at Canterbury Cathedral with additional study under John Pyke Hullah, a teacher of singing classes, and William H. Monk. Music was an avocation for Bullinger; he studied for the ministry at King's College, London, and became an able Greek and Hebrew scholar.

Composer: BULLINGER (273, p. 202)

Bunyan, John (b. Elstow, near Bedford, England, November 30, 1628; d. London, August 31, 1688) was the son of a tinker. He attended the village school and at 16 was drafted into the Parliamentary army, serving until 1647. He joined a religious community founded by John Gifford, a converted Royalist major, and after deep reflection and study of scripture, he renounced his former life, found peace, and began preaching in 1653. His preaching was forthright and powerful and caused his arrest and imprisonment during the years 1660-72. During this first term in prison, in particular the years 1660-66, he wrote 9 books, including the autobiographical *Grace Abounding to the Chief of Sinners.*

He was jailed again in 1675 at the time of the revocation of the Declaration of Indulgence and during his 6 months in prison began *Pilgrim's Progress,* published in 1678. This was followed by *The Holy War,* 1682, and the second part of *Pilgrim's Progress,* 1684.

Bunyan, as a Baptist in later life, renounced his youthful love for "bell-ringing, dancing and reading tales," yet upheld those who among the nonconformists favored the singing of hymns in church. In his *Solomon's Temple Spiritualized,* 1688, he speaks of hymn singing as a divine institution. Bunyan has been frequently referred to among nonconformists as "Bishop Bunyan," which speaks of his profound influence in the late seventeenth and early eighteenth centuries.

Isaac Watts's *Divine and Moral Songs,* 1715, is modeled after Bunyan's *Country Rhymes for Children,* 1686.

Author: He Who Would Valiant Be (155)

Burke, Christian Caroline Anna (b. Camberwell, England, September 18, 1857; d. Saffron Walden, Essex, England, March 4, 1944) contributed verse to various periodicals. Her collected verse was published in *The Flowering of the Almond Tree and Other Poems,* 1896 and 1901.

Author: Lord of Life and King of Glory (517)

Burleigh, William Henry (b. Woodstock, Conn., February 2, 1812; d. Brooklyn, N.Y., March 18, 1871) was an influential journalist and abolitionist. In 1836 he began lecturing for the American Anti-slavery Society, and in 1837 he became publisher of the *Christian Witness* and *Temperance Banner.* In 1843 he became editor of the *Christian Freeman* later known as *Charter Oak.*

Burleigh's poems were published in 1841. His hymns have had wide use in England, having been introduced through the collection *Lyra Sacra Americana,* 1868.

Author: Lead Us, O Father, in the Paths of Peace (269)

Burnap, Uzziah Christopher (b. Brooklyn, N.Y., June 17, 1834; d. Brooklyn, December 8, 1900) studied music in Paris as a young man and served as organist for 37 years at the Reformed Church in Brooklyn Heights. By profession he was a prominent Brooklyn dry goods merchant.

Burnap composed and adapted many hymn tunes, collaborating with John K. Paine of Harvard in compiling *Hymns and Songs of Praise,* 1874, and was music editor of the Reformed Church hymnal, *Hymns of the Church: with Tunes,* 1870.

William J. Reynolds has furnished the biographical information on Burnap.

Arranger: ARTHUR'S SEAT (243, p. 284)
SERENITY (158, p. 236)

Burns, James Drummond (b. Edinburgh, Scotland, February 18, 1823; d. Mentone, France, November 27, 1864) was a graduate of the University of Edinburgh with an M.A. degree. He was ordained in 1845 and became the minister of the Free Church at Dunblane at the time of the "disruption." Ill health caused him to seek a warmer climate, and in 1848 he was appointed minister of the Presbyterian church, Funchal, in the Madeira Islands.

Burns served as minister of London's Hampstead Presbyterian Church, 1855-63, and during that time he published 2 collections of hymns and 39 translations of German hymns. The eighth edition of *Encyclopaedia Britannica* contains an article by Burns on hymns.

Author: At Thy Feet, Our God and Father (498)

Burrowes, Elisabeth Havens (b. Detroit, Mich., January 13, 1885) is the daughter of an old New Jersey family. She was educated at Peddie Institute, Hightstown, N.J., and attended Vassar. She is the author of 2 books for children, *Little Thunder* and *Good Night,* and numerous poems, hymns, and articles. Her hymn "O God, Send Men" was sung at the one-hundredth anniversary of the Pacific School of Religion in 1966 at Berkeley, Calif., where she presently resides.

Author: God of the Ages, by Whose Hand (206)

Burt, Bates Gilbert (b. Wheeling, W.Va., December 21, 1878; d. Edgewood, Md., April 5, 1948) was educated at Kenyon College (M.A. 1901) and as a special student at Seabury Divinity School in 1902. He was ordained deacon in 1903, priest in 1904, and was dean of St.

Paul's Cathedral in Marquette, Mich., during the years 1904-17 and 1920-22. He served as chaplain in France, 1918-19. From 1922 until his retirement in 1947 he was rector of All Saints' Church, Pontiac, Mich.

Burt wrote numerous Christmas carols in collaboration with his son Alfred S. Burt, as well as hymn tunes and settings for the chants *Venite* and *Benedictus es, Domine.* In 1946 he was named a member of the joint commission on the revision of the Episcopal *Hymnal 1940.*

Composer: SHADDICK (**186, 252**, pp. 357-58)

Byrne, Mary Elizabeth (b. Dublin, July 1, 1880; d. Dublin, January 19, 1931) was educated at the Dominican convent in Dublin and at the University of Ireland (M.A. 1905). She worked as a researcher on the Board of Intermediate Education and was a contributor to the *Old and Mid-Irish Dictionary* and *Dictionary of the Irish Language,* as well as one of the compilers of the *Catalogue* of the Royal Irish Academy. For her treatise on *England in the Age of Chaucer* she received the chancellor's gold medal in the Royal University.

Translator: Be Thou My Vision (**256**)

Camidge, John (b. York, England, 1735; d. York, April 25, 1803) was the first of a line of family of musicians who supplied the organists of Yorkminster for a century. John, Sr., was the pupil of Samuel Green and G. F. Handel. He assumed the Yorkminster post in 1756 upon the resignation of his teacher James Nares. Camidge retired from the cathedral in 1799 and was succeeded by his son Matthew.

Composer: Lift Up Your Hearts (**842**, p. 451)
O Lord, Open Thou Our Eyes (**798**, p. 457)

Campbell, Jane Montgomery (b. Paddington, England, 1817; d. Bovey Tracey, South Devonshire, England, November 15, 1878) was the daughter of the rector at St. James's, in Paddington. She taught music in the parish school there and from this experience published *Handbook for Singers,* a series of musical exercises. She assisted Charles S. Bere in the preparation of *Garland of Song, or an English Liederkranz,* 1861, and *Children's Choral Book,* 1869, to which she contributed a number of translations from German hymns and poems.

Translator: We Plow the Fields (**513**)

Canitz, Friedrich Rudolph Ludwig, Freiherr von (b. Berlin, November 27, 1654; d. Berlin, August 11, 1699) studied at the universities of Leyden and Leipzig, and traveled extensively in Europe and England. He was appointed groom of the bedchamber to Frederick William, Elector of Brandenburg. In 1680 he became councilor of legation, later privy councilor, and finally baron of the empire. His hymns, numbering about 24, were published anonymously as *Nebenstunden unterschiedener Gedichte,* 1700.

Author: Come, My Soul, Thou Must Be Waking **(258)**

Canning, Thomas (b. Brookville, Pa., December 12, 1911) was educated at Oberlin (B.M. 1936) and Eastman School of Music (M.M. 1940). He taught at Morningside College in Iowa, 1936-42, Indiana State Teachers College, 1945-46, the Royal Conservatory of Music, Toronto, 1946-47, and Eastman School of Music, 1947-62. At present he holds the position of associate professor of music and composer in residence at West Virginia University in Morgantown.

His published compositions include a fantasy for string orchestra, 1944, works for organ, vocal ensembles, and instruments. He was commissioned in 1961 by the Board of Education of The Methodist Church to compose a choral setting of John Wesley's Covenant Service.

Composer: COVENANT HYMN (**508**, p. 144)

Carr, Benjamin (b. London [?], England, September 12, 1768; d. Philadelphia, Pa., May 24, 1831) received his musical training from Samuel Arnold, editor of Handel's works, and Charles Wesley, Jr.

Joseph Carr, Benjamin's father, had been a music publisher in London, and when the family came to Philadelphia in 1793, he continued his work. It is claimed that he established the first music store in America, bearing the name Carr's Musical Repository. The family also had stores in Baltimore and New York. Always leaders in the printing of patriotic music, the Carrs published *The Federal Overture,* 1794, a medley of 9 tunes, including "Yankee Doodle"; "Hail Columbia," 1798; and "The Star Spangled Banner," published in 1814 and set to the tune "Anacreon in Heaven."

Benjamin founded the musical weekly *Musical Journal* in 1800, announcing that for his selections of vocal and instrumental music he would draw on "a regular supply of new music from Europe and the assistance of men of genius in this country." As such, Carr is an important figure in the transmission of European tradition and the development of American talent.

After 1800 Carr's interests turned also to teaching and church music. For 30 years he was in charge of music at St. Peter's Roman Catholic Church in Philadelphia and was in a position to influence a generation of church musicians. He was cofounder of the Musical Fund Society of Philadelphia, 1820, and served as one of its first conductors.

Carr was one of the most influential and versatile promoters, publishers, and performers of his day. His works include an opera, ballads, songs, keyboard works, and 2 sacred collections: *Masses, Vespers, Litanies, Hymns* . . . , 1805, and *A Collection of Chants,* 1816.

Arranger: SPANISH HYMN (77, p. 137)

Carter, Russell Kelso (b. Baltimore, Md., November 18, 1849; d. Catonsville, Md., August 23, 1926) graduated in the first class from Pennsylvania Military Academy in Chester, 1867, where he was an outstanding athlete. His various careers included teacher of science, engineering, and mathematics; sheep-raiser; Methodist minister, ordained in 1887 and active in the Holiness movement and camp meetings; publisher, author, editor; composer of gospel hymns and tunes; and a practicing physician in Baltimore. With A. B. Simpson he edited *Hymns of the Christian Life* in 1891, to which he contributed 52 texts and 44 tunes.

William J. Reynolds has supplied the biographical information on Carter.

Author and composer: Standing on the Promises (PROMISES) (221)

Caswall, Edward (b. Yately, Hampshire, England, July 15, 1814; d. Edgbaston, Birmingham, England, January 2, 1878) was the fourth son of the vicar of Yately. He was educated at Marlborough, and at Brasenose College, Oxford (B.A. 1836, M.A. 1838) and was ordained priest in 1839. He served as curate at Bishop's Norton and Milverton, Somerset, and in 1840 was named perpetual curate of Stratford sub Castle, near Salisbury, and remained there until he became a Roman Catholic under the influence of Cardinal Newman. After the death of his wife, Caswall was re-ordained in 1852 and remained at the Oratory of St. Philip Neri at Edgbaston until his death.

Caswall is second only to John Mason Neale in the number of hymns translated from Latin, about 200 in all. His works include *Lyra Catholica, Containing the Hymns at Vespers, Compline and Benediction, with Those in the Office of the Blessed Virgin and in the Missal,* 1849; *The Masque of Mary and Other Poems,* 1858; *A May Pageant and Other Poems,* 1865; and *Hymns and Other Poems,* 1873.

John Julian has written that Caswall's faithfulness to the rhythm of the Latin in his translations make them very suitable for congregational song. Yet, less than a dozen of either his translations or poems are found in today's hymnals.

> Translator: Earth Has Many a Noble City (405)
> Jesus, the Very Thought of Thee (82)
> When Morning Gilds the Skies (91)

Cennick, John (b. Reading, Berkshire, England, December 12, 1718; d. London, England, July 4, 1755), though born of Quaker parents, was brought up in the Church of England. He worked as a surveyor, but in 1739 gave up his work to join the Wesleys. John Wesley appointed him teacher at Kingswood School, Bristol. He left Wesley on doctrinal grounds and joined George Whitefield, but in 5 years left to join the Moravians. He traveled and preached in Germany and Ireland. He was buried in the Moravian Cemetery, Chelsea.

Cennick's published works include *Sacred Hymns for the Children of God in the Days of Their Pilgrimage,* 1741, *Sacred Hymns for the Use of Religious Societies,* 1743, and *Hymns to the Honour of Jesus Christ,* 1754. The Moravian Collection of 1789 contains some of his unpublished hymns.

> Author: Be Present at Our Table, Lord (518)
> Children of the Heavenly King (300)

Challinor, Frederic Arthur (b. Longston, Staffordshire, England, November 12, 1866; d. Paignton, England, December 1, 1952) worked as a laborer in a brickyard, as a coal miner, and in a china factory during his early years. Later he pursued a musical education, gaining a diploma from the Royal College of Music and the B.M. degree in 1897 and the Mus.D. degree in 1903 from the University of London.

Challinor published over 1,000 compositions including 3 cantatas: *Judah in Babylon, The Gardens of the Lord,* and *Bethany.* He often wrote his own verse to hymns and part songs (usually under a pen name), and a number of his poems were published. His *Ode to Art,* written for the Stoke on Trent Historical Pageant and the Josiah Wedgwood Bicentenary, was performed by chorus and orchestra in 1930.

Winifred A. Webb, the granddaughter of Challinor, has provided the biographical information and gives as his birthplace Stoke on Trent. The *Musical Messenger,* published in 1905, provides a detailed biography.

Composer: STORIES OF JESUS (**88,** p. 388)

Chambers, John David (b. London, England, 1805; d. Westminster, England, August 22, 1893) was educated at Oriel College, Oxford (B.A. 1827). In 1831 he entered church law and served as recorder of New Sarum (Salisbury) beginning in 1842. There he devoted much study to the work of Osmund (c. 1006-1099), bishop of Salisbury, 1078-99, and to the development of the cathedral's divine office and rules.

Chambers published a translation of *The Psalter, or Seven Ordinary Hours of Sarum, with the Hymns for the Year, and the Variations of the York and Hereford Breviaries,* 1852, and also *Lauda Syon, Ancient Latin Hymns of the English and Other Churches, Translated into Corresponding Metres,* 1857-66.

Translator: To Thee Before the Close of Day (**814,** p. 463)

Chao Tzu-ch'en (b. Hso-tsun, China, February 14, 1888) received his B.A. degree from Soochow University and did further work at Vanderbilt University (M.A. 1916, B.D. 1917). Princeton University conferred upon him the D.D. degree. He taught sociology at Soochow University.

During the years 1926-51 Chao was chaplain of Yenching University and dean of the school of religion. Originally a Methodist, he entered the Anglican-Episcopalian Union in 1938 and served as minister of Chung Hwa Shen Kung Hui parish. Chao was a delegate to 3 conferences of the International Missionary Council: Jerusalem in 1929, Madras in 1938, and Whitby in 1947. He served as a consultant at the first assembly of the World Council of Churches, Amsterdam, 1948. He resigned as one of the presidents of the World Council in June of 1951, apparently as a form of protest for the Central Committee's endorsement of the United Nations' defense of South Korea.

Chao ranks first among Chinese Christian thinkers and writers both in quality and in influence. His major books, all in Chinese, are *A Philosophy of the Christian Religion*, 1925, *Life of Jesus*, 1926, *Life of Paul*, 1947, and *An Interpretation of Christianity*, 1948. Articles in English appeared in the *Chinese Recorder*, the *China Christian Year Book*, and *International Review of Missions*. He is the author of several poems, many of them collected in the volume entitled *Fishing*, 1931. In 1926 he translated and published *Christian Fellowship Hymns*, 150 texts from Western sources. Wishing to provide indigenous hymns for the Christian movement in China, he published 50 in *Hymns for the People*, 1931.

Recent information is not available on Chao, but it is thought that he probably retired from teaching in 1956.

Author: Ne'er Forget God's Daily Care (**519**)
Rise to Greet the Sun (**490**)

Chapin, Lucius (1760-1842) was one of the members of a family frequently cited in Southern tunebooks. Lucius, from Massachusetts, enlisted as a fifer in the Revolutionary army and settled in the Shenandoah Valley of Virginia where he became a singing master, 1787. Irving Lowens states that no fewer than 7 Chapins were involved in composing and compiling music in the post-Revolutionary period.

Attributed composer: TWENTY-FOURTH (**789**, p. 462)

Charles, Elizabeth Rundle (b. Tavistock, Devonshire, England, January 2, 1828; d. Hampstead Heath, near London, England, March 28 or April 1, 1896) was a painter, poet, translator, musician, and author, who in later life assumed the name of Rundle-Charles. Mrs. Charles was educated by tutors at her home and began her literary work in 1850 with a translation of a hymn by Joachim Neander. Her interest in translating extended beyond German to include Latin and Swedish.

She is best known for her numerous works in fiction and history, the latter field including works on English religious history, the German Reformation, and the Wesleys and their times. Her best-known work in America at the turn of the century was *The Chronicles of the Schönberg-Cotta Family*, 1863. Her hymns for the most part are included in *Voice of Christian Life in Song*, 1864, and *Songs Old and New*, 1882.

Author: Never Further Than Thy Cross (**430**)

509

Chatfield, Allen William (b. Chatteris, Cambridgeshire, England, October 2, 1808; d. Much-Marcle, Herefordshire, England, January 10, 1896) was educated at Charterhouse School and Trinity College, Cambridge, where he took top classical honors (B.A. 1831). Ordained in 1832, he served as vicar at Stotfold, Bedfordshire, 1833-47, and at Much-Marcle until his death.

His most important work was the rendering into Greek in various meters of the litany, *Te Deum,* and other parts of the English Church offices. Some of his sermons were published. He published *Songs and Hymns of the Earliest Greek Christian Poets, Bishops and Others, Translated into English Verse,* 1876, and *Collected Psalms and Hymns.*

Translator: Lord Jesus, Think on Me **(284)**

Chesterton, Gilbert Keith (b. Kensington, London, England, May 29, 1874; d. Beaconsfield, England, June 14, 1936) was educated at St. Paul's School, London, and studied at the Slade School of Art. His reviews of art in the *Bookman* and the *Speaker* gained the attention of the literary world. During the years 1905-30 he contributed to the *Illustrated London News* and also illustrated the books of Hilaire Belloc, the man most responsible for Chesterton's becoming a Roman Catholic in 1922.

Chesterton was sometimes called the "Prince of Paradox," and his vigorous writing became known throughout the English-speaking world. In America he is noted for his delightful detective stories, featuring the priest-hero Father Brown. His poems were published in 1927, and he provided important biographical studies of Francis of Assisi, Robert Browning, Charles Dickens, and G. B. Shaw. Chesterton's religious views espoused the thirteenth century as the socio-religious ideal, and in the face of an emerging Democratic Socialism in England he advocated a return to the trade-guild system.

He was not inclined to go out of his way to express kind thoughts about others and their views, and his contemporaries at times responded in like measure. His critics' preoccupation with facets of his personal life tends to gloss over the fact of his literary genius. His writings encompass a period of 40 years.

Author: O God of Earth and Altar **(484)**

Chorley, Henry Fothergill (b. Blackley, Lancashire, England, December 15, 1808; d. London, England, February 16, 1872) was born of Quaker parents. Instead of going into business as his family wished, he moved into literature and musical journalism, and ranks with James William Davison (1813-1885) as one of the leaders in the field of nineteenth-century musical criticism. Chorley traveled widely and was variously active as a dramatist, translator, art critic, poet, novelist, and journalist. He was employed on the staff of the London *Athenaeum*, 1831-68, and also wrote musical criticism for many years for the London *Times*. Basically a voice of the Mendelssohn-Spohr musical ideal, he resisted innovation by openly attacking the efforts of Chopin, Schumann, and Wagner.

Chorley's *Autobiography, Memoir and Letters* (2 vols., 1873) was edited in part by Henry Gay Hewlett.

Author: God the Omnipotent (544)

Christierson, Frank (Frederick) von (b. Lovisa, Finland, December 25, 1900) came to America at the age of 5. He was educated at Stanford University (B.A. 1923) and San Francisco Theological Seminary (B.D. 1929, M.A. 1930). He has served Presbyterian pastorates at Calvary Presbyterian Church in Berkeley, Calif., 1929-44, Trinity Community Presbyterian Church in North Hollywood, 1944-61, and Celtic Cross United Presbyterian Church in Citrus Heights, 1961-66. Christierson has held the position of moderator of the San Francisco and Los Angeles presbyteries and positions of leadership in interdenominational work. He is presently assistant minister at the First Presbyterian Church in Marysville, Calif.

Seven prizewinning hymns of his are in print.

Author: As Men of Old Their First Fruits Brought (511)
Break Forth, O Living Light of God (356)

Clark, Alexander (b. Jefferson County, Ohio, March 10, 1834; d. Atlanta, Ga., July 6, 1879) was an important figure in the Methodist Protestant Church. Educated largely by his father, a classical scholar, he began a teaching and journalism career at the age of 17. He was editor and publisher of the *School Visitor,* later named *Schoolday Magazine* and 20 years later merged with *St. Nicholas*. Clark served until his death as editor of the *Methodist Recorder,* the editorial voice of the northern and western groups of the Methodist Protestant Church. At the time of reunion of the Methodist and Methodist Protestant churches in 1877, he traveled widely in the West and South, seeking support for both the *Recorder* and the *Methodist Protestant.*

Clark was a widely recognized preacher, lecturer, and author of several books including a small book of poems. He was a member of the committee which prepared *The Voice of Praise,* 1871, a hymnal for use in the Methodist Protestant Church.

> Author: Heavenly Father, Bless Me Now (95)

Clark, Jeremiah (b. London, England, c. 1669-73; d. London, December 1, 1707) was a chorister in the Chapel Royal under John Blow. During the years 1692-95 he was organist at Winchester College, succeeding Blow in 1693 as master of the choristers at St. Paul's Cathedral. He was made organist of St. Paul's in 1695 and gentleman-extraordinary of the Chapel Royal in 1700. In 1704 he and William Croft were made joint organists of the Chapel Royal.

Clark collaborated on 2 operas. He wrote incidental music for plays, a cantata, an ode, anthems, songs, and hymn tunes. He is sometimes referred to as the father of the modern English hymn tune, and most of his tunes appear in the 2 chief editions of Henry Playford, *The Divine Companion or David's Harp New Tun'd,* 1701 and 1707.

Despondency over an unhappy love affair led to his suicide.

> Composer: ST. MAGNUS (458, p. 393)

Claudius, Matthias (b. Reinfeld, near Lübeck, Holstein, August 15, 1740; d. Hamburg, January 21, 1815), the son of a Lutheran pastor, entered the University of Jena in 1759 where he studied for the ministry. At the university he was attracted to the rationalism of the day, and because of its influence and partly as a result of a serious illness that would have impeded his ministry, he changed his course of study to law and language. For many years he edited the *Wandsbecker Bote,* and in 1788 he was appointed auditor of the Schleswig-Holstein Bank at Altona.

John Julian writes that "much of his poetry was distinctly Christian in its spirit, and many of his pieces might rank as popular sacred songs.

Yet he wrote no hymns designed for use in church." His complete works appeared in 8 volumes entitled *Asmus omnia sua secum portans,* 1775-1812.

Author: We Plow the Fields (513)

Clausnitzer, Tobias (b. Thum, Saxony, c. February 5, 1619; d. Weiden, May 7, 1684) was graduated from the University of Leipzig (M.A. 1643) and appointed chaplain to the Swedish army in 1644. After the Peace of Westphalia in 1649, he accepted the newly established pastorate at Weiden in the Upper Palatine and served there until his death.

Three of his hymns have come into English use: "Lord Jesus! May Thy Grief and Pain," a passion hymn sung between each of 12 sermons, found in his *Passions-Blume,* 1662; "Blessed Jesus, at Thy Word," for use before the sermon; and "We [all] believe in one True God," for Trinity Sunday.

Author: Blessed Jesus, at Thy Word (257)
    We Believe in One True God (463)

Clement of Alexandria (b. Athens, Greece [?], c. 160; d. Palestine [?], c. 215) was the successor to Pantaenus as the leader of the famous Catechetical School in Alexandria. Pantaenus probably led Clement away from stoicism and eclecticism to Christianity. Clement put forth no complete theological system as such; this was to become the task of his pupil Origen. Clement's 3 most important works are *Exhortation to the Heathen; Instructor,* the first treatise on Christian conduct; and *Stromata* or *Miscellanies,* a collection of his thoughts on religion and theology.

Philosophy was regarded by Clement as religion's handmaid. Williston Walker has written that at Alexandria

a union of what was best in ancient philosophy, chiefly Platonism and stoicism, was effected to a degree nowhere else realized in orthodox circles, and the result was a Christian Gnosticism. Clement of Alexandria was typical of this movement. At the same time he was a presbyter in the Alexandrian Church, thus serving as a connecting link between the church and the school.

Author: O Guide to Every Child (84)
    Shepherd of Eager Youth (86)

Clephane, Elizabeth Cecilia (b. Edinburgh, Scotland, June 18, 1830; d. Melrose, Roxburghshire, Scotland, February 19, 1869), a humanitarian and poet, gained the name of "Sunbeam" from the poor of the area around Melrose. Her works, 8 poems in all, were published as "Breathings on the Border" in the *Family Treasury,* 1772-74, a magazine edited by the Free Church minister William Arnett. Arnett describes the poems as expressing "the experience, the hopes and longings of a young Christian lately released."

Author: Beneath the Cross of Jesus **(417)**

Coffin, Henry Sloane (b. New York, N.Y., January 5, 1877; d. Lakeville, Conn., November 25, 1954) was educated at Yale (B.A. 1897, M.A. 1900) with study at New College, Edinburgh, 1897-99, and Union Theological Seminary in New York (B.D. 1900). He was ordained a Presbyterian minister in 1900, serving 5 years at the Bedford Park Church in New York City. During the years 1905-26 he was pastor at the Madison Avenue Presbyterian Church and served as associate professor of practical theology at Union Theological Seminary. He was president of Union 1926-45, and in 1943 he served a one-year term as moderator of the General Assembly of the Presbyterian Church U.S.A.

For many years Coffin taught hymnology at Union and served as coeditor of *Hymns of the Kingdom of God,* 1910. He is the author of 15 books, including *In a Day of Social Building,* the Lyman Beecher Lectures at Yale in 1918.

Translator: O Come, O Come, Emmanuel **(354)**

Conkey, Ithamar (b. Shutesbury, Mass., May 15, 1815; d. Elizabeth, N.J., April 30, 1867) was a versatile musician. After serving as organist at the Central Baptist Church in Norwich, Conn., 1849-50, he went to New York City where he had a distinguished career as a church soloist and in oratorio. Conkey served as bass soloist at both Calvary and Grace Episcopal churches. From 1861 until his death he sang bass and directed the quartet choir at the Madison Avenue Baptist Church.

Composer: RATHBUN **(416,** p. 239)

Converse, Charles Crozat (b. Warren, Mass., October 7, 1832; d. Highwood, N.J., October 18, 1918) was educated at the academy at Elmira, N.Y., and at the Leipzig Conservatory with Richter, Hauptmann, and Plaidy, 1855-59. Upon his return to America, he studied law and graduated from Albany University in 1861. Most of his life was spent in Erie, Pa., though he retired to Highwood, N.J. Rutherford College in North Carolina conferred the LL.D. degree upon him in 1895.

Converse was a man with wide interests which included philosophy and philology, as well as music. He composed string quartets, quintets, patriotic overtures, cantatas, various vocal compositions, chorales, and hymn tunes, often using the pen names of Redan, Nevers, or Revons. His associations with Sunday school hymnody included William B. Bradbury and Ira D. Sankey.

Composer: CONVERSE (261, p. 426)

Cook, Joseph Simpson (b. Durham County, England, December 4, 1859; d. Toronto, Canada, May 27, 1933) was educated at Wesleyan College of McGill University, Montreal. He became a Methodist minister and later served in the United Church of Canada.

Author: Gentle Mary Laid Her Child (395)

Copenhaver, Laura Scherer (b. Marion, Va., August 29, 1868; d. Marion, December 18, 1940), a leader in southern mountain work, was credited with the beginnings of the missionary effort to the mountain people under the sponsorship of the United Lutheran Church in America. Her talents included handicrafts, especially handwoven coverlets and hooked rugs. For 30 years she taught English literature at Marion College, a women's school founded by her father in 1873. A number of her pageants and articles were widely circulated.

Author: Heralds of Christ (406)

Copes, Vicar Earle (b. Norfolk, Va., August 12, 1921) was educated at Davidson College in Davidson, N.C. (B.A. 1940) and Union Theological Seminary in New York City (M.S.M. 1944, B.D. 1945). He has served as minister of music at Highland Park Methodist Church, Dallas, Tex., 1946-49, professor of organ and church music at Hendrix College in Conway, Ark., 1949-56, and at Cornell College in Mt. Vernon, Iowa, 1956-58. During the years 1958-67 he was music editor of the General Board of Education of The Methodist Church in Nashville, Tenn., where he was responsible for the monthly periodical *Music Ministry*. Since 1967 he has been the head of the department of organ and church music at Birmingham Southern College.

During Copes's editorship of *Music Ministry* he assisted in the denominational effort that has attempted since 1952 to raise educational and performance standards in music, particularly music as related to the local church program of Christian education. Active in professional and interdenominational committees on church music, in the summer of 1962 he was selected as 1 of the 9 American church musicians by the government of West Germany to participate in a 4-week study tour of German church music.

As a special consultant to the committee for the 1964 revision of the Methodist hymnal, Copes served on the subcommittee on hymn tunes and made a significant contribution to the music of the hymnal. Several of his anthems are in print.

    Composer: EPWORTH CHURCH (**422,** p. 375)
         KINGDOM (**314,** p. 181)
         VICAR (**161,** p. 218)
  Harmonizer: ANCIENT OF DAYS (**459,** pp. 89-90)
         BRADBURY (**121,** p. 366)
         IN DULCI JUBILO (**391,** p. 204)
         ITALIAN HYMN (**292, 352,** p. 129)
         OLD 113TH (**9, 39,** pp. 234-35)
         SALZBURG (**295, 319,** p. 224)
         SEYMOUR (**94,** p. 166)
         ROYAL OAK (**34,** p. 86)

Copley, Robert Evan (b. Liberal, Kan., March 22, 1930) was educated at Denver University (B.M. 1952) and Michigan State University (M.M. 1954, Ph.D. 1958). He taught organ and music theory at Iowa Wesleyan College, 1958-65, and since 1965 has taught at Oklahoma State University. Copley has composed symphonies, overtures, piano and organ literature, and many choral works.

  Composer: Amen (**821,** p. 442)

Cosin, John (b. Norwich, England, November 30, 1594; d. Westminster, England, January 15, 1672) was educated at Caius College, Cambridge. He was ordained and served as chaplain to the bishop of Durham, 1624. He became archdeacon of East Riding (Yorkshire), 1625, master of Peterhouse, Cambridge, 1635-39, and vice-chancellor of the university, 1639-40. The Puritan Long Parliament drove him from his position, and he served as chaplain to the exiled royal family resident in France. After the Restoration he was made bishop of Durham, and under his tenure extensive renovation was made to the cathedral and its library.

Cosin was involved in the 1662 revision of *The Book of Common Prayer*. His most important work was *Collection of Private Devotions in the Practice of the Ancient Church Called the Hours of Prayer*, 1627.

Translator: Come, Holy Ghost, Our Souls Inspire (467)

Coster, George Thomas (b. Chatham, Kent, England, October 3, 1835; d. Rotherham, Yorkshire, England, August 29, 1912) was 1 of 13 children, all of whom entered some form of social or religious work. George was educated at New College and was ordained a Congregational minister in 1859. According to Robert G. McCutchan, Coster also served Wesleyan Methodist churches before he retired in 1902. His ministerial career was marked by chronic ill health, but in spite of this disability, he championed humanitarian enterprises including the founding of Victoria Hospital for children at Hull and a local branch of the Guild of Brave Poor Things. Coster's writings include *Poems and Hymns*, 1882, *Collected Poems*, 1890, *Hessle Hymns*, 1901, and numerous sermons and devotional literature.

Author: March On, O Soul, with Strength (243)

Cotterill, Thomas (b. Cannock, Staffordshire, England, December 4, 1779; d. Sheffield, England, December 29, 1823) was educated at the Free School, Birmingham, and St. John's College, Cambridge (B.A. 1801). Ordained in 1803, he served as curate at Tutbury, incumbent of Lane End, Staffordshire, 1808-17, and perpetual curate of St. Paul's, Sheffield, 1817-23.

At Sheffield, 1819, Cotterill created a controversy by introducing his *Selection of Psalms and Hymns for Public and Private Use* (1810; 8th ed., 1819) for use in worship. Those of the congregation who preferred the exclusive use of psalms persuaded the archbishop of York to prohibit the use of hymns. Another collection, dated 1820, was given approval and as such became the first hymnal given official sanction by church authorities.

> Author: In Memory of the Savior's Love (**319**)
> Adapter: By Thy Birth and by Thy Tears (**113**)

Cowper, William (b. Berkhampstead, Hertfordshire, England, November 15, 1731; d. East Dereham, Norfolk, England, April 25, 1800) was the son of the prominent clergyman John C. Cowper. He was educated at Westminster School where he studied law. In 1754 he was called to the bar, but he never practiced.

Beginning with his childhood he periodically suffered deep depressions and felt that he was spared death by a merciful God. Some of his most lucid and productive years were spent with John Newton, curate at Olney, where they collaborated on the famous *Olney Hymns,* completed in 1779 with 67 of Cowper's hymns in the collection.

Cowper was regarded by many as the supreme poet of his day, especially for his translation of Homer in 1791. As a poet he marks the transition from Pope to Burns and Wordsworth. His complete works are available in several editions. There is also a concordance and biography by David Cecil. Armin Haeussler has written of Cowper: "Cowper reflects in his poetry something of his leisured existence, his love of nature, his simple tastes and pleasures, his gentle ways and promptings of an almost feminine sensibility."

> Author: God Moves in a Mysterious Way (**215**)
> Jesus, Where'er Thy People Meet (**98**)
> O For a Closer Walk with God (**268**)
> Sometimes a Light Surprises (**231**)
> There Is a Fountain Filled with Blood (**421**)

Cox, Frances Elizabeth (b. Oxford, England, May 10, 1812; d. Headington, England, September 23, 1897) contributed 56 translations from the German in *Sacred Hymns from the German,* 1841, which contained the original text and notes on the authors. A second edition,

Hymns from the German, appeared in 1864. Miss Cox's friend Baron Bunsen was instrumental in suggesting to her texts he assessed as worthy of translation.

Translator: Sing Praise to God Who Reigns Above (4)

Coxe, Arthur Cleveland (b. Mendham, N.J., May 10, 1818; d. Clifton Springs, N.Y., July 20, 1896) was the son of the prominent Presbyterian minister Samuel Cox. Upon entering the Episcopal Church, the boy altered his name to Coxe. He was educated at the University of the City of New York and General Theological Seminary. Ordained in 1842, he served as rector in churches in Connecticut, Maryland, and finally in New York City at Calvary Church. He was elected bishop coadjutor of western New York in 1865.

Coxe was a strong voice of the theologically conservative Anglican, opposing the views of men such as Phillips Brooks. His poetry was written early in life and collected in *Advent,* 1837, *Christian Ballads,* 1840, and *Athanasion,* 1842. Though he was a member of the 1866-74 hymnal commission, he would not allow his poems to be included in the 1871 Episcopal *Hymnal.* Other writings include *Impressions of England,* 1855, *Sermons on Doctrine and Duty,* 1855, and a commentary on the history of the Church of England, *L'Episcopat de l'occident,* 1874.

Author: How Beauteous Were the Marks Divine (80)
O Where Are Kings and Empires Now (308)

Croft, William (baptized at Nether Eatington, Warwickshire, England, December 30, 1678; d. Bath, England, August 14, 1727) was a chorister in John Blow's choir at Chapel Royal, 1700, and was co-organist with Jeremiah Clark in 1704. Upon Clark's death, Croft was made organist. In 1708 he was named as Blow's successor at Westminster Abbey, while maintaining the position of master of the children and composer at Chapel Royal. Oxford awarded him the Mus.D. degree in 1713, after his 2 odes, *Musicus Apparatus Academicus,* had been approved. In 1725 he helped organize the Academy of Vocal Music.

In early life Croft composed for the theater. His most important sacred publication is the 2-volume *Musica Sacra,* 1724. This was the first church music engraved in score on plates. Many of his psalm tunes are contained in *The Divine Companion or David's Harp New Tun'd* (London, 1707) and the 1708 Supplement and mark the transition to the eighteenth-century style of English psalmody.

Erik Routley in *Companion to Congregational Praise* has judged Croft as the "greatest English composer of hymn-tunes between Lawes and Parry" on the strength of only 2 of his hymn tunes—HANOVER and BINCHESTER.

> Composer: Out of the Deep (**671**, p. 458)
> We Praise Thee, O God (**665**, pp. 464-65)
> Attributed composer: HANOVER (**409**, p. 436)
> ST. ANNE (**28, 308**, p. 313)
> ST. MATTHEW (**457**, p. 143)

Croly, George (b. Dublin, Ireland, August 17, 1780; d. Holborn, England, November 24, 1860) was a graduate of the University of Dublin (M.A. 1804). He was ordained in the Church of Ireland and ministered in Ireland until 1810 when he went to London where he pursued a brilliant literary career. Croly was a political and religious conservative sharply critical of what he considered the latitudinarianism of his day. In 1835 he became rector of the united benefices of St. Bene't Sherehog and St. Stephen's, Walbrook, and his bold preaching attracted great numbers of people from a broad cross section of society. In 1831, the University of Dublin conferred the LLD. degree upon him.

> Author: Spirit of God, Descend upon My Heart (**138**)

Crosby, Fanny Jane (b. Southeast Putnam County, N.Y., March 24, 1820; d. Bridgeport, Conn., February 12, 1915) was blind at 6 weeks of age but began writing verse at the age of 8. At 12 she entered the New York City School for the Blind, where she later taught grammar, rhetoric, and Roman and American history. In 1858 she was married to the blind musician Alexander Van Alstyne and shortly afterward began her amazing hymn-writing career.

The total output of her religious verse has been estimated at 8,500, and for 100 years her poems have served as the norm for "successful" gospel hymn writing. William J. Reynolds states that "much of her writing was done to order. For Biglow and Main she produced three hymns a week for an indefinite period of time."

Her songs reached England by way of the Moody-Sankey revivals, and she supplied a great number of texts for gospel hymn composers such as Bradbury, Doane, Lowry, Sankey, Kirkpatrick, and others. Much of her writing was published under a pen name including Ella Dale, Mrs. Kate Grinley, and Miss Viola V. A.

Mrs. Van Alstyne was a lifelong Methodist and spent most of her life in New York City.

> Author: All the Way My Savior Leads Me (205)
> Blessed Assurance, Jesus Is Mine (224)
> I Am Thine, O Lord (159)
> Jesus Is Tenderly Calling (110)
> Jesus, Keep Me Near the Cross (433)
> Pass Me Not, O Gentle Savior (145)
> Rescue the Perishing (175)
> Savior, More Than Life to Me (226)
> Thou My Everlasting Portion (176)

Crotch, William (b. Green's Lane, Norwich, England, July 5, 1775; d. Taunton, England, December 29, 1847) displayed extraordinary musical talent as a small child. At the age of 4 he gave public recitals in London; at 11 he studied at Cambridge with John Randall, whom he assisted at the organs at Trinity and King's colleges, and he began theological studies when only 13. In 1790 Crotch became organist of Christ Church, graduating with a B.M. degree in 1794 and a Mus.D. degree in 1799. During the years 1797-1807 he served there as professor of music. He moved to London and was made principal of the newly founded Royal Academy of Music, 1822-32.

Crotch is best known for his chants, numbering 74. He also composed 2 oratorios—*The Captivity of Judah,* 1789, and *Palestine,* 1812—10 anthems, 3 organ concertos, piano sonatas, an ode, a glee, and the motet *Methinks I Hear the Full Celestial Choir.* His theoretical works include *Elements of Music Composition,* 1812, 1833, 1856, and *Practical Thorough Bass.* A list of his compositions was compiled by John S. Bumpus and printed in *Musical News,* April 17 and 24, 1897.

> Composer: Blessed Art Thou, O Lord (668, p. 442)
> Blessed Be the Lord God of Israel (666, p. 443)
> Arranger: ST. MICHAEL (16, 114, 277. 477, 810, 812, p. 221)

Crüger, Johann (b. Grossbreesen bei Guben, Prussia, April 9, 1598; d. Berlin, February 23, 1662) was educated at the Jesuit College of Olmütz and at Regensburg. At Regensburg he studied with the cantor Paul Homberger and served as cantor at St. Nicholas' Church in Berlin, 1622-62, during which time he founded and directed the famous choir. Crüger's *Praxis Pietatis Melica,* first published in 1647, went through several editions. Four additional collections of tunes and texts reflect an intense interest on the part of this remarkable composer and compiler for the promotion of congregational singing. His musical abilities also found expression in the standard seventeenth-century forms as well as several theoretical works.

> Composer: GRÄFENBERG (134, 262, 340, 341, p. 142)
> HERZLIEBSTER JESU (412, p. 70)
> JESU, MEINE FREUDE (220, p. 249)
> NUN DANKET (49, p. 298)
> SCHMÜCKE DICH (318, p. 165)

Crum, John Macleod Campbell (b. Mere Old Hall, Cheshire, England, October 12, 1872; d. Farnham, Surrey, England, December 19, 1958) was educated at Eton and New College, Oxford (B.A. 1895, M.A. 1901). He was domestic chaplain to Francis Pager, bishop of Oxford, and served as vicar at Mentmore with Ledburn, Buckingham, rector of Farnham, 1913-28, and canon of Canterbury, 1928-43.

Crum's publications include *Road Mending on the Sacred Way,* 1924, *The Original Jerusalem Gospel,* 1927, *St. Mark's Gospel, Two Stages of Its Making,* 1936, and several works for children (he had 6 of his own). In 1930 he published *Notes on the Old Glass of the Cathedral of Christ Church, Canterbury,* which reflected his intense interest in the history and architecture of the cathedral.

> Author: Now the Green Blade Riseth (441)

Cummings, William Hayman (b. Sidbury, Devonshire, England, August 22, 1831; d. London, England, June 6, 1915), a widely acclaimed singer and antiquarian, was instrumental in the founding of the Purcell Society and in 1882 authored Purcell's biography. He was a celebrated oratorio tenor in England and America and at the age of 16 sang in the premiere performance of Mendelssohn's *Elijah* with the composer conducting.

Cummings composed the cantata *The Fairy Ring*, 1873, some church music, glees, and part songs. In 1900 the University of Dublin conferred the Mus.D. degree upon him.

Adapter: MENDELSSOHN (388, pp. 210-11)

Cuninggim, Maud Merrimon (b. Raleigh, N.C., March 7, 1874; d. Knoxville, Tenn., May 2, 1965) was the daughter of United States Senator Augustus S. Merrimon. As a young girl her interests included literary and musical expressions. She once sang in the White House during the administration of Grover Cleveland. Her formal education included the diploma from Peace Institute in Raleigh, 1892, and Scarritt College, Nashville, Tenn. (B.A. 1926, M.A. 1930).

Mrs. Cuninggim was a prolific writer of poems, hymns, articles for newspapers and denominational publications. She and her husband devoted the bulk of their lives to Scarritt College, where he was president.

Author: O Living Christ, Chief Cornerstone (349)

Cutler, Henry Stephen (b. Boston, Mass., October 13, 1824; d. Boston, December 5, 1902) studied music in America and Europe and was greatly influenced by English cathedral music. He returned to Boston in 1846 and served as organist at Grace Church and the Church of the Advent. At the latter church he organized a choir of men and boys, the first surpliced choir in America, reflecting the influence of the Oxford Movement upon him. From Boston he went to Trinity Church in New York City and remained during the years 1858-65. Later he served churches in Brooklyn, Providence, Philadelphia, and Troy, before retiring to Boston in 1885. In 1864 Columbia University conferred upon him the Mus.D. degree.

Cutler's publications include *Trinity Psalter*, 1864, and *Trinity Anthems*, 1865. Leonard Ellinwood in *The History of American Church Music* has provided a detailed description of the influence of the Oxford Movement upon Anglican church music in this country, and in particular the work of Cutler.

Composer: ALL SAINTS NEW (419, p. 400)

Cutts, Peter Warwick (b. Birmingham, England, June 4, 1937) was educated at Clare College, Cambridge (B.A. 1961, M.A. 1965) and Mansfield College, Oxford (B.A. 1963, theology). He has held positions in the music department of Huddersfield College of Technology and in the music and religious studies departments of Oastler College of Education in Huddersfield. Presently he is lecturer in music at Bretton Hall College of Education near Wakefield, Yorkshire.

He is the composer of several hymn tunes.

Composer: WYLDE GREEN (**62**, p. 193)

Damon (Daman), William (b. c. 1540; d. c. 1590) was one of Queen Elizabeth's musicians and probably the earliest composer to set the psalms in the vernacular to part music. His work appeared from the presses of John Day (*The Psalms of David in English Metre,* 1579) and Thomas Est (*The Former Book of Music of M. William Daman,* 1591), with words from the Sternold-Hopkins version of the psalter, printed in 4 separate part books.

Source: SOUTHWELL (**284**, pp. 276-77)
WINDSOR (**414, 428**, pp. 114-15)

Daniel ben Judah (Jehuda) Dayyan (late fourteenth century [?]) is presumed to be the arranger of the Hebrew Yigdal or doxology, for use by precentor and congregation in antiphonal singing.

Source: Praise to the Living God (**30**)

Darwall, John (b. Haughton, Staffordshire, England, baptized January 13, 1731; d. Walsall, England, December 18, 1789) was educated at Manchester Grammar School and Brasenose College, Oxford (B.A. 1756). Darwall became curate and in 1769 vicar of Walsall. His musical compositions include 2 volumes of sonatas for the piano and tunes for all 150 psalms (*New Version*), in 3 volumes.

Composer: DARWALL'S 148TH (**483**, p. 358)

Davies, Henry Walford (b. Oswestry, Shropshire, England, September 6, 1869; d. Wrington, Somerset, England, March 11, 1941) was born of nonconformist Welsh parentage. At the age of 12 he became a chorister at St. George's Chapel, Windsor. During the years 1885-90 he was assistant to the organist Walter Parratt. His positions include teacher at the Royal College of Music, 1895-1903, conductor of the London Bach Choir, 1903-7, and the London Church Choir Association, 1901-13; organist of Temple Church, 1890-1919, and professor of music at the University of Wales, 1919-26. He was knighted in 1922. In 1934 he succeeded Edward Elgar as Master of the King's Music. Oxford conferred the Mus.D. degree upon him in 1935.

Though a prolific composer, editor, and writer, Davies is better remembered for his pioneer work in educational radio. Erik Routley in *Twentieth-Century Church Music* has written that Davies' "most remarkable contribution to church music was his advocacy of 'speech-rhythm' chanting of the Psalms: hardly less important was his championship of congregational hymn-singing." Davies and his students at the University of Wales experimented considerably in hymn-tune writing.

Among Davies' many publications are *The Church Anthem Book* with H. G. Ley, 1933, and *Music and Worship* with Harvey Grace, 1935. H. C. Colles wrote his biography in 1943.

> Composer: CHILDHOOD (525, pp. 178-79)
> God Be in My Head (813, pp. 447-48)

Davis, Katherine Kennicott (b. St. Joseph, Mo., June 25, 1892) was educated at Wellesley College (B.A.) and studied privately with Stuart Mason, Nadia Boulanger, and Thomas Whitney Surette. At Surette's Concord Summer School of Music, founded in 1914, in Miss Davis' words, "[Surette] first aroused my enthusiasm for choral music. He did the same for hundreds of others."

Miss Davis' works include 2 operettas, an Easter musical drama, 10 choral collections, and hundreds of choral and piano arrangements and original settings. Her 3 hymn tunes appearing in the hymnal were requested by the hymnal committee, and they are her first to be included in any denominational hymnal.

> Composer: MASSACHUSETTS (485, p. 184)
> SURETTE (408, p. 132)
> WACHUSETT (96, p. 231)

Davis, Ozora Stearns (b. Wheelock, Vt., July 30, 1866; d. en route from Topeka to Kansas City, Kan., March 15, 1931), Congregational minister, educator, and theologian, was educated at Dartmouth, where he received the B.A. in 1889, Hartford Theological Seminary, and the University of Leipzig, where he was awarded the M.A. and Ph.D. in 1896. He served Congregational churches in New England before his election as president of Chicago Theological Seminary, 1909-20. During the years 1927-29 he acted as moderator of the National Council of Congregational Churches.

Davis was the author of several books on preaching and the social aspects of the gospel.

> Author: At Length There Dawns the Glorious Day (189)
> We Bear the Strain of Earthly Care (202)

Day (Daye or Daie), John (b. Dunwich, Suffolk, England, 1522; d. Walden, Essex, England, July 23, 1584) was the printer of the first church music book in English—*Certain Notes Set Forth in Four and Three Parts to Be Sung*, 1560. According to the *Dictionary of National Biography*, "He is the first English letter-founder of whom we possess authentic records, and his new Anglo-Saxon, Italic, Roman and Greek types are remarkably fine."

> Source: ST. FLAVIAN (313, p. 109)

Dearle, Edward (b. Cambridge, England, March 2, 1806; d. Camberwell, London, England, March 20, 1891) was educated at Cambridge (B.M. 1836, Mus.D. 1842) and served as organist in Blackheath, Wisbech, and at St. Mary's, Warwick. During the years 1835-64 he was the organist at the parish church and master of the song school at Newark upon Trent.

Dearle composed hymn tunes, anthems, oratorios, and some service music.

> Composer: PENITENTIA (327, p. 215)

Dearmer, Percy (b. Somerset House, Kilburn, Middlesex, England, February 27, 1867; d. Westminster, England, May 29, 1936) was educated at Westminster School and Christ Church, Oxford (B.A. 1890,

M.A. 1896) . He was ordained deacon in 1891, priest in 1892. Dearmer served several curacies before becoming vicar of St. Mary's, Primrose Hill, London, 1901-15; secretary of the London branch of the Christian Social Union, 1891-1912; chairman of the League of Arts; and chaplain in World War I to the British Red Cross in Serbia, during which time he received the Serbian Red Cross Decoration. He became professor of ecclesiastical art at King's College, London, and in 1931 was made canon of Westminster.

Dearmer wrote several books on the history of worship. With Ralph Vaughan Williams he edited *The English Hymnal,* 1906. With Martin Shaw and Vaughan Williams he produced *Songs of Praise,* 1925, *The Oxford Book of Carols,* 1928, and *Songs of Praise Enlarged,* 1931. He was the compiler of *Songs of Praise Discussed,* 1933, the handbook to *Songs of Praise.* About 10 of his translations and hymns are in common use.

Dearmer's interests were wide and extended over 50 publications dealing with history, language, and the arts. He ranks as one of the most influential leaders in the field of twentieth-century English hymnody.

> Author: Book of Books, Our People's Strength (370)
> Translator: Father, We Praise Thee (504)
> Adapter: He Who Would Valiant Be (155)

DeLamarter, Eric (b. Lansing, Mich., February 18, 1880; d. Orlando, Fla., May 17, 1953) studied with George Fairclough and Wilhelm Middelschulte in this country and with Félix Alexandre Guilmant and Charles Marie Widor in France. He was the organist at various Chicago churches, assistant conductor of the Chicago Symphony, 1918-36, and music critic for several Chicago newspapers.

DeLamarter composed many works for orchestra, organ, and solo voice.

> Composer: Amen (822, p. 442)

Dexter, Henry Martyn (b. Plympton, Mass. August 13, 1821; d. Boston, Mass., November 13, 1890) was educated at Yale (B.A. 1840), received the B.D. from Andover Theological Seminary in 1844, and was ordained the same year for the Congregational ministry. He served pastorates in Manchester, N.H., and at the Berkeley Street Congregational Church in Boston, 1849-67. The foremost historian of American Congregationalism, Dexter was also editor of the *Congregationalist and Recorder.*

According to his son Morton Dexter, Dexter "never regarded himself as a poet and never gave much attention to versifying." Only one hymn translation was ever published, but it has been in common use for over 125 years.

Translator: Shepherd of Eager Youth (86)

Dietterich, Philip Richard (b. Buffalo, N.Y., September 17, 1931) was educated at Ohio Wesleyan University (B.M. 1955), Boston University School of Theology (S.T.B. 1958), and Union Theological Seminary School of Sacred Music in New York (M.S.M. 1966). He has served as director of music at Trinity Methodist Church in Youngstown, Ohio, 1959-62, and at First Methodist Church in Westfield, N.J., since 1962.

As a consultant to the service music subcommittee of the 1964 hymnal committee, Dietterich assisted in the selection of music for that portion of the hymnal. He is the composer of many anthems and arrangements for church school publications and is an authority on music for children and youth, and lectures on this subject at Union Theological Seminary School of Sacred Music. He has served as jurisdictional representative and vice-president of the National Fellowship of Methodist Musicians and is a ministerial member of the New Jersey Annual Conference.

Composer: Communion Service in E Minor (833–837, p. 444)

Dix, William Chatterton (b. Bristol, England, June 14, 1837; d. Cheddar, Somersetshire, England, September 9, 1898) was educated at Bristol Grammar School. Language and poetry were an avocation for Dix; he was a businessman in Glasgow in marine insurance. He translated hymns from Greek and Ethiopian and wrote a number of original ones, the latter published in *Hymns of Love and Joy,* 1861, and *Altar Songs, Verses on the Holy Eucharist,* 1867.

Author: As with Gladness Men of Old (397)
       To Thee, O Lord, Our Hearts We Raise (524)
       What Child Is This (385)

Doane, George Washington (b. Trenton, N.J., May 27, 1799; d. Burlington, N.J., April 27, 1859) prepared for a career in law at Union College, Schenectady, N.Y. (B.A. 1818), but turned to theological study at the newly formed General Theological Seminary in New York City. He was ordained priest in 1823 and served as assistant at Trinity Church, Hartford, Conn. He was professor of rhetoric and belles-lettres at Washington (Trinity) College, Hartford, Conn., assistant and then rector of Trinity Church in Boston, 1828-32, and was consecrated bishop of New Jersey in 1832.

Doane was a man of great energy and administrative ability and a principal promoter of the missionary movement and of educational institutions. He published an American edition of John Keble's *Christian Year* in 1834. Many of his hymns were included in *Songs by the Way, Chiefly Devotional,* published by him in 1824 and reprinted in 1859 and 1875. He ranks as one of the first American writers and supporters of hymns and hymn singing as distinguished from psalmody.

Author: Softly Now the Light of Day (494)
Thou Art the Way: To Thee Alone (75)

Doane, William Croswell (b. Boston, Mass., March 2, 1832; d. Albany, N.Y., May 17, 1913) was the son of George Washington Doane. He was educated at Burlington College in New Jersey (B.A. 1850, M.A. 1852). He later received another M.A. from Trinity College in 1863. After ordination he became his father's assistant at Burlington in 1853, then rector at St. John's Church in Hartford, Conn., 1860-64, and at St. Peter's Church in Albany, N.Y., 1867-69.

Doane became the first bishop of Albany in 1869 and was highly regarded by all of the churches. He served as chairman of the commission which prepared the Episcopal *Hymnal* of 1892. Later he wrote the biography of his father, from whom he inherited an intense devotion for foreign missions and social betterment of all men.

He was awarded honorary degrees by Trinity, Columbia, Hobart, Union, and Pennsylvania, and by Oxford, Cambridge, and Dublin.

Author: Ancient of Days (459)

Doane, William Howard (b. Preston, Conn., February 3, 1832; d. South Orange, N.J., December 24, 1915) collaborated with Fanny

Crosby and the Moody-Sankey evangelistic enterprise in providing the musical settings for hymns and in editing collections. He was a cotton manufacturer and a Baptist layman of considerable religious and civil influence in Cincinnati from 1860 until the turn of the century. He wrote more than 2,200 tunes, and over 40 of his collections were used widely in revival and Sunday school meetings. As a benefactor of Denison University, Ohio, Doane was given the Mus.D. degree in 1875.

Composer: EVERY DAY AND HOUR (226, p. 367)
I AM THINE (159, p. 225)
MORE LOVE TO THEE (185, p. 287)
NEAR THE CROSS (433, p. 246)
PASS ME NOT (145, p. 352)
PRECIOUS NAME (87, p. 385)
RESCUE (175, p. 360)

Doddridge, Philip (b. London, England, June 26, 1702; d. Lisbon, Portugal, October 26, 1751) was the son of a London merchant. His mother was of Lutheran parentage. His life parallels Isaac Watts's in that he chose to be schooled at one of the dissenting academies at Kibworth in Leicestershire. At the age of 21 he began to preach and eventually became the head of an academy in Northampton, where he remained for 22 years. His writings include *The Rise and Progress of Religion in the Soul,* 1745, and some 400 hymns, all published after his death, which, like Watts's, were used as extensions of the sermon topic of the day.

Bernard Manning has described Doddridge as the "scholarly saint and sweet singer of Israel." Louis F. Benson has accounted Doddridge the "first scholar in the school of Watts."

Author: Awake, My Soul, Stretch Every Nerve (249)
Great God, We Sing That Mighty Hand (509)
How Gentle God's Commands (53)
Let Zion's Watchmen All Awake (335)
O Happy Day, That Fixed My Choice (128)
See Israel's Gentle Shepherd Stand (312)
The King of Heaven His Table Spreads (325)

Douglas, Charles Winfred (b. Oswego, N.Y., February 15, 1867; d. Santa Rosa, Calif., January 18, 1944), the son of a schoolteacher, had his first experiences in church music at the age of 16 as organist in the local Presbyterian church. He entered Syracuse University (B.M. 1891) and sang in the cathedral choir there and was organist at a mission parish. After graduation, he was for a time an instructor in vocal music at Syracuse University before he moved to New York City in 1892 as organist-choirmaster of the Church of Zion and St. Timothy. He returned to Syracuse for seminary training at St. Andrew's Divinity School and was ordained deacon in 1893. His health broke, and he retired to Evergreen, Col. Here he served in a limited capacity at the Cathedral of St. John in the Wilderness, Denver, in the meantime founding the Mission of the Transfiguration at Evergreen and pursuing further theological study at St. Matthew's Hall in Denver. He was ordained priest in 1899 and did further preparation in music and liturgy in England, France, and Germany, 1903-6.

Canon Douglas' first wife was a physician, Mary Josepha Williams. They met at Evergreen when she assisted in his recovery from a severe lung malady. Together they provided the land for the mission at Evergreen. She died in 1938.

Douglas' travel and leadership in regard to music and liturgy were divided for the most part between Evergreen and its annual school of church music and the Community of St. Mary, Kenosha, Wisc., and the Community of St. Mary in Peekskill, N.Y. He was canon residentiary, later honorary canon of St. Paul's Cathedral in Fond du Lac. Wisc., and St. John's Cathedral in Denver. He served as vicar of the Mission of the Transfiguration at Evergreen, 1937-43. Various societies and professional organizations honored him for his service, and Nashotah Seminary in Wisconsin conferred upon him the Mus.D. degree in 1917.

Few individuals in American church music have so successfully pursued so many aspects of the profession as did Douglas. For a period of almost 40 years his work dominated the liturgical, linguistic, and musical life of the Protestant Episcopal Church. He served as musical editor of the *New Hymnal,* 1916 (music edition 1918) , and of its successor *The Hymnal 1940.* Douglas' unique contribution in the field of plainsong is widely acknowledged, and his settings and adaptations were published in the definitive *Monastic Diurnal,* 1932, with the music edition nearly complete on his death. As both priest and musician he effected a bridge between the 2 professions unparalleled in

American Protestant Episcopal church music. His Hale Lectures at Seabury-Western Seminary, 1935, were published in 1937 as *Church Music in History and Practice* (revised by Leonard Ellinwood in 1962). At his request in 1941 he was relieved of the work begun in 1939 as chairman of the *The Hymnal 1940 Companion,* and his widow Anne Woodward Douglas and Leonard Ellinwood continued his work.

Douglas had a wide range of interests which included the study of Indian culture and artifacts. He was program annotator for the Denver Symphony Orchestra during the years 1937-41. He also edited music for general church music publications.

The resolution of the joint commission on the revision of the *Hymnal 1940* sums up Douglas' work:

He was Catholic in the complete sense of the word, a member of the Universal Church who was happily at home in all parts of it, and who entered with the same sympathy and fidelity into the translation of Latin Office Hymns and of Evangelical Chorales derived from the Protestant Reformation in Germany.

A generation after his death, Douglas' influence is still evident in the present liturgical and hymnological renewal evidenced in non-Anglican churches in this country.

Composer: ST. DUNSTAN'S (155, p. 214)
Arranger: CONDITOR ALME (78, p. 161)
DIVINUM MYSTERIUM (357, pp. 345-46)
FAR-OFF LANDS (85, 512, p. 335)

Draper, William Henry (b. Kenilworth, Warwickshire, England, December 19, 1855; d. Clifton, Bristol, England, August 9, 1933) received his education at Cheltenham College and Keble College, Oxford. He was ordained in 1880 and served various churches as curate, vicar, and rector, becoming master of the Temple in London, 1919-30. His publications include *The Victoria Book of Hymns,* 1897, *The Way of the Cross, Hymns for Tunes by Orlando Gibbons,* 1925, and many translations of Greek and Latin hymns.

Translator: All Creatures of Our God and King (60)

Duffield, George, Jr. (b. Carlisle, Pa., September 12, 1818; d. Bloomfield, N.J., July 6, 1888), was the son of a prominent Presbyterian minister. He was educated at Yale (B.A. 1837) and Union Theological Seminary in New York. He served pastorates in Bloomfield, N.J.; Philadelphia, Pa.; Adrian, Mich.; Galesburg, Ill.; and Ann Arbor and Lansing, Mich. Knox College conferred the D.D. degree upon him in 1871.

Duffield was independently wealthy and spent his means in the establishment of small congregations and in evangelistic endeavors.

Author: Stand Up, Stand Up for Jesus **(248)**

Dwight, Timothy (b. Northampton, Mass., May 14, 1752; d. Philadelphia, Pa., January 11, 1817) was a grandson of Jonathan Edwards. This foremost hymnologist of his day was educated at Yale, graduating at the age of 17. He was a tutor at Yale during the years 1771-77, and during the Revolutionary War he served as chaplain and gained the admiration of George Washington. He was a Congregational minister at Fairfield, Conn., 1783-95, where he also administered an academy. Called to the presidency of Yale, he served with distinction as an administrator, teacher, and chaplain. His chapel preaching on *Theology Explained and Defended* deeply influenced the religious life of Yale and other campuses in New England.

Dwight's revision of Isaac Watts's *Psalms of David* was published in 1801. It was popularly titled *Dwight's Watts,* but the title-page read:

THE PSALMS OF DAVID, imitated in the language of the New Testament, and applied to the Christian use and worship. By I. Watts, D.D. A new edition, in which the Psalms omitted by Dr. Watts are versified, local passages are altered, and a number of Psalms are versified anew, in proper metres. By Timothy Dwight, D.D., President of Yale-College. At the request of the General Association of Connecticut. To the Psalms is added a Selection of Hymns. Hartford; 1801.

Author: I Love Thy Kingdom, Lord **(294)**

Dykes, John Bacchus (b. Kingston upon Hull, Yorkshire, England, March 10, 1823; d. Ticehurst, Sussex, England, January 22, 1876) was educated at Cambridge (B.A. 1847) where he helped to found the University Musical Society. He was ordained deacon in 1847 and later priest at Malton, Yorkshire. Moving in 1849 to Durham, he became minor canon and precentor, receiving the Mus.D. degree from the

University of Durham in 1861. He was given the parish of St. Oswald's, Durham, which he served until the year of his death.

Besides his 300 hymn tunes, Dykes composed Service in F, a musical setting of Psalm 23, anthems, and part songs. He remains of all the Victorian composers of hymn tunes the most representative and successful; his tunes are standard repertory for all major denominational hymnbooks in this country, over 100 years after their introduction by *Hymns Ancient and Modern*. Erik Routley in *The Music of Christian Hymnody* has written that among "Victorians, Dykes is a man of great moderation and musical sense." Arthur Hutchings appraises Dykes in this way: "His failures as well as his successes show him to have been a priest first and a composer a long way afterwards," which is to say that Dykes wrote in popular style for popular taste and was the best of those who did just that.

For a complete biography on Dykes, see J. T. Fowler, *The Life and Letters of John Bacchus Dykes*, 1897.

> Composer: BLAIRGOWRIE (173, p. 344)
> DOMINUS REGIT ME (67, p. 395)
> KEBLE (146, 152, p. 182)
> LUX BENIGNA (272, pp. 263-64)
> MELITA (407, 538, p. 168)
> NICAEA (26, p. 217)
> ST. AGNES (82, 193, 516, p. 208)
> VOX DILECTI (117, p. 226)

Dyson, George (b. Halifax, Yorkshire, England, May 28, 1883; d. September 28, 1964) studied at the Royal Academy of Music, where he won the Mendelssohn prize and for 47 years was the recipient of this traveling scholarship. He was a distinguished educator, writer, lecturer, and composer, and was knighted in 1941. During the years 1937-52 he served as director of the Royal College of Music.

Dyson's compositions were written for orchestra, strings, and piano. He composed some church music, including 3 oratorios, *The Canterbury Pilgrims*, 1932, *Nebuchadnezzar*, 1935, and *Quo Vadis*, 1949. His books include *The New Music*, 1924, *The Progress of Music*, 1932, and an autobiography, *Fiddling While Rome Burns; A Musician's Apology*, 1954.

> Composer: Let Thy Word Abide in Us (796, p. 451)

Ebeling, Johann Georg (b. Lüneburg, July 8, 1637; d. Stettin, Pomerania, March, 1676) was appointed the successor to Johann Crüger at St. Nicholas' Church and served as a faculty member of the Graues Kloster Gymnasium in 1662. In 1668 he became professor of music at the College of St. Charles in Stettin, also serving as cantor of the school. His most important work was his setting of 120 texts (113 tunes) of Paul Gerhardt's work in *Das andere Dutzend geistlicher Andachtslieder Herrn Paul Gerhardts mit neuen Melodien,* 1666-67, and *Evangelischer Lustgarten Herrn Pauli Gerhardt's* in 1669.

Composer: WARUM SOLLT ICH MICH DENN GRÄMEN (379, p. 78)

Edgar, Mary Susanne (b. Sundridge, Ontario, Canada, May 23, 1889) was educated at Havergal College and the University of Toronto and through correspondence courses at the University of Chicago. She is a graduate of the National Training School of the Y.W.C.A. in New York City. For many years she was associated with camp work and with the Y.W.C.A. in Canada. In 1922 she founded Camp Glen Bernard for Girls in northern Ontario.

Miss Edgar traveled widely until her retirement to Toronto in 1955. Her published works include 5 hymns written for interfaith and camping situations, the collected poems *Woodfire and Candlelight,* 1945, the book of essays *Under Open Skies,* 1955, and *A Christmas Wreath of Verse,* 1965.

Author: God, Who Touchest Earth with Beauty (273)

Edmeston, James (b. Wapping, London, England, September 10, 1791; d. Homerton, Hackney, Middlesex, England, January 7, 1867) was a prominent architect, surveyor, and teacher. During his life he composed over 2,000 hymns, many for his family's Sunday devotions. His concern for orphaned children led him to visit regularly the London Orphan Asylum, for whose children he wrote *Sacred Lyrics,* 1820, and *Infant Breathings,* 1846.

Author: Savior, Breathe an Evening Blessing (496)

Edson, Lewis, Sr. (b. Bridgewater, Mass., January 22, 1748; d. Mink Hollow [Woodstock], Conn., 1820) was of the second generation of the musical Edson family. An Anglican and a Tory, he moved to an obscure section of western Massachusetts after the French and Indian Wars, having served with his father in the British army. He was a blacksmith by trade but learned music, perhaps from his brother Obed. He was widely known for his singing voice. In 1769 he was leading music in a local singing school and led congregational music in an Anglican parish in Lanesboro, Mass. At this time he probably began writing tunes.

Edson's tunes came to the attention of the compilers of *The Chorister's Companion,* 1782, and Edson's 3 famous tunes appear there. Other tunes of his appear in *Federal Harmony,* 1790, and Lewis Edson, Jr.'s *Social Harmonist,* 1801.

In his book *Music and Musicians in Early America,* 1964, Irving Lowens has devoted a chapter to a discussion of the Edson family, and of this family he writes: "The Edsons are prototypes of an American civilization as yet unexcavated."

Composer: LENOX (**100, 122,** p. 97)

Ellerton, John (b. London, England, December 16, 1826; d. Torquay, Devonshire, England, June 15, 1893) was educated at King William's College on the Isle of Man and Trinity College, Cambridge (B.A. 1849, M.A. 1854). He was ordained priest in 1851 and served as curate at St. Nicholas', Brighton, 1850-52, vicar at Crewe Green, 1852-60, and as rector at Hinstock, 1860-72, at Barnes, Surrey, 1872-76, and at White Roding, Essex, 1876-86. Upon the break of his health in 1886, he spent some time in Switzerland and Italy, but later returned to White Roding.

Ellerton was active in hymn writing and hymnal compilation beginning with the first hymns he wrote for children in his Brighton parish and continuing through the 1889 edition of *Hymns Ancient and Modern.* Books of his hymns include *Church Hymns,* 1871, and *The London Mission Hymn Book,* 1884. He assisted Mrs. Carey Brock with *The Children's Hymn Book,* 1881. He wrote 68 hymns, most of them on the subject of special days and observances, and translated some, many of which are included in *Hymns, Original and Translated,* 1888.

John Julian has written of Ellerton:

The subjects of Mr. Ellerton's hymns, and the circumstances under which they were written, had much to do with the concentration of thought and terseness of expression by which they are characterized. The words which he uses are usually short and simple; the thought is clear and well stated; the rhythm is good and stately. Ordinary facts in sacred history and in daily life are lifted above the commonplace rhymes with which they are usually associated, thereby rendering the hymns bearable to the cultured and instructive to the devout.

No better description of the poetic ideal of the Victorian hymn has been stated.

> Author: Behold Us, Lord, a Little Space (549)
> God the Omnipotent (544)
> Savior, Again to Thy Dear Name We Raise (236)
> The Day Thou Gavest, Lord, Is Ended (500)
> Translator: Welcome, Happy Morning (452)

Elliott, Charlotte (b. Clapham, London, England, March 18, 1789; d. Brighton, East Sussex, England, September 22, 1871) was an invalid for the last 50 years of her life, during 40 of which she carried on an intimate "spiritual" correspondence with the Genevan evangelist César Malan. Miss Elliott's published verse, some 150 hymns, is contained in *The Invalid's Hymn Book*, 1834; *Psalms and Hymns for Public, Private, and Social Worship*, 1835-48, edited by her brother Henry; *Hours of Sorrow*, 1836; *Hymns for a Week*, 1839; and *Thoughts in Verse on Sacred Subjects*, 1869.

James Davidson in John Julian's *Dictionary of Hymnology* has written that "her verse is characterized by tenderness of feeling, plaintive simplicity, deep devotion, and perfect rhythm. For those in sickness and sorrow she has sung as few others have done."

> Author: Just as I Am, Without One Plea (119)
> O Holy Savior, Friend Unseen (144)

Ellor, James (b. Droylsden, Lancashire, England, 1819; d. Newburgh, N.Y., September 27, 1899) was a hatter by trade and choir director in the Wesleyan chapel at Droylsden. He migrated to America in 1843.

> Composer: DIADEM (72, p. 77)

Elvey, George Job (b. Canterbury, England, March 27 or 29, 1816; d. Windlesham, Surrey, England, December 9, 1893) was born into a musical family. He was a chorister at Canterbury Cathedral and studied with his brother Stephen and at the Royal Academy of Music. In 1838 he was awarded the B.M. from New College, Oxford, and by special action of the chancellor, the Mus.D. in 1840. In the meantime he had taken the position as organist of St. George's Chapel, serving from 1835 until 1882. He was knighted in 1871.

Elvey's works include 2 oratorios—*The Resurrection and Ascension,* 1840, and *Mount Carmel,* 1886—and odes, glees, anthems, and service music.

Composer: DIADEMATA (184, 250, 288, 455, p. 162)
ST. GEORGE'S WINDSOR (522, p. 158)

Emerson, Luther Orlando (b. Parsonsfield, Me., September 29, 1820; d. Hyde Park, Mass., October 1, 1915) was educated at Parsonsfield Seminary and at Effingham Academy and in medicine at Dracut Academy. His interest in music stemmed from his family, and he rejected a career in medicine to study music with I. B. Woodbury. He served as teacher and choir director in Salem, Mass., and after 8 years moved to a position with the publishing firm of Oliver Ditson Company, Boston. Emerson compiled more than 70 collections and conducted over 300 musical conventions. Findlay College in Ohio conferred the honorary Mus.D. degree upon him.

Harmonizer: AR HYD Y NOS (497, p. 201)

Est (or *Este, East,* or *Easte*), *Thomas* (b. London, England, c. 1540; d. London, January, 1608) was licensed to print in 1565. He published William Byrd's *Psalms, Sonnets and Songs of Sadness and Piety,* probably in 1587, and was the assignee of Byrd's printing patent. Est also published works by a number of other Tudor composers.

His *Whole Book of Psalms,* 1592, was unique in 2 ways: It was the first to be printed in full score rather than separate books for each voice, and the tunes were identified by specific names. The most famous publisher of his time, Est printed in 1603 the *Triumphs of Oriana,* a compilation of madrigals honoring Queen Elizabeth. Through his publishing he introduced into England the Italian School, thereby laying the groundwork for the English madrigal, which became so popular in Elizabethan England.

Source: WINCHESTER OLD (54, 70, 131, 394, pp. 139-40)

Evans, David (b. Resolven, Glamorganshire, Wales, February 6, 1874; d. Rhosllan-nerchrugog, near Wrexham, May 17, 1948) was educated at Arnold College, Swansea, the University College, Cardiff, and Oxford University where he received the Mus.D. degree. He served as organist of the Jewin Street Welsh Presbyterian Church in London. During the years 1903-39 he was professor of music at the University College in Cardiff and leading judge of the National Eisteddfod. From 1916 to 1921 he was editor of *Y Cerddor,* the Welsh musical periodical.

Hymnals have been enriched through Evans' hymn tunes and harmonizations. He served as music editor for the 1927-30 edition of the *Church Hymnary.* Evans composed cantatas, anthems, and services, including a cantata for chorus and orchestra, *The Coming of Arthur,* and *Alcestis,* for chorus and string orchestra.

> Harmonizer: LLANFAIR (443, p. 244)
> NYLAND (230, p. 237)

Evans, William Edwin (b. Baltimore, Md., July 11, 1851; d. Richmond, Va., May 22, 1915) was educated at Randolph-Macon College, where he later became chaplain. He was a Methodist minister, with membership in the Baltimore Annual Conference and then in 1872 in the Virginia Annual Conference, where he served various churches. In 1892 he became an Episcopal rector and served the Church of the Advent in Birmingham, Ala.

> Author: Come, O Thou God of Grace (352)

Everest, Charles William (b. East Windsor, Conn., May 27, 1814; d. Waterbury, Conn., January 11, 1877) was graduated from Trinity College, Hartford, in 1838. He was ordained in 1842 and served as rector of the Episcopal church in Hampden, Conn., for 31 years. In addition to his duties as rector, he was in charge of a school. One of Everest's hymns still in common use was adapted from a poem in a collection Everest published at the age of 19, *Visions of Death and Other Poems.*

> Author: Take Up Thy Cross (160)

Ewing, Alexander (b. Old Machar, Aberdeen, Scotland, January 3, 1830; d. Taunton, Somersetshire, England, July 11, 1895) studied law at Marischal College in Aberdeen and some music at Heidelberg University. While not a professional musician, he was skilled at several instruments and sang in the Aberdeen Haydn Society and Harmonic Choir. At the outbreak of the Crimean War in 1855, Ewing took an army post in the commissariat department and served at Constantinople. In 1867 he married the celebrated authoress of children's books, Juliana Horatia Scott-Gatty. After further service in Australia and China, Ewing retired to Taunton in 1883. Only one musical composition is known to have been written by Ewing.

Composer: EWING (303, p. 243)

Faber, Frederick William (b. Calverly, Yorkshire, England, June 28, 1814; d. London, England, September 26, 1863) was educated at Balliol and University colleges, Oxford University (B.A. 1836). He was elected a fellow of University College in 1837. After ordination into the Church of England he was made rector of Elton, Huntingdonshire, in 1842. At one time he was a staunch supporter of the Anglican view of its own catholicity, but in 1845 he seceded to Rome and established in London a branch of the Priests of the Congregation of St. Philip Neri, of which John Henry Newman was superior.

Faber viewed his own contribution to hymnody as the Roman Catholic counterpart of William Cowper and John Newton, writing hymns with strong popular appeal. Erik Routley in *Hymns and the Faith* points out, however, that there was another aspect of Faber's writing. These lines from a hymn written for the Roman Catholics in 1849 illustrate a style and subject matter foreign to the hymns that have survived:

> Ill masters good; good seems to turn
> To ill with greatest ease;
> And worst of all, the good with good
> Is at cross-purposes.

Faber wrote 150 hymns, all published after he became a Roman Catholic. His works include *Jesus and Mary—Catholic Hymns for Singing and Reading,* 1849 and 1852, *All for Jesus, or the Easy Ways of Divine Love,* 1853, and *Oratory Hymns,* 1854.

Author: Faith of Our Fathers (151)
There's a Wideness in God's Mercy (69)

Farrant, Richard (b. c. 1530; d. Windsor, England, 1581) was a gentleman of the Chapel Royal during the reign of Edward VI. In 1564 he became master of the choristers and lay clerk and organist of St. George's Chapel, Windsor. Farrant is an important figure in Elizabethan music. His sacred music is in use today and includes several anthems and Service in A Minor.

Composer: It Is a Good Thing to Give Thanks (**667**, p. 450)

Farrington, Harry Webb (b. Nassau, B.W.I., July 14, 1879; d. Asbury Park, N.J., October 25, 1931) was educated at Darlington Academy in Maryland, Dickinson Seminary, Syracuse University (B.A. 1907), and the Boston University School of Theology (S.T.B. 1910). He later received his M.A. degree from Harvard. A man of unusual talent and energy, Farrington was a pioneer in the field of weekday Christian education, inaugurating programs in 1914 in Gary, Ind., and in New York City, 1916. He was an ordained Methodist minister and served churches in the New York and New England conferences. During World War I he was recognized for his efforts in the physical education of the French military, 1918-19. During the years 1920-23 he was pastor of Grace Church in New York City, and until 1928 lectured in the public schools of New York City and was director of education for the Methodist Church Welfare League.

Farrington's publications and writings include 7 volumes of his poems, collected into 2 volumes by his widow in 1932, various books about leading figures in American history, and an autobiography of his youth, *Kilts to Togs,* 1930. Of his 29 hymns only 1 is in common use today.

Author: I Know Not How That Bethlehem's Babe (**123**)

Fawcett, John (b. Lidget Green, near Bradford, Yorkshire, England, January 6, 1739/40; d. Hebden Bridge, Yorkshire, England, July 25, 1817) as a 16-year-old apprentice to a tradesman in Bradford was deeply impressed by George Whitefield's preaching. He joined the Methodists for a time but united with the Baptists at Bradford in 1758. Fawcett began preaching in 1763, serving churches at Wainsgate, Yorkshire, and at Hebden Bridge. At Hebden Bridge he converted a portion of his home into a school for neighborhood children.

He declined offers to preach at Carter's Lane Chapel, London, and the presidency of the Baptist academy at Bristol, preferring to remain at Hebden Bridge. In 1811 Brown University, Providence, R.I., honored him with the D.D. degree.

In the Isaac Watts tradition Fawcett wrote hymns as an expression and exposition of the sermon. He was the author of many works of prose and poetry, the best known of which is *Devotional Commentary on the Holy Scriptures*, 1811. In 1782 more than 160 hymns of his were published as *Hymns Adapted to the Circumstances of Public Worship and Private Devotion.*

> Author: Blest Be the Tie That Binds (**306**)
> Lord, Dismiss Us with Thy Blessing (**165**)

Featherstone, William Ralph (b. Montreal, Quebec, Canada, July 23, 1846; d. Montreal, May 20, 1873) was a member of the Wesleyan Methodist Church in Montreal. According to William J. Reynolds, no information other than his parentage seems to be available.

> Author: Lord Jesus, I Love Thee (**166**)

Findlater, Sarah Laurie Borthwick (b. Edinburgh, Scotland, November 26, 1823; d. Torquay, Devonshire, England, December 25, 1907) was the sister of Jane Borthwick, with whom she published *Hymns from the Land of Luther*, 1854-62. Of the 122 translations Sarah produced 31.

> Translator: God Calling Yet! Shall I Not Hear (**105**)

Fink, Gottfried Wilhelm (b. Sulza, Thuringia, March 7, 1783; d. Halle, August 27, 1846) was an illustrious minister, editor, critic, and teacher. He studied at Leipzig during the years 1804-8 and began writing for the *Allgemeine musikalische Leitung* in 1808 and served as editor 1827-41. His publications include *Musikalischer Hausschatz der Deutschen* (Leipzig, 1843), *Die deutsche Liedertafel* (Leipzig, 1846), and many historical and theoretical works.

> Composer: BETHLEHEM (**343**, pp. 78-79)

Finlay, Kenneth George (b. London, England, February 3, 1882), a school music teacher, was educated at Robert Gordon's College in

Aberdeen, the Merchiston Castle School in Edinburgh, the Royal College of Music in London, and the Teacher's Training College in Jordanhill, Glasgow. A shipbuilder until 1928, he was a teacher of class-singing at Irvine, Ayrshire, 1930-47. He has published papers about safety of life at sea, 2 cantatas—*The Savior's Birth,* 1928, and *Before the Dawn,* 1938—hymn tunes, part songs, carols, and anthems.

Composer: AYRSHIRE (157, 255, p. 99)
GLENFINLAS (791, p. 450)

Fischer, William Gustavus (b. Baltimore, Md., October 14, 1835; d. Philadelphia, Pa., August 12, 1912) developed an interest in music and singing by attending singing schools while yet a small boy. Later he studied music while at the same time working in J. B. Lippincott's book bindery. He became widely acclaimed as a teacher of theory and director of choral festivals. During the years 1858-68 he was professor of music at Girard College in Philadelphia. Later he and John E. Gould established a retail piano business and music store. At an 1876 Moody-Sankey revival meeting in Philadelphia he conducted a chorus of 1,000 voices, and for the bicentennial of the landing of William Penn he led the chorus of the combined Welsh Societies.

Fischer wrote 200 tunes and published some Sunday school songs under the firm name Fischer and Gould.

Composer: COMING TO THE CROSS (116, p. 225)
HANKEY (149, p. 229)
THE ROCK OF REFUGE (245, p. 334)

Flemming, Friedrich Ferdinand (b. Neuhausen, Saxony, February 28, 1778; d. Berlin, May 27, 1813) prepared for the medical profession at Wittenberg, Jena, Vienna, and Trieste. A successful physician in Berlin, Flemming was also an amateur composer for male choral groups.

Composer: FLEMMING (144, p. 318)

Fortunatus, Venantius Honorius (b. Treviso, Italy, c. 530; d. Poitiers, France, c. 609) studied oratory and poetry at Ravenna. Tradition is that he was almost blind and that he received back his sight by anoint-

COMPANION TO THE HYMNAL

ing his eyes with oil from a lamp that burned before the altar of St. Martin of Tours in Ravenna. In 656 while on a pilgrimage to the tomb of St. Martin of Tours, he met Queen Rhadegonda. She persuaded Fortunatus to settle at Poitiers near a convent she had founded. He was admitted to the priesthood and in 599 became bishop of Poitiers. His literary output includes a collection of 250 poems.

Author: Welcome, Happy Morning (452)

Fosdick, Harry Emerson (b. Buffalo, N.Y., May 24, 1878; d. New York, N.Y., October 5, 1969), the distinguished American clergyman, was educated at Colgate University (B.A. 1900), Union Theological Seminary in New York City (B.D. 1904), and Columbia University (M.A. 1908). He was the recipient of many honorary degrees. Ordained a Baptist minister in 1903, he became pastor of First Baptist Church, Montclair, N.J., 1904-15. During the years 1908-15 he was a teacher of homiletics at Union and occupied the chair of practical theology, 1915-46. He served as pastor of the First Presbyterian Church, New York City, 1919-26, and at Park Avenue and Riverside churches, 1926-46.

Fosdick was at the center of the "liberal controversy" for over 30 years and was very influential in shaping the religious belief and thought of a generation of Protestant America. His radio broadcasts and writings, including 32 books, extended his preaching ministry far beyond the pulpit of Riverside Church, an interdenominational church built by John D. Rockefeller, Jr. His autobiography, *The Living of These Days*, was published in 1956.

Author: God of Grace and God of Glory **(470)**

Francis of Assisi (b. Assisi, Italy, c. 1182; d. Assisi, October 4, 1226) was the founder of the monastic order which bears his name. Born in wealth, he spent a frivolous youth until a serious illness caused him to dedicate his life to the imitation of Christ's life in prayer, poverty, and service to mankind. He was at home in the natural world of flowers, birds, and animals. His use of the French or Provençal troubadour style of song combined with his employment of the Italian vernacular is claimed by some scholars as the beginning of the Italian *laudi*.

Author: All Creatures of Our God and King **(60)**

Franck, Johann (b. Guben, Brandenburg, June 1, 1618; d. Guben, June 18, 1677) was educated at the University of Königsberg, the only major school to survive the Thirty Years' War. Here he was encouraged in his writing by Simon Dach and Heinrich Held. Returning to his home, he was elected to the town council and in 1661 became mayor. Franck was highly respected as a lawyer and public servant and was appointed to many positions of trust, including deputy from Guben to the Diet of Lower Lusatia in 1671. He did some translating from Latin, but his fame rests on his 100 pietistic hymns published in 1674, *Deutsche Gedichte, bestehend im geistlichen Zion.*

Author: Deck Thyself, My Soul, with Gladness (318)
Jesus, Priceless Treasure (220)

Franz, Ignaz (b. Protzau, Silesia, October 12, 1719; d. 1790) was a German Catholic hymnologist and compiler. He studied at Glaz and Breslau. Ordained priest at Olmütz in 1742, he served as chaplain at Gross-Glogau in 1753 and until his death was assessor at the apostolic vicar's office in Breslau. Among his published collections are *Katholisches Gesangbuch,* 1774 (?), and a tunebook, dated 1778, both important to eighteenth-century Catholic hymnody.

Attributed author: Holy God, We Praise Thy Name (8)

Frazier, Francis Philip (b. Santee, Neb., June 2, 1892; d. Yankton, S.D., September 29, 1964) was a third generation full-blooded Sioux Congregational minister and missionary. He was educated at the Santee Mission, Yankton Academy, and attended Mt. Herman School in Massachusetts and Dartmouth College. Frazier served in the A.E.F. in France and Germany, 1917-19. After war service he entered Oberlin College (B.A. 1922) and attended Garrett Seminary, Evanston, and Chicago Theological Seminary (B.D. 1925). Oberlin honored him with the D.H.L. degree in 1960 and Dartmouth the D.D. degree in 1964.

Frazier's service in the cause of Indian missions included Quaker missionary to the Kickapoo Indians in Oklahoma, 1924-32, superintendent of Native Churches, North Dakota, 1932-37, local church work at Ponca Creek, S.D., 1937-43, and at the Los Angeles Indian Center, 1943-47, Quaker missionary to the Osage Indians in Hominy, Okla.,

1947-56, and supervisor to five churches on the Standing Rock Indian Reservations, 1956 until his death in 1964.

See *Music Ministry,* June, 1968, for an extensive article about Frazier. His widow, Susie M. Frazier, has written a monograph on Frazier's life and work.

Author: Many and Great, O God (40)

Gardiner, William (b. Leicester, England, March 15, 1770; d. Leicester, November 16, 1853) was the son of a hosiery manufacturer and made his living in that same work. Besides his business pursuits he devoted his life to music, in particular the introduction of the music of Beethoven, Haydn, and Mozart into England. Business travels in Europe made it possible for Gardiner to know first hand the musicians and music of the early eighteenth century. His *Sacred Melodies,* 1812-15, containing hymn tune adaptations of melodies from eighteenth-century classics, became a sourcebook for nineteenth-century English hymnals. Lowell Mason adapted Gardiner's tunes and arranging methods for his collections.

Gardiner's *Music and Friends* (3 vols., 1838-53) contain reminiscences of his travels and contact with musicians. He also translated from the French Marie-Henri Beyle's *Lives of Haydn and Mozart* and wrote an important book on the science of acoustics, *The Music of Nature,* 1832. Erik Routley in *The Music of Christian Hymnody,* pp. 112-13, discusses the influence of Gardiner's adaptation of the classics in hymn tunes.

Source: GERMANY (**36, 160, 204, 351,** p. 169)

Gauntlett, Henry John (b. Wellington, Shropshire, England, July 9, 1805; d. Kensington, London, England, February 21, 1876) was a prolific composer of hymn tunes (some 10,000), church organist, and reformer in the field of organ construction. He was trained in both law and music. Gauntlett's activity in the fields of organ design, Gregorian music, and congregational song ranks him as an important figure in English Victorian church music, though Erik Routley in *The Music of Christian Hymnody* dismisses him as a "true and inspired master of the commonplace."

Gauntlett's work in the field of congregational song at Union Chapel, Islington, resulted in the "psalmody-class" as a way of training lay singers. Many of his tunes are contained in *The Congregational Psalmist* (1st ed., 1858).

Adapter: STUTTGART (63, 65, 334, 405, 496, p. 167)

Gawler, William (b. Lambeth, London, England, 1750; d. London, March 15, 1809) was the organist of the Royal Female Orphan Asylum at Lambeth. Here he compiled *Hymns and Psalms Used at the Asylum or House of Refuge for Female Orphans*, 1785-88, for use of the girls' choir.

Source: ST. MICHEL'S (171, p. 330)

Gay, Annabeth McClelland (b. Ottawa, Kan., April 18, 1925) is the daughter of a Presbyterian minister. Mrs. Gay was educated at Knox College (B.M.E. 1947) and Union Theological Seminary School of Sacred Music in New York City (M.S.M. 1949). She has served as choir director in Ohio churches served by her husband, a minister of the United Church of Christ.

Composer: SHEPHERDS' PIPES (202, p. 419)

George, Graham (b. Norwich, Norfolk, England, April 11, 1912) received his early musical training under Alfred Whitehead during the years 1932-36, who then was organist of Christ Church Cathedral, Montreal. From the University of Toronto George earned the B.M. in 1936 and the Mus.D. in 1939. He is an associate and fellow of the Canadian College of Organists, and his advanced studies include composition with Hindemith at Yale and conducting with Willem van Otterloo in Holland. Presently he is professor of music and resident musician at Queen's University, Kingston, Ontario, where he is director of student operatic, orchestral, and choral groups.

George has written for most media: 2 operas, 2 ballets, orchestral works, a concerto for flute and strings, quartets, and other chamber works, including the 1943 award-winning *Variations for Strings*. In addition to his music studies, his interest in philosophy has led to formal training in that field.

Composer: GRACE CHURCH, GANANOQUE (240, p. 177)
THE KING'S MAJESTY (425, p. 360)

Gerhardt, Paul (b. Gräfenhainichen, Saxony, March 12, 1607; d. Lübben, Saxe Merseburg, May 27, 1676) was the son of the mayor of the city. He was educated in the Elector's school at Grimma, 1622-27, and at the University of Wittenberg, 1628-42. He moved to Berlin about 1643 and became a tutor in the home of Andreas Barthold and later married Barthold's daughter, Anna Maria, in 1655. He preached in Berlin and was ordained in 1651, serving as pastor in Mittenwalde during the years 1651-57, as deacon at St. Nicholas' Church, 1657-66, and archdeacon and later as pastor at Lübben. Gerhardt's early life was deeply influenced by tragedy and marked by the Thirty Years' War. Four of his children died in infancy, and his wife died in 1668. During the years 1666-68 he was the center of theological and political controversy because of his refusal to sign the edict of Elector Frederick William I, which set limits on the discussion of Lutheran and Reform issues.

Gerhardt's hymns reflect a deep and abiding trust in a providential and loving God and mark the transition in German hymnody from confessional and ecclesiastical hymns to those of subjective pietistic and devotional content. The great popularity of his hymns, 132 in all, can be attributed to their timely appeal to a church and a people crushed by war and controversy. Many of his hymns appear in Johann Crüger's 1648 edition of *Praxis Pietatis Melica;* the composer was Gerhardt's associate at St. Nicholas'. Crüger's successor, Johann G. Ebeling, published many settings of Gerhardt's texts in his *Das andere Dutzend geistlicher Andachtslieder Herrn Paul Gerhardts mit neuen Melodien,* 1666-67. The first English translation of his works appears to be by John Wesley, 1739-40.

Catherine Winkworth, translator of 20 of his hymns, believed that in Gerhardt's work "the religious song of Saxony finds its purest and sweetest expression" and in evaluating his influence, stated that he was the "typical poet of the Lutheran Church as Herbert is of the English."

Author: All My Heart This Night Rejoices (379)
Give to the Winds Thy Fears (51)
Holy Ghost, Dispel Our Sadness (132)
Jesus, Thy Boundless Love to Me (259)
Translator: O Sacred Head, Now Wounded (418)

Gesius, Barthölomäus (b. Müncheberg, near Frankfort, c. 1555; d. Frankfort, c. 1613) had thorough training in both theology and music. A prolific writer, his compositions cover the full range of Lutheran liturgical music, including 10 collections of hymns and a setting of the *St. John Passion,* 1588. He was the cantor at Frankfort from 1592 until his death during the plague. He was also the author of a theoretical work, *Synopsis musicae practicae,* editions in 1609, 1615, and 1618. Gesius' family name is also spelled Göss or Gese.

Composer: DU FRIEDENSFÜRST, HERR JESU CHRIST (491, p. 390)

Giardini, Felice de (b. Turin, Italy, April 12, 1716; d. Moscow, June 8, 1796), a chorister at the Cathedral of Milan, studied violin with G. B. Somis. He was popular as a violinist and toured Germany and joined the Italian opera in London as concertmaster and conductor, becoming impresario in 1756. Giardini conducted the three Choirs Festival, 1770-76, and was concertmaster at the Pantheon Concerts, 1774-80. After additional tours of Italy and England, he traveled to Moscow, where he died. Giardini was a prolific composer of operas, string quartets, sonatas, overtures, concertos, and violin sonatas; yet he died penniless, seeming always to live beyond his means.

Composer: ITALIAN HYMN (3, 292, 352, pp. 129-30)

Gibbons, Orlando (baptized at Oxford, England, December 25, 1583; d. Canterbury, England, June 5, 1625) was a chorister at King's College at Cambridge, 1596. He was appointed organist of the Chapel Royal, 1601, and remained there the rest of his life. In 1606 he received the B.M. from Cambridge and in 1622 the honorary Mus.D. He was the outstanding organist of his time, as well as the composer of 40 anthems and services. In 1623 he was also named organist of Westminster Abbey where he conducted the music for the funeral of King James I, 1625.

In the field of hymnody, Gibbons' significant effort is contained in the 16 tunes and basses (the harmonizations were added by E. H. Fellowes and others) he provided for George Wither, *The Hymns and Songs of the Church*, 1623. None of Wither's texts have survived. (See John Julian's *Dictionary of Hymnology*, pp. 1289-90.) Some of Gibbons' tunes have survived and usually carry the numerical designation provided in the 1623 collection.

Composer: CANTERBURY (135, 311, 430, 530, pp. 130-31)
SONG 46 (229, p. 353)

Gill, Thomas Hornblower (b. Birmingham, England, February 10, 1819; d. Grove Park, Kent, England, March 4, 1906) was educated at King Edward's School. For many years he was a Unitarian, but later, because of study of Isaac Watts's hymns, he accepted more orthodox ways and aligned himself with the Anglican Evangelicals.

Gill wrote about 200 hymns and other published works: *The Golden Chain of Praise Hymns*, 1869, and *Luther's Birthday*, 1883. In the preface to *The Golden Chain* he wrote:

Hymns are not meant to be theological statements, expositions of doctrine, or enunciations of precepts; they are utterances of a soul in its manifold moods of hope and fear, joy and sorrow, love, wonder, and aspiration. . . . The best and most glorious hymns cannot be more exactly defined than as divine love songs.

Gill's hymns enjoyed great popularity during his lifetime, with over 80 in use in Britain and in America. Now only one remains in common use in contemporary American hymnals.

Author: We Come unto Our Fathers' God (58)

Gillman, Frederick John (b. Devizes, Wiltshire, England, February 25, 1866; d. Jordans, Beaconsfield, Buckinghamshire, England, February 18, 1949) was trained in the grocery trade and later became private secretary to the president of Rountree and Company, cocoa manufacturers. Gillman was originally a Congregationalist but in 1916 helped found the Society of Friends in England. He also was active in adult education, serving as national president of the Adult School

Movement, 1927-28. He was a founder-member of the Hymn Society of Great Britain and Ireland and joint chairman in its early years.

On the whole self-educated, Gillman did publish several important books on hymnology including *Evolution of the English Hymn,* 1927, *The Story of Our Hymns,* 1921, and *The Songs and Singers of Christendom,* 1911. He served as editor of *The Fellowship Hymn-Book,* 1909 and 1933.

Gillman's daughter, N. Mary Lawson, has furnished the biographical information on this author.

Author: God Send Us Men (**191**)

Gilmore, Joseph Henry (b. Boston, Mass., April 29, 1834; d. Rochester, N.Y., July 23, 1918) was educated at Phillips Andover Academy, Brown University (B.A. 1858), and Newton Theological Seminary, where he taught Hebrew, 1861-62. He preached in Philadelphia for a short time. Gilmore was an ordained Baptist minister, serving churches in New Hampshire and New York. He was editor of the Concord, N.H., *Daily Monitor,* 1864-65, and professor of English at the University of Rochester, 1868-1908. During the years 1870-78 he wrote editorials for the New York *Examiner.* His other publications include *The Art of Expression,* 1876, *Outlines of English and American Literature,* 1905, and *He Leadeth Me, and Other Religious Poems,* 1877.

Author: He Leadeth Me: O Blessed Thought (**217**)

Gladden, Washington (b. Pottsgrove, Pa., February 11, 1836; d. Columbus, Ohio, July 2, 1918) was educated at Owego Academy and Williams College. In 1860 he was ordained into the Congregational ministry and served churches in New York and Massachusetts before accepting the call to the First Congregational Church in Columbus, Ohio, where he served during the years 1882-1914.

As an early advocate of the social gospel, Gladden was editor of the *Independent* and contributed to much of the writing of social protest. His social creed, as declared in his *Recollections,* 1909, is as follows:

Because the Christian life is the noblest life; because it is more blessed to give than to receive, and better to minister than to be ministered unto;

because the good life is not found in separating yourself from your fellows, but by identifying yourself with them—therefore, let us be Christians. If the church would dare to preach and practice the things which Jesus Christ commanded, she would soon regain her lost power.

Gladden was moderator of the National Council of Congregational Churches, 1904-7.

Author: O Master, Let Me Walk with Thee (170)

Gläser, Carl Gotthelf (b. Weissenfels, May 4, 1784; d. Barmen, April 16, 1829) received his musical training from his father and at St. Thomas' School, Leipzig. An extraordinary violinist and teacher, he taught at Leipzig and Barmen. He composed many church compositions and was widely recognized as a choral director.

Composer: AZMON (1, 278, p. 254)

Gordon, Adoniram Judson (b. New Hampton, N.H., April 19, 1836; d. Boston, Mass., February 2, 1895) was educated at Brown University and Newton Theological Seminary. After ordination into the ministry in 1863 he served as pastor at the Baptist church at Jamaica Plain, Mass. In 1869 he went to the Clarendon Street Baptist Church, Boston. Gordon was active in evangelistic music and a close friend of Dwight L. Moody.

Two hymnals were edited by Gordon—*The Service of Song for Baptist Churches,* 1871, and *The Vestry Hymn and Tune Book,* 1872.

Composer: GORDON (166, p. 276)

Goss, John (b. Fareham, England, December 27, 1800; d. London, England, May 10, 1880) was the son of a parish organist. Goss trained with John Stafford Smith at the Chapel Royal and later with Thomas Attwood. He was organist of Stockwell Chapel, 1821-24, St. Luke's, Chelsea, 1824-37, and St. Paul's, London, succeeding Attwood in 1838 and serving until 1872. During the years 1827-74 he was professor of harmony at the Royal Academy of Music. Upon his retirement he was knighted, and an honorary Mus.D. degree was conferred by Cambridge in 1876.

Goss's compositions include anthems and glees. In 1826 he published *Parochial Psalmody;* in 1841 257 *Chants, Ancient and Modern;* with James Turle a 2-volume collection of cathedral services and anthems in 1846; was musical editor of W. Mercer, *Church Psalter and Hymn Book,* 1854; and in 1833 *Introduction to Harmony and Thorough-Bass.*

Goss is second only to Samuel S. Wesley in effecting reforms in cathedral music and congregational song.

Composer: ARTHUR'S SEAT (243, p. 284)
LAUDA ANIMA (18, p. 388)

Gottschalk, Louis Moreau (b. New Orleans, La., May 8, 1829; d. Rio de Janeiro, Argentina, December 18, 1869) was an important American composer, pianist, and conductor. Though he wrote in the prevailing European eighteenth-century style, particularly his piano pieces, he is among the first to incorporate "new world" themes and rhythmic intricacies. Well trained and highly regarded in his day, he still remains an important American figure for his use of Creole and Caribbean folk music in his compositions. Through his published articles on this music, Gottschalk has left a contemporary account of the "raw" performance of this folk idiom.

Composer: MERCY (494, p. 376)

Goudimel, Claude (b. Besançon, France, c. 1505; d. Lyons, France, August 27, 1572) was providing polyphonic settings of Geneva psalms for use by Roman Catholic and Protestant choirs as early as 1551. Sometime before 1565 he joined the Huguenots. His harmonized psalters, *Les CL Pseaumes de David* (Paris, 1564) and *Les Pseaumes mis en rime* (Geneva, 1565) are the base from which various later harmonizations of psalter tunes were adapted. Other compositions include motets, chansons, masses, and magnificats. Even though he composed for the Roman rites, there is no factual basis to indicate that he was either schooled or directly influenced by the sixteenth-century Italians.

Goudimel was murdered by Roman Catholics in the St. Bartholomew's Day massacres.

Composer: OLD 107TH (468, pp. 397-98)

Gould, John Edgar (b. Bangor, Me., 1822; d. Algiers, Africa, March 4, 1875) was a composer, publisher, and merchant in New York City. He moved to Philadelphia about 1868 and opened a piano and music business with William G. Fischer, composer of the tune for "I love to tell the story." With Edward L. White he compiled *The Modern Harp,* 1846, *The Wreath of School Songs,* 1847, *The Tyrolian Harp,* 1847, and *The Sunday School Lute,* 1848. Later he compiled *Harmonia Sacra,* 1851, and *Songs of Gladness for the Sabbath School,* 1869.

Gould died while on an extended journey of England, Europe, and Africa.

Composer: PILOT (**247**, p. 249)

Gower, John Henry (b. Rugby, Warwickshire, England, May 25, 1855; d. Denver, Col., July 30, 1922) was talented musically as a child, serving as assistant organist at Windsor Castle at the age of 12. He later studied at Oxford (B.M. 1876, Mus.D. 1883) and became organist and music master at Trent College, Nottingham, 1876-87. He was noted as a recitalist, conductor, and teacher. He moved to America to pursue a mining career. In 1887 he became organist-choirmaster of the Cathedral of St. John in the Wilderness, Denver, later at the Central Presbyterian and the Unity churches. During the Columbian World Exposition in Chicago in 1893, Gower was organist at the Church of the Epiphany. He published *Original Tunes,* 1890.

Composer: MEDITATION (GOWER) (**312**, p. 369)

Grant, Robert (b. Bengal, India, 1779; d. Dalpoorie, India, July 9, 1838) was educated at Magdalene College, Cambridge (B.A. 1801, M.A. 1804), and was called to the bar in 1807. He was elected to Parliament in 1818 and in 1833 initiated a bill to remove civil restrictions imposed against Jews. Grant was made judge advocate general in 1832, was appointed governor of Bombay and knighted in 1834. He contributed hymns to the *Christian Observer,* 1806-15, and to H. V. Elliott's *Psalms and Hymns,* 1835. His elder brother, Lord Glenelg, gathered 12 of his hymns and published them as *Sacred Poems,* 1839.

Author: By Thy Birth and by Thy Tears (**113**)
O Worship the King (**473**)

Greatorex, Henry Wellington (b. Burton on Trent, Staffordshire, England, December 24, 1813; d. Charleston, S. C., September 18, 1858) after early training in England moved to Hartford, Conn., in 1839, where he became organist of Center Church and later St. John's Church. About 1846 he went to St. Paul's Church in New York City and later served as organist-choirmaster of Calvary. He moved to Charleston in 1853.

Greatorex's *Collection of Psalm and Hymn Tunes, Chants, Anthems and Sentences for the Use of the Protestant Episcopal Church in America* (Boston, 1851) contained 37 original tunes and many adaptations and arrangements. Robert G. McCutchan in *Our Hymnody* writes that Greatorex's book "passed through many editions and generally had a wholesome effect on church music, especially in the larger cities."

> Composer: Glory Be to the Father **(792, p. 447)**
> Arranger: SEYMOUR **(94, p. 166)**
> Source: MANOAH **(403, p. 417)**

Gregory the Great (Gregory I) (b. Rome, Italy, 540; d. Rome, 604) was born of wealthy parents. He became a monk, turning his inherited fortune to monastic work. Elected pope in 590, he was influential in spreading the Roman Catholic Church to England by way of Augustine at Canterbury in 597.

Gregory was a strong advocate of the monastic ideal and greatly shaped the future of Western church music and liturgy. The system of chant which bears his name gradually displaced almost all other types of chant in the Western Church.

> Attributed author: Father, We Praise Thee **(504)**

Greiter, Matthäus (b. Aichach, Bavaria, c. 1490; d. Strassburg, December 20, 1550 or 1552) studied to be a singer and a monk at Strassburg Minster and in 1524 became a Lutheran minister there. He served as assistant pastor at St. Martin's and pastor at St. Stephen's, directing the choir-school beginning in 1548. Before death by the plague, Greiter recanted and returned to the Roman Catholic Church.

Greiter placed 7 melodies in his *Strassburger Kirchenamt,* 1525. More significant is that he served as music editor to Calvin's first psalter (Strassburg, 1539). Calvin spent the years 1538-41 preaching and teaching in Strassburg and was greatly impressed with the ideals of congregational song so adequately realized in the Lutheran churches of that city.

Attributed composer: OLD 113TH (9, 39, pp. 234-35)

Grobel, William Kendrick (b. Cresco, Iowa., April 24, 1908; d. Nashville, Tenn., February 2, 1965) was a New Testament scholar and interpreter of the writings and thought of Rudolf Bultmann. He was educated at Yankton College, S.D. (B.A. 1928, B.M. 1929), the University of Chicago (M.A. 1932), the Chicago Theological Seminary (B.D. 1932), and the University of Heidelberg, Germany (Th.D. 1934).

Grobel began his teaching career as instructor in New Testament at the Hartford Theological Seminary, 1934-36, then served 2 Congregational Christian churches as pastor: Stafford Springs, Conn., 1936-43, and Randolph, Vt., 1944-47. During the war years of 1934-44 he worked with refugees in Lisbon, Portugal, under the American board of Unitarian Service Commission. At Vanderbilt University Divinity School he held the positions of associate professor of biblical theology, 1947-52, professor of biblical theology, 1952-55, and professor of New Testament, 1955-65. During his Vanderbilt years he served as Fulbright lecturer in the University of Oslo, Norway, 1951-52, and guest professor at the United Theological College, Bangalore, South-India, 1959-60.

At the time of his death Grobel was the executive secretary of the Society of Biblical Literature. He is the author of several books and many articles contributed to learned journals, periodicals, encyclopedias, and dictionaries such as the *Encyclopaedia Britannica,* Hastings' *Dictionary of the Bible,* and *The Interpreter's Dictionary of the Bible.*

Translator: O Guide to Every Child (84)

Gruber, Franz Xaver (b. Unterweizberg, near Hochburg, Upper Austria, November 15, 1787; d. Hallein, June 7, 1863) was the son of a linen weaver who wanted the boy to stay in the trade. Franz secretly studied violin and in 1805 went to study organ with Georg Hartdobler at Burghausen. He taught school at Arnsdorf during the years 1807-29 and served frequently as the organist at the Roman Catholic parish of St. Nicholas' Church at nearby Oberndorf. From 1833 until his death he was headmaster at Berndorf and organist at Hallein. Gruber wrote more than 90 compositions but is remembered for the one hymn tune which employs only 3 chords—tonic, subdominant, and dominant.

Composer: STILLE NACHT (393, p. 372)

Gurney, Dorothy Frances Blomfield (b. London, England, October 4, 1858; d. Kensington, England, June 15, 1932) was the daughter of Frederick George Blomfield, rector of St. Andrew's Undershaft, London. She married Gerald Gurney in 1897, and they were received into the Roman Catholic Church in 1919. Two volumes of her poetry were published.

Author: O Perfect Love (333)

Hamilton, Mary C. D. No information is available concerning this author. Research tends to relate her to the Hamilton family of Walter Kerr Hamilton (d. 1869), bishop of Salisbury. Bishop Hamilton's eldest son, Sir Edward Walter Hamilton, died in 1908, and his will divides money among his sisters but does not specify by name; therefore, the family relationship is uncertain.

Author: Lord, Guard and Guide the Men Who Fly (541)

Handel, George Frederick (b. Halle, February 23, 1685; d. London, England, April 14, 1759) was the famous composer of Italian opera and considerable orchestral and choral music. He became a British subject in 1727, residing in England from 1712 until his death. He is best known in the field of oratorio, such as his *Messiah*, 1741, which, however, is not the best representation of his work. His success in producing oratorio, beginning in 1730, laid the patterns for all that was to be English choral music until Victorian times and later. Handel also composed anthems and settings for some of the psalms and the *Te Deum*.

An acquaintance of the Wesleys, Handel wrote 3 hymn tunes about 1746 for Charles Wesley's texts written in 1746 for *Festival Hymns:* CANNONS for "Sinners, obey the gospel Word," FITZWILLIAM for "O

Love divine," and GOPSAL for "Rejoice, the Lord is King." These were discovered by Charles's son, Samuel, in 1826. Tunes from Handel's operas and oratorios were reworked and used extensively in eighteenth- and nineteenth-century evangelical tunebooks. Probably the first such use of a Handel tune was in John Wesley's *Foundery Collection,* 1742, where a march from *Riccardo Primo* appears. See Erik Routley, *The Music of Christian Hymnody,* for a discussion of the Methodist use of operatic tunes.

Considerable biography on Handel is available. The Percy M. Young *Handel* (London, 1946) is a good starting point. See also the bibliographical listings in *Baker's Biographical Dictionary of Musicians,* pp. 652-53.

Composer: ANTIOCH (**392,** p. 260)
CHRISTMAS (**249,** p. 107)
HALIFAX (**456, 476,** p. 93)
JUDAS MACCABEUS (**450,** p. 406)

Hankey, Arabella Catherine (Katherine) (b. Clapham, London, England, 1834; d. Westminster, England, May 9, 1911) was the daughter of Thomas Hankey, a banker and member of the sect led by William Wilberforce, the Clapham Sect of Evangelicals. Young Kate came under this influence and began Bible classes for girls in London. A trip to Africa made her aware of the great financial needs of the mission field. In her late years all of her income derived from literary work went to foreign missions. Her collection of poems *Heart to Heart,* 1870, went through several editions.

Author: I Love to Tell the Story (**149**)

Harding, James Procktor (b. Clerkenwell, London, England, May 19, 1850; d. Islington, London, England, February 21, 1911) was an amateur musician and church organist, and a civil service clerk in the Inland Revenue Department, 1867-1909. He was organist for 35 years at St. Andrew's Church in Islington and during that time composed a great amount of church music, in particular for the children's choir festivals at the Gifford Hall Mission in London, of which his brother was principal benefactor. Harding's secular compositions and part songs were written for the musical activities of the civil service which he served for many years.

Composer: MORNING STAR (**400**, pp. 124-25)

Harkness, Georgia Elma (b. Harkness, N.Y., April 21, 1891), educator, author, and theologian, was educated at Cornell University (B.A. 1912) and Boston University (M.A. 1920, M.R.E. 1920, Ph.D. 1923), with postdoctoral work and special study at Harvard University, 1926, Yale Divinity School, 1928-29, and Union Theological Seminary in New York, 1936-37. She has been awarded honorary degrees from several schools including the D.Lit. in 1962 from Elmira College in New York. Dr. Harkness was professor of philosophy at Elmira College, 1922-37, professor of religion at Mount Holyoke College, 1937-39, professor of applied theology at Garrett School of Theology, 1939-50, and at the Pacific School of Religion, Berkeley, 1950-61. She taught at the newly formed Japanese International Christian University, 1956-57.

Dr. Harkness is the recipient of several awards in contests sponsored by the Hymn Society of America and is the author of the centennial hymn of the Pacific School of Religion. Of her 28 books, 3 are collections of her poems or prayers and poems.

Author: Hope of the World (**161**)
Composite author: This Is My Song (**542**)

Harlow, Samuel Ralph (b. Boston, Mass., July 20, 1885) received the B.A. from Harvard, the M.A. from Columbia, and the Ph.D. from Hartford Theological Seminary. He was ordained into the Congregational Christian Church in 1912. He served as chaplain and teacher of sociology at International College, Smyrna, Turkey, until 1922. During World War I he served with the A.E.F. in France as a religious director of the Y.M.C.A. During the years 1919-22 he was general director of the Student Volunteer Movement for the Near East. From 1923 until his retirement he was professor of religion and social ethics at Smith College.

Harlow is the author of many books including *The Life and Teachings of Jesus,* written in collaboration with Mary Jenness, 1929.

Author: O Young and Fearless Prophet (**173**)

Harper, Earl Enyeart (b. Coffey, Mo., March 28, 1895; d. St. Petersburg, Fla., March 1, 1967) was educated at Nebraska Wesleyan (B.A. and music certificate 1918) and Boston University School of Theology (S.T.B. 1921), with additional study at Harvard and the University of Chicago. He was a ministerial member of the New England Conference of The Methodist Church. Harper served as pastor of the Centenary Methodist Church, Auburndale, Mass., 1921-27, and at the Boston University School of Theology as instructor in church music and worship, 1923-27. At Boston he founded the Seminary male choir. He also taught music at Lasell Junior College, 1924-27. During the years 1927-36 he was president of Evansville College in Indiana, and of Simpson College, Iowa, 1936-38. He was director of the school of fine arts and the Iowa Memorial Union, 1938-63.

Harper served his church as precentor of the Methodist Episcopal General Conferences of 1924, 1932, and 1936. He was a member of the joint commission which revised the Methodist hymnal of 1935 and a member of the hymnal committee and chairman of the executive-editorial subcommittee which produced the present 1964 revision. He was active in the Hymn Society of America and served on the music committee of the National Council of Churches of Christ in the U.S.A. The author of several books, including *Church Music and Worship,* 1924, he was also editor of *The Abingdon Hymnal,* 1928.

The contribution of Earl Harper to the work of revising the 1935 and 1964 Methodist hymnals is unique. He was a tireless worker, innovator, and administrator, who nevertheless possessed a very practical mind and who was willing to accommodate his ideas to others when he felt his were not reflective or in the best interests of those he served. One example illustrates this point. Harper was an engaging foe of "gospel hymns." When the list of gospel hymns to be included in the 1964 hymnal was presented at a meeting of the subcommittee on texts, there had been no opportunity for the editor to expose the list for reactions before the session began. After the list of 24 hymns had been presented, including "The Old Rugged Cross" and "How Great Thou Art," Harper was the first to speak. "Mr. Chairman," he spoke in his characteristic clear tenor voice, "I move we accept the entire list without debate." There was considerable debate, but finally 18 of the list were approved.

Composer: SHIRLEYN (**123**, p. 226)

Harrell, Costen Jordan (b. Holly Grove, Gates County, N.C., February 12, 1885) was educated at Duke (B.A. 1906) and Vanderbilt universities (B.D. and M.A. 1910). He is the recipient of many honorary degrees, including the D.D. from Emory University in 1957. Ordained an elder in 1914, Harrell served pastorates in Methodist churches in Raleigh, N.C., 1910-13; Durham, N.C., 1913-19; Atlanta, Ga., 1920-25; Norfolk, Va., 1925-29; Richmond, Va., 1929-33; and Nashville, Tenn., 1933-44. In 1944 he was elected bishop and served the Birmingham, Ala., 1944-48, and Charlotte, N.C., 1948-56, areas until his retirement.

Harrell is the author of 14 books, including his most recent, *The Wonders of His Grace,* 1966.

Author: Eternal God and Sovereign Lord (351)

Harrington, Karl Pomeroy (b. Somersworth, N.H., June 13, 1861; d. Berkeley, Calif., November 14, 1953) was educated at Wesleyan University (B.A. 1882, M.A. 1885) and became a well-known teacher of Latin, teaching at Wilbraham Academy, 1885-87, Wesleyan University, 1889-91 and 1905-29, the University of North Carolina, 1891-99, and the University of Maine, 1899-1905. Wesleyan conferred the Mus.D. degree in 1946.

Harrington was organist in local churches near or in the schools where he taught. He was director of the Festival Chorus, Bangor, Me., founder and director of the Chapel Hill Choral Society in North Carolina, and director of the Middlesex Musical Association. With Peter C. Lutkin he was musical editor of the 1905 Methodist hymnal, which contained 12 of his hymn tunes and responses. He also served on the committee which produced the 1935 Methodist hymnal and was musical editor of 6 hymn and song collections, as well as the author of *Education in Church Music,* 1931. Many of his choral works, including songs, anthems, and responses, remain unpublished.

Composer: CHRISTMAS SONG (380, p. 404)

Harrison, Ralph (b. Chinley, Derbyshire, England, September 10, 1748; d. Manchester, Lancashire, England, November 4, 1810) was the son of the dissenting minister William Harrison. Ralph was educated at Warrington Academy, a Unitarian school. After leaving school about 1769 he served an Independent chapel at Shrewsbury and then was called in 1771 to Cross Street Chapel, Manchester, where he served until his death. There he helped establish a boys' school and Manchester Academy in 1786. He served as classical tutor at the academy, 1786-89.

Harrison published *The Rudiments of English Grammar,* 1777, and *Sacred Harmony,* 1784, and in 1791 a second volume of his 1784 collection. As an amateur musician he exerted considerable influence on the shaping of Independent collections of hymn and psalm tunes.

Composer: CAMBRIDGE (24, p. 152)

Hart, Joseph (b. London, England, 1712; d. London, May 24, 1768). Little is known of Hart's early life and education. He became a teacher in London and was converted at the Moravian meetingplace Fetter Lane, London, on Whitsunday, 1757. From 1759 until his death he was the greatly loved minister of Jewin Street Independent Chapel, London. A strict Calvinist, he was a frequent critic of John Wesley's theology, at one time writing a tract on "The Unreasonableness of Religion, Being Remarks and Animadversions on the Rev. John Wesley's Sermon on Romans 8:32." Next to Isaac Watts, Hart was the most popular of Independent hymn writers. His hymns are contained in *Hymns Composed on Various Subjects, with the Author's Experience,* 1759.

Author: Come, Ye Sinners, Poor and Needy (104)

Hassler, Hans Leo (b. Nuremberg, October 25, 1564; d. Frankfort, June 8, 1612) was the most famous of the 3 musical sons of Isaak Hassler. Leo took an early interest in organ and was the first Bavarian to study in Italy. He became a pupil of composition with Andrea Gabrieli and a friend of Giovanni Gabrieli. Upon his return to Germany he served as Count Octavian Fugger's private organist, 1585-1600, then as organist of the Frauenkirche and director of the Nuremberg town band, 1601-9, and finally as organist to the Elector of Saxony at Dresden until his death. While serving at Prague, about 1602, he also manufactured and installed musical clocks.

Hassler used Italian methods of composition to found the German school of choral art, and as such his work forms the base for indigenous German national art. His collections include *Cantiones Sacrae* (Augsburg, 1591), *Neue Deutsche Gesang*, 1596, 8 masses (Nuremberg, 1599), *Psalmen und christliche Gesang*, 1607, *Kirchengesänge, Psalmen und geistliche Lieder*, 1608, and motets, litanies, and organ works.

Composer: PASSION CHORALE (**418**, p. 333)

Hastings, Thomas (b. Washington, Litchfield County, Conn., October 15, 1784; d. New York, N.Y., May 15, 1872) was the son of a physician. The family moved to the frontier at Clinton, N.Y., in 1786. Hastings, though an albino and extremely nearsighted, taught himself music and began directing choirs and compiling hymn collections. While directing the Oneida County Musical Society, he compiled the *Utica Collection*, 1816, later titled *Musica Sacra*, which went through many printings. He moved to Utica in 1828 to be the editor of the religious weekly the *Western Recorder*. After he moved to New York City in 1832, he joined Lowell Mason in publishing *Spiritual Songs for Social Worship*. Here he directed choirs, including the Bleecker Street Presbyterian Church choir, and founded the *Musical Magazine*, 1836. New York University conferred the Mus.D. degree in 1858.

Hastings, through his composing, directing, teaching, and publishing, is second only to Lowell Mason in establishing in church music the "European norm" of theory, notation, and taste. Though he did harmonize Indian melodies in *Indian Melodies,* 1845, he was constantly on the attack against other folk music, including shaped-note music and notation. He was an apostle of "scientific" theory, composition, and criticism so influential in the mid-nineteenth century.

Hastings is said to have written 600 hymns, 1,000 tunes, and compiled 50 collections including the influential *Mendelssohn Collection* with Bradbury. As a resident of New York City for about 40 years, he was influential in shaping both its public and church music, and helped establish the centrality of that city in nineteenth-century American music education and publishing.

Composer: ORTONVILLE (**83**, p. 282)
RETREAT (**232**, p. 184)
TOPLADY (**120**, p. 364)
Alterer: Come, Ye Disconsolate (**103**)

Hatch, Edwin (b. Derby, England, September 4, 1835; d. Oxford, England, November 10, 1889) was the son of nonconformist parents. He was educated at King Edward's School in Birmingham and at Pembroke College, Oxford (B.A. 1857). In 1853 he was confirmed into the Church of England and was ordained priest in 1859. He served briefly as parish priest in East London before moving to Toronto, Canada, where he became professor of classics at Trinity College. He later served as rector at one of the high schools in Quebec, 1859-66. In 1867 he returned to Oxford as vice-principal of St. Mary's Hall. He became rector at Purleigh, Essex, in 1883 and university reader in ecclesiastical history, 1885-89. Hatch was widely acclaimed in Europe for his Bampton Lectures, 1880, and Hibbert Lectures, 1888.

Author: Breathe on Me, Breath of God (133)

Hatton, John (b. Warrington, England, date unknown; d. St. Helen's, England, December, 1793). Percy Dearmer in *Songs of Praise Discussed* writes that Hatton "resided in St. Helen's, in the township of Windle, in a street whose name he gave to the one tune by which his name is known." Others state that his funeral sermon was preached at the Presbyterian church, December 13, 1793. Nothing more is known about this person.

Composer: DUKE STREET (14, 23, 472, 550, pp. 143-44)

Havergal, Frances Ridley (b. Astley, England, December 14, 1836; d. Oystermouth, Glamorganshire, Wales, June 3, 1879) was the youngest child of William Henry Havergal. At the age of 7 Frances began writing verse. Chronic poor health prevented her from receiving a formal education, but through travel and private study she mastered the modern languages and Hebrew and Greek.

Miss Havergal was deeply religious, and as John Julian states, "Her poems are permeated with the fragrance of her passionate love of Jesus." Her poems were printed first in tracts and leaflets, and later published. She also composed a number of hymn tunes.

Author: Lord, Speak to Me (195)
Master, Speak! Thy Servant Heareth (274)
Take My Life, and Let It Be Consecrated (187)
Truehearted, Wholehearted, Faithful and Loyal (179)
Composer: HERMAS (452, p. 424)

Havergal, William Henry (b. Chipping Wycombe, Buckinghamshire, England, January 18, 1793; d. Leamington, Warwickshire, England, April 19, 1870) began his education at Princes Risborough in 1801, and continued at the Merchant Taylors' School in 1806, and at St. Edmund's Hall, Oxford (B.A. 1815, M.A. 1819). He was ordained deacon in 1816, priest in 1817, assigned curate at Astley, and was made rector in 1829. A serious accident forced him to inactive status. During recuperation he pursued the study of church music.

In 1845 Havergal reissued Thomas Ravenscroft's *Whole Book of Psalms,* adding an introduction. His own compilation, *Old Church Psalmody,* 1847, contained tunes from a variety of sources, including the adaptation of chorale melodies set to English meters. The importance of this work is somewhat diminished since his German sources were dull versions of chorales. His other publications include *A History of the Old Hundredth Psalm Tune,* 1854, and *A Hundred Psalm and Hymn Tunes,* 1859. After his death his efforts were continued by his daughter Frances and son, Henry.

In 1841, after his health was restored, Havergal became rector of St. Nicholas', Worcester, honorary canon of Worcester Cathedral in 1845, and vicar of Shareshill, Wolverhampton, 1860. His retirement came in 1867.

Composer: EVAN **(6, 338, 368,** pp. 119-20)
Arranger: FRANCONIA **(141, 182, 276,** p. 118)
WINCHESTER NEW **(102, 429,** p. 152)

Haweis, Thomas (b. Redruth, Cornwall, England, January 1, 1733, "Old Calendar Style"; d. Bath, Somersetshire, England, February 11, 1820) was educated at Truro Grammar School and apprenticed to a surgeon. In 1755 he entered Christ Church, Oxford, and Magdalen Hall, and was ordained in 1757. Haweis served as chaplain and curate of various churches, but Methodism attracted him to become Martin Madan's assistant at the Lock Hospital Chapel in London. In 1764 until his death he was rector of All Saints', Aldwinkle, Northamptonshire. He graduated from Cambridge with an LL.B. in 1772.

Haweis was also chaplain to Selina, Countess of Huntingdon, and became her trustee and executor. A champion of interdenominational missions, he worked for the founding of the London Missionary Society. He published *Carmina Christo, or Hymns to the Saviour*, 1792, and several hymn tunes.

Composer: RICHMOND (**12, 130,** p. 338)

Hawks, Annie Sherwood (b. Hoosick, N.Y., May 28, 1835; d. Bennington, Vt., January 3, 1918) was a longtime resident of Brooklyn and a member of the Hanson Place Baptist Church. Her pastor, Robert Lowry, encouraged her in her early hymn-writing ventures. Of her more than 400 hymns, only one remains in common use, but it has been translated into numerous languages.

Composer: I Need Thee Every Hour (**265**)

Haydn, Franz Joseph (b. Rohrau, Austria, March 31, 1732; d. Vienna, Austria, May 31, 1809) was Kapellmeister in the court of Prince Paul Esterhazy and the great creative genius of the late eighteenth century in Austria and England. His works include 100 symphonies, 22 operas, 4 oratorios, masses and settings of the Latin liturgy, and much chamber music. He contributed 6 hymn tunes to William Tattersall's *Improved Psalmody*, 1794. See the article on Haydn in *Grove's Dictionary of Music and Musicians* and the biography by Geiringer, *Joseph Haydn*, 1946.

Composer: AUSTRIA (**42, 239,** p. 187)
CREATION (**43,** pp. 400-401)
HAYDN (**258,** p. 147)
ST. ANTHONY'S CHORALE (**6,** p. 423)

Haydn, Johann Michael (b. Rohrau, Austria, September 14, 1737; d. Salzburg, August 10, 1806) was the younger brother of Franz Joseph. He became Kapellmeister at Grosswardein in 1757, and from 1762 until his death he was musical director to Archbishop Sigismund of Salzburg.

Johann devoted his life to Roman Catholic Church music and wrote a number of hymn tunes for Catholic congregations. Many of his other melodies have been made into hymn tunes. Erik Routley in *The Music of Christian Hymnody* writes: "Haydn's best work was done in writing popular music, often adapted from traditional tunes, for Catholic congregations." More than 400 of his works (the bulk of which is still unpublished) were for the church, including oratorios and choral works, and those for organ and orchestra.

Composer: LYONS (473, p. 343)
SALZBURG (295, 319, p. 224)

Hearn, Marianne (b. Farningham, Kent, England, December 17, 1834; d. Barmouth, Merionethshire, Wales, March 16, 1909) was a Baptist writer and poet who wrote under the pen name Marianne Farningham. She was a member of the editorial staff of the *Christian World* and editor of the *Sunday School Times*. Her collected works, based upon her contributions to the *Christian World*, were published in 20 volumes.

Author: Just As I Am, Thine Own to Be **(169)**

Heath, George (b. c. 1750; d. 1822) was educated at the dissenting academy at Exeter. He served as pastor of the Presbyterian church in Honiton, Devonshire, but in time was dismissed when he proved unworthy of his office. He later entered the Unitarian ministry. He published *Hymns and Poetic Essays Sacred to the Public and Private Worship of the Deity,* 1781, and *A History of Bristol,* 1797.

Author: My Soul, Be on Thy Guard **(246)**

Heber, Reginald (b. Malpas, Cheshire, England, April 21, 1783; d. Trichinopoly, India, April 3, 1826) was educated at Brasenose College, Oxford. He was named a fellow of All Souls' College in 1805 and during the years 1807-23 served as rector at Hodnet, Shropshire, his family's parish. During these years his hymns were written and appeared, beginning in 1811, in the *Christian Observer.*

The success of Congregational song as practiced by Methodists and Baptists moved Heber to suggest the authorization of a hymnal structured along lines of special days and the Christian Year. To this end he began to compile a hymnbook, enlisting the aid of poets such as Sir Walter Scott, Henry Milman, and Robert Southey. The bishop of London refused to authorize its publication, and Heber's election as bishop of Calcutta and untimely death on a visit to Trichinopoly eliminated any further pursuit of the project by him, though his wife published it in 1827 under the title *Hymns Written and Adapted to the Weekly Service of the Church Year*. This collection was reprinted in America and went into a second revised edition in England in 1827. It is as important to nineteenth-century Anglican hymnody as is John Wesley's 1737 Charleston *Collection* to eighteenth-century evangelical hymnody.

It is generally agreed that Heber's poems mark a transition from the evangelical writings of Wesley, Newton, and Cowper (Heber used *Olney Hymns* in his parish) to the hymns produced by the Oxford Group, culminating in the production of *Hymns Ancient and Modern,* 1860. In attempting to relate hymnody to contemporary poetry, Louis Benson questions not the success of the "descriptive hymn," celebrating the events chronicled in the Christian Year, but writes that in "the hymn of spiritual experience the literary motive seems to invite inquiry whether its intrusion has lowered the spiritual temperature, and whether its welcome involves any sacrifice of spiritual reality or depth." John Julian comments that Heber's hymns "have not the scriptural strength of our best early hymns, nor the dogmatic force of the best Latin ones. They are too flowing and florid, and the conditions of hymn composition are not sufficiently understood. But as pure and graceful devotional poetry, always true and reverent, they are an unfailing pleasure." A by-product of Heber's poetry was the necessity for the composition of new tunes to express texts cast in meters such as 98.98.84. or 11 12.12 10.

> Author: Bread of the World (320, 322, 323)
> Brightest and Best (400)
> God, That Madest Earth and Heaven (497)
> Holy, Holy, Holy! Lord God Almighty (26)
> The Son of God Goes Forth to War (419)

Hedge, Frederic Henry (b. Cambridge, Mass., December 12, 1805; d. Cambridge, August 21, 1890) was a Unitarian minister and educator. He spent several years studying in Germany and Holland, beginning at the age of 14. In 1829 he was ordained and served churches in Maine and Massachusetts. While minister of the Brookline Unitarian Church, 1857-72, he served at Harvard as professor of ecclesiastical history, 1857-76, and professor of German, 1872-84.

Hedge was an important figure in the Transcendental movement and a brilliant scholar of German literature and biography. With F. Dan Huntington, he compiled *Hymns for the Church of Christ*, 1853.

Translator: A Mighty Fortress Is Our God (20)

Heermann, Johann (b. Raudten, Silesia, October 11, 1585; d. Lissa, Posen, February 17, 1647), the only surviving child of his parents, studied at Wohlau, Fraustadt, Breslau, and Brieg. Illness caused him to forsake a teaching career, and he became pastor at Koeben, 1611-34. He continued limited pastoral duties until 1638 when he retired to Lissa. Koeben was the scene of much plunder and horror during the Thirty Years' War, and as a resident he came close to death several times and lost all his possessions.

Heermann is acknowledged as the greatest hymn writer between Martin Luther and Paul Gerhardt. Most of his hymns were written for family devotions.

Author: Ah, Holy Jesus, How Hast Thou Offended (412)

Heins, Francis Donaldson (b. Hereford, Herefordshire, England, February 19, 1878; d. Toronto, Canada, January 5, 1949) was educated in Leipzig and London. He moved to Ottawa, Canada, in 1902 and directed the instrumental music program in the public schools. In 1927 he joined the faculty of the Toronto Conservatory of Music and served as assistant to Ernest MacMillan with the Toronto Symphony. Heins was a celebrated teacher, composer, violinist, and conductor.

Composer: HEREFORD (362, p. 404)

Helmore, Thomas (b. Kidderminster, Worcestershire, England, May 7, 1811; d. Westminster, England, July 6, 1890) graduated from Magdalen Hall, Oxford (B.A. 1840, M.A. 1845). He served as curate, then vicar at Lichfield Cathedral, moving in 1842 to St. Mark's College, Chelsea, as vice-principal and precentor, where he stayed until 1877. He became master of the choristers of the Chapel Royal at St. James's in 1846.

An important figure in the restoration of plainsong, Helmore was musical editor of John Mason Neale's translations of Latin hymns.

He wrote an important article on plainsong in the *Dictionary of Musical Terms,* 1881, and assisted in the editing of carols and plainsong in various collections, including *The Hymnal Noted,* 1851-54. His harmonizations of plainsong melodies cast them into quasi-hymn tunes. In time Helmore's efforts were influential in rediscovering this rich source of ancient church song and along with Neale's fresh translations mark an important contribution to nineteenth-century English hymnody.

Adapter: VENI EMMANUEL (354, p. 305)

Hemy, Henri Frederick (b. Newcastle upon Tyne, England, November 12, 1818; d. Hartlepool, Durham, England, 1888) was born of German parents and served for a while as organist of St. Andrew's Roman Catholic Church at Newcastle. Later he became professor of music at St. Cuthbert's College in Ushaw, Durham.

Hemy's collections of sacred music, arranged from many sources, were widely used, in particular his *Crown of Jesus Music,* 1864. His book on piano methods, *Royal Modern Tutor for the Pianoforte,* 1858, was reprinted several times.

Composer: ST. CATHERINE (151, 259, 344, p. 139)

Herbert, George (b. Montgomery Castle, England, April 3, 1593; d. Bemerton, near Salisbury, England, March 1, 1633) was educated at Westminster School and Trinity College, Cambridge (B.A. 1611, M.A. 1615). In 1619 he was named orator for the university. Herbert served 2 parishes for 3 years each. His friend Izaak Walton published his biography.

Herbert's most famous work, *The Temple,* was published in 1633 and was widely read in the seventeenth century, then ignored for a time until John Wesley made extensive use of it. Wesley included over 40 poems from *The Temple* in various hymn collections, including the 1737 Charleston *Collection.* Ralph Vaughan Williams' *Five Mystical Songs from George Herbert* for solo baritone voice, 1911, is based on Herbert's *Temple.*

Author: Let All the World in Every Corner Sing (10)

Herbst, Martin (b. Rothenbach, January 15, 1654; d. Eisleben, 1681) studied at St. Lorenz's School, Nuremberg, and at Altdorf and Jena. In 1680 he was appointed rector of the gymnasium at Eisleben and pastor of St. Andreas'. He is probably the composer of 4 melodies in *Nürnbergisches Gesangbuch* (Nuremberg, 1676-77).

Attributed composer: AUS DER TIEFE (**95**, p. 214)

Hermann, Nicolaus (b. Altdorf, near Nuremberg, c. 1490; d. Bergstadt, Bohemia, May 3, 1561) spent most of his life as pastor, educator, and musician in the Latin school at Joachimsthal. The school was supervised by Johann Matthesius, and Hermann used Matthesius' sermons as the basis for hymns, setting them to his own tunes. He published 2 volumes of *Cantica Sacra,* 1554 and 1558, and other collections.

Hermann is an important figure in Christian education, most of his hymns having been written for the children of the school at Joachimsthal. He published a book on the education of children, *Ein gestrenges urteil Gottes,* about 1526.

Composer: LOBT GOTT, IHR CHRISTEN (**389, 510,** p. 267)

Hérold, Louis Joseph Ferdinand (b. Paris, France, January 28, 1791; d. Thernes, France, January 19, 1833) entered the Paris Conservatory in 1806 and won first prize in the piano competition of 1810. He moved to Italy and continued his study of composition. In Naples he produced his first opera, *La gioventó di Enrico Quinto,* 1815. The bulk of his work was done in Paris in opera as chorusmaster of the Italian opera, 1824, and then with the Grand Opera, 1827, where he was commissioned to write for ballet productions.

Hérold has been placed in the ranks of successful French operatic composers. He also wrote much piano music, including sonatas, caprices, rondos, divertissements, fantasies, and variations.

Composer: MESSIAH (**187,** p. 385)

Hewitt, James (b. Dartmoor, England, June 4, 1770; d. Boston, Mass., August 1, 1827) was the son of a British sea captain. James entered naval service but retired later to study and perform orchestral music.

John Heart, of the old American Company, brought Hewitt to New York in 1792. He led the first performances in the New World of compositions by Haydn, Ignaz Pleyel, and Johann Stamitz, including Haydn's *Seven Last Words*. He entered publishing in 1798 as branch owner of Carl's Musical Repository. According to Irving Lowens, "Hewitt was apparently dissatisfied with New York as a center of his activities. At one time or another, he seems to have visited practically every orchestral pit on the Atlantic seaboard, proceeding as far south in his journeys as Augusta, Georgia."

Moving to Boston in 1810, Hewitt played the organ at the Federal Street Theater. He composed several operas, an overture, piano music, and a new setting for "The Star-Spangled Banner" which never became popular. His *Harmonia Sacra*, 1812, is a compilation of his own tunes and tunes adapted from Handel, Thomas Ravenscroft, Jeremiah Clark, Boyce, and others. It is significant that no tunes of Americans such as Billings, Holden, French, Ingalls, Edson, or Read are included. (See Robert Stevenson, *Protestant Church Music in America*, 1966.)

For more information on Hewitt, see John Tasker Howard, "The Hewitt Family in American Music," *Music Quarterly*, XVII (January, 1931), 28.

Source: CHRISTMAS (249, p. 107)

Hine, Stuart Wesley Keene (b. London, England, July 25, 1899) was educated at the Coopers Company School, London. He passed a local examination for entrance into Oxford University, but did not continue his education. During World War I he served in France.

During the years 1923-32, Hine and his wife served as missionaries in east Poland; 1932-39 in Ruthenia, east Czechoslovakia. They have carried on extensive work among displaced persons in Britain, whose languages they speak, and have published evangelical literature in the various languages.

Hine has written and published a number of popular hymns.

Translator: O Lord My God! When I in Awesome Wonder (17)

Hodges, Edward (b. Bristol, Gloucestershire, England, July 20, 1796; d. Clifton, Gloucestershire, England, September 1, 1867) received the Mus.D. from Cambridge in 1825 and served as organist at Bristol and Clifton. In 1838 he moved to Canada and became organist of Toronto

Cathedral. He stayed one year and moved to New York City, where he was organist of St. John's, 1839-46, and Trinity Church, 1846-63. He returned to England in 1863.

Hodges' works include anthems and hymn tunes and the books *An Apology for Church Music and Musical Festivals,* 1834, and *An Essay on the Cultivation of Church Music,* 1841. The Library of Congress acquired his extensive music library, including his own manuscripts, in 1919.

Arranger: HYMN TO JOY (38, 41, 440, pp. 260-61)

Hodges, John Sebastian Bach (b. Bristol, Gloucestershire, England, 1830; d. Baltimore, Md., May 1, 1915) was the son of Edward Hodges. He came to this country in 1845 and was educated at Columbia University (B.A. 1850, M.A. 1853). In 1854 he was ordained deacon, priest in 1855. He served Episcopal churches in Pittsburgh, Pa., Chicago, Ill., and Newark, N.J. He also taught at Nashotah House, Wisc. For 35 years Hodges was the rector at St. Paul's, Baltimore, where he re-established the men and boys' choir and the parish choir school. Some authorities claim this choir school as the first established in America.

Hodges' compositions include about 100 hymn tunes and anthems. He was the compiler of *Book of Common Praise,* 1869, and the revised edition of *Hymn Tunes,* 1903. He was influential in the revision of the 1874 Episcopal *Hymnal,* a publication unique in that it was not bound to the prayerbook and marked a departure for American Anglicans from the metrical psalter. Hodges also served on the joint commission which prepared the 1892 edition.

Composer: EUCHARISTIC HYMN (320, p. 121)

Holden, Oliver (b. Shirley, Mass., September 18, 1765; d. Charlestown, Mass., September 4, 1844) was a carpenter, musician, minister, congressman, and realtor. He helped to rebuilt Charlestown, burned by the British during the Battle of Bunker Hill. After acquiring considerable property, he opened a general store about 1790. He built the Puritan church in Charlestown and served as its preacher. For several years he represented the town in the Massachusetts House of Representatives. The small organ used by Holden in composing and editing is now in the Bostonian Society, Old State House, Boston.

Holden's publications include *The American Harmony,* 1792, *Union Harmony,* 1793, *The Massachusetts Compiler,* with Hans Gram and Samuel Holyoke, 1795, *The Worcester Collection* (6th rev. ed. by Holden, 1797), *Sacred Dirges, Hymns and Anthems,* 1800, *The Modern Collection of Sacred Music,* 1800, *Plain Psalmody,* 1800, and *The Charlestown Collection of Sacred Songs,* 1803.

Composer: CORONATION (71, pp. 76-77)

Holland, Henry Scott (b. Ledbury, Herefordshire, England, January 27, 1847; d. Oxford, England, March 17, 1918) was educated at Balliol College, Oxford (B.A. 1870, M.A. 1873). He was ordained in 1874 and served as select preacher at Oxford, 1879-80 and 1894-96; canon of St. Paul's, London, 1884-1910; and lecturer and regius professor of divinity, Oxford, 1911-18. Aberdeen conferred the D.D. degree in 1903.

Holland was editor of the *Commonwealth* and assisted in editing *The English Hymnal,* 1906, and the *New Cathedral Psalter.* His preaching and writing reflected his identification with the social aspects of the gospel. His sermons and some autobiographical material are contained in *A Bundle of Memories,* 1915.

Author: Judge Eternal, Throned in Splendor (546)

Holland, Josiah Gilbert (b. Belchertown, Mass., July 24, 1819; d. New York, N.Y., October 21, 1881) prepared for a career in medicine and practiced in Springfield, Mass. After a short time he embarked upon a literary career and joined the Springfield *Republican* as the author of the "Timothy Titcomb" letters. He assisted in the establishment of *Scribner's Magazine* and beginning in 1870 served as its editor until his death. His *Complete Poetical Writings* were published in 1879.

Author: There's a Song in the Air (380)

Holmes, John Haynes (b. Philadelphia, Pa., November 29, 1879; d. New York, N.Y., April 3, 1964) was educated at Harvard (B.A. 1902, S.T.B. 1904). He was ordained a Unitarian minister and was called to the Church of the Messiah in New York City where he remained for 42 years. The church withdrew from the denomination in 1919 and renamed itself the Community Church. From this pulpit and through his writings and community action Holmes was one of the most persistent advocates of pacifism and civil rights in the country. He was the recipient of many honors and honorary degrees.

Holmes's several books, including his biography *I Speak for Myself,* 1959, contain a sense of urgency for the church to become involved in the world through direct action. His *Collected Hymns* was published in 1960.

Author: The Voice of God Is Calling (**200**)

Holmes, Oliver Wendell (b. Cambridge, Mass., August 29, 1809; d. Boston, Mass., October 7, 1894) graduated from Harvard in 1829 and began to study medicine. He entered practice in Boston, but after advanced studies in Europe he turned to teaching and taught anatomy and physiology at Dartmouth, 1839-47, and Harvard, 1847-82. At Harvard he wrote the anniversary poems for his alma mater, 1851-89.

Holmes was a man of extraordinary writing ability. He was intimate with the New England group, Longfellow, Bryant, Lowell, and Whittier. Instrumental in the founding of the *Atlantic Monthly,* 1857, he contributed many delightful articles under the captions *The Autocrat of the Breakfast Table* and *The Professor at the Breakfast Table.* Commenting on his religious faith, he once said that he "believed more than some and less than others."

Author: Lord of All Being (**64**)
O Love Divine, That Stooped to Share (**270**)

Holst, Gustav Theodore (b. Cheltenham, Gloucestershire, England, September 21, 1874; d. Ealing, near London, England, May 25, 1934) studied with C. V. Stanford at the Royal College of Music, 1893-98, supporting himself by playing trombone in the Carl Rosa Opera Company and organ at various churches. He had an interest in Hindu literature and in 1899 learned Sanskrit in order to create his own librettos from Vedic hymns. He was music instructor at James Allen Girls' School, 1903-20, St. Paul's Girls' School, 1905-34, and at the Morley College for Working Men and Women, 1907-24. During World War I he went to Asia Minor as music teacher to several army camps, often performing the great sixteenth-century choral literature. In 1923 he visited America when he conducted the Ann Arbor Festival, and again in 1932 to lecture at Harvard. Holst's daughter Imogen wrote the biography *Gustav Holst,* 1938, and compiled his compositions, *The Music of Gustav Holst,* 1951.

Holst's music represents a distinct break from Victorian musical sounds and forms. In a sense he is far more "twentieth century" than Ralph Vaughan Williams. His principal works were 5 operas, 2 suites, choral hymns, the large sacred work *Hymn of Jesus,* 1917, various vocal and instrumental chamber works, incidental music, and settings of English and Welsh folk songs. Eleven of his tunes appear in *Songs of Praise,* 1925 and 1931.

Composer: CRANHAM (376, p. 238)

Hopkins, Edward John (b. Westminster, England, June 30, 1818; d. St. Pancras, London, England, February 4, 1901) was a chorister at the Chapel Royal and during the years 1843-98 was organist at Mitcham Parish Church, at St. Peter's, Islington, at St. Luke's, Berwick Street, and at the Temple Church. He was the recipient of many honors, including degrees from the Archbishop of Canterbury and Trinity College, Toronto. In conjunction with Edward F. Rimbault, he published *The Organ: Its History and Construction,* 1855. His anthems, hymn tunes, and settings of chants have been widely used in both England and America.

Composer: ELLERS (236, p. 365)

Hopkins, John Henry, Jr. (b. Pittsburgh, Pa., October 28, 1820; d. Hudson, N.Y., August 14, 1891) was educated at the University of Vermont (B.A. 1839, M.A. 1845) and at General Theological Seminary in New York City, 1850. A man of many talents, he became the first instructor in church music at the seminary, 1855-57, and founded and edited the *Church Journal,* 1853-68. Ordained priest in 1872 he served as rector of Trinity Church, Plattsburg, N.Y., until 1876, and Christ Church, Williamsport, Pa., 1876-87.

Hopkins was also a member of the New York Ecclesiological Society, with particular talents in creating and reproducing church *ornamenta.* Leonard Ellinwood in *The Hymnal 1940 Companion* writes that he "was one of the great leaders in the development of hymnody in the Episcopal church during the mid-nineteenth century."

Author and composer: We Three Kings (KINGS OF ORIENT) (402)

Hopper, Edward (b. New York, N.Y., February 17, 1816 or 1818; d. New York, April 23, 1888) was educated at New York University and Union Theological Seminary in New York City, 1842. A Presbyterian minister, he served in Greenville, N.Y.; Sag Harbor, Long Island; and his last pastorate was at the Church of the Sea and Land, New York City. Lafayette College conferred the D.D. degree in 1871.

Author: Jesus, Savior, Pilot Me (247)

Horne, Charles Silvester (b. Cuckfield, Sussex, England, April 15, 1865; d. Toronto, Canada, May 2 or 4, 1914) was educated at Newport Grammar School, the University of Glasgow, and Mansfield College, Oxford, where he was a member of the first class of the college, 1886. He was a forceful preacher, and while yet a student was called and ordained at Allen Street Church, Kensington, in 1889. He remained there until 1903 when he became superintendent of Whitefield's Tabernacle, Tottenham Court Road. He served as chairman of the Congregational Union, 1910-11, as member of Parliament, 1910, and president of the National Brotherhood Council, 1913. He died en route from Niagara to Toronto shortly after having given the Lyman Beecher Lectures on preaching.

Author: For the Might of Thine Arm We Bless Thee (534)

Horsley, William (b. London, England, November 15, 1774; d. London, June 12, 1858) studied music privately and became organist of Ely Chapel, Holborn, 1794, and assistant to John Callcott, organist of the Asylum for Female Orphans. He succeeded Callcott in 1802 and married Callcott's daughter in 1813.

An important figure in early nineteenth-century English music, Horsley wrote many anthems, glees, and catches for the "Concentores Sodales," a choral society he and Callcott founded in 1798. He was also a founder of the Philharmonic Society of London, 1813, and a friend of Mendelssohn. He published 5 albums of glees, 1801-7, hymn tunes, 1820, piano pieces, a theoretical work, *An Explanation of Musical Intervals,* 1825, and the first book of William Byrd's *Cantiones Sacrae.*

Composer: HORSLEY (**218, 225,** p. 275)

Hosmer, Frederick Lucian (b. Framingham, Mass., October 16, 1840; d. Berkeley, Calif., June 7, 1929) was educated at Harvard (B.A. 1862, M.A. 1869) and was ordained into the Unitarian ministry. He served pastorates in Northboro, Mass.; Quincy, Ill.; Cleveland, Ohio; St. Louis, Mo.; and Berkeley, Calif. He was a leader in hymnic and liturgical renewal among Unitarians. *The Thought of God in Hymns and Poems,* with W. C. Gannett, 1885, contains 50 of Hosmer's hymns.

Author: God, That Madest Earth and Heaven (**497**)
O Thou, in All Thy Might So Far (**12**)

Houghton, James Russell (b. Davenport, Iowa, April 11, 1899) was educated at the University of Iowa, Harvard University. Simpson College in Iowa conferred the Mus.D. He possessed a natural singing voice and after undergraduate study served for 3 years as soloist with the Harvard Club, Archibald T. Davison, conductor. Houghton apparently was headed for an operatic career, but instead decided to teach at Boston University. For 37 years he taught sacred music and served as chairman of the voice department. He also served as director of the university chorus and the glee club. He toured Europe with the latter group in 1952 and Alaska in 1955. He retired from Boston University in 1964.

Houghton's contribution to Methodist music has been unique in that over a thousand seminary students were introduced to the ministry of music during the years 1927-64 through participation in the Boston University School of Theology Seminary Singers. Houghton served on the revision committees which were responsible for editing *The Book of Worship,* 1944 and 1964 and the 1935 and 1964 editions of Methodist hymnals. He was director of music for the General Conferences of The Methodist Church, 1939-60. His collection of *101 Hymns for Men to Sing* was published in 1939.

Arranger: Out of the Deep (**672**, p. 459)

Housman, Laurence (b. Bromsgrove, Worcestershire, England, July 18, 1865; d. Glastonbury, Somersetshire, England, February 20, 1959) was the brother of the poet A. E. Housman. He was educated at Bromsgrove School and South Kensington. Housman's career included positions as art critic for the *Manchester Guardian,* book illustrator, playwright, poet, and author. He is best remembered for his series of plays *Little Plays of St. Francis,* 45 in all, 1922-31, and *Victoria Regina,* 1934. At times he enjoyed the reputation of England's most censored playwright.

Though confirmed in the Church of England, he was attracted to Roman Catholicism. In later years his pacifist views brought him close to the Quakers. Housman wrote his own obituary notice and sold it to the *Manchester Guardian* who published it with explanatory notes.

Author: Father Eternal, Ruler of Creation (469)

How, William Walsham (b. Shrewsbury, Shropshire, England, December 13, 1823; d. Leenane, County Mayo, Ireland, August 10, 1897) was educated at Wadham College, Oxford (B.A. 1845, M.A. 1847), and Durham. He was ordained priest in 1847 and served in Kidderminster, Whittington, and Oswestry. In 1879 he became suffragan bishop of East London and was nicknamed the "poor man's bishop." In 1888 How became the first bishop of Wakefield. His publications include *Daily Prayers for Churchmen,* 1852, *Psalms and Hymns* (1st ed., 1854) with Thomas B. Morrell, and with John Ellerton, editor of *Church Hymns,* 1871, with Arthur Sullivan as music editor. His 54 hymns are characterized by their simplicity and directness.

Author: For All the Saints (536, 537)
O Jesus, Thou Art Standing (108)
O Word of God Incarnate (372)
We Give Thee But Thine Own (181)

Howard, Samuel (b. London, England, c. 1710; d. London, July 13, 1782) was a chorister at the Chapel Royal under William Croft and later a pupil of Johann Christoph Pepusch, Handel's rival. He held concurrent posts as organist at St. Clement Danes, Strand, and at St. Bride's, Fleet Street. He set the music for a Drury Lane pantomime, *The Amorous Goddess,* 1744, and composed many songs and cantatas. Howard also assisted William Boyce in compiling the collection *Cathedral Music,* 1760-78. Cambridge conferred the Mus.D. degree upon him in 1769.

Composer: ST. BRIDE (51, 339, 465, p. 174)

Howe, Julia Ward (b. New York, N.Y., May 27, 1819; d. Newport, R.I., October 17, 1910) was a poet and social worker. She was greatly devoted to her husband's efforts among the blind and other humanitarian causes. In 1870 Mrs. Howe attempted to organize a worldwide campaign among women to end war and preparations for war. She was an active Unitarian and often occupied the pulpit in Unitarian and other churches in the cause of abolition. As a writer she published 3 volumes of poetry: *Passion Flowers,* 1854, *Words of the Hour,* 1856, and *Later Lyrics,* 1866.

Author: Mine Eyes Have Seen the Glory (545)

Hoyle, Richard Birch (b. Cloughfold, Lancashire, England, March 8, 1875; d. London, England, December 14, 1939) was a Baptist minister and scholar. He served as minister in several English churches before moving in 1934 to the United States to teach at Western Theological Seminary, 1934-36. Hoyle was a close friend of Suzanne Bidgrain who first collected the hymns for *Cantate Domino,* which eventually became the hymnbook of the World Student Christian Federation.

Translator: Thine Is the Glory (450)

Hu Te-ai (b. China, c. 1900). No information is available on this person, according to Bliss Wiant, except that her given name, Te-ai, means "virtuous love" and is representative of names given to Chinese Christians, especially girls.

Composer: LE P'ING (490, p. 362)

Hughes, John (b. Dowlais, Wales, 1873; d. Llantuit Fardre, Pontypridd, Wales, May 14, 1932) as a boy worked as doorboy at a local mine in Llantuit Fardre. He later became a clerk and an official in the traffic department of the Great Western Railway. He was a lifelong member of the Salem Baptist Chapel, succeeding his father as deacon and precentor. Hughes composed a number of Sunday school marches, anthems, and hymn tunes.

Composer: CWM RHONDDA (271, 470, p. 196)

Hull, Eleanor Henrietta (b. Manchester, England, January 15, 1860; d. London, England, January 13, 1935) was the founder and a secretary of the Irish Text Society, 1899, and served for a time as president of the Irish Literary Society of London. She is the author of several books on Irish literature and history, and was instrumental in the renewed interest in ancient Gaelic culture.

Versed: Be Thou My Vision (256)

Hunter, John (b. Aberdeen, Scotland, July 12, 1848; d. Hampstead, London, England, September 15, 1917) attended elementary schools in Aberdeen, but his family could not afford to send him to the university, and the 13-year-old boy was apprenticed to a draper. The revival of 1859-61 persuaded him that he should enter the ministry, and he attended what is now Mansfield College, Oxford. Hunter served Congregational churches at Salem Chapel, York; Wycliffe Chapel, Hull; Trinity Church, Glasgow; and King's Weigh House Church, London, before he returned to Trinity House in 1904 and remained until 1913. While in retirement in London he preached weekly at Aeolian Hall.

Hunter's pioneer work in public worship and his publication on the subject, *Services for Public Worship,* 1886, were very influential. He published *Hymns of Faith and Life,* 1889, which contained radically altered classic texts.

Author: Dear Master, in Whose Life I See (254)

Husband, Edward (1843-1908) was educated at St. Aidan's College, Birkenhead, and ordained priest in 1867. He served as curate at Atherton, 1866-72, curate and later vicar at St. Michael and All Angels' Church, Folkestone. Here he lectured on church music and gave organ recitals. Husband published *The Mission Hymnal,* 1874. He was editor of *Supplemental Tunes to Popular Hymns,* 1882, and *An Appendix for Use at the Church of St. Michael and All Angels, Folkestone,* 1885.

Composer: ST. HILDA (108, p. 320)

Hutchinson, Albert H. No information has been found on this author.

Author: For All the Blessings of the Year (525)

Hutton, Frances A. (1811-1877). No information is available on this author except that she lived in England.

Alterer: In the Hour of Trial (237)

Ingalls, Jeremiah (b. Andover, Mass., March 1, 1764; d. Hancock, Vt., April 6, 1828) was a farmer, cooper, tavern keeper, and singing master, who no doubt did his instruction at least in part in his own tavern, a common practice of the day. For a time he served as choir director in the Congregational church at Newbury, Vt. His hymn tunes, few of which are used today, appeared in several collections. He was the compiler of an important collection of folk hymns, *The Christian Harmony* (Exeter, N.H., 1805).

Attributed composer: FILLMORE (527, 528, p. 92)

Irons, William Josiah (b. Hoddesdon, Hertfordshire, England, September 12, 1812; d. London, England, June 18, 1883) was the son of a nonconformist preacher and hymn writer. Irons was educated at Queen's College, Oxford (B.A. 1834, M.A. 1835, B.D. 1842, and D.D. 1854). After ordination in 1835 he served several churches including St. Mary-Woolnoth, formerly served by John Newton. From 1860 until his death he was prebendary of St. Paul's Cathedral. He gave the Bampton Lectures in 1870, entitled *Christianity as Taught by St. Paul.*

Irons's hymns and translations date from 1835 and are contained in 4 collections: *Metrical Psalter,* 1857, *Appendix to the Brampton Metrical Psalter,* 1861, *Hymns for Use in Church,* 1866, and *Psalms and Hymns for the Church,* 1873, 1875, and 1883.

Author: Sing with All the Sons of Glory (440)

Jackson, Robert (b. Oldham, Lancashire, England, 1842; d. Oldham, 1914) was the son of the parish organist of St. Peter's Church. He studied at the Royal Academy of Music and was organist of St. Mark's, Grosvenor Square, for a time. In 1868 he succeeded his father at St. Peter's in Oldham and directed the Oldham Musical Society and the Werneth Vocal Society. The combined tenure of father and son of 96 years seems to be a record of sorts. Jackson wrote many hymn tunes.

Composer: TRENTHAM (133, p. 124)

Jacobi, John Christian (b. Thuringia, 1670; d. London, England, December 14, 1750) was appointed keeper of the Royal German Chapel, 1708, and held that post until his death. His translations are included in 2 important collections which also contain the hymn tune and Thorough-bass: *A Collection of Divine Hymns, Translated from the High Dutch,* 1720, and *Psalmodia Germanica, or a Specimen of Divine Hymns,* about 1722. The second collection is a revision of the first.

Translator: Holy Ghost, Dispel Our Sadness (132)

Jeffery, John Albert (b. Plymouth, England, October 26, 1855; d. Brookline, Mass., June 4, 1929) studied with his father and succeeded him at St. Andrew's Cathedral in Plymouth. With additional study in Germany, under Liszt and Reinecke, he received an unprecedented honorary Mus.D. degree from the conservatory at Leipzig.

In 1876 Jeffery settled in America and in 1878 became the head of the music department at St. Agnes' School, Albany, N.Y., and ultimately organist at All Saints' Cathedral. He moved to Yonkers in 1893 where he was organist of the First Presbyterian Church. In 1900 he settled in Boston, teaching piano at the New England Conservatory of Music and serving as organist of the North Cambridge Universalist Church.

Composer: ANCIENT OF DAYS (459, pp. 89-90)

John of Damascus (c. 675–c. 749) was a Greek theologian, hymn writer, and a Father of the Greek Church born near the beginning of the eighth century at Damascus. The Italian monk and hymn writer Cosmas was his first teacher. Later he entered the monastery of St. Sabas, near Jerusalem, about 730, after having served in a civil capacity under the Mohammedan Caliph.

John's theological, liturgical, and hymn-writing activity marks him as the most important dogmatist of the Eastern Church. His influence spread into the Latin Church of the thirteenth century through the scholastics and the nineteenth-century English Church in the work of the translator John Mason Neale. John is also credited with the organization of "Eastern" chants similar to the work of Gregory's in the West. He composed 6 "canons" for the great festivals and set them to music. He was also a significant spokesman for those favoring the use of pictures and images as aids to the worshiper.

Author: Come, Ye Faithful, Raise the Strain (446, 448)
The Day of Resurrection (437)

Johnson, Erastus (b. Lincoln, Me., April 20, 1826; d. Waltham, Mass., June 16, 1909) was at various times a schoolteacher, rancher, farmer, and oil man. He lived a vigorous life as a resident of Maine, California, Washington, Pennsylvania, and Massachusetts. His interest in the Bible stemmed from his early years as a schoolteacher and when a student at Bangor Theological Seminary. Johnson played the organ, was a fluent speaker, and wrote poetry.

Robert G. McCutchan in *Our Hymnody* quotes from Johnson's diary as he makes reference to his brothers and sisters: "Of the thirteen, not one ever took a glass of intoxicating drink, nor used tobacco, nor got rich, nor used profane word."

Author: O Sometimes the Shadows Are Deep (245)

Jones, William (b. Lowick, Northamptonshire, England, July 30, 1726; d. Nayland, England, January 6, 1800) was an influential churchman and musical theoretician who was educated at Charterhouse and University College, Oxford. In 1777 he was appointed perpetual vicar at Nayland and became known as "Jones of Nayland." In 1793 he established the *British Critic*. His publications include *Treatise on the Art of Music,* 1784 and 1827, *Ten Church Pieces for the Organ with Four Anthems in Score,* 1789, *The Catholic Doctrine of the Trinity,* 1756, and *Physiological Disquisitions,* 1781.

Composer: ST. STEPHEN (296, 353, 356, p. 123)

Jude, William Herbert (b. Westleton, Suffolk, England, September, 1851; d. London, August 8, 1922) was the organist at the Blue Coat Hospital at Liverpool and after 1889 at the Stretford Town Hall near Manchester. Jude was an active recitalist and lecturer in England and Australia. He edited several important musical periodicals including *Monthly Hymnal* and 2 hymn collections: *Mission Hymns,*

1911, and *Festival Hymns,* 1916. In addition to songs and anthems, he wrote an operetta, *Innocents Abroad.*

Composer: GALILEE (**107,** p. 243)

Keble, John (b. Fairford, Gloucestershire, England, April 25, 1792; d. Bournemouth, Hampshire, England, March 29, 1866) was tutored by his father, the vicar of Coln St. Aldwin's. Keble graduated from Corpus Christi College, Oxford (B.A., 1810, M.A. 1813). He was ordained in 1815 and remained at Oxford as a tutor and examiner and served local parishes. During the years 1831-41 he was professor of poetry at Oxford. His *Assize Sermon,* preached at Oxford in 1833, dealt with national apostasy and is credited by John Henry Newman as the beginning of the Oxford Movement. Keble wrote several of the tracts in the series *Tracts for the Times,* 1833-41, which were influential in the movement.

Keble's most influential work was *The Christian Year: Thoughts in Verse for the Sundays and Holidays Throughout the Year,* first published anonymously in 1827. During his lifetime 96 editions were published, with royalties going toward the restoration of his church at Hursley, near Winchester. He was vicar there during the years 1836-63. Other published works include *Lyra Innocentium,* 1846, *Psalter or Psalms of David in English Verse,* 1839, and *Life of Bishop Wilson,* 1863. Twelve volumes of sermons, his *Letters of Spiritual Counsel,* and *Miscellaneous Poems* were published after his death.

Author: Blest Are the Pure in Heart (**276**)
New Every Morning Is the Love (**499**)
Sun of My Soul, Thou Savior Dear (**502**)

Kelly, Thomas (b. Kellyville, Stradbally, County Queens, Ireland, July 13, 1769; d. Dublin, Ireland, May 14, 1855) was the son of an Irish judge. He was educated at Trinity College, Dublin (B.A. 1789), for the bar but instead took holy orders in 1792. His friendship for Walter Shirley, a cousin of Lady Huntingdon, and sympathies for the evangelical movement led the archbishop of Dublin to prohibit him from preaching in the Dublin diocese and led to his becoming an Independent minister. An excellent preacher, he was also well-to-do and devoted his energies and money to helping the poor. He built churches at Athy, Portarlington, and Wexford.

Kelly's 765 hymns were published in *A Collection of Psalms and Hymns* (Dublin, 1800), *Hymns on Various Passages of Scripture* (1st ed., 1804), and *Hymns by Thomas Kelly, Not Before Published,* 1815. He also composed a set of tunes which were issued as a companion volume to be used with his hymns.

Author: Look, Ye Saints! The Sight Is Glorious (453)
The Head That Once Was Crowned with Thorns (458)

Ken, Thomas (b. Little Berkhampstead, Hertfordshire, England, July, 1637; d. Longleat, Wiltshire, England, March 19, 1710, "Old Calendar Style") at the age of 9, after the death of his parents, was provided a home by Izaak Walton and was educated later at Winchester College and Hart Hall, Oxford. He became a fellow of New College in 1657 (B.A. 1661, M.A., 1664). After his ordination in 1662 for a brief time he was rector of Little Easton, Essex, but returned to Winchester as domestic chaplain to Izaak Walton's friend Bishop Morley. In 1666 he was elected a fellow of Winchester and for the next 3 years served as curate of Brightstone on the Isle of Wight. He moved back to Winchester in 1669, having been named prebendary. His work for 10 years was with the cathedral college and as the bishop's chaplain.

Ken was appointed chaplain to Princess Mary (later queen), wife of William of Orange who resided at The Hague. He visited Rome in 1674. Previous to this, he returned to Winchester in 1683 and accompanied the fleet to Tangier as chaplain. Ken was consecrated bishop of Bath and Wells in 1685. He was sent to the Tower with 6 other bishops in 1688 for refusing to subscribe to James II's Declaration of Indulgence. He was acquitted but resigned the bishopric in 1691 and retired to the home of Lord Weymouth at Longleat.

His *Manual of Prayers for the Use of the Scholars of Winchester College* was edited and published at Winchester in several editions. In 1721 his poetical works were published, and volume I was reprinted in 1868 as *Bishop Ken's Christian Year, or Hymns and Poems for the Holy Days and Festivals of the Church.*

Author: All Praise to Thee, My God, This Night (493)
Awake, My Soul, and with the Sun (180)
Praise God, from Whom All Blessings Flow (809)

Kennedy, Benjamin Hall (b. Summer Hill, England, November 6, 1804; d. Torquay, Devonshire, England, April 6, 1889) was an important nineteenth-century educator, hymn writer, compiler, and translator. Only one of his translations is in common use in twentieth-century English hymnody.

Translator: Ask Ye What Great Thing I Know (124)

Kennedy, Gerald Hamilton (b. Benzonia, Mich., August 30, 1907) was educated at the College of the Pacific (B.A. 1929), the Pacific School of Religion (M.A. 1931, B.D. 1932), and Hartford Theological Seminary (S.T.M. 1933, Ph.D. 1934). He has received numerous honorary degrees. In 1932 he was ordained a Methodist minister, but served first as pastor of the First Congregational Church in Collinsville, Conn., 1932-36, then Methodist pastorates in San Jose and Palo Alto, Calif., and Lincoln, Neb. In 1948 he was elected bishop and was assigned to the Portland, Ore., area, then to the Los Angeles area where he has remained since 1952.

Kennedy has served as director of the Wesley Foundation at Stanford, 1940-42, and acting professor of homiletics, Pacific School of Religion, 1938-42. He has been on many denominational boards and agencies and served on the texts subcommittee for the present 1964 hymnal revision. In 1954 he delivered the Lyman Beecher Lectures at Yale. He is the author of 17 books.

Author: God of Love and God of Power (153)

Kerr, Hugh Thompson (b. Elora, Canada, February 11, 1872; d. Pittsburgh, Pa., June 27, 1950) was educated at the University of Toronto (B.A. 1894, M.A. 1895) and Western Theological Seminary, Pittsburgh, 1897. He was the recipient of many honorary degrees. He was ordained a Presbyterian minister in 1897 and served Presbyterian churches in Kansas and Illinois before going to Shadyside Presbyterian Church in Pittsburgh, 1913-46. A pioneer in religious radio broadcasting, Kerr preached every Sunday during the years 1922-44 over KDKA in Pittsburgh. In 1930 he was elected moderator of the General Assembly of the Presbyterian Church in the U.S.A.

In addition to writing 22 religious books, Kerr compiled several collections of children's stories and for 20 years was a contributor to the church school curriculum material. He served as chairman of the committees for the Presbyterian *Hymnal* and the Presbyterian *Book of Common Worship*.

Author: God of Our Life (47)

Kethe, William (d. 1594). The circumstances of Kethe's birth and early life are unknown. During the persecutions of Queen Mary, 1555-58, he was in exile on the continent and served as messenger to other exiles in Basel and Strassburg. It is believed that he was a Scottish minister and may have worked with the scholars who remained in Geneva after Mary's death to complete the Geneva Bible, published in 1560. In 1563 and 1569 he served as chaplain to the English troops under the Earl of Warwick. From 1561 until his death it is thought that he was rector of the church of Childe Okeford in Dorsetshire.

The Anglo-Genevan Psalter, 1561, contains 25 of his metrical psalms, which later appeared in the Scottish Psalter of 1564.

Author: All People That on Earth Do Dwell (21)

Kingsley, Charles (b. Holne Vicarage, Devonshire, England, June 12, 1819; d. Eversley, Hampshire, England, January 23, 1875). During Kingsley's education in private school at Clifton he witnessed the Bristol Riots in 1831, which profoundly impressed him and led to his later emphasis on the social responsibilities of the church. Later studies were at the grammar school in Helston, Cornwall, under Derwent Coleridge. After a short time at King's College, London, he entered Magdalene College, Cambridge (B.A. 1841). Ordained in 1842, he became the first curate and then rector of Eversley, Hampshire. In 1859 he was chaplain to the queen, in 1860 professor of modern history at Cambridge, canon of Chester, 1869-73, and canon of Winchester, 1873-75.

With F. D. Maurice, Kingsley was a leader in the Christian Socialism Movement and was temporarily prohibited by the bishop of London from preaching in the London diocese because Kingsley was suspected of Chartist views. His controversy with John Henry Newman grew out of his strong criticism of the medievalism and narrowness of the Oxford Tractarian Movement. He wrote 35 books, of which his historical novels—*Hypatia,* 1853, and *Westward Ho,* 1855—filled with skillful descriptive material, were very popular.

Author: From Thee All Skill and Science Flow (485)

Kingsley, George (b. Northampton, Mass., 1811; d. Northampton, March 13, 1884), a self-taught musician, became organist of Old South Church, Boston, and Hollis Street Church, Boston. Later he taught music at Girard College, Philadelphia, and was supervisor of music in the Philadelphia public schools. He provided more than 40 hymn tunes for Charles Everest's *Sabbath,* 1873.

Arranger: MESSIAH (**187,** p. 385)

Kingsley, George (b. Northampton, Mass., 1811; d. Northampton, England, October, 1634) apparently lived at Rushbrooke near Bury St. Edmunds, where he was musician to Sir Robert Jermyn and possibly church warden of St. Mary's. He was largely responsible for the harmonizations in Thomas Est's *Whole Book of Psalms,* 1592. In 1597 his *First Set of English Madrigals* was published.

Attributed arranger: WINCHESTER OLD (**54, 70, 131, 394,** pp. 139-40)

Kirkpatrick, William James (b. Duncannon, Pa., February 27, 1838; d. Philadelphia, Pa., September 20, 1921) received his early musical training with his father and studied with Pasquale Rondinella, Leopold Meignen, and T. Bishop. He moved to Philadelphia in 1855 where he joined Wharton Street Methodist Episcopal Church. He published a collection of camp-meeting songs, *Devotional Melodies,* in 1859 when he was only 21. During the Civil War he was a fife major with the 91st regiment of the Pennsylvania volunteers. He went into the furniture business in Philadelphia, 1862-78.

After his first wife's death in 1878, Kirkpatrick left business and devoted his full time to music, serving as music director at Grace Methodist Episcopal Church in Philadelphia, 1886-97. His first 2 wives died, and his third wife was Mrs. John R. Sweney of Williamsport, Pa. From 1880 to 1921 he had a hand in the publication of about 100 collections of gospel songs. Among his collaborators were John R. Sweney, H. L. Gilmour, and John H. Stockton. He was president of

Praise Publishing Company, Philadelphia, which published many of his collections.

Composer: TRUST IN JESUS (208, p. 413)
Arranger: NORSE AIR (304, 524, pp. 333-34)

Klug, Joseph. There seems to be no biographical information at all available on this printer. His first imprint appeared in 1524, and his last in 1552. Some sources believe that since the pestilence was widespread in Wittenberg in 1552 that he possibly died from it. His *Geistliche Lieder* appeared in 4 editions: 1529, 1533, 1535, and 1543. In the 1954 facsimile edition of *Das Klugsche Gesangbuch,* 1533, are the remarks:

Luther seems to have placed special confidence in Klug. This accounts for the fact that Klug could use Luther's crest in printing. That Luther's crest also appears on the title page permits one to suppose that Klug's hymnal had official sanction and makes Luther's direct participation in the choice of hymns most probable. . . . The first reproduction of the tune of "Ein' feste Burg"—the 1533 imprint doubtless reproduces that of 1529—had previously called attention of hymnologists to this hymnal. Its importance, however, extends far beyond this: it is the most important source for hymns of the time of the Reformation.

See the comments on EIN' FESTE BURG, p. 67.

Source: NUN FREUT EUCH (58, 84, pp. 315-16)
Probable source: EIN' FESTE BURG (20, p. 67)

Knapp, Phoebe Palmer (b. New York, N.Y., March 9, 1839; d. Poland Springs, Me., July 10, 1908) was the daughter of the Methodist evangelist Walter C. Palmer. She showed signs of musical talent early as a singer and composer of songs for children. She married Joseph Fairfield Knapp, the founder of the Metropolitan Life Insurance Company. They were members of John Street Methodist Church in New York City. When her husband died in 1891, she shared her substantial income with various charitable causes.

Mrs. Knapp's gospel hymns and tunes found acceptance in both England and America. Of the more than 500 she wrote, however, only

2 remain in common use, both with texts by Fanny Crosby—"Open the gates of the Temple" and "Blessed assurance."

Composer: ASSURANCE (224, p. 116)

Knapp, William (b. Wareham, Dorsetshire, England, 1698 or 1699; buried Poole, Dorsetshire, England, September 26, 1768) was probably of German descent. He served as parish clerk of St. James's Church in Poole for 39 years. Two collections of his were published: *A Set of New Psalm Tunes and Anthems,* 1738, and *New Church Melody,* 1753, both of which went through several editions.

For an article and portrait of Knapp, see the *Musical Times,* XLIII, 399.

Composer: WAREHAM (509, p. 205)

Knecht, Justin Heinrich (b. Biberach, Württemberg, September 30, 1752; d. Biberach, December 1, 1817) was educated at the convent of Esslingen. He played the flute, oboe, trumpet, cor anglais, violin, and organ. Classically trained, he became professor of literature for his native town, adding to his duties in 1771 the direction of music for the town. In 1807 he became director of opera and court concerts for Stuttgart, but resigned after 2 years to return to Biberach. In addition to works on music theory and piano instruction, he published with J. F. Christmann *Vollständige Sammlung . . . Choralmelodien* (Stuttgart, 1799), which contained 97 of his tunes.

Composer: ST. HILDA (108, p. 320)

Kocher, Conrad (b. Ditzingen, Württemberg, December 16, 1786; d. Stuttgart, March 12, 1872) studied piano and composition at St. Petersburg, after which he traveled in Italy and studied Catholic Church music. In 1821 he founded in Stuttgart a sacred vocal music society and in 1827 became director of music in the collegiate church in Stuttgart, continuing until 1865. He received an honorary doctorate at the University of Tübingen in 1852.

Kocher's compositions include 2 operas, an oratorio, and smaller works. He also published a piano method, a treatise on church music, *Die Tonkunst in der Kirche,* 1823, and a collection of chorales, *Zionsharfe,* 1855.

Composer: DIX (35, 397, p. 100)

König, Johann Balthasar (baptized Waltershausen, near Gotha, January 28, 1691; buried Frankfort, April 2, 1758) at the age of 12 went to Frankfort as a chorister. During the years 1711-21 he trained under Georg Philipp Telemann. Eventually he succeeded Telemann as director of the municipal music and was in charge of music at Barfüsserkirche and St. Catharine's, Frankfort.

König's *Harmonischer Liederschatz* . . . , 1738, was the largest and most influential collection of tunes published in the eighteenth century. Of the 1,784 tunes in the main section of the book, 361 were new.

Composer: FRANCONIA (141, 182, 276, p. 118)

Kremser, Edward (b. Vienna, April 10, 1838; d. Vienna, November 26, 1914) in 1869 became the choral director of the Vienna Männergesangverein. He composed operettas, works for piano and voice, and several works for male chorus and orchestra, of which *Sechs altniederländische Volkslieder* was the best known. In 1912 and 1913 he published 2 volumes of *Wiener Lieder und Tänze* in Vienna.

Arranger: KREMSER (59, p. 420)

La Feillée, François de was a priest associated with the choir of Chartres Cathedral. Nothing about his birth and death dates is available. He published a shortened version of the Roman Antiphonary and a manual of plainsong entitled *Nouvelle Méthode de plain-chant,* first published in 1745. The 1777 edition was dedicated to the bishop of Poitiers. The book is important for its representation of the musical changes of the era, from modes to tonal harmony, and free to isometric rhythm. Most of the tunes are in major and minor keys, and are measured.

Source: CHRISTE SANCTORUM (504, p. 176)

Lampe, Johann Friedrich (later *John Frederick*) (b. Saxony, 1703; d. Edinburgh, Scotland, 1751) went to England at the age of 23 where his talents as a bassoon player got him a position at Covent Garden Theatre and in Handel's orchestra. John Rich, proprietor of the Theatre Royal, introduced Lampe to Henry Carey, and the 2 men collaborated in writing many successful dramas with music, the most successful being *The Dragon of Wantley,* a clever skit based on the absurdities of Italian opera.

In 1745 Lampe came under the influence of John Wesley and developed a close friendship with Charles. He set 24 of Charles's hymns to music in 1746, entitled *Hymns on the Great Festivals, and Other Occasions*. Although the tunes were in the popular florid style of the stage and difficult to sing, they became very popular with Methodists, and Thomas Butts's *Harmonia Sacra* included 20 of them. In 1748-49 Lampe accompanied John Wesley to Ireland, where he published *A Collection of Hymns and Sacred Poems* (Dublin, 1749). He died during a professional engagement at the Theatre Royal, Edinburgh.

Composer: KENT (350, p. 220)
Probable arranger: IRISH (56, 282, p. 309)

Landsberg, Max (b. Berlin, February 26, 1845; d. Rochester, N.Y., December 8, 1928) was educated by his father, the rabbi of Hildescheim, and at the Josephinium Gymnasium at Hildesheim and at the universities of Göttingen, Breslau, Berlin, and Halle (Ph.D. 1866). He also attended the Jewish seminary at Breslau. During the years 1866-71 he taught at the seminary for Jewish teachers in Hanover and became a rabbi in 1870. He was called the next year to the Temple B'rith Kodesh, Rochester, N.Y., where he remained for 34 years. In 1887 he published *Ritual for Jewish Worship and Hymns for Jewish Worship*. Landsberg's name is synonymous with the vigorous sweep of reform that pushed B'rith Kodesh to the front of the Jewish Reform movement in America.

Translator: Praise to the Living God (30)

Lane, Spencer (b. Tilton, N.H., April 7, 1843; d. Reedville, Va., August 10, 1903) served with the Union army during the Civil War, then studied at the New England Conservatory of Music. After teaching voice and instrumental music in New York City, he moved to Woonsocket, R.I., where he established a music store and served as organist-choirmaster at St. James's Protestant Episcopal Church for 13 years. He later served churches in Monson, Mass.; Richmond, Va.; and at Baltimore, Md., where he was at All Saints' Protestant Episcopal Church and was an associate of the Sanders & Stayman music firm.

Composer: PENITENCE (237, pp. 239-40)

Langran, James (b. London, England, November 10, 1835; d. Tottenham, England, June 8, 1909) was a student of organ with J. B. Calkin and J. F. Bridge. He did not receive his B.M. degree from Oxford until 1884, when he was 49. He was organist of St. Michael's, Wood Green; Holy Trinity, Tottenham; and St. Paul's Church, Tottenham, 1870-1909. Beginning in 1878 he was also musical instructor at St. Katherine's Training College, Tottenham.

Langran contributed several of the new tunes for *Hymns Ancient and Modern* and was music editor for the *New Mitre Hymnal*, 1875.

Composer: LANGRAN (**269**, p. 264)

Larcom, Lucy (b. Beverly, Mass., March 5, 1826; d. Boston, Mass., April 17, 1893), after the death of her father, moved to Lowell, Mass., with her mother. She began working in a mill at the age of 11. Working in the Lowell factory system was regarded as a social asset, and Lucy contributed many poems to *Lowell Offering*, published by the Improvement Circle, a factory women's organization. John Greenleaf Whittier became interested in her poetic gifts through reading the journal and became a lifelong friend.

Miss Larcom graduated from Monticello Female Seminary, Alton, Ill., and studied at Wheaton Seminary, Norton, Mass. She taught for awhile in advanced schools, but poor health forced her to retire and devote her time to writing. She collaborated with Whittier in editing several volumes of poetry and published several works independently: *Childhood Songs*, 1873, *Wild Roses of Cape Ann*, 1881, *Poetical Works*, 1885, and *Beckonings*, 1886.

Author: Draw Thou My Soul, O Christ (**188**)

Lathbury, Mary Artemisia (b. Manchester, Ontario County, N.Y., August 10, 1841; d. East Orange, N.J., October 20, 1913), the daughter of a Methodist minister, was trained and practiced as a professional artist. As a contributor to and editor of Sunday school periodicals printed by the Methodist Sunday School Union, she came to the attention of its secretary John H. Vincent. Vincent was the founder of the original Chautauqua Institution located in western New York state. Miss Lathbury became known as the "Laureate of Chautauqua" and is also remembered as the founder of the Look-Up Legion, a Methodist

Sunday school organization which was based on Edward Everett Hale's 4 rules of good conduct:

Look up, not down;
Look forward, not back;
Look out, not in,
And lend a hand.

Author: Break Thou the Bread of Life (**369**)
Day Is Dying in the West (**503**)
O Shepherd of the Nameless Fold (**304**)

Laufer, Calvin Weiss (b. Brodheadsville, Pa., April 6, 1874; d. Philadelphia, Pa., September 20, 1938) was educated at Franklin and Marshall College (B.A. 1897, M.A. 1900) and Union Theological Seminary in New York, 1900. He was ordained as Presbyterian minister and served as pastor at the Steinway (Dutch) Reformed Church, Long Island City, N.Y., 1900-5, and the First Presbyterian Church, West Hoboken, N.J., 1905-14. Because of his writing ability and interest in religious education and music, he was made a field representative of the Presbyterian Board of Publication and Sunday School Work, 1914-24, and field representative of the Presbyterian Board of Education, 1924-38. Beginning in 1925 he was also assistant editor of music publications.

In addition to several books, Laufer edited *Junior Church School Hymnal*, 1927, *Songs for Men*, 1928, *The Church School Hymnal for Youth*, 1928, *Primary Worship and Music*, 1930, *Hymn Lore*, 1932, and *When the Little Child Wants to Sing*, 1935. With Clarence Dickinson he helped edit the 1933 Presbyterian *Hymnal* and served as associate editor of the *Handbook to the Hymnal*, 1935.

Author: O Thou Eternal Christ of God (**482**)
Author and composer: We Thank Thee, Lord (FIELD) (**203**)

Leeson, Jane Elizabeth (b. London, England, 1809; d. Warwickshire, England, 1881) was an active worker in the Catholic Apostolic Church, Gordon Square, London. She sometimes improvised hymns at the services as "Prophetic utterances" which were "delivered slowly, with short pauses between the verses, a pause three times as long as any one would ordinarily make in reading." Her several books were of a devotional nature and written for children. She also contributed 9 hymns and translations to the Catholic Apostolic hymnal. Late in life she became a Roman Catholic.

Author: Savior, Teach Me, Day by Day (162)

Leisentritt, Johann (b. Olmutz, c. 1527; d. Bautzen, November 25, 1586) studied theology with Antonius Brus at Krakow. In 1561 he was appointed as administrator ecclesiasticus, a post comparable to bishop. He compiled several choral books for the Roman Catholic Church, including *Geistliche Lieder und Psalmen* in 2 parts, 1567, and *Catholisches Pfarbuch* (Cologne, 1577).

Source: AVE VIRGO VIRGINUM (448, pp. 156-57)

Lew, Timothy Tingfang (b. Wenchau, Chekiang, China, 1891; d. Albuquerque, N.M., August 5, 1947) was one of China's leading educators, authors, and editors. He was educated in China and at Columbia University in New York, where he received the M.A. and Ph.D. He received the B.D. from Yale. Lew studied at Union Theological Seminary in New York and also taught Christian education. During the years 1926-28 he lectured extensively at prominent American schools and colleges. Oberlin College conferred the S.T.D. degree.

In 1932 Lew was elected commission chairman for the preparation of the Chinese Union hymnbook, 1936, commonly called *Hymns of Universal Praise.* The music editor for this widely used hymnal was Bliss Wiant, one of Lew's colleagues at Yenching University in Peking. Lew was also coeditor of the *Union Book of Common Prayer,* used by 4 Protestant Chinese groups with membership numbering 500,000. He was the Chinese delegate to the World Council sessions, 1927 in Lausanne, 1937 in Oxford, and 1939 in Madras. From 1936 to 1941 he was a member of the national legislative body of the Chinese government.

Lew is best known for his work with Chinese Christian organizations in China and America. He resided in America during the years 1941 and 1947 and died while teaching at the University of New Mexico.

Lew's widow, Katherine Y. T. Lew, has furnished the biographical information on the composer.

Author: The Bread of Life, for All Men Broken (317)

BIOGRAPHIES

Lindeman, Ludwig Mathias (b. Trondheim, Norway, November 28, 1812; d. Christiana, Norway, May 23, 1887) studied under his father, Ole Andreas Lindeman, the organist at Our Lady's Church in Trondheim for 57 years and a successful concert pianist. Although he assisted his father at the cathedral, his main interest was theology, and he entered the seminary in Christiana, Oslo, in 1833. During his seminary days he played cello in the theater orchestra and often substituted for his brother Jacob as organist of Our Saviour's Church. In 1840, he succeeded his brother as organist and remained there for 47 years. He gave up theology and continued to teach singing and church music at the seminary and with his son, Peter, founded a conservatory of music in 1883, the Musikkonservatoriet, the only music college in Oslo. As the most outstanding recitalist in Norway, he was invited to play several recitals on the new organ in Albert Hall, London, in 1871.

Lindeman composed hymn tunes, songs, choral works, sonatas, fantasies for organ, and chamber music. He is best remembered, however, for his collections of folk music and his revision of the Lutheran hymnbook *Koralbog for den Norske Kirke*, 1871. Between the years 1840 and 1867 he collected nearly 2,000 melodies, many of which were published in his 3-volume *Older and Newer Mountain Melodies*, 1853-67.

Composer: KIRKEN DEN ER ET GAMMELT HUS (355, p. 272)

Littledale, Richard Frederick (b. Dublin, Ireland, September 14, 1833; d. London, England, January 11, 1890) was the son of a merchant and was educated at Trinity College, Dublin (B.A. 1855, M.A. 1858, LL.B. and LL.D. 1862). In 1857 he was ordained priest and served churches in Norwich and London. Ill health forced him to devote his energies to writing.

Littledale was a man of enormous literary ability, and his works encompassed theology, history, liturgy, and hymnody. Though a high churchman, he warned against a return to Rome in *Plain Reasons for Not Joining the Church of Rome*, 1880. His hymnological works include translations from Danish, Swedish, Greek, Latin, Syriac, German, and Italian, as well as some original hymns, metrical litanies, and the book *Carols for Christmas and Other Seasons*, 1863.

Translator: Come Down, O Love Divine (466)

597

Littlefield, Milton Smith (b. New York, N.Y., August 21, 1864; d. Corona, Long Island, N.Y., June 12, 1934) was educated at Johns Hopkins, 1888-89, and Union Theological Seminary in New York, 1889-92. He served churches in New York City, Brooklyn, and Corona, Long Island. Originally a Presbyterian, he was a Congregationalist for the last 23 years of his life. During the years 1911-20 he was the district secretary of the Congregational Education Society, and 1927-28 was the president of the Hymn Society of America. In addition to lecturing on hymnology and writing several books, he compiled *The School Hymnal,* 1920, *Hymns of the Christian Life,* 1925, and *Hymnal for Young People,* 1927.

Author: O Son of Man, Thou Madest Known **(197)**

Lloyd, William (b. Rhos Goch, Llaniestyn, Caernarvon, Wales, 1786; d. Caernarvon, Wales, 1852) was a cattleman and farmer and a self-educated musician with a good singing voice. His home became a gathering place for singing schools, and he conducted singing societies in various parts of the Lleyn Promontory.

Composer: MEIRIONYDD **(200,** p. 402)

Longfellow, Samuel (b. Portland, Me., June 18, 1819; d. Portland, October 3, 1892) was educated at Portland Academy, Harvard University (B.A. 1839), and Harvard Divinity School (B.D. 1846). He was ordained into the Unitarian ministry and served churches in Fall River, Mass.; Brooklyn, N.Y.; and Germantown, Pa. With Samuel Johnson, a fellow student at Harvard, he edited *A Book of Hymns for Public and Private Devotions,* 1846, and *Hymns of the Spirit,* 1864. He also published *Vespers,* 1859, hymns used at services in Brooklyn, and *A Book of Hymns and Tunes,* 1860. He wrote a biography of his famous brother, Henry Wadsworth Longfellow, published in 1886.

Author: Father, Give Thy Benediction **(815,** p. 444)
       God of the Earth, the Sky, the Sea **(36)**
       Holy Spirit, Truth Divine **(135)**
       I Look to Thee in Every Need **(219)**
       Now, on Land and Sea Descending **(505)**
       O God, Thou Giver of All Good **(515)**
       One Holy Church of God Appears **(296)**

Longstaff, William Dunn (b. Sunderland, England, January 28, 1822; d. Sunderland, April 2, 1894) was the son of a wealthy ship and land owner. When Longstaff's friend, the Reverend Arthur A. Rees, left the Anglican Church to establish Bethesda Free Chapel, Longstaff served as treasurer for the chapel and provided for needed alterations and additions to the building. Dwight L. Moody, Ira D. Sankey, and William Booth of the Salvation Army were his close friends and frequent visitors in his home, and Bethesda was the second church in England to permit Moody to preach in its pulpit.

Author: Take Time to Be Holy (**266**)

Lovelace, Austin Cole (b. Rutherfordton, N.C., March 26, 1919) was educated at High Point College, High Point, N.C. (A.B. 1939), and Union Theological Seminary School of Sacred Music (M.S.M. 1941, D.S.M. 1950). High Point College honored him with the Mus.D. degree in 1963. He has taught at the University of Nebraska and Queens College in Charlotte, N.C., and served local churches in Lincoln, Charlotte, and Greensboro, N.C., before serving for 10 years as minister of music at First Methodist Church in Evanston, Ill., 1952-62, and 2 years at Christ Church Methodist in New York City, 1962-64. Since 1964 he has been minister of music at Montview Boulevard Presbyterian Church in Denver, Col. While at Evanston, Lovelace was associate professor of church music at Garrett Theological Seminary. From 1962 to 1964 he was lecturer in hymnology at Union Theological Seminary. He was an adjunct faculty member at Iliff School of Theology in Denver, 1964-69, and presently he teaches organ at Temple Buell College, Denver.

A leader in Methodist and interdenominational church music, Lovelace has been active in the Hymn Society of America and the American Guild of Organists. He was the organizing chairman and first president of the National Fellowship of Methodist Musicians, 1955-57. He was organist for the Second Assembly of the World Council of Churches, 1954, and director of music for the General Conference of The Methodist Church in Pittsburgh, 1964. A prolific composer with over 250 compositions for choir, organ, and solo voice, Lovelace is also the author of 4 books on church music, including *The Organist and Hymn Playing*, 1962, *The Anatomy of Hymnody*, 1965, and with William C. Rice, *Music and Worship in the Church*, 1960. His hymn tunes are found in Baptist, Presbyterian, and Lutheran hymnals. As chairman of the subcommittee on hymn tunes for the 1964 revision of the Methodist hymnal, Lovelace, more than any single person, shaped the musical materials for the hymnal.

Composer: HINMAN (86, p. 371)
     Come, Bless the Lord (783, pp. 443-44)
     I Was Glad (786, pp. 449-50)
     O Send Out Thy Light (797, p. 457)
Adapter: ANGEL VOICES (2, p. 93)
Alterer: MELCOMBE (499, p. 296)
    O JESU (219, p. 228)
Versed: Jesus, We Want to Meet (487)
Harmonizer: AMAZING GRACE (92, p. 89)
      ARMENIA (196, 301, pp. 81-82)
      AUS TIEFER NOT (526, pp. 351-52)
      BEALOTH (137, p. 378)
      CLONMEL (189, p. 103)
      CORMAC (534, pp. 181-82)
      DAVIS (129, p. 339)
      DETROIT (32, p. 397)
      ELLESDIE (251, p. 245)
      FILLMORE (527, 528, p. 92)
      GARTON (375, p. 280)
      GLORIA (374, p. 95)
      HALIFAX (456, 476, p. 93)
      HAYDN (258, p. 147)
      KEBLE (146, 152, p. 182)
      LOBT GOTT, IHR CHRISTEN (389, 510, p. 267)
      MAINZER (139, pp. 104-5)
      MORNING SONG (190, 481, p. 106)
      PISGAH (142, 302, pp. 142-43)
      ROCKINGHAM (MASON) (206, 213, 329, p. 198)
      SANKEY (514, p. 203)
      SHIRLEYN (123, p. 226)
      SPANISH HYMN (77, p. 137)
      TRUE HAPPINESS (227, p. 319)
      W ZLOBIE LEZY (396, p. 240)
      WEDLOCK (211, p. 194)

Lowell, James Russell (b. Cambridge, Mass., February 22, 1819; d. Cambridge, August 12, 1891), poet and essayist, graduated from

Harvard (B.A. 1838) and practiced law until 1855 when he became the Smith Professor of Modern Languages at Harvard. He retired as professor emeritus in 1886. He was the United States minister to Spain, 1877-80, and ambassador to England, 1880-85.

While Lowell wrote many poems with moral themes in which he spoke out against such issues as slavery and the Mexican War, he did not write any hymns per se. Among his outstanding works are *The Vision of Sir Launfal*, 1848, and *The Biglow Papers*, 1848 and 1867. During the years 1857 to 1862 he edited the *Atlantic Monthly*, and the *North American Review*, 1863 to 1872.

> Author: Once to Every Man and Nation (242)

Lowry, Joseph C. William J. Reynolds cites the research of Harry Eskew into nineteenth-century music printing in Virginia in which he found a little information on Lowry. Apparently Lowry was a "gentleman teacher" in Virginia. He is mentioned in the second edition of Ananias Davisson's *Kentucky Harmony*, c. 1815. No other information is available on this person.

> Attributed composer: PISGAH (142, 302, pp. 142-43)

Lowry, Robert (b. Philadelphia, Pa., March 12, 1826; d. Plainfield, N.J., November 25, 1899) graduated from Bucknell University in 1854. He served as a Baptist minister in Pennsylvania, New York City, and Brooklyn. While at Lewisburg, Pa., 1869-75, he also taught at Bucknell and received the D.D. from that institution in 1875. He was a popular preacher and orator. From 1875 until his death Lowry served as pastor of the Park Avenue Baptist Church in Plainfield, N.J., and became involved in hymn writing and the composition of gospel hymn tunes—in particular with the publishing company Biglow and Main.

> Author and composer: Low in the Grave He Lay (CHRIST AROSE) (444)
> Composer: ALL THE WAY (205, p. 84)
> NEED (265, p. 230)
> SOMETHING FOR JESUS (177, p. 368)

Luther, Martin (b. Eisleben, Saxony, November 10, 1483; d. Eisleben, February 18, 1546) was the son of a miner. Luther was educated at Magdeburg and Erfurt (M.A. 1505). In 1505 he entered the Augustinian convent at Erfurt and was ordained priest in 1507. At Wittenberg he assisted in the university in 1508 and began to preach. After he received the Th.D. from Wittenberg, he started teaching and formulating his ideas concerning current practices of the church. While on a trip to Rome in 1510-11 he was shocked by the appalling corruption of the church. In 1517 he requested debate on the matter of the sale of indulgences in Saxony by the Dominican monk Tetzel. On October 31, 1517, Luther posted his 95 theses or articles, which began a long, open struggle with Rome, culminating in his defense of his writings before the imperial Diet of Worms, 1521. He refused to retract his writings and openly broke with Rome, emerging in time as the leader and spokesman for the Reformation.

Luther translated the Bible into German, 1521-34, and prepared the way for the first German hymnbook, 1524, and his own contributions to congregational song through paraphrases of biblical texts and translations from Latin set to his adaptations of plainsong and folk music. The 37 hymns and paraphrases he wrote are in simple, plain, and sometimes rough phrases. Most English translations tend to detract from rather than transmit his vigorous and bold style. The sixteenth-century chorale melody as it was harmonized in the eighteenth century by J. S. Bach and others lost its rhythmic qualities. Consequently, the real excitement of early German hymnody, particularly Luther's, is for the most part unknown to the last 100 years of English-speaking congregations.

Luther's positive attitude toward music and congregational song is summarized by W. E. Buszin, *Musical Quarterly*, XXXII, 80-97.

Author and composer: A Mighty Fortress Is Our God (EIN' FESTE BURG) (20)

Author: Christ Jesus Lay in Death's Strong Bands (438)
Out of the Depths I Cry to Thee (526)

Attributed composer: AUS TIEFER NOT (526, pp. 351-52)
VOM HIMMEL HOCH (281, p. 196)

Lvov (Lwoff), Alexis Feodorovich (b. Revel, now Tallinn, Estonia, June 5 or 6, 1799; d. Romanovo, Lithuania, December 28, 1870) was educated by his father, who was the director of the imperial court chapel at St. Petersburg, and at the Institute of Road Engineering, 1818. He served in the Russian army and attained the rank of major-general. In 1837 he succeeded his father at the chapel and held the post for 24 years. During that time he edited a collection of music for the church year in the Eastern Orthodox Church.

Lvov was an excellent violinist and toured Europe with his own string quartet. He composed a violin concerto as well as several operas. Deafness forced his retirement in 1867.

Composer: RUSSIAN HYMN (544, p. 202)

Lyon, Meyer (or *Meier Leon*) (b. 1751; d. Kingston, Jamaica, 1797). His given name Leon Chazzan means singer or precentor. The latinized form of his name was used by Lyon while singing opera. He was a singer and leader of music in various London synagogues, including the Great Synagogue, 1768-72. He began singing in opera but was unsuccessful because he refused to sing on Friday evenings and during religious festivals, and because he was a poor actor. In 1787 the Ashkenazic congregation in Kingston, Jamaica, needed a cantor. Lyon was hired and remained there until his death.

Arranger: LEONI (30, p. 356)

Lyon, Percy Hugh Beverley (b. Darjeeling, India, October 14, 1893) was educated at Rugby School, 1907-12, and Oriel College (B.A. and M.A. 1912-14 and 1919-21), where he won the Newdigate prize for poetry. During World War I he served in the 6th Durham Light Infantry as a master commandant and became a prisoner of war. During the years 1921-26 he was assistant master at Cheltenham College, then rector of Edinburgh Academy, 1926-31, head master of Rugby School, 1931-48, and director of the Public Schools Appointments Bureau, 1950-60. His writings include *Turn Fortune* and *The Discovery of Poetry.*

Author: O God, Before Whose Altar (486)

Lyte, Henry Francis (b. Kelso, Scotland, June 1, 1793; d. Nice, France, November 20, 1847) was born of English parents and educated at Enniskillen and Trinity College, Dublin (B.A. 1814). Three times he gained honors for his poetry. He took holy orders in 1815 and after several appointments was named perpetual curate at Lower Brixham, Devonshire, in 1823. His 24-year ministry in the fishing village had a strong evangelical center, but the rigors of the priesthood were too much for his failing health. Lyte's published works include *Tales on the Lord's Prayer in Verse*, 1826, *Poems, Chiefly Religious*, 1833, and 1845, and *The Spirit of the Psalms*, 1834.

Author: Abide with Me (289)
       Jesus, I My Cross Have Taken (251)
       Praise, My Soul, the King of Heaven (66)
Alterer: As Pants the Hart for Cooling Streams (255)

McCutchan, Robert Guy (b. Mt. Ayr, Iowa, September 13, 1877; d. Claremont, Calif., May 15, 1958) was educated at Park College, Parkville, Mo., and Simpson College, Indianola, Iowa (B.M. 1904). He began teaching voice at Baker University, Baldwin, Kan., in 1904 and later organized the conservatory of music there. In 1910 he took time out from teaching to study music privately in Berlin and Paris. From 1911 to 1937 he was the dean of the school of music at DePauw University. During this time and continuing after his retirement he was very active in summer music institutes and as a director of hymn festivals in many parts of the country. He also was a special lecturer and visiting professor at several colleges and universities, including Perkins School of Theology at Southern Methodist University, 1954-55. Simpson College conferred the Mus.D. degree in 1927. Other honorary degrees include the D.Sac.Litt. in 1935 from Southern Methodist University, the D.Litt. from Southwestern University in 1943, and the Mus.D. from DePauw in 1956.

The revision of the 1905 Methodist hymnal began with the Methodist Episcopal commission on the revision of the hymnal and psalter, 1924-28. In December of 1931 the joint commission (the Methodist Episcopal and Methodist Episcopal, South, later joined by the Methodist Protestant) elected McCutchan editor. He had been heading the subcommittee on tunes. After the work of the commission was complete, he and John W. Langdale, book editor of the Methodist Episcopal Church, in consultation with certain other commission members, began moving the hymnal towards publication. The 3 churches had for various reasons, not the least of which was the grave economic depression of the times, little enthusiasm for the actual publication of the hymnal. Amos Thornburg stated:

There was a time in the finishing of the work that the committee had no more time to meet, and the entire task of finishing the work was for

[McCutchan] to achieve. This included text and tune and other matters where decision and responsibility are usually shared. But the task left to him was achieved because of his energy and faithfulness. He was responsible for detail and decision far above the knowledge of most of those who have praised him for his work.

While at work on the hymnal, McCutchan was assiduously acquiring and organizing materials relevant to the text and tunes of its hymns, so that in 1937 the handbook *Our Hymnody* was published. William J. Reynolds has stated: "It was the first significant hymnal handbook produced in America. Here are revealed the years of his careful research, his understanding of the broad field of hymnology, and occasional glimpses of his keen wit and humor. In many respects this was a pioneer venture, and those who have since prepared hymnal handbooks have been much in his debt, to an even greater extent than they have sometimes admitted."

McCutchan's other published works include *American Junior and Church School Hymnal,* of which he was music editor, 1928, *Aldersgate 1738-1938,* published in 1938, *Hymns in the Lives of Men,* 1945, *Hymns of the American Frontier,* 1950, and *Hymn Tune Names: Their Sources and Significance,* 1957. With others he produced *Better Music in Our Churches,* 1925, and *Music in Worship,* 1927. He was also author of many monographs and articles including the unpublished article on American Methodist Hymnody for John Julian's *Dictionary of Hymnology.*

For the 1935 Methodist hymnal McCutchan composed and arranged 7 hymn tunes and several responses. The 3 composed while he was on the hymnal commission were submitted under the pen name "John Porter" since he said, "It would simply not do for it to be known that the editor was their composer." Of these tunes ALL THE WORLD has proved the most popular. The text and tune are included in many hymnals and children's songbooks.

McCutchan's motto might well have been the first line of the hymn "Let all the world in every corner sing." He devoted himself to bringing hymns into men's lives. Besides his Methodist work, he was particularly active in Congregational, Brethren, and Adventist church music and was constantly at work in interpreting the 1935 hymnal at conventions, pastors' schools, and conferences. His particular concern came to be with the local church. His "common touch" is cited by William J. Reynolds:

He knew the practices and problems of local churches and was sharply critical of those who wrote about church music from lofty towers, familiar only with the services of metropolitan cathedrals and oblivious and unconcerned about the thousands of small churches across the nation where the multitudes worship each week. He loved to walk the unfamiliar paths of hymns and tunes and share their wealth with the common man in the pew. He taught the joy of hymn singing, not in the stilted style of a classroom professor, but as one whose love for hymnic expression was a vital part of abundant Christian living.

During his lifetime of interest in hymnody and in his travels in every state, McCutchan was always in search for American songbooks and hymnbooks. In attics, at auctions, in little secondhand bookshops, he picked up quaint and rare, as well as contemporary, items. Thus was assembled a library of some thousands of volumes dating from pre-Civil War times. This hymnological collection is housed at the Honnold Library serving the associated colleges of Claremont and is available to students, professors, and any serious scholar who wishes to use it.

Death came to McCutchan after 3 years of suffering from cancer, during which time he continued writing. His remarkable wit and sense of humor, according to his widow, "came to his aid and those who cared for him through all the difficult days." His ashes were placed at his wish beside those of his first wife, Carrie, in the mausoleum at Forest Hill Cemetery, Greencastle, Ind.

Composer: ALL THE WORLD (10, p. 266)
Harmonizer: CAMPMEETING (111, pp. 145-46)

McDonald, William (b. Melmont, Me., March 1, 1820; d. Monrovia, Calif., September 11, 1901) was of Scottish descent. He became a member of the Maine Conference of the Methodist Episcopal Church in 1843, transferring to the Wisconsin Conference in 1855 and to the New England Conference in 1859. A prominent member of the National Holiness Association, he was editor of the *Advocate of Christian Holiness* for 15 years. From 1870 until his death he was active in evangelistic work. He published 10 volumes on religious subjects and either edited or coedited 7 collections of gospel songs.

Author: I Am Coming to the Cross (116)

MacMillan, Ernest Campbell (b. Mimico, Ontario, Canada, August 18, 1893) was the son of the editor of the *Hymnary of the United Church of Canada,* 1930, Alexander MacMillan. Ernest was educated at the University of Toronto, the University of Edinburgh, and Oxford University (B.M. 1910). While he was visiting the Wagner Festival, in Bayreuth, 1914, World War I began, and he was held at Ruhleben prison camp for 4 years. During this time he composed *England,* a work for chorus, soloists, and orchestra which won him the Mus.D. degree from Oxford. During the years 1926-52 he served as director of the Toronto Conservatory of Music and was conductor of the Toronto Symphony, 1931-56. He was knighted by King George V in 1935 for recognition of his work in Canada, as composer, teacher, conductor, and organist.

MacMillan is now retired except for occasional radio engagements. He serves as president of the Composers, Authors, and Publishers Association of Canada and the Canadian Music Centre. *Music Across Canada,* Vol. I (July–August, 1963), featured the life and work of MacMillan.

Arranger: TEMPUS ADEST FLORIDUM (**395, 442,** p. 185)

Madan, Martin (b. Hertingfordbury, England, 1726; d. Epsom, Surrey, England, May 2, 1790) was the brother of the bishop of Peterborough and a cousin of William Cowper. Madan studied at Westminster School and Christ Church, Oxford (B.A. 1746). In 1748 he was admitted to the bar and sent by his convivial club to hear John Wesley preach so that he could caricature him before the members. However, he was converted by Wesley's preaching, gave up law, and was ordained for the ministry. As chaplain at Lock Hospital, an "institution for the restoration of unhappy females," Madan was so disturbed by the problems of the patients that he wrote the treatise *Thelyphthora,* 1780, in which he advocated polygamy as a solution. The storm of criticism forced him to retire to Epsom.

Madan did not write any original hymns, but he was successful in piecing together the works of others. In 1760 he published a miscellaneous collection of hymns, *A Collection of Psalms and Hymns,* by various authors and reissued it with an appendix in 1763. Immensely popular, his versions came to be the form accepted in the eighteenth century.

Probable alterer: Hail, Thou Once Despised Jesus (**454**)

Besides writing hymns he was also a printer, carpenter, mechanic, and artist. In 1826 the University of Glasgow honored him with the D.D. degree.

Malan wrote more than 1,000 hymns, setting them to his own tunes. His hymns are identical in spirit to those springing from the English Calvinistic reaction to the Wesleys. In John Julian we read that they have a "marked didactic tone, necessitated by the great struggle of the Réveil for Evangelical doctrine; and an emphatic Calvinism, expressing itself with all the despondency of Newton and Cowper, but in contrast to them, in bright assurance, peace, and gladness." H. Leigh Bennett has written that Malan is the "greatest name in the history of French hymns." One tune is all that remains extant in contemporary English hymnody.

Composer: HENDON (124, p. 101)

Mann, Arthur Henry (b. Norwich, Norfolk, England, May 16, 1850; d. Cambridge, England, November 19, 1929) was educated at Norwich Cathedral and New College, Oxford (B.M. 1874, Mus.D. 1882). While a chorister at Norwich he was capable of playing the cathedral service when he was only 8. After serving as organist at St. Peter's, Wolverhampton, 1870, Tettenhall parish church, 1871-75, and a few months at Beverley Minster, 1875, he went to King's College Chapel, Cambridge, where he was organist for 53 years.

An acknowledged authority on Handel and a skillful boy choir trainer, Mann was musical editor for Charles D. Bell's *Church of England Hymnal*, 1895. He wrote many anthems, organ pieces, and hymn tunes.

Composer: ANGEL'S STORY (164, p. 320)

Mann, Newton (b. Cazenovia, N.Y., January 16, 1836; d. Chicago, Ill., July 25, 1926) was educated at the Cazenovia Seminary and was ordained for the Unitarian ministry in 1865. He served churches in Kenosha, Wisc., Troy and Rochester, N.Y., and Omaha, Neb. Mann published works in many fields including *The Evolution of a Great Literature* and *Natural History of the Jewish and Christian Scriptures*, 1905. He wrote several poems on religious and philosophical themes, but is best known for his translation of the Yigdal.

Translator: Praise to the Living God (30)

Marlatt, Earl Bowman (b. Columbus, Ind., May 24, 1892) is the son of a Methodist minister. He was educated at DePauw University (B.A. 1912) and Boston University (S.T.B. 1922, Ph.D. 1929), with further study at Harvard, Oxford, and the University of Berlin. He has served as associate professor of philosophy, then professor, 1925-38, and later dean, 1938-45, at Boston University. From 1946 to 1957 he was professor of philosophy of religion and religious literature at Perkins School of Theology, Southern Methodist University. He served as curator of the Treasure Room and Hymn Museum, Interchurch Center, New York City, 1960-62.

Marlatt was the associate editor of *The American Student Hymnal,* 1928. He continues his active concern for hymnology. Several volumes of his poetry have been published.

> Author: Are Ye Able (413)
> Spirit of Life, in This New Dawn (462)

Marriott, John (b. Cottesbach, England, September 11, 1780; d. St. Giles in the Fields, Middlesex, England, March 31, 1825) was educated at Rugby School and Christ College, Oxford, where he was an outstanding student. He was ordained in 1804 and spent 4 years at Dalkeith Palace as tutor to George Henry, Lord Scott. He was also domestic chaplain to the fourth duke of Buccleuch, who appointed him rector at Lawford in Warwickshire. Ill health caused him to move to Devonshire where he served several churches.

Marriott was a close friend of Sir Walter Scott, who dedicated the second canto of *Marmion* to him. A modest man, he would not allow the publication of his hymns during his lifetime, although some were published without his permission.

> Author: Thou, Whose Almighty Word (480)

Marsh, Simeon Butler (b. Sherburne, N.Y., June 1, 1798; d. Albany, N.Y., July 14, 1875) was raised on a farm. He had little musical training until the age of 16, yet 3 years later began teaching in singing schools. He was encouraged in his work by Thomas Hastings whose singing school he attended in Geneva, N.Y., in 1818. For 30 years he conducted similar schools in the churches of the Albany Presbytery. Besides teaching voice, violin, and piano, he served as choir director and Sunday school superintendent in the Presbyterian church in Sherburne.

In 1837 Marsh founded the *Intelligencer* in Amsterdam, N.Y., and edited it for 7 years. Later he published the Sherburne *News*. He used his knowledge of printing to set the type and layout of the 3 children's songbooks he published.

Composer: MARTYN (126, p. 248)

Martin, Civilla Durfee (b. Jordan, N.J., August 21, 1866; d. Atlanta, Ga., March 9, 1948) was a village schoolteacher with some formal musical training. She worked with her husband Walter Stillman Martin in evangelistic campaigns and collaborated with him in writing gospel songs.

Author: Be Not Dismayed (207)

Martin, Walter Stillman (b. Rowley, Mass., 1862; d. Atlanta, Ga., December 16, 1935) was educated at Harvard University. He was ordained a Baptist minister, but later became a member of the Disciples of Christ. For a time he taught Bible at Atlantic Christian College in North Carolina. In 1919 he took up residence in Atlanta which served as a base of operations for Bible conferences and evangelistic meetings he held in all parts of the country.

Composer: MARTIN (207, p. 110)

Mason, Harry Silvernale (b. Gloversville, N.Y., October 17, 1881; d. Torrington, Conn., November 15, 1964) was educated at Syracuse University (B.M. 1911) with graduate study at Boston University, 1924-26. Syracuse later honored him with the Mus.D. He served as organist of Auburn Theological Seminary, 1916-39, instructor of music there, 1917-35, and assistant professor of fine arts and religion, 1935-39. He was organist of First Presbyterian Church in Auburn, and later of Second Presbyterian, where he served for 27 years.

Composer: BEACON HILL (413, p. 96)

Mason, Lowell (b. Medfield, Mass., July 8, 1792; d. Orange, N.J., August 11, 1872) was born into the sixth generation of a family which settled in America in 1653. Following musical instruction by local musicians, he began directing choirs and singing schools at the age of 16. When he was 20, he moved to Savannah, Ga., to work as a bank clerk. In addition to his bank duties he played the organ and directed the choir of the First Presbyterian Church, while studying theory with F. L. Abel. In an attempt to find a publisher for his hymn tunes and the book of church music he had compiled, he returned to Boston and interested G. K. Jackson of the Boston Handel and Haydn Society. The society sponsored the publication Boston *Handel and Haydn Society Collection of Church Music,* 1821. Erik Routley calls it the "most influential publication in the history of American hymnody." Commenting on Mason's contribution as a composer, Routley in *Companion to Congregational Praise* writes:

The hymn tunes of Mason are of cardinal importance in the history of American hymnody; if their musical content is often lower than we now think desirable for our own hymn-singing, it is worth remembering that Mason's object was deliberately to write his music in a restrained fashion in order to counteract the prevailing tendency to wild extravagance and sentimental vanity which was abroad in American church music of the time.

The success of the collection was immediate, and when the compiler's name was made public, Mason was invited to move from Savannah to Boston in 1827. There he was elected president and served as conductor of the Handel and Haydn Society during the years 1827-32 and directed music for 14 years in the Bowdoin Street Church where Lyman Beecher was pastor. In addition to these responsibilities he became interested in the field of music education and resigned his position with the Handel and Haydn Society to devote more time to children's music and instruction. He founded the Boston Academy of Music with G. J. Webb in 1832 after studying in Europe the Pestalozzian method of teaching. While he was in Germany, he became acquainted with Johann Nägeli, the publisher of the works of Beethoven and Clementi, and brought back to America many publications and copies of English, German, and French music then unknown in Boston. By 1834 he had established teacher-training classes and music conventions, and gave lectures, which were the primary means of the music education of teachers prior to the Civil War. Employing Pestalozzian educational principles, Mason inaugurated a music curriculum for the

Boston public schools in 1838. He returned to Europe, 1851-53, to lecture, and in 1855 New York University honored him with an honorary Mus.D. degree.

Mason's significant publications greatly enlarged his sphere of influence. Leonard Ellinwood in *The Hymnal 1940 Companion* has written: "The full scope of his influence may be realized if we recall that America had been settled a little over 300 years. . . . For 60 full years Lowell Mason was a dominating factor in church and school music, and in the pedagogy and philosophy of musical education."

The biographer Arthur L. Rich in *Lowell Mason: the Father of Singing Among the Children* (Chapel Hill, 1946) credits Mason as being compiler or collaborator in at least 80 publications, the most important being *Carmina Sacra*, 1852, which sold an estimated half million copies. Mason's grandson, Henry L. Mason, lists in *Hymn Tunes of Lowell Mason*, 1944, his output at 1,126 original tunes and 497 arrangements.

> Composer: BETHANY (**263**, p. 294)
> BOYLSTON (**150**, p. 65)
> DORT (**480**, p. 411)
> HAMBURG (**435**, p. 431)
> HEBRON (**128, 365, 471**, p. 170)
> LABAN (**246**, p. 293)
> MALVERN (**98**, p. 259)
> OLIVET (**143**, pp. 290-91)
> ROCKINGHAM (MASON) (**206, 213, 329**, p. 198)
> Arranger: ANTIOCH (**392**, p. 260)
> ARIEL (**168**, p. 306)
> AZMON (**1, 278**, p. 254)
> DENNIS (**53, 306, 336**, pp. 90-91)
> EVAN (**68, 338, 368**, pp. 119-20)
> MENDEBRAS (**488**, p. 307)
> NAOMI (**140**, p. 174)
> SABBATH (**489**, p. 365)

Massie, Richard (b. Chester, Cheshire, England, June 18, 1800; d. Pulford Hall, Coddington, England, March 11, 1887) was the son of the rector of St. Bride's Church, Chester, where he spent his childhood. He was apparently self trained in German. Massie joined with Frances E. Cox, Henry J. Buckoll, Arthur T. Russell, Catherine Winkworth, and others in the translations of German hymns. In 1854 he published translations from Martin Luther's spiritual songs; in 1860 a translation of Carl Johann Philipp Spitta's *Psalter und Harfe* under the title *Lyra Domestica,* first series. Four years later he published a second series of Spitta's texts together with an appendix of translations from other German sources.

Translator: Christ Jesus Lay in Death's Strong Bands (438)

Masterman, John Howard Bertram (b. Tunbridge Wells, Kent, England, December 6, 1867; d. Devonport, Devonshire, England, November 5, 1933) was educated at Weymouth College and St. John's College, Cambridge (B.A. 1893, M.A. 1897, honorary D.D. 1923). He was ordained deacon in 1893, priest in 1894. Masterman held various positions, including lecturer in church history at St. John's College, 1893-95; vicar of St. Aubyn's in Devonport, 1896-99; principal of the Midlands Classical College in Edgbaston, 1899-1901; warden of Queen's College, Birmingham, 1901-7; vicar of St. Michael's College Church, Coventry, 1907-12; canon of Coventry, 1912-22. In 1923 he was consecrated suffragan bishop of Plymouth.

Masterman wrote 13 books on history, doctrine, and New Testament studies.

Author: Lift Up Our Hearts, O King of Kings (194)

Matheson, George (b. Glasgow, Scotland, March 27, 1842; d. North Berwick, Scotland, August 28, 1906) was the son of a prosperous Glasgow merchant. He suffered from poor eyesight and was almost completely blind by the time he was 18. In spite of this affliction, he was an outstanding student, graduating from Glasgow Academy, 1852, and Glasgow University (B.A. 1861, M.A. 1862). He attended the Divinity School of Glasgow University in 1862 and was licensed to preach in the Presbyterian Church in 1866. He served churches in Glasgow, Innellan, Argyllshire, and in 1866 became the minister of St. Bernard's in Edinburgh where he retired in 1899 because of ill health.

Matheson received an honorary D.D. from Edinburgh University in 1879 and an LL.D. from Aberdeen University in 1902 in recognition of his outstanding ability as a preacher and author of theological studies. His only volume of verse, *Sacred Songs,* was published in 1890.

Author: Make Me a Captive, Lord (184)
O Love That Wilt Not Let Me Go (234)

Maurus, Rhabanus (also *Hrabanus Magnentius Marcus* and *Rabanus Maurus*) (b. Mainz, 776; d. Winkel, February 4, 856) became a monk at Fulda. In 802 he studied at Tours with Alcuin who gave him the name "Maurus." In 803 he was made director of the Benedictine school at Fulda. He was ordained in 814 and made a pilgrimage to the Holy Land shortly thereafter. He was named abbott at Fulda, 822-42, and in 847 was made archbishop of Mainz.

Maurus wrote works on theology and poems. His works were widely read during the Middle Ages.

Attributed author: Come, Holy Ghost, Our Souls Inspire (467)

Medley, Samuel (b. Cheshunt, Hertfordshire, England, June 23, 1738; d. Liverpool, Lancashire, England, July 17, 1799) as a youth served in the Royal navy. Converted upon reading an Isaac Watts sermon, Medley joined the Eagle Street Baptist Church (now Kingsgate Church) in London. He served as pastor of the Baptist churches in Watford, 1767-72, and Liverpool, 1772-99. In Liverpool the Byron Street Church prospered under his leadership, and a new building was erected in 1790.

In addition to hymns which appeared in magazines and 48 sacramental hymns which were published in *A Memoir* by his daughter Sarah in 1833, Medley published *Hymns,* 1785, *Hymns on Select Portions of Scripture,* 1785 and 1787, *Hymns,* 1794, and *Hymns: The Public Worship and Private Devotions of True Christians, Assisted in Some Thoughts in Verse: Principally Drawn from Select Passages of the Word of God,* 1800.

Author: I Know That My Redeemer Lives (445)
    O Could I Speak the Matchless Worth (168)

Meineke (also *Meinecke* and *Menicke), Christoph* (b. Oldenburg, May 1, 1782; d. Baltimore, Md., November 6, 1850) was the son of Karl Meinecke, the organist to the duke of Oldenburg. About 1810 Christoph moved to England from Germany and in 1820 established residence in Baltimore, Md., where he was organist at St. Paul's Episcopal Church until his death. His *Music for the Church . . . Composed for St. Paul's Church, Baltimore, by C. Meineke, Organist,* 1844, is the source of his minor contributions to church music.

Composer: Glory Be to the Father (794, pp. 446-47)

Mendelssohn, Jakob Ludwig Felix (b. Hamburg, February 3, 1809; d. Leipzig, November 4, 1847) was the son of a Jewish banker and a grandson of the Jewish philosopher Moses Mendelssohn. His mother was an artist, pianist, and singer. From her he received his first training. In 1811 the family moved to Berlin during the French occupation of Hamburg and became communicants of the Lutheran Church. The name "Bartholdy" was added at the time to indicate they were Christians.

By the age of 12 Mendelssohn had composed 5 symphonies and numerous other works. Discovering the music of J. S. Bach, which had been in eclipse for decades, he conducted a performance of Bach's *St. Matthew Passion* in 1829, the first since Bach's death. His enormous output included 2 oratorios—*St. Paul*, 1836, and *Elijah*, 1846. Many of his harmonizations and arrangements of chorales have been mined for use in hymnals from *St. Paul*. In 1833 he became the town music director at Düsseldorf, then moved to Leipzig in 1835 where he built the Gewandhaus Orchestra into the first of the great modern symphony orchestras. He also founded the Leipzig Conservatory in 1843.

Composer: CONSOLATION (**264**, p. 383)
MENDELSSOHN (**388**, pp. 210-11)
Arranger: MUNICH (**167, 201, 372**, p. 293)
NUN DANKET (**49**, p. 298)

Merbecke (also *Marbeck* and *Marbecke*), *John* (b. England, 1523; d. England, c. 1585) by 1541 was a lay clerk, chorister, and organist of St. George's, Windsor. A biblical scholar interested in the principles of the Reformers, he studied Calvin's works and started work on a concordance, which was discovered in his home by church commissioners hunting for heretics. Merbecke was tried and convicted with 3 other men who were hanged in 1543, but he escaped death through the intervention of Bishop Gardiner of Winchester and was pardoned by Henry VIII.

In 1550, one year after the appearance of the First Prayer Book of Edward VI, Merbecke produced his *Book of Common Prayer Noted* and also his concordance, the first complete one of the English Bible. In his setting of the English text for Morning Prayer and Holy Communion he was instructed by Archbishop Thomas Cranmer to set the English text "not full of notes, but, as near as may be, for every syllable a note, so that it may be sung distinctly and devoutly." His adaptation was based on early plainchant with most of the settings truncated to fit the English text. Even though he wrote regretfully of his "study of Musike and playing Organs wherein I consumed vainly the greatest part of my life," he continued in office at Windsor and managed to survive the Marian turmoil. During Queen Elizabeth's reign he wrote several controversial tracts espousing the Reformed cause.

Composer: Glory Be to God on High (**800**, p. 445) (**840**, p. 445)
Holy, Holy, Holy (**830B**, pp. 448-49)
Lift Up Your Hearts (**841**, p. 451)
Lord, Have Mercy upon Us (**838**, pp. 452-53)
O Lamb of God (**830C**, pp. 456-57)
Praise Be to Thee (**801**, p. 459)

Merrill, William Pierson (b. East Orange, N.J., January 10, 1867; d. New York, N.Y., June 19, 1954) at the age of 11 joined the Belleville Congregational Church in Newburyport, Mass. Two years later he transferred to the Second Dutch Reformed Church in New Brunswick, N.J. After his education at Rutgers College (B.A. 1887, M.A. 1890) and Union Theological Seminary (B.D. 1890), he was ordained a Presbyterian minister in 1890 and served pastorates at Chestnut Hill, Pa., 1890-95, and Chicago, Ill., 1895-1911. In 1911 he went to Brick Presbyterian Church in New York City and spent the rest of his ministry there, retiring in 1938. Beginning in 1915, he was president of the trustees of the Church Peace Union.

An eminent preacher, Merrill was also the author of 10 books, including *Liberal Christianity*, 1925, *Prophets of the Dawn,* 1927, and *We See Jesus,* 1934. Columbia University honored him with the S.T.D degree in 1927.

Author: Not Alone for Mighty Empire (**548**)
Rise Up, O Men of God (**174**)

Messiter, Arthur Henry (b. Frome, Somersetshire, England, April 12, 1834; d. New York, N.Y., July 2, 1916) took his early education with private tutors, with 4 years of musical study at Northampton. Coming to America in 1863, he sang for a time in the choir at Trinity Church, New York City. After a short time as organist at Poultney, Vt., and Philadelphia, he became organist at Trinity Church in New York, where he served with distinction, 1866-97, maintaining the high standards of the English men and boys' choir tradition. In addition to being an editor of one of the music editions of the Protestant Episcopal *Hymnal,* 1893, he edited a *Psalter,* 1889, *Choir Office-Book,* 1891, and authored *A History of the Choir and Music of Trinity Church,* 1906.

Composer: MARION (233, p. 359)

Milligan, James Lewis (b. Liverpool, England, February 1, 1876; d. Scarborough Township, York County, Ontario, Canada, May 1, 1961) attended Anglican schools until the age of 12 when he went to work in the building trades. He continued his study privately and was a contributor to the London papers. In 1910 he won the Hemans prize for lyrical poetry at the University of Liverpool, and the same year a collection of his verse was published in London. In 1911 he emigrated to Canada and became lay preacher on a Methodist circuit in Hastings County, Ontario. In 1913 Milligan became editor of the Peterborough *Daily Review* and soon thereafter joined the editorial staff of the *Toronto Globe.* Later he became an editorial writer for the Stafford *Beacon-Herald.* He served as editor and publicity director for the Presbyterian Bureau of Literature and Information during the days when the Canadian Church union movement was underway and helped to bring the union to fruition. Milligan's second book of verse, *The Beckoning Skyline,* was published in 1920, and a play, *Judas Iscariot,* in 1930.

Author: There's a Voice in the Wilderness Crying (362)

Milman, Henry Hart (b. London, England, February 10, 1791; d. London, September 24, 1868) was educated at Eton and at Brasenose College, Oxford (B.A. 1814, M.A. 1816, B.D. and D.D. 1849). He was ordained in 1816 and was named professor of poetry at Oxford in 1821. He gave the Bampton Lectures in 1827. In 1835 he was made rector of St. Margaret's and canon of Westminster, remaining there until he was made dean of St. Paul's Cathedral in 1849.

Milman's literary works include *History of the Jews,* 1829, *Selection of Psalms and Hymns,* 1837, *History of Latin Christianity,* 1854, and

Annals of St. Paul's, published posthumously. Milman was a friend of Reginald Heber, and Heber's *Hymns Written and Adapted to the Weekly Service of the Church Year,* 1827, contained 13 of Milman's poems.

Author: Ride On, Ride On in Majesty (425)

Milton, John (b. London, England, December 9, 1608; d. Artillery Walk, St. Giles, England, November 8, 1674) was educated at St. Paul's School and Christ's College, Cambridge (B.A. 1629, M.A. 1632). For 6 years he lived at Horton with his parents, then traveled in Europe, 1638-39, before settling in Aldersgate Street. He married in 1643 but his wife died in 1653, the year Milton became blind. During Cromwell's rule he was named Secretary for Foreign Tongues in the Council of State, holding the translator's post during the years 1649-59.

Milton's 19 metrical psalms were not intended for singing, but for devotional reading. His influence as a poet extended to the Wesleys. Henry Bett in *Hymns of Methodism* wrote that this influence is "visible everywhere in the hymns. The great Puritan poet is the source of many of their striking phrases, and his influence upon the poetry of the Wesleys is greater, perhaps, than that of any other writer."

Author: Let Us with a Gladsome Mind (61)
The Lord Will Come and Not Be Slow (468)

Mohr, Joseph (b. Salzburg, Austria, December 11, 1792; d. Wagrein, Austria, December 4, 1848) as a boy sang as a chorister in the cathedral at Salzburg. Because his father, a mercenary musketeer, was away from home much of the time, a priest, Domvikar J. N. Hiernle, became his foster father. He was ordained into the Roman Catholic priesthood in 1815 and served in many capacities in various parishes in the diocese of Salzburg. During the years 1817-19 he was an assistant priest of St. Nicholas' Church, Oberndorf, where he wrote his famous carol. His last post was as vicar of Hintersee from 1828 until his death.

Author: Silent Night, Holy Night (393)

Moment, John James (b. Orono, Ontario, Canada, February 1, 1875; d. Plainfield, N.J., May 11, 1959) was a graduate of Princeton University (B.A. 1896) and Hartford Theological Seminary (B.D. 1906). He was awarded a D.D. from Washington and Jefferson College.

During the years 1898-1904 he taught at Lawrenceville School and thereafter served Presbyterian pastorates in East Orange, N.J., 1906-8; Jersey City, N.J., 1908-11; Newark, 1911-18; and from 1918 until his retirement as pastor of Crescent Avenue Presbyterian Church in Plainfield, N.J.

Moment collaborated with Charlotte Lockwood Garden, organist at Plainfield, in writing texts for many anthems and oratorios. He was a member of the hymnal committee which produced the Presbyterian U.S.A. *Hymnal* of 1933.

Author: Men and Children Everywhere (11)

Monk, Edwin George (b. Frome, Somersetshire, England, December 13, 1819; d. Radley, Berkshire, England, January 3, 1900) studied under Henry Field, George Field, John P. Hullah, Henry Phillips, and George A. Macfarren. He entered Oxford in 1847 (B.M. 1848, Mus.D. 1856). After his first appointment as organist at Midsomer Norton parish church, he went as first precentor and master of music at St. Columba's, Rathfarnham, Dublin, the first Protestant public school in Ireland. After conducting the University Motet and Madrigal Society at Oxford, he became organist and master of music of St. Peter's College in Radley. During the years 1858-83 he was organist at Yorkminster, where he succeeded John Camidge. For 12 years he was examiner in music at Oxford University.

Monk's publications included several editions of chants and hymns, and he provided the librettos for 3 of Macfarren's oratorios. An amateur astronomer, he was elected a fellow of the Royal Astronomical Society.

Composer: We Praise Thee, O God (665, pp. 464-65)

Monk, William Henry (b. Brompton, London, England, March 16, 1823; d. London, March 1, 1889), after training with Thomas Adams, J. A. Hamilton, and G. A. Griesbach, began at the age of 18 to serve as organist in various London churches. He was choir director in 1847, organist in 1849, and professor of vocal music in 1874 at King's College. In 1852 he became organist of St. Matthias' Church, Stoke Newington, and continued in this position until his death. He also served as professor of music at the School for the Indigent Blind, the National

Training School for Music, and Bedford College, London. Durham University awarded him the Mus.D. degree in 1882.

Monk's most important contributions were made as editor of the *Parish Choir,* 1840-51, and as music editor of *Hymns Ancient and Modern,* 1861 and 1868. He collaborated with others on the 1875 and 1880 music editions of the same hymnal, to which he contributed 50 tunes and arrangements. He assisted in the editing of other collections, including *The Book of Common Prayer, with Plain Song and Appropriate Music.*

Composer: DIX (35, 397, p. 100)
EVENTIDE (289, pp. 68-69)
INNOCENTS (61, p. 268)
Arranger: RATISBON (401, 463, p. 135)
VICTORY (447, p. 401)
Harmonizer: STEPHANOS (99, p. 98)

Monsell, John Samuel Bewley (b. St. Colomb's, Londonderry, Ireland, March 2, 1811; d. Guildford, England, April 9, 1875), the son of the archdeacon of Londonderry, was educated at Trinity College, Dublin (B.A. 1832, LL.D. 1856). He was ordained priest in 1835 and held various positions, such as chaplain to Bishop Mant, chancellor of the diocese of Connor, rector of Ramoan, vicar of Egham, and rector of St. Nicholas' at Guildford.

Monsell published 11 volumes of poetry, including nearly 300 hymns. He urged that hymns be "more fervent and joyous. We are too distant and reserved in our praises; we sing, not as we should sing to Him who is Chief among ten thousand, the Altogether Lovely." He was accidentally killed by falling stonework at St. Nicholas', which was being rebuilt.

Author: Fight the Good Fight (240, 241)
God Is Love, by Him Upholden (62)
Light of the World, We Hail Thee (398)
What Grace, O Lord, and Beauty Shone (178)

Montgomery, James (b. Irvine, Ayrshire, Scotland, November 4, 1771; d. Sheffield, Yorkshire, England, April 30, 1854) was the son of John Montgomery, an Irish Moravian minister, and James was intended by his parents for the Moravian ministry. His parents left him with the

COMPANION TO THE HYMNAL

Moravian settlement at Bracehill near Ballymena and went in 1783 as missionaries to Barbados and Tobago, West Indies, where they died, 1790-91. The boy attended school at Fulneck, near Leeds, but was dismissed because of his preoccupation with writing poetry and was apprenticed to a baker. He ran away in 1787 and found employment in a chandler's shop at Mirfield, near Wakefield. With a desire to publish his poetry, he traveled to London, but failed to find a publisher there. The publisher-owner of the *Sheffield Registrar,* Joseph Gales, took an interest in the youth and hired him as his assistant. In 1794 the controversial Mr. Gales left the country to avoid prosecution for his anti-Tory opinions and writings. James assumed the ownership of the paper, changed its name to the *Sheffield Iris,* and continued its controversial writings for 31 years. Some of his hymns were first published in the *Iris.* Twice he was fined and imprisoned, once for printing a song which celebrated the fall of the Bastille and again for reporting a political riot at Sheffield. He was a champion of many liberal causes, including the abolition of slavery, and often lectured in support of foreign missions and the British and Foreign Bible Society.

Montgomery worshiped at the Wesley chapel in Sheffield, and from at least 1814 he maintained a close relationship to Methodism. One of the Wesley chapels in Sheffield bears his name. His interest in the question of hymn singing in Anglican worship is seen in his support of Thomas Cotterill, bishop of St. Paul's Church in Sheffield, in Cotterill's attempt to introduce hymns to his congregation. Montgomery later became a communicant of St. George's, where hymn writer William Mercer was vicar.

Montgomery wrote many poems and articles and about 400 hymns, which were collected in 1853. Some 20 to 25 are in use today.

> Author: According to Thy Gracious Word (316)
> Angels, from the Realms of Glory (382)
> Be Known to Us in Breaking Bread (313)
> Go to Dark Gethsemane (434)
> God Is My Strong Salvation (211)
> Hail to the Lord's Anointed (359)
> In the Hour of Trial (237)
> Pour Out Thy Spirit from on High (337)
> Prayer Is the Soul's Sincere Desire (252)
> Stand Up and Bless the Lord (16)

Moore, Thomas (b. Dublin, Ireland, May 28, 1779; d. London or Sloperton, Devizes, Wiltshire, February 25, 1852) attended Trinity College, Dublin, and studied law in London. In 1803 Moore was appointed admiralty registrar in Bermuda. This relationship led to a series of financial difficulties which plagued him for the rest of his life. He traveled to New York in 1840 and toured America and Canada.

Moore was a very popular and versatile writer. His works include *A Selection of Irish Melodies*, 1807-34, *Odes upon Cash, Corn, Catholics and Other Matters*, 1828, and the editing of Lord Byron's letters, 1830. Moore's only connection with hymnody is contained in *Sacred Songs*, 1816, containing 32 texts.

Author: Come, Ye Disconsolate (**103**)

Morey, Lloyd (b. Laddonia, Mo., January 15, 1886; d. Urbana, Ill., September 29, 1965) was educated at the University of Illinois (B.A. and B.M. 1911, C.P.A. 1916). He began working in the university's controller's office after graduation and began teaching in 1917. During the years 1916-53 he was controller of the university, and during the years 1953-54 he served as president. Morey was advisor to many educational and governmental agencies and the recipient of many honorary degrees and awards.

From 1911 to 1940 Morey was organist-choir director of the Trinity Methodist Church in Urbana. His choir was made up of a select group of 16 music students. He composed much service music for use in the church during the pastorates of James C. Baker and Paul Burt.

Composer: All Things Come of Thee (**807**, p. 441)

Morison, John (b. Cairnie, Aberdeenshire, Scotland, 1749; d. Canisbay, Caithness, Scotland, June 12, 1798) was educated at the University of Aberdeen (M.A. 1771). In 1780 he became minister at Canisbay, Caithness. His early poetry was published in the *Edinburgh Weekly Magazine* with the signature of "Musaeus." He was a member of the General Assembly committee for the revision of the Scottish *Translations and Paraphrases*, 1781, to which he had earlier contributed 7 paraphrases.

Author: The People That in Darkness Sat (**361**)

Mote, Edward (b. London, England, January 21, 1797; d. Horsham, Sussex, England, November 13, 1874) was the son of the keeper of a public house. Edward grew up without religious training in the streets. Apprenticed to a cabinetmaker, he began to attend church and was influenced by John Hyatt, who preached at Tottenham Court Road Chapel, one of Lady Huntingdon's chapels. Settling in Southwark near London, Mote became a cabinetmaker and reporter for the press. In 1852 he became a Baptist minister and preached at Horsham, Sussex, with great success for 21 years. *Hymns of Praise, A New Selection of Gospel Hymns* (London, 1836)—the first use of the term "gospel hymn"—contained more than 100 of his hymns.

Author: My Hope Is Built (222)

Moultrie, Gerard (b. Rugby, England, September 16, 1829; d. Southleigh, England, April 25, 1885) was the son of an Anglican minister. His great-grandfather left South Carolina after the outbreak of the American Revolution and returned to England. Moultrie's great-grand-uncle was General William Moultrie, elected governor of South Carolina in 1785, and for whom Fort Moultrie was named.

Gerard was educated at Rugby School and Exeter College, Oxford (B.A. 1851, M.A. 1856). After being ordained into the Anglican priesthood he became a master and chaplain of Shrewsbury School, 1869, vicar of Southleigh, 1869, and warden of St. James's College, Southleigh, 1873.

Among his publications are *Hymns and Lyrics for the Seasons and Saints' Days of the Church*, 1867, and the preface to *Cantica Sanctorum*, 1880. The latter contained 103 hymns, mostly on themes not previously covered in hymns. His fame rests primarily on his excellent translations of Greek, Latin, and German hymns.

Translator: Let All Mortal Flesh Keep Silence (324)

Murray, James Ramsey (b. Andover, Mass., March 17, 1841; d. Cincinnati, Ohio, March 10, 1905) was born of Scottish parentage. He received musical instruction from Lowell Mason, George F. Root, William B. Bradbury, and George J. Webb. During the years 1856-59 he studied at the Musical Institute in North Reading, Mass. During the Civil War he served as a Union soldier. Later he was employed by the

Chicago publishing firm of Root & Cady, where he edited the monthly periodical the *Song Messenger*. The Chicago fire of 1871 destroyed the publishing firm, and he returned to Andover to teach music. From 1881 until his death he was employed by a Cincinnati publisher, the John Church Company, and headed their publishing department and edited the monthly magazine the *Musical Visitor*.

Murray composed many Sunday school songs, gospel songs, and anthems, and compiled and edited many collections, the most popular being *The Prize, Royal Gems, Pure Diamonds, Murray's Sacred Songs,* and *Dainty Songs for Little Lads and Lasses.*

William J. Reynolds in *Hymns of Our Faith* is the first to research Murray's life and work.

Composer: AWAY IN A MANGER (384, pp. 108-9)

Nägeli, Johann (Hans) Georg (b. Wetzikon, near Zurich, Switzerland, May 26, 1768 or 1773; d. Wetzikon, December 26, 1836) was a writer, teacher, and composer. He founded a publishing firm in 1792 and published in his *Répertoire de clavecinistes,* beginning in 1803, the first printings of Beethoven's sonatas, Op. 31. Nägeli was an important exponent of Pestalozzian teaching methods and deeply influenced Lowell Mason in this regard.

Composer: DENNIS (53, 306, 336, pp. 90-91)
NAOMI (140, 268, p. 174)

Neale, John Mason (b. London, England, January 24, 1818; d. East Grinstead, Sussex, England, August 6, 1866) was the only son of the Reverend Cornelius and Susanna Neale, who were both of Evangelical persuasion. He graduated from Trinity College, Cambridge in 1840 and became a fellow of Downing College and acting chaplain and tutor. While at Cambridge, Neale became identified with the Oxford Movement and was one of the founders of the Cambridge Camden Society. He was ordained priest in 1842; chronic ill health and his Anglo-Catholic leanings kept him out of the parish priesthood. Instead, in 1846 he became warden of Sackville College, East Grinstead, a home for old men. The remainder of his life was spent in research and writing. He was a champion of social welfare, and he founded a nursing sisterhood and extended the ministry of Sackville College to include orphans and young women.

Neale's primary achievements are his translations and paraphrases from Greek and Latin authors. Within the existing English traditions of psalmody and hymnody, he single-handedly introduced the Eastern Christian liturgical and didactic writings, which were up until that time unknown. The publication of *Hymns of the Eastern Church,* 1862, was the culmination of 12 years of research. His principal collections containing his translations from the Latin are *Mediaeval Hymns and Sequences,* 1851 and 1863, *Hymns, Chiefly Mediaeval, on the Joys and Glories of Paradise,* 1865. *The Hymnal Noted,* 1851 and 1854, contained many of his own hymns as well as translations of Latin texts. The "trial" or first edition of *Hymns Ancient and Modern,* 1859, contained many of his texts. Today his hymns and translations are found in all hymnals.

A paradox concerning Neale's work is the lack of official English recognition given his achievement. However, he received an inscribed copy of an ancient liturgy from the Metropolitan of Russia in 1860, and Trinity College, Hartford, Conn., honored him with degrees.

Translator: All Glory, Laud, and Honor (424)
Art Thou Weary, Art Thou Languid (99)
Christ Is Made the Sure Foundation (298)
Christian, Dost Thou See Them (238)
Come, Ye Faithful, Raise the Strain (446, 448)
Creator of the Stars of Night (78)
Good Christian Men, Rejoice (391)
Jerusalem the Golden (303)
O Come, O Come, Emmanuel (354)
O Sons and Daughters, Let Us Sing (451)
Of the Father's Love Begotten (357)
The Day Is Past and Over (491)
The Day of Resurrection (437)
To Thee Before the Close of Day (814, p. 463)

Neander, Joachim (b. Bremen, 1650; d. Bremen, May 31, 1680) received his education in the Pädagogium where his father was master and at the Gymnasium Illustre. He was descended from a long line of clergymen. As a student at the gymnasium, he joined in the riotous, rebellious student life. At the age of 20 he joined a group of students to attend St. Martin's Church, Bremen, to criticize and make fun, but was moved by the preaching of the pastor Theodore Under-Eyck and was converted later under his guidance. After serving as a tutor at Frankfort and Heidelberg, he was appointed rector of the Latin school at Düsseldorf in 1674. The school was Calvinistic, and Neander's close association with P. J. Spener and the Pietists led to his suspension. It is reported that he lived for some months in a cave near Mettman on the Rhine in the valley where Neanderthal man was later found. This valley was named for him. In 1679 he returned to Bremen as assistant preacher at St. Martin's Church. He died of tuberculosis.

Neander wrote about 60 hymns for which he also provided tunes.

> Author: Praise to the Lord, the Almighty (55)
> Composer: ARNSBERG (788, p. 448)
> UNSER HERRSCHER (7, 13, 153, p. 197)

Nelson, Ronald Axel (b. Rockford, Ill., April 29, 1927) was educated at St. Olafs College (B.M. 1949) and the University of Wisconsin (M.M. 1959). He has taught public school music and directed Lutheran Church choirs in Rockford, Ill., and St. Louis Park, Minn. Since 1955 he has been director of music, Westwood Lutheran Church, St. Louis Park. Nelson has several choral compositions in print.

> Composer: God Be Merciful unto Us (804, p. 448)

Neumark, Georg (b. Langensalza, Thuringia, March 16, 1621; d. Weimar, July 18, 1681) was the son of a clothing merchant. Neumark studied at the gymnasia of Schleusingen and Gotha. In 1640 or 1641 he set out with a caravan to study law at Königsberg, but on the way there was robbed by highwaymen. Left with a prayerbook and a few coins, which were sewed into his clothing, he sought employment in 4 cities before securing a tutorship in Kiel in the family of Judge Stephan Henning. In 2 years he had saved enough money to return to Königsberg, where he studied law. After graduation he again was unable to secure employment until 1652 when he was appointed court poet, librarian, and registrar at Weimar, and finally secretary of the ducal archives. He became blind in his last year. Most of Neumark's 34 hymns were written during times of trial and suffering.

> Author and composer: If Thou But Suffer God to Guide Thee (WER NUR
> DEN LIEBEN GOTT) (210)

Newman, John Henry (b. London, England, February 21, 1801; d. Edgbaston, England, August 11, 1890) was educated at Ealing and at Trinity College, Oxford (B.A. 1820). He became a fellow of Oriel in 1822 and was ordained in 1824. After a short curacy at St. Clement's, he was appointed vicar of St. Mary's, Oxford, 1828. During the years 1832-33 he traveled abroad with Hurrell Froude, and it was during this voyage that he wrote most of his poems, which were published in *Lyra Apostolica,* 1836. His famous *Tracts for the Times* began in 1833, and 10 years later he retired to Littlemore and became a Roman Catholic in 1845. In 1848 he was appointed to the oratory of St. Philip Neri, Edgbaston, and remained there the rest of his life.

Newman was not entirely trusted by the Catholic hierarchy and felt that his efforts in behalf of the Roman Catholic Church were unappreciated. He was made a cardinal in 1879.

Author: Lead Kindly Light (272)

Newton, John (b. London, England, July 24, 1725; d. London, December 21, 1807) was the son of a shipmaster. He went to sea with his father at the age of 11. He later was imprisoned on a man-of-war, escaped to work on a slave-trading ship, and led a rough life as master of a slaveship. At Liverpool he was greatly influenced by George Whitefield and the Wesleys. As a result of their influence and his reading of Thomas à Kempis' *Imitation of Christ,* he retired from active sea duty and during 1755-60 was tide-surveyor at Liverpool. At the same time he studied Hebrew and Greek, in preparation for ordination.

Newton became the curate at Olney and was ordained in 1764. With lay reader William Cowper he produced the *Olney Hymns* in 1779. Newton contributed 281 hymns to the collection to Cowper's 67. In 1780 he left Olney to become rector at St. Mary's, Woolnoth, in London, and remained there until his eightieth year.

His correspondence with contemporaries was very heavy, and he is looked upon as the leader of the evangelical wing of the Church of England. *Olney Hymns* can be judged as the first and most important of Anglican hymnbooks printed for parish use. Though a former slaveship captain, he was an ardent abolitionist.

His life is best summed up by his own epitaph:

John Newton, clerk
once an infidel and libertine,

A Servant of slaves in Africa:
Was by the rich mercy of our Lord and Saviour, Jesus Christ,
   Preserved, restored, pardoned,
   And appointed to preach the Faith
   He had labored long to destroy.
Near sixteen years at Olney in Bucks;
And twenty-seven years in this Church.

Author: Amazing Grace! How Sweet the Sound (92)
   Glorious Things of Thee Are Spoken (293)
   How Sweet the Name of Jesus Sounds (81)
   May the Grace of Christ Our Savior (334)
   Safely Through Another Week (489)

Niceta, Bishop of Remesiana (d. after 414) was a missionary bishop of Remesiana to Dacia (now Yugoslavia) from 392 to 414. He was a friend of Aurelius Clemens Prudentius and a contemporary of St. Jerome. A letter of Pope Innocent I, dated December 13, 414, indicates that Niceta was still living at that time.

Attributed author: We Praise Thee, O God (665, pp. 464-65)

Nichol, Henry Ernest (b. Hull, Yorkshire, England, December 10, 1862; d. Aldborough, Skirlaugh, Yorkshire, August 30, 1926) was apprenticed to the study of civil engineering in 1877. He changed his study to music in 1885 and received his B.M. degree from Oxford in 1888. Nichol's 130 tunes were written primarily for Sunday school anniversary services. He used the pen name "Colin Sterne" for those texts for which he also wrote the tune.

Author and composer: We've a Story to Tell to the Nations (MESSAGE) (410)

Nicolai, Philipp (b. Mengeringhausen, Waldeck, August 10, 1556; d. Hamburg, October 26, 1608) was the son of a Lutheran pastor and was educated at Erfurt and Wittenberg. He was ordained at 20 years of age and first assisted his father, then became preacher of Herdecke. Here and in his following positions at Niederwildungen, Altwildungen, and Unna, Westphalia, he was embroiled in controversies with Catholics, Sacramentarians, and Calvinists. During his ministry in Unna the town was devastated by pestilence. In 1601 he went to his final charge as chief pastor of St. Katherine's Church in Hamburg, where he died of a fever.

Author and composer: O Morning Star, How Fair and Bright (WIE
SCHÖN LEUCHTET DER MORGENSTERN) (399)
Wake, Awake, for Night Is Flying (WACHET
AUF) (366)

Niedling, Johann (b. Sangerhausen, Saxony, 1602; d. Altenburg, February 14, 1668) was educated at Altenburg. From 1638 until his death he taught at the gymnasium in Altenburg. Niedling compiled 6 collections of poems and hymns, including *Lutherisch Handbüchlein,* which went through 6 printings.

Source: Lord Jesus Christ, Be Present Now (784, pp. 453-54)

Noel, Caroline Maria (b. London, England, April 10, 1817; d. London, December 7, 1877) was the daughter of a poet and clergyman. She began writing hymns at an early age but stopped at the age of 20. During a sickness in 1857 she began to write again, and in 1861 *The Name of Jesus and Other Verses for the Sick and Lonely* was published. Other poems of hers were published after her death, in 1878.

Author: At the Name of Jesus (76)

North, Frank Mason (b. New York, N.Y., December 3, 1850; d. Madison, N.J., December 17, 1935) was educated at Wesleyan University (B.A. 1872, M.A. 1875) and was ordained into the ministry of the Methodist Episcopal Church in 1872. He served churches from 1872 to 1892 in Florida, New York, and Connecticut. He was editor of the *Christian City* and corresponding secretary of the New York Church Extension and Missionary Society of the Methodist Episcopal Church, 1892-1912. In 1919 North became secretary of the Board of Foreign Missions and was president of the Federal Council of Churches of Christ in America, 1916-20. He received many honorary degrees.

North's writings are housed at Drew University, Madison, N.J.

Author: O Master of the Waking World (407)
Where Cross the Crowded Ways of Life (204)

Oakeley, Frederick (b. Shrewsbury, Worcester, England, September 5, 1802; d. Islington, London, England, January 29, 1880) was educated at Christ Church, Oxford (B.A. 1824), and became a fellow of Balliol in 1827. He was a prebendary of Lichfield Cathedral, a preacher at Whitehall, and minister of Margaret Chapel, London (now known as All Saints', Margaret Street). At Margaret Chapel Oakeley translated Latin hymns and was otherwise closely related to the Oxford Group, especially John Henry Newman. In 1845, at Littlemore, Oakeley became a Roman Catholic. He spent many years ministering to the poor in Westminster and in 1852 was made canon of the Westminster Procathedral. In 1865 he published the preface on antiphonal chanting in Richard Redhead's *Laudes Diurnae, Lyra Liturgica.*

Translator: O Come, All Ye Faithful (**386**)

Oakeley, Herbert Stanley (b. Ealing, Middlesex, England, July 22, 1830; d. Eastbourne, East Sussex, England, October 26, 1903) was the son of a clergyman. He was educated at Rugby and Christ Church, Oxford (B.A. 1853, M.A. 1856). He studied music further at Leipzig, Dresden, and Bonn. During the years 1865-91 he was Reid Professor of Music at Edinburgh and was influential in the musical life of Scotland. He was the recipient of honorary degrees from 9 universities. In 1876 he was knighted, and in 1881, he was named composer to the queen.

Oakeley composed much choral and instrumental music, including the cantata *Jubilee Lyric.* As an organist, he was skilled at improvisation.

Composer: ABENDS (**501**, p. 102)

Oliver, Henry Kemble (b. Beverly, Mass., November 24, 1800; d. Salem, Mass., August 12, 1885) was educated at Boston Latin School, Phillips Andover Academy. He spent 2 years at Harvard but graduated from Dartmouth, 1818. Harvard granted him a B.A. and M.A. in 1862, and included his name in the class of 1818. He taught school at Salem, Mass., for 24 years and served on the committee which drew up plans for the organization which was the forerunner of the National Educational Association. Oliver's varied career included adjutant-general of the Massachusetts militia, 1844-48, superintendent of the Atlantic Cotton Mills at Lawrence, 1848-58, state treasurer, 1860-65, first head and director of the Massachusetts Bureau of Statistics of Labor, 1869-73, and mayor of Salem, 1877-80.

Oliver also founded the Salem Oratorio Society, the Salem Glee Club, and the Mozart Association, of which he was president, organist, and director. He was organist of St. Peter's, Barton Square, and North Church in Salem for 24 years, and of the Unitarian church in Lawrence for 12 years. His publications include *The National Lyre,* with Samuel P. Tuckerman and S. A. Bancroft, 1848, *Oliver's Collection of Hymn and Psalm Tunes,* 1860, and *Original Hymn Tunes,* 1875.

Composer: FEDERAL STREET (105, 118, pp. 191-92)

Olson, Ernst William (b. Skane, Sweden, 1870; d. Chicago, Ill., October 6, 1958) came to America with his parents in 1875. He graduated from Augustana College in Rock Island and served as editor of various Swedish weeklies for about 12 years. He was named office editor of the Engberg-Holmberg Publishing Company in Chicago, 1906-11, and held a similar position with the Augustana Book Concern, 1911-49.

Olson possessed unusual literary gifts. He authored several works including "A History of the Swedes in Illinois." In 1922 he was awarded a prize for Swedish poetry. He contributed 28 translations and 4 original English hymns and paraphrases to the *Augustana Hymnal,* 1925. He served as a member of the committee responsible for the *Service Book and Hymnal,* 1958. In 1926 Augustana College awarded him the L.H.D.

E. E. Ryden has furnished the biographical information on this person.

Translator: Children of the Heavenly Father (521)

Olude, Abraham Taiwo Olajide (b. Ebute-Metta, Lagos, Nigeria, July 16, 1908) received his professional education for teaching and as a minister at Wesley College, Ibadan, and journalistic study at a Mindola training school. His interest in the use of indigenous African compositions in worship began as a student in 1925. Olude has been a pioneer in the movement to throw off the European base of congregational song and to exploit native drums and other indigenous instruments in both choir and congregational music. He has written many hymns in the folk idiom and has toured with his own choir in Nigeria demonstrating this music during the years 1937-50. As a pastor and district superintendent he has served various school and institutional causes.

Olude has written dramas and music for public and private schools, all using the African style of performance and the Nigerian language base. He states his view concerning the necessity of incorporating both these elements in Christian worship: "It is my attempt to make singing more meaningful at worship than singing words to English tunes which make nonsense of the words used."

Olude has received many honors including the Order of the Niger, and an honorary Mus.D. degree from the University of Nigeria, 1967.

Author and composer: Jesus, We Want to Meet (NIGERIA) (487)

Owen, William (b. Bangor, Caernarvonshire, Wales, 1814; d. 1893) like his father, worked in the Penrhyn slate quarries and was noted for his singing. At the age of 18 he wrote his first tune for a popular hymn. He was criticized for writing a new tune for an old text and was admonished to write new tunes for new texts. In 1886 he published *Y Perl Cerddorol,* a collection of anthems and hymn tunes. In Wales he is called "Prysgol."

Composer: BRYN CALFARIA (364, 453, p. 271)

Oxenham, John (b. Cheetham, Manchester, England, November 12, 1852; d. High Salvington, Sussex, England, January 23, 1941) was born William Arthur Dunkerly. He took his pen name from the Elizabethan sea dog in *Westward Ho!* which a Sunday school teacher gave to him to read. He was educated at Old Trafford School and Victoria University in Manchester, 1861-69. During the years 1872-81 he was in business with his father, a wholesale merchant, and traveled in Europe and America. His early writings were so successful that he turned to full-time literary work, producing 41 novels, 3 short story books, 8 poems, and 11 volumes of religious works. He was a Congregationalist of deep faith and edited the *Christian News-Letter* during

World War II and later became a deacon at Ealing Congregational Church, London, where he taught a Bible class.

Author: In Christ There Is No East or West (192)
Mid All the Traffic of the Ways (225)

Page, Kate Stearns (b. Brookline, Mass., August 21, 1873; d. New York, N.Y., January 19, 1963) taught at Dennison House Settlement School in Boston and at the Parke School in Brookline. During the years 1933-41 she taught the preschool music classes at the Diller-Quaile School of Music in New York City. Mrs. Page collaborated with Angela Diller, one of the founders of the school, in writing *9 Pieces to Be Learned by Rote, A Pre-School Music Book, Diller-Page Carol Book, Diller Page Song Books I and II, Rote Pieces for Rhythm Band,* and the *Schubert Band Book.*

Author: We, Thy People, Praise Thee (6)

Palestrina, Giovanni Pierluigi Sante da (b. Palestrina, Italy, 1525; d. Rome, Italy, February 2, 1594) was the son of a wealthy father in Palestrina. He was given the name "da Palestrina" to designate his birthplace. In 1544 he was appointed organist and choirmaster in his native town, and in 1551 his bishop, having become Pope Julius III, called him to the Capella Giulia at Rome. There he spent the rest of his life writing masses, motets, and madrigals, and serving various positions in papal and Roman churches and chapels. His complete works, published by Breitkopf & Härtel, 1862-1903, fill 33 volumes.

Composer: VICTORY (447, p. 401)

Palmer, Ray (b. Little Compton, R.I., November 12, 1808; d. Newark, N.J., March 29, 1887) was the son of Judge Thomas Palmer. He was educated at Phillips Andover Academy and Yale University (B.A. 1830). In 1835 he was ordained into the Congregational ministry and served churches in Bath, Me., 1835-50, and Albany, N.Y., 1850-65. He was appointed corresponding secretary of the American Congregational Union in 1865, working in New York City until his retirement.

Palmer contributed 15 original and translated hymns from Latin for Edward A. Park and Austin Phelps's *Sabbath Hymn Book,* 1858.

Included in his publications were *Hymns and Sacred Pieces,* 1865, *Hymns of My Holy Hours,* 1868, and the complete *Poetical Works,* 1876.

> Author: My Faith Looks Up to Thee (143)
> With Thine Own Pity, Savior (340)
> Translator: Jesus, Thou Joy of Loving Hearts (329)

Park, John Edgar (b. Belfast, Ireland, March 7, 1879; d. Cambridge, Mass., March 4, 1956) was educated at Queen's College in Belfast, the Royal University in Dublin, and at the universities of Edinburgh, Leipzig, Munich, Oxford, and Princeton. He was ordained a Presbyterian minister in 1902 and worked in the lumber camps of the Adirondacks. Changing to the Congregational Church, he served for 19 years at the Second Congregational Church in West Newton, Mass. In 1925 he taught at Boston University School of Theology and in 1926 became president of Wheaton College in Norton, Mass., retiring in 1944. He was the author of numerous books.

> Author: We Would See Jesus (90)

Park, Roswell (b. Lebanon, Conn., October 1, 1807; d. Chicago, Ill., July 16, 1869) was educated at Union College and West Point Military Academy, 1831. He served in the United States Army Corps of Engineers, was professor of chemistry at the University of Pennsylvania, and eventually was ordained in the Protestant Episcopal Church after beginning the study of theology in 1842. During the years 1852-63 he was president and chancellor of Racine College in Wisconsin, then moved to Chicago where he established a school.

> Author: Jesus Spreads His Banner o'er Us (331)

Parker, Edwin Pond (b. Castine, Me., January 13, 1836; d. Hartford, Conn., May 28, 1925) was educated at Bowdoin College and Bangor Theological Seminary. For 50 years he was pastor of the Center Congregational Church in Hartford, Conn. He was a musician as well as a pastor. He wrote more than 200 hymns and composed and arranged many tunes in his work of compiling several hymnals.

> Arranger: MERCY (494, p. 376)

Parker, William Henry (b. New Basford, Nottingham, England, March 4, 1845; d. Nottingham, December 2, 1929) was apprenticed as a boy in the machine construction department of a New Basford lace-making plant. Later he headed an insurance company. He was a member of the Chelsea Street Baptist Church in Nottingham and was active in Sunday school work. Most of Parker's hymns were written for Sunday school anniversaries. Fifteen of his hymns appear in the National Sunday School Union's *Sunday School Hymnary*, 1905.

Author: Tell Me the Stories of Jesus (88)

Parkin, Charles (b. Felling on Tyne, England, December 25, 1894) was educated at schools in Durham and at Oxford (A.A. 1911). During World War I he served in the British army, 1915-19, and he was secretary of the northern branch of the British Poetry Society, 1920-21. He came to America in 1922. In 1927 he was ordained elder in the Maine Conference of the Methodist Episcopal Church and served churches in Orr's Island, Brunswick, Farmington, Bangor, Portland, and Rumford. During the years 1952-64 he was director of the Advance Department, Division of National Missions in Philadelphia, where he also wrote articles on studies on Methodist missions. In 1961 he was a delegate to the World Methodist Conference in Oslo, Norway.

Parkin has published hymns with the Hymn Society of America and in various denominational publications.

Author: See the Morning Sun Ascending (7)

Parry, Joseph (b. Merthyr Tydfil, Wales, May 21, 1841; d. Cartref, Penarth, Wales, February 17, 1903) was born into a very poor family and had to work in the puddling furnaces before he was 10. His parents moved to Danville, Pa., in 1854, and he had his first music study in a class conducted by other Welsh workers in the iron works. He won a prize for composition in 1860 and was able to go to a normal music school in Genesco, N.Y., in the summer of 1861. Returning to Wales, he won several Eisteddfod contests, prizes in Swansea in 1863, Llandudno in 1864, and Chester in 1866. He studied at the Royal Academy of Music, 1868-71, under William Sterndale Bennett and Charles Steggall.

Parry conducted a private music school in Danville, Pa., 1871-73.

Returning to Wales he became professor of music at the Welsh University College at Aberystwyth. Later he taught at the University College in Cardiff, from 1888 until his death. His compositions include 2 oratorios, several cantatas, and about 400 hymn tunes, as well as *Blodwen*, 1880, the first Welsh opera.

Composer: ABERYSTWYTH (125, 358, pp. 247-48)

Peace, Albert Lister (b. Huddersfield, Yorkshire, England, January 26, 1844; d. Liverpool, Lancashire, England, March 14, 1912) was a child prodigy, gifted with perfect pitch. He became organist at the parish church of Holmfirth, Yorkshire, at the age of 9. After his graduation from Oxford University (B.M. 1870, Mus.D. 1875), he succeeded William T. Best as organist at St. George's Hall, Liverpool, in 1897 and remained there until his death. He played the opening recitals on the organs at Canterbury Cathedral, 1886, Victoria Hall, Hanley, 1888, and Newcastle Cathedral, 1891, and was known for his brilliant pedal techniques.

Peace was the editor of several Church of Scotland collections: *The Scottish Hymnal*, 1884, *Psalms and Paraphrases with Tunes*, 1886, *The Psalter with Chants*, 1888, and *The Scottish Anthem Book*, 1891.

Composer: ST. MARGARET (234, p. 328)

Peek, Joseph Yates (b. Schenectady, N.Y., February 27, 1843; d. Brooklyn, N.Y., March 17, 1911) was a carpenter, farmer, and druggist's clerk. He served with the Union army in the Civil War. From 1881 to 1904 he worked as a florist, with music as an avocation. He became a Methodist lay preacher in 1904, preaching in Maine, Florida, and California, and was fully ordained less than 2 months before his death. Peek had no formal musical training but played the violin, banjo, and piano.

Composer: PEEK (156, p. 232)

Pennefather, William (b. Dublin, Ireland, February 5, 1816; d. Muswell Hill, London, April 30, 1873) was the son of Richard Pennefather, the baron of the Irish Court of Exchequer. William was educated at Westbury College, near Bristol, and Trinity College, Dublin (B.A. 1840). Ordained in 1841, he was made curate of Bally-macugh, Kilmore, and became vicar of Mellifont, near Drogheda, in 1844. He moved to England in 1848, with livings at Walton near Aylesbury; Christ Church, Barnet, Hertfordshire; and St. Jude's, Mildmay Park, London, where he established the famous Mildmay Religious and Benevolent Institution, a center for religious work. His hymns, written for his conferences, were collected in *Hymns Original and Selected,* 1872, and *Original Hymns and Thoughts in Verse,* 1873.

Author: Jesus, Stand Among Us (**791,** p. 450)

Pennewell, Almer Mitchell (b. Middletown, Mo., June 23, 1876) entered the Methodist ministry as a circuit rider in 1900. He became a member of the Missouri Conference and was appointed to St. Catherine's Circuit. In 1901 he was appointed to Warrenton, Mo., and remained there until 1905, during which time he attended Central Wesleyan College (B.A. 1905). After receiving his B.D. from Garrett Biblical Institute in 1908, he spent the next 2 years in the Adirondack Mountains in Wanakena, N.Y., where he recuperated from an illness and supplied a Presbyterian church there. He returned to Illinois in 1910 and transferred to the Rock River Conference and was appointed to a Methodist church in Maywood, Ill. Pennewell has served churches in Oak Park, Morris, Evanston, Wheaton, and St. John's Methodist in Chicago from which he retired from the duties of a full-time active pastorate in 1947. He served as central U.S. representative for the Spiritual Mobilization Movement, 1947-49.

Pennewell's writings include *The Methodist Movement in Northern Illinois,* 1942, and a collection of poems entitled *Sing, Parson, Sing,* 1949. Garrett honored him with the D.D. degree in 1925.

Author: So Lowly Doth the Savior Ride (**422**)

Perronet, Edward (b. Sundridge, Kent, England, 1726; d. Canterbury, England, January 2, 1792). The Perronet family came as Huguenots to England from Switzerland in 1680. Vincent Perronet (b. 1693), vicar of Shoreham, was greatly esteemed by the Wesleys. Edward, his son, as a Methodist preacher, emerged in 1758 as a spokesman advocating administration of the Lord's Supper by Methodist preachers. In 1757 he authored *The Mitre,* a poetic satire upon the established church. He greatly offended the Wesleys and the Countess of Huntingdon, and vacated the leadership of the Countess' chapel in Canterbury to become a minister of an Independent church in the same city.

Author: All Hail the Power of Jesus' Name (71, 72, 73)

Pfautsch, Lloyd Alvin (b. Washington, Mo., September 14, 1921) was educated at Elmhurst College (B.A. 1943) and Union Theological Seminary (M.S.M. 1948, B.D. 1946). Elmhurst College honored him with the Mus.D. degree in 1959.

He served as director of choral music at Illinois Wesleyan University, 1948-58. Beginning in 1958 he initiated a program of graduate studies in church music at Southern Methodist University. There he has served as the associate dean of the School of Arts and chairman of the music division, 1964-67, and director of choral activities. Pfautsch has had extensive experience as a soloist, choral conductor, and teacher. He has many compositions in print for choir, organ, and instruments, including 2 cantatas: *God with Us* and *Seven Words of Love.*

Composer: EUCLID (280, p. 231)
WALDA (238, p. 136)

Phelps, Sylvanus Dryden (b. Suffield, Conn., May 15, 1816; d. New Haven, Conn., November 23, 1895) was educated at Connecticut Literary Institute, Brown University (B.A. 1844), and Yale Divinity School. He was ordained into the Baptist ministry and served First Baptist Church in New Haven, Conn., for 28 years, and Jefferson Street Baptist, Providence, R.I., from 1874 to 1876. He left the latter post to become editor of the *Christian Secretary.* Brown University honored him with a D.D. degree in 1854.

Author: Savior, Thy Dying Love (177)

Pierpoint, Folliott Sandford (b. Bath, Somersetshire, England, October 7, 1835; d. Newport, England, March 10, 1917) was educated at the grammar school at Bath and at Queen's College, Cambridge (B.A. 1857). For some time he was classical master at Somersetshire College. Pierpoint was a contributor to *Lyra Eucharistica,* wrote some hymns for the canonical hours in *The Hymnal Noted*, and published several collections of poems.

Author: For the Beauty of the Earth (35)

Pierpont, John (b. Litchfield, Conn., April 6, 1785; d. Medford, Mass., August 26, 1866) graduated from Yale in 1804. He tutored for a time in South Carolina, then studied law and practiced in Newburyport before entering the dry-goods business in Boston and attempting to establish a chain of stores. Failing all these, he entered the ministry after graduating from Harvard Divinity School. Pierpont served as minister of Hollis Street Unitarian Church in Boston for 26 years, but after a dispute over temperance, slavery, and a host of other issues, he was ousted. He then served the First Unitarian Church in Troy, N.Y., for 4 years, and First Unitarian Church in West Medford, Mass., for 9 years. Then he volunteered and was a chaplain at the age of 76 with the 22nd Massachusetts volunteers in the Civil War before Senator Charles Sumner persuaded him to resign the post and become a clerk in the Treasury Department. His second daughter, Juliet, became the mother of J. Pierpont Morgan.

Author: On This Stone Now Laid with Prayer (348)

Pilsbury, Amos (dates of birth and death unknown) was a singing master in Charleston, S.C. His collection *The United States Sacred Harmony* was published in Boston in 1799. No other information seems to be available on him.

Source: KEDRON (191, p. 200)

Pleyel, Ignace Joseph (b. Ruppersthal, near Vienna, Austria, June 1, 1757; d. near Paris, France, November 14, 1831) was the twenty-fourth child of a village schoolmaster. He studied with J.B. Wanhal and Haydn and lived with the latter for 5 years. He took further study in Rome, 1777-81, and again in 1783. In 1789 he became Kapellmeister at the Strassburg Cathedral but was forced to leave during the revolution. He conducted concerts in England, 1791-93, and returned to Strassburg, but was further bothered by the revolutionists. Afterwards he went to Paris and founded the piano firm now known as Pleyel et Cie.

Pleyel was a prolific instrumental composer in Haydn's style. Hymn tunes which bear his name are arrangements from his 45 string quartets.

Composer: PLEYEL'S HYMN (300, 348, p. 129)

Plumptre, Edward Hayes (b. London, England, August 6, 1821; d. Wells, Somersetshire, England, February 1, 1891) was educated at King's College, London, and at University College, Oxford (B.A. 1844, M.A. 1847). He was elected a fellow of Brasenose College. Ordained in 1846, he won fame as a scholar, theologian, and preacher. He held various positions, including chaplain of King's College, 1847-68; professor of pastoral theology, 1853-63; professor of New Testament exegesis, 1864-81; and he was assistant preacher of Lincoln's Inn, dean of Queen's College at Oxford, prebendary of St. Paul's, rector of Pluckley, Kent, vicar of Bickley, Kent, and dean of Wells.

Plumptre wrote a biography of Bishop Thomas Ken, 1888, several volumes of poetry, and translations from the classics. He was a member of the Old Testament Company for the revision of the Authorized Version of the Bible.

Author: Rejoice, Ye Pure in Heart (233)

Pollard, Adelaide Addison (b. Bloomfield, Iowa, November 27, 1862; d. New York, N.Y., December 20, 1934) was given the name "Sarah" by her parents, but adopted the name "Adelaide." Her schooling included Denmark Academy in Denmark, Iowa, a school in Valparaiso, Ind., and 3 years of study in elocution and physical culture at the Boston School of Oratory. During the 1880's she taught in several girls' schools in Chicago. Her interest in evangelistic work led to assisting Alexander Dowie in healing and 8 years of teaching at the Missionary Training School, Nyack-on-the-Hudson. Prior to World War I, she served for a few months as a missionary in Africa, then in Scotland during the war. Her last years were spent in New England and New York, where she was attracted to extreme sects. She was in poor health much of her life and lived the life of a mystic, returning to her Presbyterian family home only occasionally to regain her strength.

Author: Have Thine Own Way, Lord (154)

Pollock, Thomas Benson (b. Strathallan, Isle of Man, May 28, 1836; d. Birmingham, England, December 15, 1896) was educated at Trinity College, Dublin (B.A. 1859, M.A. 1863), where he won the vice-chancellor's prize for English verse. He began study for medicine but was ordained in 1861, serving as curate of St. Luke's at Leek, St. Thomas' at Stamford Hill in London, and finally at St. Albans', Bordesley, Birmingham, where he assisted his brother for 30 years, succeeding him as vicar. He refused opportunities to go to wealthier parishes, and spent his entire life working with the poor in Birmingham in educational and social welfare work.

Pollock published *Metrical Litanies for Special Services and General Use,* 1870, and was a member of the committee which compiled *Hymns Ancient and Modern.*

Author: Jesus, with Thy Church Abide (311)

Pond, Sylvanus Billings (b. Milford, Vt., April 5, 1792; d. Brooklyn, N.Y., March 12, 1871) was a composer of Sunday school songs, conductor of the New York Sacred Music Society, and the New York Academy of Sacred Music. He joined and reorganized one of the principal music houses—Firth, Pond, and Company, which published Stephen Foster's compositions.

In 1838 Pond edited and published *Union Melodies,* the *United States Psalmody* in 1841, and *The Book of Praise* in 1866 for the Reformed Dutch Church in America.

Composer: ARMENIA (301, 196, pp. 81-82)

Pott, Francis (b. Southwark, London, England, December 29, 1832; d. Speldhurst, England, October 26, 1909) was a translator of Latin hymns and a member of the committee that prepared the original edition of *Hymns Ancient and Modern,* 1861. He received his education at Brasenose College, Oxford (B.A. 1854, M.A. 1857). Ordained in 1856, he served as rector at Norhill, Ely, 1866-91, but deafness and ill health caused his resignation from the parish ministry, and he applied his talents to study and translations. *Hymns Fitted to the Order of Common Prayer, and Administration of the Sacraments and Other Rites and Ceremonies of the Church, According to the Use of the Church of England, to Which Are Added Hymns for Certain Local*

Festivals, first edition published in 1861, and *Free Rhythm Psalter,* 1898, reflected his interest in the return of chanting.

Author: Angel Voices, Ever Singing (2)
Translator: The Strife Is O'er, the Battle Done (447)

Powell, Robert Jennings (b. Benoit, Miss., July 22, 1932) was educated at Louisiana State University (B.M. 1954) and Union Theological Seminary School of Sacred Music (M.S.M. 1958). He also received the Choirmaster and Fellowship certificates in the American Guild of Organists. He was assistant organist and choirmaster at the Cathedral of St. John the Divine in New York City, 1957-59, and afterwards was organist-choir director at St. Paul's Episcopal Church in Meridian, Miss., for 6 years, director of music at St. Paul's School in Concord, N.H., for 3 years. Presently he is organist-choir director at Christ Church (Episcopal) in Greenville, S.C. Powell is a prolific composer of organ and choral literature.

Composer: AUTHOR OF LIFE (315, p. 105)

Praetorius, Michael (b. Kreutzburg, Saxe-Weimar, February 15, 1571; d. Wolfenbüttel, February 15, 1621) was educated at the Latin school of Torgau and the University of Frankfort-on-Oder, where he was organist of St. Mary's Church. In 1589 he became organist of the Castle Church in Groningen for Bishop Heinrich Julius. In 1594 he moved to Wolfenbüttel, where he was court organist and Kapellmeister, having his own home from 1612 until his death. When the duke dedicated a new Beck organ in 1596, 50 well-known organists came to Groningen to play the new instrument, giving Praetorius an opportunity to meet the leading German organists.

Largely self taught, he became one of the leading figures of the early Baroque period. Praetorius was recognized as an organist, choir director, theorist, composer, author, and editor. His published work was enormous, including *Musae Sioniae,* 1605-10, and *Syntagma Musicum* in 4 parts, 1615-20.

Adapter: PUER NOBIS NASCITUR (515, p. 313)

Prentiss, Elizabeth Payson (b. Portland, Me., October 26, 1818; d. Dorset, Vt., August 13, 1878) was educated in the public schools of

Portland. She began contributing poetry and prose to the *Youth's Companion* when she was only 16. After teaching for some years in Portland, Me., Ipswich, Mass., and Richmond, Va., she married Dr. George Lewis Prentiss, a Congregational minister who later became professor of homiletics and polity at Union Theological Seminary in New York.

Among Mrs. Prentiss' many published books was *Stepping Heavenward,* 1869, her best-known work.

Author: More Love to Thee, O Christ **(185)**

Prichard, Rowland Hugh (b. Graienyn, near Bala, North Wales, January 14, 1811; d. Holywell, Flintshire, Wales, January 25, 1887) spent most of his life in Bala, moving to Holywell in 1880 where he worked as an assistant loomtender. He was an amateur precentor. His tunes were published in many Welsh periodicals and are marked by both power and simplicity. His *Cyfaill y Cantorion* (The Singer's Friend) was published in 1844.

Composer: HYFRYDOL **(132, 360, 548, p. 155)**

Procter, Adelaide Anne (b. London, England, October 30, 1825; d. London, February 2, 1864) was the daughter of Bryan Waller Procter who went under the pen name of "Barry Cornwall" and who was a friend of Charles Lamb and Dickens. Her first poems were published in *Household Words,* edited by Dickens, under the name "Mary Berwick." In addition to publishing *Legends and Lyrics,* 1858 and 1862, she was the author of many popular songs, including "The Lost Chord." She became a Roman Catholic when she was 26. Her unselfish philanthropic work among the poor led to her loss of health, with 15 months of suffering before her death.

Author: My God, I Thank Thee **(50)**

Prudentius, Aurelius Clemens (b. Spain, 348; d. c. 413). From a short biography in verse, which he prefixed to his poems, it is known that Prudentius came from a good Spanish family, had a good education, practiced law, was a judge in 2 cities, and was made chief of the imperial bodyguard of the Emperor Honorius. When he was 57, he moved into a monastery where he spent his time in devotion and meditation, writing sacred poems and hymns. His chief works were *Liber Cathemerinon* (hymns for the hours of the day) and *Liber Peristephanon* (14 hymns praising important martyrs) .

Author: Earth Has Many a Noble City (405)
Of the Father's Love Begotten (357)

Purday, Charles Henry (b. Folkestone, Kent, England, January 11, 1799; d. Kensington, London, England, April 23, 1885) was a music teacher and publisher in London, and a pioneer in using program notes at concerts. He was also involved in amending laws governing music copyrights. He was a precentor at the Scottish Church, Crown Court, Covent Garden, and was one of those who sang at Queen Victoria's coronation. Purday was a contributor to *Grove's Dictionary of Music and Musicians,* and he published books on chanting as well as several collections of tunes. In 1854 he published *Crown Court Psalmody,* which contained "101 popular tunes and chants," a number which he maintained was sufficient for any book.

Composer: SANDON (47, p. 198)

Quaile, Robert Newton (b. County Limerick, Ireland, 1867; d. Mallow, County Cork, Ireland, July 26, 1927) was the son of an Irish Methodist minister. He was an amateur musician engaged in business at Mallow, County Cork. During the political and economic turmoil in Ireland, all his possessions were burned in 1920. Three of his tunes were included in the English Methodist *Sunday School Hymnal,* 1910.

Composer: OLDBRIDGE (523, p. 324)

Rankin, Jeremiah Eames (b. Thornton, N.H., January 2, 1828; d. Cleveland, Ohio, November 28, 1904) was educated at Middlebury College, Vermont, and Andover Theological Seminary. He was ordained into the Congregational ministry in 1855 and served churches in New York, Vermont, Massachusetts, Washington, D.C., and New Jersey. In 1889 he became president of Howard University, Washington, D.C. He compiled and edited many gospel songbooks.

Author: God Be with You Till We Meet Again (539, 540)

Mainzer, Joseph (b. Treves, March 7, 1801; d. Salford, Manchester, England, November 10, 1851) was a singing teacher and journalist. He sang at Treves Cathedral and studied at Darmstadt, Munich, and at Vienna. In 1826 he was ordained priest in Germany and taught in a seminary there. For political reasons he moved to England in 1839, after having lived in Brussels for 6 years. He immediately began a crusade to teach sightsinging to the general public and centered his work in Edinburgh, 1842-47. He moved to Manchester and continued publication of *Mainzer's Music Times and Singing Circular*, which became the *Musical Times* in 1844. For more information about Mainzer, see Percy A. Scholes, "The Mainzer Movement" in the *Mirror of Music*, I (London, 1947), 3-10.

    Composer: MAINZER (139, pp. 104-5)

Maker, Frederick Charles (b. Bristol, Gloucestershire, England, 1844; d. Bristol, 1927) was an important figure in Free Church music. He began his music training as a chorister in Bristol Cathedral. He studied organ with Alfred Stone and later contributed tunes to Stone's *Bristol Tune Book* and its Supplement, 1881. During the years 1882-1910 he served as organist of the Milk Street Free Methodist Church, the Clifton Downs Congregational Church, and the Redland Park Congregational Church. He was also visiting professor of music at Clifton College and conductor of the Bristol Free Church Choir Association. Maker is the composer of anthems, hymn tunes, and the cantata *Moses in the Bulrushes.*

    Composer: REST (235, p. 164)
            ST. CHRISTOPHER (417, p. 116)
            WENTWORTH (50, p. 291)

Malan, Henri Abraham César (b. Geneva, Switzerland, July 7, 1787; d. Vandoeuvres, Switzerland, May 18, 1864) received his M.A. from the College of Geneva and was ordained in 1810 into the National Church of Geneva, where he became a popular preacher. He took exception to the Unitarian and formalist leanings of the church and was attracted to current evangelical-Calvinistic movements. He subsequently founded a chapel in his own garden where he preached for 43 years. During this time he made lengthy evangelistic tours into Belgium, Scotland, and England. Malan was a man of many talents.

Rawnsley, Hardwicke Drummond (b. Shiplake, England, September 28, 1851; d. Grasmere, England, May 28, 1920), the son of Canon Rawnsley, was educated at Uppingham and Balliol College, Oxford (B.A. 1875, M.A. 1883). Ordained in 1875, he served as curate of St. Barnabas', Bristol, 1875-78; vicar at Low Wray, Lancashire, 1878-83; vicar at Crosthwaite, 1883-1917; and honorary canon of Carlisle, 1893. He was founder and secretary of the National Trust for Places of Historic Interest and Natural Beauty. In addition to many books including poetry, he published several hymns for special occasions.

Author: O God, Whose Will Is Life (411)

Read, Daniel (b. Rehobeth, now Attleboro, Mass., November 16, 1757; d. New Haven, Conn., December 4, 1836) served in John Sullivan's expeditions to Rhode Island in 1777 and in 1778 during the American Revolution. After the war he went into partnership with Amos Doolittle, an engraver, in publishing and selling books. He also was an ivory comb manufacturer, taught singing schools, composed anthems and hymn tunes, and edited hymnals. His first publication was *The American Singing Book*, 1785, with 47 of his own tunes. Other books were *An Introduction to Psalmody*, 1790, which was an instruction book for children in vocal music, *The New Haven Collection of Sacred Music*, 1817, and *The Columbian Harmonist*, 1793. He also began the *American Musical Magazine*, 1786, the first of its kind in America. In 1832 at the age of 73 he compiled another collection, *Musica Ecclesia*, which he offered to the American Home Missionary Society, the proceeds to go to missions in the United States. The offer was not accepted, and the collection was never published. See Irving Lowens' *Music and Musicians in Early America*, pp. 159-77, for a discussion of Read's correspondence.

Composer: WINDHAM (80, p. 220)

Redhead, Richard (b. Harrow, Middlesex, England, March 1, 1820; d. Hellingly, England, April 27, 1901) received early musical training which included study with the organist Walter Vicary and as a chorister at Magdalen College, Oxford. As organist of Margaret Street Chapel, London, 1839-59, and at the new church named All Saints' Church on Margaret Street, he conducted daily choral services until

1864. During the years 1864-94 he was organist of St. Mary Magdalene, Paddington.

Redhead's *Laudes Diurnae* with H. S. Oakeley, 1843, and *Church Hymn Tunes, Ancient and Modern,* 1853, contributed to the Victorian revival of Latin plainsong. He composed a good deal of vocal music and edited *The Cathedral and Church Choir Book, Parochial Church Tune Book,* and *The Universal Organist.* See Erik Routley, *The Music of Christian Hymnody,* pp. 115-21, for a discussion of English adaptations of Gregorian chant.

> Composer: REDHEAD 76 (113, 434, pp. 126-27)
> Harmonizer: ORIENTIS PARTIBUS (162, p. 367)

Redner, Lewis Henry (b. Philadelphia, Pa., December 15, 1830; d. Atlantic City, N.J., August 29, 1908) was educated in the public schools of Philadelphia. He became a wealthy real estate broker and was active in church work, serving as organist in 4 different Philadelphia churches, including tenure at Holy Trinity Episcopal when Phillips Brooks was rector. He also was a Sunday school superintendent for 19 years, during which time attendance increased from 36 to over 1,000.

> Composer: ST. LOUIS (381, p. 321)

Reed, Andrew (b. Westminster, England, November 27, 1787; d. Hackney, London, England, February 25, 1862) was the son of a watchmaker. He entered Hackney College at the age of 16 and trained for the Congregational ministry. Ordained in 1811, he was the first pastor at the New Road Chapel, St. George's in the East, until 1861, and during that time built Wycliffe Chapel. He visited American churches in 1834 and was awarded the D.D. degree by Yale. Reed was instrumental in the founding of several institutions: the London Orphan Asylum at Clapton, the Reedham Orphanage at Coulsdon, an asylum for idiots at Earlswood, the Royal Hospital for Incurables at Putney, and the Eastern Counties Asylum at Colchester.

He published his first edition of *Hymn Book* in 1817 as a supplement to Isaac Watts's *Psalms and Hymns,* to which he contributed 21 hymns. *Wycliffe Supplement,* 1872, contains hymns by Reed and his wife.

> Author: Spirit Divine, Attend Our Prayers (461)

Reed, Edith Margaret Gellibrand (b. London, England, March 31, 1885; d. London, June 4, 1933) was educated at Clifton High School, St. Leonard's School, St. Andrews', and the Guildhall School of Music in London. She was an associate of the Royal College of Organists and assisted Percy Scholes in editorial work on *The Music Student, Music and Youth,* and *Panpipes.* She wrote 2 Christmas mystery plays and *Story Lives of the Great Composers.*

Paraphrased: Infant Holy, Infant Lowly (**396**)
Arranger: ᴡ ᴢʟᴏʙɪᴇ ʟᴇᴢʏ (**396**, p. 240)

Rees, Bryn Austin (b. Chelsea, London, England, September 21, 1911) was educated at Neath Grammar School and was trained for the Congregational ministry at Hackney and New College, London. He has held pastorates at Sawbridgeworth, Hertfordshire, 1935-40; Ipswich, Suffolk, 1940-45; Felixstowe, Suffolk, 1945-50; and Muswell Hill Congregational Church in London, 1950-62. Since 1962 he has been minister of Woodford Green United Free Church in the London borough of Redbridge.

Rees is the author of texts for 3 cantatas by Lloyd Webber: *The Savior, The Meeting Race,* and *The Good Samaritan.*

Author: Have Faith in God, My Heart (**141**)

Reinagle, Alexander Robert (b. Brighton, East Sussex, England, August 21, 1799; d. Kidlington, England, April 6, 1877). Alexander's grandfather, Joseph Reinagle, Sr., was "trumpeter to the king," and his father was an accomplished cellist. His uncle came to America in 1786 and for 2 decades was a leading conductor, composer, teacher, and theatrical manager in Baltimore and Philadelphia. Alexander was organist at St. Peter's Church in the East, Oxford, 1822-53. In addition to books of instruction for the violin and cello, he published 2 collections of hymn tunes in 1836 and 1840.

Composer: ꜱᴛ. ᴘᴇᴛᴇʀ (**81, 192, 349, 520,** p. 224)

Rendle, Lily (b. London, England, May 14, 1875; d. Eastbourne, East Sussex, England, July 27, 1964) was educated in London and Paris. She won a gold medal with an associateship in the Guildhall School of music instead and was organist at St. Nicholas' for 20 years. One of his organ students was William T. Best.

Cardinals Newman and Wiseman and Pope Pius IX made presentations honoring him for his distinguished service to the Roman Catholic Church. In 1875 his wife and children died during an epidemic. His health broke 2 years later, and he retired to his birthplace an invalid.

Arranger: ST. BERNARD (75, p. 408)

Ridout, Daniel Lyman (b. Chestertown, Md., April 21, 1899) was a graduate of Princess Anne Academy and Chicago Law School. He studied music education at Ithaca Conservatory of Music and piano at the Sternbury School of Music in Philadelphia. Allen University conferred the Mus.D. in 1960. He was director of music at Maryland State College and Princess Anne Academy before he became a pastor and district superintendent in the Delaware Conference. He then served as special assistant to Bishops John Wesley Lord and Edgar A. Love and is now superintendent of the Chestertown district, the Peninsula Conference.

Ridout founded and directed the Baltimore Great Hymns Choir. He was a charter member of the National Fellowship of Methodist Musicians and served on its council, 1955-59. He is the author of *Verses from a Humble Cottage, A Young Man Enters the Ministry,* and *Twelve Negro Spiritual Interpretations.* A member of the 1964 hymnal committee, he served as secretary of the subcommittee on texts.

Arranger: BALM IN GILEAD (212, p. 402)
STAND BY ME (244, p. 432)

Riley, John Athelstan Laurie (b. London, England, August 10, 1858; d. Isle of Jersey, England, November 17, 1945) was educated at Eton and at Pembroke College, Oxford (B.A. 1881, M.A. 1883). He traveled in Persia, Turkey, and Kurdistan, where he gained material for articles on various Eastern Christian churches and a book, *Athos, or the Mountain of the Monks,* 1887. He was a compiler of the 1906 *English Hymnal,* contributing 3 original hymns and 7 translations of Latin hymns. Most of his life he was a member of the House of Laymen of the province of Canterbury.

Author: Ye Watchers and Ye Holy Ones (19)

Rinkart (also *Rinckart*), *Martin* (b. Eilenburg, Saxony, April 23, 1586; d. Eilenburg, December 8, 1649) was educated at the Latin school in Eilenburg and St. Thomas' School in Leipzig, where he was a foundation scholar and a chorister. He studied theology at the University of Leipzig. He became cantor and later deacon at Eisleben, pastor at Ardeborn, and archdeacon at Eilenburg in 1617. During the Thirty Years' War, 1618-48, many flocked to the walled city of Eilenburg for safety, and in spite of his frail physique, Rinkart ministered heroically. He is said to have buried nearly 5,000 persons, including his wife, during the pestilence of 1637.

Rinkart was a good musician and wrote voluminously, including a cycle of 7 dramas on the Reformation for the centenary in 1617.

Author: Now Thank We All Our God (49)

Rippon, John (b. Tiverton, Devonshire, England, April 29, 1751; d. London, England, December 17, 1836) joined the Baptist Church at the age of 16 and was educated for the ministry at Bristol Baptist College. In 1772, when he was 21, he accepted the interim pastorate of the Baptist Church at Carter Lane, London, and the following year became its permanent pastor, serving for 63 years.

Rippon was an authority on the hymns of Isaac Watts, and among his significant contributions is his *Selection of Hymns from the Best Authors, Intended to Be an Appendix to Dr. Watts's Psalms and Hymns,* 1787. *A Selection of Psalms and Hymn Tunes,* 1791, with the earlier collection became standard sources for early nineteenth-century hymnals published in England and America. As a pastor and the editor of the *Baptist Annual Register,* 1790-1802, Rippon was one of the most influential and important Baptist ministers of his time. His numerous books and publications brought him considerable income. One of the weaknesses in his efforts in the field of hymnody was his failure to identify in his collections his own reconstruction of the texts of others, or in some instances failure to identify the author or composer.

Alterer: All Hail the Power of Jesus' Name (71, 72, 73)
Source: How Firm a Foundation (48)

Rist, Johann (b. Ottensen, Holstein, March 8, 1607; d. Wedel, near Hamburg, August 31, 1667), the son of a clergyman, studied at

Rinteln and Rostock. He became a pastor and a physician at Wedel. Rist suffered greatly during the Thirty Years' War and lost all his personal property. In 1645 he was made poet laureate by Emperor Ferdinand III.

Rist wrote a number of plays and secular poems. Few of his hymns were popular during this lifetime except in his circle of friends since he did not make use of them in worship in the Wedel church. The hymns, numbering 680, extend over the range of religious experience. For the most part they are well represented in 6 collections published 1641-56.

Author: Break Forth, O Beauteous Heavenly Light (373)

Robbins, Howard Chandler (b. Philadelphia, Pa., December 11, 1876; d. Washington, D.C., March 20, 1952) was educated at Yale (B.A. 1899) and the Episcopal Theological Seminary (B.D. 1903). After his ordination he served churches in Morristown, N.J.; Englewood, N.J.; and New York City where he was dean of the Cathedral of St. John the Divine, 1917-29. During the years 1929-41 he was professor of pastoral theology at General Theological Seminary and from 1942 to 1944 was visiting preacher at St. John's, Lafayette Square, Washington, D.C.

Robbins was a member of the joint commission on the revision of *The Hymnal 1940*, to which he contributed 5 original hymn texts, 1 translation, and 1 hymn tune. He was the author or editor of several works, including associate editor of *New Church Hymnal*, 1937, co-author of *The Eternal Word in the Modern World*, 1937, and author of *Preaching the Gospel Today*, 1939.

Author: And Have the Bright Immensities (456)

Roberts, Daniel Crane (b. Bridgehampton, Long Island, N.Y., November 5, 1841; d. Concord, N.H., October 31, 1907) graduated in 1857 from Kenyon College in Gambier, Ohio, and served as a private in the 84th Ohio volunteers during the Civil War. He was ordained deacon in 1865, priest in 1866 in the Protestant Episcopal Church, and served parishes in Vermont and Massachusetts before going as vicar to St. Paul's Church in Concord, N.H., for the last 29 years of his life. Although he claimed, "I remain a country Parson, known only within my own small world," he served as president of the New Hampshire State Historical Society, as chaplain of the New Hampshire department of the Grand Army of the Republic, and was active in the Knights Templar on both local and national levels.

Author: God of Our Fathers (552)

Roberts, John (Gwyllt, Ieuan) (b. Tanrhiwfelen, Penllwyn, near Aberystwyth, Wales, December 22, 1822; d. Vron, Caernarvon, Wales, May 6, 1877) was a Welsh musician, editor, teacher, composer, and Calvinistic Methodist minister. As a boy he was a pupil of Richard Mills, a leader of congregational singing schools. Roberts began preaching in 1856, was ordained in 1859, and served churches in Aberdare and Capel Cock. He founded the singing festival Cymanfâu Ganu, 1859, and edited the Calvinistic Methodist hymnal *Llyfr Tonau Cynulleidfaol*, 1859. Erik Routley states in *Companion to Congregational Praise* that Roberts' "hymn-tunes are to Wales what those of Croft are to England—the very backbone of their hymnody at its finest."

Source: ST. DENIO (**27**, p. 235)

Robinson, Robert (b. Swaffham, Norfolk, England, September 27, 1735; d. Birmingham, England, June 9, 1790) was apprenticed to a barber after his father's death. In 1752, upon hearing George Whitefield preach on "The Wrath to Come" (Matthew 3:7) , he was greatly impressed. For 3 years he "struggled" and in 1755 found "joy and peace in believing." Thereupon he began to preach, first in a Calvinistic Methodist chapel at Mildenhall, Suffolk, then on to an Independent congregation which he founded at Norwich. During the years 1761-90 he pastored the Stone Yard Baptist Church in Cambridge. His later years were influenced by the Unitarian philosopher and theologian Joseph Priestly. Robinson's many publications include *History of the Baptists,* 1790.

Author: Come, Thou Fount of Every Blessing (**93**)

Röntgen, Julius (b. Leipzig, Germany, May 9, 1855; d. Utrecht, September 13, 1932) studied music under Franz Lachner, Moritz Hauptmann, E. F. Richter, and C. Reinecke. He succeeded J. J. H. Verhulst as conductor of the Society for the Advancement of Musical Art in 1886, following 8 years as professor in the conservatoire at Amsterdam. In 1918 he became director of the conservatoire. Röntgen was a friend of Liszt, Brahms, and Grieg, and was well known as a distinguished pianist, conductor, composer, musicologist, and editor.

Arranger: IN BABILONE (69, 454, p. 207)

Rossetti, Christina Georgina (b. London, England, December 5, 1830; d. London, December 29, 1894) was the daughter of Gabriele Rossetti, an Italian refugee who became professor of Italian at King's College, London. She broke her engagement to the artist James Collinson because he was a Roman Catholic. Later she was asked by Charles B. Cayly to marry, but faith and finance prevented the marriage. Poor health bothered her from the age of 16, but she found solace from all her disappointments and sorrows in intense religious devotion and in writing many volumes of poetry and prose. Her exceptionally beautiful face was the model for several portraits of the madonna, including the ones by Millais and her brother, Dante Gabriel.

Author: In the Bleak Midwinter (376)
Love Came Down at Christmas (375)

Rowland, May (Mary Alice) (b. Woodstock, Oxfordshire, England, September 21, 1870; d. Eastbourne, East Sussex, England, February 17, 1959) was educated at Somerset. She moved to Eastbourne in 1902. She resided in Maresfield for a short time, beginning in 1943, but returned to Eastbourne. For many years she was a faithful teacher of young people and a parish worker with a special interest in missions at All Souls' Church in Eastbourne. She first published her historic and patriotic poems in newspapers and magazines, then began writing sacred verse including the award-winning "Hymn for Airmen" in a contest sponsored by the Hymn Society of America in 1928. She wrote a history of the parish of All Souls' Church and composed the "Jubilee Hymn" in 1932. She and Lily Rendle collaborated in producing 3 hymns which appeared in the 1935 Methodist hymnal.

Eric G. Wells, vicar of All Souls', 1946-57, writes that Miss Rowland "was a cultured lady with a very great gift of language and poetry. In addition to her literary gifts, she was a very shrewd judge of people and circumstances, and for myself, I never hesitated to seek her guidance in matters where I was in any doubt."

Author: The Day Is Slowly Wending (506)

Rumbaugh, Vida Faye (b. Lisbon, Iowa, January 23, 1927) was educated at Coe College, Cedar Rapids (B.A. 1941, B.M. 1947), and at the School of Sacred Music at Union Theological Seminary in New York City (M.S.M. 1949). Under the auspices of the Presbyterian Church she served as musical missionary to Thailand, 1949-58. During the years 1958-65 she was director of personnel at the United Fire and Casualty Company in Cedar Rapids. She is presently staff assistant at St. Michael's Episcopal Church in Cedar Rapids, with assignments in music and education.

Translator: The Righteous Ones Shall Be Forever Blest (214)

Russell, Arthur Tozer (b. Northampton, England, March 20, 1806; d. Southwick, Brighton, England, November 18, 1874) was the son of the Reverend Thomas Clout, a Congregational minister who changed his name to Russell. He was educated at St. Saviour's School in Southwark, the Merchant Taylors' School in London, Manchester College in York, and St. John's College, Cambridge. Ordained in 1829 he became curate of Great Gransden, Hunts; vicar at Caxton, 1830; at Whaddon, 1852; at Toxteth Park, Liverpool, 1866; at Wrackwardine Wood, Wellington, Shropshire, in 1867; and Southwick, Brighton, 1874.

Russell was deeply involved in the struggles of the Oxford Movement as an effective critic of the high church *Tracts* and the broad church *Essays*. His study of Augustine moved him from the high church position to a moderate Calvinist. He wrote about 140 hymns and in 1840 published *Hymn Tunes, Original and Selected, from Ravenscroft and Other Musicians* and in 1851 *Psalms and Hymns, Partly Original, Partly Selected, for the Use of the Church of England.*

Translator: Let All Together Praise Our God (389)

Ryden, Ernest Edwin (b. Kansas City, Mo., September 12, 1886) was educated at Augustana College and Augustana Seminary. He was ordained in 1914 and served many years as pastor of Gloria Dei Lutheran Church in St. Paul, Minn. He is presently pastor of the Emmanuel Lutheran Church in North Grosvenordale, Conn.

Ryden was chairman of the hymnal committee of the Augustana Synod, coeditor of the *Augustana Hymnal,* 1925, and secretary of the joint commission which prepared the common hymnal, *Service Book and Hymnal,* 1945-58. His editorial work and writing include also editor of the periodical *Lutheran Companion,* 1934-61, author of *The Story of Our Hymns,* 1935, *The Story of Christian Hymnody,* 1958, and the article "Lutheran Hymnbooks Since the Reformation" in the *Lutheran Encyclopedia,* 1964. He is the translator and author of many hymns.

Augustana College honored him with the D.D. in 1930 and in 1949 the Swedish government bestowed upon him the Royal Order of the North Star, in recognition of his efforts in bringing Scandanavian hymnody to the attention of the English-speaking churches.

Author: How Blessed Is This Place (**350**)

Sammis, John H. (b. Brooklyn, N.Y., July 6, 1846; d. Los Angeles, Calif., June 12, 1919) at the age of 23 moved to Logansport, Ind., where he became a successful businessman. After working with the Y.M.C.A. for several years, he decided to enter the ministry and attended McCormick and Lane theological seminaries, graduating from Lane in 1881. He was ordained into the Presbyterian ministry in 1880 and held pastorates in Iowa, Indiana, Michigan, and Minnesota. During the latter part of his life he was on the faculty of the Los Angeles Bible Institute.

Author: When We Walk with the Lord (**223**)

Sankey, Ira David (b. Edinburgh, Pa., August 28, 1840; d. Brooklyn, N.Y., August 13, 1908) was born on a farm and moved to Newcastle, Pa., in 1857 where he later joined the Methodist Episcopal Church and became a Sunday school superintendent and choir leader. He served in the Union army during the Civil War. At a Y.M.C.A. meeting in Indianapolis, Ind., in 1870 he met Dwight L. Moody and joined him 6 months later as his music leader. He not only led singing but often sang gospel solos, accompanying himself on a portable reed organ.

In 1872 Sankey and Moody went to England, and the response to his songs (still in manuscript then) led him to publish *Sacred Songs and Solos*, 1874 (?) , with Morgan & Scott, English publishers. The 1903 edition of this work contained 1,200 songs, and the book in all editions is said to have sold 80 million copies. Returning to America, he persuaded Philip P. Bliss, who had published *Gospel Songs* in 1874, to combine their collections, and the famous *Gospel Hymns and Sacred Songs* was published in 1875. Six more volumes were published culminating in *Gospel Hymns Nos. 1-6 Complete,* 1894, containing 739 hymns.

For comments concerning music for evangelism by Sankey, see Erik Routley, *Church Music and Theology,* pp. 72 ff.

Composer: SANKEY (514, p. 203)

Schein, Johann Hermann (b. Grünhain, Saxony, January 20, 1586; d. Leipzig, November 19, 1630) was the son of a Lutheran pastor. On the death of his father, the boy sang in the electoral chapel choir at Dresden, with further study at the gymnasium of Schulpforta, 1603-7, and the University of Leipzig. He became Kapellmeister at Weimar, 1615, and succeeded Seth Calvisius as cantor of St. Thomas' Church in Leipzig, 1616.

Schein was among the first to adapt chorales as the base for organ compositions, and with Schütz and Praetorius he introduced to German music the monody and instrumental style of the Italian school. His most important work is *Cantional oder Gesangbuch Augsburgischer Konfession* (1627; 2nd ed. 1645) for 4- and 6-part settings, 312 in all, of German and Latin sacred psalms and songs. Breitkopf & Härtel published his works, in 7 volumes edited by Arthur Prüfer, 1901-23.

Composer: EISENACH (46, 172, p. 127)

Schlegel, Katharina Amalia Dorothea von (b. October 22, 1697) was a member of the group who wrote the so-called *Cöthnische Lieder.* Some 29 other hymns appear in the collections of 1744 and 1752. James Mearns in John Julian's *Dictionary of Hymnology* conjectures that she may have been one of the women attached to the Cöthen court. Only one of her hymns has been translated.

Author: Be Still, My Soul (209)

Schmolck, Benjamin (b. Brauchitzchdorf, Silesia, December 21, 1672; d. Schweidnitz, Silesia, February 12, 1737) was the son of the Lutheran pastor at Brauchitzchdorf. He studied in the gymnasium at Laubau and at the University of Leipzig. After his ordination he became his father's assistant. In 1702 he was appointed deacon of the Friedens-kirche at Schweidnitz, a post he held the rest of his life. Schmolck wrote more than 900 hymns.

Author: My Jesus, As Thou Wilt (167)
Open Now Thy Gates of Beauty (13)

Schop, Johann (b. c. 1590; d. Hamburg, between 1664 and 1667) was noted as a performer on the lute, trumpet, violin, and zinke. He was an intimate friend of Johann Rist and a member of the court orchestra at Wolfenbüttel. At the time of his death he was director of "Rats-musik" in Hamburg.

Composer: ERMUNTRE DICH (373, p. 122)

Schütz, Johann Jakob (b. Frankfort, September 7, 1640; d. Frankfort, May 22, 1690) was trained in law at Tübingen. He was a close friend of P. J. Spener who founded Pietism, and like many of the pietists, Schütz, under the influence of J. S. Petersen, left the Lutherans in 1686 and became a Separatist. In 1675 he published *Christliches Gedenckbüchlein*.

Author: Sing Praise to God Who Reigns Above (4)

Schulz, Johann Abraham Peter (b. Lüneburg, March 31, 1747; d. Schwedt, June 10, 1800) was the son of a baker who wanted his son to be a minister, but Johann preferred music. At the age of 15 he ran away from home and went to Berlin to study with Kirnberger, whom he persuaded to be his teacher. During the years 1768-73 he toured Germany, France, and Italy in the entourage of the Polish

Princess Sapieha. He directed music in the French theater in Berlin, 1776-80, when he became Kapellmeister to Prince Henry of Prussia, and held a similar post at the King of Denmark's court in Copenhagen, 1787-95. Schulz composed operas, church music, instrumental music, and collected sacred and secular German songs, published between 1785 and 1790.

Composer: WIR PFLÜGEN (513, p. 422)

Schumann, Robert Alexander (b. Zwickau, Saxony, June 8, 1810; d. Endenich, near Bonn, July 29, 1856) was the son of a bookseller and publisher. He was brought up in a literary atmosphere and showed musical talent early, for he began composing at the age of 7. He studied with Friedrich Wieck, whose daughter, Clara, he later married. As an accomplished pianist, Clara made Schumann's music widely known. Schumann developed mental instability and in 1854 attempted to take his life by drowning and afterwards was committed to an asylum where he died.

Schumann wrote symphonies and chamber music, but was best known for his piano and vocal works. His style was that of the romantic school of the nineteenth century, and he was one of the first to acclaim the genius of Chopin and Brahms. He helped found and edited for 10 years *Die neue Zeitschrift für Musik,* a periodical that raised the music level of the time.

Composer: CANONBURY (195, 197, p. 278)

Schwedler, Johann Christoph (b. Krobsdorf, Silesia, December 21, 1672; d. Niederwiese, January 12, 1730) was a popular preacher and hymn writer and a friend of Count Zinzendorf and Johann Mentzer. He was educated at the University of Leipzig (M.A. 1697) and served first as an assistant, then as pastor from 1701 until his death at Niederwiese, near Greiffenberg. The founding of an orphan's home was one of his many humanitarian interests. He wrote hundreds of hymns, but only one has been translated into English.

Author: Ask Ye What Great Thing I Know (124)

Scoggin, Robert Edward (b. Mercury, Tex., April 30, 1930) was educated at Texas Tech, Midwestern University (B.M. 1951), and

Perkins School of Theology at Southern Methodist University (B.D. 1954). He has received additional study at Union Theological Seminary, New York City, 1953, and in Europe, 1962-63. Scoggin has served as minister of music in Dallas and Wichita Falls, Tex., including the University Park Methodist Church in Dallas, 1956-63. He presently serves the First Methodist Church in Rochester, Minn.

Composer: Enter into His Gates (785, p. 444)

Scott, Clara H. (b. Elk Grove, Ill., December 3, 1841; d. Dubuque, Iowa, June 21, 1897) attended the first musical institute in Chicago taught by C. M. Cady. In 1859 she began teaching music in the Ladies' Seminary at Lyons, Iowa, and 2 years later she married Henry Clay Scott. Horatio R. Palmer encouraged her writing, and she contributed many songs to his collections. Her *Royal Anthem Book,* 1882, was the first collection of anthems published by a woman.

She met an accidental death when she was thrown from a buggy by a runaway horse, while visiting in Dubuque.

Author and composer: Open My Eyes, That I May See (OPEN MY EYES) (267)

Scott, Robert Balgarnie Young (b. Toronto, Canada, July 16, 1899) graduated from Knox College (B.D.) and the University of Toronto (B.A., M.A., Ph.D.). After a year of study in Europe, he was ordained in 1926 as a minister of the United Church of Canada. After a brief ministry in Long Branch, Ontario, and as professor of Old Testament at Union College in Vancouver, he taught Old Testament at United Theological College, McGill University, Montreal, 1931-55. During World War II he served as honorary flight lieutenant and chaplain of the Royal Canadian Air Force. For 4 years he was president of the Fellowship for a Christian Social Order, during which time he wrote hymns for the group's use. In 1955 Scott was named professor of religion at Princeton and chairman of the department in 1963. Before his retirement he was Danforth Professor of Religion.

All his life Scott has been active in the field of social reform. He is an Old Testament scholar and the author of several books, including *The Relevance of the Prophets,* 1944, *Treasures from Judean Caves,* 1955, *The Psalms as Christian Praise,* 1958, and with Gregory Vlastos,

Towards the Christian Revolution, 1936. His hymns are contained in 20 hymnals.

Author: O Day of God, Draw Nigh (**477**)

Scott-Gatty, Alfred (b. Ecclesfield, Yorkshire, England, April 26, 1847; d. London, England, December 18, 1918) was the son of the sub-dean of York Cathedral. He was given royal license to take the additional surname "Scott" from his mother's family. His 2 main interests were heraldry and composing music for children. In 1886 he founded the Magpie Madrigal Society. He wrote several musical plays, including the operetta *Tattercoats,* 1900. Scott-Gatty was knighted and appointed to the office of Garter Principal King-of-Arms in 1904.

Composer: WELWYN (**199, 371,** p. 302)

Scriven, Joseph Medlicott (b. Seapatrick, County Down, Ireland, September 10, 1819; d. Bewdley, Rice Lake, Ontario, August 10, 1886) entered Trinity College at Dublin in 1835 but decided on an army career and became a cadet at Addiscombe Military College, Surrey, 1837. Poor health forced him to give up the idea of an army career, and he returned to Trinity College, graduating in 1842. His Irish fiancée accidentally drowned the evening before their wedding. At the age of 25 he moved to Canada, where he taught school for awhile in Woodstock and Brantford and served as a tutor to the family of Lieutenant Pengelley near Bewdley. Miss Eliza Roche, a relative of the Pengelley family, died suddenly after a brief illness before Scriven was to marry her.

Scriven was a member of the Plymouth Brethren and devoted most of his time to doing menial work for the physically handicapped and financially destitute, accepting no remuneration. He was an eccentric, and in later years failing health, meager income, and fear of becoming helpless pushed him into great depression. His body was found near Rice Lake, and it is not clear whether his drowning was suicide or accidental.

Scriven's small collection of poems, *Hymns and Other Verses,* was published in 1869.

Author: What a Friend We Have in Jesus (**261**)

COMPANION TO THE HYMNAL

Seagrave, Robert (b. Twyford, Leicestershire, England, November 22, 1693; d. c. 1759) was educated at Clare College, Cambridge, in 1714 and took holy orders in the Church of England in 1715. Becoming greatly interested in the work of the Wesleys and George Whitefield, he issued a series of pamphlets between 1731 and 1746 to arouse clergymen to a deeper interest in their work. He was the Sunday evening lecturer at Loriner's Hall, London, 1739-50, and also preached frequently at Whitefield's Tabernacle. Seagrave's *Hymns for Christian Worship* (1st ed. 1742) included 50 of his own hymns.

Author: Rise, My Soul, and Stretch Thy Wings (474)

Sears, Edmund Hamilton (b. Sandisfield, Mass., April 6, 1810; d. Weston, Mass., January 16, 1876) was educated at Union College in Schenectady, N.Y., 1834, and Harvard Divinity School, 1837. He was ordained into the Unitarian ministry in 1839 and held pastorates at Wayland, Lancaster, and Weston, Mass. Although a Unitarian with a Swedenborgian bent, he wrote to Bishop E. H. Bickersteth, "I believe and preach the divinity of Christ." He retired because of ill health and spent his time writing.

Among Sears's works are *Regeneration,* 1854, *Pictures of the Olden Time,* 1857, *Athanasia, or Foregleams of Immortality,* 1858, *The Fourth Gospel, the Heart of Christ,* 1872, and *Sermons and Songs of the Christian Life,* 1875. Most of his hymns were first published in the *Monthly Religious Magazine* when he was its coeditor.

Author: It Came upon the Midnight Clear (390)

Shackford, John Walter (b. Walkerton, King and Queen County, Va., January 10, 1878) was educated at Randolph-Macon College (B.A. 1900) and Vanderbilt University (B.D. 1903). He served as pastor and presiding elder in the Virginia Conference, Methodist Episcopal Church, South, before becoming secretary of Missionary Education and later general secretary at the General Sunday School Board of the Methodist Episcopal Church, South, in Nashville, Tenn., 1922-30. Both as a pastor and denomination leader, he has led in the field of educational and social reforms. His work resulted in the unification of the church's educational program on the local church level, 1930, the acceptance of the Social Creed of the Methodist Episcopal Church by the 1914 General Conference, and the establishment of the Board of Temperance and Social Service, 1918. Shackford also served on the Virginia State Interracial Commission for 10 years. He is the author of numerous training texts used by education and mission study groups.

Author: O Thou Who Art the Shepherd (201)

Shaw, Martin Fallas (b. Kensington, London, England, March 9, 1875; d. Southwold, Suffolk, England, October 24, 1958) was the son of the organist of Hampstead Parish Church and the elder brother of Geoffrey Shaw. He studied at the Royal College of Music under Charles V. Stanford, C. H. H. Parry, and Walford Davies. After touring Europe as a conductor, he became organist at Primrose Hill, London, in 1908, at St. Martin's in the Fields in 1920, and then at the Guild-house in London. He was a co-founder of the Summer School of Church Music, which became the Royal Society of Church Music, and director of music for the diocese of Chelmsford, 1935-45. In 1932 he and his brother Geoffrey received the Lambeth degree of Mus.D.

Shaw published *Additional Tunes,* 1915, and was editor of *The Oxford Book of Carols,* 1928. With Ralph Vaughan Williams, he served as musical editor for *Songs of Praise,* 1925. He composed over 100 songs, many anthems, and service music, all possessing "dignity, massiveness, and reserve."

Harmonizer: FRENCH CAROL (441, p. 299)

Shepherd, Thomas (b. England, 1665; d. Bocking, Essex, England, January 29, 1739) was ordained into the Church of England, but left it in 1694 to become pastor of the Independent Castle Hill Meeting House at Nottingham, where Philip Doddridge later became pastor. Moving to Bocking, near Braintree, Essex, in 1700, he preached for 7 years in a barn before a small chapel was built. He served as pastor of the congregation for 39 years.

Composite author: Must Jesus Bear the Cross Alone (183)

Sheppard, Franklin Lawrence (b. Philadelphia, Pa., August 7, 1852; d. Germantown, Pa., February 15, 1930) graduated from the University of Pennsylvania in 1872 with highest honors and as a charter member of the Phi Beta Kappa chapter. In 1875 he went to Baltimore in charge of his father's foundry, Isaac A. Sheppard & Company, the manufacturer of stoves and heaters. He was organist and vestryman of Zion Protestant Episcopal Church, Baltimore. Later he joined Second Presbyterian in Baltimore and became the music director. He was a delegate to the General Assembly many times and a member and later president of the Presbyterian Board of Publication. He edited the Presbyterian Sunday school songbook *Alleluia*, 1915, and served on the editorial committee for the 1911 Presbyterian *Hymnal*.

Composer: TERRA BEATA (45, pp. 406-7)

Sherwin, William Fiske (b. Buckland, Mass., March 14, 1826; d. Boston, Mass., April 14, 1888) was a student of Lowell Mason. He directed choirs as a young man and joined the faculty of the New England Conservatory of Music in Boston. He was a Baptist, but his abilities as a director of amateur singers caused him to be chosen by John H. Vincent as musical director of Methodism's Chautauqua Institution in western New York State.

Composer: BREAD OF LIFE (369, pp. 123-24)
CHAUTAUQUA (503, p. 163)

Shrubsole, William (b. Canterbury, England, 1760; d. London, England, January 18, 1806) was the son of a blacksmith. He took his early musical training during the years 1770-77 as a chorister in the cathedral at Canterbury. In 1782 he was appointed organist of Bangor Cathedral, but his association with Methodists and dissenters caused his dismissal in 1784. He returned to London and resumed his role as a private teacher of music. Later he was engaged to play the organ in Lady Huntingdon's Spa Fields Chapel. Here he remained until his death. Shrubsole was a close friend of Edward Perronet and was named the executor of his will.

Composer: MILES' LANE (73, p. 77)

Shurtleff, Ernest Warburton (b. Boston, Mass., April 4, 1862; d. Paris, France, August 29, 1917) was educated at Boston Latin School, Harvard University, New Church Theological Seminary, and Andover Theological Seminary. As a student at Andover, he played the organ at Stone Chapel of Phillips Academy for boys. He held Congregational pastorates at Ventura, Calif., Old Plymouth and Palmer, Mass., and at Minneapolis, Minn., from 1898 to 1905, when he organized the American Church at Frankfort, Germany. In 1906 he became director of student activities at the Academy Vitti in Paris. He and his wife served during World War I in relief work.

Author: Lead On, O King Eternal (478)

Sibelius, Jean (b. Tavastehus, Finland, December 8, 1865; d. Järvenpää, Finland, September 20, 1957) was the greatest of all Finnish composers. According to the citation read at the conferring of the Mus.D. at Yale University, June 17, 1914, "What Wagner did for the ancient German legends, Dr. Sibelius has, in his own magnificent way, done for the Finnish myths in Finland's national epos."

His works include symphonic poems, 7 symphonies, 86 songs, 20 choral works, and in sacred music *Musique religieuse,* 1927, and *Five Christmas Songs,* 1895. After 1929 he ceased to compose. He was the last of the nineteenth-century nationalist romantics.

Composer: FINLANDIA (209, 542, p. 112)

Simpson, Robert (b. Glasgow, Scotland, November 4, 1790; d. Greenock, Scotland, July or August, 1832) was a weaver by trade but well educated. He led the singing in Dr. Wardlaw's Congregational church in Glasgow. In 1823 he became precentor and session clerk of the East Parish Church, Greenock. He died of cholera in 1832.

Adapter: BALLERMA (461, 535, p. 209)

Small, James Grindlay (b. Edinburgh, Scotland, 1817; d. Renfrew on the Clyde, Scotland, February 11, 1888) was educated at the Royal High School and the University of Edinburgh. He joined the Free Church of Scotland in 1843, becoming pastor at Bervie, near Montrose, in 1847. Besides his 2 volumes of poems, he published *Hymns for Youthful Voices,* 1859, and *Poems and Sacred Songs,* 1866.

Author: I've Found a Friend (163)

Smart, Henry Thomas (b. London, England, October 26, 1813; d. London, July 6, 1879) studied with his father and W. H. Kearns and attended Highgate. He was organist in several London churches, 1836-65, and at St. Philip's, London, and St. Pancras Church, 1865 until his death. Smart was self taught in both organ playing and composition, and also designed organs for churches in Glasgow and Leeds. His works include an opera, 4 cantatas, many songs, part songs, anthems, some organ music, a morning and evening service, as well as many hymn tunes, 7 of which are still in general use.

Composer: LANCASHIRE (342, 437, 478, pp. 187-88)
REGENT SQUARE (66, 298, 382, p. 94)

Smith, Henry Percy (b. England, 1825; d. Christchurch, London, 1898) was educated at Balliol College, Oxford (B.A. 1848, M.A. 1850). He was ordained deacon in 1849, priest in 1850, and served as curate to Charles Kingsley at Eversley, 1849-51. He became perpetual curate of St. Michael's, York Town, Camberley, Surrey, 1851-68, and vicar of Great Barton, Suffolk, 1868-82. Smith was also chaplain of Christ Church, Cannes, France, 1882-95, and beginning in 1892 was canon of the cathedral at Gibraltar.

Composer: MARYTON (170, 462, p. 329)

Smith, Samuel Francis (b. Boston, Mass., October 21, 1808; d. Boston, November 16, 1895) was educated at Boston Latin School, Harvard University, and Andover Theological Seminary. He was editor of the *Baptist Missionary Magazine* for a year and a half, then became pastor of the Baptist church at Waterville, Me., 1834-42. He was also professor of modern languages at Waterville College (now Colby College). After 12 years as pastor of the Newton, Mass., Baptist church, he became editorial secretary of the American Baptist Missionary Union in 1854, holding the post for 15 years. Inspired by the work of Adoniram Judson, he toured the mission fields in Asia and Europe in 1880, writing *Rambles in Mission Fields,* 1884. His son, Dr. A. W. Smith, became a Baptist missionary in Burma and was president of the seminary at Rangoon.

With Baron Stowe, Smith compiled *The Psalmist,* 1843, widely used in Baptist churches in his day. He was an intimate friend of

666

Lowell Mason and contributed songs to Mason's *Juvenile Lyre*. Most of his 100 hymns were written for special occasions.

Smith's classmate and close friend, Oliver Wendell Holmes, wrote a poem for a class reunion at Harvard:

> And there's a nice youngster of excellent pith,
> Fate tried to conceal him by naming him Smith,
> But he shouted a song for the brave and the free,
> Just read on his medal, "My country, of thee."

Author: My Country, 'Tis of Thee (547)

Smith, Walter Chalmers (b. Aberdeen, Scotland, December 5, 1824; d. Kinbuck, Perthshire, Scotland, September 20, 1908) was educated at the University of Aberdeen and New College, Edinburgh. He was ordained into the Free Church of Scotland and served as pastor at the Free Church, Chadwell Street, Islington, London; Orwell Free Church, Milnathort; Free Tron Church, Glasgow; and finally the Free High Church of Scotland, Edinburgh, 1876-94. In 1893 he was elected moderator of the Free Church of Scotland. Among his published works are *Hymns of Christ and the Christian Life*, 1867, and *Poetical Works*, 1902.

Author: Immortal, Invisible, God Only Wise (27)

Sowerby, Leo (b. Grand Rapids, Mich., May 1, 1895; d. Cleveland, Ohio, July 7, 1968) studied at the American Conservatory in Chicago (M.M. 1918) and served with the 332nd Field Artillery Band in England and France during World War I. He received the Prix de Rome in 1921 while a fellow at the American Academy there. Sowerby was head of theory and composition at the American Conservatory, 1923-63, and organist and choirmaster at St. James's Episcopal Church, Chicago, 1927-63. The University of Rochester awarded him the Mus.D. degree in 1934. He was the director of the College of Church Musicians, Washington Cathedral, 1962 until his death.

Sowerby composed symphonies, concertos, organ works, service music, cantatas, and anthems. In 1946 his oratorio *Canticle of the Sun* received the Pulitzer Prize. A member of the joint commission on the revision of the Episcopal hymnal, he served on the tunes committee. Two tunes and 3 arrangements are included in *The Hymnal 1940*.

See *Music,* October, 1968, for a symposium on Sowerby's life and work.

Composer: PERRY (321, p. 116)

Sparrow-Simpson, William John (b. London, England, June 20, 1859; d. Great Ilford, Essex, February 13, 1952) was educated at Trinity College, Cambridge (B.A. 1882, M.A. 1886, B.D. 1909, D.D. 1911). He was ordained deacon in 1882, priest in 1883, and served various churches. In 1904 he became the chaplain at St. Mary's Hospital, Great Ilford.

Simpson compiled the libretto for John Stainer's *Crucifixion,* 1887, and hymns from this work have appeared in several collections. His other writings are in the liturgical and historical aspects of the Anglo-Catholic revival with general books in the fields of church history and theology.

Author: Cross of Jesus, Cross of Sorrow (426)

Spohr, Louis (baptized **Ludwig**) (b. Brunswick, April 5, 1784; d. Cassel, October 22, 1859) was born of musical parents, and he showed musical talent early. After extensive study, he became a famous violin virtuoso. He composed oratorios, operas, violin concertos, and chamber music. Spohr was critical of Beethoven and Weber, but he championed Wagner by producing 2 of Wagner's operas in Cassel in 1842 and 1853, despite the opposition of the court.

Composer: GERALD (279, p. 232)

Stainer, John (b. London, England, June 6, 1840; d. Verona, Italy, March 31, 1901) was the son of a schoolmaster and was educated at Christ Church, Oxford, and at St. Edmund's Hall. He was a chorister at St. Paul's Cathedral, London, 1847-56. In 1860 he became the organist at Magdalen College and in 1872 succeeded John Goss as organist at St. Paul's Cathedral, but retired in 1888 because of failing eyesight. He was knighted by Queen Victoria in 1888 upon his return to Oxford University, where he taught until his death.

Stainer wrote more than 150 hymn tunes. He was coeditor of *A Dictionary of Musical Terms,* author of *The Music of the Bible,*

1879, and musical editor of *The Church Hymnary,* 1898. His book on organ playing was a classic for many years.

Composer: Amen (**825,** p. 442)

Stead, Louisa M. R. (b. Dover, England, c. 1850; d. Penkridge, near Umtali, Southern Rhodesia, January 18, 1917) was converted at the age of 9. She wanted to be a foreign missionary. In 1871 she traveled to America and lived with friends in Cincinnati. At a camp meeting in Urbana, Ohio, she offered her life as a missionary but was not sent because of her poor health. After her husband drowned while trying to rescue a child off Long Island, N.Y., she and her daughter moved to South Africa to work as missionaries in the Cape Colony, which she served for 15 years. There she married Robert Wodehouse, a native of South Africa. In 1895 they returned to America, and he became a Methodist minister. Her health improved, and they returned to the Methodist mission at Umtali, Southern Rhodesia, in 1901, where she retired in 1911. Her missionary efforts were continued in the work of her daughter, Mrs. D. A. Carson.

Author: 'Tis So Sweet to Trust in Jesus (**208**)

Stebbins, George Coles (b. East Carlton, N.Y., February 26, 1846; d. Catskill, N.Y., October 6, 1945). His music interest was whetted at the age of 13 when he attended a singing school. He studied music in Buffalo, Rochester, and New York, and at the age of 23 moved to Chicago where he was with Lyon & Healy Music Company and music director of the First Baptist Church. In 1874 he went to Clarendon Street Baptist Church in Boston as music director and 2 years later accepted a position at Tremont Temple. However, he joined the Moody-Sankey revival team in the summer of 1876 and was active in evangelistic work as a song leader. With Sankey and James McGranahan he edited and compiled the third through the sixth editions of *Gospel Hymns,* 1878-91. He composed hundreds of songs and compiled many gospel song collections. His *Memoirs and Reminiscences* was published in 1924.

Composer: ADELAIDE (**154,** p. 212)
FRIEND (**163,** p. 241)
HOLINESS (**266,** p. 386)

JESUS IS CALLING (110, pp. 245-46)
TRUEHEARTED (179, p. 415)

Steele, Anne (b. Broughton, Hampshire, England, 1716; d. Hampshire, England, November 11, 1778) was a semi-invalid from childhood and spent her entire life at Broughton, where her father was a timber merchant and an unsalaried Baptist preacher. She was deeply affected by the accidental drowning of her fiancé a few hours before they were to be married. The author of 144 hymns, 34 metrical psalms, and 30 poems, she did not consent to any publication until 1760, and then only under the pen name "Theodosia." Some of her poems were printed in the *Spectator* with only the name "Steele," and Richard Steele was falsely credited with some of her works. Miss Steele was the first of the English women hymn writers, following in the Isaac Watts's style of writing.

Author: Father of Mercies, in Thy Word (367)

Stennett, Samuel (b. Exeter, England, 1727; d. London, England, August 24, 1795). The Stennett family held a prominent place in the Seventh Day Baptist Church of England. Samuel's father was pastor of the Baptist church in Exeter at the time of Samuel's birth, and in 1737 the family moved to London. Because his family were nonconformists, Samuel could not attend any university, but he became an excellent scholar under John Hubbard of Stepney and John Walker of the academy at Mile End. In 1747 he was named assistant to his father at the church at Little Wild Street, Lincoln's Inn Fields, and became pastor when his father died in 1758. He was called in 1767 to the Sabbatarian Baptist Church where his grandfather had been pastor for 23 years. He did not accept the call, but did preach every Saturday morning for 20 years while holding down his other post.

At the age of 36, Stennett was granted the honorary degree of D.D. by King's College, Aberdeen, in recognition of his scholarship. He was a personal friend of King George III and John Howard, the noted philanthropist and prison reformer. He contributed 38 hymns to John Rippon's *Selection of Hymns*, 1787.

Author: Majestic Sweetness Sits Enthroned (83)
On Jordan's Stormy Banks I Stand (291)

Stocking, Jay Thomas (b. Lisbon, N.Y., April 19, 1870; d. Newton Center, Mass., January 27, 1936) was educated at Amherst College (B.A. 1895), Yale Divinity School (B.D. 1901), and the University of Berlin, 1902-3. In 1901 he was ordained a Congregational minister, serving churches in New England, New Jersey, Missouri, and Washington, D.C. He served on the Commission on International Justice and Good Will of the Federal Council of Churches of Christ in America, and was moderator of the Congregational Council, 1934-35. He wrote many books of stories for children.

Author: O Master Workman of the Race (171)

Stockton, John Hart (b. New Hope, Pa., April 19, 1813; d. Philadelphia, Pa., March 25, 1877) was born of Presbyterian parents. He was converted at the age of 21 at a Methodist camp meeting in Paulsboro, N.J. Licensed as an exhorter and preacher, 1844-46, he was made a full member of the New Jersey Conference of the Methodist Episcopal Church in 1857. Ill health caused his removal from the active ministry in 1874, though he maintained an interest in evangelistic work. He assisted Dwight L. Moody and Ira D. Sankey in their Philadelphia meetings and wrote a number of songs used by them, published in *Salvation Melodies No. 1*, 1874, and *Precious Songs*, 1875.

Author and composer: Come, Every Soul by Sin Oppressed (STOCKTON) (101)

Stone, Lloyd (b. Coalinga, Calif., June 29, 1912) received his B.A. and M.A. from the University of Southern California. He moved to Hawaii in 1936 and taught in the public schools and at the University of Hawaii. Stone is the author of 10 books of poetry and 2 children's books. He has served as Honolulu chapter president of the National Society of Arts and Letters.

Composite author: This Is My Song (542)

Stone, Samuel John (b. Whitmore, Staffordshire, England, April 25, 1839; d. Charterhouse, England, November 19, 1900) was educated at Charterhouse School and Pembroke College, Oxford (B.A. 1862, M.A. 1872). He was ordained for the ministry in the Church of England in 1862 and served as curate at Windsor and, following his

671

father, at St. Paul's Church, Haggerston, London, before his appointment as rector of All Hallows on the Wall, London, in 1890, where
he remained until his death. The author of many books, he served as
a member of the committee which prepared the 1909 edition of *Hymns
Ancient and Modern.* His *Collected Poems and Hymns* were published posthumously by F. G. Ellerton.

Author: The Church's One Foundation (297)

Stowe, Harriet Beecher (b. Litchfield, Conn., June 14, 1812; d. Hartford, Conn., July 1, 1896) was the daughter of Lyman Beecher and
the sister of Henry Ward Beecher. The family moved to Cincinnati
in 1832 when her father became president of Lane Seminary. In 1836
she married Calvin E. Stowe, professor of language and biblical literature at the seminary, and later at Bowdoin College and Andover
Theological Seminary. Her concern over the abolition of slavery led
to the writing of *Uncle Tom's Cabin,* 1852, bringing her to national
fame. She published more than 40 volumes of prose and 1 volume of
poetry. Three of her hymns were included in Henry Ward Beecher's
Plymouth Collection, 1855.

Author: Still, Still with Thee (264)

Stowell, Hugh (b. Douglas, Isle of Man, England, December 3, 1799;
d. Salford, England, October 8, 1865) was the son of Hugh Stowell,
rector of Ballaugh. He was educated at St. Edmund's Hall, Oxford
(B.A. 1822, M.A. 1826). Ordained into the Church of England in
1823, he served as curate of Shepscombe and became rector of Christ
Church, Salford, in 1831, remaining there until his death. He became
honorary canon of Chester in 1845 and in 1851 was chaplain to the
bishop of Manchester. Stowell published *A Selection of Psalms and
Hymns Suited to the Services of the Church of England,* 1831, to
which he contributed 50 hymns in this and subsequent editions.

Author: From Every Stormy Wind That Blows (232)

Studdert-Kennedy, Geoffrey Anketell (b. Leeds, Yorkshire, England,
June 27, 1883; d. Liverpool, England, March 7 or 8, 1929) received
his education from Trinity College, Dublin, and Ripon Clergy Col-

lege. He was ordained in 1908 and served as curate of St. Mary's, Leeds, and in 1914 as vicar of St. Paul's, Worcester. Famous as "Woodbine Willie," he was a chaplain in World War I and received the Military Cross. After the war he served several London parishes and devoted much time to travel, writing, and, in particular, the work of the Industrial Christian Fellowship.

Studdert-Kennedy was a forthright and popular preacher. His published works include *Rough Rhymes of a Padre, Lies, Food for the Fed-Up,* and *I Believe.* Honored as chaplain to the king, he has been called by William Temple "one of God's greatest gifts to our generation."

Author: Awake, Awake to Love and Work **(190)**

Stutsman, Grace May (b. Melrose, Mass., March 4, 1886) was educated at Boston University and the New England Conservatory of Music. At the latter she won the Endicott prize in song composition and received a scholarship for graduate study toward a career as a concert pianist and music educator. Her compositions include a symphony, string quartets, choruses, and songs. For 25 years she was the music critic for the *Christian Science Monitor,* and she also has written for *Musical America* and other periodicals.

Author and composer: In Bethlehem Neath Starlit Skies (WAITS' CAROL) **(377)**

Su Yin-lan (b. Tientsin, China, 1915; d. Tientsin, 1937) graduated from the music department of Yenching University in Peking in 1935 with honors. She was married soon after and returned to Tientsin to live. When the Japanese army of occupation bombed Tientsin in the summer of 1937, she had just given birth to a son. Being of an exceedingly timid and sensitive nature, she was literally frightened to death by the terrible noise of the bombs.

Composer: SHENG EN **(317,** p. 389)

Sullivan, Arthur Seymour (b. Bolwell Terrace, Lambeth, England, May 13, 1842; d. Westminster, England, November 22, 1900) studied with Sterndale Bennett, Goss, Moritz Hauptmann, David, and Moscheles. Beginning as a chorister in the Chapel Royal under Thomas Helmore, he developed an intense interest in church music, though he wrote little. He is best known for his operettas, and his church music comprises but a small part of his great creative work. His hymn tunes composed early in his career reflect a stoutness so unlike the easy-going melodies of the *Mikado,* 1885, or *Pinafore,* 1878. Sullivan composed some large choral works, among them *The Light of the World,* 1873, *The Golden Legend,* 1886, and he was musical editor of *The Hymnary,* 1872, and *Church Hymns with Tunes,* 1874. He was knighted by Queen Victoria in 1883.

H. J. Staples in an article in the *Choir,* XXXI (1940), 68-70, discusses Sullivan's hymn tunes, and James T. Lightwood in the *Choir,* XIX (1928) and XX (1929) discusses his choral music.

Composer: ANGEL VOICES (2, p. 93)
ST. EDMUND (188, p. 166)
ST. GERTRUDE (305, p. 349)
ST. KEVIN (446, p. 157)

Swain, Joseph (b. Birmingham, England, 1761; d. Walworth, London, England, April 14, 1796) was an orphan as a child and was apprenticed to an engraver. Purchasing a Bible, he began a serious study of the scriptures and was converted and baptized under the preaching of John Rippon. At the age of 30 he was given charge of a Baptist mission in Walworth, England. His hymns, begun early with his interest in religion, were published in his second year at Walworth in a collection called *Walworth Hymns,* 1792.

Author: O Thou, in Whose Presence (129)

Symonds, John Addington (b. Bristol, England, October 5, 1840; d. Rome, Italy, April 19, 1893) was a brilliant scholar who was educated at Harrow and at Balliol College, Oxford. He became a fellow of Magdalen College, Oxford. He suffered from ill health all his life and developed tuberculosis from overwork, moving in 1877 to Switzerland, where he built a home at Davos Platz.

Symonds published several important books, including *History of the Italian Renaissance,* 1875-86, in 6 volumes. He also translated autobiographies of Benvenuto Cellini and Count Carolo Gozzi, and sonnets of Michelangelo and Campanella.

Author: These Things Shall Be (198)

Synesius of Cyrene (b. Cyrene, c. 375; d. 430) was born of wealthy parents. He studied under the neoplatonist Hypatia at Alexandria. In 397 he went to Constantinople in a vain attempt to convince the Emperor Arcadius that the Gothic invasion was serious. He married a Christian wife in 403, and a few years after his conversion to Christianity he was popularly elected bishop of Ptolemais in 409 or 410. An orator, philosopher, poet, musician, and statesman, Synesius was better known for his cultural interests than for his religious zeal.

Author: Lord Jesus, Think on Me (284)

Tallis (also *Tallys* and *Talys*), *Thomas* (b. probably Leicestershire, England, c. 1505; d. Greenwich, England, November 23, 1585) was an organist and composer who successfully survived the varying political-religious climate of the reigns of Henry VIII, Edward VI, Mary, and Elizabeth. One of the most distinguished Tudor musicians, he is often referred to as the father of English cathedral music. Tallis had little difficulty in accommodating his musical gifts to both Protestant and Catholic rulers. He prepared the music for the Responses and Litany for the Second Prayer Book of Edward VI. Under Queen Mary he wrote Latin motets and masses, and the queen leased him the manor of Minster in Thanet. Apparently he pleased Elizabeth, for she granted to him and William Byrd the exclusive right to print music and music paper for 21 years. Byrd and Tallis published in 1575 a collection of Latin motets, *Cantiones quae ab argumento sacrae vocantur.* Nine tunes by Tallis in 4-part harmony were printed in Archbishop Matthew Parker's *Whole Psalter Translated into English Metre,* 1561-67. In 1577 he and Byrd were named joint organists of the Chapel Royal.

Recent reprints of his works include anthems, masses, magnificats, and other service music. His most elaborate composition was *Spem in alium non habui,* written for eight 5-part choirs, or 40 separate voice parts.

Composer: Ferial (**850**, pp. 463-64)
  Festal (**806**, pp. 463-64)
  Lord, Have Mercy upon Us (**827**, p. 452)
  TALLIS' CANON (**180, 216, 493**, pp. 83-84)
  TALLIS' ORDINAL (**316, 367, 411**, p. 69)
  Thanks Be to Thee (**799**, p. 460)

Tans'ur, William (b. Dunchurch, Warwickshire, England, 1706 [?];
d. St. Neots, England, October 7, 1783) was the son of a laborer who
was probably named Edward Tanzer. Little of Tans'ur's life is known
except that he was an organist, traveling teacher of music and director
of group singing, and bookseller. As a theoretician, he is described by
Irving Lowens as a "much maligned figure whose presentation of the
theoretical aspects of music is in fact not unskillful." He published
many important collections of tunes and theoretical works, some of
which have been reprinted in America.

See Irving Lowens and Allen P. Britton, *Papers of the Biographical
Society of America* (1955), pp. 340-54.

Composer: BANGOR (**427**, p. 87)
  ST. MARTIN'S (**507**, pp. 144-45)

Tappan, William Bingham (b. Beverly, Mass., October 24, 1794; d.
West Needham, Mass., June 18, 1849) was apprenticed at the age of
12 to a Boston clockmaker. He moved to Philadelphia in 1815, where
he made and repaired clocks. In 1822 he became interested in the
American Sunday School Union and retained a connection with the
organization the rest of his life. He was licensed as a Congregational
minister in 1840 and became a successful evangelist. Tappan published 10 volumes of verse.

Author: 'Tis Midnight, and on Olive's Brow (**431**)

Tarrant, William George (b. Pembroke Dock, South Wales, July 2,
1853; d. Wandsworth, England, January 15, 1928). Tarrant's father
died when William was only 1, and his mother when he was 6. He
was sent to an orphanage in Birmingham and received his early instruction in the Free Industrial School there. During the years 1867-74
he was apprenticed to a silversmith in Birmingham. He entered the

Unitarian Home Missionary College in Manchester in 1879 and earned his B.A. in 1883 from Manchester New College, London. Ordained for the Unitarian ministry, he was the pastor of the Unitarian Christian Church, Wandsworth, London, for 37 years.

Tarrant's literary skill led him to the editorship of the Unitarian weekly the *Inquirer,* 1887-97, 1918-27. He wrote tunes for many of his hymns and was coeditor of the *Essex Hall Hymnal,* 1890. He also published *Songs of the Devout,* 1912.

Author: Now Praise We Great and Famous Men (532)

Tate, Nahum (b. Dublin, Ireland, 1652; d. Southwark, London, England, August 12, 1715) was the son of an Irish clergyman. He received his B.A. from Trinity College, Dublin, in 1672. He moved to London in 1668, where he wrote for the stage, chiefly adapting the works of others. Tate never really succeeded in making a significant contribution to the stage except perhaps *King Lear.* In 1692 he was made poet laureate, in 1702 royal historiographer.

His most significant work is *The New Version of the Psalms of David,* 1696, which he produced with Nicolaus Brady as an alternative to the "Old Version" of Sternhold and Hopkins. In 1698 a Supplement was produced which contained in addition to the psalms, the canticles, the Apostles' Creed, the Lord's Prayer, the Communion, *Veni Creator,* and 6 additional hymns. The success of Tate and Brady's work, later bound with *The Book of Common Prayer,* extended well into Victorian times.

Tate died in a debtor's refuge, the mint of Southwark.

Author: While Shepherds Watched Their Flocks by Night (394)
Source: As Pants the Hart for Cooling Streams (255)
          O Lord, Our Fathers Oft Have Told (54)
          Through All the Changing Scenes of Life (56)

Tattersall, William de Chair (b. 1752; d. 1829) was educated at Westminster and at Christ Church, Oxford (M.A. 1777). He was ordained into the Anglican ministry and became rector of Westbourne, Sussex. In 1794 he published his *Improved Psalmody,* the musical edition of John Merrick's *Psalms.* Tattersall succeeded in getting Haydn, who was in London at the time, to contribute 4 tunes to the collection and to become one of the paying subscribers.

Source: SICILIAN MARINERS (165, 517, p. 273)

Taylor, Sarah Ellen (b. Stockport, England, December 30, 1883; d. Pawtucket, R.I., October 5, 1954) was the daughter of a Primitive Methodist preacher, William B. Taylor. She was brought to America in 1892. Educated at Brown University (B.A. 1904, M.A. 1910), she was a schoolteacher all her life, teaching first in mission schools in Alabama and Virginia. She later taught in Massachusetts and for 32 years in the high schools of Central Falls and Pawtucket, R.I., from which she retired in 1949. A lifelong member of the Primitive Methodist Church, she taught Sunday school for 55 years and served as a member of the denomination's Foreign Mission Board.

Several of Miss Taylor's hymns won prizes in contests sponsored by the Hymn Society of America, and she was the author of the Rhode Island state song.

Author: O God of Light, Thy Word, a Lamp Unfailing (371)

Taylor, Virgil Corydon (b. Barkhamsted, Conn., April 2, 1817; d. Des Moines, Iowa, January 30, 1891) was a descendant on his mother's side of the Pilgrim, William Brewster. He led singing schools, held institutes, and taught music. He served as organist in Hartford, Conn., Poughkeepsie, Brooklyn, and Niagara Falls, N.Y., and Des Moines, Iowa. Taylor published several song collections, including *The Sacred Minstrel,* 1846, in the style of Thomas Hastings and Lowell Mason, both of whom he greatly admired.

Composer: LOUVAN (64, p. 277)

Taylor, Walter Reginald Oxenham (b. Portsmouth, England, August 1, 1889) was educated at the school of the China Inland Mission, Chefoo, North China, and at the University of Durham in England, where he received his M.A. Ordained a priest in the Church of England, Taylor served with the Church Missionary Society in China, 1924-49. With Bliss Wiant he served on the committee which prepared the Chinese Union hymnal, *Hymns of Universal Praise.* During

World War II he remained in occupied China, where T. T. Lew's hymn was often sung in prison camps. In a recent letter he comments that the hymnbooks used in the Church of England presently do not contain translated Chinese hymns: "I am quite certain I shall never hear it sung in English—though we often used it in China."

Taylor, now retired, lives at Sevenoaks, Kent, England.

Translator: The Bread of Life, for All Men Broken (317)

Tennyson, Alfred (b. Somersby, Lincolnshire, England, August 6, 1809; d. Aldworth, Surrey, England, October 6, 1892), the son of the rector of Somersby, was educated at Louth Grammar School and Trinity College, Cambridge. As a student he became well known for his poetry, and after the publication of *In Memoriam* he was named poet laureate when William Wordsworth died in 1850. He was elevated to the peerage in 1884 under the title of Baron Tennyson of Aldworth and Farringford. Tennyson wrote about 20 major works, of which *Idylls of the King*, 1859, was one of the most popular. He was buried in Westminster Abbey.

Author: Strong Son of God, Immortal Love (146)

Tersteegen, Gerhardt (b. Mörs, Netherlands, November 25, 1697; d. Mühlheim, Rhenish Prussia, April 3, 1769). Tersteegen's father died when Gerhardt was only 6, and his mother was unable to afford the necessary education for the Reformed Church ministry. He studied at Mörs Gymnasium, then became a silkweaver. Tersteegen shared his meager wages with the poor, and the consequent malnutrition and privation caused a serious mental depression for 5 years. Afterwards he wrote a new covenant with God, signing it with his own blood. He devoted himself entirely to Christian work outside the Reformed Church which he thought had lost its evangelical zeal. His home was called "The Pilgrim's Cottage" and became a retreat for persons seeking a new way of life. Strongly attracted to mysticism, he ceased attendance at Reformed services after 1719 and translated books by medieval mystics. He wrote 111 hymns.

Author: God Calling Yet! Shall I Not Hear (105)
God Himself Is with Us (788, p. 448)
Thou Hidden Love of God, Whose Height (531)

Teschner, Melchior (b. Fraustadt, Silesia, 1584; d. Oberprietschen, Posen, December 1, 1635) was appointed cantor and schoolmaster of the Zum Kripplein Christi Lutheran Church in his home town of Fraustadt in 1609. He moved to nearby Oberprietschen in 1614, where he served as pastor. His son and grandson succeeded him in this position.

Composer: st. theodulph (424, p. 74)

Theodulph of Orleans (b. probably Spain, c. 750; d. Angers, September 18, 821) was born of a noble Gothic family, probably in Spain. He became abbot of a monastery in Florence and in 781 was taken to France by Charlemagne where he was appointed abbot of Fleury and bishop of Orleans, becoming the king's chief theologian upon Alcuin's death. After Charlemagne's death, in 818 he was accused of conspiring with King Bernard of Italy against Louis I and was imprisoned in Angers. He died 3 years later, probably from poison. Although the tune named for him is called st. theodulph, there is no evidence that he was ever sainted.

Author: All Glory, Laud, and Honor (424)

Thomas, Edith Lovell (b. Eastford, Conn., September 11, 1878) was educated at Boston University (B.R.E., S.R.E., and M.Ed.) and the School of Sacred Music at Union Theological Seminary in New York City, with additional study at Wellesley College. Miss Thomas has served as professor of music and worship at Boston University, and minister of music in New York, New Jersey, and Connecticut. For many years she was director of church school music, Christ Church Methodist, in New York City and lectured on music education in private schools in the greater New York area.

A pioneer in the field of music in Christian education, she has compiled several important collections, including *First Book in Hymns and Worship,* 1922, *Singing Worship,* 1935, *Sing, Children, Sing,* 1939, *The Whole World Singing,* 1950, *Martin and Judy Songs,* 1951, and the book *Music in Christian Education,* 1953. Scores of musicians and teachers have been introduced to the vast potential of the arts in Christian education through the teaching and writing of this gifted and gracious woman. She lives in "active retirement" in Claremont, Calif.

Arranger: ST. ANTHONY'S CHORALE (**6**, p. 423)

Thompson, Will Lamartine (b. East Liverpool, Ohio, November 7, 1847; d. New York, N.Y., September 20, 1909) was educated at Mt. Union College, Ohio. He attended a music school in Boston and studied in Leipzig, Germany. He established Will L. Thompson & Company, East Liverpool and Chicago, a highly successful music publishing firm. He was famous for his numerous gospel songs as well as his secular and patriotic songs, and his work was much admired by Dwight L. Moody.

Author and composer: Jesus Is All the World to Me (ELIZABETH) (**97**)

Thomson (also *Thompson*), *Mary Ann* (b. London, England, December 5, 1834; d. Philadelphia, Pa., March 11, 1923). Armin Haeussler quotes Mrs. Thomson: "I am an English woman and was born, baptized, and confirmed in London, and I am, and for many years have been, a member of the Church of the Annunciation, Philadelphia. I am the wife of John Thompson, the librarian of the Free Library of Philadelphia, and he is the Accounting Warden of the Church of the Annunciation."

She contributed more than 40 hymns and poems to the *Churchman,* New York, and the *Living Church,* Chicago. Her husband was the first librarian of the Free Library.

Author: O Zion, Haste! Thy Mission High Fulfilling (**299**)

Threlfall, Jeannette (b. Blackburn, Lancashire, England, March 24, 1821; d. Westminster, England, November 30, 1880) was the daughter of a Blackburn wine merchant and a socially prominent lady whose parents disapproved of the marriage. She was left an orphan early in life. She lived with an uncle and aunt in Blackburn, then at Leyland. Miss Threlfall was accidentally lamed and mutilated, leaving her an invalid for life; nevertheless, she was not bitter and was known for her cheerfulness and courage.

Her verses, published in various periodicals, were collected in *Wood-*

sorrel, or Leaves from a Retired Home, 1856, and *Sunshine and Shadow,* 1873.

Author: Hosanna, Loud Hosanna (423)

Thring, Godfrey (b. Alford, Somersetshire, England, March 25, 1823; d. Shamley Green, Guildford, Surrey, England, September 13, 1903) was educated at Shrewsbury School and Balliol College, Oxford (B.A. 1845). He was ordained deacon in 1846, priest in 1847, and served several curacies. In 1858 he succeeded his father as rector of Alford and in 1876 was named prebendary of Wells. Thring's publications include *Hymns and Other Verses,* 1866, *Hymns Congregational and Others,* 1866, and *A Church of England Hymn Book, Adapted to the Daily Services of the Church Throughout the Year,* 1880. This latter collection appeared revised in 1882 as *The Church of England Hymn Book.*

John Julian in *A Dictionary of Hymnology,* pp. 1173-74, makes considerable comment on Thring's output and poetic style.

Author: Crown Him with Many Crowns (455)

Thrupp, Dorothy Ann (b. London, England, June 20, 1779; d. London, December 14, 1847) wrote several hymns for W. Carus Wilson's *Friendly Visitor* and *Children's Friend,* often under the pen name "Iota." Later she contributed several hymns signed "D.A.T." to Mrs. Herbert Mayo's *Selection of Hymns and Poetry for Use of Infants and Juvenile Schools and Families,* 1838. She edited *Hymns for the Young,* about 1830, in which all the hymns were unsigned.

Attributed author: Savior, Like a Shepherd Lead Us (121)

Tillett, Wilbur Fisk (b. Henderson, N.C., August 25, 1854; d. Nashville, Tenn., June 4, 1936) was educated at Trinity College in North Carolina, Randolph-Macon College (B.A. 1877), and Princeton University (M.A. 1879). He attended Princeton Theological Seminary and received honorary degrees from Randolph-Macon College, Wesleyan University, Southwestern University, and Northwestern University. After a 2-year pastorate in Danville, Va., he went to Vanderbilt University in 1882 where he served successively as chaplain and tutor in theology, adjunct professor and professor of systematic theology, professor of Christian doctrine, dean of the faculty, and vice-chancellor of the university. He became dean emeritus in 1919.

In 1889 Tillett published *Our Hymns and Their Authors,* and in 1911 he and Charles S. Nutter collaborated on *Hymns and Hymn Writers of the Church,* a handbook to the 1905 Methodist hymnal. He served on 3 hymnal committees for the Methodist Episcopal Church, South—1886, 1904, and 1930. He was chairman of the committee on selection of new hymns for the joint hymnal of 1935.

Author: O Son of God Incarnate (85)

Tindley, Charles Albert (b. Berlin, Md., July 7, 1851; d. Philadelphia, Pa., July 26, 1933) was the son of slave parents. His mother died when he was 4, and he was separated from his father when only 5. He was 17 when by sheer determination he learned to read and write. Soon afterward he moved to Philadelphia where he worked as a hod carrier and janitor of a small church while attending night school and taking a correspondence course from the Boston School of Theology. Ordained into the Methodist ministry, he joined the Delaware Annual Conference in 1885 and served churches in South Wilmington, Odessa, Ezion, and Wilmington, Del., and Cape May, N.J. He was presiding elder of the Wilmington District, 1899-1902.

In 1902 Tindley returned as pastor to Calvary Methodist Episcopal Church in Philadelphia, where he had served as janitor. His ministry was highly successful, and a new building was built. The name of the church was changed, over his protests, to Tindley Temple Methodist Church. The leadership of the church included Negroes, Italians, Jews, Germans, Norwegians, Mexicans, and Danes.

Tindley wrote both words and music to many gospel songs, including "I'll overcome some day," written in 1901 and adapted in part to become the civil rights song "We shall overcome," made popular by the work of Martin Luther King, Jr.

William J. Reynolds has furnished information for this biography.

Author and composer: When the Storms of Life Are Raging (STAND BY ME (244)

Tisserand, Jean (birth information not available; d. Paris, France, 1494) was a preaching friar of the Franciscan order in Paris. He founded an order for penitent women and is possibly the author of an office commemorating Franciscans martyred in Morocco in 1220. His famous hymn was published posthumously in a small collection of religious pieces.

Author: O Sons and Daughters, Let Us Sing (451)

Tomer, William Gould (b. October 5, 1833; d. Hunterdon[?], N.J., September 26, 1897). Tomer's musical training consisted of attending singing schools and of singing in the choir at Finesville, N.J. During the Civil War he served in the 153rd Pennsylvania infantry and on the staff of General Oliver O. Howard, for whom Howard University was named. After the war he was a federal employee for 20 years in Washington, D.C., and served as music director for Grace Methodist Episcopal Church. He spent the last years of his life in New Jersey as a schoolteacher.

Composer: GOD BE WITH YOU (539, pp. 190-91)

Toplady, Augustus Montague (b. Farnham, Surrey, England, November 4, 1740; d. London, England, August 11, 1778) was educated at Westminster School in London, and Trinity College, Dublin (B.A. 1760). He was converted in a Dublin barn under James Morris, a Methodist lay preacher. Ordained into the Church of England in 1762, he first served as curate in Blagdon and Farleigh, then was named vicar at Broadhembury, Devonshire, in 1766. In 1775 he moved to London where he preached at the French Calvinist Church in Leicester Fields.

Toplady was strongly Calvinist and carried on a running public feud for years with John Wesley in sermons, pamphlets, letters, tracts, and hymns, including *Psalms and Hymns for Public and Private Worship,* 1776. In poor health most of his life, he died of tuberculosis.

Author: If, on a Quiet Sea (147)
Rock of Ages, Cleft for Me (120)

Towner, Daniel Brink (b. Rome, Pa., March 5, 1850; d. Longwood, Mo., October 3, 1919) was the son of J. G. Towner, a well-known singer and music teacher, and Daniel studied under him. Later he studied with John Howard, George F. Root, and George J. Webb. He served as music director for Centenary Methodist Episcopal Church, Binghamton, N.Y., 1870-82; York Street Methodist Episcopal Church, Cincinnati, Ohio, 1882-84; and at Union Methodist Episcopal Church, Covington, Ky., 1884-85. In 1885 he joined Dwight L. Moody in his evangelistic campaigns and in 1893 became head of the music department of Moody Bible Institute, Chicago. The University of Tennessee awarded him the Mus.D. degree in 1900 in recognition of his influence in training music leaders and evangelistic singers. He wrote more than 2,000 songs and was associated with the publication of 14 collections.

Composer: TRUST AND OBEY (223, p. 432)

Troutbeck, John (b. Blencowe, Cumberland, England, November 12, 1833; d. London, England, October 11, 1889) was a translator for Novello and Company of London. He was a graduate of Oxford (B.A. 1856, M.A. 1858) and precentor of Manchester Cathedral, 1865-69. He was also chaplain and priest in ordinary to the queen.

Troutbeck published *The Manchester Psalter*, 1868, *Manchester Chant Book*, 1871, *Hymn Book for Use in Westminster Abbey*, 1883, and *Church Choir Training*, 1879. His translations for Novello also included librettos of German, French, and Italian operas as well as works such as Bach's *Christmas Oratorio*, from which "Break forth, O beauteous heavenly light" is taken.

Translator: Break Forth, O Beauteous Heavenly Light (373)

Tucker, Francis Bland (b. Norfolk, Va., January 6, 1895), the son of an Episcopal bishop, was educated in the public schools of Lynchburg, Va., the University of Virginia (B.A. 1914), and Virginia Theological Seminary (B.D. 1920, D.D. 1942). He served as a private in France during World War I. Ordained deacon in 1918 and priest in 1920, he was rector of Grammar parish, Lawrenceville, Va., 1920-25; St. John's Church in Georgetown, Washington, D.C., 1925-45; and at Christ Church, Savannah, Ga., since 1945. John Wesley served the latter parish during the years 1736-37. Tucker was a member of the joint commission which produced the 1940 edition of the Episcopal *Hymnal*, which contained 6 of his hymns and translations.

Author: All Praise to Thee, for Thou, O King Divine (74)
Translator: Alone Thou Goest Forth (427)
Father, We Thank Thee, Who Hast Planted (307)

Turner, Herbert Barclay (b. Brooklyn, N.Y., July 17, 1852; d. Washington, Conn., May 1, 1927) was educated at Amherst College and Union Theological Seminary in New York. He became a Congregational minister and served churches in Massachusetts and Connecticut. He was chaplain of Hampton Normal and Agricultural Institute in Virginia, 1892-1925. While there he edited *Hymns and Tunes for Schools,* 1907, with William Bindle. Turner also compiled 2 other collections for Sunday School use, including *Carmina,* 1894. Amherst College honored him with the D.D. degree in 1905.

Composer: CUSHMAN (**90,** p. 423)

Tweedy, Henry Hallam (b. Binghamton, N.Y., August 5, 1868; d. Brattlebury, Vt., April 11, 1953) was of Scottish ancestry through his father and a descendant of William Bradford and William Pratt through his mother. He was educated at Phillips Andover Academy, Yale University (B.A. 1901, M.A. 1909), Union Theological Seminary in New York, and the University of Berlin. Ordained into the Congregational ministry in 1898, he served Plymouth Church, Utica, N.Y., 1898-1902, and South Church, Bridgeport, Conn., 1902-9. From 1909 to 1937 he was professor of practical theology at Yale Divinity School. In addition to authoring many books, including *The Minister and His Hymnal,* he compiled the hymnal *Christian Worship and Praise* for Barnes & Company in New York City, 1939. Always interested in poetry and hymn writing, he won several hymn contests sponsored by the *Homiletic Review* and the Hymn Society of America.

Author: Eternal God, Whose Power Upholds (476)
O Gracious Father of Mankind (260)
O Spirit of the Living God (136)

Twells, Henry (b. Ashted, England, March 13, 1823; d. Bournemouth, England, January 19, 1900) was educated at King Edward's School in Birmingham and at St. Peter's College, Cambridge (B.A. 1848, M.A. 1851). He was ordained deacon in 1849, priest in 1850, and served as sub-vicar of Holy Trinity, Stratford on Avon, 1851-54; master of St.

Music. She was a pianist, singer, and composer and taught at Bechstein Hall, London, for 20 years. Her final concert in London included 18 songs for which she wrote both words and music.

She cared for her invalid mother during the years 1922-44 at Eastbourne and did not pursue her musical career. After her mother's death she taught a few pupils at Eastbourne.

Composer: VESPER HYMN (RENDLE) (506, p. 391)

Reynolds, William Jensen (b. Atlantic, Iowa, April 2, 1920), the nephew of the prominent Baptist musician Isham E. Reynolds, was educated at Oklahoma Baptist University, Southwest Missouri State College (B.A. 1942), Southwestern Baptist Seminary (M.S.M. 1945), North Texas State University (M.M. 1946), and George Peabody College for Teachers (Ed.D. 1961). He served as minister of music in Ardmore and Oklahoma City before joining the church music department of the Baptist Sunday School Board in 1955.

Reynolds is a composer and arranger, and the author of *A Survey of Christian Hymnody*, 1963. He served on the hymnal committee for the 1956 *Baptist Hymnal* and wrote the companion to that hymnal, *Hymns of Our Faith*, 1964. In 1968 he prepared a reprint of the 1859 edition of *The Sacred Harp*, which has provided an important source for the study of nineteenth-century American folk hymnody. He was also instrumental in the 1966 revision of *The Sacred Harp*, the definitive songbook used by present-day "shaped-note" singers.

A friend of the Methodist hymnologist Robert G. McCutchan, Reynolds was deeply influenced by him in hymnological research. Reynolds stands perhaps as the hymnologist with the most latitude of musical and theological interests produced by the Southern Baptists. He is a member of the Hymn Society of America.

Composer: SIMS (533, p. 185)

Richardson, John (b. Preston, Lancashire, England, December 4, 1816; d. Preston, April 13, 1879) was educated in Roman Catholic day schools. He became a chorister of St. Wilfrid's Roman Catholic Church and attracted attention for his beautiful alto voice. At the age of 13 he went to Liverpool where he sang in the choir of St. Nicholas' Church. He was apprenticed to a house painter but turned to church

Andrew's School in Wells, Somerset; and headmaster of Godolphin School in Hammersmith, 1856-70. For the remainder of his life he served in various capacities—as rector at Waltham on the Wolds, 1871-90, rural dean of Framland II, and honorary canon of Peterborough Cathedral. His last years were spent in Bournemouth where he was at times priest in charge, giving generously of both his funds and failing health in the building of St. Augustine Church.

Twells was one of the editors of the Supplement to the revised edition of *Hymns Ancient and Modern,* 1889.

Author: At Even, ere the Sun Was Set (501)

Vail, Silas Jones (b. Brooklyn, N.Y., October 6, 1818; d. Brooklyn, May 20, 1884) was a hatter and clerk by trade, later a successful businessman. An amateur composer, in 1863 Vail compiled *The Athenaeum Collection* which contained 10 previous unpublished songs by Stephen Foster. The prohibitionist Horace Waters engaged Vail and W. F. Sherwin to compile *Songs of Grace and Glory,* 1874.

Composer: CLOSE TO THEE (176, p. 410)

Van Dyke, Henry (b. Germantown, Pa., November 10, 1852; d. Princeton, N.J., April 10, 1933) was educated at Brooklyn Polytechnic Institute, Princeton University (B.A. 1873), and Princeton Theological Seminary. He was ordained into the Presbyterian ministry and served as pastor of the United Congregational Church, Newport, R.I., 1879-83, and pastor of Brick Presbyterian Church in New York City, 1883-99. Beginning in 1899 he was Murray Professor of English Literature at Princeton for 23 years. He was appointed United States minister to the Netherlands and Luxemburg by his friend President Woodrow Wilson and served during the years 1913-16. During World War I he served as lieutenant-commander in the United States Navy Chaplain Corps.

Van Dyke was chairman of the committee which prepared the Presbyterian *Book of Common Worship* in 1905 and a member of the committee which prepared the 1932 revision. He was a prolific writer, publishing some 25 books.

Author: Joyful, Joyful, We Adore Thee (38)

687

Vaughan Williams, Ralph (b. Down Ampney, Gloucestershire, England, October 12, 1872; d. St. Marylebone, England, August 26, 1958) was the son of the Reverend A. Vaughan Williams, vicar of Christ Church in Down Ampney. His mother was a descendant of Josiah Wedgewood and a niece of Charles Darwin. Ralph had early training in piano, violin, and theory, continuing private study for 5 years at a preparatory school in Rottingdean. He was educated at Charterhouse School, 1887-89, the Royal College of Music, 1890-92, and Trinity College, Cambridge (B.M. 1894, B.A. 1895, Mus.D. 1901). He also studied under Max Bruch in Berlin and Maurice Ravel in Paris. During the years 1895-98 he was church organist of St. Barnabas', South Lambeth, where he also directed the choir, gave recitals, and conducted a choral and orchestral society which he organized at the church. After his return from Paris, he gave up the church post to devote his time to composition.

He joined the Folk-Song Society in 1904 and helped to collect a large body of folk music of the British Isles. Much of his material, which he arranged with great skill, first appeared in *The English Hymnal,* 1906, for which he was invited to be the musical editor by Percy Dearmer. Vaughan Williams wrote in his *Musical Autobiography,* 1910, that "two years of close association with some of the best (as well as the worst) tunes in the world was a better musical education than any amount of sonatas and fugues." *The English Hymnal* almost singlehandedly changed the direction of English hymnody because of Vaughan Williams' belief that the choice of tunes is a "moral rather than a musical issue." Such tunes as DOWN AMPNEY, RANDOLPH, and SINE NOMINE set a new style and standard for hymn tunes. With Martin Shaw and Percy Dearmer he edited *Songs of Praise,* 1925 and 1931. The results of his interest in folk music and carols are also seen in the distinctive collection *The Oxford Book of Carols,* 1928.

More than anyone else, Vaughan Williams established a folk base for congregational song. His harmonizations and original tunes are represented in most American hymnals, and the success of his work has inspired others in England and America to adapt folk music and compose tunes in the folk idiom.

Vaughan Williams enlisted as an orderly in the Royal Army Medical Corps at the age of 41 when World War I started. He served in England, Salonika, and France, receiving a commission in 1918. He was honored with a Mus.D. degree from Oxford in 1919, appointed professor of composition at the Royal College of Music and conductor of the Bach Choir in 1920, and awarded the Order of Merit by King George V in 1935. In 1922 he visited the United States and conducted his *Pastoral Symphony* in the Norfolk, Conn., festival.

Although Vaughan Williams' major interest is reflected in vocal music, the standard orchestral repertory contains many of his orchestral compositions, including fantasies for strings and 6 symphonies. In addition, he wrote operas, ballets, film music, chamber music, and 3 preludes for the organ on Welsh hymn tunes. The folk music of East Anglia and Herefordshire in particular is widely represented in his works. His work also reflects the influence of the Tudor composers and Henry Purcell. He must be ranked as England's greatest composer since Purcell.

> Composer: DOWN AMPNEY (**466**, p. 137)
> KING'S WESTON (**76**, p. 103)
> RANDOLPH (**540**, p. 191)
> SINE NOMINE (**74, 536**, p. 82)
> Harmonizer: FOREST GREEN (**33, 37**, p. 72)
> KING'S LYNN (**484**, p. 311)
> LASST UNS ERFREUEN (**60**, p. 73)

Venua, Frédéric Marc-Antoine (b. Paris, France, 1786; d. 1872) was born of Italian parents. He enrolled at the Paris Conservatory in 1800 and went to London in 1805 to study violin and composition. He stayed nearly 60 years. At one time he was musical director of the ballet at the King's Theatre. William Gardiner, who introduced Venua's tune into American hymnody in his *Sacred Melodies,* 1812, said that it was "an adagio dance by Venua who formerly led the ballet in the Opera."

> Composer: PARK STREET (**25**, p. 204)

Vulpius, Melchior (b. possibly at Wasungen, Thuringia, c. 1560; buried Weimar, August 7, 1615) served as cantor at Weimar from 1602 until his death. He composed contrapuntal settings of existing melodies and published *Cantiones Sacrae,* 1602-4, *Kirchengesänge und geistliche Lieder,* 1604, and *Ein schönes geistliches Gesangbuch,* 1609.

He also composed a setting of the *St. Matthew Passion*, 1612-14, and published a German translation and revision of Heinrich Faber's *Musicae Compendium* in 1610.

Composer: CHRISTUS, DER IST MEIN LEBEN (44, 178, pp. 325-26)
GELOBT SEI GOTT (449, p. 203)

Wade, John Francis (b. c. 1710; d. Douay, France, August 16, 1786) was an English layman who lived in Douay, France, a Roman Catholic center with an English college and a haven for English refugees of the Jacobite rebellion of 1745. He was a teacher of music and a music copyist specializing in plainchant and hymn collections for use in private chapels of English Roman Catholic families.

Composer: ADESTE FIDELES (386, p. 303)

Walch, James (b. Edgerton, near Bolton, England, June 21, 1837; d. Llandudno, Caenarvonshire, Wales, August 30, 1901) studied music with his father and Henry Smart. He was organist at Duke's Alley Congregational Church in Bolton, 1851; Walmsley Church, 1857; Bridge Street Wesleyan Chapel, 1858; and St. George's Parish Church, Bolton, 1863. He conducted the Bolton Philharmonic Society during the years 1870-74. From 1877 until his death he was music dealer in Barrow in Furness.

Composer: TIDINGS (299, p. 345)

Walford, William (b. Bath, Somersetshire, England, 1772; d. Uxbridge, England, June 22, 1850) was educated at Homerton Academy and ordained into the Congregational ministry, serving several pastorates at Sowmarket, Suffolk, 1798-1800; Great Yarmouth, Norfolk, 1800-13; and Uxbridge, 1824-31 and 1833-48. Between his last 2 appointments he was classical tutor at Homerton, and apparently he suffered from some form of mental illness during the years 1831-33.

While it is uncertain that Walford wrote "Sweet hour of prayer," he did write *The Manner of Prayer*, 1836. Joseph F. Green, Jr., in a careful study of the book suggests that there are strong similarities between the hymn and the book. However, there is no direct evidence confirming William Walford's authorship of the hymn. See comments on the text.

Possible author: Sweet Hour of Prayer (275)

Walker, William (b. near Cross Keys, S.C., May 6, 1809; d. Spartan-
burg, S.C., September 24, 1875) was born of Welsh descent. He was
a devout Baptist and showed an early talent for singing which earned
him the nickname "Singin' Billy" Walker. At the age of 24, he married
Amy Golightly, and they had 10 children. Benjamin Franklin White,
who married Amy's sister, Thurza, joined with Walker in making a
collection of traditional tunes as they were sung in the Southern
Appalachians. But after Walker went to New Haven, Conn., with the
manuscript of *Southern Harmony,* it was published in 1835 without any credit listed for B. F. White. As a result, White moved to
Harris County, Ga., where he brought out an equally famous collection, *The Sacred Harp,* 1844.

Walker taught singing schools, using his book as a tool. At first the
books were printed in the 4 shaped-note system (see below). The
system was borrowed from one introduced in 1800 by William Little
and William Smith of Albany, N.Y. Later Walker turned to the 7
shaped-note system for his *Christian Harmony* (see below). As Walker
toured the mountain areas of the South, he collected tunes wherever
he went. The result was one of the best collections of early American
folk hymns, made up primarily of traditional melodies from Wales,
Scotland, Ireland, and England, recast in the shaped-note format.

Fa	Sol	La	Mi			
Do	Re	Mi	Fa	Sol	La	Ti

Composer: COMPLAINER (398, p. 270)

Wallace, William Vincent (b. Waterford, Ireland, June 1, 1812; d.
Château de Bages, France, October 12, 1865) was of Scottish descent.
He studied music with his father who was a bassoon player and bandmaster. Becoming an accomplished violinist, he gave his first concert
in Dublin at the age of 15. After a marriage which ended in divorce,
he spent some time wandering in Australia, New Zealand, India, and
South America. In 1845 he presented his opera *Maritana* at Drury

Lane, London, and in 1847 a second opera, *Matilda of Hungary*. Wandering again in the United States, Mexico, and South America, he concertized, accepting as payment anything of market value. In 1850 he married the pianist Helena Stoepel. He completed 7 operas, 1 cantata, and many piano pieces. Failing eyesight forced him to give up writing. Following another successful concert tour of the United States, he retired on his doctor's orders to the Pyrenees.

Composer: SERENITY (158, p. 236)

Walter, Howard Arnold (b. New Britain, Conn., August 19, 1883; d. Lahore, India, November 1, 1918) was educated at Princeton, Hartford Theological Seminary, and universities in Edinburgh, Glasgow, and Göttingen. His hymn was written at the age of 23 when he was teaching English at Waseda University in Tokyo. After a period as assistant minister of Asylum Hill Congregational Church, Hartford, he applied to become a missionary but was rejected because of his weak heart. However, in 1913, after joining the executive staff of the Y.M.C.A. at the urging of John R. Mott, he went to India for the Y.M.C.A. and worked among Mohammedan students in Foreman Christian College in Lahore. He died during an influenza epidemic.

Author: I Would Be True (156)

Walter, Samuel (b. Cumberland, Mo., February 2, 1916) is the son of a clergyman. He was educated at Marion College in Marion, Ind. (B.A. and B.S. 1939), the New England Conservatory of Music (B.M. 1942, M.M. 1943), Boston University (M.A. 1943), and Union Theological Seminary in New York City (D.S.M. 1957). He has served as organist in many churches in New England and New York City, as well as instructor in organ and chapel organist at Boston University, 1948-55, and instructor in theory at Union Theological Seminary School of Sacred Music. He is presently professor of music at Rutgers.

Walter has studied composition with Nadia Boulanger, organ with Marcel Dupré, and liturgical music with Everett Titcomb. He has many published compositions for choirs, voice, and organ, as well as 2 books: *Basic Principles of Service Playing*, 1963, and *Music Composition and Arranging*, 1965.

Composer: HIGH POPPLES (511, p. 98)

Walter, William Henry (b. Newark, N.J., July 1, 1825; d. New York, N.Y., 1893) as a boy played the organ at the Presbyterian and Episcopal churches in Newark. He studied with Edward Hodges and became the organist of St. John's Chapel, St. Paul's Chapel, and Trinity Chapel, New York. He was granted an honorary Mus.D. from Columbia in 1864, and the following year he was appointed organist for the school. His publications include *Manual of Church Music*, 1860, *The Common Prayer, with Ritual Song*, 1868, and numerous anthems, masses, and services.

Composer: FESTAL SONG (**174**, p. 362)

Walther, Johann (b. Cola, Thuringia, 1496; d. Torgau, April 24, 1570) was the bass singer at the court of Frederick III, elector of Saxony. He also served as Kapellmeister at Dresden. He collaborated with Martin Luther in producing both the *Geistliches Gesangbüchlein*, 1524, and the German mass. Walther wrote several hymns: 3 are translated, and 1 is in present use in Lutheran hymnals in America. His most important work was in the adaptation of old melodies as chorale tunes.

Source: AUS TIEFER NOT (**526**, pp. 351-52)
CHRIST LAG IN TODESBANDEN (**438**, p. 132)

Walton, James George (b. 1821; d. 1905). Nothing is known about this person except that he edited *Plain Song Music for the Holy Communion Office*, 1874.

Adapter: ST. CATHERINE (**151, 259, 344**, p. 139)

Walworth, Clarence Alphonsus (Augustus) (b. Plattsburg, N.Y., May 30, 1820; d. Albany, N.Y., September 19, 1900) graduated from Union College, Schenectady, 1838, and was admitted to the bar in 1841. He studied for the Episcopal ministry at General Theological Seminary in New York in 1845, but was ordained a priest of the Roman Catholic Church. In 1866 he was named rector of St. Mary's in Albany and helped to found the order of Paulists in the United States. Walworth took the name Alphonsus when he became one of the founders of the Paulist congregation. He was blind the last 10 years of his life.

Translator: Holy God, We Praise Thy Name (**8**)

Ward, Samuel Augustus (b. Newark, N.J., December 28, 1847; d. Newark, September 28, 1903) studied with Jan Pychowski and other teachers in New York City. He began a successful music store in Newark. In 1880 he followed Henry S. Cutler as organist at Grace Episcopal Church in Newark. Ward also founded the Orpheus Club of Newark in 1889, serving as its director until 1900.

Composer: MATERNA (543, p. 301)

Ware, Henry, Jr. (b. Hingham, Mass., April 21, 1794; d. Framingham, Mass., September 25, 1843) was the son of a Unitarian pastor and teacher. He graduated from Harvard in 1812 and was named to the faculty of Exeter Academy in New Hampshire. In 1815 he was licensed a Unitarian minister and was ordained in 1817 at Second Unitarian Church in Boston. Because of his failing health, he was assigned an assistant pastor, Ralph Waldo Emerson, in 1829. During the years 1830-42 he was professor of pulpit eloquence and pastoral care at Cambridge Theological School and served as editor of the *Christian Disciple*, which became the *Christian Examiner* in 1824. In 1834 Harvard honored him with the D.D. degree. Some 4 volumes of his works were collected by Chandler Robbins in 1846.

Author: All Nature's Works His Praise Declare (343)
Happy the Home When God Is There (516)

Waring, Anna Laetitia (b. Plas-y-Velin, Neath, Glamorganshire, Wales, April 19, 1823; d. Clifton, Bristol, England, May 10, 1910) was brought up in the Society of Friends. She joined the Church of England and was baptized in 1842. Nineteen of her hymns were published in *Hymns and Meditations by A. L. W.*, 1850, a collection which was enlarged to include 39 hymns in the tenth edition, 1863. Her social concerns were revealed in visits to the prisons in Bristol and in supporting the Discharged Prisoners' Aid Society.

Author: In Heavenly Love Abiding (230)

Warren, George William (b. Albany, N.Y., August 17, 1828; d. New York, N.Y., March 17, 1902) was educated at Racine College, Wisconsin. Largely a self-taught organist, he held posts at St. Peter's Episcopal Church, 1846-58, and St. Paul's Church, 1858-60, both in Albany;

Holy Trinity in Brooklyn, 1860-70; and St. Thomas' in New York, 1870-90. His collection *Warren's Hymns and Tunes as Sung at St. Thomas' Church,* 1888, is the source for his only surviving tune.

Composer: NATIONAL HYMN (406, 552, p. 197)

Watts, Isaac (b. Southampton, England, July 17, 1674; d. Stoke Newington, England, November 25, 1748), the first of 9 children, was born of dissenter parents. He learned Greek, Latin, and Hebrew at the grammar school in Southampton, and was offered the opportunity to prepare for the Anglican priesthood but declined and went instead to study at the nonconformist academy at Stoke Newington, 1690-94. After graduation he returned home and wrote most of the hymns contained in *Hymns and Spiritual Songs,* 1707, 1709. For a period of 6 years at Stoke Newington he was tutor to the son of Sir John Hartopp. Here, he engaged in such intense theological and philosophical study that his health was burdened, but this did not prevent his ordination and appointment as pastor of Mark Lane Independent Chapel, London, in 1702. In failing health, he called an assistant to share in the pastoral responsibility. From 1712 until his death Watts lived in semi-retirement in the home of Sir Thomas Abney, serving as chaplain to the family. In spite of his full pastoral duties, he found the time and energy to do a great deal of writing and to keep up a voluminous correspondence with contemporary leaders of religion. During this time he wrote around 60 books covering many fields.

Watts's most famous theological and philosophical works are *The Improvement of the Mind,* 1741, *Logic,* for many years an Oxford University textbook, *Catechisms, Scripture History,* 1732, and *The World to Come,* 1745. His 600 hymns are contained in 7 collections: *Horae Lyricae* (2 collections, 1706 and 1709), *Hymns and Spiritual Songs,* 1707, 1709. *The Psalms of David, Imitated in the Language of the New Testament,* 1719, *Sermons with Hymns,* 1721-27, *Reliquiae Juveniles,* 1734, and *Remnants of Time,* 1736.

Watts is called the "father of English hymnody." The influence of his hymns dominated congregational song in the nineteenth century and continues through the present day. He succeeded in maintaining that hymns be unique in function as distinguished from the strict paraphrase of psalms and scripture. Hymn singing was identified with preaching, worship, and the education of children. He used only a few basic meters and attempted to use the plain, simple language of the people. He was largely responsible for breaking the dull psalm-singing tradition and establishing the foundation for English hymnody represented in its golden era, dating roughly from Charles Wesley to James Montgomery. Watts is to English hymnody as Ambrose is to the medieval office hymn and Luther is to the German chorale. Millar Patrick in *The Story of the Church's Song* has written:

He set forever the example of what the congregational hymn should be. What made his own hymns so popular was their fidelity to Scripture, their consistent objectivity and freedom from introspection, and their exact suitability, in ideas and in the limpid clearness of their language, for giving voice to the religious thought and emotion of the average believer; these qualities make his best hymns perfect for the expression of a congregation's worship. He showed also that a good hymn for popular use should have a single theme, organic unity, boldness of attack in the opening line and a definite progression of thought throughout to a marked and decisive climax. Also, it should be short. His hymns are brief, compact, direct and telling. Reasons like these justified James Montgomery in saying that Watts was the "real founder of English hymnody."

For more information on Watts, see Harry Escott, *Isaac Watts, Hymnographer* (London, 1961), and A. P. Davis, *Isaac Watts, His Life and Works,* 1948.

Author: Alas! and Did My Savior Bleed (415)
Am I a Soldier of the Cross (239)
Before Jehovah's Awful Throne (22)
Come, Holy Spirit, Heavenly Dove (134)
Come, Sound His Praise Abroad (24)
Come, Ye That Love the Lord (5)
Give Me the Wings of Faith (533)
Great God, Attend, While Zion Sings (25)
I Sing the Almighty Power of God (37)
I'll Praise My Maker While I've Breath (9)
Jesus Shall Reign (472)
Joy to the World (392)
Let All on Earth Their Voices Raise (39)
O God, Our Help in Ages Past (28)
The Heavens Declare Thy Glory, Lord (365)
The Lord Jehovah Reigns (31)
This Is the Day the Lord Hath Made (789, pp. 461-62)

To God the Only Wise (**810**, p. 462)
When I Survey the Wondrous Cross (435)
Composite author: From All That Dwell Below the Skies (14)

Webb, George James (b. Wiltshire, England, June 24, 1803; d. Orange, N.J., October 7, 1887). His father, a wealthy farmer, wished George to enter the ministry, but he chose music and studied with Alexander Lucas at Salisbury. He was organist for a short time at a Falmouth church, then emigrated to Boston in 1830 where he was organist of the Old South Church for 40 years. With Lowell Mason he was appointed professor at the Boston Academy of Music in 1833. He was also president of the Boston Handel and Haydn Society in 1840. He joined Mason in New York in various musical ventures in 1870 and lived there and in New Jersey until his death.

Webb's publications include *The Massachusetts Collection of Psalmody,* 1840, and *The American Glee Book,* 1841; and with Mason as coeditor, *The Psaltery,* 1845, *The National Psalmist,* 1848, *Cantica Laudis,* 1850, and *Cantica Ecclesiastica,* 1859. He also edited 2 periodicals for brief periods: the *Music Library* and the *Musical Cabinet.*

Composer: WEBB (**248**, p. 381-82)

Webbe, Samuel, Sr. (b. London, England, 1740; d. London, May 25, 1816) was apprenticed to a cabinetmaker until about the age of 20, when he decided to study music. Webbe's job as music copyist for the London publisher Welcker brought him to the attention of the organist Carl Barbandt, who became his teacher. His formal education is not a matter of record, but he did study music, including composition, and Latin, French, Italian, German, Greek, and Hebrew. The Roman Catholic chapels at the Sardinian and Portuguese embassies in London employed Webbe as the organist beginning in 1776. He was the secretary of the Catch Club, 1784-1816, and won 27 prizes in the club's composition contests.

Webbe published *A Collection of Sacred Music as Used in the Chapel of the King of Sardinia in London,* c. 1793, *A Collection of Masses for Small Choirs,* 1792, *A Collection of Motets and Antiphons,* with his son Samuel, 1792, *Antiphons in Six Books of Anthems,* 1818, as well as catches, glees, a harpsichord concerto, divertissement for wind band, and hymn tunes, including some adaptations and harmonizations.

Composer: CONSOLATOR (103, pp. 155-56)
MELCOMBE (499, p. 296)
TANTUM ERGO (546, p. 261)

Weber, Carl Maria Friedrich Ernst von (b. Eutin [northern Germany], November 18, 1786; d. London, England, June 5, 1826) as a boy lived in many places since his father was a traveling theatrical impresario. His teachers included Johann Michael Haydn and Abt Vogler. At various times he was conductor of municipal theaters in Breslau, Stuttgart, Prague, and Dresden. His operas, *Der Freischütz, Preciosa, Euryanthe,* and *Oberon,* made him famous, but he also wrote symphonies, masses, cantatas, and chamber music.

Composer: SEYMOUR (94, p. 166)

Weimar, Georg Peter (b. Stotternheim, December 16, 1734; d. Erfurt, December 18, 1800) was trained in Erfurt at the gymnasium. He later was cantor at Zerbst and in 1763 was appointed cantor of the Kaufmannskirche at Erfurt. In 1774 he was made music director of the Erfurt Gymnasium. His *Choral-Melodienbuch,* published posthumously in 1803, included 5 of his melodies.

Composer: ALLGÜTIGER, MEIN PREISGESANG (285, p. 327)

Weissel, Georg (b. Domnau, Prussia, 1590; d. Königsberg, Prussia, August 1, 1635) was the son of Johann Weissel, mayor of Domnau, near Königsberg. Georg's chief study was at the University of Königsberg with short terms at Wittenberg, Leipzig, Jena, Strassburg, Basel, and Marburg. He became pastor of the Altrossgart Church in Königsberg in 1623 and remained there until his death. The majority of his hymns, about 20 in all, were written for the greater festivals of the church year.

Author: Lift Up Your Heads, Ye Mighty Gates (363)

Wellesley, Garret (or *Garrett*) (b. Dangan Castle, County Meath, Ireland, July 19, 1735; d. Kensington, England, May 22, 1781) was the son of Richard Colley, first baron Mornington who changed his name to Wesley when he succeeded to the estates of a Garrett Wesley after Charles Wesley declined to become the adopted heir of his Irish kinsman. He became a baron upon his father's death and was raised to the peerage in 1760 and granted the titles of Viscount Wellesley of Dangan Castle and Earl of Mornington. Three of his sons attained distinction and honor, with Arthur Wellesley, the first duke of Wellington, gaining the spectacular victory at Waterloo. The family name was changed from Wesley to Wellesley about 1790. Lord Mornington was a regular visitor at the Charles Wesley home and participated frequently in private subscription concerts which Charles's 2 sons, Charles and Samuel, gave in their father's home before fashionable audiences.

Robert G. McCutchan has written:

He was a well-known writer of madrigals, glees, and other part songs, some of which, being for the church, may be found in the choir books in St. Patrick's Cathedral, Dublin. In 1757 he founded an amateur singing society known as the Academy of Music, in which women sang in the chorus—an innovation at that time. He lived most of his life at Dublin, Ireland, where he was Professor of Music, Trinity College, Dublin University.

Composer: MORNINGTON (310, pp. 257-58)

Wells, Marcus Morris (b. Cooperstown, Otsego township, N.Y., October 2, 1815; d. near Hartwick, N.Y., July 17, 1895) was converted as a youth in a Buffalo, N.Y., mission. He spent most of his life near Hartwick as a farmer and maker of farm implements. A New York state highway marker marks the site of the Wells farm, and a window in the Baptist church at Hartwick commemorates the writer and the hymn for which he is remembered.

Author and composer: Holy Spirit, Faithful Guide (FAITHFUL GUIDE) (106)

Werner, Johann Gottlob (b. Hayn, near Leipzig, 1777; d. Merseburg, July 19, 1822) was the organist at Frohburg, beginning in 1798. In 1808 he was assistant to Christian Tag, cantor of Hohenstein, and organist and director at Merseburg, 1819-22. Noted as a teacher, he published several method books for organ and piano as well as a harmony book. His *Choralbuch zu den neuen protestantischen Gesangbüchern* was published in Berlin in 1815. Some chorale preludes and 40 organ pieces for beginners were also published.

Composer: RATISBON (**401, 463,** p. 135)

Wesley Family. Wesley is the most significant family name in eighteenth- and nineteenth-century English hymnody. The name was originally Welswe from the Somerset region in the mid-tenth century. It continued as Westley of Westleigh, Devonshire. The present spelling of the name evolved through Wellesley. A full family tree traced forward from about 938 has been furnished by G. J. Stevenson in *Memorials of the Wesley Family,* 1876. To help clarify the dates of the better-known Wesleys of the eighteenth and nineteenth centuries, the following chart is prepared. See also Erik Routley, *The Musical Wesleys,* 1969.

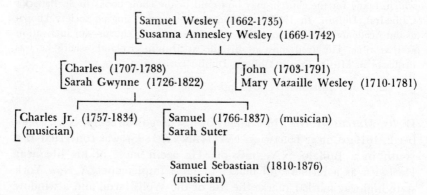

Samuel Wesley (1662-1735)
Susanna Annesley Wesley (1669-1742)

Charles (1707-1788)
Sarah Gwynne (1726-1822)

John (1703-1791)
Mary Vazaille Wesley (1710-1781)

Charles Jr. (1757-1834) (musician)

Samuel (1766-1837) (musician)
Sarah Suter

Samuel Sebastian (1810-1876) (musician)

Wesley, Charles (b. Epworth, Lincolnshire, England, December 18, 1707; d. Marylebone, London, England, March 29, 1788) was the eighteenth child and youngest son of Samuel and Susanna Wesley, and the brother of John. His parents were his early teachers, and in 1716 he went to Westminster School where his room and board were provided by his brother Samuel, an usher at the school. During this time a wealthy Irishman offered to adopt Charles and make him his heir, but was refused (see the biographical comment on Garret Wellesley). In 1721 he was elected a king's scholar, which provided free board and education. In 1726 he was elected to a Westminster studentship at Christ Church, Oxford, where his brother John studied. He received his B.A. in 1730, his M.A. in 1732, and became a college tutor. Charles is properly called the first "Methodist," since he, along with John and George Whitefield, formed the Oxford Holy Club and helped shape its disciplined approach to Bible study, worship, visitation to the sick and imprisoned, and frequent Communion.

With some reluctance on his part he was ordained deacon and elder in the Church of England on succeeding Sundays in September of 1735. Later that fall, John convinced Charles and Benjamin Ingham of the Holy Club to accompany him as missionaries to the Georgia colony. In Georgia Charles worked at St. Simon's Island as General Oglethorpe's secretary but became disillusioned and in July of 1736 departed for England via Boston. In Boston, he was received by the leaders of the community and preached in several churches, including what is now Old South Church.

Back in London, he reunited with his family and friends and made friends with William Law, Count Zinzendorf, and Peter Böhler. These 3 men greatly influenced his life. His conversion on Whitsunday, May 21, 1738, is marked among other ways by the writing of the hymn "Where shall my wondering soul begin." Frank Baker in *The Representative Verse of Charles Wesley* has shown, however, that Charles was more of a poet prior to this occasion than has generally been thought. Baker has written: "He was already, I am convinced, a matured poet. Already he had written hundreds of competent poems, mainly versifications of the classics in the manner of Dryden or Pope." And, "The picture may seem slightly overdrawn, but this will serve to underline the fact that Charles Wesley's art of versification was quite consciously an *art,* and a carefully practiced art, long before he was fired with religious inspiration."

Beginning in 1738 John and Charles set about to proclaim the "good news" to England, Ireland, and Wales. While John was the organizing genius of Methodism, Charles gave it wings and developed its practical theology with his hymns. Frederick Gill has written: "He, no less than John, established Methodism. Their work was indivisible. John organized; Charles provided the impulse. . . . Charles gave wings to his brother's work, spreading it with a rapidity and gaining for it a popularity it could never otherwise have known." For a period of 6 months, 1738-39, although not licensed by the bishop, Charles served

701

as curate of St. Mary's, Islington, which became a center of early Methodist activity. At the urging of Whitefield, he began field preaching. In 1749 he took up residence in Bristol and married Sarah Gwynne, and they had 8 children, 3 of whom survived. Their two sons, Samuel and Charles, distinguished themselves in music. In 1771 he returned to London.

John and Charles, though candidly objective in their criticisms of each other, greatly admired and respected each other's work. Charles took exception to John's increasing "separation" from the Church of England, including John's practice of allowing preachers to dispense the sacraments, his ordaining of ministers, and permitting the holding of Methodist services at the same time that stated worship services of the local Anglican churches were being conducted. He remained loyal to the Anglican Church throughout his life.

As a poet, Charles's output was extraordinary, probably exceeding 6,500 texts. He used the hymn as a means of expressing the broad range of Christian experience subjectively. A master of meter, he used at least 45 iambic meters to give the right feel to the subject matter, a versatility rivaled only by Shelley. New music was called for to express the unconventional lines of 66.66.88.; 76.76.D.; or 77.44.7.D. His hymns are shot through with biblical allusions, and of the books in the Bible, only Obadiah, Nahum, Zephaniah, and John III are not used for illustrative material.

During Charles's lifetime 64 collections were published, many of which contained only his work. They are listed in John Julian's *Dictionary of Hymnology*, pp. 1259-60. In 1868-72 George Osborn collected and arranged *The Poetical Works of John and Charles Wesley*, in 13 volumes. Bernard Manning's *Hymns of Wesley and Watts*, 1942, is a classic study of eighteenth-century hymnody and sets forth the continuing relevance of these texts for twentieth-century Christians.

Author: A Charge to Keep I Have (150)
All Praise to Our Redeeming Lord (301)
And Are We Yet Alive (336)
And Can It Be That I Should Gain (527)
Arise, My Soul, Arise (122)
Author of Faith, Eternal Word (139)
Author of Life Divine (315)
Blest Be the Dear Uniting Love (338)
Blow Ye the Trumpet, Blow (100)

Praise the Lord Who Reigns Above (15)
Rejoice, the Lord Is King (483)
See How Great a Flame Aspires (464)
Servants of All, to Toil for Man (186)
Servant of God, Well Done (288)
Sing to the Great Jehovah's Praise (510)
Sing We to Our God Above (811, p. 460)
Sinners, Turn: Why Will You Die (112)
Soldiers of Christ, Arise (250)
Spirit of Faith, Come Down (137)
Talk with Us, Lord (262)
'Tis Finished! The Messiah Dies (429)
Thou Hidden Source of Calm Repose (89)
What Shall I Do My God to Love (130)
What Shall I Render to My God (196)
Where Shall My Wondering Soul Begin (528)
Ye Servants of God (409)
Composite author: Jesus Christ Is Risen Today (443)

Wesley, John Benjamin (b. Epworth, Lincolnshire, England, June 17, 1703; d. London, England, March 2, 1791) was the son of the Anglican clergyman Samuel and Susanna. When a small child, John (Jackie) was dramatically pulled from the flaming rectory in 1709, and his mother considered this a sign of his being saved for God's purposes. He was educated at Charterhouse School and Christ Church, Oxford (B.A. 1724, M.A. 1726-27), and became a fellow of Lincoln in 1727. Ordained priest on September 22, 1728, he served as curate to his father until 1729 when he returned to Oxford as tutor. Here he joined his brother Charles in the disciplined activities of the Holy Club (see the biographical comment on Charles Wesley, above). Under the sponsorship of the Society for the Propagation of the Gospel he and others in the club, including Charles, went as missionaries to Savannah, Ga. John had the specific task of parish priest (the parish he served is now Christ Church, Savannah). As priest he became the center of controversy and was brought to court, but departed for England before the case was closed.

In 1737 at Charleston, John published *A Collection of Psalms and Hymns,* the first of English hymnals. The book reflected an extraordinary grasp of 4 hymnic traditions: English psalm paraphrase, English devotional poetry, English hymns, and German hymnody. He had gained an interest in the latter because of his shipboard contact with

Moravians en route to America. His German translations remain the best of the eighteenth century and can be compared favorably with the finest of the nineteenth.

After returning to England in February of 1738, John was again deeply influenced by the Moravians. On Wednesday evening, May 24, 1738, while attending a society meeting on Aldersgate Street, he "felt [his] heart strangely warmed." Aldersgate as an "experience" is one of dozens cited by Wesley, but is seldom mentioned in his writings. To view Aldersgate as the norm of his religious experience is to make Wesley appear more of a dissenter than Anglican, when, in fact, the Methodist movement was for at least 3 decades, 1739-69, a militant, organized, evangelical wing of the Anglican Church. His debt to the Moravians ended at this point, and after a visit to Herrnhut he broke openly with them.

During the course of the Methodist revival Wesley published books, tracts, sermons, and hymns, all of which emerged as instrumental in the revival's continuing impact. The Wesleys' poetical publications cover 53 years and 64 hymnbooks. That the hymns are not always identified as John's or Charles's work has caused continued speculation in hymnological circles. Henry Bett has concluded that in the 1780 *Collection of Hymns for the Use of the People Called Methodists,* nine-tenths of the hymns were written by Charles. However, in the process of hymn-book compilation, editing was a joint venture until well into the 1760's, as was much of the organizational activity of the Methodist societies. This fact disputes the well-worn legend that John did the preaching and organizing, and Charles wrote the hymns. John's ability in editing was unique. John Julian has written:

With that wonderful instinct for gauging the popular mind, which was one element in his success, [John] saw at once that hymns might be utilized, not only for raising the devotion, but also for instructing and establishing the faith of his disciples. He intended the hymns to be not merely a constituent part of public worship, but they were also a kind of creed in verse.

A good example of this is the 1745 collection *Hymns on the Lord's Supper,* bound with John's reduction of Daniel Brevint's writings.

In his "Directions for Singing" (see the 1964 edition of the Methodist hymnal, p. viii), Wesley expresses a concern for vital congregational song. Folk music and any other melody at hand sufficed to express Charles's texts, but after the publication of the error-filled collection of tunes, *Foundery Collection,* 1742, John narrowed the field of choice. With the publications of Thomas Butts's *Psalmodia Sacra,* 1753, *Sacred Melody,* 1761, and certainly with the Lock Hospital collections of 1769 and 1792, there is enough evidence to support Erik Routley's view that "we must accept the fact that the generous and hospitable Gospel of the Wesleys allowed a good deal of bogus music to slip in." In particular, Wesley employed popular operatic melodies in distorted forms, while all the time dismissing the fuging tune as being unable to move passions. Unfortunately, folk music and Wesley texts never had a chance to live together in England after 1742. Early nineteenth-century American tunebooks did match them up, and American and English Methodists have 2 distinct musical traditions for the expression of Wesleyan hymnody.

The 1780 *Collection* is the supreme hymnbook of the eighteenth century, containing the "proved" hymns published by Wesley since 1739 and organized along lines which reflected the matured needs of the Methodist societies. His preface to the hymnbook is one of the great religious documents of English church hymnody. The full text is printed on pp. 30-32 in the article "The Psalms and Hymns of the Church."

Author: To God the Father (812, p. 462)
We Lift Our Hearts to Thee (492)
Translator: Give to the Winds Thy Fears (51)
Jesus, Thy Blood and Righteousness (127)
Jesus, Thy Boundless Love to Me (259)
O Thou, to Whose All-Searching Sight (213)
Thou Hidden Love of God, Whose Height (531)
Alterer: Before Jehovah's Awful Throne (22)
I'll Praise My Maker While I've Breath (9)
O God, Our Help in Ages Past (28)

Wesley, Samuel (b. Whitechurch, Dorsetshire, England, 1662; d. Epworth, Lincolnshire, England, April 25, 1735) was born, as was his wife Susanna, of nonconformist parents, but study convinced him of the shortcomings of dissent. He took his degrees at Exeter College, Oxford. Ordained in 1689, after a brief tenure at South Ormsby he became rector in 1697 at Epworth and remained there until his death. His tenure was constantly marked by controversy and troubles. These difficulties included at least 2 rectory fires, the last one in 1709 which destroyed the residence, and time spent in Lincoln prison for debts. Toward the end of his life his parishioners valued him as a conscientious parish priest and good husband and father.

Wesley's poetic works are now eclipsed by those of his sons, John, Charles, and Samuel, and his daughters, Emilia and Mehetabel. It is unfair, however, to dismiss his influence as simply the father of a large and creative family. He dedicated 3 literary works to 3 queens, including his last *Dissertations on the Book of Job* to Queen Caroline in 1735. Deeply interested in congregational song and no doubt influential in developing the thought and sensitivities in his sons, he expressed criticism of the "Old Version" of the psalter. He attacked the boring singing of the psalms at Epworth in *Athenian Oracle* and *Advice to a Young Clergyman*. He championed the cause of contemporary poetic expression in *An Epistle to a Friend Concerning Poetry*, 1700. Other works include *Heroic Poem on the Life of Our Blessed Lord and Saviour Jesus Christ*, 1693, and *The History of the Old and New Testament*.

For more information on Wesley, see L. Tyerman, *Life and Times of Samuel Wesley* (London, 1866).

Author: Behold the Savior of Mankind (428)

Wesley, Samuel Sebastian (b. London, England, August 14, 1810; d. London, April 19, 1876) was the son of Samuel, Charles's son (see the chart under Wesley family). His father was his first teacher. He was a chorister at the Chapel Royal, 1820-26. Wesley served several London churches as organist, 1826-32; Hereford Cathedral, 1832-35; Exeter Cathedral, 1835-42; Leeds Parish Church, 1842-49; Winchester Cathedral, 1849-65; and Gloucester Cathedral until his death. Oxford conferred the Mus.D. in 1839, excusing him from the Bachelor's exam. In 1850 he was made professor of organ at the Royal Academy of Music.

Wesley was among the first cathedral organists to insist on the installation of a full pedal board. This is but one of the reforms he sought and explains to some extent his various moves from one church position to another. Most of his professional views are contained in *A Few Words on Cathedral Music and the Musical System of the Church, with a Plan of Reform*, 1849.

Though he was considered the outstanding performer of his time, Wesley's compositions brought him considerable fame also. His hymn tunes, some 131, are contained in *The European Psalmist,* 1872, and are characterized by both marked innovation and sturdy, yet unconventional, writing. Other works include 4 church services, 2 psalm settings, 27 anthems, glees, *Ode to Labour,* 1864, and some organ and vocal compositions.

Composer: AURELIA (**297**, p. 390)
Lead Me, Lord (**802**, p. 450)
Arranger: CAMBRIDGE (**24**, p. 152)

West, Robert Athow (b. Thetford, England, 1809; d. Georgetown, D.C., February 1, 1865) came to America in 1843 and was the official reporter of the 1844 Methodist Episcopal General Conference. This conference, some 6 weeks long, resulted in the split into the northern and southern churches. At the 1848 General Conference of the Methodist Episcopal Church, North, a hymnal committee of 7, including West, was appointed. The hymnal was published in 1849 and served that segment of the church until 1876. West also served as editor of *Columbia Magazine,* 1846-49, and the *New York Commercial Advertiser,* after 1858. His books include *Sketches of Methodist Preachers,* 1848, and *A Father's Letters to His Daughter,* 1865.

Author: Come, Let Us Tune Our Loftiest Song (**23**)

White, Henry Kirke (b. Cheapside, Nottingham, England, March 21, 1785; d. St. John's College, Cambridge, England, October 19, 1806) was the son of a butcher. At the age of 17 he was articled to Messrs. Coldham and Enfield, Solicitors, of Nottingham, where he studied law diligently. He taught himself several modern languages as well as Latin and Greek, and was skilled in music and drawing. He entered St. John's College and planned to prepare for holy orders, but fell ill from over-study and died at the age of 21. White published *Clifton Grove and Other Poems,* 1806.

Author: The Lord Our God Is Clothed with Might (**32**)

Whitefield, George (b. Gloucester, England, December 16, 1714; d. Newburyport, Mass., September 30, 1770) was educated at St. Mary le Crypt School and Pembroke College, Oxford. He joined the Oxford

Holy Club in 1735 (see the biographies of Charles and John Wesley, above), was ordained into the Church of England in 1736, and began preaching for the Methodists in 1737. He first visited America in 1738 and divided his time between the colonies and England for the rest of his life. In 1741 he separated from the Wesleys over doctrinal differences, yet remained their friend.

Like the Wesleys, Whitefield used hymn singing effectively in his meetings and introduced the hymns of Isaac Watts to America during the period of the Great Awakening. He published *Collection of Hymns for Social Worship,* for use in his Tabernacle on Tottenham Court Road and brought the book to American shores where it was reprinted several times. He was buried under the pulpit of Old South Presbyterian Church in Newburyport.

Alterer: Hark! the Herald Angels Sing (**387, 388**)

Whiting, William (b. Kensington, England, November 1, 1825; d. Winchester, England, May 3, 1878) was educated at Clapham and at Winchester College. For more than 30 years he was master of Winchester College Choristers' School. He published *Rural Thoughts and Other Poems,* 1851, but wrote only one hymn.

Author: Eternal Father, Strong to Save (**538**)

Whittier, John Greenleaf (b. Haverhill, Mass., December 17, 1807; d. Hampton Falls, N.H., September 7, 1892) was an American Quaker born of rural New England stock. Whittier was largely self-educated except for a short time of study at Haverhill Academy. His early poems were published by the abolitionist William Lloyd Garrison, and Whittier emerged, in time, as the eloquent spokesman for the abolitionist cause. He edited various publications including the *American Manufacturer* and the *New England Review,* and he was on the staff of the antislavery paper *National Era.*

Whittier's poems are deeply devotional and express his abiding optimism and a Quaker's apprehension for formal religion. He disclaimed any ability at hymn writing, but about 50 hymns have been drawn from his poems by others.

For a full treatment of Whittier, see the *Hymn,* VII, 105-10.

Author: All Things Are Thine (347)
   Dear Lord and Father of Mankind (235)
   I Know Not What the Future Hath (290)
   Immortal Love, Forever Full (157, 158)
   O Brother Man, Fold to Thy Heart (199)

Wiant, Bliss (b. Dalton, Ohio, February 1, 1895) was educated at Wittenberg College, Ohio Wesleyan University (B.A. 1920), Boston University (M.A. 1936), and Peabody College (Ph.D. 1946), with additional study at Harvard, 1928-29, and Union Theological Seminary in New York City, 1941-42. He was ordained an elder and joined the Ohio Conference of the Methodist Episcopal Church in 1923. In the years 1923-51, with some interruptions, he headed the department of music at Yenching University in Peking, China. After his return from China, he was pastor of St. Paul's Church in Delaware, Ohio, 1953-55, minister of music at Mahoning Methodist Church in Youngstown, 1955-57, and director of music at the Methodist Board of Education and executive secretary of the National Fellowship of Methodist Musicians, Nashville, Tenn., 1957-61. Since that time he served as director of music at Scarritt College, 1961-62, director of music for the Ohio Council of Churches, 1962-63, professor of music at Chung Chi College of the Chinese University of Hong Kong, director of music programming for the National Council of Churches of Christ in the U.S.A. in Hong Kong, and lecturer in the theological schools of South East Asia, 1963-65.

Wiant served as music editor for *Hymns of Universal Praise,* 1936, and has compiled many collections of Chinese music; he and his wife Mildred provided the translations. He served as a consultant on the tunes subcommittee for the revision of the 1964 Methodist hymnal. His doctoral thesis, *Character and Function of Music in Chinese Culture,* was published in 1966. He has lectured widely on Chinese music, and his lectures are illustrated with his own performance on the indigenous instruments. One of Wiant's remembrances is having served as organist at the funeral of Sun Yat-sen in 1925.

Translator: Rise to Greet the Sun (490)
 Arranger: SHENG EN (317, p. 389)
    WIANT (519, pp. 294-95)
Harmonizer: LE P'ING (490, p. 362)

Wiant, Mildred Kathryn Artz (b. Lancaster, Ohio, June 8, 1898) graduated from Ohio Wesleyan University in 1920 where she was elected to Phi Beta Kappa. She married Bliss Wiant in the fall of 1922 and went to Boston, Mass., where she continued her vocal training for one year. The next year she left with her husband for Yenching University in Peking, China, and became associate professor of voice there. While on missionary furloughs, she continued voice training in Boston and was a special student of Marie Sundelius, Metropolitan Opera Company prima donna.

Mrs. Wiant has served as instructor in vocal music at Scarritt College, 1942-46 and 1961-62, a teacher at the Biennial Convocations of the National Fellowship of Methodist Musicians, 1957-61, instructor of vocal music at Chung Chi College, Chinese University of Hong Kong, 1963-65. She is the translator of 50 Chinese indigenous hymns into English, most of which are contained in the booklet "Worship Materials from the Chinese," published by the National Council of Churches of Christ in the U.S.A., 1969.

She is the mother of 4 children, all born in Peking.

Composite translator: Rise to Greet the Sun (**490**)

Wile, Frances Whitmarsh (b. Bristol, N.Y., December 2, 1878; d. Rochester, N.Y., July 31, 1939) was educated in the public schools of Webster, N.Y., and the Normal School at Genesco. According to her daughter, Mrs. Dorothy M. W. Bean, the author was to a great extent self-taught. She was an avid reader and was active in the cause of woman suffrage and other civic affairs. During the years 1898-1921 she was active in the Unitarian church at Rochester, where she assisted William Channing Gannett with his "Boys' Evening Home." She turned to theosophy in 1921, and this interest superceded her earlier interest in Unitarianism.

Many of her poems were published in the local papers.

Author: All Beautiful the March of Days (**33**)

Williams, Aaron (b. London[?], England, 1731; d. London, 1776) was a music teacher, publisher, and music engraver. At Scots Church, London Wall, he served as clerk. His publications include *The Universal Psalmodist,* 1763, *The Royal Harmony,* 1766, *The New Univer-*

sal Psalmodist, 1770, *Harmonia Coelestis* (6th ed. 1775) , *Psalmody in Miniature,* 1778. The 1763 book was reprinted several times, including an American edition published in 1769 in Newburyport, Mass., by Daniel Bailey and entitled *The American Harmony or Universal Psalmodist.*

Source: ST. THOMAS (5, **294, 492,** pp. 159-60)

Williams, Peter (b. Llansadurnin, Carmarthenshire, Wales, January 7, 1722; d. Llandyfeilog, Wales, August 8, 1796) was educated at the Carmarthen Grammar School. He was converted under George White-field and ordained in 1744 and afterwards was appointed to the parish of Eglwys Cymmyn, where he began a school. In 1746 Williams left the Church of England and joined the Welsh Calvinistic Methodists and became one of the most prominent itinerant leaders of the Methodist revival in Wales. Later he was expelled by the Methodists for heresy and founded his own chapel on Water Street, Carmarthen. His publications include a Welsh hymnbook, a Welsh Bible with annotations, 1773, a concordance, 1773, and *Hymns on Various Subjects,* 1771.

Composite translator: Guide Me, O Thou Great Jehovah (271)

Williams, Robert (b. Mynydd Ithel, Anglesey County, North Wales, c. 1781; d. Mynydd Ithel, 1821) was born blind on the island of Anglesey and spent his life there as a skilled basketmaker.

Composer: LLANFAIR (443, p. 244)

Williams, Thomas. No information is available on this person.

Source: TRURO (198, 346, 363, 445, p. 227)

Williams, Thomas John (b. Ynysmeudwy, Swansea Valley, Glamor-ganshire, Wales, 1869; d. Llanelly, Wales, 1944) was a pupil of David Evans. He was organist-choirmaster of Zion Church, Llanelly, 1903-13, and at Calfaria Church, Llanelly, from 1913 until his death.

Composer: EBENEZER (242, 460, p. 192)

Williams, William (b. Cefn-y-coed, near Llandovery, Wales, February 11, 1717; d. Pantycelyn, Wales, January 11, 1791) was known as the "Sweet Singer of Wales." He was the son of a prosperous Welsh farmer and went to Llwynllwyd Academy (later the Presbyterian College) at Carmarthen to study medicine. A sermon by the revivalist Howell Harris in 1738 led him to enter the ministry. Although ordained by the bishop of St. David's, he resigned the established church after 3 years to join David Rowlands and Harris in their evangelistic campaigns in the Welsh Calvinistic Methodist Church. He composed 800 hymns in Welsh and more than 100 in English. His hymns were collected and published by his son John in 1811.

> Author and probably partial translator: Guide Me, O Thou Great Jehovah (**271**)

Willis, Richard Storrs (b. Boston, Mass., February 10, 1819; d. Detroit, Mich., May 7, 1900) was educated at Chauncey Hall and Yale (B.A. 1841). He studied in Germany with Xavier Schnyder and Moritz Hauptmann, and was a close friend of Felix Mendelssohn. In 1848 he returned to the United States and served as music critic for the *New York Tribune*, the *Albion*, and the *Musical Times*. During the years 1852-64 he edited the *Musical Times*, the *Music World*, and *Once a Month*. Willis' publications include *Church Chorals and Choir Studies*, 1850, *Our Church Music*, 1856, *Waif of Song*, 1876, and *Pen and Lute*, 1883.

> Composer: CAROL (**390**, pp. 240-41)
> Arranger: ST. ELIZABETH (**79**, pp. 171-72)

Wilson Hugh, (b. Fenwick, Ayrshire, Scotland, c. 1764 or 1766; d. Duntocher, August 14, 1824) was the son of a shoemaker and was apprenticed to his father's trade. He studied music and mathematics in his spare time and designed sundials as an avocation. He was a part-time precentor at the Secession Church at Fenwick, teaching writing, arithmetic, and music to the villagers. Before 1800 he moved to Pollokshaws to work in William Dunn's mill as a draughtsman and calculator. He was active in the church and helped extend its ministry through the efforts of several laymen to establish the first Sunday school at Duntocher. At the time of his death many manuscripts of hymn tunes are believed to have been destroyed. Only MARTYRDOM has survived.

Composer: MARTYRDOM (328, 415, p. 71)

Winchester, Caleb Thomas (b. Montville, Conn., January 18, 1847; d. Middletown, Conn., March 24, 1920) graduated from Wesleyan University in 1869 and served as librarian at the school during the years 1869-73, was made professor of rhetoric and English literature, 1873, and became professor of English in 1890. Wesleyan conferred upon him the LL.D. degree in 1892.

Winchester was a member of the joint commission which compiled the 1905 Methodist hymnal. In 1906 he published *The Life of John Wesley,* widely acclaimed for its scholarship.

Author: The Lord Our God Alone Is Strong (346)

Winkworth, Catherine (b. London, England, September 13, 1827; d. Monnetier, Savoy, July 1, 1878) spent most of her life near Manchester but moved to Clifton in 1862 where she lived with her father and sisters. She was very active all her life in educational and social work.

Miss Winkworth remains the foremost English translator of German hymns. They are contained in her publication *Lyra Germanica,* 1855 and 1858. In 1863 her *Chorale Book for England* appeared, which had as its music editors William Sterndale Bennett, founder of the Bach Society in 1849, and Otto Goldschmidt, German-born pianist-composer and husband of Jenny Lind, who founded the Bach Choir in 1875. Miss Winkworth also published *Christian Singers of Germany* in 1869.

Translator: All My Heart This Night Rejoices (379)
Blessed Jesus, at Thy Word (257)
Deck Thyself, My Soul, with Gladness (318)
If Thou But Suffer God to Guide Thee (210)
Jesus, Priceless Treasure (220)
Lift Up Your Heads, Ye Mighty Gates (363)
Lord Jesus Christ, Be Present Now (784, pp. 453-54)
Now Thank We All Our God (49)
O Morning Star, How Fair and Bright (399)
Open Now Thy Gates of Beauty (13)
Out of the Depths I Cry to Thee (526)
Praise to the Lord, the Almighty (55)

Wake, Awake, for Night Is Flying (366)
We Believe in One True God (463)

Wolcott, Samuel (b. South Windsor, Conn., July 2, 1813; d. Longmeadow, Mass., February 24, 1886) was educated at Yale and Andover Theological Seminary. During the years 1840-42 he served as missionary to Syria, but returned to America because of ill health and served several Congregational churches in Rhode Island, Massachusetts, Chicago, and Cleveland. For several years he was secretary of the Ohio Home Missionary Society.

Wolcott's first hymns were written at the age of 56. Only 1 of the 200 he wrote has remained in common use.

Author: Christ for the World We Sing (292)

Woodbury, Isaac Baker (b. Beverly, Mass., October 23, 1819; d. Charleston, S.C., October 26, 1858) studied in Boston, Paris, and London. He taught music in Boston until 1849 when he moved to New York and directed the music at Rutgers Street Church. He was editor of the *New York Musical Review* and the *Musical Pioneer.* His health broke in 1858, and he moved to Charleston, where he died 3 days later.

Woodbury helped compile the musical edition, 1857, of *The Methodist Hymn Book,* 1849, and edited many popular tunebooks: *The Choral,* 1845, *The Timbrel,* 1848, *The Anthem Dulcimer,* 1850, *The Lute of Zion,* 1853, *The Harp of the South,* 1853, *The Cythera,* 1854, *The Casket,* 1855, and *The New Lute of Zion.*

Composer: SELENA (420, p. 328)

Woodward, George Ratcliffe (b. Birkenhead, England, December 27, 1848; d. St. Pancras, England, March 3, 1934) was educated at Gonville and at Caius College, Cambridge (B.A. 1872, M.A. 1875). He received the Lambeth Mus.D. degree in 1924.

Woodward was a clergyman, musician, editor, and translator. In 1922 he published *Hymns of the Greek Church,* translations with the original Greek. His other publications include an edition of *Piae Cantiones,* 1910, *An Italian Carol Book,* 1920, and *The Cambridge*

715

Carol Book; and with Charles Wood, he edited *The Cowley Carol Book,* 1901, and *Songs of Syon,* 1904 and 1923.

Harmonizer: PUER NOBIS NASCITUR (515, pp. 313-14)

Wordsworth, Christopher (b. Lambeth, England, October 30, 1807; d. Harewood, England, March 20, 1885) was the youngest son of the Reverend Christopher Wordsworth and the nephew of William Wordsworth. He was educated at Winchester School and Trinity College, Cambridge, where he excelled in scholarship and athletics. His positions include headmaster of Harrow School, canon of Westminster Abbey, vicar of Stanford in the Vale cum Goosey, Berkshire, archdeacon of Westminster, and bishop of Lincoln. His *Holy Year, or Hymns for Sundays and Holydays* (new ed., 1862) contained hymns for every season and festival of the Christian year.

Author: O Day of Rest and Gladness (488)
O Lord of Heaven and Earth and Sea (523)

Work, John Wesley, III (b. Tullahoma, Tenn., June 15, 1901; d. Nashville, Tenn., May 18, 1967), the prolific composer, arranger, and authority on Afro-American music and culture, was the oldest son of 7 children of John Wesley Work, Jr., and Agnes Haynes Work. While John was still an infant, his parents returned to Nashville, Tenn., the native home of his father, for the latter to assume a position at Fisk University, the alma mater of both himself and his wife, Agnes. Young John was enrolled in the kindergarten at the Daniel Hand Training School at Fisk, and he continued and completed his entire primary, elementary, preparatory, and college training at Fisk University (B.A. 1923), with further study at the Institute of Musical Art in New York City. Upon the death of his father, John became the head of the family, assuming responsibility for his widowed mother, his 2 younger sisters, and his youngest brother. He resumed his study in New York in 1927, and it was during this period that he again met his former Fisk classmate, Edith McFall of Charleston, S.C. In 1928 they were married. They returned to Fisk in the fall of 1928, and Work resumed the task begun by his mother, the training of choral groups. He continued his graduate study at Columbia University and received the M.M.Ed. in 1930.

716

During the late 1920's and 1930's Work trained and directed the famous Fisk Men's Glee Clubs which gained national popularity. From 1948 to 1957 he directed the Fisk Jubilee Singers in the tradition of his parents, directors 1901-16. In 1931 he was the recipient of a fellowship for further study at Yale University, where he received his B.M. in 1933. It was during these years that he increased his production of compositions and the arranging of spirituals that were to bring him fame as a composer. He had begun his career in composing at the early age of 17 when he wrote his first song, "Mandy Lou," for which his father wrote the lyrics. From the 1920's until 1965 he composed and published approximately 115 compositions, some of which have been performed by such groups as the Harvard and Yale glee clubs, the First International University Choral Festival, as well as choirs all over America. His works include anthems and spirituals for choir and solo voice, the choral cycle *Isaac Watts Contemplates the Cross,* 1964, and the book *American Negro Songs and Spirituals,* 1940.

Work was a member of several professional fraternities and clubs, and he was the recipient of numerous honors and awards. Perhaps the most significant of these was the first-place award given by the Fellowship of American Composers in 1946 for his cantata *The Singers,* performed at the Detroit convention the same year. In 1963 Fisk University conferred upon him the Mus.D. degree.

He was beloved by his students and was an inspired and inspiring teacher. The warmth and love which were the very essence of his home were extended to a host of friends, hundreds of Fisk alumni, and generations of Fisk students whose good fortune it was to share his and his wife's hospitality.

Adapter and arranger: Go, Tell It on the Mountain (GO, TELL IT ON THE MOUNTAIN) (404)

Wreford, John Reynell (b. Barnstaple, England, December 12, 1800; d. St. Marylebone, England, 1881) was educated at Manchester College, York, for the Unitarian ministry. After 5 years at New Meeting, Birmingham, he retired in 1826, when his voice failed. Thereafter he opened a school at Edgbaston. His later years of retirement were in Bristol.

Wreford's writings include *A Sketch of the History of Presbyterian Nonconformity in Birmingham,* 1832, and *Lays of Loyalty,* the latter published in 1837 to celebrate Queen Victoria's ascension to the throne. He wrote 55 hymns for J. R. Beard's *Collection of Hymns for Public and Private Worship,* 1837, a book which rejected all Trinitarian and evangelical hymns.

Author: Lord, While for All Mankind We Pray (551)

Wyeth, John (b. Cambridge, Mass., March 31, 1770; d. Philadelphia, Pa., January 23, 1858) was a printer and publisher who spent most of his life in Harrisburg, Pa., as editor of the Federalist paper *Oracle of Dauphin.* Though not a musician, he published *Repository of Sacred Music,* 1810, and *Repository of Sacred Music, Part Second,* 1813. This latter publication contained many folk and fuguing tunes already in print and was used in revivals and camp meetings. Though Unitarian in religious persuasion, Wyeth actively sought opportunities to print tunebooks of various denominations and ethnic groups, including German-speaking sects active in Pennsylvania during the early decades of the nineteenth century.

For more information concerning Wyeth and his work in printing music books, see Irving Lowen's introduction to the reprint of *Repository of Sacred Music, Part Second* (Da Capo Press, 1964) .

Source: DAVIS (**129,** p. 339)
   MORNING SONG (**190, 481,** p. 106)
   NETTLETON (**93,** p. 154)

Young, Carlton Raymond (b. Hamilton, Ohio, April 25, 1926) was educated at the College of Music and the University of Cincinnati (B.S. in music education 1950), and Boston University School of Theology (S.T.B. 1953). He was ordained an elder in The Methodist Church in 1953 and served as minister of music at the Church of the Saviour, Cleveland Heights, Ohio, 1953-56, and at Trinity Methodist Church, Youngstown, Ohio, 1956-59. In 1959 he began the program of music publishing and distribution as director of church music at Abingdon Press in Nashville, Tenn. Since 1964 he has been associate professor of church music at Perkins School of Theology and the School of the Arts at Southern Methodist University, Dallas, Tex.

Young has been active in local, state, national, and interdenominational music. He was the first recording secretary of the National Fellowship of Methodist Musicians, 1956-58, and in 1960 was named to the hymnal committee for the revision of the Methodist hymnal. In September of 1960 he was elected editor by the hymnal committee and served as editor of the 1964 revision of the Methodist hymnal until publication date, July 1, 1966. In 1966, 1968, and 1970 he served as director of music for the General Conferences, including in 1968, the Uniting Conference of the Evangelical United Brethren and Methodist Churches, which resulted in The United Methodist Church. Ohio Northern University conferred the Mus.D. degree in 1969.

His writings include many articles on music in Christian education, worship, and hymnody, as well as the article "American Methodist Hymnody—A Survey" in *A History of American Methodism,* 1964, *An Introduction to the Methodist Hymnal,* 1966, and 45 published music compositions.

Composer: The Lord Is in His Holy Temple (787, pp. 460-61)
Arranger: ARFON (MAJOR) (464, p. 368)
BRYN CALFARIA (364, 453, p. 271)
CANDLER (529, pp. 150-51)
CHARLESTOWN (426, pp. 161-62)
COMPLAINER (398, p. 270)
FOUNDATION (48, p. 222)
LASST UNS ERFREUEN (19, p. 73)
LET US BREAK BREAD (330, pp. 267-68)
NAOMI (140, 268, p. 174)
SLANE (256, pp. 112-13)
WONDROUS LOVE (432, p. 429)

Young, John Freeman (b. Pittston, Me., October 30, 1820; d. New York, N.Y., November 15, 1885) was educated at Wesleyan University and Virginia Theological Seminary in Alexandria. Ordained in 1845, he served churches in Florida, Texas, Mississippi, Louisiana, and New York. In 1867 he was elected the second bishop of Florida and served in that capacity for 18 years.

Young published *Hymns and Music for the Young,* 1860-61. His *Great Hymns of the Church* was published posthumously by John Henry Hopkins, Jr., in 1887. His interests also included architecture and establishing schools.

For more information on Young, see the *Hymn,* VIII (October, 1957), 123-30.

Composite translator: Silent Night, Holy Night (393)

Zinzendorf, Nicolaus Ludwig von (b. Dresden, May 26, 1700; d. Herrnhut, May 9, 1760) was born to nobility. He was raised by an aunt and grandmother and was educated at A. H. Francke's Adelspädagogium in Halle and Wittenberg University in law. Zinzendorf was deeply moved by a picture of Christ crowned with thorns, inscribed "This have I done for Thee, what hast thou done for me?" and he purchased an estate in Saxony in 1722 called "Herrnhut" which became a haven for persecuted Moravians. In 1737 he was consecrated a Moravian bishop. He was banished from Saxony and established Moravian colonies in Germany, England, the Baltic area, Holland, and North America.

Between 1712 and 1760 Zinzendorf wrote more than 2,000 hymns. John Wesley visited Herrnhut in 1738 and was influenced by the Moravians' hymns and pietism, yet rejected their "quietism."

Author: Jesus, Thy Blood and Righteousness (127)
O Thou, to Whose All-Searching Sight (213)

Zundel, John (b. Hochdorf, Germany, December 10, 1815; d. Cannstadt, Germany, July, 1882) was born and educated in Germany. He spent 7 years in St. Petersburg where he was organist of St. Anne's Lutheran Church and bandmaster of the imperial horse guards. He traveled to America in 1847 and served as organist at First Unitarian, Brooklyn; St. George's, New York; and Plymouth Congregational Church, Brooklyn, where Henry Ward Beecher was its famous minister. He retired 3 times, the last in 1878 after having served 28 years when he was to become organist for only a few months at Central Methodist Episcopal Church in Detroit.

With Henry and Charles Beecher, Zundel prepared the *Plymouth Collection of Hymns,* 1855, for which he wrote 28 tunes. He edited various collections and books of instruction on organ playing and harmony.

Composer: BEECHER (283, 479, p. 279)

Part IV
BIBLIOGRAPHY AND INDEXES

BIBLIOGRAPHY

Handbooks

Covert, William C., and Laufer, Calvin W. *Handbook to the Hymnal.* Philadelphia: Presbyterian Board of Christian Education, 1935.

Dearmer, Percy, and Jacob, Archibald. *Songs of Praise Discussed.* London: Oxford University Press, 1933.

Douglas, Charles Winfred; Ellinwood, Leonard; and others. *The Hymnal 1940 Companion.* New York: The Church Pension Fund, 1949.

Frost, Maurice, ed. *Historical Companion to Hymns Ancient and Modern.* London: William Clowes & Sons, 1962.

Haeussler, Armin. *The Story of Our Hymns.* St. Louis: Eden Publishing House, 1952.

Hostetler, Lester. *Handbook to the Mennonite Hymnary.* Newton, Kan.: General Conference of the Mennonite Church of North America Board of Publications, 1949.

Kelynack, William S. *Companion to the School Hymn-Book of the Methodist Church.* London: Epworth Press, 1950.

Lightwood, James T. *The Music of the Methodist Hymn-Book.* London: Epworth Press, 1935.

McCutchan, Robert Guy. *Our Hymnody: A Manual of the Methodist Hymnal.* Nashville: Abingdon-Cokesbury Press, 1937.

Martin, Hugh, ed. *The Baptist Hymn Book Companion.* London: Psalms and Hymns Trust, 1962.

Moffatt, James, and Patrick, Millar. *Handbook to the Church Hymnary.* London: Oxford University Press, 1935.

Nutter, Charles S., and Tillett, Wilbur F. *The Hymns and Hymn Writers of the Church.* New York and Cincinnati: The Methodist Book Concern, 1911.

Parry, K. L., and Routley, Erik. *Companion to Congregational Praise.* London: The Independent Press, 1953.

Polack, W. G. *The Handbook to the Lutheran Hymnal.* St. Louis: Concordia Publishing House, 1942.

Reynolds, William Jensen. *Hymns of Our Faith.* Nashville: Broadman Press, 1964.

Ronander, Albert C., and Porter, Ethel K. *Guide to the Pilgrim Hymnal.* Philadelphia: United Church Press, 1966.

Telford, John. *The Methodist Hymn-Book Illustrated in History and Experience.* London: Epworth Press, 1934.

Hymnology

Bäumker, Wilhelm. *Das katholische deutsche Kirchenlied.* 4 vols. Freiburg: Herder'sche Verlagshandlung, 1886-1911.

Baker, Frank. *Charles Wesley's Verse*. London: Epworth Press, 1964.

———, ed. *The Representative Verse of Charles Wesley*. Nashville: Abingdon Press, 1963.

Benson, Louis F. *The English Hymn*. New York: George H. Doran, 1915.

Bett, Henry. *The Hymns of Methodism in Their Literary Relations*. Enlgd. ed. London: Epworth Press, 1945.

Buchanan, Annabel Morris. *Folk Hymns of America*. New York: J. Fischer & Brother, 1938.

Diehl, Katharine S. *Hymns & Tunes, An Index*. New York: Scarecrow Press, 1966.

Escott, Harry. *Isaac Watts, Hymnographer*. London: The Independent Press, 1962.

Flew, R. N. *Hymns of Charles Wesley*. London: Epworth Press, 1953.

Foote, Henry Wilder. *Three Centuries of American Hymnody*. Cambridge, Mass.: Harvard University Press, 1940.

Frost, Maurice. *English and Scottish Psalm and Hymn Tunes*. London: Oxford University Press, 1953.

Gill, Frederick C. *Charles Wesley: The First Methodist*. Nashville: Abingdon Press, 1965.

Hutchings, Arthur. *Church Music in the Nineteenth Century*. London: Oxford University Press, 1967.

Idelsohn, Abraham Z. *Jewish Music: In Its Historical Development*. New York: Schocken Books, 1929.

Julian, John. *A Dictionary of Hymnology*. 2 vols. New York: Dover Publications, 1907.

Liemohn, Edwin. *The Chorale*. Philadelphia: Muhlenberg Press, 1953.

Lightwood, James T. *Hymn-Tunes and Their Story*. London: Charles H. Kelly, 1905.

McCutchan, Robert Guy. *Hymn Tune Names*. Nashville: Abingdon Press, 1958.

Manning, Bernard L. *The Hymns of Wesley and Watts*. London: Epworth Press, 1942.

Nuelson, John L. *John Wesley und das deutsche Kirchenlied*. Zurich: Christliche Vereinsbuchhandlung, 1938.

Patrick, Millar. *Four Centuries of Scottish Psalmody*. London: Oxford University Press, 1949.

———. *The Story of the Church's Song*. Rev. ed. by James R. Sydnor. Richmond: John Knox Press, 1962.

Phillips, Charles S. *Hymnody Past and Present*. New York: The Macmillan Company, 1937.

Pidoux, Pierre *Le Psautier Huguenot du XVIe Siècle*. Basel: Edition Bärenreiter, 1962.

Pocknee, Cyril E. *The French Diocesan Hymns and Their Melodies*. New York: Morehouse-Gorham, 1954.

Pratt, Waldo S. *The Music of the French Psalter of 1562*. New York: Columbia University Press, 1939.

————. *The Music of the Pilgrims: A Description of the Psalm-book Brought to Plymouth in 1620.* Boston: Oliver Ditson, 1921.

Rattenbury, J. E. *The Eucharistic Hymns of John and Charles Wesley.* London: Epworth Press, 1948.

————. *The Evangelical Doctrines of Charles Wesley's Hymns.* London: Epworth Press, 1941.

Report of the Hymnal Committee of the Commission on Worship to the 1964 General Conference of The Methodist Church. Nashville: The Methodist Publishing House, 1964.

Reynolds, William Jensen. *A Survey of Christian Hymnody.* New York: Holt, Rinehart and Winston, 1963.

Routley, Erik. *Church Music and Theology.* Philadelphia: Fortress Press, 1960.

————. *Hymns and the Faith.* Grand Rapids: Eerdmans Publishing Co., 1968.

————. *Hymns Today and Tomorrow.* Nashville: Abingdon Press, 1964.

————. *I'll Praise My Maker.* London: The Independent Press, 1957.

————. *The Music of Christian Hymnody.* London: The Independent Press, 1957.

————. *Twentieth-Century Church Music.* New York: Oxford University Press, 1964.

————. *Words, Music, and the Church.* Nashville: Abingdon Press, 1968.

Ryden, Ernest E. *The Story of Christian Hymnody.* Rock Island, Ill.: Augustana Press, 1959.

Stevenson, Robert. *Protestant Church Music in America.* New York: W. W. Norton, 1966.

Sydnor, James R., ed. *A Short Bibliography for the Study of Hymns.* New York: Hymn Society of America, Paper XXV, 1964.

Wackernagel, Philipp, ed. *Das deutsche Kirchenlied.* 5 vols. Leipzig: B. G. Teubner, 1864-77.

Wesley, John. *A Collection of Psalms and Hymns.* Charleston, S. C.: Printed by Lewis Timothy, 1737. A facsimile with additional material ed. by Frank Baker. London: Wesley Historical Society, 1964.

Zahn, Johannes. *Die Melodien der deutschen evangelischen Kirchenlieder.* . . . 6 vols. Gütersloh: C. Bertelsmann, 1889-93.

General

Baker, Theodore. *Baker's Biographical Dictionary of Musicians.* 5th ed. rev. by N. Slonimsky. New York: Schirmer, 1958.

Blom, Eric, ed. *Grove's Dictionary of Music and Musicians.* 10 vols. New York: St. Martin's Press, 1954.

Blume, Friedrich. *Geschichte der evangelischen Kirchenmusik.* Cassel: Bärenreiter-Verlag, 1965.

Dictionary of American Biography. 22 vols. New York: Charles Scribner's Sons, 1928-58.

Dictionary of National Biography. 27 vols. London: Oxford University Press, 1917-59.

Douglas, Charles W. *Church Music in History and Practice.* New York: Charles Scribner's Sons, 1937. Rev. 1962 by Leonard Ellinwood.

Dreves, Guido M., ed. *Analecta Hymnica Medii Aevi.* 55 vols. Leipzig, 1886-1922.

Ellinwood, Leonard. *The History of American Church Music.* New York: Morehouse-Gorham, 1953.

Grout, Donald Jay. *A History of Western Music.* New York: W. W. Norton, 1960.

Jackson, George P. *White and Negro Spirituals.* New York: J. J. Augustin, 1944.

————. *White Spirituals in the Southern Uplands.* Chapel Hill, N. C.: University of North Carolina Press, 1933.

Koch, Eduard E. *Geschichte des Kirchenlieds und Kirchengesangs.* 8 vols. 3rd ed. Stuttgart, 1866-76.

Lang, Paul Henry. *Music in Western Civilization.* New York: W. W. Norton, 1941.

Lowens, Irving. *Music and Musicians in Early America.* New York: W. W. Norton, 1964.

Raby, F. J. G. *A History of Christian Latin Poetry.* Oxford: Clarendon Press, 1927.

Scholes, Percy A. *The Oxford Companion to Music.* London: Oxford University Press, 1938.

Walker, Williston, *A History of the Christian Church.* Rev. ed. by C. C. Richardson and others. New York: Charles Scribner's Sons, 1959.

Wellesz, Egon. *A History of Byzantine Music and Hymnody.* Oxford: Clarendon Press, 1949.

Westrup, J. A., *et al. New Oxford History of Music.* London: Oxford University Press, 1957.

Work, John W. *American Negro Songs and Spirituals.* New York: Bonanza Books, 1940.

GENERAL INDEX

(Bold face numbers refer to major comments.)

726

TUNE INDEX

(Bold face numbers refer to major comments.)

INDEX OF CANTICLES WITH MUSIC, SERVICE MUSIC, AND COMMUNION MUSIC

766

THE AUTHORS

Fred D. Gealy, distingui… …minary professo… …sultant en liturgic… …Methodist hymnal.

Austin C. Lovelace is minister … Montview Boulevard Presbyterian … in Denver, Colorado, and teaches org… Temple Buell College, Denver. He is th… author of *Music and Worship in the Church* (with William C. Rice), *The Organist and Hymn Playing, The Youth Choir,* and *The Anatomy of Hymnody.*

Carlton R. Young, editor of *The Methodist Hymnal,* is associate professor of church music, Perkins School of Theology and the School of the Arts, Southern Methodist University, Dallas, Texas.

CONSULTING EDITOR

Emory Stevens Bucke is Senior Edi… of Abingdon Press.